GLOBE FEARON

Global Studies

GLOBE FEARON EDUCATIONAL PUBLISHER
A Division of Simon & Schuster
Upper Saddle River, New Jersey

Director of Editorial and Marketing, Secondary Supplementary: Nancy Surridge
Executive Editor: Jean Liccione
Senior Editor: Karen Bernhaut
Project Editor: Lynn Kloss
Assistant Editor: Brian Hawkes
Editorial Assistants: Derrell Bradford, Ryan Jones, Kathleen Kennedy
Market Manager: Rhonda Anderson
Production Director: Kurt Scherwatzky
Manufacturing Buyer: Tara Felitto
Production Editor: Alan Dalgleish
Art Directors: Pat Smythe and Mimi Raihl
Interior Design: Margarita Giammanco and Mimi Raihl
Cover Design: Marsha Cohen
Cover Art: Friedrich Fischbach, Owen James, N. Simakoff
Editorial Development: WestEd, Ink
Electronic Page Production: *aegis*

Printed in the United States of America   4 5 6 7 8 9 10   00 99 98

ISBN 0-835-92201-4

GLOBE FEARON EDUCATIONAL PUBLISHER
A Division of Simon & Schuster
Upper Saddle River, New Jersey

REVIEWERS

Daniel Berman
Social Studies Coordinator
Fox Lane Middle
and High School
Bedford, New York

David Crumley
Social Studies Department
Coordinator
Belzer Middle School
Indianapolis, Indiana

Bruce Ferrara
Social Studies Department
Chairperson
Roosevelt Jr. High School
Oakland, California

Pamela L. Halter
World Studies Teacher
Clarksville Middle School
Jeffersonville, Indiana

Russell Maruna
Director of Social Studies
Cleveland Public Schools
Cleveland, Ohio

John McLaughlin
World Cultures Teacher
Garfield High School
Garfield, New Jersey

Dr. Sheldon Shuch
Director of Instruction and
Professional Development
Community District 5
New York, New York

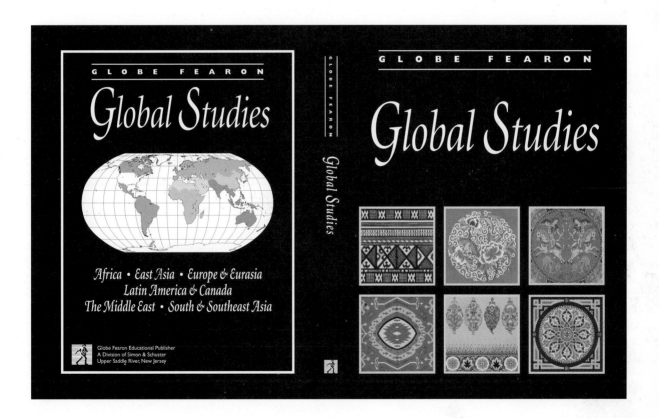

ABOUT THE COVER: The designs on the front cover are common motifs of the cultures presented in *Global Studies*. From left to right, they are (top) Africa, East Asia, Europe and Eurasia, (bottom) Latin America, South & Southeast Asia, and the Middle East. As you read this book, you will learn more about the art of the world's cultures. The globe on the back cover highlights the regions presented in the units of the book.

CONTENTS

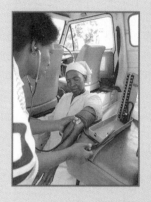

v

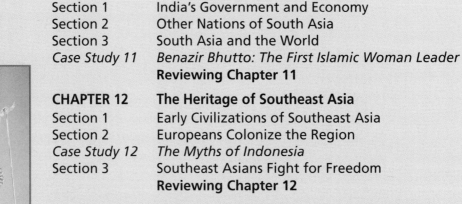

UNIT 3   FOCUS ON EAST ASIA   204

UNIT 6   FOCUS ON EUROPE AND EURASIA   498

MAPS

ATLAS

CHARTS, GRAPHS, AND TIME LINES

TO OUR READERS

WELCOME TO THE GLOBAL VILLAGE

Think globally; act locally. If you've seen this message on bumper stickers or television commercials, you may have wondered just what people mean when they use the word *global*. This word refers to the whole world—a world in which people cooperate with one another and think of themselves as members of a global village. In a global village, people around the world communicate, share experiences, and depend on one another.

Today, computers, fax machines, satellites, and jet aircraft are bringing people from all corners of the globe closer together. For example, students in Moscow, Russia, can now communicate with students in Boston, Massachusetts, through the Internet in a matter of minutes.

Because the world is getting smaller, the chance that you'll meet people from other cultures is increasing. Some of these people may share your views and values. Others may have customs and beliefs that are very different from your own. Understanding and respecting the values, customs, and views of people from different cultures makes it easier to interact with them.

INTRODUCING GLOBAL STUDIES

Global Studies is a book about the world's cultures. As you read this book, you will meet people from different regions of the world. You will learn about their values, customs, and beliefs. You will discover how their physical environment shapes their lives. You will explore the ways in which history, politics, and economics affect their experiences.

Global Studies contains six units. Each unit focuses on one of the following regions:

- Africa
- South and Southeast Asia
- East Asia
- Latin America and Canada
- The Middle East
- Europe and Eurasia

In each unit, there are chapters on culture, geography, history, politics, and economics. As you read and learn about each one, think about the connections between these important facets of life.

CULTURE: DEFINING OURSELVES

Culture is a way of life of a group of people. It includes the group's ideas, customs, skills, and arts. These areas define a culture and make it unique.

As you read about each culture, think about ways in which that culture is similar to and different from your own. This will help you remember that culture's unique features.

GEOGRAPHY: INTERACTING WITH OUR ENVIRONMENT

Geography is the study of the earth and the way in which people interact with the earth. In this book you will read about each region's physical features—its mountains, rivers, plains, and plateaus.

When you read about a region's physical features, think about how they affect people's lives. Consider how these physical features determine a culture's customs and ways of life. Consider, as well, the ways in which the physical features of your surroundings affect you and your community.

HISTORY: STUDYING THE PAST, PRESENT, AND FUTURE

Each unit in this book also presents the history of the region. When studying history, you might ask yourself these questions: "How am I connected to those in the past?" and "How has the world changed and how might it change in the future?" Learning the answers to these questions helps you to adapt to an ever-changing world.

POLITICS AND GOVERNMENT: PEOPLE RULING PEOPLE

The study of politics allows you to look at ways in which people are governed. Each unit of *Global Studies* examines the recent political history of major countries. This information will help you to recognize how political power is gained and used throughout the world.

As you read *Global Studies*, explore the connections between culture, history, and recent political events. Consider how U.S. culture and history affects politics and government in your community, state, and the country as a whole.

ECONOMICS: BALANCING RESOURCES AND HUMAN NEEDS

Economics is the study of the production, distribution, and consumption of goods and services. Economic needs often shape the politics of a region and force cultures to make difficult choices. As you read this book, think about the different economic systems countries use to balance their resources with the needs and desires of their people.

BECOMING A MEMBER OF THE GLOBAL VILLAGE

By studying other countries and cultures of the world, you become better able to see the connections between your life in the United States and the lives of people in far-off places. You learn to understand and respect the things that make each culture unique. You learn to recognize the common experiences that link all people. These discoveries will help you become an informed member of the global village.

We hope you enjoy reading about the cultures of the world. Everyone who put this book together worked hard to make it interesting as well as useful. The rest is up to you. We wish you well in your studies. Our success is in your accomplishment.

One aspect of culture is the way people relate to each other. Teenagers in the United States tend to relate to each other in casual ways. What does this tell us about their culture?

The World and Its Cultures

Why is it important to learn about the world's cultures?

Looking at Key Terms

- **culture** the way of life of a group of people, including their ideas, customs, skills, and arts
- **cultural diversity** having a variety of cultures
- **global village** a term that refers to the entire modern world where diverse people communicate, share experiences, and depend on one another for resources
- **extended family** the family unit in most traditional societies, consisting of three or four generations living in one household
- **nuclear family** the family unit in most developed societies, consisting often of a father, mother, and children
- **cultural diffusion** the spread of new ideas and new ways of doing things from one society to others
- **interdependent** the state of being dependent on one another for support or survival

On Assignment...

Formulating Questions: Asking good questions will help you determine the main ideas of subjects you study. As you read this chapter, write questions you would like answered about the regions of the world. Look for On Assignment hint boxes to help you formulate your questions. When you are finished reading the chapter, you will finalize your list of questions.

1

SECTION 1

Focus on Cultures

To what extent does culture determine who we are and how we behave?

- In the United States, people greet one another by shaking hands. In Thailand, people greet one another by bowing low, with their palms pressed together.

- People in some societies, such as the Muslims of Pakistan, do not eat pork. People in other societies, such as the Hindus of India, do not eat beef.

- In some places, such as the United States, people measure wealth by the size of their homes. In other places, such as Papua New Guinea, wealth is measured by the number of pigs a person owns.

A World of Many Cultures

All these differences are differences between **cultures**. Culture is the way of life of a group of people. You may think of culture as what people add to the natural world. All people have a culture.

The people who share a particular culture may or may not live in a single country. For example, people of the Jewish faith live in many countries of the world, including the United States, South Africa, Mexico, and Israel.

One country may contain more than one culture. The United States is a country with people from many different cultures. Therefore, we say that the United States is a country of **cultural diversity**.

The cultural diversity of the United States provides a good reason for us to learn about other parts of the world. By learning about different world cultures, we learn more about ourselves. We learn to appreciate the richness of our heritage.

The World as a Global Village You may have heard people say that the world is becoming a smaller place every day. What they mean is that it is becoming easier to communicate with people around the world. Recent advances in technology have made communication and transportation much easier. As an example, consider the journey of Ferdinand Magellan—the first person to sail completely around the world. In the 1500s, Magellan's journey took three years. Today, airplanes can circle the globe in less than 24 hours. During the American Revolution, it took months for letters from the leaders of the 13 colonies to reach leaders in England. Today, world leaders can communicate instantly by using the telephone, fax, or Internet.

All these changes have created a world that many people refer to as a **global village**. This term refers to the way in which diverse people from around the world communicate, share experiences, and depend on one another for resources.

What Is Culture? When some people think of culture, they think of a symphony orchestra or a dance festival. Culture embraces far more than the arts, however. For instance, if you put on jeans in the morning, listen to rock music, go to school five days a week, and watch football games on television on weekends, you are participating in U.S. culture. On the other hand, if you herd cattle, speak the Setswana language, play soccer, and wear tribal garments, you might be part of the Tswana culture in Botswana.

Culture examines how humans live on earth. It answers such questions as:

- What is family life like in a certain culture?

- How do the people of a certain culture make a living?

- What religions do the people of a certain culture practice?

- What sort of government do they have?
- How does their culture affect the way they interact with the land?

Learning a Culture Culture is learned. However, it is not learned the way you learn algebra or biology. You begin learning your culture the minute you are born. You learn to eat certain foods, wear certain clothes, and speak a certain language. You learn appropriate ways to behave. You learn certain beliefs and customs.

Beliefs and Customs Every culture has specific beliefs and customs. For example, in many Asian cultures, people believe that it is the sons' responsibility to care for their parents as they age. Therefore, families tend to be large. This increases the chance that there will be many sons. Generally, the beliefs and customs of a culture are deeply related to its religion.

Religion Most cultures have religions. Religion is a belief in a superhuman power or powers to be obeyed and worshipped as creators and rulers of the universe. A religion usually includes a set of beliefs and practices that govern behavior. Examples of religions around the world are Christianity, Islam, Judaism, Hinduism, and Buddhism.

Members of a religious group hold similar beliefs about how people should treat one another. They hold similar beliefs about how the world came into existence. Many religious groups believe that there is some kind of life after death.

Language A shared language is one of the most important elements of a culture. Without it, people in a culture would not be able to communicate.

All cultures have languages. These languages express thoughts, beliefs, feelings, and questions. Most people are born with the ability to learn to speak a language. However, the actual language they speak is determined by their culture.

Family Organization In most cultures, the family is the most important unit of life. The family teaches young people how they are expected to behave.

In many cultures, three or four generations of a family live together in a single home or compound. This type of family organization is known as the **extended family**.

In traditional farming societies, a large extended family is necessary to help the family meet its needs. The young and middle-aged men and women of the family farm the land, while older members often look after and teach the children. In other

The nuclear family, such as this one in Thailand, includes a wife, a husband, and their children. Nuclear families can be large or small, depending on the number of children.

In traditional societies, families or villages produce nearly all that they need to survive. In northern Nigeria, villagers trade or sell bowls they have made and goods they have grown.

societies, the extended family is a sign of the culture's respect for its elderly. Families are expected to live with and care for their older members.

In some cultures, the typical family includes a wife, husband, and their children. This organization is known as the **nuclear family**. The nuclear family is common in developed countries. Developed countries have economies based on industry and technology. Families in developed countries often do not need to be large to meet the needs of everyday living. However, a nuclear family is not necessarily small. A nuclear family can have many children.

Economies and Governments

All societies have economic and political systems. Economic systems determine what goods should be produced, how much should be produced, and what the goods are worth. Political systems are ways of organizing government.

Ways of Meeting Economic Needs In traditional societies, families or villages produce nearly all the goods they need to survive. The members of these societies hunt and farm for food. They make their own clothes and build their own homes. If they produce more than they need, they might trade what is left over for other goods.

In modern societies, individuals tend to specialize in the type of work they do. Because people do not make all that they need, they use money to buy and sell goods and services.

Whether a society is traditional or modern, it has to deal with the scarcity of resources. *Scarcity* means "not enough." In economics, it refers to the availability of natural resources, such as water, or resources made by humans, such as housing. Reasons for scarcity vary. For example, food can be scarce if a region has been hit by drought. Sometimes, one group in society gains power and purposely makes resources scarce for another group.

The economies of many modern societies are organized into free enterprise systems. People are able to start and run almost any business they choose. The governments of such countries make few decisions about what is produced and how much goods cost.

Some countries organize their economies in a way called central planning. Here, the government makes almost all of the decisions about what goods are produced and how much they will cost. Governments that use central planning usually own and operate most of the nation's industries.

Most nations today, including the United States, have mixed economies. In a mixed economy, private ownership of business is combined with government control. A mixed economy allows the government to make laws to control the economy and protect the public. Most businesses are owned by individuals and will succeed or fail based on their ability to make a profit.

Government When people live together, they need rules and laws for solving problems. Governments serve this purpose. Governments are made up of people who have the power to create and enforce the rules and laws of society.

There are various ways to organize a government. Below, you will read about three types of governments: democracies, monarchies, and dictatorships.

In a democracy, citizens have the right to participate in government. In many democracies, citizens vote for people to represent them in government. This is the way democracy works in the United States. The main feature of a democracy is that people have the power to shape their government through voting or other means.

In a monarchy, a king or queen heads the government and holds absolute power. Heredity determines who holds the crown. Today, a number of countries have constitutional monarchies. In a constitutional monarchy, the king or queen holds little real power. A body of elected officials, such as a parliament, makes the laws. Britain has such a government.

In a dictatorship, a leader or a group holds power by force. People who express their opposition to the government are usually punished harshly. The country of Iraq is a dictatorship ruled by Saddam Hussein.

Cultures Change Cultures are always changing, although some cultures change faster than others. U.S. culture has changed rapidly in recent years. Other cultures have had few changes in hundreds of years. For example, among the San people of Africa's Kalahari Desert, ways of life have changed little. The San still use simple tools in gathering wild plants and hunting animals.

Cultures borrow items or ideas from other cultures. Blue jeans are an example of this borrowing. Jeans were originally developed in San Francisco in the mid-1800s. These sturdy pants originally were made for gold miners. Less than 100 years later, people all over the globe wear jeans for comfort and for fashion.

Cultural Diffusion The spread of new ideas and new ways of doing things from one society to others is called **cultural diffusion**. The popularity of reggae music is an example of cultural diffusion. Reggae music began in Jamaica. In the 1970s, Bob Marley and other musicians played reggae to audiences in the United States and Europe. The popularity of reggae spread and influenced the rock music of the 1980s, especially in Britain.

A Global System

The world relies on a global economic system. Valuable resources such as oil and iron are not spread evenly. One place might be rich in many resources. Another might be rich in only one. Therefore, the people of the world must trade with one another to meet their needs.

People rely on one another for more than just goods and services. As you read earlier, the world is sometimes called a global village. It can also be said that the people of the world are **interdependent**. *Interdependent* means "people depend on one another." An event on one side of the globe can affect lives on the other side.

With interdependence comes responsibility. Today, conflict between faraway cultures can affect our lives. By understanding other cultures, we can make the differences that separate us count less and the similarities that connect us count more. By cooperating with one another, we can keep our world at peace and in balance.

Section 1 Review

1. What is culture?
2. **Inferring** The United States is often called a multicultural society. The prefix *multi-* means "many." What do you think multicultural means? Why do you think the United States is called a multicultural society?

SECTION 2

Focus on Places

How does a knowledge of geography help in understanding world cultures?

Geography, especially cultural geography, is an important part of global studies. Understanding where people live helps to create an understanding of who they are and why their culture developed as it did.

Two questions geographers ask are:
• Where do people live?
• Why do they live there?

To answer these questions, geographers look at five basic themes—location, place, interaction, movement, and regions.

Location

To study a place, geographers begin by finding out where it is located. A place's location is its position on the earth's surface. Location can be expressed in two ways: absolute location and relative location.

Absolute location is an exact, precise place on the earth. You give an absolute location when you use longitude and latitude. For example, New York City's absolute location is 41° North, 74° West.

Relative location is where a place is in relation to other places. You give a relative location when you say you live 12 miles (19 km) southeast of Columbus, Ohio.

Place

All places on the earth have distinct features that make them unique. Geographers use natural features and cultural features to describe places.

Natural Features When you visit a place, you might notice the sandy beaches, the warm weather, and the tall palm trees. These are natural, or physical, features. Another way to think of natural features is to think of them as the environment.

Take a special look at the environment of places you study because the environment affects how people live. You can identify environment if you look at climate, land, and water.

Climate includes all the elements that make up the weather over a period of time—especially precipitation, temperature, and wind. Climate influences the kinds of crops that grow in a certain region and the type of homes and buildings people make there. It determines the clothing people wear and the types of work people can do.

Land includes the soil, vegetation, mountains, and mineral resources of a region. Land affects crops, animal life, and the work people do.

Water is the third essential part of the environment. Water includes rivers, lakes, and oceans. Water is a vital part of all people's lives. Without it there can be no farming or irrigation. Water can aid transportation and it powers electrical generators.

Cultural Features When you visit a city or country, you might talk about it by describing its delicious food or by describing graceful old buildings that stand by a river. These are cultural features.

Cultural features are the part of the landscape that people add. When you know something about the natural and cultural features of a place, you know what makes it different from other places on earth.

Interaction

The theme of interaction helps geographers understand the relationship between people and their environment.

Every place on earth has advantages and disadvantages for the people who live there. Usually places with many advantages contain large populations. These places are often near water and are flat enough for easy farming. Other advantages might include an

People of all cultures are affected by the environment in which they live. These nomads of southern Jordan have found ways to adapt to the vast desert that is their home.

On Assignment. . .

What would you like to know about the relationship of people and the environment throughout the world? Think of questions you would like to ask.

abundance of natural resources that can build an economy.

Fewer people live where it proves more difficult to survive. But people are problem solvers and find ways to interact with their environment. Humans have learned to build aqueducts to bring water to dry areas. They have also carved terraces into mountains so that they can farm the land.

Movement

Geographers use the theme of movement to find out how people, ideas, and products move from place to place.

Many places are made up of people who have moved there from other places. Movement explains why many Vietnamese people live in Texas and California. Some people move because they want to live somewhere with better job opportunities or because they want to escape from a bad situation.

Movement explains the worldwide popularity of blue jeans. Products move when people want something that they do not have. Movement also shows how the religion of Islam spread from the Arabian Peninsula to Africa, Asia, and the United States. Goods and ideas move when people move.

The theme of movement helps you to understand how and why people from one place in the world interact with people from many other areas.

Region

The basic unit of geographic study is the region. A region is a part of the world that has natural or cultural features distinct from other regions. The study of regions helps you compare areas of the world. It helps you to see the earth as a system of places that are related in different ways.

You are probably most familiar with political regions. A nation, state, or city is a political region. Regions can be defined by other natural or cultural features. For example, Florida is part of a plains region, a tourist region, and a tropical climate region.

Section 2 Review

1. What are the five themes of geography? How do they help organize the study of geography?
2. **Analyzing** Why is an understanding of geography important in global studies?

SECTION 3

Focus on Change

What changes affect the world's environment?

Geographers and scientists are often called upon to guess the changes that may occur in a region. Predicting these changes helps people plan for the future, avoid catastrophes, and make wise use of resources. One thing geographers and scientists cannot do is stop change from happening.

Some changes result from new inventions and new ways of doing things. For example, fertilizers, pesticides, and farm machines have changed how food is grown. Jets and bullet trains have sped up transportation. Computers have changed how people work and communicate.

Change can be both good and bad. Chemical fertilizers and insecticides improve crop yield but may damage the environments in which birds and fish live. Jets greatly decrease travel time but cause air pollution

and noise pollution. Computers and computer-controlled robots make work more efficient but may cause people to lose jobs.

Making Choices

As the world changes, individuals face choices about whether they should support or oppose these changes. They must decide whether to move to cities, use computers, and spray crops with insecticides. You, too, face choices about change. If there are homeless people in your community, you may urge your local government to provide housing for them. If there is air pollution where you live, you may choose to use public transportation instead of traveling by car.

Studying how people of other cultures have changed in both good and bad ways will help you make your own decisions. Learning about other cultures and regions will help you learn about yourself, your own community, and your own culture. You will also discover new things about your relationship to the rest of the world. All of these things are important in preparing you for your role in the global village of the future.

Section 3 Review

1. What are some changes that have had good and bad results?
2. **Predicting** What choices do you think you will make about your community's environment in the future?

On Assignment. . .

Formulating Questions: Change is a part of life in our times. As you know, change can be both good and bad. Jot down three questions you have about how the cultures of the world are changing. Then make a list of questions you have about how your community is changing. You might want to ask community leaders what new problems and opportunities face your community.

I. Reviewing Vocabulary

Match each word on the left with the correct definition on the right.

1. culture
2. extended family
3. nuclear family
4. cultural diffusion
5. interdependent

a. the spread of new ideas and ways of doing things from one society to others
b. a family unit consisting often of parents and children
c. being dependent on one another for support or survival
d. the way of life of a group of people
e. a family unit consisting of three or four generations living in one household

II. Understanding the Chapter

Answer the questions below on a separate piece of paper.

1. What do people mean when they describe the world as a "global village"?
2. Describe how a person learns his or her culture.
3. What is scarcity of resources and why does it exist?
4. Give one example of the geographic theme of movement.

III. Building Skills: Identifying Central Issues

Review pages 6 and 7 of this Introduction. Then answer the question below on a separate sheet of paper.

What is the difference between the geographic themes of location and place? Give one example of each.

IV. Working Together

Form a small group. Predict one way that technology may change your life. First, choose a type of technology, such as computers, satellites, or high-speed aircraft. Go to the library to research information about advances in the technology your group has chosen. Then write a brief report that describes the important ways this technology may affect your lives. Read your report to the class.

On Assignment...

Formulating Questions: Keep a journal of questions you wrote as you read this Introduction. When you find facts and examples in this book that answer your questions, write the answers in your journal. If more questions occur to you as you progress through this book, add them to your list.

FOCUS ON

Africa

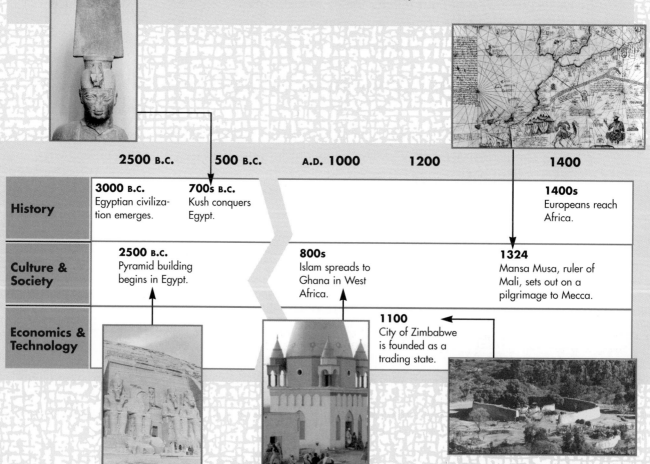

	2500 B.C.	500 B.C.	A.D. 1000	1200	1400
History	**3000 B.C.** Egyptian civilization emerges.	**700s B.C.** Kush conquers Egypt.			**1400s** Europeans reach Africa.
Culture & Society	**2500 B.C.** Pyramid building begins in Egypt.		**800s** Islam spreads to Ghana in West Africa.		**1324** Mansa Musa, ruler of Mali, sets out on a pilgrimage to Mecca.
Economics & Technology				**1100** City of Zimbabwe is founded as a trading state.	

PREVIEWING THE UNIT

Study the time line. On a separate sheet of paper answer the questions below.

1. When did Egyptian civilization emerge?

2. About how many years after Islam reached West Africa did Mansa Musa go on his pilgrimage?

3. How long did the Atlantic slave trade last?

4. How many years after the establishment of apartheid was Nelson Mandela elected president of South Africa?

5. How many years after the Portuguese set up trading posts did Europeans begin to colonize Africa?

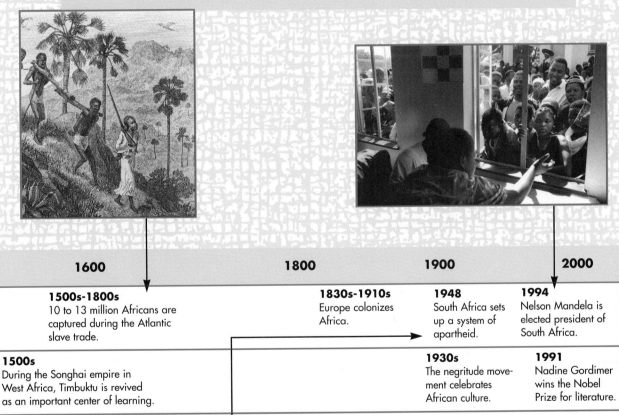

1600   **1800**   **1900**   **2000**

1500s-1800s
10 to 13 million Africans are captured during the Atlantic slave trade.

1830s-1910s
Europe colonizes Africa.

1948
South Africa sets up a system of apartheid.

1994
Nelson Mandela is elected president of South Africa.

1500s
During the Songhai empire in West Africa, Timbuktu is revived as an important center of learning.

1930s
The negritude movement celebrates African culture.

1991
Nadine Gordimer wins the Nobel Prize for literature.

1500s
The Portuguese set up trading posts along the African coast.

1869
The Suez Canal is built in Egypt.

Population in Africa
Reading Population Pyramids

Africa's population is growing at a rapid rate. Africa also has a young population. A population pyramid shows the age of a country's population. Below are population pyramids for Kenya, Nigeria, and the United States. Study the pyramids. On a separate sheet of paper, answer the questions below.

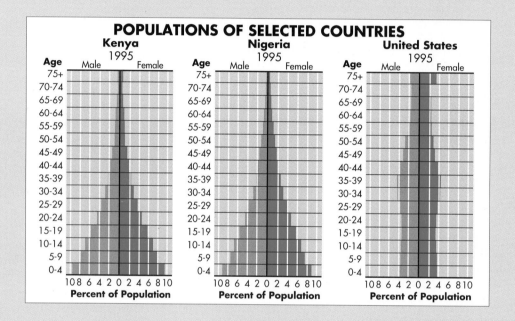

POPULATIONS OF SELECTED COUNTRIES

Kenya 1995 · Nigeria 1995 · United States 1995

Age groups: 75+, 70-74, 65-69, 60-64, 55-59, 50-54, 45-49, 40-44, 35-39, 30-34, 25-29, 20-24, 15-19, 10-14, 5-9, 0-4

Male | Female

10 8 6 4 2 0 2 4 6 8 10
Percent of Population

Did You Know

- Africa is the third most populated and the fastest growing region in the world. (See Chapter 1.)

- Young Africans are streaming into the cities in record numbers. (See Chapter 5.)

- Rapid population growth in Africa is a problem for countries plagued with high unemployment and crowded cities. (See Chapter 6.)

1. **Reading the Pyramids** (a) What do the numbers on the left and bottom of the pyramids represent? (b) What does the shading inside the pyramids show?

2. **Thinking About the Pyramids** (a) What do the populations of Kenya and Nigeria have in common? (b) How is the population of the United States different from the populations of Kenya and Nigeria?

3. **Going Beyond the Pyramids: Making Inferences** Think about your answer to 2b, above. How do you think having a large population of young people affects education in Kenya and Nigeria?

CHAPTER 1

The Land and People of Africa

What is unique about the land and people of Africa?

In Africa, traditional and modern ways often blend. In this photograph, men in the ancient country of Mali conduct business in traditional garb.

Looking at Key Terms

- **plateau** a large area of flat land that is higher than the surrounding land
- **fault** a crack in the earth's crust caused by movements in that crust
- **hydroelectric power** electricity created by water
- **delta** a broad area of soil deposits near the mouth of a river
- **savanna** a grassy plain with scattered trees and bushes
- **desertification** a process that turns a dry grassland into desert through overgrazing and lack of rain
- **landlocked** having no outlet to the sea
- **ethnic group** a group of people who have a common history, language, culture, and way of life

On Assignment...

Creating Posters: This chapter describes the land and peoples of Africa. Imagine that you are working for the United Nations to create an exhibit about Africa. An important part of the exhibit will be a poster display. Your assignment is to design two or three of those posters. They can be about the beauty and variety of Africa or about some of the problems found there. As you read this chapter, look for the On Assignment boxes. These boxes contain ideas for your posters.

The Continent of Africa

What geographic features influence life in Africa?

Africa has a fairly smooth coastline with few bays, gulfs, or peninsulas. As a result, Africa does not have many good harbors.

AFRICA'S PHYSICAL FEATURES

15°W · 0° · 15°E · EUROPE · 30°E · 45°E

Strait of Gibraltar

ATLAS MOUNTAINS

Mediterranean Sea

ASIA

30°N

S A H A R A

Tropic of Cancer

AL-JUF PLATEAU

L. Nasser

Nile R.

Red Sea

N
W · E
S

15°N

Niger R.

L. Chad

White Nile

Blue Nile

Mt. Cameroon

Gulf of Guinea

Zaire (Congo) R.

ZAIRE BASIN

RUWENZORI MOUNTAINS

GREAT RIFT VALLEY

Mt. Kenya

L. Victoria

Mt. Kilimanjaro

0° Equator

ATLANTIC OCEAN

L. Tanganyika

INDIAN OCEAN

15°S

KATANGA PLATEAU

L. Malawi (L. Nyasa)

Zambezi R.

Madagascar

Tropic of Capricorn

KALAHARI DESERT

NAMIB DESERT

30°S

DRAKESBERG MTS.

0 · 500 · 1,000 Miles
0 · 500 · 1,000 Kilometers

Africa straddles the equator. About half the continent lies to the north of the equator and about half lies to the south. Thus the seasons are reversed in the two parts of Africa. When it is winter in North Africa, it is summer in Southern Africa.

The oldest human bones ever discovered were found in Olduvai Gorge in Kenya. These findings and others in Southern Africa give Africa its title as "the birthplace of humankind."

Forty years ago, countries such as Tanzania, Zimbabwe, Zambia, and Namibia did not exist as independent countries. Today, they are mentioned almost daily in newspapers. There are more than 50 independent countries in Africa. This is more than on any other continent. About 680 million people call Africa their home.

Africa's geography is really divided into two regions. Between the two regions is the vast desert of the Sahara, which stretches eastward from the Atlantic Ocean to the Red Sea. North of the Sahara, the people are mainly Arabs with a way of life much like that of Middle Eastern peoples. South of the Sahara, there is a great variety of peoples and cultures.

Mount Kilimanjaro (kil•uh•muhn•JAHR•oh) is Africa's highest mountain. This snowcapped mountain, which is near the equator, is one of Africa's most dramatic and beautiful sights. Kilimanjaro is a volcano that rises sharply from the plains below. Its lower slopes are fertile farmland. At a higher level, a dense tropical rain forest begins. A great variety of wildlife calls Kilimanjaro's rain forest home. Above the rain forest is a mountain meadow. Higher still, the climate gets colder and vegetation disappears. Kilimanjaro's peak is always covered with snow.

The Zaire (zah•EER) River is not as long or well known as the Nile River in Egypt. However, it carries more water than the Nile and more than any river in Africa. The Zaire River, which was known as the Congo River, is fed by seven large rivers and many smaller streams. It begins in Central Africa, flowing north and west in a huge arc before reaching the Atlantic Ocean.

The Land

Think of a giant table that is tilted and you'll get a rough idea of what the land of Africa looks like. The lower edge of the table lies in the west. To the east, the land gradually becomes higher. Most of Africa lies on this "table," which is actually a series of **plateaus**. A plateau is a large area of flat land that is higher than the surrounding land.

In the east and south, Africa's highest plateaus rise more than a mile (1.6 km) high. In the west, the plateaus range from 1,000 to 3,000 feet (305 to 915 m) above sea level.

In most places, Africa's plateaus reach almost to the sea. This means that most of Africa's coastal plains are very narrow. Often they are less than 20 miles (32 km) wide. Only in a few places are they more than 100 miles (161 km) wide.

Africa's Mountains   The highest mountains in Africa are on the eastern coast. This range contains Africa's two tallest peaks. Mount Kilimanjaro is more than 19,000 feet (5,795 m) above sea level. Mount Kenya reaches an altitude of more than 17,000 feet (5,185 m). Although both are located almost on the equator, they are so high that ice and snow blanket their peaks year round.

The Atlas Mountains in the far north of Africa run for 1,500 miles (2,535 km) through Morocco, Algeria, and Tunisia. The Atlas Mountains are actually part of a giant range that continues under the Mediterranean Sea and includes the Alps in Europe.

The Great Rift Valley   Powerful natural forces have pushed and pulled at the African continent. These forces have created a long rift, or trench. Called the Great Rift Valley, this spectacular series of deep valleys stretches from north to south through most of eastern Africa. It begins in Asia, then runs through East Africa into Southern Africa for 4,000 miles (6,440 km). That is almost one sixth of the earth's diameter.

The Great Rift Valley was formed millions of years ago when movements in the earth's crust produced a **fault**, or crack in the earth's crust. The Great Rift Valley is so deep that more than 30 Grand Canyons would fit inside it!

The Lakes of Africa   Some huge lakes have formed in the Great Rift Valley. Snow from the mountains provides some of the water for the lakes. Several of Africa's largest lakes are near the southern end of the Great Rift Valley. The largest, Lake Victoria, is about the size of Lake Superior, the largest of the Great Lakes in North America.

The Rivers of Africa   Rivers have always been important to humans. Their waters irrigate farmland, provide fish for

The Great Rift Valley cuts through East Africa from north to south. The Rift Valley contains some of Africa's richest farmland. This portion of the valley is located in Kenya.

food, and act as highways for transport. In modern times, humans have used flowing river water to produce electric power.

Africa's largest rivers begin in the rainy plateaus of the interior. On these plateaus, the rivers are broad and deep in many places. Before they reach the sea, the rivers often descend in roaring rapids and falls. In addition, sandbars often form where the rivers flow into the sea.

Africa's best known river is the Nile. At 4,100 miles (6,600 km) long, it is the longest river in the world. The Nile begins as two rivers, the White Nile and the Blue Nile. The White Nile begins in the mountains of Ethiopia, while the Blue Nile begins in the highlands of Uganda. The two branches of the river meet in Sudan. The Nile then flows northward into Egypt, finally emptying into the Mediterranean Sea.

Until the 1970s, the Nile flowed freely to the sea. Each year it overflowed its banks, bringing with it soil and minerals from the mountains of Africa. This provided farmers with natural fertilizers to enrich the soil.

The flooding ended when Egypt built the Aswan Dam. The dam controls the flow of the Nile. It has created a huge lake that provides water for farmers year round. It also produces **hydroelectric power**. Hydroelectric power is electric power that is created by flowing water.

The Zaire River is the main river in Central Africa. The Niger is West Africa's most important river. Like the Zaire River, the Niger carries more water than the Nile. It forms a large **delta** where it reaches the sea. A delta is a broad area of soil deposits near the mouth of a river. The Niger delta is the largest delta in Africa.

Traveling in Africa

Lakes and rivers allow travel within the African interior. But travel from the coast to the interior is more difficult for a few reasons. Africa's rivers form rapids that plunge down from the plateau to the coast. Boats must stop at the rapids. Furthermore, the

On Assignment...

Use words and pictures to describe the geography of Africa in one or two of your posters. You might highlight the plateaus of Africa, the Great Rift Valley, the rivers of Africa, or the mountains near the equator.

mouths of many African rivers are difficult to navigate because of the deltas and sandbars.

In addition, it is very difficult to reach Central Africa by crossing the Sahara from the north. Water is scarce in the desert and the heat is intense.

Travel is also difficult because much of the African coastline is smooth and straight. There are few harbors where boats can stop. All these barriers have created great difficulties in travel and communication in Africa.

The Regions of Africa

Africa is the world's second largest continent. Only Asia is larger. Africa is more than three times the size of the United States. Geographers divide this vast land into five main regions. They are North Africa, West Africa, East Africa, Central Africa, and Southern Africa.

North Africa North Africa consists of five countries that border on the Mediterranean Sea and include a large part of the Sahara. From east to west they are Egypt, Libya, Tunisia, Algeria, and Morocco. Several groups claim control of a sixth territory, called Western Sahara.

The Sahara, the largest desert in the world, is the most important geographic feature of North Africa. However, few people live in the Sahara. Most of the people in North Africa live along the Mediterranean coast. This is the only part of North Africa where rain falls regularly.

Even though almost no rain falls in the valley of the Nile River, it has the most dependable water supply in North Africa. An ancient historian called Egypt the "gift of the Nile." He meant that without the Nile River, all of Egypt would be a desert.

West Africa West Africa consists of 16 countries and more than 200 million people. That is about half of Africa's population south of the Sahara. The giant of the region is Nigeria. With more than 110 million people, it has the largest population of any country in Africa. No other country in West Africa has more than 15 million people.

A belt of rain forest hugs the coastline of West Africa. The rain forest is fed by the showers that fall almost every day of the year. Some of this rain forest has been cut down as the population has grown.

Inland, a wide belt of grassland, or **savanna**, crosses West Africa. A savanna is a grassy plain with scattered trees and bushes. North of the savanna is a semi-desert belt called the Sahel (suh•HEL). In recent years, lack of rain and overgrazing have caused the Sahel to expand southward across the savanna. Scientists call this process **desertification**.

East Africa East Africa stretches from Sudan and Eritrea (eh•ruh•TREE•uh) on the Red Sea to Tanzania on the Indian Ocean. It includes four island nations. One of these is the large island of Madagascar.

The Serengeti (seh•ren•GET•ee) Plain in Tanzania is the largest game reserve in the world. During the migration season, zebras and other animals thunder across the plain in seemingly endless herds. Sudan, East Africa's largest country, is also the largest country in Africa.

Central Africa The countries of Central Africa vary greatly in size and population. Zaire is Africa's second largest country. It is about one fourth as large as the United States. The group of islands that make up the country of São Tomé and Príncipe (sow TOO•may and PRIN•ceh•pay) could fit comfortably within the U.S. city of Indianapolis.

Most of Central Africa is covered by tropi-

The African continent contains a great variety of wildlife. The Serengeti Plain in Tanzania supports elephants, baboons, zebras, giraffes, lions, and gnus.

cal forests or savanna. Africa's largest rain forest is located around the waters that make up the Zaire River system. Heavy rains wash away many nutrients in the tropical rain forests. This means that the rain forests do not have good farmland. Despite this, the rain forests face destruction. Logging companies that seek valuable woods have increased their harvesting. Large cocoa, rubber, and palm oil plantations have been set up in the rain forest.

Southern Africa Southern Africa covers about 20 percent of the African continent. The two largest countries in the region are South Africa and Angola. Each is only slightly smaller than the state of Texas.

Of the ten countries in the region, six are **landlocked**. This means that they have no outlet to the sea. For access to the sea, they depend on railroads and ports in countries such as Mozambique and South Africa. Because of this, events in one country significantly affect neighboring countries.

Most of Southern Africa is covered by savannas and grasslands. Although the eastern coast receives adequate rain, much of the rest of the region is very dry. The Namib desert is among the driest places on earth. Just to the east is the Kalahari (kahl•uh•HAH•ree) desert, where only scrubby vegetation grows.

Southern Africa has some of the most beautiful scenery in the world. Victoria Falls in northwest Zimbabwe (zim•BAHB•way) is the world's tenth largest waterfall—and one of the most spectacular.

Climate

The equator runs through the middle of Africa. As you probably know, temperatures near the equator tend to be warm. However, it is always cooler in the highlands than at sea level. Therefore, parts of tropical Africa are cooler than you might expect because they lie at high elevations.

Tropical Rain Forest Climate Within the rain forests, it is always hot and rainy. The treetops are so thick that they form an "umbrella" that blocks sunlight from reaching the forest floor.

Tropical Wet-and-Dry Climate The single largest climate zone in Africa is found in the savannas. Here, it is warm all year long. Rain falls during the rainy season of summer. It is dry during the winter dry season.

Some parts of the savanna have many trees. Others are almost treeless. The savanna is home to most of Africa's large animals. Elephants, giraffes, zebras, and antelope all roam the savanna. They gather at water holes throughout the region.

Desert Climate North and south of the savannas are deserts. In the deserts, days are extremely hot. However, nights can be extremely chilly. That is because there are no clouds to keep the day's heat from escaping. While the Sahara receives almost no rain,

The mist and noise of the crashing waters gave Victoria Falls its original name. Africans who lived near the falls called it Mosi-oa-Tunya (MOH•see wa TOON•yuh), which means "smoke that thunders."

parts of the Kalahari may receive as much as ten inches (25 cm) a year.

Mediterranean Climate A few areas along Africa's northern and southern coasts have what is called a Mediterranean climate. Mediterranean winters are cool and rainy and summers are warm and dry. Dense shrubs, some grasses, and scattered trees all grow in this pleasant climate.

Section 1 Review

1. Why is it difficult to travel from the coast to the interior of Africa?

2. **Comparing and Contrasting** How is the climate in the Sahara different from the climate of the rain forest?

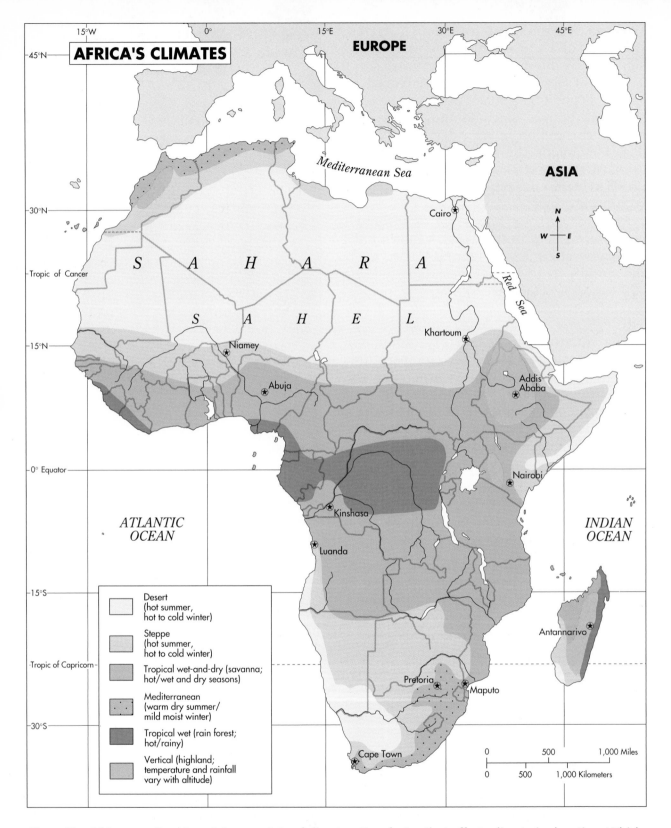

AFRICA'S CLIMATES

EUROPE

ASIA

Mediterranean Sea

Cairo

Red Sea

S A H A R A

Tropic of Cancer

S A H E L

Niamey

Khartoum

Abuja

Addis Ababa

ATLANTIC OCEAN

0° Equator

Nairobi

Kinshasa

Luanda

INDIAN OCEAN

Antannarivo

Tropic of Capricorn

Pretoria

Maputo

Cape Town

Legend:
- Desert (hot summer, hot to cold winter)
- Steppe (hot summer, hot to cold winter)
- Tropical wet-and-dry (savanna; hot/wet and dry seasons)
- Mediterranean (warm dry summer/mild moist winter)
- Tropical wet (rain forest; hot/rainy)
- Vertical (highland; temperature and rainfall vary with altitude)

0   500   1,000 Miles
0   500   1,000 Kilometers

Place The African continent contains a variety of climates. One factor that affects climate is elevation. Which parts of Africa have a vertical climate? What is the climate of Cairo?

SECTION 2

The People of Africa

What ethnic groups live in Africa?

It is morning on the continent of Africa, and people are beginning the day. On a high plateau in East Africa, herders round up their cattle and drive them out to graze in the open grassland beyond their village. In a coastal town along the Indian Ocean, a shopkeeper prepares for the day. Facing north, he kneels on a small mat and chants his morning prayers to Allah. *Allah* is the Islamic word for God.

In Johannesburg (joh•HAHN•ihs•burg) in South Africa, a young computer expert guides her car through the busy morning traffic. She works for one of Africa's largest commercial banks.

Along the Zaire River, fishers cast delicately woven nets into the water. As they begin the day's fishing, they call on the spirits of the river to bring many fish.

In southwestern Nigeria, women walk to the fields outside their town. They are going to begin the harvest of millet, their most important crop. Meanwhile, in a city not far away, the son of one of these women prepares for an examination. A student at the university there, he hopes someday to be an engineer.

These are some of the people of Africa, who are of many cultures and who practice many different traditions. In this chapter, you will learn about where and how Africa's people live. You will also learn about some of their similarities and differences.

Africa's Diversity

Africa is the third most populated—and the fastest-growing—region in the world. It is a region of great diversity, or variety. Because of climate and geographic conditions, Africa's population is not distributed evenly across the continent. Large areas of Africa's deserts and rain forests have almost no people. Most Africans live in highlands, along river banks and lakes, and along the coasts. About three in ten Africans live in large towns and cities.

Africa has more than 2,000 different **ethnic groups**. An ethnic group is a group of people who have a common history, language, culture, and way of life.

Each ethnic group has its own cultural characteristics, customs, and traditions. The way that African people live can be very different from group to group. This is especially true for those who live in traditional rural communities.

Most of the people of North Africa are Arabs, people who speak the Arabic language. The Berbers (BEHR•bers) are another major ethnic group in North Africa. Like the Arabs, most Berbers are Muslims. They live in settled or nomadic groups from Morocco to Egypt.

About 570 million of Africa's 680 million people live in the region south of the Sahara. Most countries south of the Sahara have several ethnic groups living within their borders. In Nigeria, for example, there are more than 250 ethnic groups. Having so many people with different languages and customs in one country has often led to ethnic conflict. For example, between 1967 and 1970, the Ibo people fought unsuccessfully to leave Nigeria and set up their own country.

People of one ethnic group may be found in more than one nation. For example, the Somali (soh•MAH•lee) people live not only in Somalia, but also in neighboring countries. This came about because the European powers controlled parts of Africa and set boundaries as they pleased. Many of these boundaries cut across the lands traditionally held by ethnic groups. The borders of many present-day African nations are based on these colonial patterns.

Besides black African groups and Arabs, small numbers of Asians, white Africans, and people of mixed heritage live in Africa, primarily in the Republic of South Africa.

More than 80 percent of the people of Mozambique work as farmers. Many grow food mainly for their own use. Others grow cash crops, including cassava, corn, wheat, peanuts, potatoes, and beans. Only 4 percent of the land in Mozambique is used for farming. The government of Mozambique is introducing programs to increase the amount of farmland and to help farmers practice efficient farming methods.

About 278 million Africans—including most of the people of North Africa—are Muslims. Muslims are followers of the Islamic religion, which is the official religion in the countries of North Africa. It is also a major religion in several countries in both West and East Africa. Islam came to Africa when Arab armies conquered North Africa in the 600s and 700s. Muslims founded important cities in northern Africa. Islam's influence spread to sub-Saharan Africa through trade and commerce. In early African empires, non-Muslim rulers used Muslims as officials and advisers. Today Islamic houses of worship, called mosques, are common in several parts of Africa.

Nairobi, in Kenya, is one of East Africa's important cities. Cities in Africa have grown rapidly in recent decades. Africa's cities are a mixture of old and new. The newer parts of the cities have modern skyscrapers, supermarkets, movie theaters, and large shops. In older neighborhoods, open air markets and houses line crowded streets.

There are about 300 million Christians in Africa. Christianity dates back to the first century in Africa, when people in Egypt accepted the new religion. Today's Coptic Christians in Egypt are descendants of people who did not convert to Islam after the Arab conquest. There are large Christian communities in most sub-Saharan nations, such as Nigeria. Ethiopia also has a large Coptic community that dates back many centuries.

The Languages of Africa

There are about 1,000 different languages spoken in Africa. These languages fall into five major categories: Semitic, Afro-Asiatic, Niger-Congo, Nilo-Saharan, and Khoisan (KOI•sahn) languages.

Semitic and Afro-Asiatic languages are spoken in North Africa and in parts of East Africa. Arabic is a Semitic language. About 100 million Africans speak Arabic. Berber is an Afro-Asiatic language.

Niger-Congo is by far the largest language group in Africa. It includes many languages spoken in West Africa. It also includes the large Bantu group. About 300 different Bantu languages are spoken in parts of East Africa and throughout Central and Southern Africa.

One of the Bantu languages that is best known outside Africa is Swahili (swah•HEE•lee). Swahili has been heavily influenced by Arabic. It is a major language in Eastern Africa and Southern Africa, and is spoken by about 100 million people. Swahili is one official language of Kenya and Tanzania.

Nilo-Saharan languages are spoken in parts of East and West Africa. The Maasai people of Kenya speak a Nilo-Saharan language.

The Khoisan languages are also called "click" languages. This is because their words include clicking sounds. Khoisan languages are spoken mainly in Southern Africa. The San of the Kalahari speak a click language.

Other languages widely spoken in Africa are those of the former European colonial powers. The most widely spoken European languages are French and English. French is the official language of African countries such as Chad and Mali. Both were once French colonies. Along with Swahili, English is the official language of Kenya and Tanzania. English is the only official language of Nigeria. Kenya, Tanzania, and Nigeria all are former British colonies. Angola was once a colony of Portugal. Today Portuguese is the official language of that country.

Traditional Religions of Africa

About half the African people south of the Sahara practice traditional African religions. There are many different forms of traditional religions in Africa. Most religious groups believe that God gave to all living and nonliving things a life force, or spirit, that cannot die. In addition, they believe that everything, living and nonliving, is connected to every other living thing.

African traditional religions are systems of belief that give their followers a moral philosophy. They teach what is right and what is wrong. They teach how to live a good life and how to avoid anything that is evil or harmful. Most traditional religions include reverence for ancestors. They believe that spirits of ancestors can be called on to ask God to help the living. In some African religions, the spirits associated with nature, such as thunder, water, soil, and crops, are believed to be always present and are part of everyday life. You will read more about traditional religions in Chapter 3.

Section 2 Review

1. Why do members of a single African ethnic group often live in several neighboring countries?

2. **Identifying Relationships** What is the relationship between Nigeria's history and the fact that English is spoken there today?

Disease in Equatorial Africa

The environment of Africa affects its population and economy. Nowhere is this more true than in equatorial Africa, the part of Africa that is nearest to the equator. Equatorial Africa's hot and wet climate attracts animals that carry many serious diseases. These diseases have affected the way people live.

One of the most serious diseases in equatorial Africa is malaria. It is carried by mosquitoes that thrive in warm, moist climates. These mosquitoes pass on the disease by biting their victims. Malaria weakens adults and leaves them unable to work. Young children who get the disease often die. Those who survive carry the disease into adulthood.

Another dangerous disease, called sleeping sickness, affects both humans and animals. The disease is so named because people or animals who have it fall asleep just before they die. Sleeping sickness is spread by tsetse flies, which live in the savanna. Animals bitten by tsetse flies usually die after a few days. Human beings live longer. They may survive for weeks, but they steadily grow weaker and weaker.

These and other diseases have prevented economic development and slowed progress in equatorial Africa. Infected cattle cannot be used for food and milk. Infected horses and oxen cannot be used for transportation or plowing. This means that in large parts of Africa, people cannot keep cattle and horses. This makes it much harder for the people of equatorial Africa to feed themselves.

The nations of equatorial Africa have undertaken massive efforts to control and prevent these destructive diseases. International organizations such as the World Health Organization have offered aid. In recent years, the people of equatorial Africa have begun to hope that the deadly insect-borne diseases will someday be wiped out.

Case Study Review

1. What disease is spread by tsetse flies?
2. **Cause and Effect** How does disease make it more difficult for the nations of equatorial Africa to develop their economies?

I. Reviewing Vocabulary

Match each word on the left with the correct definition on the right.

1. fault
2. delta
3. savanna
4. plateau

a. a large area of flat land that is higher than the surrounding land
b. a grassy plain with scattered trees and shrubs
c. a crack in the earth's crust formed by movement of that crust
d. a broad area of soil deposits near the mouth of a river

II. Understanding the Chapter

Answer the questions below on a separate sheet of paper.

1. Why has Egypt been called the "gift of the Nile"?
2. How did the Great Rift Valley form?
3. Which parts of Africa are most heavily populated? Which parts are least heavily populated?
4. How have insects, like tsetse flies, affected life in equatorial Africa?

III. Building Skills: Reading a Map

Study the map on page 593 and answer the following questions.

1. Which African countries border on the Mediterranean Sea?
2. Through which African countries does the equator run?
3. Which African country lies farthest north? Which is farthest south? Farthest east? Farthest west?
4. Which large country in Central Africa has a very narrow outlet to the Atlantic Ocean?

IV. Working Together

With a small group, write a letter to students in an East African country. Tell them what you have learned about their country. Tell them how life here is similar to, and different from, life in their country. Display the letters on a classroom bulletin board.

On Assignment . . .

Creating Posters: Review the notes you took and the sketches you created as you read this chapter. Choose two or three of your sketches from which to create your posters. Add descriptive captions to your posters based on the notes you took.

Thousands of years ago, Egyptian kings, called pharaohs, built huge stone pyramids in which they were buried. Today, tourists visit these tombs to see the riches hidden inside.

CHAPTER 2

The Early History of Africa

What significant events shaped the history of Africa?

Looking at Key Terms

- **monument** something that is built to honor a person or event
- **rapids** a place where a river falls sharply and flows very quickly
- **mummy** a dead body treated with chemicals and wrapped so that it does not decay
- **scribe** a member of the class of people in ancient Egypt whose job was to write
- **devout** very religious
- **caravan** a group of travelers who band together for safety

On Assignment...

Creating a Storyboard: A storyboard is a plan of action in pictures. It is made up of a series of cartoons or sketches. Filmmakers use storyboards to plan the scenes of a movie. At several points in this chapter, there are hints to help you sketch storyboard panels about the early history of Africa. Each hint will deal with a different early civilization that developed in Africa. When you have finished reading this chapter, you will be asked to put your storyboard together.

Ancient Civilizations of Africa

What were the accomplishments of the ancient civilizations of Egypt, Kush, and Axum?

About ten miles (16 km) south of Cairo, Egypt's capital, is a dusty plateau. The plateau overlooks the western bank of the Nile River. A huge stone building towers over the plateau's hot sands. It is built in six layers, like a giant layer cake. Each layer is smaller than the one below it. This huge layer cake of stone is more than 200 feet (60 m) high. It is called the Step Pyramid.

The Step Pyramid was built more than 4,600 years ago. When it was finished, it was the largest building in the world. It was a mighty symbol of the power of the kings of ancient Egypt.

The pyramids built after the Step Pyramid were even more impressive. They had smooth sides from top to bottom. Many were much larger than the Step Pyramid. The pyramid of a king named Khufu is 481 feet (146 m) high. Its base is a square that measures 756 feet (230 m) on each side. This means that the pyramid is as high as a 48-story building and that each side is almost as long as two and a half football fields.

Khufu's pyramid is made of 2.3 million stone blocks. The average block weighs about two and a half tons.

The Egyptians who built the pyramids were among the greatest builders of the ancient world. They built the pyramids as burial places for their kings. Experts think that about 10,000 men worked to build a typical pyramid. Khufu's pyramid took 23 years to build.

The ancient Egyptians created one of the first civilizations in the world. Their pyramids, temples, and the other **monuments** still remind us of what they achieved thousands of years ago. A monument is something that is built to remember a person or event.

Early Egyptian Civilization

For many centuries before the pyramids were built, farming villages existed in the valley along the Nile River. By about 3200 B.C., the people living in the Nile valley had a system of writing. With their knowledge of mathematics, they could measure and weigh things accurately. Some people worked in crafts and other jobs. The Egyptians also had a well-developed religion and a highly organized form of government.

The land of ancient Egypt began at the Nile delta and stretched about 750 miles (1,200 km) southward to the first of several **rapids** along the Nile. Rapids are places where a river falls sharply and therefore flows very quickly. A series of cities governed by local rulers formed along the Nile.

Ancient Egypt was protected from invaders by deserts to its east and west. The Nile rapids protected Egypt from invaders from the south. The Mediterranean Sea protected the country in the north.

While the desert, rapids, and sea made it difficult to invade Egypt, they did not prevent trade and other contacts between Egypt and its neighbors.

In about 3100 B.C., a king named Menes (MEE•neez) conquered the Nile valley from the rapids to the delta. He unified Egypt for the first time.

Egyptian Religion

Religion was a very important part of ancient Egyptian civilization. Much of Egypt's government, art, medicine, literature, and science was connected to its religion. The Egyptian religion had many gods. Egyptians believed that the spirits of these gods lived in the sun, sky, and earth and in other things in nature.

The Egyptians also believed in an afterlife, or a life after a person dies. They believed that if a person lived a good life, his or her soul would find happiness in the afterlife.

The Egyptians spent a great deal of time and effort preparing for the afterlife. They learned how to make mummies to give the soul a resting place. A **mummy** is a dead body that is treated with chemicals and wrapped so that it does not decay. The mummies of kings and nobles were buried with rich treasures that they could use in the afterlife. They were buried in carefully built tombs to prevent grave robbers from stealing the treasures. The greatest tombs were the pyramids built for the kings.

A Strong Central Government

Like many other ancient peoples, the Egyptians believed that their king was a god. His name was rarely spoken aloud. Instead, the Egyptians called their king *pharaoh* (FAHR•oh). The word *pharaoh* means "great house" or "palace."

The pharaoh had absolute power. He made the laws and appointed officials to carry them out. He owned all the land in Egypt and everything on it. When people were brought to meet the pharaoh, they first threw themselves to the ground. They then crawled toward the king while praising his greatness.

Egypt's pharaohs tried to provide justice and order. At the same time, they expected absolute obedience from their subjects.

Social Structure

Egypt's society can be described as a pyramid. At the top of the pyramid was the pharaoh. Directly beneath the pharaoh were his family and other nobles. This tiny group enjoyed a life of luxury. They hunted animals, took boat trips on the Nile, and enjoyed fine foods. At their parties, musicians and dancers entertained them.

Most Egyptians were at the bottom of the social pyramid and lived much harder lives. These Egyptians were peasants who lived in mud houses in crowded and dirty villages.

During most of the year, they farmed the land. Peasants used simple wooden plows drawn by oxen. Much of the food they raised was used to pay taxes to the pharaoh.

Thousands of peasants also had to work for months at a time as the pharaoh ordered. They built Egypt's huge pyramids, palaces, and temples. Many of them suffered serious injuries or were killed moving heavy blocks of stone without machinery.

Egyptian Writing

One of Egypt's most important achievements was its system of writing. Egyptians believed that writing was invented by one of the gods. Only a tiny percentage of the population could read and write. That skill was reserved for a special class called **scribes**.

Young boys learned to become scribes in special schools. After a scribe graduated, he could enter government service. Talented scribes could become important officials. As one ancient text said, "The scribe orders the destinies of everyone."

After about 1100 B.C., Egypt's power gradually declined. Local rulers challenged the pharaoh's power. This weakened Egypt and left the country unable to defend itself against foreign powers. It fell under a series of foreign rulers. The Kushites, Assyrians, Babylonians, Persians, and Greeks in turn all conquered Egypt. In 30 B.C., Rome took control of Egypt.

The Kingdoms of Kush and Axum

While Egypt was becoming powerful, another African civilization was developing south of the Nile rapids. The kingdom of

On Assignment . . .

Based on the words and pictures in this chapter, pick a scene to sketch for your storyboard. You might want to sketch a scene about the building of pyramids, the lifestyles of Egypt's nobles and peasants, or the work of scribes.

The kingdom of Kush thrived from about 1000 B.C. to A.D. 350. The Kushites built pyramids, created gold jewelry, and made fine pottery and sculpture.

Kush was located in present-day Sudan. At first, the people of Kush, called Kushites, traded with Egypt and adopted many Egyptian ways. At times, Egyptian pharaohs sent armies to raid or conquer the region. But the people of Kush always won back their independence.

Trade and warfare spread Egyptian culture southward to Kush. The Kushites worshiped Egyptian gods, built Egyptian-style buildings and pyramids, and used the Egyptian form of writing.

In the 700s B.C., Kush conquered Egypt. Kushite kings ruled Egypt for almost 100 years. In the 600s B.C., conquerors from Asia called Assyrians drove the Kushites out of Egypt. The Kushites could not match the iron weapons of the Assyrians.

Soon the Kushites also learned how to make iron tools and weapons. They made use of iron deposits near their new capital city, Meroë (MEHR•uh•wee). The furnaces of Meroë began producing iron for weapons and tools. Meroë became the first African center of iron manufacturing. Trade may have spread this iron technology into West Africa.

With iron plows, the Kushites were able to produce ample amounts of food. With iron spears, they were able to protect their trade routes to the Red Sea. At trading posts on the Red Sea, they traded goods they had gathered from a wide region of Africa—ivory, gold, ostrich feathers. In return, they received luxuries from India, the Arabian Peninsula, Greece, and Rome. Kush became wealthy from the trade.

As Kush prospered, the spirit of Southern Africa grew stronger in Meroë. The Kushites developed their own artistic styles. Animals such as lions and elephants that were rarely seen in Egyptian art began to appear in Kushite art. The Kushites also developed their own system of writing.

In the A.D. 300s, the kingdom of Axum, which was located in the highlands of Ethiopia, conquered Kush. Axum soon became a powerful trading state. During the 300s, its people converted to Christianity.

Axum reached the height of its power in the A.D. 400s and 500s. At its height, it reached from the mountains of Ethiopia to the shores of the Red Sea. The people of Axum commanded a trade network that linked Africa, India, and countries along the Mediterranean Sea.

Axum lost power when Arab conquests spread Islam to North Africa. Its valuable trade routes disappeared. However, the people of Axum refused to give up Christianity. To this day, many Ethiopians practice Christianity.

Section 1 Review

1. What geographic features protected Egypt from invasion?

2. **Analyzing Information** Explain how Egypt's social structure resembled a pyramid.

SECTION 2

Empires South of the Sahara

How did the gold-salt trade lead to the growth of strong empires in West Africa?

Mansa Musa (MAHN•suh MOO•suh) was the ruler of the West African empire of Mali (MAH•lee). He was a **devout** Muslim, a believer in the religion of Islam. In 1324, he set out on a pilgrimage to the Islamic holy city of Mecca, in Arabia. This was no ordinary pilgrimage. His **caravan** consisted of 6,000 people! A caravan is a group of travelers who band together for safety. Among the people traveling with Mansa Musa were his rivals. By taking them along on the pilgrimage, he kept them from threatening his power at home while he was gone. Mansa Musa was well-supplied with money. Each of his 80 camels was loaded with hundreds of pounds of gold dust.

Stories of Mansa Musa's fabulous pilgrimage spread far and wide. Mali became known as one of West Africa's great kingdoms— kingdoms that rivaled those of Europe at the time. As a result of Mansa Musa's journey, Mali appeared on the first European maps of West Africa as a place of fabulous wealth. In this section, you will read about Mali and two other important empires of West Africa, Ghana and Songhai.

The empires that developed in West Africa are sometimes called the "kingdoms of gold and salt." This is because trade in gold and salt was very important to their development.

For the people of West Africa, salt was a necessity. Like other people in desert climates, they sweated away body salts and had to replace them by eating salty food. They also used salt to preserve foods. Therefore, they traded the gold from the south for the salt from North Africa.

Ghana

If there was one word that meant more than any other in Ghana, it was gold. In fact, the name *Ghana* came to mean gold. At Ghana's most powerful point, around A.D. 1000, the ruler was called "king of gold."

The kingdom of Ghana was established shortly after A.D. 600. It was located north and west of the modern nation of Ghana, in an area now occupied by parts of the nations of Mali and Mauritania. (See the map on page 32.)

Ghana lay along one of the most important routes across the Sahara. Because of its location, it became a major center of trade. The people of Ghana, like the Kushites, knew how to make iron tools and weapons. With their iron swords, they were able to conquer their neighbors, who were equipped only with wooden weapons.

The king of Ghana taxed all goods bought or sold in his country. Thus, as trade grew, the king of Ghana became very wealthy. The king's servants carried swords decorated with gold. Guard dogs standing near the king had collars made of gold.

Ghana's kings also used their wealth to keep up a large army to control their territory. They could call on 200,000 warriors to fight their battles.

In the 8th century, Islam spread to Ghana. Muslim traders and scholars settled in cities throughout the kingdom. They built mosques and introduced Arabic learning. Most of Ghana's farmers and members of the ruling class kept their old religious beliefs. In the 1000s, however, Muslims from North Africa conquered Ghana. After that conquest, Ghana never regained its power.

The Empire of Mali

After Ghana declined, a new empire, called Mali, arose in West Africa. Timbuktu was at its center. Mali won control of important trade routes across the Sahara. It also controlled rich gold-producing areas in West Africa.

Mali reached the height of its power under the emperor Mansa Musa, whose pilgrimage to Mecca you read about at the beginning of this section.

While in Cairo, Mansa Musa spent his gold at an incredible rate. There seemed to be no end to his wealth. Mansa Musa spent so much that the price of gold in Cairo fell and stayed low for many years.

While Mansa Musa was in Mecca, he persuaded some of Islam's finest scholars and architects to return with him to Mali. They helped enlarge and enrich the city of Timbuktu. Mansa Musa built new buildings and opened several Islamic universities. Timbuktu became a center of learning and culture. Students came from across Africa to study at Timbuktu. The city became a lively center of West African trade.

After Mansa Musa's death in 1332, the empire of Mali began to fall apart. Raiders from neighboring lands attacked its cities. In addition, local rulers broke away from the empire to set up their own kingdoms. In the mid-1400s, the rulers of one city led a revolt and began to build the empire of Songhai (sahn•HY).

The Empire of Songhai

Like Ghana and Mali, the empire of Songhai grew rich from trade. Its main trade goods were gold and ivory. Unlike the two earlier empires, however, Songhai expanded its trade network to Europe and Southwest Asia. Some of Songhai's gold was sent by desert caravan to Egypt, which then shipped it to other areas. In turn, Egypt shipped to Songhai goods made on the east coast of Africa, such as cloth, copper, and beads.

The person who turned Songhai into a great empire was Sunni Ali (SOO•nee AH•lee). He reigned from 1464 to 1492. During his rule, Sunni Ali enlarged Songhai so that it spanned most of West Africa. After Sunni Ali's death, one of his generals seized power. His name was Askia Muhammad.

In 1493, Askia began a 35-year rule that brought Songhai to the height of its power. Through military conquests, he greatly expanded the empire. He also brought more Islamic scholars to Timbuktu, making it once again an important center of learning.

The empire of Songhai was even larger than Mali. However, Songhai had serious

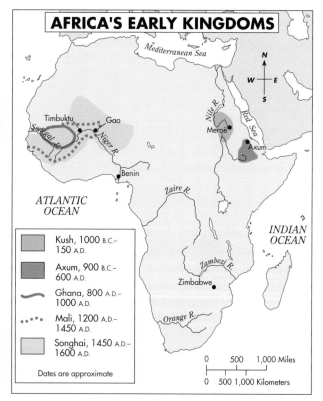

Location Great kingdoms developed across the African continent. Which were located near the Atlantic Ocean? Which city was located in Kush?

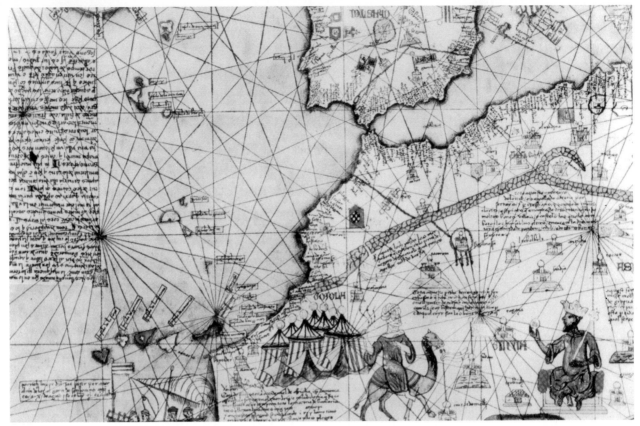

This map from an atlas created in the late 1300s, shows Mansa Musa on a throne in West Africa. Europeans found out about Mali and Mansa Musa when the king made a pilgrimage to Mecca.

weaknesses. There was tension between the ruling classes who were Muslims and the common people who practiced their traditional African religions. In 1591, an army from Morocco crossed the desert in search of gold. The soldiers of Songhai, who fought with bows and arrows, were no match for the Moroccans, who had guns. Songhai quickly fell to the invaders.

On Assignment. . .

Based on what you have read in this section, pick a scene to sketch for your storyboard. You might want to sketch a scene about Mansa Musa's caravan, the trade in gold and salt, or the city of Timbuktu.

Benin and Other West African Societies

The West African empires were not the only kingdoms in the region. Smaller kingdoms grew up in the rain forest region near the coast.

One of those kingdoms was Benin, at the delta of the Niger River. The people of Benin were famous for their sculpture. They made beautiful statues and other objects out of bronze, wood, and ivory.

City-States of East Africa

To the east, small trading communities grew up along the coast or on islands off the coast. At first Kushites lived there. Later, Bantu-speaking people moved in. Their main trading partners were Arabs.

Great Zimbabwe, shown here, is one of the finest examples of stone building in Southern Africa. It stands as evidence of an advanced city-state in East Africa.

Around the 10th century, Arabs settled along the East African coast. They intermarried with local people and converted them to Islam. A new language developed in East Africa. The new language, Swahili, was a mixture of Arabic and Bantu languages.

In time, some East African trading communities became larger and more powerful. Like kingdoms of West Africa, these kingdoms served as marketplaces for gold, copper, ivory, and slaves. Large sailing ships loaded with cloth, carpets, and other goods from Arabia, India, and even China pulled into East African ports. Equally large African ships headed eastward.

By the end of the 1100s, Kilwa had become the center of the East African gold trade. Kilwa was a walled city with wide streets, impressive palaces, and beautiful mosques.

The Walled City of Zimbabwe

Far to the south was the inland kingdom of Zimbabwe (zim•BAHB•way). It was in a rich region where there were large amounts of gold, copper, and iron. The people of Zimbabwe built up a large trade with the coastal regions of East Africa.

The city of Zimbabwe was founded around 1100. Its people built large stone buildings throughout the region. In fact, *Zimbabwe* means "great stone house."

The builders of Zimbabwe worked without mortar or cement. With great care and skill, they fit the stones together so they would stay in place by themselves.

The greatest building project in Zimbabwe was a huge wall and temple for the king. Most of the wall is more than 25 feet (7 m) high. In some parts the wall is about 15 feet (5 m) thick.

Section 2 Review

1. What were the two main products upon which the trade of Ghana, Mali, and Songhai was built?

2. **Cause and Effect** What effect did new weapons have on the history of Songhai?

Africa, the Outside World, and Slavery

How did the slave trade rob Africans of their human rights?

Just before dawn broke, wooden drums sounded the alarm. Enemies had surrounded the village. Warriors grabbed their weapons, but it was too late. Intruders armed with heavy wooden clubs, spears, and bows and arrows overran the village. Some villagers fled. Others fought back. Many fell, stunned by well-aimed blows to the head. When the battle ended, the invaders joined the captured villagers together neck to neck with heavy logs and ropes.

The villagers had fallen victim to African slave traders from the Atlantic coast. The traders forced them to march barefoot over mountains, through forests, and along rivers. Those who rebelled were killed. Those who fell ill were left to die along the trail. At a village on the coast, the captives were put on boats. As the boats sailed away, the captives got their last look at Africa.

The Growth of the Slave Trade

Two groups of outsiders participated in expanding the slave trade—Arabs and Europeans. The Arab trade operated mainly from Oman on the Arabian Peninsula, and worked along the East African coast. Africans captured by the Arabs carried gold and ivory out of Africa. The Africans were then sold on the coast or on the island of Zanzibar and sent to Arabia. This trade was heaviest in the 1700s and 1800s. Some experts think that 10 or 11 million African people were enslaved by the Arabs.

Arrival of the Europeans

In 1441, a ship left Lisbon, Portugal, and set out along the West African coast. The boat sailed down the coast to Senegal. There, sailors seized nine people and some gold dust and returned to Portugal.

More ships followed and went further south. By 1482, the Portuguese reached the mouth of the Congo River, now known as the Zaire River. The Portuguese were trying to sail around Africa and reach India. They finally succeeded in 1498.

As the Portuguese moved along the African coast, they set up trading posts. They also raided and looted cities along the coast. During the late 1400s, they captured Africans to use as slaves.

Eventually, other European nations sent ships to compete with Portugal for the African trade. At first, they traded for gold, ivory, nuts, and other African products. Then the European nations explored and began to settle North and South America. They needed laborers for the mines and plantations in the Americas. The Atlantic slave trade from Africa was about to begin.

The Atlantic Slave Trade

At first, the Portuguese dominated the Atlantic slave trade. Then the Dutch, English, French, and Americans entered the market.

Very few Europeans actually captured people for slavery. Instead, they built forts along the coast of Africa and depended on the rulers there to capture people who lived inland. The Europeans gave these rulers guns, ammunition, and other products in return for slaves.

The people who were captured inland were chained together and marched to the coast. There they were kept locked up until they were sold. Finally, they were squeezed onto cramped and filthy ships for the voyage to slavery in the Americas.

Many of the enslaved Africans never completed the journey. Millions died on the brutal march to the coast or while locked up. Still others died on the terrible voyage across the ocean.

The Atlantic slave trade had a devastating effect on the civilizations of West Africa. Entire communities disappeared as people were traded for guns and other goods.

The Atlantic slave trade lasted for about 400 years. Experts believe that between 10 to 13 million people were captured in Africa and sold into slavery in the Americas.

Effects of the Slave Trade

For about 400 years, the slave trade plundered West Africa. The area suffered an enormous loss of population. At least one African died for every one who reached the coast alive. African slave traders eager for European manufactured goods captured more and more people over the years. Local warfare spread, and professional armies arose. Wars were fought for the sole purpose of gaining captives to sell as slaves. By the mid-1700s, gun makers in England were making more than 100,000 guns a year for the trade with the kingdom of Guinea (GIN•ee) alone. The splendor that was Africa under the empires of Ghana, Mali, and Songhai had been destroyed.

The exchange of humans for manufactured goods affected Africa's economy for many centuries. The cheap goods that Europeans exchanged for slaves made it unnecessary for West Africans to develop any additional manufacturing.

When Europe's interest in colonies grew in the 1800s, West Africa did not have the economic strength to resist. Europe needed the raw materials available in West Africa, and West Africa benefited from this trade. Thus, as a result of the African slave trade, millions of people were killed. In addition, it delayed economic development in Africa for more than 300 years.

Section 3 Review

1. Why did the African slave trade hurt Africa's economy?

2. **Summarizing** What lasting effect do you think the slave trade had on Africans who remained in Africa?

On Assignment. . .

Based on the words and pictures in this section, pick a scene related to the slave trade to sketch for your storyboard.

A Prince Is Forced Into Slavery

What was it like to become a slave? Of the millions of Africans who were enslaved, only a few got to tell their story. Abd al-Rahman Ibrahima was one of those few.

Abd al-Rahman Ibrahima was born in 1762 in a farming region of the present-day country of Guinea. Ibrahima was a member of the powerful Fula people. As a son of one of nine chieftains, he was expected to become a leader of his people when he became an adult.

When Ibrahima was 12, he was sent to Timbuktu to study. Timbuktu was a center of learning in West Africa. The city attracted scholars in medicine, mathematics, law, and religion from Africa, Europe, and Asia. Young Ibrahima was raised in the Muslim tradition and received a well-rounded education.

When he returned home, Ibrahima was ready to take his place as a leader. In his twenties, he became a leader of Fula troops who were at war with the neighboring Mandingo people. During a battle, Ibrahima's soldiers attacked the Mandingo. The enemy retreated into the forested mountains. Ibrahima's men chased them, but soon found that they had stepped into a trap. Ibrahima was in the middle of battle when something smashed against his head and knocked him out.

When he came to, he tried to move his arms but they were tied with a heavy rope. He was now a prisoner. The Mandingos pushed him into file with other captives. They then began a long trip that took them to the sea. When they reached the sea, the captives were put into irons and loaded onto a ship.

The ship was already crowded with African captives. The sailors on the ship looked very strange to the captured Africans. Most of the Africans had never seen white men before. The whites had long hair, red faces, and spoke a language the Africans had never heard before. Ibrahima and the others were shoved toward an open hatch.

The area was dark and the smell overpowering. The captives lay all day, gasping for air. Their muscles cramped. Iron cut into their legs and wrists. In those close quarters, many died. After a three-week journey, the ship landed at what is today the city of Biloxi, Mississippi. Within two days, Ibrahima was sold to a Virginia planter and began his life as a slave in a strange land.

Case Study Review

1. Where did Ibrahima receive his education?
2. **Identifying Points of View** Why do you think the sailors on the slave ship looked "strange" to the enslaved Africans?

REVIEWING CHAPTER 2

I. Reviewing Vocabulary

Match each word on the left with the correct definition on the right.

1. mummy
2. scribe
3. caravan
4. devout

a. a member of the class of people in ancient Egypt whose job was to write

b. a dead body treated with chemicals and wrapped so that it does not decay

c. a group of travelers who band together for safety

d. very religious

II. Understanding the Chapter

Answer the questions below on a separate sheet of paper.

1. Why did the ancient Egyptians make mummies and bury them in tombs along with rich treasures?
2. Why were the kingdoms of West Africa called the "kingdoms of gold and salt"?
3. Describe how Africans were captured for the Atlantic slave trade.
4. What lasting impact did the slave trade have on West Africa?

III. Building Skills: Identifying Primary and Secondary Sources

Documents that are produced by people who were present at a historic event are called primary sources. Writings by historians who depend on others for their information are called secondary sources. On a piece of paper, make two columns with the headings "Primary Source" and "Secondary Source." List each item below under the correct heading. Beside each item, give a brief explanation of why you placed it where you did.

1. a description of his or her capture written by an African who was enslaved
2. a piece of writing from ancient Kush
3. an encyclopedia article about the walled city of Zimbabwe

IV. Working Together

Divide into small groups. Each group should choose a separate African kingdom that was discussed in this chapter. With your group, write a report that discusses important facts about the kingdom you chose. Include information about people, events, and developments discussed in the chapter. Draw a picture to illustrate the kingdom you selected.

On Assignment . . .

Creating a Storyboard: Review the sketches that you made as you read the chapter. Create final storyboard panels of the scenes that you have sketched. Use them to create a presentation on Africa's history. Write an introduction that links the three panels. Tell what you find interesting about African history. Display your storyboards to the class while you read your narration to them.

The Maasai are a nomadic people who live in Kenya and Tanzania. They have maintained many of their traditions. This jumping ceremony is held to celebrate the birth of a new child.

CHAPTER 3

Traditional Patterns of Life in Africa

What are the traditional ways of life of people in Africa?

Looking at Key Terms

- **griot** an African storyteller
- **proverb** a short saying that expresses some well-known fact or common experience
- **clan** a group made up of many extended families
- **age set** in some African societies, a group made up of boys or girls of the same age
- **subsistence farming** type of farming that produces just enough food for people to survive
- **nomad** a person who moves from place to place in search of food

On Assignment . . .

Creating a Collage: A collage is a large picture made from various types of objects like pictures from newspapers and magazines, cloth, and pressed flowers. When pasted together on a poster board, a collage communicates an idea or theme. At several points in this chapter, there are hints to help you prepare a collage about traditional patterns of life in Africa. At the end of the chapter, you will be given final instructions for putting your collage together.

Growing Up in Traditional African Society

What role does the family play in traditional African life?

It is night in a West African village. The villagers gather around the fire to listen to the **griot** (GREE•oh), their best storyteller. Tonight he tells the story of why bats live apart from other animals. The storyteller tells of a time long ago when Bat's poor mother was very ill. Bat went to Antelope for medicine, but Antelope sent him to Joba, the sun. Each day for six days, Bat asked for help and each day Joba refused. On the seventh day, Bat's mother died. Bat asked the animals to help bury his mother. They refused. They said that because Bat's mother has wings, she is obviously a bird. Bat asked the birds for help, but they turned him away too. They told Bat that since his mother has teeth, she cannot be a bird. In the end, Bat announced to the beasts and the birds: "I am not a beast and not a bird. I will live by myself and never look on you in the daylight, for none will claim me and Joba, the Sun, refused to help me."

Through stories of animals, birds, and insects, young people in Africa learn many things. They learn about bats and how they live. More importantly, they learn to have respect for their parents. Bat's devotion to his mother is an important part of the story. Respect for one's parents is one of the most important values of traditional African society.

The Importance of Family

Many African **proverbs** speak about families. A proverb is a short saying that expresses some well-known fact or common experience. One African proverb says: "A man without kin is as good as dead." It suggests that a person's family is one of the most important things in life. In the United States and other Western countries, when we think of family, we usually think about our immediate family: mother, father, and children. This group is called a nuclear family.

In traditional African societies, the immediate family includes the nuclear family as

Young African girls learn responsibility early in life. In rural parts of Africa, girls might go to school for a few years. After that, they help their families earn a living.

well as all uncles, aunts, cousins, and grandparents. This larger immediate family is called an extended family. In the extended family system, aunts and uncles share with the parents responsibility for rearing the children. Cousins are regarded almost like sisters and brothers. Grandparents are respected and looked up to as "parents" of the whole family.

Clans, Tribes, and Nations The family is the basic unit of African society. The family works together for the good of everyone. But relationships in traditional Africa do not stop with the extended family.

Each person is also a member of another group called a **clan**. A clan is made up of many extended families that live together in a village. A third group that Africans typically belong to is called a tribe. There are more than 800 tribes in Africa today. Some have as few as 200 members, while others have more than 20 million. The tribe is made up of a collection of clans. The clans in a tribe usually speak the same language and share the same customs. Finally, an African is also a member of a group called a nation. An African nation is an association of tribes.

Responsibilities Each person in an African village has a job to do. In most cases, the father heads the family and makes most of the family's decisions. The mother, sons, and daughters obey the father, but they also perform tasks that are essential to the family and the village.

Anna Apoko is a member of the Acholi tribe, whose home is in northern Uganda. The Acholi people are mostly farmers. In this traditional society, the men plant the seeds. The women tend the fields and harvest the crops.

Like other African women, Acholi women work very hard. Several times a day, Anna goes to the well to fetch the water her family needs. All the water for cooking and washing must be carried from the well.

Anna also grinds grain into flour and bakes bread for her family. Acholi

women—like women in most traditional societies—prepare the meals and do all the cooking. They are also responsible for keeping the home clean.

The most important job of women in traditional societies is feeding and caring for the children. The ideal woman is one who marries and has many children. Girls learn their responsibilities at a very young age. When Anna was in elementary school, she already had many chores to do. She cared for her younger brothers and sisters and helped her mother fetch water. Anna helped spread out peas and grains to dry. By age eight or nine, she could help grind the grains and collect firewood.

Girls like Anna are usually much less free to do what they want than boys are. Mothers and fathers warn their daughters to stay close to home and to obey. Even Anna's older brother can tell her what to do.

Age Sets

African children are considered adults at about the age of 14 or 15. Before they are considered adults, however, they must go through an initiation ceremony. (See the Case Study on page 43.) Initiation ceremonies are much more common for boys than for girls.

Often several boys who are the same age are initiated at the same time. The boys are part of the same **age set**. These boys develop a strong and lasting relationship. If one member of the age set needs help, he knows he can count on the others in the group to help him. During the initiation, one of the boys may emerge as the leader. He will be the leader of his age set for his whole life. Age sets are most important in East Africa. Among cattle herders, the age set may be an important bond for life.

Traditional Religious Beliefs

Like family, religion has always played an important role in African life. In areas where life has not changed very much, people still practice traditional African religions. It is hard to make generalizations about African religions because there are so many. But there are certain beliefs that almost all African religions have in common.

The first is the idea of God as Creator of the world. The second is the belief in lesser gods who live in rivers, caves, forests, mountains, or even animals. Traditional Africans believe the forces of nature such as lightning, thunder, and floods are controlled by these gods.

A third shared characteristic is the belief in ancestral spirits. Many traditional Africans believe that even when people die, their spirits linger on. According to believers, these spirits can punish the living if they forget to honor the dead.

Finally, followers of traditional African religions believe that certain people in the clan have special powers. Some people believe the medicine man or woman has the power to heal. Healers usually know a lot about herbs and fruits and use them to cure the sick.

Although many people in Africa still practice traditional religions, many Africans today are either Christians or Muslims. Christianity came to northeast Africa in about A.D. 300. It did not come to the rest of Africa until Spanish and Portuguese explorers and missionaries arrived in the 1400s and 1500s. Today, there are over 300 million Christians in Africa.

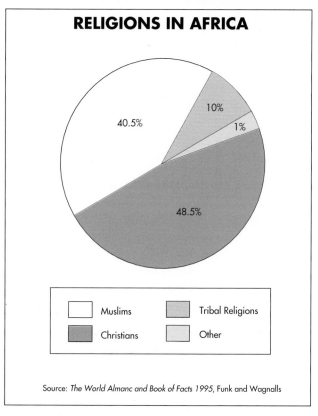

RELIGIONS IN AFRICA

40.5%
10%
1%
48.5%

Muslims   Tribal Religions
Christians   Other

Source: *The World Almanc and Book of Facts 1995*, Funk and Wagnalls

Most people in Africa are either Christians or Muslims. What percentage of Africans are Christian? Are there more Christians or Muslims in Africa?

More than 278 million Africans are Muslims. Islam was introduced in North Africa during the 600s and 700s. Traders brought the new religion across the Sahara (See Chapter 2.) By the 1000s, most of West Africa was controlled by Muslims.

On Assignment . . .

Section 1 talks about family and religion. Think about what you want to show in your collage about traditional African family life and religious beliefs. Look for pictures and other objects that will help you express your message.

Section 1 Review

1. What characteristics do traditional African religions have in common?

2. **Comparing and Contrasting** Compare and contrast the ideal woman in traditional African society with the ideal woman in U.S. society.

An Initiation Ceremony

In many cultures, a special ritual marks the time when children become adults. In many African societies, young men are initiated into manhood in an elaborate ceremony.

Damany is a member of the Fali people of Cameroon. When he was a young boy, he spent his days in a carefree manner. Now that he is almost 14, he knows his days of play are coming to an end. Soon he will assume his role as an adult member of his clan.

Damany is one of several boys to be initiated. All of them are about the same age. Three days before the initiation, Damany moves to the home of his friend, Camara. Camara is seven years older than Damany. Since Damany was about two, Camara had looked after him. Among the Fali people, Camara is known as a *Yum*. The *Yum* is the person responsible for watching a younger child if the parents are busy. The *Yum's* duty stops after initiation. But he plays an important part during the ceremony.

Damany lives in Camara's home for three days. During those three days, neither of them can have any contact with women. They are not allowed to eat meat or drink wine. At sunset of the day before the initiation, Damany and the other boys being initiated are given wine to drink. They are then told to go out and look for a man wearing a special mask. This mask represents the founder of the clan.

The day of the initiation begins with Camara shaving Damany's head. The removal of the hair represents the shedding of childhood. The clan priest pulls a feather from each of twenty chickens and places the feathers on an altar. Tremendous drum rolls summon all of the clan's ancestors. Their presence at the ceremony is symbolized by two dancers. As the dancers circle, the priest pushes Damany and the other boys into the dance.

The next day, all the members of Damany's father's clan come together. They argue about whether Damany has the right to become a full clan member and decide that he does. Damany has proven his worth to the clan. The final step in the initiation is a ritual bath. The bath symbolically washes away Damany's boyhood. Now he is finally ready to assume his role as an adult clan member.

Case Study Review

1. Why is Damany's head shaved?
2. **Comparing and Contrasting** What are the rites of passage from childhood to adulthood in U.S. society? How are they similar to and different from those of the Fali people?

SECTION 2

Leadership in Traditional Africa

What kind of political structure does traditional Africa have?

For hundreds of years, people who did not live in Africa knew very little about its history or culture. Today we know that Africa has a rich history. It had thriving cities long before European cities developed. It had great centers of learning before universities were founded in countries like England or Germany. During the Middle Ages when Europe was divided into hundreds of warring factions, Africa had great kingdoms with courts of law.

In Chapter 2, you read about the West African empires of Ghana, Mali, and Songhai. The kings of these empires had absolute power and were considered godlike. Their power came from several sources. First, each king's subjects believed that he had special connections to their ancestors. Second, the king controlled a vast army. For example, the King of Ghana had an army of 200,000 warriors that helped unify a large area of land.

Third was the king's ability to govern a large area effectively. The great Songhai leader, Askia, divided his empire into provinces. Each province was ruled by a governor appointed by the king. Askia had a group of ministers who helped him govern. They included a treasurer, a chief of the navy, a chief tax collector, and chiefs of forests, woodcutters, and fishermen. Since the empire was so large, the king appointed judges to every large district. These judges helped apply the law and keep order.

In many African states today, there is an elected head of state, usually a president. This person has the formal power to govern. Most countries are democracies with elected representatives who make the law. (You will read more about today's African governments in Chapter 6.) Nevertheless, traditional leadership still exists. Kings and chiefs still hold considerable power. The new African governments are located in the capital cities of the nation. In the rural areas, people tend to look toward their traditional chiefs for leadership more than to the officials of the national government.

The Council of Elders

Almost every African village has a Council of Elders. The council is made up of older people from different families of the clan. The Council of Elders shows that older people are valued and respected in traditional African society. The elders are the wisest members of the village. They solve most of the village's everyday problems. The council generally rules by consensus. This means that council members discuss and debate an issue and reach a decision together.

The Council of Elders is a part of life in many African villages. The elders of the tribe make decisions based on general agreement. The elder in this picture welcomes a new chief.

Think about how you might show the traditional power of kings and chiefs in your collage. What symbols could you use to represent their power?

Section 2 Review

1. How did African kings maintain their power?

2. **Analyzing** The Council of Elders rules by consensus. What do you think are some advantages of ruling by consensus?

SECTION 3

Economic Patterns in Traditional Africa

How do most African villagers support themselves?

Today, about 80 percent of all Africans live in villages. Some make their living as craft-workers, but most farm or raise livestock. A typical African village is built around a central square. The square is the center of village activity. It is used as a meeting place. Important business such as settling disputes and collecting taxes is conducted there.

The square is surrounded by small homes. The houses are built of materials that are available locally. In some parts of Africa, houses are built of bricks made of sun-dried mud. The roofs are often made of metal.

Larger villages have community facilities. For example, in drier regions there may be a large tank to collect and store rainwater. There may also be a medical clinic. A few small shops may also be found.

Surrounding the village are farmlands. The Wolof people of Senegal plant their crops in three ring-shaped areas with the village in the center. The innermost circle contains vegetable gardens and other small plots. The middle circle is used to grow peanuts. The outermost ring contains fields for such grains as millet and sorghum. Millet and sorghum are often grown in areas with limited amounts of rain.

In places with wetter climates like Sierra Leone, rice is a major crop. Another crop which can be found in wetter climates is cassava. Cassava is a little like a potato. Before it can be eaten, it must be peeled and soaked in water. Then, it is pounded until it looks like a lump of dough. It is eaten in place of bread or potatoes. You may be familiar with tapioca. Tapioca is made from the cassava plant.

Subsistence Agriculture

The type of agriculture practiced in most areas of Africa is **subsistence farming**. Subsistence farmers grow food on small farms for their own families' use. If more food is produced than is needed, the surplus may be traded or sold. In subsistence agriculture, tools are usually simple hand tools like hoes. Machinery like tractors and combines (a machine that helps farmers harvest grains) are too expensive and too large for traditional farms. In many areas of Africa, subsistence farming is the village's main economic activity.

Livestock Herding

The traditional way of life for some people in Africa is not farming, but herding. The Maasai people of Africa's Great Rift Valley are **nomads**. They move from place to place in search of food for their cattle. The Maasai believe "you cannot be a Maasai unless you have cattle."

The Maasai measure their wealth not by how much money they have, but by how

In rural parts of Africa, people practice traditional crafts such as basket weaving. Selling baskets to other villages provides much-needed income.

many animals they own. They depend on their cattle for survival. Milk is an important part of the Maasai diet. They use the animal's hides in building their homes as well as for clothes and for mats to lie on.

Many Maasai live in Kenya. The Kenyan government would like the Maasai to settle down and become farmers. Most, however, prefer their traditional way of life and do not want to change. The Maasai believe after God created the world, he gave the Maasai "all the cattle upon the Earth." Many believe that it is a sin to "turn the land upside down" to plow it.

Of course, the Maasai are not Africa's only herders. In the desert regions of Africa, people raise camels. In other parts of Africa,

goats and sheep as well as cows are raised. Village people usually have a pen to keep the animals from roaming at night.

The Village Market

From the smallest villages to the largest, the market plays a central role in the lives of Africans. Most villages have markets every few days. They are usually held outside. People buy, sell, and trade factory-made goods, food products, and livestock. Also for sale is art, jewelry, cloth, and pottery. The market is also the traditional meeting place. People can socialize and catch up on the news. It is a place where young people looking for marriage partners can meet.

On Assignment...

What symbols could you use in your collage to show the importance of farming, herding, and the marketplace in African cultures?

Section 3 Review

1. What is subsistence farming?
2. **Analyzing** How do the beliefs of the Maasai conflict with those of the Kenyan government?

I. Reviewing Vocabulary

Match each word on the left with the correct definition on the right.

1. clan
2. griot
3. nomad
4. subsistence farming

a. a group made up of many extended families
b. type of farming that produces just enough food for people to survive
c. a person who travels from place to place in search of food
d. an African storyteller

II. Understanding the Chapter

Answer the questions below on a separate sheet of paper.

1. How do extended families in traditional African societies differ from nuclear families in the United States?
2. What responsibilities do women have in traditional African families?
3. What role does the Yum play in Fali culture?
4. How do most traditional Africans earn their living?

III. Building Skills: Interpreting a Quotation

Read the following quote and answer the questions that follow. "Government officials usually do not want traditional culture recorded, pictured or revealed."

1. Rewrite the quotation in your own words.
2. Why might a government feel this way?
3. Write a letter to the government of an African nation explaining whether you agree or disagree with the practice described in the quote.

IV. Working Together

Form a small group. With the group, make up a chart. On the left side, show some of the ways your life is similar to traditional life in Africa. On the right side, list some of the ways your life is different. Share your chart with the class.

On Assignment . . .

Creating a Collage: Put together the various ideas you have for your collage. Find images from magazines, newspapers, and other sources that convey your ideas. Present your finished collage to the class. Explain why you included what you did. Help others understand the symbols you used to express your message.

CHAPTER 4

Modern History of Africa

How did European imperialism affect the African continent?

The nation of Mali gained its independence in 1960. Here Mali children celebrate independence day. Study the maps on pages 50 and 56. From what country did Mali gain its independence?

On Assignment. . .

Writing Diary Entries:
Imagine that you are going on a trip to Africa. However, this is no ordinary trip. You'll be traveling back in time to witness turning points in African history. On your trip, you will keep a diary of your thoughts and feelings about what you see and hear. Take notes as you read this chapter. At the end of the chapter, you'll be asked to write three diary entries about imperialism in Africa. Look for hint boxes throughout the chapter to help you write your diary entries.

Looking at Key Terms

- **missionary** a person who is sent to do religious work in a territory or foreign country
- **protectorate** a country with its own government whose policies are controlled or directed by a more powerful country
- **imperialism** a policy of conquering and taking over foreign territory
- **colonialism** the policy of taking over foreign lands usually to exploit them economically
- **nationalism** a strong devotion to and pride in one's country
- **pan-Africanism** the belief that people of African descent have common interests and should work together for freedom
- **boycott** a refusal to buy or use certain goods or services
- **legacy** something handed down from the past

SECTION 1

Africa Falls Into European Hands

How did European nations gain control of Africa?

David Livingstone came from Britain to Africa in 1841. Livingstone was a **missionary**—a person who is sent to do religious work in a territory or foreign country. Through his work, Livingstone came to know many African people. He developed a deep respect for their cultures. As Livingstone's fascination with the land and people of Africa grew, he began to journey into the African interior. Soon he was heading into regions no other white person had ever seen.

David Livingstone was a Scottish doctor who volunteered for missionary work in Africa. His explorations opened the African interior to Europeans.

On Assignment...

In your diary, you may wish to write about Livingstone. What are your impressions of Livingstone? How do you think Livingstone's explorations helped to spark European interest in Africa?

In 1849, Livingstone became the first white person to cross the vast Kalahari desert and see Lake Ngami. Two years later, he journeyed with his wife and children into the Africa interior. Together they reached the Zambezi River. On another trip in 1855, he came to a great waterfall that he named Victoria Falls. Livingstone's writings about the African continent made him the most famous European explorer of Africa.

In 1866, Livingstone set out on his most ambitious trip. He wanted to find the source of the Nile River. He began his journey at Cape Town at the southern tip of Africa and traveled slowly northward. For several years, little was heard from or about him. Many feared that Livingstone had died or had gotten lost.

Then, in 1869, U.S.–British newspaper reporter Henry Stanley was given the following assignment: "Find Livingstone." Stanley reached Africa in 1871 and traveled for 126 days in search of the doctor. One day he reached the town of Ujiji on Lake Tanganyika. Stanley's newspaper account describes what happened next.

> *The expedition at last comes to a halt. . . . As I come nearer I see the white face of an old man. . . .We raise our hats and I say: "Dr. Livingstone, I presume?" and he says, "Yes."*

Stanley had found Livingstone. He had also decided that he wanted to continue exploring the continent of Africa.

Exploring Africa

Livingstone and Stanley were among the first Europeans to venture into the African interior. Their journeys sparked European interest in the continent. Before explorers opened the interior, Europeans were familiar only with North Africa and the areas along the African coast. North Africa is located close to southern Europe and the Middle East. (See the map below.) For hundreds of years, European and Arab traders had exchanged goods and slaves. European explorers had also established trading posts along the coast. Few attempts had been made to explore the vast interior of Africa. In Europeans' imaginations the continent was a dark mystery.

There were several geographical reasons why the interior remained unexplored. One reason was that the deserts made travel by

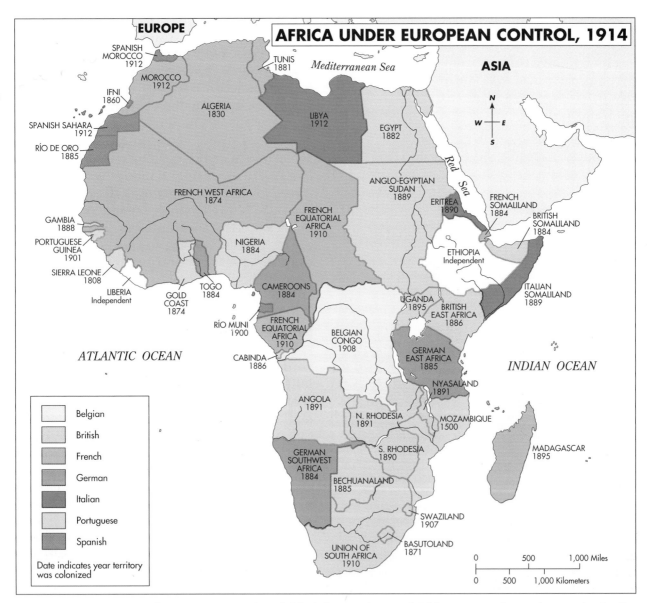

AFRICA UNDER EUROPEAN CONTROL, 1914

EUROPE

SPANISH MOROCCO 1912
MOROCCO 1912
IFNI 1860
SPANISH SAHARA 1912
RÍO DE ORO 1885
TUNIS 1881
Mediterranean Sea
ALGERIA 1830
LIBYA 1912
EGYPT 1882
ASIA
FRENCH WEST AFRICA 1874
GAMBIA 1888
PORTUGUESE GUINEA 1901
SIERRA LEONE 1808
LIBERIA Independent
GOLD COAST 1874
TOGO 1884
NIGERIA 1884
FRENCH EQUATORIAL AFRICA 1910
ANGLO-EGYPTIAN SUDAN 1889
Red Sea
ERITREA 1890
FRENCH SOMALILAND 1884
BRITISH SOMALILAND 1884
ETHIOPIA Independent
ITALIAN SOMALILAND 1889
CAMEROONS 1884
RÍO MUNI 1900
FRENCH EQUATORIAL AFRICA 1910
CABINDA 1886
BELGIAN CONGO 1908
UGANDA 1895
BRITISH EAST AFRICA 1886
GERMAN EAST AFRICA 1885
NYASALAND 1891
ATLANTIC OCEAN
ANGOLA 1891
N. RHODESIA 1891
MOZAMBIQUE 1500
INDIAN OCEAN
MADAGASCAR 1895
GERMAN SOUTHWEST AFRICA 1884
BECHUANALAND 1885
S. RHODESIA 1890
SWAZILAND 1907
BASUTOLAND 1871
UNION OF SOUTH AFRICA 1910

Legend:
- Belgian
- British
- French
- German
- Italian
- Portuguese
- Spanish

Date indicates year territory was colonized

0   500   1,000 Miles
0   500   1,000 Kilometers

Interaction and Region The European powers divided the continent of Africa among themselves at the Berlin Conference in 1884–85. Which European nations controlled portions of Africa by 1914?

land difficult. Another reason was that the many rivers that cross Africa are nearly impossible to navigate because of their many rapids and waterfalls. Sea travel was also difficult. The coasts of Africa have few large harbors in which ships can dock.

European Interest Builds

During the 1800s, several developments encouraged Europeans to brave the elements and explore Africa's interior. The most important development was the Industrial Revolution. During the Industrial Revolution, European nations built new industries based on new technology and work methods. Raw materials, such as coal, iron ore, gold, silver, tin, and copper, were needed to fuel new European factories. Many of these raw materials could be found in Africa. As the Europeans saw it, Africa was a huge treasure box—theirs for the taking. The Europeans cared little for African cultures that were hundreds or thousands of years old.

Shipping routes were another reason Europeans became interested in Africa. In 1869, a French company built the Suez Canal in Egypt. The canal connects the Mediterranean Sea to the Indian Ocean by way of the Red Sea. The opening of the canal revolutionized world shipping. Ships no longer had to travel around the tip of South Africa to reach Asia. The trip from London, England, to Bombay, India, was shortened by more than 4,000 miles (6,400 km)!

In 1875, the British government bought controlling interest in the Suez Canal company. At the time, the British also controlled India. The British became concerned about losing control of the canal, so they sent an army into Egypt. A few years later, the British made Egypt a **protectorate**. As a protectorate, Egypt stayed independent, but its foreign policy was controlled by Britain.

The Scramble for Africa

The policy of conquering and ruling other lands is called **imperialism**. Generally, imperialism means a powerful nation controls a weaker one. There were many reasons for the rise of imperialism in Africa and elsewhere. Again, one reason was the Industrial Revolution. European countries wanted unlimited access to the raw materials they needed to fuel their factories at home. They took colonies in Africa that had those raw materials. **Colonialism** is a term for the policy of taking over foreign lands in order to exploit them economically.

Another reason for imperialism was national pride. Some countries sought colonies because they thought an empire would make them look important in the eyes of the world. King Leopold of Belgium sent Henry Stanley to the Congo to make treaty arrangements with the local leaders. Stanley was very successful. By 1884, Belgium, one of the smallest countries in Europe, controlled an area in Africa that equaled the size of all of Western Europe. Belgium gained much wealth and prestige from its colony.

A third cause of imperialism was a military build-up throughout Europe. Many European countries were increasing the size and power of their navies. Sea power was vital for controlling important trade routes and protecting economic interests. Britain's takeover of the Suez Canal is an example of this type of imperialism. Many other European nations also used their colonies in Asia and Africa to provide and store supplies for their navies.

Another cause of imperialism had nothing to do with wealth or power. It was the belief that westerners were superior to other people. Many Europeans looked down on traditional African culture. They believed that Africans were backward and uncivilized. Europeans thought that it was their responsibility to bring Christianity and Western culture to Africa.

Europeans Divide the Continent

In the mid- to late 1800s, one European nation after another began to claim portions of Africa. Then the nations of Europe began to squabble with one another over lands they claimed. In 1884–85, the European powers attended a conference in Berlin, Germany. The purpose of the Berlin Conference was to settle the disputes of European nations that held territory in Africa. Although the nations of Europe were discussing the fate of Africa, no representatives from Africa were invited to the conference. At the Berlin Conference, the European powers divided the African continent into colonies. By 1910, only Liberia and Ethiopia remained independent. (See the map on page 56.)

During the 1800s, Ethiopia's leader, King Menelik II, had modernized his country and its army. In 1896, Italy tried to conquer Ethiopia but lost in battle to the Ethiopian army. After that battle, the European powers recognized Ethiopia's independence.

Liberia had been established by the American Colonization Society to resettle African Americans who had won freedom from slavery. Due to its ties to the United States, Liberia's independence was recognized by European nations.

Section 1 Review

1. Why was the interior of Africa unexplored by Europeans for so long?
2. **Determining Bias** Why do you think there were no representatives from Africa present at the Berlin Conference?

On Assignment...

You might note in your diary your impressions of the Berlin Conference. What are your thoughts about the outcome of the conference? If you had attended the conference, what suggestions might you have made?

The Effects of European Imperialism: Resistance and Defeat

How did the Zulus react to European expansion in Southern Africa?

"I hear the sound of the feet of a great white people. They will tread this land flat." Shaka, king of the Zulus, uttered these words on his deathbed. The Zulus are a people from Southern Africa. Zululand, the area controlled by Shaka and the Zulus, took up most of what is today the country of South Africa. Shaka was a military genius with a gift for organization. He was also a cruel and ruthless leader. By 1823, his empire stretched over an area of 100,000 square miles (260,000 sq. km). He had defeated all of the African tribes that had opposed him. Just five years later, he lay dying, killed by his own brother, Dingaan.

Europeans in Southern Africa

Like other Africans, the Zulus opposed European expansion into their territories. A small group of Dutch settlers had arrived in what is now Cape Town on the southern coast of Africa in 1652. The Dutch farmers soon began claiming lands that belonged to the African groups in the region, including the San and the Khoi Khoi. There were constant clashes.

When the British captured Cape Town in 1806, many of the Dutch left and headed northward. They called themselves *Boers*—the Dutch word for "farmers." During the 1830s and early 1840s, thousands of Boers journeyed into the African interior on what is called the *Great Trek*. As the Boers trekked northward into Zulu territory, conflict between the Boers and the Zulus became certain.

In 1838, the land-hungry Boers crossed the Drakensberg Mountains. They went to

Zulus resisted Boer expansion into Zulu territory in the 1800s. They fought many wars, but in the end were defeated. Pictured here are Zulu headmen, or chiefs. Today, there are about two million Zulus living in South Africa.

see the Zulu king to ask for permission to settle there. The king was Shaka's brother Dingaan. Dingaan invited a group of the Boers to a feast. There were many hours of dancing, eating, and drinking. When the Boers got up to leave, they were attacked by Zulu warriors. All 70 Boers who attended the feast were killed. In the next days and weeks, Zulu raiders attacked the many Boer families that had settled on the land.

The Boers refused to leave the land and decided to seek revenge on the Zulu king. With 500 soldiers, the Boers arrived on the banks of the Buffalo River where they waited for the Zulus to attack. On December 16, 1838, thousands of warriors attacked. The battle raged for six hours. But the Zulu spears and courage were no match for the Boers' guns. The Zulus were defeated and the Boers took the land.

For a while, an uneasy peace settled over the land, but trouble soon began again. Europeans had little respect for or knowledge of Zulu customs and culture. A new Zulu king said that he wished to be friends with the Boers. However, the king believed that the European settlers had no right to tell him how he should rule his people. Tensions between the Zulus and the Boers increased.

The British Defeat the Zulus In December 1878, the British, who were taking control of more of South Africa, demanded that the Zulu army be disbanded. The British knew the Zulus would not accept this demand. On the morning of January 11, 1879, the British forces crossed into Zululand.

The British commander had an army of nearly 18,000 officers and men. Each carried a single-shot rifle. They faced a Zulu army of about 25,000 men. Their chief weapon was the assegai, a short stabbing spear.

On January 22, 1879, Zulu warriors wiped out a British regiment. It was the biggest defeat ever suffered by a European force in South Africa. Despite this success, the final outcome was never in doubt. For all their bravery, the Zulu warriors could not hold off the British army. In July, the British captured and burned the Zulu capital. The Zulu

On Assignment...

Note in your diary your opinion of the Zulus, the Boers, and the British. How did the Europeans treat the Zulus?

leader was brought to England and punished. As Shaka predicted, the Zulu nation had been crushed by "the feet of a great white people."

The Effects of European Rule

The Zulu war represents one of the worst effects of imperialism. The Zulus tried to defend their land from foreign invaders. The Europeans viewed and treated African people as inferior, as people of little importance or value. They had little respect for African cultures or customs. Africans were often treated as second-class citizens in their own countries. In almost every African colony, some form of discrimination existed.

Another negative effect of imperialism was economic exploitation. This means that the Europeans used the African people to make a profit for themselves. The purpose of colonialism was to produce wealth for the colonizing power. Natural resources such as minerals, lumber, and rubber were exported from Africa to Europe. Large plantations in Africa produced cotton and other cash crops.

Africans worked hard, but received none of the profit. The traditional subsistence system of farming was practically destroyed. African workers were also taken advantage of by their European bosses. Working conditions were very harsh. Workers were sometimes treated like slaves. They were not allowed to leave their jobs and were severely punished if they broke the rules.

Another way the Europeans exploited Africans was by forcing them to pay taxes. The people of European countries did not want to pay taxes to help support their African colonies. Africans who did not pay the taxes could be fined or arrested. Often the only way to earn enough money to pay the taxes was to work as a farmhand, servant, or miner for the Europeans. Sometimes, the jobs were far from workers' homes and villages. The distance separated family members and weakened traditional African family and village life.

The family and village were not the only institutions that changed as a result of imperialism. Africa's traditional political and religious systems were also affected. The chiefs lost the power and respect they had once had. In the past, it was believed that the chiefs held power through their connection with the tribe's ancestors. Under European rule, many Africans became Christians. They no longer believed in the chief's power. European-style governments replaced traditional African rule.

Improvements in Africa European rule did bring some improvements to the colonies. However, few of the improvements were made because they were good for Africans. Most were carried out because they made the colonies more profitable and easier to manage.

Using African labor, the colonial powers built a network of roads and railroads. The roads and railroads made the transport of natural resources from the interior of Africa to the coast more efficient. From Africa these resources were shipped around the world. Later, Europeans introduced telegraph and telephone service to improve communication. After African nations won independence, these roads and telephone lines helped African nations build their economies.

Europeans also brought modern medicine and health practices to Africa. The primary reason for this was to help protect themselves from disease. Hospitals and clinics did help bring some of the terrible diseases that had killed many Africans under control, as well.

Colonial governments sent a number of Africans to school in Europe. Again, these educational programs were designed to help maintain colonial rule. Some Africans were trained to fill minor positions in colonial governments. Others received training so they could work in industries controlled by the colonial powers.

Section 2 Review

1. How did European rule change traditional African ways of life?
2. **Cause and Effect** Decide whether each of the following are causes or effects of imperialism:
   a. need for raw materials;
   b. roads and telegraph lines are built in Africa;
   c. Africans work in mines and on European-owned plantations;
   d. hospitals and clinics are built in Africa.

SECTION 3

The Rise of Nationalism in Africa

What factors led to the demand for independence in Africa?

Nationalism refers to the love a people have for their country. Nationalism was an important political force in European countries during the 1800s. It was one of the causes of imperialism.

After World War II, nationalism swept across the continents of Africa and Asia. The people of these lands had fought for their colonial rulers during the war. Now that the war was over, many Africans believed they had earned the right to rule themselves.

Africans were tired of being governed by non-Africans. They wanted higher wages and lower taxes. They needed new roads, better

transportation, improved health care, and more schools.

The strongest push for independence came from the Africans who had been educated in Europe and the United States. There, they saw that people had freedom of speech and religion. They also had the right to vote. Africans rightfully believed that they, too, should enjoy the same freedoms in Africa.

The Roots of African Nationalism

Many African nationalists believed in an idea called **pan-Africanism**. Pan-Africanism is the belief that people of African

Kwame Nkrumah led Ghana in its fight for independence. Nkrumah believed in African unity. He played a key role in the formation of the Organization of African Unity.

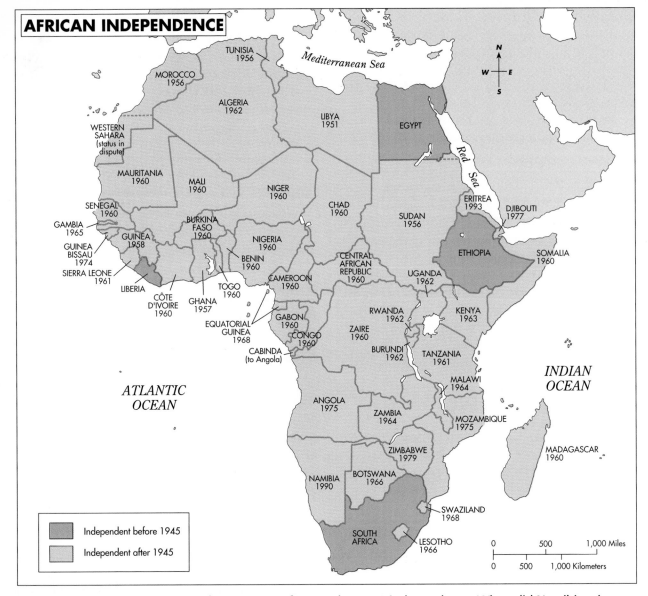

AFRICAN INDEPENDENCE

TUNISIA 1956
MOROCCO 1956
ALGERIA 1962
LIBYA 1951
EGYPT
Mediterranean Sea
WESTERN SAHARA (status in dispute)
MAURITANIA 1960
MALI 1960
NIGER 1960
CHAD 1960
SUDAN 1956
ERITREA 1993
DJIBOUTI 1977
Red Sea
SENEGAL 1960
GAMBIA 1965
GUINEA BISSAU 1974
GUINEA 1958
SIERRA LEONE 1961
LIBERIA
BURKINA FASO 1960
NIGERIA 1960
BENIN 1960
CÔTE D'IVOIRE 1960
TOGO 1960
GHANA 1957
CAMEROON 1960
CENTRAL AFRICAN REPUBLIC 1960
UGANDA 1962
ETHIOPIA
SOMALIA 1960
EQUATORIAL GUINEA 1968
GABON 1960
CONGO 1960
ZAIRE 1960
RWANDA 1962
BURUNDI 1962
KENYA 1963
TANZANIA 1961
CABINDA (to Angola)
MALAWI 1964
ATLANTIC OCEAN
ANGOLA 1975
ZAMBIA 1964
MOZAMBIQUE 1975
INDIAN OCEAN
ZIMBABWE 1979
MADAGASCAR 1960
NAMIBIA 1990
BOTSWANA 1966
SWAZILAND 1968
SOUTH AFRICA
LESOTHO 1966

Independent before 1945
Independent after 1945

0   500   1,000 Miles
0   500   1,000 Kilometers

Region After World War II, one African nation after another won independence. When did Namibia win freedom? When did Zimbabwe? During what decade did most African nations gain independence?

descent have common interests and should join together to fight for freedom at home and abroad. Pan-Africanists fought against imperialism in Africa. The pan-African movement was begun in 1900 by West Africans and African Americans. A leader of pan-Africanism was W.E.B. Du Bois. Du Bois was an African American writer and teacher. Another person who influenced African nationalists was Marcus Garvey. He began the Universal Negro Improvement

Association (UNIA) in 1914. Garvey promoted two basic ideas. The first was that African Americans should return to Africa and build a country of their own.

Garvey's second idea was expressed by the slogan "Black is beautiful." Garvey believed that African Americans should not try to be like whites. Garvey was unsuccessful in getting many African Americans to resettle in Africa. But the idea that blacks should be proud of their African heritage

On Assignment...

In your diary, discuss your feelings about African independence. What do you think it was like to be in an African nation such as Ghana on independence day?

still inspires African Americans today. Garvey's ideas were so powerful that the newspaper he published was banned by colonial governments in Africa.

In South Africa, a strong voice for African nationalism was the African National Congress. It was founded in 1912 to lobby for political rights for blacks. You will read more about South Africa's struggle for equal rights in Chapter 6.

New Nations Emerge

As demands for independence grew, Britain and France began giving Africans more of a say in government. Africans were allowed to elect some members of the colonial parliaments. Some Africans were appointed to important government positions. But these changes were too little and too late. Africans wanted to be completely free of European rule.

Ghana Wins Freedom As time passed, Africans grew impatient. The tensions boiled over first in the British colony called the Gold Coast—now known as Ghana. In 1948, nationalists organized a **boycott** of European-owned shops. African people refused to buy European-made goods. Later, there was rioting in major towns. Britain responded by appointing an all-African committee to write a new constitution. This was not enough to satisfy the nationalists.

Kwame Nkrumah, leader of the nationalists, was typical of African nationalists. Educated in European-style colonial schools, he went on to earn three degrees in universities in the United States. In 1949, he founded a political party, the Convention People's Party (CPP). He told his followers: "We want to be able to govern ourselves in this country of ours without outside interference, and we are going to see that it is done!" The CPP won big majorities in every election between 1951 and 1960. In 1957, Ghana became the first country in West Africa to gain independence.

Colonial Powers Let Go Britain realized that it could no longer hold on to its other colonies in West Africa. Nigeria, the largest African country, won independence in 1960, along with 16 other countries. Sierra Leone was one of three countries granted independence in 1961. In 1965, Gambia became the last British colony to win independence.

France was not as willing to give up control of its African empire. It gave Morocco and Tunisia independence in 1956. But Algeria won independence after a long and bitter seven-year war. In 1962, it too became independent.

Meanwhile, the former Belgian and German colonies also gained their freedom. Portuguese Angola and Mozambique won independence in 1975. The last African colony to win its independence was Namibia in 1990.

Section 3 Review

1. What is pan-Africanism?

2. **Drawing Inferences** The year 1960 was labeled "The Year of Africa." Why do you think this is so?

Jomo Kenyatta, African Freedom Fighter

The stern judge looked down on the tall African man standing before him.

"Jomo Kenyatta, before I sentence you, do you have anything to say?" the judge asked.

"Yes I do, your honor," the man answered. "This case has been arranged to strangle the only African political organization which fights for the rights of the African people. We have done our level best to find ways by which the community in this country can live in harmony. But what we have objected to—and we shall continue to object to—is discrimination in the government of this country. We look forward to the day when peace shall come to this land and that the truth shall be known that we as African leaders have stood for peace."

With those words, Jomo Kenyatta explained the cause he had been fighting for all his life. His words had no impact on the British judge. Kenyatta was sentenced to seven years of hard labor in a remote prison.

Kenyatta went to prison because the British accused him of being a leader of a secret, violent group called the Mau Mau. The Mau Mau was a group of Africans who vowed to rid Kenya of all whites. Many Mau Mau members belonged to the Kikuyu people.

The Seeds of Conflict

White settlers and the Kikuyu were in bitter conflict over land. The British wanted to farm the rich land of southwestern Kenya. These lands had been the homeland of the Kikuyu for centuries. The Kikuyu believed that the land still belonged to them. To the Kikuyu, land could not be bought and sold. It could pass from one owner to another only with formal religious ceremonies. Most importantly, the land of the Kikuyu could never be sold to foreigners.

The British believed they owned the land. Determined to keep it, they set up a government that gave them total power over the Africans. The British controlled huge amounts of land. They built grand houses. They forced the Africans to work for them for very low wages. They made racist laws and enforced segregation of whites and Africans. Africans were not allowed in hotels, restaurants, or shops. It was even against the law for Africans to hold public meetings in areas where whites lived.

"The Land Is Ours"

Jomo Kenyatta was one of the Kikuyu leaders who believed in nonviolence. He believed that the British had something to offer Kenya. He admired their modern farming methods. Kenyatta felt that if the British would grant equal rights to the Africans, they could live together in peace.

For 22 years, Kenyatta led peaceful protests against British rule. He made several trips to London to plead the Kikuyu cause to the British government. He helped plan the Pan-African Conference of 1945. At that conference, African and African American leaders discussed independence movements throughout Africa.

During these years of protest, Kenyatta spoke strongly against British rule. "The land is ours," he told other Kikuyu. "When the Europeans came, they kept us back and took our land. We want self-government. Don't be afraid to spill your blood to get the land."

The Fight for Freedom

In 1952, terrible violence began. Mau Mau bands murdered both British and Kenyans. In response, British rule became even harsher. Thousands of Kikuyu were arrested, including Jomo Kenyatta.

Mau Mau violence continued while Kenyatta was in jail. The British were determined to end the revolt. By January 1960, the British succeeded. But the price was terrible. More than 11,500 Kenyans suspected of being Mau Mau were killed.

The British victory could not silence the Africans' cry for independence. From every corner of the land came the chant of *Uhuru!* In Swahili, *Uhuru* means "Freedom!" Pressure on the British grew. When Kenyatta's prison term ended, he was released and continued his struggle. At last, the British realized they had no choice. In 1960, they gave voting rights to Africans.

Kenyatta was elected president of the newly formed Kenya African National Union (KANU). In May 1963, this party won the national election in Kenya. The KANU had the right to establish a new government to replace British control. Kenya officially became independent of British rule on December 12, 1963. The next year, Kenya became a republic, and Kenyatta became its president. He held the office for the next 14 years, until his death in 1978. Kenyatta was a respected leader.

Case Study Review

1. Why was Jomo Kenyatta sentenced to prison?
2. **Formulating an Argument** If you could have defended Kenyatta during his trial, what one statement would you have made on his behalf?

SECTION 4

The Challenge of Independence

What were some of the challenges newly-independent countries in Africa faced?

Once African nations won freedom from European powers, they faced the challenge of building modern nations. In many ways, winning independence was easier than building a nation. Almost all Africans supported independence. Various African ethnic groups were willing to set aside their differences to fight against imperialism. Once the enemy was defeated, ethnic differences reemerged.

The Colonial Legacy

For more than 100 years, Europeans controlled the African continent. The Europeans left a lasting **legacy** in Africa. A legacy is something handed down from the past. One legacy was the borders Europeans drew when they divided Africa. As you read in Chapter 3, there are hundreds of ethnic and cultural groups in Africa. When the Europeans divided Africa in the 1800s, they did so without any regard for the ethnic and cultural differences among Africans. European imperialists drew borders that were convenient for them. However, these borders were not convenient for the tribes that lived within them. Sometimes, European boundaries separated the members of a single tribe. Other times, the boundaries mixed together enemy tribes or tribes that spoke different languages. Once African nations gained freedom, African leaders had to work to help people overcome their differences.

Imperialism greatly weakened many elements of African culture. Colonial governments took away farm and pasture lands that had been used by African tribes. This meant that many families were no longer able to farm. Traditional family ties were broken as fathers and brothers were forced to work in faraway mines or on plantations. Other families left their villages to try to find work in cities.

By taking land away from Africans, the Europeans also destroyed the traditional idea of land ownership. Africans had thought of the land as belonging to the entire clan or village. They shared the land. Europeans introduced the idea of individual land ownership.

Imperialism also put an end to the traditional legal system of Africa. This system was based on respect for elders and the chief. The Europeans introduced the idea of a legal code. A code is made up of formal laws and rules. The Europeans forced Africans to follow the legal code. This weakened an important part of African culture.

With the destruction of their traditional cultures, Africans were faced with building countries based on European ideas of government and economics. However, few Africans had experience running governments and economies of this type. Under European rule, few Africans had been given a chance to take part in politics.

As a result, when Africans assumed leadership positions, they made many mistakes. As you will read in Chapter 6, African nations experimented with various types of governments and economies. Throughout the 1970s, 1980s, and 1990s, African nations struggled to find ways to improve the lives of their citizens.

Section 4 Review

1. Why did the leaders of the newly independent African countries lack political experience?
2. **Summarizing** What is the legacy of the many years of colonial rule in Africa?

I. Reviewing Vocabulary

Match each word on the left with the correct definition on the right.

1. missionary   **a.** strong devotion to and pride in one's country
2. imperialism   **b.** a policy of conquering and taking over foreign territory
3. nationalism   **c.** refusal to buy or use certain goods or services
4. boycott   **d.** a person who is sent to do religious work in a foreign country

II. Understanding the Chapter

Answer the questions below on a separate sheet of paper.

1. What were three causes of European imperialism?
2. Name four European countries that had colonies in Africa.
3. What were two negative effects of imperialism?
4. How did imperialism nearly destroy traditional African culture?

III. Building Skills: Interpreting a Primary Source

Below is part of a speech given by Jomo Kenyatta, the first president of Kenya, at its independence ceremonies in 1964.

Today, we have freedom and unity as pillars of the state. That is what republic means. The Republic is the people of Kenya. All through the colonial days, for the purpose of divide and rule, we were constantly reminded that we were Kikuyu or Wakamba. . . or Maasai or English. . . But now, the Republic has embodied those features of equality and respect which cut through any differences of race or tribe.

1. What did Kenyatta mean by "divide and rule"?
2. How does Kenyatta define the word *republic?*
3. What is Kenyatta's main idea?

IV. Working Together

Work with two or three other students to complete a study chart of several African nations. First, choose three or four nations. Then, using library or classroom resources, fill out a chart that lists the following items for each country: colonizing power, type of government, main languages, and problems and challenges.

On Assignment. . .

Writing Diary Entries: Put together the notes you took as you read the chapter. Then organize your notes into three diary entries about imperialism and nationalism in Africa. Keep in mind that a diary entry should read as if you were witnessing the events you describe. Share your diary entries with a classmate.

CHAPTER 5

Changing Patterns of Life in Africa

How has life in Africa changed in recent times?

In towns and cities across Africa, the religion of Islam is growing in popularity. Muslims gather many times a day at this beautiful mosque in the city of Omdurman in the Sudan.

On Assignment . . .

Creating a Fact Sheet:
In this chapter, your assignment is to work with several classmates to design a "Country Fact Sheet" for three or four countries in Africa. A fact sheet lists key information, including population and location. Study the map on page 593 and choose three or four countries in Africa. Then as you read the chapter, think about the kind of information you want to show on your fact sheet. Look for hint boxes that contain information that will help you decide what kinds of categories to include. You will also need to use library and classroom resources to complete the assignment.

Looking at Key Terms

- **Koran** the holy book of Islam
- **fundamentalism** a movement or point of view that opposes modern ideas and favors a return to strict religious values
- **literate** able to read and write
- **urbanization** the movement of people from the countryside to cities
- **bartering** trading goods or services without exchanging money
- **shantytown** a slum on the outskirts of a city
- **apartheid** the South African policy of strict separation of the races

SECTION 1

Cultural Changes Since Independence

How have cultural traditions changed in modern Africa?

The students sit cross-legged on mats on the tiled floor. They listen carefully to the teacher. He is teaching them to read and write in Arabic. The young people are eager to learn Arabic because they want to study the **Koran**. The Koran is the holy book of Islam. According to Muslims, it contains God's words as spoken to the prophet Muhammad. The Koran will help the students understand Islamic law and religion.

Suddenly, the sound of a muezzin (myoo•EZIN), or holy crier, is heard. The children stop what they are doing. They get on their knees and turn toward Mecca, the holy city in Saudi Arabia. They begin to pray. Muslims are required to pray at least five times a day.

You might think this scene is taking place somewhere in the Middle East—maybe Syria, Iran, or Iraq. In fact, it could easily be taking place in any of the countries of North or East Africa where the majority of people are Muslim. Islam—with about 278 million followers—is the fastest growing religion in Africa.

Islamic Fundamentalism

In the 1980s, Iran and Iraq were at war. During this war, thousands of teenage Iranian boys died. They had no weapons. As Iraqi soldiers approached, the Iranian boys rushed the enemy troops. The boys wore headbands that read "Warriors of God" in blood-red letters. They also carried small metal keys that their leader, Ayatollah Khomeini, promised would allow them to enter heaven.

The kind of passion the young volunteer soldiers displayed is an example of **fundamentalism**. Fundamentalism refers to a movement or point of view in which people oppose modern ideas and favor a return to strict religious values. All fundamentalists, whether Christian, Jewish, or Muslim, share a common approach. They believe in the absolute truth of their religion's own holy writings. For Christians, this means the Bible; for Jews, the Torah; and for Muslims, the Koran. Fundamentalists believe that their holy book should govern all aspects of life.

Islamic fundamentalists believe in the Sharia. The Sharia is the code of Islamic law. It offers a complete guide to Muslims on how to lead their lives. It covers such topics as cleanliness, diet, and dress.

Fundamentalism is usually strongest in countries that have developing economies and that have undergone a great deal of change in recent times. It often appeals to people who feel hostile toward modern, Western society. Many fundamentalists believe that Western ideas are destroying the traditional values of their society. Twenty-one-year-old Hussein Abdel-Meguid, a medical student at Cairo University, speaks for many young fundamentalists. He says, "Every time I turn on the television, I see the same things; guns, money, and violence. We get these shows from America. It is very bad for young people to be watching these things."

Islamic fundamentalism in Africa is strongest in the North African countries of Egypt, Algeria, and Tunisia. In these countries, some people are frustrated with governments that seem unwilling or unable to improve the lives of the people. People's frustration is fueled by widespread poverty and the lack of jobs. The fundamentalists promise a society free from foreign influences and corruption.

Some fundamentalist groups promote violence as a way to rid their countries of what they consider evil modern ways. But most fundamentalists are not violent. They attract followers by providing services such as medical care, schools, and religious teaching. They offer people a strong sense of what is right and wrong. They appeal to people's national pride.

Even though fundamentalists have not taken over the governments of any African countries, they have influenced governments to adopt some of their ideas. For example, the Algerian government has restricted the use of alcohol. Elected political leaders make a point of going to Mecca on a pilgrimage as required by the Koran. Egyptian television now includes many more religious programs.

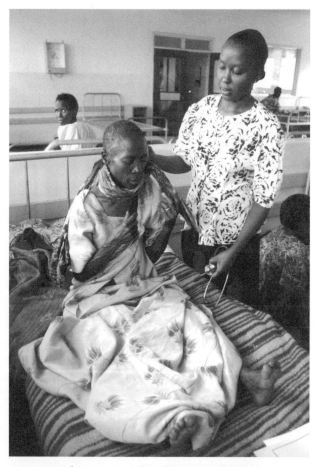

In many African countries, the roles of women are changing. More and more women are entering the work force. Here, a woman doctor treats a patient in a hospital in Uganda.

On Assignment . . .

You may wish to include information about women on your fact sheet. In the African countries you have chosen, what percentage of the population is made up of women? How many women are in the work force?

The Changing Role of Women

One major concern of Islamic fundamentalism is women. The lives of many women in Africa, like the lives of women everywhere, are changing. In Egypt, women make up 40 percent of the work force. Egypt has women doctors, scientists, and teachers. In some African countries, women are well-represented in the government.

These women hardly fit the traditional image of African women. All over Africa, but especially in the cities, many women look and live very much like women in the United States. Some women own their own homes. They dress in Western fashions. They drive cars. They work at a variety of jobs. Some work in factories. Others work in such fields as photography, electronics, dry cleaning, construction, and machine repair. A few own their own businesses. The selling of food and other goods in Ghana is controlled and operated primarily by women.

This is in sharp contrast to rural Africa. Here the role of women has changed only a little. In rural areas, women are considered a lifelong source of free labor. They walk miles every day to gather firewood and water. They cook the food, clean the house, and wash the clothes. Of course, they also bear and raise the children. Africa has the highest birthrate in the world. In some countries, the average woman has eight children.

As many countries shift from subsistence farming to cash-based economies, the men in rural areas often take jobs far away from home. This has increased the burden on women. According to the United Nations,

On your fact sheet, indicate what percentage of the people in your countries complete elementary school, high school, and college. For comparison, find out how many people in the United States have completed education at each level.

women perform up to 75 percent of all the farm work in Africa. Their average workday may be as long as 18 hours.

More Than One Wife

Many African societies practice polygamy. Under polygamy, a person may have two or more spouses. In African cultures, as in many cultures that practice polygamy, it is the men who take more than one wife. Since most families have incomes of less than $500 a year, wives are very valuable. A family's economic survival may depend on the income of all of the wives. In rural areas, a man and all of his wives may live within the same compound.

A wealthy man may have a farm in the country and a house in the city. He may then have one wife who attends social functions with him while another wife takes care of the farm.

The editor of a magazine for Kenyan women tries to explain polygamy from a woman's point of view. She says that some "women would rather marry a man who has some money and be one of his wives than to be the only wife of a poor man. The poorer the man, the less likely it is that he will have more than one wife."

Despite the tradition of polygamy, more and more men are opting for just one wife. For example, in Kenya, nearly two thirds of all married men have just one wife.

The Role of Education

In many parts of Africa, especially in remote villages, education is still very tradi-

tional. Children learn the skills they need to survive by watching their parents and other adults. Like children everywhere, African children play "house" and "store." They learn by playing the roles they will perform as adults.

During the age of imperialism, Europeans introduced Western-style education. At first this kind of education was offered to only a few people. In 1960, when much of Africa gained independence, only 9 percent of the people were **literate**, or able to read and write. After independence, many countries began literacy programs. They needed to train people to take over the jobs in industry and government that had been filled by Europeans. The governments built many schools, trained teachers, and developed job-training programs for adults.

Today, education is still a high priority. More than half of all African children attend primary school. More high schools and universities are being built. In 1990, the literacy rate in Africa was over 40 percent.

Parents often have to make great sacrifices to send just one child to school. They must work hard to earn enough extra money to pay school fees. The lucky child who is chosen to receive an education is usually a boy. As a result, nearly two thirds of the people in Africa who cannot read or write are women.

Young Africans who attend school receive an education that stresses work-related skills. African nations suffer from a shortage of skilled workers. This means that receiving an education almost guarantees a good job.

Section 1 Review

1. Why do you think many young people in Africa are attracted to Islamic fundamentalism?

2. **Compare and Contrast** How are the lives of African women in rural areas and in cities similar? How are they different?

SECTION 2

Growing Cities

Why are more Africans moving to the cities and what effect will this movement have?

In most African countries people live mainly in villages. They depend on farming for a living. It is a way of life that has not changed much in hundreds of years. Even today, 70 percent of African people live in rural areas. That way of life, however, is rapidly changing. Thousands of Africans are flocking to the cities. This movement of people from the countryside to the cities is called **urbanization**. In 1950, only two African cities had more than a million people. Experts believe that by the year 2000, there will be 37 African cities with populations over a million.

North Africa is the most urbanized part of Africa. In countries that border the Mediterranean Sea, most people live in cities of 20,000 or more. West Central Africa is not as urbanized. For example, only 8 percent of Burkina Faso's people live in cities. Yet

On Assignment . . .

What percentage of the people in your African countries live in cities? What are the largest cities in your countries? This is information you might include on your fact sheet.

in Guinea, nearly 60 percent live in urban areas. East Africa is the least urbanized part of Africa.

In most African countries, there is usually only one main city. It is the center of government and the hub of transportation and communication. Often, it dominates the economy because it is a major market as well as a manufacturing and financial center. Dakar, the capital of Senegal, is a good example. Nearly 75 percent of Senegal's business people and manufacturing workers work in Dakar. Over half the country's transportation and administrative workers work there, as well. While only 16 percent of Senegal's people live in Dakar, the city uses 95 percent of all the electricity in the country.

The thriving city of Dakar is one of the most important ports in Africa. With modern facilities, Dakar has become a major fishing and fish processing center for all of Africa.

Why People Move to Cities

People move to cities for many economic and social reasons. One economic cause of urbanization is the lack of opportunity in the countryside. In many rural areas, the farmlands have been overused and are no longer productive. In addition, large families do not have enough land to distribute to each child. Once children grow up, there is very little land for them to farm.

Another economic cause of urbanization is the desire for money. In the villages, most people raise all the food they require. If a person needs something his neighbor has, he would trade goods or services for it. This system is known as **bartering**. Today, many young people want electronic goods such as radios and televisions. Buying these goods requires money. Cities offer the best hope of earning money.

There are also social reasons that explain why young Africans are streaming to the cities. Some wish to break the strict bonds that traditional rural society places on them. Farming in the village is hard work. There is little time for fun. City life, in contrast, seems to be exciting. Cities offer amusements like movies and sporting events that are not available in rural villages.

The Effects of Urbanization

The movement of people off the land has had some serious effects on African countries. Generally, food production has declined. In Africa, having fewer farmers generally means less food. In the early 1990s, nearly 150 million Africans in 22 countries faced hunger and malnutrition. The situation is getting worse. In 1970, sub-Saharan Africa produced nearly all the food it needed. Today, the same region has to import nearly 20 percent of the grain it needs. However, urbanization is only one reason for the shortage of food. Disease, civil war, and drought are other reasons.

Another effect of urbanization is high unemployment. The lure of the city is strongest for young men. Unfortunately, there are not enough jobs for all of them. Many African countries have a high male unemployment rate. People who are unable to find jobs often become desperate. Some turn to alcohol and crime.

Urbanization also puts a great strain on family life. To provide for their families, men often seek jobs in the cities. Long periods go by before family members see each other again. As a result, women often have to learn to support themselves. Children grow up without fathers. Strong family ties are broken.

Tradition is often lost as people move to cities. Children who are born and raised in cities live very differently from those who grow up in traditional villages. City dwellers have little regard for the authority of their elders. They lose contact with their family's ancestral home.

On the other hand, the movement to the cities has had one positive effect. As more and more people move to urban areas, they come in contact with people of different clans and races. In this way, they learn about the customs and beliefs of other people. This has sometimes worked to relieve tensions between ethnic groups.

Much of Africa in the late 1990s has become more westernized. If you were to travel to most African capitals today, you would find tall buildings, big department stores, and heavy automobile traffic. African city dwellers are concerned with many of the same things we are. They worry about their jobs, and they work hard to try to buy a home or a car. They are very concerned about their children's education. At night, they may sit down to watch television, just as westerners do.

Section 2 Review

1. What are three reasons people in Africa are moving to cities?

2. **Making Inferences** Why do you suppose most educated Africans prefer city life to village life?

Lagos, Nigeria: A Small Village Grows Into a Large City

At night, driving along the marshy flats outside the city of Lagos, Nigeria, it seems that you are in a land without people. In the distance, the lights of the city flicker and glow like the last embers of a fire. But around you, there are no lights. Yet the flats are home to hundreds of thousands of people. Most have recently left their villages so they could live in the city. Living without electricity, their homes are not visible from the modern highways that surround Lagos.

Once Lagos was a small, quiet village. Two hundred years ago, it was a major slave trading post. Large numbers of Africans were shipped from the port of Lagos to the Americas. It was an ideal trading post for slavers because it was an island. This made is easy to defend. Lagos grew slowly and became a major city in Nigeria after independence.

Today, Lagos is Nigeria's leading commercial and manufacturing city—and one of Africa's fastest growing cities. Between 1970 and 1990, its population doubled to about 1.5 million people. Experts believe that by the year 2025, it may be one of the five largest cities in the world.

Henry Okukenu is one of the many Nigerians who have contributed to Lagos's rapid growth. Henry had long wanted to go to Lagos. He finally decided to leave his village when his friend Moses Murtela returned from the city with enough money to buy a herd of 50 goats.

Soon after, Henry left for Lagos with hardly a penny in his pocket. He walked the 100 miles of muddy roads in four days. Arriving in the city, he found lodging with cousins in a modern housing project built on one of Lagos's islands. Henry was used to living in cramped quarters. Among the Yoruba people, extended families live in small family compounds in large towns. From these towns, they often travel long distances to reach their farms during the growing seasons.

Henry's first view of Lagos convinced him that God must have built this city. In the downtown district on Lagos and Victoria islands, he saw huge buildings, expensive hotels, and wealthy private homes. He marveled at double-decker buses and lights that sparkled from dusk to dawn.

After Henry got a job in a small tourist shop on Victoria Island, he decided to build a house on the salt flats. His cousins helped him put up a shack made of corrugated iron, wood scraps, and mud. Mud is a readily available resource on the flats. At night, after the rains, Henry sinks ankle deep into the mud as he approaches his shack from the road.

Today Lagos is a sprawling city. The city has grown with no obvious planning. Residential areas mix with business and industrial areas. Sidewalks are filled with stalls. Crowded districts are located near modern high-rise office buildings. As more and more people pour into Lagos, finding housing becomes a big problem. Many of these people, like Henry, are forced to live in **shantytowns**, or slums, on the outskirts of the city.

Traffic jams in Lagos are world famous. There are not many buses or trains. People either drive their own cars or use private buses known as *molves*. These buses are often in poor condition and jam-packed. They break down constantly, tying up traffic. There are only three bridges that connect the city's crowded islands to the mainland. Each day at least 200,000 workers travel across the bridges. They travel either on foot, by bicycle, by motorbike, or by car or bus. The result is that it takes hours to make a relatively short trip. Sitting in traffic has become a permanent feature of life in Lagos. A large number of "hawkers" have taken advantage of these long traffic jams. While drivers sit captive in their cars, hawkers try to sell them everything from clocks to books to live chickens.

Despite its problems, Lagos is an exciting city. It is a huge commercial center. Its port handles more cargo than any other port on the west coast of Africa. As one writer describes it: "there is a zest for life that keeps the city thriving."

Henry Okukenu feels this zest for life every day in the city. He loves the bustle of canoes and ferries in the waterways. At lunch time, he likes to watch the boats entering and leaving the giant harbor. After work, he marvels at the mass of shopkeepers and street vendors.

Henry has saved money and has been able to buy furniture for his shack. Although he would be a rich person if he returned to his village, he doesn't think he will ever leave Lagos. The excitement of the city has become a part of his life.

Case Study Review

1. Why is traffic congestion such a big problem in Lagos?
2. **Understanding Points of View** Despite all of its problems, why do you think Lagos still attracts more and more people?

Literature and the Arts

What roles do literature, art, and music play in African life?

When we think of literature, we usually think of stories or poetry written by an author. Much of Africa's literature has been oral, or passed down from one generation to the next by word of mouth. A valued member of each community is the griot, or storyteller. The griot learns stories from the elders and in turn passes them on to younger members of the clan. In this way, the griot helps preserve traditional culture.

The Oral Tradition

In traditional Africa, storytelling involves more than listening. The griot may call on the audience to sing songs that are part of the story. Often listeners are expected to comment on the story. The storyteller may ask questions. The griot's purpose is both to educate and entertain.

African stories often teach a lesson or carry a moral. The story of the bat that you read in Chapter 3 is an example of such a tale. When telling a tale that involves animals, the storyteller may act out the roles. Often these kinds of stories tell of small creatures like spiders who use their intelligence to outwit bigger and stronger animals.

Besides stories, another form of oral literature is the proverb. A proverb is a short saying that expresses some well-known fact or common experience. Almost every culture has its favorite proverbs. Benjamin Franklin wrote down many of the more familiar U.S. proverbs. For example, he wrote, "A penny saved is a penny earned." African proverbs have similar messages. For example, "The one with the sharp knife will eat meat." This means that the person who is best prepared will get the reward. Another proverb states: "One does not follow a snake into its hole." The message warns listeners not to take unnecessary risks.

Written Literature

The oral tradition is still popular in Africa today. However, a growing number of writers are producing books. African writers publish their work in various African languages as well as in French, English, and Portuguese. Many of the new writers were educated in colonial schools and continue to write in the language of their former rulers.

One of the first great modern novelists of sub-Saharan Africa was Thomas Mofolo. He was born in Lesotho and wrote in the Sotho language in the 1920s and 1930s. His novel, *Pitsens*, tells the story of a young African growing up during the age of imperialism. Another novel, *Chaka*, is a story based on the life of a famous Zulu chief.

In the 1930s, a number of African writers were members of the negritude movement. This movement celebrated African culture. Negritude writers held that African culture was more in harmony with nature and life than was Western culture. They praised Africans' love for their land and their respect for their ancestors and their history.

A number of African authors focus on the problems of modern Africa. A common theme is the clash of old and new values. One writer who explores this theme is Chinua Achebe (CHIN•oo•ah ah•CHAY•bay). In his novel, *Things Fall Apart*, Achebe describes traditional African life in conflict with colonial rule and westernization.

Other African writers explore the experiences of young people. Topics include life in the cities, friendship, dating, and finding work. These African writers give us insights into life in contemporary Africa.

South African writers, both black and white, have written many books about life under **apartheid**. Apartheid was a policy of racial segregation and discrimination against nonwhites in South Africa. You will read more about apartheid in South Africa in Chapter 6. Books by writers such as Nadine Gordimer alerted people all around the world to the injustice of apartheid. Gordimer was awarded the Nobel Prize for literature in 1991.

Theater and Film in Africa

Traditional theater in Africa combines acting and singing. The actors often speak directly to the audience. People in the audience sometimes call out to the actors, answering questions the actors have asked.

Theater is often part of important festivals. Actors practice for months to learn the complicated dance steps and songs of a particular play. On the day of the festival, they dress in colorful costumes. Often the costumes include masks carved of wood. Plays are usually about the traditional history of a tribe. Actors who wear the masks and perform the songs and dances represent spirits. The spirits may be those of ancestors or important historical figures. The audience does not just sit by and watch quietly, however. The men, women, and children often join the "masks," turning the play into a community event.

Film In recent years, African films have grown into an important art form. Films from the United States and other countries are quite popular, but many Africans prefer films written by other Africans. Not surprisingly, these films focus on the real lives of African people. The problem for African filmmakers is that their films are poorly distributed both in Africa and abroad. A film that is not distributed to many theaters cannot be profitable. As a result, few films are made.

Visual Arts in Africa

Art in Africa is closely tied to the traditional beliefs and values of the African people. Painting, sculpture, and crafts are all part of everyday life. From ancient times to the present, Africans have used various art forms. Art is everywhere in Africa. It decorates everyday objects like clothing, baskets, boats, jewelry, and homes.

The staffs of tribal chiefs are made from beautifully hand-carved wood. The buses that carry people to work in the cities have colorful paintings splashed on them. Even in remote villages, women wear elegantly designed necklaces and bracelets.

African artists use many materials for their work. In the ancient kingdom of Benin, sculptors perfected a technique for making beautiful bronze figures. Other artists made beautiful works out of clay. Carved wooden objects are still created for everyday use. Wooden spoons for cooking as well as bowls used for serving food are carved with graceful designs. In Africa, art is not normally produced as something to be sold. Instead, it is created as an expression of beauty and culture.

Worldwide Influence In the last hundred years, African art has had a strong influence on Western art. In the 1900s, French painters living in Paris began to imitate African art objects. At the time, most Western art tried to show people and nature as realistically as possible. The French painters admired the abstract nature of African art. In abstract art, the finished work may not look at all like an actual object. They liked that African sculpture simplified the most important features of a figure. Africans seemed to be more interested in showing an idea rather than an actual person. Among the modern artists who were influenced by African art were Pablo Picasso of Spain and Henri Matisse of France.

Music and Dance

Music and dance are part of everyday life in Africa. There are traditional dances for rain, for a good harvest, and for a successful hunt. Like people in the United States, Africans dance at weddings and other celebrations. Sometimes they dance just for the fun of it. Dance is an important part of community life. Usually everyone participates. Africans almost always dance in groups. The dancers move their bodies to the rhythms being played by drums and rattles made from gourds.

African music has had a great influence on the world. During the time of slavery, many Africans were captured and forced to go to other countries. In the United States, the music of the enslaved Africans formed a basis for jazz. Gospel music and the blues also reflect African influences. Much of the music people in the United States enjoy today, including rhythm and blues and rock-and-roll, has African roots.

The best-selling album of 1986 and the winner of the Grammy award for album of the year was *Graceland*. This album featured Paul Simon and a ten-member South African group by the name of Ladysmith Black Mambazo. It exposed millions of listeners to the sound of African music. It also began a movement called "Afropop" or "worldbeat."

Much of the music that came out of South Africa was protest music against apartheid. It originated in urban shantytowns. The lyrics called for justice and freedom. The music combined the rapid beat of traditional drums with the sound of Western bass guitars and saxophones. The music lifted the spirits of black South

Africans during the era of apartheid. As one South African musician remarked, "Music, like prayer, is a healing force."

Section 3 Review

1. What is a common theme in modern African writing?

2. **Interpreting a Quote** Would you agree with the quote: "In Africa, art is not separate from everyday life"? Explain.

Rhythm is highly developed in African music. Thus, various types of drums are often used by African musicians. Above, a musical group performs in Cameroon.

I. Reviewing Vocabulary

Match each word on the left with the correct definition on the right.

1. Koran
2. fundamentalism
3. urbanization
4. literate

a. able to read and write
b. a movement that opposes modern ideas and favors a return to strict religious values
c. the holy book of Islam
d. the movement of people from rural areas to cities

II. Understanding the Chapter

Answer the questions below on a separate piece of paper.

1. Why do Islamic fundamentalists believe that the Koran should govern all aspects of life?
2. What effect has urbanization had on food production?
3. How is traditional African literature different from Western literature?
4. What are three challenges the city of Lagos faces?

III. Building Skills: Identifying Cause and Effect

In each pair below, tell which is the cause and which is the effect.

1. **a.** Millions of Africans flood into cities. **b.** The countryside is crowded and farming and grazing areas are already overused.

2. **a.** African cities grow. **b.** Traditional family ties are weakened.

3. **a.** Many people turn to alcohol and crime. **b.** People are unable to find jobs.

IV. Working Together

Work with three or four classmates to create a pamphlet for an art and literature museum exhibit that celebrates African culture. Use library and classroom resources to decide on at least five writers and five artists you will highlight in your exhibit. Then describe your choices in a pamphlet to attract people to the museum.

On Assignment . . .

Creating a Fact Sheet: It is now time to organize your group and complete your fact sheet. First decide what categories to include. Your sheet should contain at least five categories. Use almanacs, encyclopedias, and other books to gather your facts. Present your completed fact sheet to the class.

Leon Maurice Anoma Kanié, author of "All That You Have Given Me, Africa," was born in Ivory Coast and grew up under French rule. In his poetry, Kanié celebrates the beauty of Africa and his African culture.

Like Kanié, Léopold Senghor writes poetry that reflects his love of Africa and his pride in his African heritage. Senghor was both a fine writer and a respected political leader. He was born in 1906 in Senegal, a part of French West Africa, and was educated in France. Senghor was one of the most important figures of the negritude movement. This movement was formed by Africans who strongly opposed European colonialism and wished to preserve African traditions. The poems you are about to read, "The Prebend Garden" and "Interior" reflect Senghor's pride in Africa and his attempt to come to terms with European culture.

Somali painter Abdim Dr No shows respect for tradition and reverence of African culture. *Days End* shows Somali women returning to their village after a day of work.

All That You Have Given Me, Africa

Leon Maurice Anoma Kanié
(translated by Kathleen Weaver)

All that you have given me, Africa
Lakes, forests, misted lagoons[1]
All that you have given me,
Music, dances, all night stories around a fire
All that you have etched in my skin
Pigments[2] of my ancestors
Indelible[3] in my blood
All that you have given me Africa
Makes me walk
With a step that is like no other
Hip broken under the weight of time,
Feet large with journeys,
All that you have left to me
Even this lassitude[4] bound to my heels,
I bear it with pride on my forehead
My health is no more to be lost
And I go forward
Praising my race which is no better
Or worse than any other.
All that you have given me Africa,
Savannahs[5] gold in the noonday sun
Your beasts that men call wicked,
Your mines, inexplicable[6] treasures
Obsession of a hostile world
Your suffering for lost paradises,
All that, I protect with an unforgiving hand
As far as the clear horizons
So that your heaven-given task
May be safe forever.

---

[1]**lagoons** (luh-GOONZ) *n. pl.* bodies of water which are bounded by sandbars or coral reefs
[2]**pigments** (PIHG-muhnts) *n. pl.* substances used to give color
[3]**indelible** (ihn-DEHL-uh-buhl) *adj.* permanent
[4]**lassitude** (LAS-ih-tood) *n.* feeling of exhaustion or weakness
[5]**savannahs** (suh-VAN-uhz) *n. pl.* flat, treeless grasslands of warm regions
[6]**inexplicable** (ihn-EHK-splih-kuh-buhl) *adj.* not capable of being explained

The Prebend Gardens

Léopold Sédar Senghor

Prebend[7] gardens
You touched my shoulder
As I walked by your green gates,
Indifferent . . .

But today you are my friend
On this October afternoon
—It is night, it is day in the streets and underbrush—
On this October afternoon
Where in my usual daze I can barely hear
Lamenting[8] and searching its way in some lost clearing in me
A muted[9] trumpet.

Interior

Léopold Sédar Senghor

We bathe in an African presence
Of sparkling soft carpets from Timbuktu,[10]
Moorish[11] cushions,
Musky fragrances,
Dark, heavy furniture from Guinea and the Congo,
Mats thick with silence,
Authentic, primitive masks
On the primitive, solid walls.
And, friendly lamp, your tenderness
Softens my obsession[12] with this presence so
Black, brown, and red, Oh! red as African soil.

---

[7]**Prebend** (PREE-behnd) *n.* land owned by the Church of England
[8]**lamenting** (luh-MEHNT-ing) *v.* feeling or expressing great sorrow
[9]**muted** (MYOOT-uhd) *adj.* muffled or softer in sound
[10]**Timbuktu** (tihm-buhk-TOO) *n.* town in West Africa
[11]**Moorish** (MOOR-ihsh) *adj.* of the Moors, especially those Muslim people of northern Africa who invaded Spain in the 8th century A.D.
[12]**obsession** (uhb-SEHSH-uhn) *n.* a thought or emotion that occupies the mind continually

Africans are moving their nations forward by bringing economic change while preserving their culture. Here, a student reads English medical books in a Nigerian Library.

Making Connections

1. What aspects of African culture—both past and present—are presented in the poems?

2. **Interpreting Poetry** Choose one poem. What words and images does the poet use to express his pride in his African identity? What words and images does the poet use to express his opposition to European colonialism?

CHAPTER 6

Economic and Political Trends

How are Africans meeting the economic and political challenges of today?

Denied basic human rights, blacks in South Africa fought segregation bitterly. In 1994, the years of struggle were finally rewarded with an open election for all South Africans.

On Assignment. . .

Creating a Mural: A mural is a wall painting that shows a variety of activities and characters. Working in small groups, create a mural about Africa today. Choose a few countries in different parts of the continent to highlight in your mural. As you read through the chapter, look for the On Assignment boxes. The boxes will contain ideas for your mural.

Looking at Key Terms

- **coup** a takeover of government
- **subsidy** assistance that a government provides to consumers or industries
- **multinational** having operations in many countries
- **diversify** to make more varied; to give additional options
- **federal system** system of government in which the central government shares power with lower-level governments
- **secede** to withdraw, as a state or region withdraws from a larger nation
- **multiracial** made up of many races

Political Choices

Has democracy been successful in Africa?

There was a happy glow in the crowd as if people were at a major sports event or a street fair. Long lines snaked through the streets. Vendors sold food and cold drinks. Knowing they would have to wait for hours, many people sat in folding chairs they had brought and used umbrellas to fend off the sun. Some were still in line long after dark.

The place: Soweto (soh•WEHT•oh), South Africa. The time: April 1994. For the first time, black South Africans were voting in a free national election. One man said: "We've been waiting five hours. But other people have been waiting 40 years." The result of the election was a stunning victory for Nelson Mandela—and for democracy. Mandela, head of the African National Congress (ANC), had spent 28 years in prison because he had fought against a white-ruled South Africa.

Africa's independence movements had their first successes in the 1950s. Since then, democracy has made progress on the continent. Throughout Africa, democratic elections became more frequent in the 1990s. Voters chose governments in such nations as Benin (beh•NEEN), Malawi, Mozambique (moh•zahm•BEEK), and Zambia.

But the trend was a mixed one. Dictators still ruled in Zaire and a few other nations. Soldiers controlled the government in such countries as Nigeria and Sierra Leone.

Building National Unity

Tanzania (tan•zuh•NEE•uh), in East Africa, has 120 ethnic groups, speaking dozens of languages. Since Tanzania gained independence in 1961, its people have lived together in harmony. In 1995, they elected a president in free elections.

Next door to Tanzania are Rwanda and Burundi. They have just two main ethnic groups—the Hutu (HOO•too) and the Tutsi (TOOT•see). In the 1990s, both Rwanda and Burundi were torn by civil wars. People of one group massacred those of the other. Under such conditions, free elections were an impossible dream.

Building national unity is a goal of all African nations. It is a job that is complicated by the continent's ethnic variety and by its history of rule by colonial powers.

The Impact of Colonialism Some of Africa's ethnic feuds have long and bloody histories. Almost all were twisted into their current shapes by the period of colonial rule. Under colonial rule, Africans lost control of their own destinies. Old ways of life crumbled. Old methods for making group decisions no longer worked.

As you read in Chapter 4, colonial borders did some of the damage. They grouped different cultures together in strange new ways. They split tribes and clans that had once been together. Colonial rule also broke up old political systems. Local leaders lost status and power. Colonial capitals became the chief centers of power and influence.

Colonial rulers often played favorites among ethnic groups. They gave some groups special privileges, like jobs in colonial government. They punished other groups—especially groups that put up resistance.

Trying to Forge New Ties Imagine that an outside power has conquered Maine and Quebec. It abolishes all local governments and creates new ones. Call the new colony Norvonia. It spans the U.S.–Canadian border. Its rulers jail all opponents. They keep a tight grip on the news media. They ban the use of English or French in public life. People have to learn a new language. They begin to forget the old ways. After a hundred years, the outsiders pull out. What will happen to Norvonia? Will it hold together? How will its people rule themselves?

COUNTRIES OF AFRICA

Country	Capital	Area (Square miles)	Population (Millions of people)	Population Under Age 15 (Percent)
NORTH AFRICA				
Algeria	Algiers	919,590	27.3	44
Egypt	Cairo	384,380	58.3	39
Libya	Tripoli	679,360	4.9	50
Morocco	Rabat	172,320	28.0	40
Sudan	Khartoum	917,370	27.4	46
Tunisia	Tunis	59,980	8.6	37
Western Sahara (status in dispute)	Al Aaiún	103,00	0.2	not available
CENTRAL AFRICA				
Burundi	Bujumbura	9,900	5.8	46
Cameroon	Yaoundé	179,690	12.8	45
Central African Republic	Bangui	240,530	3.1	42
Chad	N'Djamena	486,180	5.4	41
Congo	Brazzaville	131,850	2.4	44
Equatorial Guinea	Malabo	10,830	0.4	43
Gabon	Libreville	99,490	1.1	33
Rwanda	Kigali	9,530	7.4	49
São Tomé and Príncipe	São Tomé	370	0.1	42
Zaire	Kinshasa	875,520	41.2	43
SOUTHERN AFRICA				
Angola	Luanda	481,350	9.5	45
Botswana	Gaborone	218,810	1.4	48
Lesotho	Maseru	11,720	1.9	41
Malawi	Lilongwe	36,320	10.0	48
Mozambique	Maputo	302,740	15.3	44
Namibia	Windhoek	317,870	1.6	46
South Africa	Pretoria	471,440	39.0	40
Swaziland	Mbabane	6,640	0.8	47
Zambia	Lusaka	287,020	8.6	49
Zimbabwe	Harare	149,290	10.7	45

Africa's population of more than 600 million people is young and getting younger.

Country	Capital	Area (Square miles)	Population (Millions of people)	Population Under Age 15 (Percent)
WEST AFRICA				
Benin	Porto-Novo	42,710	5.1	46
Burkina Faso	Ouagadougou	105,710	10.0	48
Cape Verde	Cidade de Praia	1.560	0.4	45
Côte d'Ivoire	Abidjan	122,780	13.4	48
Gambia	Banjul	3,860	0.9	44
Ghana	Accra	88,810	16.4	45
Guinea	Conakry	94,930	6.2	44
Guinea-Bissau	Bissau	10,860	1.0	43
Liberia	Monrovia	37,190	2.8	46
Mali	Bamako	471,120	8.9	46
Mauritania	Nouakchott	395,840	2.2	44
Niger	Niamey	489,070	8.5	49
Nigeria	Abuja	351,650	95.1	45
Senegal	Dakar	74,340	7.9	47
Sierra Leone	Freetown	27,650	4.5	44
Togo	Lomé	21,000	4.1	49
EAST AFRICA				
Comoros	Moroni	860	0.5	48
Djibouti	Djibouti	8,960	0.5	45
Eritrea	Asmara	45,300	3.2	not available
Ethiopia	Addis Ababa	425,100	56.7	49
Kenya	Nairobi	219,960	27.7	49
Madagascar	Antananarivo	224,530	13.3	47
Mauritius	Port Louis	710	1.1	30
Reunion	St. Denis	970	0.6	30
Somalia	Mogadishu	242,220	9.5	46
Seychelles	Victoria	100	0.1	35
Tanzania	Dar-es-Salaam	342,100	27.8	47
Uganda	Kampala	77,050	18.1	49

In how many African countries are more than one out of three people under the age of 15?

When independence came to Africa's colonies, the new leaders faced similar questions. Though they were unhappy with the borders left by the colonial powers, they had no choice but to work to build African nations on the European pattern. They simply didn't know any other way. They chose national anthems and designed flags. Getting people to salute the flags, however, was easier than getting them to believe that they all really belonged to one nation.

Keeping Old Ties Imagine that you belong to a rural farm family in Rwanda. You may be Hutu or Tutsi. Either way, you believe that you cannot depend on the national army to protect you. After all, army units had participated in massacres of both Tutsi and Hutu in 1994. To whom can you turn for safety? Only to those who belong to your own ethnic group, you believe.

In most African countries, ethnic ties remain strong. People of an ethnic group often support one another in business. Also, they may find jobs through members of their group who hold public office. Officeholders often direct government money to personal friends and to members of their own ethnic groups.

The First Years of Independence

When African nations first became independent, most of them formed governments based on a European model. They had legislatures. They had systems for electing national leaders. But many of democracy's support structures were missing. African countries had only a small educated class. There was no tradition of a free press to inform people of public issues. There were no trained opposition leaders to take turns holding power. Thus, democracy proved weak in the early years of independence.

One-Party Rule Many African nations adopted a system of one-party rule. Guinea, a former French colony in West Africa, was an example. Its party was the Democratic Party of Guinea.

Guinea's president was Sékou Touré (SAY•koo too•RAY). Touré did not allow rival parties. He thought they would only stir trouble between different groups.

Touré's party had bases in every village. At first, party leaders listened to ordinary people's ideas and tried to carry them out. But as time passed, the party's leaders became set in their ways. Leaders at the top set the rules. People at the local level—even local party leaders—had little say.

Many African nations adopted this one-party system. Some claimed that it was patterned after traditional African ways. In some nations, one-party rule did promote national unity. However, in other nations like Mozambique it contributed to violent divisions.

Military Rule In some African nations, democracy gave way to military rule. Military officers were often among the few people who had advanced training or education. They also had powerful weapons. They could stage a military **coup** (koo), or takeover. Often, military officers took power because they believed that civilian rule had failed. Many civilian governments were riddled with corruption. Leaders got rich by stealing public funds or taking bribes. Military leaders promised to "clean up the mess" and restore order.

A Swing to Democracy Neither one-party rule nor military rule solved the problems that African nations faced. People in African nations had expected great gains

On Assignment . . .

Skim this section by reading the heads and subheads. Write down the issues that are most important to understanding the history of democracy in Africa. Draw a sketch for your mural showing how democracy is working in Africa.

Other African nations took steps toward democracy in the 1990s. They included Malawi, Mozambique, Zambia, Benin, Ethiopia, and, of course, South Africa.

Section 1 Review

1. Why did the military take control of governments in many African countries after independence?

2. **Making Connections** What are some traditions that keep democracy alive in the United States?

SECTION 2

Economic Choices

How are African nations trying to strengthen their economies?

In Tanzania, the word the government used to describe its economy was *"ujamaa"* (oo•jah•MAH). It means "pulling together." The government used this slogan to stir support for its program of "African socialism." Tanzania's government owned most industries. It even established government-owned farms. This policy of government ownership is known as *socialism*.

In Ivory Coast, the term that described its economy was *free enterprise*. Free enterprise is an economic system in which most decisions are made by private individuals who are trying to make a profit. For years, Ivory Coast's government was one of the few in Africa to favor a system in which government was not too deeply involved in the economy.

Since the 1980s, Tanzania, like many other governments, has turned away from African socialism and toward free enterprise. The reason is simple: the old ways weren't

Throughout Africa, from the Mediterranean to the Cape of Good Hope, democracy is alive and vibrant. Above, a demonstration in Bamako, Mali, protests the actions of the ruling party and calls for a new government.

from independence. But they saw little improvement in their day-to-day lives.

By the end of the 1980s, many Africans had become active in the democracy movement. One such person was Djibril Coulibaly (jih•BREEL coo•lee•bah•LEE), a student in Mali. In 1991, he joined other students and government workers who were protesting in the capital city, Bamako. The demonstrators attacked soldiers and tanks. The soldiers fired their guns. At least 100 people died. But the protest brought about the end of the mili-

working. Production had declined. Prices were high. People could not get the goods they needed.

Will the new ways succeed where the old ones failed? That remains to be seen.

Mixed Economies

Most African nations today have mixed economies. Each nation uses a blend of socialist and free enterprise policies.

Leaning Toward Socialism As you have just read, countries whose governments exert a strong influence over economic decisions lean toward socialism. These governments often own all or part of major industries. They give **subsidies**, or assistance, to industries and consumers. For example, many governments set low prices for basic foods that people eat every day. These subsidies help to protect the poorest people in society from starvation.

Food subsidies are popular in urban areas, where people have to buy their food. But subsidies can cause problems, too. One problem is that they are expensive. The government may have to collect high taxes to pay for them. Another problem is that food subsidies hold down the prices that farmers receive. The subsidies set a price for the food that is lower than the price the food would get in a free market. That means farmers have less money with which to buy fertilizer and new equipment. If farmers earned more money, they would be able to improve their farms. Then they could do a better job of feeding Africa's people.

Leaning Toward Free Enterprise Governments that lean toward free enterprise take a more "hands-off" approach. They are less likely to own industries. They try to keep taxes low to encourage people to invest their money in private businesses. They have few regulations for businesses to follow. They generally leave prices free to rise or fall.

Such policies open many opportunities to people willing to risk their money. Private businesses can flourish. Private investors respond quickly to changes in the market. They start new lines of business that seem likely to make a profit. In contrast, government-owned businesses are often slow to change. Governments may refuse to close a money-losing factory, since that would put people—voters—out of work.

Many countries in Africa that used to lean toward socialism have started to change their policies. Many have sold industries to private buyers. For example, in 1994, Ghana's government sold off its shares in a major gold mining business. The move brought millions of dollars into the state's treasury. It also gave private owners the opportunity to build up industry.

In nations that lean toward free enterprise, large companies often make investments. Such companies have operations in many countries. These companies are called **multinational** corporations.

Not everyone is happy with the shift toward free enterprise. Some Africans argue that their governments no longer protect poor people. They also worry that rich business people and multinational corporations will gain too much influence.

Challenges and Problems

From the time of independence, Africa's nations have faced major economic problems. Although they have made progress in some areas, much remains to be done.

Developing Agriculture At the time of independence, most Africans were subsistence farmers. They grew food for their own families and neighbors. Because there weren't many roads, farmers had few ways to get their crops to distant markets. Even today, subsistence farming is common in rural areas. However, since independence, African governments have encouraged the spread of cash crops. A cash crop is one that is sold for money.

Some cash farmers work on a small scale. For example, women in Gambia grow vegetables for sale at city markets. Each farmer works her own land. She uses the simplest equipment. Other cash farmers have much larger operations. For example, big companies run flower farms.

Diversifying Economies Many African countries depend on one or two major crops or minerals. Zambia gets 80 percent of its income from exporting copper. Ivory Coast depends mainly on cocoa. Kenya sells coffee. Zimbabwe sells tobacco. Many countries throughout the world depend on one crop. For example, Latin American countries such as Brazil, Ecuador, El Salvador, and Colombia depend on the export of coffee.

African nations are trying to **diversify** their economies. That is, they are attempting to develop more products or services that they can sell on world markets. A nation that depends on one or two products is at the mercy of outside forces. If drought or insects

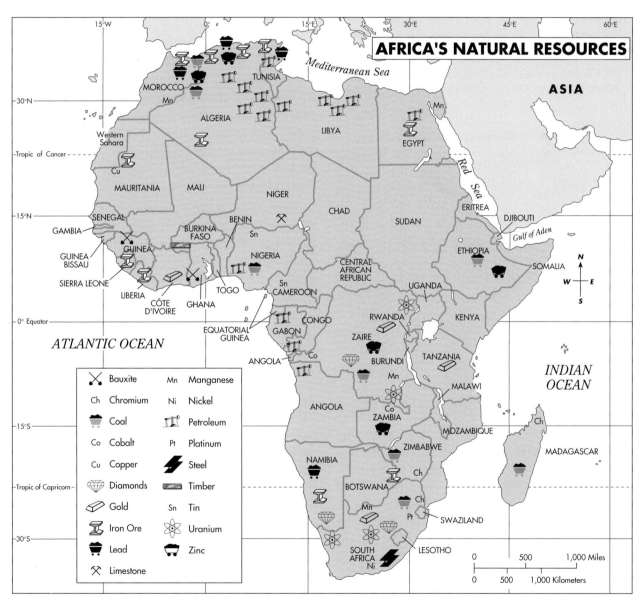

AFRICA'S NATURAL RESOURCES

Bauxite	Mn	Manganese
Ch	Chromium	Ni	Nickel
	Coal		Petroleum
Co	Cobalt	Pt	Platinum
Cu	Copper		Steel
	Diamonds		Timber
	Gold	Sn	Tin
	Iron Ore		Uranium
	Lead		Zinc
	Limestone		

Interaction Africa is rich in resources. What is Tanzania's major resource? What resource is found in countries from Algeria to Angola? Which African countries are major coal producers?

destroy the crop, there is nothing else to sell. If the world price for the crop suddenly drops, so does the nation's income.

Dealing With Drought and Famine

The people of Africa are more exposed than most people to natural disasters, such as drought. Along the equator, rain falls almost every day. But north and south of the equator, rain comes only at certain seasons. It varies greatly from year to year. Often, the rains don't come at all. Some farmers make up for poor rainfall by irrigating their crops. But most farmers have no source of water. When rains fail, they watch their crops wither. Then they go hungry.

Almost every year, famine strikes one or more countries in Africa. Most often, it is the countries on the edges of the Sahara that experience drought. There, rainfall is scant even in the best years. Countries like Sudan, Ethiopia, and Somalia had famines in the 1990s. Famines may also occur in countries where farming is disrupted by civil war.

Drought and famine have devastating effects on the economies of African nations. Agriculture is a main source of income for many Africans. Most people cannot afford to buy imported food. The world's nations often pitch in and send food in times of need. But food deliveries are often inadequate. Also, they may not reach remote areas where people are most in need.

Dealing With Rising Populations

Africa's population is fairly low. But it is increasing faster than the population of any other continent. One reason for this increase is that African parents often have many children. Traditionally this was because many African children died in the first year of life. Having many children was a way of making sure that some survived. Today, however, death rates for children are dropping because of better health care efforts. Thus, each year, Africa's population rises by about 3 percent. At that rate, the population will double every 23 years.

On Assignment . . .

How could you show in your mural the economic issues facing Africa? Write down the most important issues covered in this section. Then make sketches of them. Keep your ideas and sketches for the mural.

Is population growth good for the economy? Again, in traditional African society, it was. An African proverb held that "a child is born not only with a mouth to feed but also with two hands with which to work." In other words, more people meant more workers.

Nowadays, many government leaders see population growth as a problem for the economy. They worry about high unemployment rates and overcrowding in the cities. Many nations have started programs to encourage married couples to have fewer children.

Meeting Debt Payments

From the 1960s through the 1980s, African nations borrowed heavily to build up their economies. International agencies were eager to help. They wanted to promote economic development.

In the 1990s, many of the loans had to be paid back. African nations found themselves saddled with a large debt. Like consumers who are deeply in debt because they made an expensive purchase, African nations found it hard to get new credit. Worse yet, they had used much of their precious income to make payments on old loans. Mali, for example, spent 60 percent of its budget on debt payments.

Section 2 Review

1. What free-enterprise policies have many African countries adopted?

2. **Evaluating Information** Why do African nations want to diversify their economies?

Nigeria's Ethnic Divisions

With more than 100 million people, Nigeria, in West Africa, is the continent's most populous nation. Nigeria's population consists of more than 250 different ethnic groups. When Nigeria was a colony, the British imposed unity on the Nigerians. But since 1960, Nigeria has been independent. Its separate groups have struggled to find a system under which all of them can live together in peace.

Trying to Unite

Nigeria decided to try a **federal system**, a system in which each major region has a strong government of its own. As in the United States, the powers of the central government would be limited. But ethnic and religious disputes made everything very complicated.

Since independence, Nigeria's four largest ethnic groups have competed for power. In the southwest live the Yoruba (YOR•uh•buh). The Ibos live in the southeast. Many people in the southeast and southwest are Christians.

Two groups, the Hausas and the Fulani, live in the north. Most people there are Muslims. Northerners outnumber other Nigerians and have dominated the army. They have provided most of Nigeria's top leaders.

Civil War (1967–1970)

In the mid-1960s, Nigeria's federal government began to fall apart. A military officer gained control of the national government and declared an end to the federal system. The officer was an Ibo. His actions aroused fears among other groups.

Mobs rioted in northern Nigeria and attacked Ibos who lived there. Many Ibos were massacred. Others fled to the southeast, seeking safety in the Ibo heartland. In May 1967, eastern Nigeria **seceded**, or withdrew, from Nigeria. It set up the independent Republic of Biafra (bee•AF•ruh).

The secession touched off a civil war that lasted for three years. An estimated 1.5 million people—mostly Ibos—died in combat. A Nigerian blockade kept food and supplies from reaching Biafra. As a result, hundreds of thousands of Biafrans died of hunger and disease. Finally, Biafra gave up. Nigeria was once again united. It restored its federal system and tried again.

Who Will Rule?

After 1970, Nigeria switched between periods of civilian and military rule. Most of the time, military officers held power. They imposed strict rule. Military police arrested opponents, censored newspapers, and blocked most forms of political action.

Corruption was common under both civilian and military governments. Top leaders became rich. Officials at lower levels sought bribes in order to eke out a living. Ordinary Nigerians sometimes had to make payoffs in order to get driver's licenses or other official documents.

Wealth or Poverty?

Nigeria has the potential to be a very rich nation. It is a major oil producer. Oil wells dot many marshes and

Lagos, Nigeria is a crowded, bustling city. Nigerians move to Lagos from all over the country to find a better life.

lowlands. But since the 1970s, oil income has dropped. The amount of money entering the country has fallen dramatically.

Nigerians are struggling to find solutions to their problems. They are seeking a way to bring back civilian rule and to give people a say in the way they are governed. When censorship is lifted, Nigeria is known for its free press. It has many educated leaders. It has a strong university system. One day, Nigeria may emerge from the shadows to assume a role of leadership on the African continent.

Case Study Review

1. Why did Nigeria try a federal system of government?
2. **Understanding Points of View** If Nigeria's ethnic groups did not get along, why didn't Nigerian leaders just let Biafra declare its independence?

South Africa Ends Apartheid

What changes came to South Africa in the 1990s?

It was a thrilling moment. The date: May 10, 1994. Nelson Mandela stepped forward to take the oath of office as South Africa's president. For the first time, a black African was at the helm of Africa's richest nation.

Times had certainly changed. Until the end of the 1980s, South Africa's black citizens were like strangers in their own land. They made up three fourths of the population. Yet they were barred from voting, barred from the best jobs, and forbidden to live in the country's best residential districts.

Setting Up Apartheid

White South Africans had set up the system of apartheid in 1948. As you read in Chapter 5, apartheid was designed to oppress black South Africans. All South Africans were classified by race. They were either white, black, "colored" (mixed heritage), or Asian. Each group was assigned its own area of the country in which to live. Ten parts of the country were set apart as black homelands. Each was for a particular group, such as the Zulu or the Xhosa (KAW•suh). Blacks had to get special permission to live outside their "homelands."

Living Under Apartheid

Life was hard for nonwhites under apartheid. Everywhere they went, they had to carry a pass. The pass said where they could live and work. If they went to a "white" area to work or shop, a police officer might ask to see the pass. People who didn't have the right pass could be arrested.

Apartheid was hard on family life. Nonwhite men and women often took jobs far from home, in "white" areas. Some worked in mines or factories. Others served as domestic workers for white families. They could not bring their families to live with them. So the workers lived in dormitories or in quarters

Apartheid was backed by laws that segregated whites from other South Africans. At left, a 1976 photo shows separate restroom entrances for whites and blacks.

provided by their employers. Many saw their families only once or twice a year.

Schools and other public services were kept separate. Schools for nonwhites were inferior to those for whites. Public services for nonwhites were minimal.

Resisting Apartheid

Nonwhite South Africans formed organizations to resist apartheid. A few whites also supported this struggle.

The leading resistance group was the African National Congress. It had been working peacefully for African rights since 1912. The ANC called for a **multiracial** South Africa—a nation in which all races would have equal rights.

The ANC held demonstrations and organized boycotts against apartheid. In 1960, the police opened fire on a crowd of demonstrators in a place called Sharpeville, killing 69. Angry protests spread. The government declared a state of national emergency. It banned the ANC. After that, ANC leaders went underground. They started guerrilla groups that used guns and bombs to fight apartheid.

The leader of the ANC, Nelson Mandela, disguised himself as a window cleaner or a chauffeur. In that way, he avoided arrest while directing a campaign of sabotage against the white government. In 1962, the government captured him and sentenced him to life in prison for plotting a revolution.

Even with Mandela in prison, the ANC continued its struggle. Soon, the fight against apartheid spread to the international arena. The United Nations barred South Africa's representatives. Many nations cut off trade. South Africa became an outcast among the world's nations. By the late 1980s, pressure against the white government was mounting.

A New Beginning

Responding to the pressure, President Frederick de Klerk tried to restore harmony

On Assignment...

Read this section again. Write down the events in the struggle against apartheid that are most important. Draw a sketch of how you want them to appear in your mural.

among the people of South Africa. De Klerk made two dramatic moves early in 1990. He freed Mandela from prison and legalized the ANC. The ANC gave up its armed struggle. Then the government began repealing apartheid laws, one by one. De Klerk, Mandela, and leaders of other groups met to work on a new constitution. Their goal was clear: to turn South Africa into a democracy where people of all races have equal rights.

The solution they chose was to create a government in which many groups would have a say in government policies. At least until 1999, power would be shared among leading parties. Also, the new constitution protected basic human rights.

Free elections were held in 1994. Mandela became president. De Klerk was one of two deputy presidents. The rest of the world welcomed the "new" South Africa with open arms. Although many problems lay ahead, South Africa faced the future with a new spirit of hope and tolerance.

Section 3 Review

1. How did apartheid affect nonwhite South Africans?

2. **Formulating Questions** Imagine that it is 1990, and Nelson Mandela has been released after serving 28 years in prison. What question would you ask him about the role he wants to play in South Africa's government?

I. Reviewing Vocabulary

Match each word on the left with the correct definition on the right.

1. coup   **a.** assistance that a government provides to consumers or industries
2. secede   **b.** a takeover of government
3. subsidy   **c.** to make more varied; to give additional options
4. diversify   **d.** to withdraw from a larger nation

II. Understanding the Chapter

Answer the questions below on a separate sheet of paper.

1. How did colonial boundaries affect African groups?
2. Why did some African countries adopt one-party governments after independence?
3. Why are some nations that have had socialist economies starting to promote free enterprise?

III. Building Skills: Comparing and Contrasting

In two or three sentences, compare or contrast the items mentioned in each statement.

1. Contrast the economic systems of African states that lean toward socialism and African states that lean toward free enterprise.
2. How did the rights of white South Africans and black South Africans compare under apartheid? How do they compare now that apartheid has ended?
3. Both the United States and Nigeria have a federal system of government. What are other similarities between the two nations?

IV. Working Together

Form a small group with three or four other students. Imagine that you are advisers to an African government. Make a list of at least five problems that the government faces. For each problem, suggest ways that the government can attack the problem. Write a report that describes both the problems and your proposed solutions.

On Assignment...

Creating a Mural: Create a mural using the sketches and notes that you made as you read the chapter. You might want to include a map of Africa in your mural. Draw pictures on the parts of the map where important events occurred. The idea of the mural is to sum up information from the chapter in the form of pictures. Display your mural on a wall in your classroom.

CHAPTER 7

Africa in the World Today

What challenges and achievements do African nations face as part of the world community?

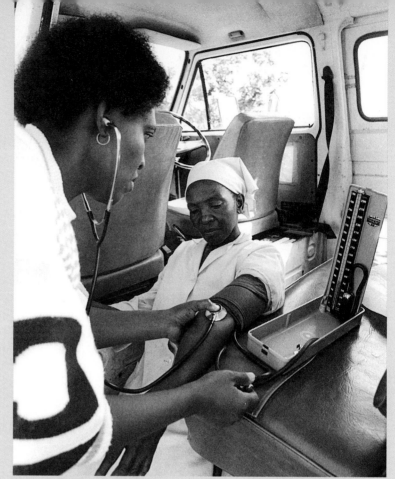

One of Africa's challenges is to improve the quality of health care. Above, a mobile health clinic provides medical services to a farming community in South Africa.

On Assignment . . .

Creating African Stories: As you have read in Chapter 5, African literature has an oral tradition. Stories are usually acted out in front of an audience. The storyteller often uses drums or rattles to accompany the story. Imagine that you are an African storyteller. You will create a story about Africa in the world today. As you read this chapter, you will find hints to help you develop your story. You might also want to use the library to find additional information to make your story more authentic.

Looking at Key Terms

- **midwife** a person who helps women during childbirth
- **hygiene** personal cleanliness
- **refugee** a person who has been forced to flee from his or her homeland for safety
- **tribalism** the allegiance of many Africans to their tribes
- **genocide** the deliberate destruction of a racial group

Challenges for African Nations

How have African nations become a part of the world community?

On a night in late January 1996, 70,000 South Africans sat in a stadium near Soweto cheering wildly for their soccer team—the Bafana Bafana or "our boys." When Bafana Bafana defeated the heavily favored team from Ghana, the crowd erupted in joy. Winning is always fun, but this victory was particularly special. Bafana Bafana was South Africa's first interracial soccer team. In the celebration that followed the win, blacks hugged whites, and whites hugged blacks. South African citizens of all colors united in pride because of the team's success.

This is not to say that South Africa has achieved perfect racial equality. It still has a way to go. However, this team and the spirit that it created shows how far South Africans have come. Ending interracial tension and establishing equality among people of all races are just two of the challenges that many African countries today are meeting. By the way, Bafana Bafana went on to win the African Nations Cup.

Africa's Regional Ties

Like the people of South Africa, many Africans have joined together to try to solve their problems. This is being done not only on a nation-by-nation basis but also through regional cooperation.

One of the organizations that promotes independence and peace in the region is the Organization of African Unity (OAU). The OAU was formed in 1963 by the independent nations of Africa. By 1994, all the nations of Africa had joined. OAU leaders drew up a blueprint for the economic revival of Africa. It called for self-sufficient food production and industrial development by the year 2000. The plan included expansion of transcontinental highways and railroads and the increase of trade among African nations.

The OAU has stopped wars and encouraged economic cooperation. For example, the OAU arranged the Lomé Agreement. This agreement permits African countries to sell goods in the European Common market without tariffs or obligations to buy. In addition, the organization fights disease and encourages agricultural improvements. It also promotes cultural links among African states and works for majority rule.

In addition to the OAU, other regional organizations are making progress in education, literacy, and health care. The Southern African Development Coordination Conference (SADCC) helped build railroads through Mozambique and Tanzania. These railroads helped link landlocked Zimbabwe, Zambia, and Botswana with seaports. The Economic Community of West African States (ECOWAS) ended customs duties. ECOWAS also supported joint transportation and energy projects.

International Ties

Although Africa is developing strong regional ties, African nations have international ties as well. Algeria, Libya, Nigeria, and Gabon are members of the powerful Organization of Petroleum Exporting Countries (OPEC).

African nations are trying to follow a policy of non-alignment, or neutrality. That is, they prefer to stay out of the struggles of major world powers. However, they recognize that they need help from economically developed countries. Some African countries maintain strong economic and cultural relations with former colonial powers. Some African nations are part of the British Commonwealth of Nations. Former French colonies still link their money to the franc and prefer French products.

As each African nation became independent, it joined the United Nations (UN). Today, African nations form the largest single voting block in the UN. Although they do not always vote together, they work for policies that help developing nations.

African countries look to the UN for help with agricultural expertise, education, and environmental conservation. The UN has responded by sending farm experts, engineers, and teachers. It has also provided emergency relief for famine, disease outbreaks, and overcrowded refugee camps.

Self-Reliance

Many people in Africa believe that the key to a better future lies in self-reliance. As a result, many African nations have started self-help programs. Tanzanian villagers in the Iringa District built a school for their children and a clinic to improve health care. "We have got to believe that we ourselves can change our lives for the better," says the village chairman.

Education will play a major role in ending dangerous diseases in Africa. In Ghana, villagers learn about the need to spray their houses to kill malaria-carrying mosquitoes.

On Assignment . . .

You may wish to take an event that you read about in Section 1 and turn it into a story. Use your creativity to invent what people might have said or done.

Section 1 Review

1. List and explain three ways African countries have established themselves in the world community.
2. **Generalizing** Why are African self-help programs effective? Give facts to support your answer.

SECTION 2

Problems and Progress for Africa's People

What are the people of Africa doing to meet challenges at home?

The simple contraption made of blue cloth, plastic, and staples hardly looks like a life-saving instrument, but it is. With ox-breath perfume as a lure, the gadget becomes a deathtrap for up to 20,000 tsetse flies a week. The tsetse fly causes sleeping sickness, an illness often fatal to humans. The disease also kills thousands of cattle, a loss that can cause starvation. Sometimes a tsetse infestation is so severe that people must abandon their villages to escape illness.

Health

In some places in Africa, life expectancy is as short as 35 years. Many children die before the age of five. The high rate of disease is one of the causes. Besides sleeping sickness, diseases like river blindness and

Education for every person is a priority for the continent of Africa. Here, students who have been driven from their homes by drought learn at a school in Mozambique.

malaria flourish. Disease makes people less productive and causes great suffering. Researchers have curbed some of these diseases and continue the struggle against others. Public health programs help to train Africans to save lives.

Batula Hassan is a **midwife** in Gizera, Somalia. A midwife helps women during childbirth. Hassan took a four-month training course to learn about **hygiene**, personal cleanliness, and how to give first aid. She learned to clean instruments, to give injections, and to use forceps to deliver babies. Since she took the classes, not one woman in Gizera has died giving birth. Batula says with quiet dignity, "I enjoy my work. Even when I am tired, I think about the ones who need my help, and I see that it is something for the community."

Since the late 1970s, AIDS has swept over many parts of the world including Africa. Millions of men, women, and children have become infected with the disease. In Africa as in other places, the cities have the highest rates of infection. Many of the victims are between the ages of 19 and 40. While Africa

has been hard hit by the disease, it also provides hope for the rest of world. In Nairobi, Kenya, a group of women have been found to be immune to the virus that causes AIDS. Scientists think that their blood may contain some specialized white blood cells called killer T-cells. These cells may be capable of destroying the HIV virus before it can cause the infection. By studying the blood of these women, researchers hope to find clues to developing a vaccine for the virus.

Education

During the colonial period, most Africans received only the most basic education. At independence, education became a priority. Parents saw learning as a "passport to life" for young people.

> *I joined the revolution. But my mind never changed about the subject of education all the time I was fighting. Without it you can't contribute anything of importance to the nation. So as soon as the war was over, I was desperate to get back to school.*

These words were spoken by 23-year-old Edmund Manyange. His statement shows that young Africans also value opportunities for higher learning.

While most Africans are pleased by this emphasis on education, some experts believe that schools should stress practical subjects. Some think that education in industry and agriculture would best serve African nations. Schools, they say, should prepare young people to live in and develop Africa's rural areas.

One nation that has made a special effort in education is Zimbabwe. Zimbabwe won its independence after a long, bloody struggle. During the war, many citizens lost their lives or became disabled. After the war, the government set up special schools for young people who are disabled. Here is how one young veteran, Lovemore Choromari, age 22, explains his feelings about the importance of education:

> *We fought this liberation war to its*
> *end, till we came back here. Then I*
> *thought the most important thing*
> *I could do was to go back to school.*
> *I'm disabled so I thought: 'If I learn,*
> *then I can work with my head.'*

In many African nations, efforts to improve education have had excellent results. Literacy has risen sharply. By the early 1990s, over 40 percent of adults were literate. This results from almost universal primary education and an increase in the number of college-educated people.

Refugees

On a January morning in 1996, a helicopter's machine guns sprayed the Hutu market in Nyabitaka, Burundi. Men, women, and children ran for cover under the flimsy stalls. Suzanne Nyahimana's arm shattered as the bullets hit, but she courageously searched for her five children. With them, she escaped to a **refugee** camp in neighboring Zaire. Refugees are people who have been forced to flee from their homeland for

Ethnic violence has ruined lives in many parts of Africa. Here, people fleeing civil war in Rwanda find refuge in neighboring Zaire.

safety. A few weeks later, Nyahimana waved the stump of her right arm emphatically and stated: "I will never go back. There is nothing left."

Nyahimana may be right. Burundi, a small, landlocked nation in central Africa, has been devastated by a civil war. Like its neighbor Rwanda, Burundi is a victim of **tribalism**. Tribalism refers to the allegiance of many Africans to their tribes. These tribal loyalties have created problems for African nationalists, who want their citizens to be devoted to the nation.

Africa has over 2,000 ethnic groups. About 1,000 languages are spoken in Africa. As you have read, European powers created colonies without regard for tribal boundaries. When the countries became independent, the borders remained. Citizens of the new nations came from many groups, often with no common language or religion and with ancient rivalries. In many cases, conflicts among the rival tribes resulted in civil war and **genocide**. Genocide is the deliberate destruction of a racial group. Many who escape the conflict become refugees. Refugees place pressure on the resources of the countries that shelter them because of the food, clothing, and housing that they require.

African nations such as Zaire, Ethiopia, Somalia, and Liberia suffered from the effects of civil wars. In the 1990s, the most serious problems existed in Rwanda and Burundi. There the Hutu challenged Tutsi domination. Although the Hutus are the majority in both countries, the Tutsi control the governments, armies, and universities. The struggle between the Hutus and Tutsis has created huge numbers of refugees, destroyed agriculture, and contributed to famine.

War in Burundi The civil war in Burundi shows how a small country's troubles can affect the rest of the world. According to human-rights workers, over 15,000 people died in the fighting between the Tutsi and the Hutu in 1995. Many of them were civilians.

Burundi's civil war began in 1993, when Tutsi soldiers assassinated Mechior Ndadaye. Ndadaye, a Hutu, was the country's first democratically elected president. The Tutsi feared that he would end their 30-year control of Burundi. Ndadaye's murder led to massive revenge killings. At least 50,000 Burundians died during the first year of the violence. In the civil war that followed, thousands of men, women, and children on both sides were killed.

In 1994, international pressure caused Burundi to form a coalition government of Hutu and Tutsi politicians. But tribal loyalties have made them unwilling to stop the fighting. In the meantime, hundreds of thousands of refugees have fled to neighboring Zaire and Tanzania. The increasing number of refugees has strained the resources of these countries.

World Reaction The crisis in Burundi caught the attention of the world. The Secretary General of the United Nations called for international action. The UN had already sent in human-rights observers. It considered sending over 100 more. The United States spent more than half a billion dollars helping refugees in 1994. In 1996, the thinking was that the money would be used better for prevention. In the meantime, the people of Burundi and the many refugees in the region continued to suffer.

Drought and Famine

War is not the only reason that African people have been forced to become refugees. Famine is another. As you read in Chapter 6, African countries often face drought and famine. In the early and mid-1980s, some African countries experienced one of the worst droughts of the century. Lack of rainfall was not the only cause of drought. Overplanting, overgrazing, unwise development programs, and population pressures also contributed to the disaster.

The drought caused starving families to abandon their farms. They escaped to cities or fled to refugee camps in a desperate effort to find food. One of the nations that was most severely affected by the drought and the famine that followed was Ethiopia. Civil wars destroyed livestock and crops. The drought made food shortages even worse. Millions starved.

The rest of the world took notice of the plight of the Ethiopians. The United Nations, the United States, France, and other countries began huge emergency relief campaigns. These campaigns saved the lives of many men, women, and children.

However, Ethiopia is only one of 22 African nations to suffer from the long-term effects of the drought. The Republic of Chad has also

Your story could focus on the challenges that Africans in many nations have had to overcome during the 1990s. Remember that not all the characters and events in your story have to be realistic. Some might symbolize an idea or a problem.

been suffering from drought, famine, and civil war. Life for the people of Chad has become a nightmare. One woman, Hawa Abdel Banat, explained her situation: "I am starving, I have not eaten for 10 days. My 15-year-old daughter starved to death a fortnight [two weeks] ago." Hawa was forced to leave her village and travel to Chad's Camp One, a compound for refugees of the drought. The family did not even have a tent, so they were forced to sleep on the ground in the winter cold.

Drought and famine continue to be important issues. Industry and agriculture have not kept pace with the increasing population. Food production has decreased in the last 25 years while population has increased. Poor transportation systems have made it difficult or impossible to deliver food to where it is needed.

More people and less food equal a crisis. Efforts by African nations to improve the transportation system have helped. Also, technicians and experts from the world community have worked with farmers to improve harvests. They have taught them new methods and have planted new crops like corn and sorghum. Still, drought and starvation are very immediate problems for many Africans.

Section 2 Review

1. What are four problems the people of Africa face?

2. **Evaluate** Which of the problems in this section do you think is the most severe? Why?

SECTION 3

Africa's Endangered Environment

How are Africans working to preserve their environment?

In the Kalahari desert, the hunter follows a special sound. When he arrives at the source, he finds what he has been looking for—a hive of bees. Carefully, he extracts the delicious honeycomb from the hive. He breaks off a piece. But, instead of eating it himself, he gives it to a small bird. Why? It was the song of this bird that pointed the way to the beehive so full of honey. When a hive is found, a hunter gives the bird some honey as a reward. Hunters in the desert understand that cooperation between people and animals is important for the survival of all species.

In recent years, people all over the world have become more aware of their environment and the need to preserve and protect it. In Africa, protecting the environment has long been important. For example, before the arrival of Europeans, the people of South Africa practiced strip mining. However, they were always sure to refill the mined areas. Throughout history, people in Africa have learned to use the environment without destroying it.

Desertification

Today Africa faces a number of environmental challenges. A great many years ago, the desert and the drier savannas supported a thriving civilization. Now they are almost uninhabitable. Part of the reason for this is the severe drought that you have already read about. Another reason is that the people of the savannas are herders. While the savanna's low grasses and trees appear to provide good food for the animals, they are easily destroyed by overgrazing.

Overgrazing occurs when there are too many animals for the amount of food available. In addition, the need for firewood for cooking and for making charcoal added to the damage. When the plants died out, there was nothing to hold the sandy ground. The soil blew away. Vast areas of the savanna lost all vegetation. This process, called desertification, turned savanna into desert. As the desert spread, animals lost their habitats and people fled to cities.

Today, some nations of the Sahel region are working to reverse desertification by planting trees and limiting grazing. However, some experts think that it will be thousands of years before the savanna will be full of life again.

Nations in other areas of Africa have begun programs to improve the environment. One of these programs is Tanzania's Roots and Shoots. The program aims to raise African children's awareness about plants and animals. Balagaye G. Balagaye, headmaster of the Mlati School, arranges for his 650 school children to plant shade trees and study the environment. He and others like him hope they are planting the seeds of future conservation. Having a program like Roots and Shoots for young conservationists has caught on in other parts of the world. The United States, Canada, Germany, Japan, and more than 20 other countries have Roots and Shoots groups.

Endangered Species

An African and an American crouch quietly near a nettle patch in Karisoke, Rwanda, home of the rare mountain gorilla. Only 15 feet ahead of them is an adolescent gorilla. She has left her group to challenge the humans. Shambling forward on her knuckles, the gorilla coughs a warning. Then she suddenly cartwheels backwards and disappears into the forest. Her companions hoot and grunt in approval. One of the humans says, "Teenagers. Same the world over." But this teenaged gorilla is different. She is one of the last of her kind.

One of Africa's greatest treasures is its wildlife. Yet this treasure may be in danger. In recent years, many species, such as the African elephant, have been hunted almost to the point of extinction.

In recent years, the competition for land between humans and animals has become critical in some smaller nations. The demand for pastures and firewood also has taken its toll on wildlife and wildlife habitats. Wars have made the problem even worse. Hunters and poachers kill animals without regard for their shrinking numbers. This has led many African countries to pass laws to help protect the natural environment, to save the habitats of Africa's many animal species, and to prevent rural areas from becoming wastelands.

In 1978, the Wildlife Conservation Society of New York, with the cooperation of the Rwandan government, established a gorilla tourism and education plan for Rwandans. This program of antipoaching, tourism, and education had a great impact on Rwanda's people. Awareness of the need to protect the forest as well as the gorillas grew. The Rwandan people became proud of their environment, and the program became a conservation success story. Four groups of gorillas were habituated, or taught to accept human observers. Gorilla watching brought in money from tourists, sometimes up to $200 an hour.

Then civil war disrupted the peaceful forest and its animals. Conservationists feared that the fighting in the area could endanger the mountain gorillas. Yet soldiers on both sides have expressed some concern for the environment. Even in the midst of the fighting, Rwandans work to help save an endangered species.

Late in the 1980s, African elephants joined the list of endangered animals. Between 1980 and 1990, hunters and poachers reduced the elephant population by half. Even in protected parks and game preserves, the slaughter continued.

Elephants were hunted for economic reasons. Their ivory tusks brought very high prices and huge profits. Farmers allowed poachers to kill the animals because sometimes the animals trampled crops. Elephants could destroy an entire season's harvest in only a few minutes.

When the plight of the African elephant came to the attention of the world, people responded. Elephants were added to the list of endangered species. The Convention on International Trade in 1989 banned shipping of elephant parts and elephant ivory. This caused prices to drop, profits to decline, and poaching to decrease.

Endangered animals are not the only environmental concerns that have received attention. Scientists have also spoken out against the loss of chimpanzee habitats, the illegal trade of chimp babies, and the ill-treatment of chimpanzees in medical research. The world has listened.

In Bujumbura, Burundi, there is a half-way house to teach chimp orphans how to live in the wilderness. Organizations in Uganda, Kenya, and Zaire have also set up homes for orphans. At these sanctuaries, keepers like Ludovic Rabasa act as parents to the chimps. Rabasa's attention helps the chimps recover from such experiences as starvation, seeing their mothers killed by

On Assignment...

Think about how you want your story to end. The ending should wrap up the events of your story. Your ending can be happy and upbeat or it can be sad. You might end your story with a tale about the African environment.

poachers, and spending their childhood in cramped cages.

Not all conservationists support this effort to save orphaned chimps. Some would prefer that the money be used to save the forests that are the chimps' natural habitat. Most feel, however, that saving habitats and building sanctuaries are equally valuable and important.

African nations are recognizing the wisdom of conservation. Not only can they preserve the natural environment, but they can also benefit financially. In Uganda, the government has taken back land that 2,000 farmers had illegally carved out of the Mgahinga National Park. To make up for their losses, villagers receive 10 percent of the tourist revenues. In addition, the park's administrators offer licenses to local people to collect medicinal plants, keep bees, and harvest bamboo inside the park grounds. These licenses allow former farmers to earn a living.

Section 3 Review

1. Describe three ways Africans preserve their environment.
2. **Analyzing** Give three reasons why Africans should work to preserve their natural environment.

Balancing the Needs of Humans and the Environment

The four men watched as a young male gorilla rubbed his injured foot. The damage had been done by a poacher's snare. The wire had cut deeply into the gorilla's toes. "It can die of infection," whispered Augustin Kambale, a guard at Virunga National Park in Zaire. "We must save it." The men decided to surround the gorilla, throw their jackets over him, and pull out the snare. The injured gorilla watched them nervously. Suddenly, a much larger male ape appeared in the bamboo. He had been protecting the injured animal. The youngster limped off, the ragged ends of the wire trailing behind him. The rescue had to wait for another day and better equipment. That would take weeks.

The large gorilla's name is *Ndungutse*, or "benefits." He was given this name because of the money in tourism he has brought to Zaire.

Political problems in Zaire and in neighboring Rwanda and Burundi have hurt the gorilla conservation program. The Zairian park rangers had habituated six gorilla groups for the tourists. However, government soldiers shoot hippos for meat within walking distance of viewing areas, so tourists are reluctant to come. Rangers like Kambale have not received a paycheck for months. They continue to work only through the help of international organizations.

The situation has been made worse by Zaire's refugee crisis. Seven huge camps spread across the hillsides near gorilla territory. Over 746,000 Hutu live in the camps. More flood in daily from war-torn Burundi. In order to get firewood to survive, the refugees have hacked down several square miles of timber in Virunga National Park. In the process, they have destroyed a world heritage site that included one of the oldest rain forests in Africa. Mountain gorillas live in these forests.

"We know the cutting is very bad," says a Rwandan park warden who escaped to Zaire. "But we have to cook to eat."

In the forest, a female gorilla holds her baby. The infant is the size of a two-year-old human. They look very gentle and harmless. "It's not just our loss if they disappear," comments a park administrator. "It's everybody's."

Case Study Review

1. How have gorillas contributed to Zaire's economy?
2. **Evaluating** Do you think the parkland should be given to the refugees and farmers or saved for the gorillas? Explain your position.

I. Reviewing Vocabulary

Match each word on the left with the correct definition on the right.

1. tribalism   **a.** the allegiance of many Africans to their tribes
2. midwife   **b.** a person who has been forced to flee from his or her homeland for safety
3. genocide   **c.** a person who helps women during childbirth
4. refugee   **d.** deliberate destruction of a racial group

II. Understanding the Chapter

Answer the questions below on a separate sheet of paper.

1. How has the Organization of African Unity worked for independence and peace?
2. What role have African nations played in the United Nations?
3. What are three ways Africa's people are improving their lives?
4. Why is desertification a problem for some African nations?

III. Building Skills: Identifying Cause and Effect Relationships

Causes are the events that make something happen. *Effects* are the results that happen because of the causes. On a separate sheet of paper, provide the missing cause or effect for each item below.

1. Cause: Drought and overgrazing of the savanna
   Effect:
2. Cause:
   Effect: Large refugee camps in Zaire and other central African nations
3. Cause:
   Effect: Increased literacy rate and better health

IV. Working Together

In a small group, choose a challenge that Africans are facing. Then come up with a solution to that challenge. Create a public service campaign that promotes your solution. For example, you might choose saving the mountain gorillas. Your group could create posters for an adopt-a-gorilla program.

On Assignment . . .

Creating African Stories: You should have a topic and notes for your story. Prepare a final draft of your story and perform it for your classmates. Add gestures and changes in your voice to make your storytelling dramatic and interesting. You might ask some friends to participate by playing musical instruments or singing choral responses.

UNIT 1 REVIEW

I. Understanding the Unit

Answer the questions below on a separate sheet of paper.

1. (a) What are the main physical features of Africa? (b) Which of Africa's physical features made it difficult for outsiders, such as European explorers, to explore the African interior?

2. Often trade and travel spread culture and technology. Give at least two examples of how trade and travel spread culture and technology in ancient North Africa, West Africa, and East Africa.

3. How did the new products traded during the Atlantic slave trade change the economies of West African civilizations?

4. (a) Describe the traditional roles of children, women, and elders in African societies. (b) How has the move to the cities changed the roles of children, women, and elders?

5. (a) What improvements did European imperial powers bring to Africa? (b) Why did they bring these improvements? (c) What effect did these improvements have on African countries after independence?

6. How do the visual arts—theater, film, painting, jewelry making, sculpture—reflect traditional African values?

7. Explain how ethnic diversity has affected the following countries: (a) Nigeria, (b) Tanzania, (c) Rwanda, and (d) Burundi.

8. Explain why many African nations are trying to diversify their economies. Give one example that shows how an African nation is diversifying its economy.

II. Thinking Critically

Answer the questions below on a separate sheet of paper.

1. **Understanding Cause and Effect** Explain how nationalism played a role in both European colonization of Africa and African independence movements.

2. **Identifying Central Issues** Six of ten countries in Southern Africa are landlocked. Look at the map on page 85. Identify these six countries and explain how being landlocked affects their economies. With which countries do you think the landlocked countries would need to cooperate in order to get to the sea to export or import goods?

III. Writing to Learn

On a separate sheet of paper, write a three-paragraph essay about the following topic.

Consider the life of a young African about your age. Based on what you know about life in rural Africa and life in African cities, how is the life of an African youth similar to and different from your life? Do you think you would have more in common with a young African from the country or the city? Explain.

IV. Practicing Skills: Interpreting Data from Tables

Read the table below. On a separate sheet of paper, answer the questions that follow.

COMMUNICATIONS IN SELECTED COUNTRIES				
Country	**Telephones** (per person)	**Televisions** (per person)	**Radios** (per person)	**Daily Newspaper Circulation** (per person)
ALGERIA	1 per 23	1 per 15	1 per 4	53 per 1,000
KENYA	1 per 67	1 per 100	1 per 6	13 per 1,000
NIGERIA	1 per 240	1 per 30	1 per 12	12 per 1,000
SOUTH AFRICA	1 per 6	1 per 11	1 per 3	48 per 1,000
UNITED STATES	1 per 1.9	1 per 1.3	1 per 0.5	255 per 1,000

Source: *Statistical Abstract of the United States, 1992*, U.S. Dept. of Commerce.

1. (a) How many radios per person does Nigeria have? (b) Which country has twice the number of radios per person that Nigeria has?

2. (a) Which African country has the most telephones per person? (b) Which has the fewest?

3. Assume that newspaper circulation is related to literacy rates. The more newspapers available, the higher the literacy rate of the country. Based on that assumption, which two countries in Africa probably have the highest literacy rates?

V. Going Beyond the Unit

Work with two or three students to create a three dimensional physical map of Africa. First, find an atlas with a detailed physical map or landform map that shows elevation. Next, decide what materials you will use to create your map, such as modeling clay or papier-mâché. You may wish to use paint or different color clay to show each landform. Use a sculpting tool to show some of Africa's major rivers. Then explain to the class what each feature on the map is and how it affected African history.

The Many Forms of Government

Looking at Key Terms

monarchy, dictatorship, democracy, majority rule, direct democracy, republics

On a cool evening in May 1994, a large group of South Africans gathered outside the city of Johannesburg for a joyous ceremony. As the new many-colored flag of democratic South Africa was raised, South Africans sang *Nkosi Sikelele iAfrika* (*God Bless Africa*), their new national anthem. The next day, Nelson Mandela was sworn in as the first leader of South Africa elected by all of the people.

A few days later and a thousand miles to the north, another African democracy was born. Voters in the Central African country of Malawi elected Bakili Muluzi president. Muluzi replaced H. Kumuzu Banda, who had held power since 1964. During much of that time, Banda had allowed no opposition. He held the title "President for Life."

However, these victories for democracy are only part of the story of government in Africa. Today, the nations of Africa are ruled by many different kinds of governments. Three African countries are ruled by kings. Others are led by military officers. In still others, small groups of civilian leaders hold total power.

There is a common pattern to all these governments—indeed to governments around the world. Governments fall into two basic groups: rule by a few people or rule by the majority of the people.

When Only a Few People Rule

A **monarchy** is a form of government in which one person rules. In a monarchy, rule is passed down from one family member to another. When a ruler dies, another member of the family takes over. At different times in different countries, monarchs have had different titles. They may have been called king or queen, emperor, maharajah, or tsar.

The tiny country of Swaziland in Southern Africa is one of Africa's three monarchies. Swaziland's king, Mswati III, has ruled since 1986. Before he came to power, his father, Sobhuza, ruled for 61 years.

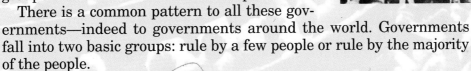

In a democracy, citizens vote to choose who will represent them in government. The 1994 elections in South Africa were special. It was the first time people of all races were free to vote.

Swaziland has shaped the monarchy to its African traditions. For example, when a Swazi king dies, the eldest son does not automatically become the new king. Rather, a secret council meets and chooses a monarch from among the dead king's sons.

A **dictatorship** is a form of government in which a few people hold power, usually by force. Power is not passed down from one family member to another. Today, many countries are dictatorships. In China, for example, a small number of high-ranking members of the Communist party controls the government.

Sometimes the people who rule are soldiers. In many countries in Africa and Latin America, groups of military officers have seized control of governments. In Nigeria, for example, military rulers ousted the elected government and took control in 1993. They then crushed all opposition with brutal force.

When a dictator dies or grows weak, there is usually a struggle for power. Kumuzu Banda in Malawi was over 90 years old when public disturbances forced him to step down. The people of Malawi forced elections for a democratic government.

When All the People Have a Say

Democracy is a system in which most of the citizens of a country have the right to participate in government. In a democracy, the final authority rests with the people. At the heart of every democracy is

majority rule. This means that the government reflects the wishes of *most* of the people, not just a few. It also means that disputes are settled peacefully. This includes elections, which are disputes about who should hold office. The issue or the candidate with the most votes wins. Everyone accepts the results.

Democracy can take many forms. In some city-states of ancient Greece, all citizens had the right to meet and vote on public matters. This is known as **direct democracy**. Today, democracies take another form, known as **republics**. In a republic, the people elect representatives. These representatives carry on the business of governing and making the laws.

When Systems Change

Today, India is by far the world's largest democracy. Of course, the United States is also a democracy. Russia is one of the world's newest democracies. Until 1991, Russia was a part of the Soviet Union. That country was a dictatorship. A few high-ranking officials of the Communist party held all power. One reason the Soviet Union broke apart was that its people wanted more democratic freedoms. The new countries that had been part of the Soviet Union became democracies.

Will democracy survive in Russia? No one can say for sure. The people of Russia do not have a tradition of democratic rule. Throughout their history, they have been led by strong rulers, such as the monarch Peter the Great or the dictators Lenin and Stalin. Democracy in Russia today is like a fragile tree that has been planted in new ground. It will take a lot of tender care—and some luck—for it to survive into the 21st century.

Review

1. What is majority rule?
2. **Comparing and Contrasting** What are the advantages and disadvantages of monarchies, dictatorships, and democracies?

*T*aking Action: Conducting a Panel Discussion

Have a panel discussion about the following forms of government: monarchy, dictatorship, and democracy. Each side should explain the way its government works and why it is beneficial to its people.

South & Southeast Asia

	2500 B.C.	500 B.C.	A.D. 1000	1200	1400
History	2500s B.C.-1500s B.C. Indus valley civilization develops.		750 The Maoris arrive in New Zealand.	1200-1526 Islamic rulers of the Delhi sultanate rule India.	
Culture & Society	1500s B.C. Hinduism begins in the Indian subcontinent.	500s B.C. Siddhartha Gautama founds Buddhism.		1112-1152 Angkor Wat is constructed in Cambodia.	
Economics & Technology	2500s B.C.-1500s B.C. The people of the Indus valley build water and sewer systems.				

PREVIEWING THE UNIT

Study the time line. On a separate sheet of paper answer the questions below.

1. According to the time line, which is the oldest religion on the Indian subcontinent?

2. When did the Maoris arrive in New Zealand?

3. How many years after it was formed did Mohandas Gandhi become leader of the Indian National Congress?

4. How did India's economy change in 1991?

5. Why did Southeast Asian countries form ASEAN?

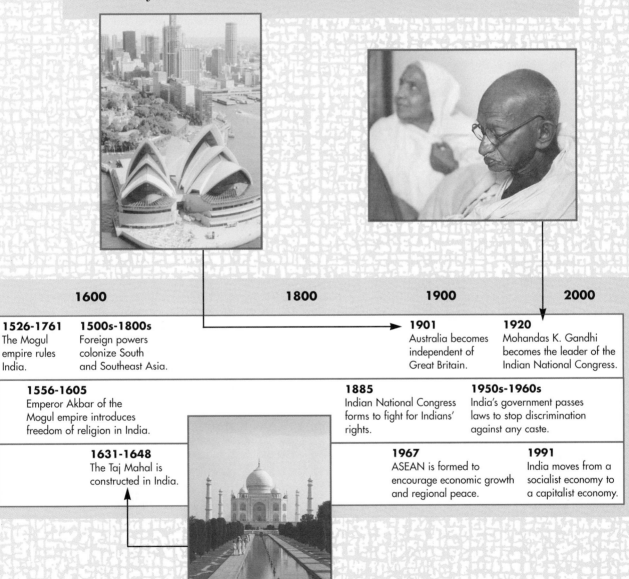

| 1600 | 1800 | 1900 | 2000 |

1526-1761
The Mogul empire rules India.

1500s-1800s
Foreign powers colonize South and Southeast Asia.

1901
Australia becomes independent of Great Britain.

1920
Mohandas K. Gandhi becomes the leader of the Indian National Congress.

1556-1605
Emperor Akbar of the Mogul empire introduces freedom of religion in India.

1885
Indian National Congress forms to fight for Indians' rights.

1950s-1960s
India's government passes laws to stop discrimination against any caste.

1631-1648
The Taj Mahal is constructed in India.

1967
ASEAN is formed to encourage economic growth and regional peace.

1991
India moves from a socialist economy to a capitalist economy.

Trade in South and Southeast Asia
Analyzing a Chart

Today, international trade is an important part of the economies of most nations in South and Southeast Asia. The chart below shows the products that the countries of the region import and export. In addition, you can see each country's major trading partners. Study the chart. On a separate sheet of paper, answer the questions below.

EXPORTS, IMPORTS, AND MAJOR TRADING PARTNERS OF SELECTED COUNTRIES OF SOUTH AND SOUTHEAST ASIA

Country	Exports		Imports		Trading Partners
	Amount Earned (in U.S. dollars)	Products Exported	Amount Spent (in U.S. dollars)	Products Imported	
Australia	$44.1 billion	coal, gold, meat, wool, aluminum, wheat, machinery and trans. equip.	$43.6 billion	machinery and transportation equip., computers, office equipment, crude oil, petroleum	Japan, United States, United Kingdom, New Zealand, Germany, South Korea, Singapore
Cambodia	$70 million	natural rubber, rice, pepper, wood	$360 million	food stuffs, fuel, consumer goods	Vietnam, Japan, India, Singapore, Malaysia, China, Thailand
India	$21.4 billion	gems and jewelry, clothing goods, engineering goods, leather, cotton yarn, fabric	$22 billion	crude oil, petroleum, gems, fertilizer, chemicals, machinery	United States, CIS*, Germany, Italy, Belgium
Indonesia	$38.2 billion	petroleum, liquid natural gas, timber, rubber, coffee, textiles	$28.3 billion	chemicals, machinery, manufactured goods	Japan, United States, Singapore, EU**
Singapore	$61.5 billion	petroleum products, rubber, manufactured goods, electronics, computers	$66.4 billion	aircraft, petroleum, chemicals, food stuffs	United States, EU**, Hong Kong, Japan

* Commonwealth of Independent States   ** European Union

Did You Know

- Today India makes steel more cheaply than any other country in the world. (See Chapter 11.)

- In 1967, ASEAN was founded to promote cooperation among member nations. (See Chapter 14.)

- Before the 1970s, Australia's main trading partner was Great Britain. After the mid-1970s, Australia developed trading relationships with Japan and other Asian nations. (See Chapter 15.)

1. **Reading the Chart** What information does each column show?

2. **Thinking About the Chart** (a) What is the difference between the amounts Australia and India earn in exports? (b) What is the difference between the earnings of Indonesia and Singapore?

3. **Going Beyond the Chart: Determining Cause and Effect** If a country earns on exports more than it spends on imports, it has a *trade surplus*. If a country spends more on imports than it earns on exports, it has a *trade deficit*. (a) How might a trade surplus affect a country's economy? (b) How might a trade deficit affect a country's economy?

CHAPTER 8

The Land and People of South and Southeast Asia

How have the land and climate affected the people of South and Southeast Asia?

Land is precious in South and Southeast Asia. Where the land is hilly, farmers cut terraces into the sides of mountains to increase the amount of land they can farm. In Bali, farmers tend their rice terraces.

Looking at Key Terms

- **subcontinent** a large landmass that juts out from a continent
- **plateau** a flat area that is higher than the land that surrounds it
- **monsoon** a seasonal wind that brings wet or dry weather
- **cyclone** a dangerous windstorm; often one that brings rain
- **delta** a triangle of land that forms where a river meets the sea
- **hydroelectricity** the power that comes from the force of rushing water
- **dialect** a regional form of a language that has its own words, expressions, and pronunciations

On Assignment. . .

Making a Brochure: In this chapter, you will learn about the land and people of South and Southeast Asia. Imagine that you are planning a brochure to attract tourists to this region. As you read, take notes about information that you might want to include in your brochure. Consider facts about the land, climate, and people. Look for On Assignment hint boxes. They will give you ideas about how to organize the brochure. At the end of the chapter, you will create your brochure.

The Lands of South and Southeast Asia

*What are the major physical features of the
Indian subcontinent and of Southeast Asia?*

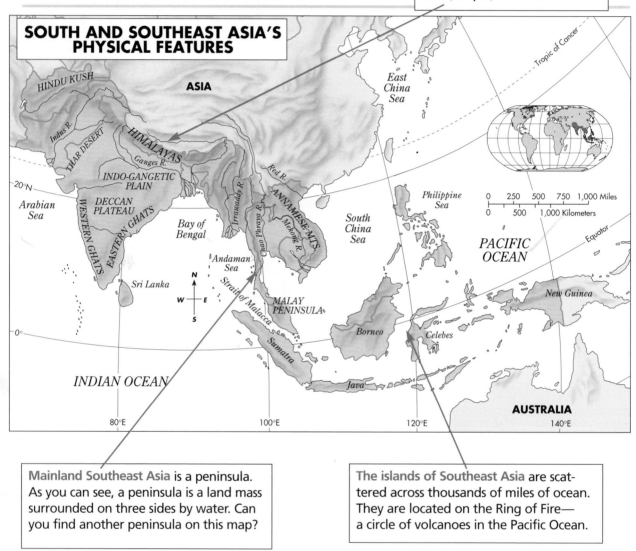

The Himalayas sweep across
the north of India and into
Tibet, Nepal, and Bhutan.

SOUTH AND SOUTHEAST ASIA'S PHYSICAL FEATURES

Mainland Southeast Asia is a peninsula.
As you can see, a peninsula is a land mass
surrounded on three sides by water. Can
you find another peninsula on this map?

The islands of Southeast Asia are scattered across thousands of miles of ocean.
They are located on the Ring of Fire—
a circle of volcanoes in the Pacific Ocean.

South and Southeast Asia are located between the Indian Ocean and the Pacific Ocean. It is a region of
densely populated cities, thinly populated deserts, high mountains, and fertile river valleys. Look at the map
and note how the region can be divided into three subregions.

The Indian **subcontinent** is the triangle of land that juts out into the Indian Ocean. Mainland Southeast
Asia is the long, thin peninsula that lies to the east of India. Island Southeast Asia is the chain of islands that
stretches out into the Pacific.

The Himalayas The Himalayan (him-uh-LAY-uhn) mountain range is more than 1,500 miles (2,400 km) long and 150 to 200 miles (240 to 325 km) wide. Towering 29,029 feet (8,848 m) into the sky, Mount Everest is the highest point on earth. The Himalayas are called by some "the rooftop of the world." The word *Himalaya* means "home of snow." The name fits.

A rice paddy in Southeast Asia Rice is vital to the people of Southeast Asia. For more than 5,000 years, people here have been growing rice to eat. It is the region's most common crop. In some places, it is common for farmers to raise three crops of rice a year. Thousands of years ago, farmers learned to grow rice on terraces that climb up the mountains. In this way, they made the most of the region's land.

The Regions of the Indian Subcontinent

The Indian subcontinent can be divided into three main geographic regions. The first region is the northern mountains. These mountains form a high, steep barrier that separates India from the rest of Asia. The northern mountains slope into the northern plain. The northern plain is the second region. Low mountains divide the plain from the third region—the Deccan Plateau.

The Northern Mountains

The Hindu Kush and the Himalayas form the northern border. These high mountain ranges form a natural wall between India and the rest of Asia. Travel across these mountains is difficult. The mountains are so high that even planes have trouble flying over them.

The Himalayas and the Hindu Kush have usually kept invaders out of the subcontinent of India. However, passage through the mountains is not impossible. There are several openings through the mountains called passes. The most famous is the Khyber (KEYE•buhr) Pass. The Khyber Pass cuts through the Hindu Kush mountains.

The most important rivers of the Indian subcontinent spring from the Himalaya Mountains. The Ganges (GAN•jeez), the Indus, and the Brahmaputra (brahm•uh•POO•truh) all begin there. They are fed by the melting snow in the mountains. These rivers water the fertile lands of the northern plain.

The Northern Plain

The northern plain is located south of the northern mountains. The plain stretches for 2,000 miles (3,200 km) across Pakistan, northern India, and Bangladesh. Rivers flowing from the northern mountains bring water to the flat land of the plain. The land is made fertile by rich topsoil that river floods bring from the mountains. The region also receives abundant rainfall.

The northern plain is the most densely populated region. Almost two thirds of the region's people live there. Most of the people are farmers. Fertile land and a good climate make the northern plain one of the largest farming areas in the world.

The Indian subcontinent is bordered in the north by two mountain ranges. The Himalayas are located in the east. The Hindu Kush lie in the west. At the right, horses graze in the highlands of Kashmir.

The Thar Desert is also part of the northern plain. Located in the plain's northwest corner, this desert is 100,000 square miles (259,000 sq km) of hot, dry land.

The Deccan Plateau

The Deccan (DEK•uhn) Plateau lies to the south of the northern plain. A **plateau** is a large area of high, flat or gently rolling land. This region is shaped like a large triangle. On the northern side of the triangle lie the Vindhya (VIN•dyuh) Mountains. The Vindhyas form the boundary between northern and southern India.

Two other mountain ranges, the Eastern Ghats and Western Ghats, form the other sides of the triangle. They are called the "Ghats" for the many ghats, or passes, that cut through them. The Ghats are too high for most rain clouds to pass over. They block rain from reaching the plateau. The lack of rain makes the Deccan Plateau a dry region that is difficult to farm. The regions between the Ghats and the sea are narrow coastal plains where rain is plentiful.

The Climate of South Asia

The climate of the Indian subcontinent ranges from bitter cold to steaming hot. The high Himalayas are cold year-round, with temperatures well below freezing. In some parts of the northern plain, however, temperatures can rise to over 100° F (38° C).

In much of India and Bangladesh, there are three seasons: hot and rainy, hot and dry, or cool. In the hot and rainy season, from June to September, people expect downpours daily. During the hot, dry season, the land becomes parched. April and May are hottest. Often no rain falls for weeks.

Monsoons are a vital part of life in South Asia. **Monsoons** are winds that blow across the subcontinent. Toward the end of May, the rain-bearing monsoon begins to blow from the southwest. The wind continues to blow across the subcontinent until the end of September or October.

The winds bring about 80 percent of the region's annual rainfall. Without the rain-bearing monsoons, the land dries and there are not enough crops. When the monsoon brings the right amount of rain, there are crops to feed the subcontinent's hundreds of millions of people.

When the monsoon brings too much rain, flooding may cost thousands of lives. In 1991, a **cyclone** hit Bangladesh at the end of the summer monsoon season. About 200,000 were killed by its winds and rains. Millions were left without homes.

In October, a second monsoon season begins. The winds from the mountains of the northeast bring cool, dry air to the subcontinent.

Mountains and Climate

The mountain ranges of the subcontinent affect the climate of the region. The high mountains of the Himalayas protect India from the cold winds of Central Asia. Also, as wet winds from the Bay of Bengal hit the cold air of the Himalayas, rain falls. The rain makes the northeast portion of the subcontinent a very wet place.

Natural Resources South Asia is rich in a number of natural resources. Mineral riches include coal, iron ore, mica, gold, diamonds, sapphires, and precious woods. Nearly all of the 70 million tons of coal mined each year fuels railroads, steel plants, and other businesses. India is a major producer of iron ore.

Perhaps South Asia's greatest natural resource is its land. About three fourths of the people are farmers. Rice is grown on about a third of the farmland. Farmers grow wheat in drier areas. Tea, sugar cane, cotton, and jute (used for rope) are other important crops.

Farmers of the subcontinent once relied on traditional methods and inferior seed. In recent years, that has changed. The use of modern methods has raised food production considerably. From 1980 to 1990, food production grew by an average of 5 percent a year.

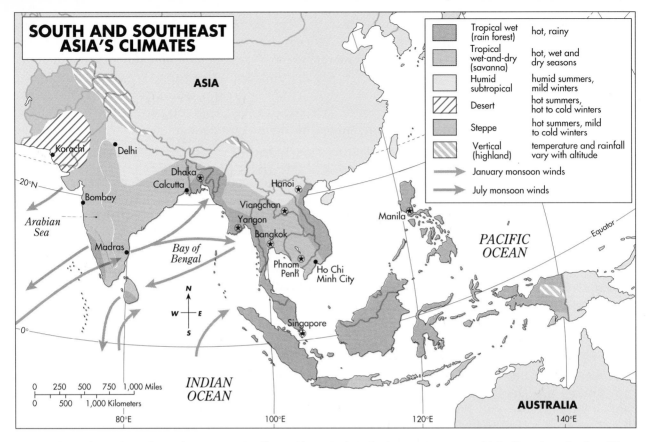

SOUTH AND SOUTHEAST ASIA'S CLIMATES

	Tropical wet (rain forest)	hot, rainy
	Tropical wet-and-dry (savanna)	hot, wet and dry seasons
	Humid subtropical	humid summers, mild winters
	Desert	hot summers, hot to cold winters
	Steppe	hot summers, mild to cold winters
	Vertical (highland)	temperature and rainfall vary with altitude
→	January monsoon winds	
→	July monsoon winds	

Place Much of South and Southeast Asia is affected by winds called monsoons. In which direction do the different monsoons blow? What climates are found on the islands of Southeast Asia?

Southeast Asia: Mainland and Islands

East of India is a region called Southeast Asia. Southeast Asia can be divided into two main parts: the mainland and the islands.

Mainland Southeast Asia Mainland Southeast Asia is made up of the nations of Myanmar (MEE•uhn•mahr), formerly Burma; Thailand; Laos; Cambodia; and Vietnam. These nations lie on a peninsula that juts out into the Indian Ocean and the South China Sea.

The northern portion of the region has high, rugged mountains. The steep highlands are lightly populated. The land and the climate make life difficult. Most of those who do live here occupy the flat, high plateaus. Nearly all of them make their living by farming.

Many people live in the river valleys that run through the mountains. There are four main river valleys: the Irrawaddy, Salween, Chao Phraya (CHOW•prah•YAH), and Mekong. These rivers often overflow their banks, leaving behind rich soil.

Near the shore, the rich soil that the rivers leave behind forms deltas. A **delta** is a triangle of land that forms where a river meets the sea. The land that forms in the delta is flat and the soil is good for growing crops. Most of the population of Southeast Asia lives in the delta region. The area's biggest cities are there. Yangon (Rangoon) in Myanmar, Bangkok in Thailand, and Ho Chi Mihn City (Saigon) in Vietnam are three of these cities.

Island Southeast Asia From above, the islands of Southeast Asia look like handfuls of scattered emeralds. These islands make up the largest group of islands in the world. They were formed long ago by volcanoes and by the earth's movement.

This region has the greatest number of active volcanoes in the world. It also has more earthquakes than just about anywhere. The volcanic eruptions, which spread ash and minerals, have made the soil on these islands rich. Most people on the islands live in the lowlands. For centuries, though, the islands' farmers have been building terraces into the mountains to grow rice.

Several countries make up island Southeast Asia. One is the tiny island country of Singapore. A location on a main shipping route and a good harbor have made Singapore a wealthy country.

Another small country is Brunei. It is located on the island of Borneo.

About 13,000 islands form the country of Indonesia. The Philippines, to the north, is a group of 7,107 islands. The country of Malaysia lies partly on the mainland and also in island Southeast Asia. Mountains form the backbone of the long, narrow strip of land located on the mainland. Most people live on the plains along the coasts.

The Climate of Southeast Asia

Southeast Asia is located near the equator. In general, its climate is steamy and hot. The temperature stays at about 80°F (25°C), except in the high mountains and in mainland Southeast Asia near China. There, the temperature is cooler.

Like the climate of South Asia, Southeast Asia's climate is affected by monsoons. The summer monsoons bring moisture and rain to the region. Farmers rely on the monsoon rains. When the monsoons don't bring rain, crops fail and people suffer.

Natural Resources

The land of Southeast Asia is rich in minerals. But to get to those resources, miners must be able to dig. People must be able to

On Assignment. . .

Think of what your brochure would tell tourists about the land and climate of Southeast Asia. What pictures would you want to include? What information would be helpful to tourists planning a trip?

build roads. Many of Southeast Asia's riches are in high mountains or dense forests that are difficult to reach.

The people of Southeast Asia have developed ways to farm in the rugged mountains. There are rice paddies and tea plantations on terraced hillsides. The cool mountains are also where the region's forests grow.

Valuable teak wood comes from the tropical rain forests. Cutting the wood, however, means destroying the rain forests. The nations of Southeast Asia face the same choices as other countries with rain forests. The countries need the income that the wood brings, but they are concerned about the destruction of their environment.

Southeast Asia is the world's largest producer of tin. Indonesia is the region's largest producer of oil. When the technology improves, Southeast Asia will find ways to harvest more of its resources in iron ore, bauxite (aluminum ore), copper, nickel, gold, and precious gems.

Section 1 Review

1. Why are monsoons important to the people of South and Southeast Asia?

2. **Determining Cause and Effect** How have volcanoes affected the farmlands of Southeast Asia?

Hinduism is a major religion in South Asia. In India, Hinduism shapes the way of life of many people. There are more than 750 million Hindus in India, making up 83 percent of the population. To Hindus, the Ganges River is sacred, or holy. Hindus bathe in its waters to purify, or spiritually cleanse, themselves.

Muslims are followers of the religion of Islam. About 300 million Muslims live on the subcontinent of South Asia. In India, about 11 percent of the population is Muslim. Bangladesh and Pakistan are Islamic countries. In Southeast Asia, Malaysia and Indonesia are mostly Muslim countries. Islam was brought to South Asia about the year 1200 and to Southeast Asia in about 900. Islam appealed to many of the region's people because it had no caste system.

City of Angels is the Thai people's name for Bangkok, their capital and largest city. About six million people live in Bangkok. On crowded streets and waterways, people on bikes, in rickshaws, in trucks, and in boats jockey for space. They rumble past new stores and ancient sites. Some people dress in Western clothes. Others dress in traditional clothing. It is a city of skyscrapers and tar paper shacks. Like most cities of the region, Bangkok is a city of contrasts.

Peace in the Village Many Southeast Asians lead lives that are much like the lives of their parents, grandparents, and great-grandparents. Families quietly tend their rice paddies. In fact, most of Southeast Asia's people still live—and farm—in small villages. They have little land, but grow enough food for their needs.

Waiting for the Rain

The sky outside Goa was a brilliant blue. Dattu Bjupal squinted into the sun. He sighed. Around him was the brown dust of his rice fields. Without the monsoon, there would be no rice.

"Here, we say that a beautiful woman has hair black as monsoon clouds," Dattu grins. "Now, I would rather have the black clouds.

"I have faith," Dattu says. "It is June 9. The next day, maybe the next. It is time. All over India, we are waiting. In Kerala, I hear they have no power. There the water makes **hydroelectricity**. There is no water, so there is no power. But soon the rains will come."

He chuckles and explains that once the monsoon season begins, "You will find me in the rain, day after day, turning the mud into rice fields. You see this dirt? Come back in August. It will all be green. You will see rice fields like green velvet."

Dattu shades his eyes and looks out. Far in the distance, clouds gather. In nearby fields, farmers look to the sky.

"Can you smell it?" Dattu asks. "It is the smell of rain. It is coming. I know. The beautiful woman is coming."

Case Study Review

1. How do the monsoons change the land and the lives of the people in India?

2. **Predicting Consequences** What do you think will happen if the monsoon is late? What will happen if it does not come at all?

SECTION 2

The People

Who lives in South and Southeast Asia?

Imagine that you are writing an advertisement in India. If you wanted to reach all of the people of India, you would have to translate the ad into the 16 official Indian languages, plus 845 other languages and **dialects**. Each dialect, or regional version of a language, has its own words, expressions, and pronunciations.

You would face the same challenge in Southeast Asia. In Indonesia alone, there are 25 languages and more than 200 dialects.

The vast number of languages shows the diversity of people who live in the region. Some of the diversity has to do with the geographic features of the region. For example, the mountain ranges worked as a barrier to keep groups of people separate.

Diversity in South and Southeast Asia

The diversity of the region has many benefits. Different people have brought different ideas about government, the economy, religion, and culture. They have brought new and sometimes better ways of doing things.

But the diversity also presents great challenges. The number of different languages has created problems. When people cannot talk to one another easily, misunderstandings often occur.

The number of religions in South Asia has created problems. Islam and Hinduism have the largest numbers of followers. These two groups have clashed violently.

Within all this diversity, there are some major groupings of people. The Dravidians (druh•VIHD•ee•uhnz) live in the south of the Indian subcontinent. The Dravidians are the original inhabitants of the subcontinent. Many historians believe that the Dravidians once lived in the north. About 1500 B.C., people called the Aryans (AIR•ee• uhnz) came

On Assignment. . .

List the information from this section that you would like to include in your brochure. Describe pictures that could illustrate your points.

out of Central Asia and pushed the Dravidians south.

Southeast Asia faces many of the same problems as South Asia. Island Southeast Asia is located on a main trade route. That means that many people have passed through this region.

Sometimes the newcomers took control of the countries they settled in. For example, in Malaysia, 55 percent of the people are Islamic Malays. The others are Chinese and Indian. The Chinese-Malaysians control most of the economy. Some Malays resent this.

In most countries of Southeast Asia, there are many culture groups. As in Malaysia, one culture group often controls the economy and the government of a particular country. For example, in Laos, the Lao people make up 50 percent of the population. Other ethnic groups include the Thai, Hmong, and Yao. The Lao control the government and the best land.

The religions of Southeast Asia include Hinduism, Buddhism, Christianity, and Islam. There are many traditional religions, however. Sometimes people have blended several religions. This blending has made the cultures of Southeast Asia unique.

Section 2 Review

1. Why is there so much diversity among the people of South and Southeast Asia?

2. **Drawing Conclusions** What challenges are created when a country has more than one or two official languages?

REVIEWING CHAPTER 8

I. Reviewing Vocabulary

Match each word on the left with the correct definition on the right.

1. cyclone
2. hydroelectricity
3. monsoon
4. plateau

a. a seasonal wind that brings wet or dry weather
b. a flat area that is higher than the land that surrounds it
c. a dangerous windstorm; often one that brings rain
d. the power that comes from the force of rushing water

II. Understanding the Chapter

Answer the questions below on a separate sheet of paper.

1. How do mountains affect India's climate?
2. Identify three important rivers in India. From where do these rivers flow?
3. How has the location of Island Southeast Asia contributed to the diversity of the region's population?
4. How have immigrants from China and India influenced Malaysia?

III. Building Skills: Identifying Cause and Effect

In each of the pairs below, identify the cause or the effect.

1. Effect: The Deccan Plateau gets little rain. What is the cause?
2. Cause: Many of the natural resources of Southeast Asia are found in steep mountains or under dense forests. What is the effect?
3. Cause: The mountain ranges in South Asia keep people separated. What is the effect?

IV. Working Together

Work with a group to create quiz questions and answers about the land and people of South and Southeast Asia. Take turns with the other groups asking and answering the questions.

On Assignment...

Making a Brochure: Study the notes that you took for your brochure about the land and the people of South and Southeast Asia. You will create a four-page brochure about the land and the people of the region. First, decide how you want to organize the information. Next, sketch the brochure deciding where you will place the pictures. Then, write the copy. Now put the pictures and copy together to create an attractive, informative brochure.

CHAPTER 9

The History of South Asia

What were the major historical developments in South Asia from early civilizations to independence?

To honor his wife, Shah Jahan built the Taj Mahal in Agra, India. Workers began the building in 1631 and finished it in 1648. The massive dome is made of white marble and inlaid gems.

Looking at Key Terms

- **descendant** a person who can trace his or her heritage to an individual or group
- **caste** a social group based on birth; the system that separates Hindus by class and job
- **meditate** to think deeply
- **reincarnated** reborn
- **nirvana** a state in which a person has achieved perfect happiness because he or she wants nothing
- **mosque** a place of worship for Muslims
- **civil disobedience** a person's refusal to follow laws that he or she believes are unjust

On Assignment. . .

Creating a Mural: By creating a mural, you can put what you learn into picture form. In each section of this chapter, you will make notes about the most important events that occurred on the subcontinent. You will also make sketches of what you want in your mural. At the end of the chapter, you will make a sketch of your mural. Then you will complete it.

SECTION 1

An Ancient Heritage: Early Civilizations of India

What were some of the early civilizations and empires of South Asia?

The scientist rubbed her hand over a small clay figure. She looked out over the Indus valley. Workers were uncovering houses and roads that had been buried for thousands of years. The scientist tried to imagine what life was like in the valley in 1500 B.C. At that time, the Indus people had been living there peacefully for 1,000 years. They had water and sewer systems, sturdy houses, and public baths. The people of the Indus were farmers and traders. They may even have been the first to weave cotton. What the Indus people didn't know, the woman thought, was that their civilization would soon come to an end.

The Aryans In about 1500 B.C., invaders arrived from the north. These invaders were the Aryans. The Aryans marched through the mountain passes in the Hindu Kush. Over the next few hundred years, waves of Aryans continued to come. Some scientists believe that the Aryan invasion contributed to the decline of Indus valley civilization. The people of the Indus valley moved south. Many historians believe that their **descendants** are the Dravidians, who live in the south of India today.

From religious writings called the Vedas (VAY•duhz), we know about the Aryans. The Vedas were written in Sanskrit, the written language developed by the Aryans. The Vedas describe the Aryans' love of war, horse-drawn chariots, music, and dance.

The Vedas also tell about Aryan religious beliefs. For example, the Aryans worshipped many gods, including Indra, Varuna, Vishnu, Siva, and Devi. They believed that the souls of people are reborn after they die.

The Aryan Caste System Another important part of Aryan society was the **caste** system. A caste is a social group based on birth. All people in Aryan society were divided into groups. At the top of the caste system were the kings and nobles. Next were the priests, or Brahmans. Third were ordinary tribesmen and herders. Fourth were the people whom the Aryans had conquered. At the bottom were the Untouchables, or the outcastes. The Untouchables did the dirty work of society. Later the order of the first and second castes switched. The priests became the first caste and the kings and nobles became the second caste.

A part of the caste system were the ideas of karma and dharma. *Karma* means "fate." According to Hindu beliefs, people who do good deeds throughout their lives can earn a good karma. This allows them to be reborn into a higher caste in their next lives.

People who are evil achieve a bad karma. They are punished by being reborn into a lower caste. Part of attaining a good karma is to follow one's *dharma*, or duty. If Hindus follow the dharma of their caste, they earn a higher caste in the next life.

As time went on, the Aryan caste system became stricter and more complex. The caste system then became an important part of Hinduism, which is the main religion of India today.

Religion in South Asia

Hinduism and Buddhism, two world religions, developed in South Asia. Islam is a third religion that is important in the region today. Islam developed in the Middle East and spread to South Asia.

Hinduism Hinduism is one of the oldest religions in the world. It has no known founder and no formal church. It developed from ancient Aryan culture and traditions. Hinduism is a system of living more than a set of beliefs. Most Hindus chant a prayer to the sun at dawn. Aside from that, there are few prayers that all Hindus say. Most

The founder of Buddhism was Siddhartha Gautama, who was an Indian prince. Siddhartha believed that people would find peace if they did good deeds and lived a good life. Shown here is a Buddhist temple in Java, Indonesia.

worship Siva, Vishnu, or Devi. They may also worship gods that are special to their town or their family.

Hinduism does not have a bible, or holy book. There are, however, sacred, or holy, Hindu texts. Among these are the Vedas and the Upanishads (oo•PAN•ih•shadz). Most Hindus are familiar with the *Mahabharata* (muh•HAH•bah•rah•tuh). The *Mahabharata,* which means "The Great Story" in Sanskrit, is a very long poem that tells the story of a 12-year war between two branches of a royal family.

The most famous section of the *Mahabharata* is the *Bhagavad-Gita* (BAHG•uh•vuhd GEE•tah). It tells of a soldier who meets the god Krishna on the eve of an important battle. Krishna advises the warrior to **meditate**, or think deeply; to do good works; and to love God. Krishna also tells him to do his duty as a soldier. In the end, the soldier is victorious.

Most Hindus do not eat meat. Hindus also believe in the caste system. They believe that people are born to their job and their status in life. If a person does his or her job well, he or she will be **reincarnated**, or reborn, into a higher caste.

Caste still rules Indian life today. The caste system divides people into classes and restricts them from certain jobs. It has been a barrier to civil rights in India. People who believe in the caste system think that sons should have the same job as their fathers and that a person in one caste may not marry a person from another caste. People in the lowest castes are often treated poorly. In the 1950s and 1960s, India's government passed laws that bar discrimination against any caste for any reason. But the laws are hard to enforce. Especially in the rural areas of India, the caste system remains strong. (See Chapter 10.)

Buddhism Buddhism is another religion that began in South Asia. It was begun in India during the 500s B.C. by a man named Siddhartha Gautama (sid•DAHRT•uh gow•TAH•muh). Siddhartha was born a prince in what is now the country of Nepal.

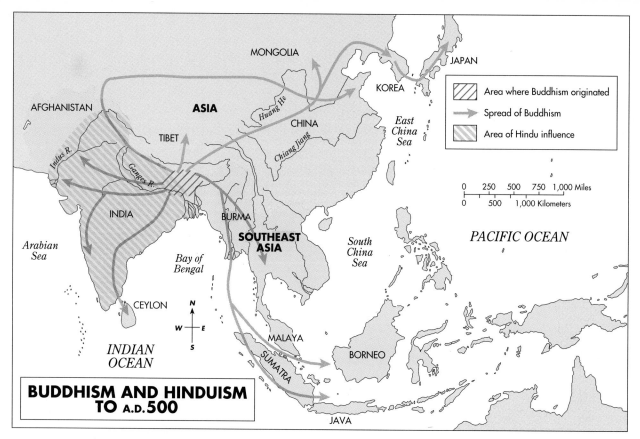

Movement and Region Buddhism and Hinduism both began in South Asia. From there, the two religions spread. To which countries did Buddhism spread? To which countries did Hinduism spread?

When he was about 30, he wandered outside of the palace and saw four things that changed his life: an old man, a sick man, a dead man, and a contented beggar. It was the first time in his life that he had seen misery. Suddenly, he realized that life is full of suffering and pain.

Siddhartha could not rest until he found the reasons for this pain and suffering. He left his wife and newborn son and wandered for six years. He looked for answers everywhere. He began to meditate. For 49 days, he sat under a tree. Then, one day the answers suddenly came to him. At that moment, Siddhartha experienced enlightenment. From then on he was known as *Buddha,* which means "Enlightened One." Buddha called the ideas that had come to him the Four Noble Truths. They are:

- Life is full of pain and suffering.

- Desire, or wanting things, causes this pain.

- The way to end pain is to end desire.

- One can learn to end desire.

Buddha believed that if people lost their desire for possessions, they would be happy. When people did good deeds and lived a good life, they would reach **nirvana** (nihr•VAH•nuh). Nirvana is a state in which a person wants nothing.

Buddha spent the rest of his life teaching his beliefs. His followers spread Buddha's teachings far and wide. Over the next thousand years, Buddhism spread throughout Asia. (See the map above.) In India, though, many of Buddha's beliefs became part of Hinduism. Today, fewer than 1 percent of the people of India are Buddhists. Although there are only 6.4 million Buddhists in India, there are about 330 million in the world.

Today, there are two main groups of Buddhists. Theravada (ther•uh•VAH•duh) Buddhists stress a solitary life as the way to reach nirvana. They believe that Buddha was a great teacher, but not a god. Mahayana (mah•huh•YAH•nuh) Buddhists believe that Buddha was a god and they worship him.

Islam The religion of Islam is important in South Asia. Islam began during the A.D. 600s in the Middle East. It first came to South Asia in the 700s. Later, in the 1200s, more people of the subcontinent converted to Islam. Followers of Islam call themselves Muslims. There are about 230 million Muslims in Pakistan and Bangladesh. In India, there are about 128 million Muslims.

Muhammad founded Islam. Muhammad, who lived in Saudi Arabia, taught that there is one God. He preached against worshiping many gods and emphasized that all people are equal before Allah. *Allah* is the Arabic word for God. Muhammad said that for Muslims to gain Allah's grace, they must obey Allah's will. In fact, the word *Islam* means "submission to Allah."

The Koran is the holy book of Islam. Muslims believe that the Koran contains the word of God. The Koran is the basis for law all over the Muslim world.

For Muslims, there are five main duties. They are known as the Five Pillars of Islam. The most important pillar is the belief in one God. The second is prayer. Muslims must pray five times a day. When they pray, they face Mecca, the birthplace of Muhammad.

Islam teaches concern for the poor. Giving charity is the third pillar. The fourth is fasting. During the holy month of Ramadan, Muslims fast during the day. At night, they feast. The fifth pillar is a pilgrimage to Mecca, the holy city in Saudi Arabia. Once in every Muslim's life, he or she is expected to go to Mecca.

The Golden Temple in Amritsar, India, is the Sikh religion's most important holy site. Built in 1604, the temple lies on an island connected to the mainland by a causeway.

Islam emphasizes that all believers are equal before God. This idea appealed to many Hindus who were trapped in low castes. From the 1200s to the 1500s, thousands in the northern regions of the Indian subcontinent converted to Islam.

Other Religions Other religions are also found in South Asia. They include Jainism (JEYEN•ihz•um), Sikhism (SEEK•ihz•um), and Christianity. Jainism began in the 500s B.C. as a reaction against Hinduism. Its followers promise to kill no living thing, to tell no lies, and to steal nothing. Jainists are strict vegetarians. Vegetarians do not eat meat. Today, there are more than three million Jains. Most live in western India.

The Sikh religion was founded by a Hindu teacher in the 1400s. Sikhs believe in one God and do not believe in the caste system. They do believe in reincarnation. Sikhs do not cut their hair, and Sikh men usually wear turbans. They do not use tobacco or alcohol. Most of the region's more than 18 million Sikhs live in the Punjab. The Punjab is located in the northwestern portion of the subcontinent.

Christian missionaries first arrived in India in the 1500s. Through the centuries, a number of Indians have converted to Christianity. Today, there are more than 22 million Christians in India.

The Empires of India

The first of South Asia's great empires was the Maurya (MAWR•yah) Empire, which was formed in about 321 B.C. by Chandragupta (chuhn•druh•GUP•tuh) Maurya. Chandragupta was king of a small northeastern region of the subcontinent. In the 300s B.C., he took over kingdoms to the north and west. Before long, the Maurya empire reached from Afghanistan in the west to the Ganges River in the east. At its height, the Maurya empire extended over all but the most southern portion of India.

The Maurya Empire The Maurya Empire had a well-organized government. Its many government officials owed their jobs to the emperor. There was also a secret police force that sent reports to Chandragupta. The secret police warned the emperor about plots against him. A huge army of 700,000 soldiers, 9,000 elephants, and 10,000 chariots helped Chandragupta maintain order.

Chandragupta worked to improve business and trade for his people. The emperor built canals to bring water to farms. He constructed roads to transport goods to market. Ships from the Maurya Empire traded with the Middle East and other parts of Asia.

The most famous Maurya emperor was Chandragupta's grandson Asoka. Asoka ruled from 273 to 232 B.C. At first, he fought to make the empire larger. In the wars that Asoka waged, more than 100,000 people died. When Asoka learned about the deaths, he was horrified. He decided to give up war and to rule through kindness and peace. Asoka became a Buddhist.

As a Buddhist, Asoka tried to rule by his good example rather than by the use of force. He built hospitals, rest houses for travelers, and wells to provide water for people to drink. Asoka sent teachers all over the empire to educate his subjects. To inspire people to do good works, Asoka carved messages of kindness on rocks and in caves throughout the empire. One message asked people to treat one another kindly and fairly.

India's Golden Age After the death of Asoka, the Maurya Empire declined. The empire split into many small kingdoms. It was not until the A.D. 300s that the next great empire arose. This was the Gupta Empire. The Gupta Empire lasted from 320 to 535.

Under the Guptas, science, mathematics, art, and literature flourished. It was during this period, called India's golden age, that Indian mathematicians developed the idea of zero. Doctors performed plastic surgery. Buildings were filled with sculptures. Poets wrote stirring works.

A Chinese Buddhist monk who traveled in India between 401 and 410 recorded what he saw in the Gupta Empire. The monk noted that the people of the empire "were prosperous and happy," and that the emperor was a fair man who punished criminals according to the seriousness of their crime. For example, the monk wrote, "even for a second attempt at rebellion the punishment is only the loss of the right hand."

Ancient India's golden age ended when invaders from Central Asia swept through the northern mountains. The Gupta Empire broke apart. For the next 1,000 years, India was divided into small warring kingdoms.

Islam in South Asia The next force to unify India was Islam. In about 1200, Islamic rulers set up a kingdom in northern

India. This kingdom, including the city of Delhi and the area around it, became known as the Delhi sultanate. It became famous as a center of Islam.

Mongols from Central Asia invaded and weakened the Delhi sultanate in 1398. In 1526, another Mongol invasion delivered the final blow to the sultanate. The invaders established the Mogul Empire. (*Mogul* is the Persian word for "Mongol." The Persians were part of the invading army.) Babur, who headed this army, became its first emperor.

Babur did not respect the Hindus. Islam, he believed, was the greatest religion. Under Babur's rule, Hindus paid heavy taxes and could not hold government jobs. Hindu temples were destroyed and looted.

Babur's grandson Akbar felt differently about Hindus. Akbar became emperor in 1556. He felt that it would be impossible to keep his empire united if he tried to make all the people live as Muslims. Akbar decided to allow people of all religions to worship as they pleased. Akbar believed that "If men walk in the way of God's will, interference with them would be unfair."

The Mogul Empire lasted for more than 300 years. Under the Moguls, great monuments, palaces, and **mosques**, or Muslim houses of worship, were built in India. The greatest of these buildings was the Taj Mahal, which was built as a monument to the wife of a Mogul emperor.

India became one of the richest countries in the world. Mogul rule extended over all but a small part of southern India.

On Assignment...

What parts of this section would you show on your mural? How might you show the religions of South Asia? How might you portray the differences between Babur and Akbar?

Eventually, weak rulers had trouble keeping the empire together. In the 1700s, civil wars and revolts caused the empire to collapse.

Section 1 Review

1. What are the Five Pillars of Islam?
2. **Inferring** How do you think Akbar's religious tolerance kept his empire unified?

SECTION 2

Europeans Arrive

How did Britain gain control of India?

Europeans had been trading with India for hundreds of years. They valued India's spices, tea, jewels, silks, and cotton. For most of those years, Italy controlled the trade routes to India. Then, in 1498, Portuguese explorers discovered an all-sea route to India that cut Italy out of the trade. Soon after, the Portuguese built trading posts in India. Other European nations followed. All competed for the control of trade with India, but by the 1700s, only Britain and France remained.

Britain and France fought a long and bitter struggle for the control of India. By the 1760s, however, the British had defeated the French and won control. The British controlled trade through the British East India Company. The East India Company was owned by a group of British business people who traded in Indian spices, silks, and dyes. The company used the decline of the Mogul Empire to gain power. As the Mogul Empire declined, India broke apart into rival kingdoms. The British encouraged rivalry between the kingdoms and forced one Indian ruler after another to sign treaties. The treaties gave the East India Company a great deal of power.

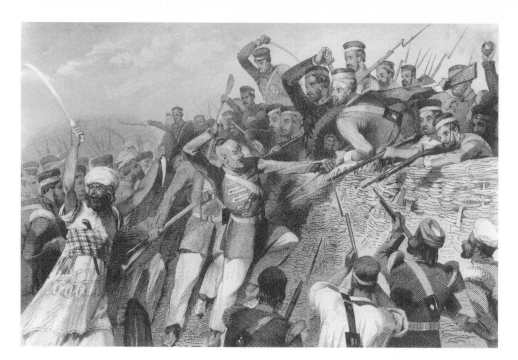

The Sepoy Rebellion (1857–1859) was a turning point in British rule over India. After the rebellion, the British decided to increase their control over the subcontinent.

The Sepoy Rebellion By the mid-1800s, the East India Company controlled most of north India. It created an army of Indian soldiers, called *sepoys*. The company also made other changes. It made English the official language of India and required Indian schools to teach European history, literature, and science. British missionaries were allowed to convert Indians to Christianity.

Indians saw their culture, language, and religious beliefs threatened by these outsiders. The final straw came when rumors spread among the sepoys that rifle cartridges had been greased with beef fat or pork fat. To use their rifles, the sepoys had to bite off part of the cartridge. Hindus believe that bulls are sacred and Muslims do not eat pork. Both groups felt that the British had insulted them and their religious beliefs. In 1857, a revolt broke out. The sepoys nearly defeated the British. In the end, however, the British crushed the revolt.

After the Sepoy Rebellion, the British government decided to end the rule of the East India Company. India had become Britain's most important colony. Britain, therefore, decided to rule it directly.

Under the new arrangement, India was divided. The British ruled about three fifths of the subcontinent directly. The rest was run by Indians, but under British control. Indians had little or nothing to say about how they were ruled.

Effects of British Rule

The chief goal of the British government in India was to help British business. The government encouraged India's farmers to grow more cotton for Britain's new cloth-making factories. Indians were not allowed to weave their own cotton into cloth or import machinery to make cloth. For hundreds of years, weaving cotton had been the way many Indian families earned their living. Now many families had no work.

At the same time, another problem arose. Many farmers who planted cotton stopped growing food crops. This resulted in a reduced amount of food available for India's fast-growing population. Low food supplies caused hunger and starvation in much of India in the late 1800s.

The British made some changes in India that improved the lives of the Indian people. Some changes helped Britain rule India more efficiently. For example, the British dammed rivers and built canals to bring water to farmlands and to grow more crops. The British built many railroads to help move food and supplies to all parts of the country. These railroads—together with new telegraph lines—helped to tie the country together. In addition, the British ended wars between the rulers of the Indian states and prevented many conflicts between Hindus and Muslims. They brought the many different peoples of India under the authority of one government.

The British also introduced changes in education and in the legal system that benefited the Indian people. The British started many schools and universities. The students in these schools learned Western ideas about freedom and democracy. It was this group of educated people that would lead the movement for freedom for India and fight for their rights in the courts.

Section 2 Review

1. How did the British East India Company take control of India?
2. **Drawing Conclusions** The British called the sepoy uprising the Sepoy Rebellion. Indians called it the First War of Indian Independence. Why do you think they had different names for it?

SECTION 3

India Wins Independence

How did India win independence from Britain?

The Indian National Congress (INC) was formed in 1885 to fight for Indians' rights. At first, it simply wanted more Indians in government. Gradually, however, the INC began to make more demands.

During World War I, Indians backed Britain with money and soldiers. More than a million Indians served in the war. Afterwards, Indians pressured Britain for more reforms. In the city of Amritsar, protests broke out and British soldiers killed almost 400 unarmed Indians and wounded 1,200.

The British government refused to punish the soldiers for firing into an unarmed crowd. The INC, however, held its own investigation, which was led by Mohandas K. Gandhi (MOH•han•dahs GAHN•dee). Gandhi was a British-educated Hindu. In 1920, Gandhi became the leader of the INC. He wanted India to achieve independence through nonviolent means.

Gandhi Urges Nonviolence

Gandhi believed in **civil disobedience**, or a person's refusal to follow laws that he or she believes are unjust. He urged Indians to refuse to pay taxes, serve in the government, and obey British laws.

The British imprisoned Gandhi for two years for breaking the law. There he went on hunger strikes to protest British rule. After his release, Gandhi's reputation grew. He became known as *Mahatma*, which means "great soul."

Gandhi continued to encourage a program of noncooperation. He also called on Indians to appreciate their own culture. He told them, "Don't pay your taxes or send your children to an English-supported school. Send them to a school where they may learn their own native language. Make your own cotton cloth by spinning the thread at home, and don't buy English-made goods." Gandhi himself wore a homespun loincloth and became a strict vegetarian. His spinning wheel became an important symbol of protest against British domination.

The British granted more self-government to India. However, Gandhi and the INC decided that India must be completely independent. When World War II broke out in 1939, Gandhi urged the Indian people not to take part unless the British granted India

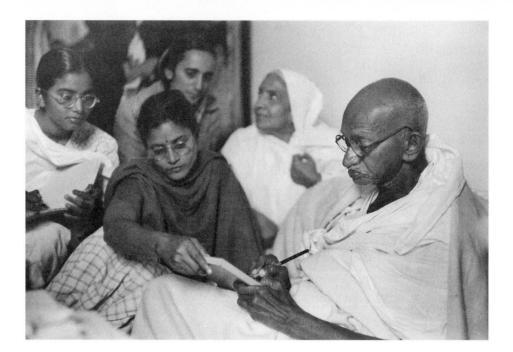

Mohandas K. Gandhi believed in the use of civil disobedience and other nonviolent methods to achieve Indian independence. Many people called him *Mahatama*, which means "great soul."

full independence. In 1942, Gandhi and other INC leaders were jailed again. Even so, more than two million Indians fought for Britain.

The end of World War II meant the end of many European empires. The British were ready to let go. The question was whether India should be one country or two. Many Muslims wanted a separate country. They felt that they could not live with the Hindus. Gandhi felt strongly that India should be united.

India Divided

In 1947, Britain granted India independence. There would be two countries. One, Pakistan, would be the home of most Muslims.

Gandhi refused to attend the Independence Day celebration. He hated the idea of India being split. As soon as the plan was decided, Hindus began to leave Pakistan. Muslims fled to Pakistan. During these flights, there were fights that killed more than a half-million people.

Gandhi began a fast to the death to stop the violence. When leaders of the groups promised to end the fighting, he ended his fast. Even so, there was more killing. In

On Assignment...

List the events or people from this section that would be most important to include in your mural. Then write how you could illustrate them. Make rough sketches of your ideas.

1948, a Hindu shot and killed Gandhi. The killer was angry that Gandhi was trying to make peace with the Muslims.

Gandhi's teachings inspired many people. In the United States, he inspired civil rights leader Martin Luther King, Jr. The startling idea that one could use peace to fight war had taken hold in the world.

Section 3 Review

1. Why was India split into two countries after it gained independence?

2. **Hypothesizing** Why do you think Gandhi was so successful?

Salt March for Freedom

Prem and his friend Ram looked down the dusty road. People began to gather on the road to watch the group coming toward them.

"I know who it is," said a woman. "It is Gandhi."

"Gandhi?" The news flew like wildfire around the village.

As the man came closer, Prem could see that it was Gandhi. That kindly face, the glasses, the bald head. Near Gandhi, a man was talking. "We are walking to the sea," he was saying. "We will not pay for British salt. We will make our own. They cannot tax that. We must prove that we do not need the British. We must prove that we want our freedom. This will do that. Will you come with us?"

Prem watched as people in the village looked at one another. Some talked. Some went to their houses and came out with bundles to take with them on the trip to the sea.

"How far is it?" called out one man. "How long?"

"We have been walking for four days," a man called back. "It is about 200 miles (320 km) to the sea. We will be there in 20 days."

Ram said to Prem, "I will go to spend this time with Gandhi and to prove that the British cannot beat us down."

In an instant, Prem made up his mind. "I will go, too."

They and several other villagers left with Gandhi. The days were long, hot, and dusty. There was little food. At night, the people slept on the road. But as the group moved on, it grew. As it grew, a sense of joy filled the thousands on the road. The slight man wearing the simple white loincloth could do that. At night, he talked to the crowds. He spoke of peace and of the rightness of the cause.

At the sea, Ram, Prem and thousands of others followed Gandhi to the salt water. They set it in dishes to let the water evaporate. The police were waiting. Gandhi went with them quietly. A light shone in his eyes as he looked to his followers. He smiled.

"Do you know," Ram said, "I do believe we will succeed."

Case Study Review

1. What did Gandhi intend to prove with the Salt March?
2. **Drawing Conclusions** Why do you think people followed Gandhi to the sea?

REVIEWING CHAPTER 9

I. Reviewing Vocabulary

Match each word on the left with the correct definition on the right.

1. caste
2. meditate
3. reincarnated
4. mosque

a. a place of worship for Muslims
b. a social group based on birth
c. to think deeply
d. reborn

II. Understanding the Chapter

Answer the questions below on a separate sheet of paper.

1. How did Aryan culture lead to the development of the Hindu religion?
2. What are the major religions of South Asia?
3. What were the causes of the sepoy uprising?
4. What were the original goals of the Indian National Congress? How did those goals change?

III. Building Skills: Identifying a Point of View

Look at each of the statements below. Then match each statement with the person or group who might have had this point of view.

1. a Buddhist
2. Gandhi
3. a British officer
4. a Muslim

a. We will succeed if we oppose the government without violence.
b. The prophet Muhammad heard the voice of God.
c. If you stop wanting things, you will be happy.
d. We have improved this country with roads, railroads, and schools.

IV. Working Together

Work with two or three classmates to create a time line that shows major events in the history of South Asia. First, review the chapter and list all of these events. Then, arrange them in chronological, or time, order. Finally, transfer your time line to a large sheet of paper and place it on the bulletin board to use as a classroom reference.

On Assignment. . .

Creating a Mural: Look at the notes and sketches that you made throughout this chapter. Think of how the pictures could tell a story from beginning to end. Now create your mural.

CHAPTER 10

Changing Patterns of Life in South Asia

How and why are traditions changing in South Asia?

In India, as elsewhere in the world, education is the key to success. These children attend a school in Gujarat, India, which has a satellite TV dish.

Looking at Key Terms

- **epidemic** an outbreak of disease
- **bustee** a poor area of a city where people live in shacks
- **stupa** a dome-shaped burial mound that serves as a Buddhist holy site
- **raga** one of the ancient melody patterns of Indian music
- **epic** a long poem that tells the story of a hero

On Assignment...

Writing Letters: Imagine that you are traveling throughout South Asia. Your assignment is to write letters home that describe the people you meet and the way they live. In your letters, you may wish to compare the way of life in South Asia to the way of life in the United States. Take notes as you read and look for hint boxes to help you write your letters. At the end of the section, you will review your notes and write one letter to your family and another to a friend about what you have observed.

India: A Land of Tradition and Change

What changes have occurred in India since independence?

"How long since you have been home?" asks Keval. He is on the dirt street of his village to the north of New Delhi. "A decade? Two? Come in! Sit down! Let me tell you how life has changed. It has changed all over India." Keval ticks off with his fingers. "First, the caste system is changed. Second, life in our village is so different. Most of my sons are gone. And, last, I must tell you about the women. The women in India today—well, you would not know them."

Keval settles in on a mat in the small mud-brick house. Most of the people in his village are farmers. "I have not decided how I feel about all these changes. Many in our village do not like it. But still—" Keval's arm sweeps the village outside. "Still people move from here. They go to the cities. There, the changes are really something. You know, in the cities,

caste does not matter so much. Sons work at different jobs than their fathers. They marry women who are not in their caste.

"Some people from the village have moved to the cities. They go to school and get an education. Then most of them do not want to follow the caste traditions. The law, too, says that everyone can vote now. Before, that was not the case. Did you hear what happened in 1990? Government jobs—27 percent—were set aside for Untouchables. Students in the cities set fire to themselves in protest. Feelings run strong, my friend."

Village Life and City Life

"Here in the village, life is different for those who stay behind. There is not enough land for everyone. My sons have left. They cannot be farmers as I am. They are in the city, learning a trade. Then," Keval shrugs, "they may be back. Or maybe not. It is sure they will not be farmers. But life is better in the village now. We have electricity. We have a hospital."

Keval stops as a young woman comes in the door. She smiles fondly at him. "Do you remember my daughter, Geeta?" Keval asks the question with pride. Geeta turns her

COUNTRIES OF SOUTH ASIA

COUNTRY	CAPITAL CITY	AREA (square miles)	POPULATION (millions of people)	POPULATION DOUBLING TIME (years)
Bangladesh	Dhaka	50,260	113.9	29
Bhutan	Thimphu	18,150	1.4	30
India	New Delhi	1,147,950	897.4	34
Maldives	Malé	120	0.2	20
Nepal	Kathmandu	52,820	20.4	28
Pakistan	Islamabad	297,640	122.4	23
Sri Lanka	Colombo	24,950	17.8	49

Source: World Population Data Sheet of the Population Reference Bureau, Inc.

The populations of the countries of South Asia are growing quickly. In how many years will the population of India double? Which country's population is due to double fastest?

Today, women in India have more opportunity than ever before to attend universities and to work outside the home. The women in this picture are nuns who work in the laboratory of a Christian mission hospital in Mahuadanr, Bihar.

large brown eyes to the visitor. She is wearing a printed cotton skirt and a white shirt. "We are looking for a husband for Geeta. She will marry someone from here, I hope. Then she will stay here. In some parts of India, women go to college. Not from this village, though. Geeta will marry a man we choose for her. And if later, they love each other. . . ." Keval shrugs.

"Father," says Geeta. "That is not so, what you said. Just last year, Saroj went to university. She will become a nurse. And now women can vote. We can buy land and sell it. All that is in the last few decades. Do not forget Indira Gandhi. She ran the whole of India. And doctors—India has more women doctors than the United States!"

Keval sighs. Then he strokes his daughter's hand. "Yes, yes," he says. "Some women do these things. But in this village, the role of wife is still most important. And do not worry. We will find you a good husband."

On Assignment. . .

Imagine that you have been the visitor in Keval and Geeta's home. What would you tell the people at home about the changes in India?

Geeta looks at her father and smiles. "Yes, father," she says. "But do not be surprised if we live in a different way."

"You see?" Keval says, laughing. "You asked what has changed. Listen to how this daughter speaks to her father!"

Section 1 Review

1. Why do people from the villages move to the cities?

2. **Summarizing** Explain the main changes that have come to Keval's village.

SECTION 2

India: Future Trends

What challenges will India face in the future?

India is the second most populous country in the world. It ranks second only to China. From 1965 to 1985, the population in India rose more than 60 percent.

To think about what that means, consider this. The United States had 248 million people in 1990, while India had 911 million. There are about 70 people per square mile in the United States. In India, there are 741 people per square mile. That means that India has 10 times as many people per square mile as does the United States.

A Growing Population

One reason India is growing so fast is that the death rate is down. Today, fewer people die from **epidemics**, or outbreaks of disease. Epidemics of smallpox and malaria used to kill many Indians.

India's government is trying to slow the growth of the population. At first, some states fined couples who had more than two children. Now, the government is trying to convince couples to have fewer children instead of punishing those who have many children. No one knows if this voluntary family planning will work.

Overpopulation has caused some serious problems in India. It is difficult to provide food, housing, jobs, and medical care for so many people. But population is only one of India's concerns.

Saving the Environment

The environment is another cause for concern. Many trees have been cut down in India's highland. When an area is cleared of trees, there is nothing to hold the soil in place. When the rains come, the soil simply washes away.

People in the highlands use a form of civil disobedience to stop loggers from cutting more trees. The people simply hug the trees. To cut down the trees, the loggers would have to hurt the tree huggers. Others around the world have used this idea to save trees.

South Asia faces other environmental problems as well. Overuse of farmland is one. Unsafe water and sewage in the cities is another. Air pollution is a big problem, too. In 1984, the name Bhopal became known to the whole world. That was the year that a leak at a chemical plant caused at least 1,500 people to die.

The Indian government has worked hard to deal with all these problems. The solutions may be years away, though.

The Move to the Cities

Most people still live in villages in India. However, farmland is becoming scarce. Many people move to the cities to find jobs. Often, that does not happen. The cities are overcrowded. In Bombay, for example, more than one million people live in **bustees**, or poor areas filled with shacks. Bombay's bustees form some of the largest shantytowns in the world. There are a half-million people who cannot even manage to live in a bustee. Those people sleep on the streets.

On a crowded street in Bombay, India, car horns blow as traffic backs up. With more than 12 million people, Bombay is India's most populous city. Like most cities, Bombay is a city of contrasts in wealth and poverty.

Bombay is not the only city in South Asia with bustees. Bustees exist in other Indian cities as well as in Kathmandu, Nepal; and Karachi, Pakistan. One of the main problems is that there are simply not enough jobs. People without jobs cannot afford housing of any sort. They live in the bustees, where cardboard or rags can make the walls of a home. Safe drinking water and public toilets are sometimes hard to find. City officials are trying to keep up with the new city dwellers and their needs, but it is hard. People keep pouring into the cities.

For the wealthy, living in a city can be good. The wealthy have large apartments. There are private schools and servants. People come to their doors to sell food. India's large middle class also finds opportunities in the cities. The cities provide access to a wide range of jobs and to schooling.

Education in India

Although wealthy and middle-class city dwellers are likely to be educated, only 43 percent of India's people can read and write. Because most high-paying jobs require literacy skills, people who cannot read and write have difficulty improving their lives. India has pledged that every child will have a free education to the age of 14. In reality, only two thirds of India's children go to school.

Why don't all children go? For most, the answer is simple. There is no school in their village. For other families, the children are too important as workers to be allowed the luxury of school. Even those who begin first grade often do not go beyond the fourth grade. Fewer girls than boys go to school. Some families in villages feel that educating girls is a waste of time.

For those who continue their education, learning English is necessary. Most teaching in high schools is in English. Because many Indians do not speak English, they are unable to attend high school. In addition, students in high school take tests at the end of every year. If they do well, they go on. If

not, their schooling is over. The amount of schooling they complete decides their future.

Recently, India has opened more technical schools. Technical skills will help India's people find answers to the problems their country faces.

Section 2 Review

1. What is a bustee?
2. **Drawing Conclusions** How is education in India different from education in the United States?

SECTION 3

The Arts and Literature in South Asia

How does religion influence the arts and literature in South Asia?

The Indian subcontinent has a rich tradition of art, literature, music, and drama. Most of it is linked to religion. Two thousand years ago, artists who worked in gold crafted figures of gods. Buddhists built **stupas** in the 200s B.C. These dome-shaped burial mounds contain the remains of holy people, including Buddha. Buddhists visit these sacred sites.

Later, Hindus built and decorated temples. Gods with many arms, marching elephants, and prancing horses cover the walls of these temples. Hindus are also known for their skillfully executed miniature paintings. These tiny, colorful paintings show scenes from Hindu stories.

Muslims brought a new style of art to the subcontinent. Islamic arches and domes appeared in mosques and other buildings. The Taj Mahal, with its arches and graceful spaces, is one example.

Dance and Music

The performing arts in India are also linked to religion. Indian dance comes from traditions that are at least 4,000 years old. It takes a minimum of ten years to train for some kinds of traditional dance. There are about 140 different poses a dancer must learn. Just as important is learning complete control over the muscles in the face, neck, and hands. Each arched eyebrow has a meaning. Indian dancers wear beautiful and rich costumes. Many of the dances are based on Hindu stories.

Indian music is based on a very complicated system of notes and melodies. Each piece of music is based on a *raga* (RAH-gah). A raga is a traditional melody that recalls an emotion or a season. There are 70,000 ragas. Indian music is often played on stringed and wind instruments. Indians also use drums in their music.

Literature

The earliest Indian literature was poetry. It was passed orally from generation to generation. Then it was written in Sanskrit. These early poems were religious. The *Mahabharata,* which is still important to Hindus, is one example of an **epic** poem. An epic is a very long poem that tells the story of a hero. Another important epic is the *Ramayana.* One lesson in this epic is that people should honor their parents.

Later works were based on themes such as love and war. Some poems were written in other languages. A romance called *The Jeweled Anklet* is a long poem that was written in the Tamil language. Both Tamil and Sanskrit are ancient Indian languages that were used to write poems, plays, and stories.

In modern times, one outstanding Indian writer was Sir Rabindranath Tagore. He lived from 1861 to 1941. Tagore wrote hundreds of popular Indian songs, in addition to poems, short stories, novels, and plays. In 1913, he was the first Asian to win the Nobel Prize for literature.

Section 3 Review

1. How did Indian literature change over the centuries?

2. **Determining Cause and Effect** What was the effect of religion on the arts in India?

Traditional Indian dance requires dancers to learn about 140 poses. To perform dances based on Hindu stories, dancers must know hand gestures called mudras.

The Hollywood of India

There is a term for most of the movies made in Bombay—*masala*. It means "spicy mixture." These movies first became popular in the 1970s. There is a beautiful woman, a handsome man who wants to win her, and a bad guy who wants to make trouble. There is comedy, action and adventure, and dancing and singing.

"Indians like to cry at the movies," Rishi Kapoor told *National Geographic Magazine*. "So our movies are like soap operas." Despite the tears, though, there is always a happy ending.

Romance is a critical part of these movies. In a land where most marriages are arranged, romance is always appealing. There's no kissing, though. Most Indians think that it is not proper to show kissing in public.

Satyajit Ray

There are some Indian and Pakistani filmmakers whose work is well known outside their countries. Perhaps the most famous is a filmmaker named Satyajit Ray. Ray began his career as an artist for an advertising agency. In the 1950s, he made *Pather Panchali* (*Song of the Road*). The movie, which Ray made without professional actors, was the first of a series of three movies that were to make him known throughout the world.

These three movies told the story of Apu, a boy whose family moves from the country to the city. The work is known as the *Apu Trilogy*. The movies were a real look at the way people live. Just before Ray died in 1992, he won an American Academy Award for his life's work.

Case Study Review

1. What does *masala* mean and why is it a good term to describe Indian movies?

2. **Comparing and Contrasting** How do you think the movies of Satyajit Ray are different from most of the movies that are made for Indian audiences?

On Assignment...

How would you describe an Indian movie to friends at home?

REVIEWING CHAPTER 10

I. Reviewing Vocabulary

Match each word on the left with the correct definition on the right.

1. bustee   **a.** a poor area of a city where people live in shacks
2. stupa   **b.** one of the ancient melody patterns of Indian music
3. raga   **c.** a long poem that tells the story of a hero
4. epic   **d.** a dome-shaped burial mound that serves as a Buddhist holy shrine

II. Understanding the Chapter

Answer the questions below on a separate sheet of paper.

1. How have women's roles changed in India?
2. What have been the results of population growth in India? How has the government tried to control population growth?
3. Why are there many Indians who do not know how to read and write?
4. Explain the difficulties involved in becoming an Indian dancer.

III. Building Skills: Comparing and Contrasting

Write a sentence comparing and contrasting the items in each pair below.

1. (a) life in villages (b) life in the cities
2. (a) the population of the United States (b) the population of India
3. (a) education for poor children in India (b) education for wealthy children in India

IV. Working Together

Work with a group to write and perform a skit about life in India. Use the story about Keval and Geeta in Section 1 as a model. Then choose a topic from the chapter and decide on the scene and characters you will portray. Possibilities include: life in a rural village, life in a bustee, training as an Indian dancer, or the movie industry in Bombay. Use library resources to find out more about your topic.

On Assignment. . .

Writing Letters: Review the notes you took as you read this chapter. You will write one letter to your family and one to a friend. What will you tell each about India in your letters?

Literature Connections

The Tiger

S. Rajaratnam

In many Southeast Asian cultures, tigers are used in stories as symbols of danger. In this short story, the author, S. Rajaratnam, uses the tiger to show how villagers feel about and interact with the natural world. Although the author lives in Singapore, the setting of "The Tiger" is Malaysia.

Fatima felt the cool yellow water of the river, a sheet of polished gold in the sunglow. The water flowed slowly around her as she clung to the bank. Then she moved further along until she stood waist deep. The wet sarong[1] clung to her brown figure, the plump body of a pregnant woman. . . .

So, when she heard the low, rumbling growl of the tiger, it only added to her dream world. But suddenly came a dull, angry roar. Fatima knew that it was not a creature of her imagination, but the real thing.

The tiger was framed by the lalang[2] and low to the ground. Fatima stared at its huge head and shoulders. It was not more than 20 yards from her. The sun gave a wicked glint to its watchful yellow eyes. Its ears were drawn back warningly. It turned its head and snarled. Around its red tongue, the yellow teeth looked like tree stumps.

Fatima was frozen into helpless fear by the glaring eyes of the tiger. The sudden stillness that fell around her made her mind numb. She dared not move. She dared not take her eyes from the watching animal. Yet the tiger, too, was still, as though it had been made motionless by the unexpected meeting with a human being.

Fatima and the animal watched one another. She was frightened; it was suspicious. Its growls continued, but became less angry each time. It showed no signs of really wanting to attack her. Instead, after a while the animal took less of an interest in her. Its huge paws stretched out in front. Now and then, the claws dug into the damp grass. Except when she moved, the animal's attention seemed to be nowhere in particular. The glare in its eyes had changed into a sullen and sometimes bored expression. Fatima noticed the surprising changes of mood in the animal's eyes. . . .

She grew desperate, as the tiger showed no signs of going away. Her hands wandered over her stomach. She was a being of two lives, she realized. She *had* to escape. She just *had* to! Her

---

[1]**sarong** (suh-RAWNG) *n.* a simple wraparound dress or skirt
[2]**lalang** (LAH-lahng) *n.* a kind of very tall, thick grass

French painter Henri Rousseau portrayed the danger of surprising a tiger. How do the villagers in this story feel about tigers?

eyes could still make out the shadowy form of the tiger in the falling light.

Fatima had studied the animal very carefully. She could tell when it was going to turn its eyes away from her. She waited, her body tense in the water with a fearful strength. Then with a desperate movement, she dived underwater. She scraped the bottom of the river as she swam toward the opposite bank, in the direction of the village. She came to the surface only when she felt that her lungs would burst for air. She felt lost in the middle of the river. When she heard the faraway growl, a fear that she had not felt even close to the tiger seized her.

She swam wildly toward the shore. Finally she saw the twinkling oil lamps of the village.

The village was in panic by the time Fatima's mother had spread an exaggerated version of the story her daughter had told her. The women gathered the children into their arms. They called out to the men to do something about the tiger. . . .

Fatima rose up from her mat. She looked out of the narrow window. The moon cast a gentle light over everything it touched. She could see the moon through the tall coconut trees. Men moved about in the moonlight, preparing for the hunt. They called out to one another. Fatima stared at them sadly.

Then the men left. Now there were only the gray trees and the whisper of the worried wind. Straining her ears, she heard the far-off sound of the river.

Somewhere out there, she thought, was the tiger. She had wondered about the animal the whole evening. She hoped that it was far out of the men's reach. . . .

Fatima scowled out of the window and listened. There was a silence over the village. Her hands, swollen and red, were knotted tightly together as she strained to hear some sound. The pound, pound of her heart echoed the noise her mother made with the wooden bowl. Then a sharp pain shot through her. Her hands went to her stomach.

"What is it, Fatima?" said her mother, looking up.

"Nothing," answered Fatima between pressed lips.

"Come away from that draft and lie down," said her mother.

Fatima went on standing by the window. She felt the pain rise and fall. She closed her eyes and pictured the tiger. It crouched in the lalang. Its eyes now red and glaring, now bored and gentle.

Then she heard the distant crack of a rifle. Another shot followed. Fatima quivered as if the shots had been aimed at her. Then came the roar of the tiger—not the growl she had heard that evening, but full of pain and anger. For a few seconds the cry of the animal seemed to fill up her heart and ears. Her face was tight with pain. Her body glistened with sweat. A moan broke between her shut lips. . . .

"I've got the pains, mother," gasped Fatima.

The old woman led the girl toward the mat. She made her lie down. . . .

Fatima lay on the mat, her eyes shut tight. Her mother boiled the water and muttered.

"Listen," said the old woman, "The men are returning. I can hear their voices."

The air suddenly was filled with the excited voices of men and women outside.

The old lady opened the door cautiously. She called out to someone.

"Hurrah for Mamood, auntie," called a youth rushing in. "He's shot the tiger. It's a big animal. No wonder it put up a good fight. And then what do you think happened?"

Fatima looked at the youth with interest. The old lady turned her tiny wrinkled head impatiently toward the boy.

"Well, what happened?"

"They said," explained the youth "that after they had killed the animal they heard noises. Then by the light of their lamps, they saw three of the tiniest tiger cubs. Their eyes were hardly open. Mamood says that they would not be more than a few hours old. No wonder the beast fought so hard."

Villagers along the rivers of Southeast Asia depend on the rain forest for food, shelter, and other basic needs. They also depend on one another for protection and support.

Fatima moaned in pain. The sweat glistened like yellow pearls on her forehead.

"Mother!" she cried.

The old woman pushed the astonished youth toward the door.

"Get the midwife, boy," she shouted. "Quick! Go! The midwife."

The youth stared, gasped, and then ran for the midwife.

Making Connections

1. How does Fatima's attitude toward the tiger change in this story?

2. **Analyzing Information** What traditions and customs of Southeast Asia do you learn about in "The Tiger"?

South Asia in the World Today

What challenges has South Asia faced since World War II?

Tea leaves are picked and then dried for brewing the flavorful beverage. India is one of the world's leading producers of tea, exporting it around the world.

Looking at Key Terms

- **martial law** temporary rule by the military
- **militant** a person who believes in using violence to promote a cause
- **communism** an economic system in which the government owns and controls most property and industry
- **non-alignment** a policy of not being allied with other nations on a regular basis, but of deciding each question of foreign policy individually
- **neutrality** a policy of refusing to take sides in a conflict
- **pact** an agreement
- **coup** a revolt, often by military leaders, against a nation's government

On Assignment...

Creating an Illustrated Time Line: In this chapter, you will organize the information you learn by making an illustrated time line that shows key events in South Asia from the 1940s to the present. Time lines list events in the order in which they occurred. Three or four events on your time line will be accompanied by pictures. Look for hint boxes to help you choose items for your time line.

India's Government and Economy

What challenges have India's government and economy faced since independence?

India is the world's largest democracy. Its government is patterned after Britain's government. In both countries, a prime minister is the most powerful government official. India has a president and a vice president, but their jobs are mostly ceremonial. They do not hold much real power.

In the United States, Congress makes the laws. Like the United States, India has a lawmaking body that is divided into two houses. The Indian lawmaking body is a parliament.

All Indian citizens who are 18 and over are permitted to vote. There are no restrictions based on caste or education. Because almost half of India's voters cannot read or write, symbols are used to represent the different parties. For example, the Praja Socialist party's symbol is a thatched hut. The symbol of the National Congress party is a team of oxen.

In India, as in Great Britain and other countries, people in each district vote for representatives to parliament. The party that wins the most seats chooses the prime minister.

The National Congress Party

For its first 20 years, India was controlled by the same political party, the National Congress party. For much of this time, the party was led by Jawaharlal Nehru (jah•WAH•hahr•lahl NAY•roo). Nehru was a leader during India's fight for independence. He became president of the Independent Congress party (INC) in 1929. INC became the National Congress party after independence.

Nehru led the Congress party and remained prime minister of India until his death in 1964. During his time in office, Nehru led his new country well. He introduced an economic plan that helped farmers produce more food. He also helped India to build new industries.

After Nehru died, Lal Bahadur Shastri became leader of the Congress party. He soon faced a huge problem. In 1965, India and Pakistan went to war. Both claimed Kashmir, in the northwest. Within a few weeks, the war ended. The following year, Shastri signed a peace treaty with Pakistan's leader. A few hours later, Shastri died of a heart attack.

India's next leader was Nehru's daughter, Indira Gandhi. The fact that a woman was chosen as leader surprised many. It seemed to say that India was moving into a new era. At first, Gandhi faced tough times. India's economy was in a shambles. People were hungry and were loudly protesting against the government. The country was suffering from drought, a period during which there is little or no rain. By 1969, though, India was producing more food. In addition, the birth rate was lower, so there were fewer mouths to feed.

Gandhi's greatest problem was the continuous fighting between India's religious and ethnic groups. At one point, she declared **martial law**. When a country is under martial law, its military enforces all laws and maintains order. In addition, Gandhi put some of her opponents in jail and restricted a number of freedoms. It seemed as if India's democracy was being replaced by a dictatorship.

In 1977, Gandhi held an election, which she lost. For the first time, India was ruled by a party other than the Congress party. The Janata party won the election and its leader, Morarji Desai, became prime minister. That didn't last, though. In three years, Gandhi was back in power.

Gandhi and the Sikhs

In the early 1980s, the Sikhs in Punjab began to demand their own country. They wanted to create an independent state in Punjab. In 1984, the conflict exploded into

Rajiv Gandhi waves to a crowd. Behind him are pictures of India's great leaders. From left to right are Indira Gandhi, Mohandas Gandhi, and Jawaharlal Nehru.

violence. Sikhs took over the Golden Temple at Amritsar, their holiest place. Gandhi sent soldiers to drive the Sikhs out of the temple. More than 600 Sikhs were killed in the fighting. India's population of 14 million Sikhs was outraged. Sikhs serving in the Indian army rebelled. On October 31, 1984, several Sikh bodyguards shot and killed the prime minister.

More Trouble Indira Gandhi's son Rajiv became the next head of the Congress party. In 1987, he sent Indian troops to neighboring Sri Lanka to keep the peace. Different groups in that country were fighting for control. (See Section 2.) Gandhi left office in 1989, but he decided in 1991 to try to return to power. While campaigning for that election, he was assassinated by a bomb planted by a Sri Lankan group.

In 1991, P.V. Narasimha Rao took office. He became prime minister during a troubled time in India. The economy was in decline and the Soviet Union, one of India's allies, was collapsing. In addition, Rao seemed an unlikely choice for prime minister. He did not seem ambitious and his health was not good.

Rao, however, surprised people. He worked with intelligence and firmness to address India's problems. In economics and foreign policy, he boldly ended outdated policies, replacing them with new ones.

In 1993, Rao faced new challenges when Hindu **militants** destroyed a 16th-century Islamic mosque. A militant is a person who believes in using violence as a way to promote a cause. The militants said that the mosque had been the site of a Hindu temple. Riots broke out. Almost 2,000 people were killed.

Today, the different faiths and peoples of India maintain an uneasy peace. Yet there is much hope for the future.

Economic Challenges

India faces serious economic challenges. It has a high potential for industrial and electric power development. There are large deposits of valuable minerals, such as iron ore and coal. However, India has not been able to reach its potential. It is one of the world's poorest countries. More than one half of its people cannot read or write. Why is India in this situation?

Agriculture employs about 70 percent of India's people. Indian farmers need water for their crops to grow. These workers are building a canal in Durgapur, India, that will direct water to the fields.

Agriculture Farming is the occupation of 70 percent of India's people. Most still farm their land the way their parents, and their grandparents, did. There is much to be said for these traditional ways of farming, though. If climate conditions are right, India can usually raise enough food for its ever-growing population.

India's farmers, however, face serious problems. One problem is the destruction that is caused by plant diseases and rats. Also, many farmers do not have enough fertilizer or water for their crops. All this means that the amount of food per acre that farmers can grow is smaller than in other countries.

Debt is another problem for Indian farmers. They borrow during bad years and have trouble repaying the loans.

Economists think that resolving these problems can increase the amount of food that Indian farmers harvest. The government has built dams and has tried to get more modern equipment for farmers. Many of the government's plans have been successful. Farmers grow much more food now. In fact, India exports more food than it imports.

Industry When the British ran India, there were many factories. They produced rubber, glass, paper, cotton, and steel. During World War II, those plants became very important. They made war goods, such as airplanes and ships.

When India won its independence from Britain, its main goal was building industry. India built new cotton mills and steel plants. Today India boasts that it makes steel more cheaply than any country in the world. Mining coal has been important. Coal is burned for electricity. Homes are heated and factories are run by coal energy.

India has a long history of "cottage industries," or businesses whose goods are produced by people working at home. Spinning and weaving cotton are cottage industries. About 6.3 million people work in

On Assignment. . .

Note the important events in this section on your time line. Also note any ideas for illustrations.

manufacturing industries. However, more than 20 million work in cottage industries.

India's industries have greatly increased production since World War II. Basically, though, India is still a farming country. Only one fifth of the money in India comes from mining and manufacturing goods. Much of the rest comes from agriculture.

Section 1 Review

1. What are the problems farmers face in India?

2. **Analyzing Information** Imagine that you are India's leader right after World War II. Which problem would you tackle first? Why?

Other Nations of South Asia

Why did Pakistan and Bangladesh separate?

"You want to know about Pakistan?" Aziz is sitting at a small cafe in Karachi. He is stirring his tea with a tiny spoon. "It is a story of bloodshed. It is a story of drama. Bangladesh, too. Talk to my friend Ali. He is from Bangladesh. He will tell you." Ali, a thin, serious-looking man, nods.

Pakistan and Bangladesh

"Pakistan and Bangladesh were once one country," Aziz says. "And once, we were all part of India. After World War II, India won

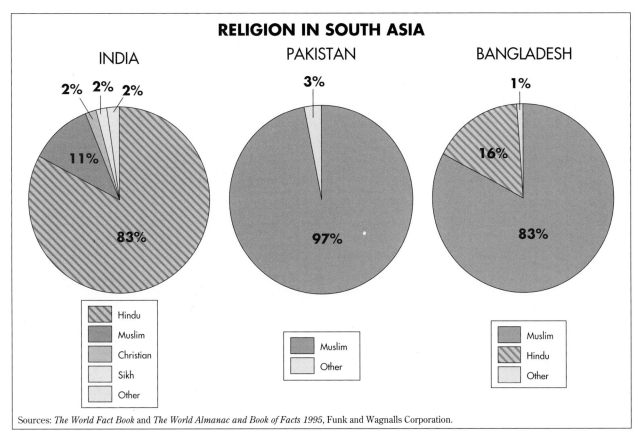

RELIGION IN SOUTH ASIA

INDIA — 2% 2% 2%, 11%, 83%

Hindu, Muslim, Christian, Sikh, Other

PAKISTAN — 3%, 97%

Muslim, Other

BANGLADESH — 1%, 16%, 83%

Muslim, Hindu, Other

Sources: *The World Fact Book* and *The World Almanac and Book of Facts 1995*, Funk and Wagnalls Corporation.

Hinduism and Islam have the largest number of followers in South Asia today. Which country has the largest percentage of Hindus? Which country has the largest percentage of Muslims?

its independence. A man named Muhammad Ali Jinnah would not let Pakistan become part of India. Ali Jinnah was from what is now Pakistan. He was part of the Congress party of India.

"He and I—most Pakistanis—are Muslim, you see. Most people in India are Hindu. In the 1930s, Ali Jinnah began to argue that the Hindus paid no attention to the problems of the Muslims. He quit the Congress party and became president of the Muslim League. He understood that we needed our own state. Ali Jinnah was stubborn. He would not let India take us. So Pakistan became its own country in 1947."

Aziz keeps stirring his tea, and sighs. "Things might have been different if Ali Jinnah had not died in 1948. Then, Liaquat Ali Khan became Pakistan's president. He had headaches. Many headaches." Aziz counts the headaches on his fingers. "There was Kashmir. Both India and Pakistan claimed it. Then there was the fact that East Pakistan and West Pakistan were separated by about 1,000 miles.

"The worst thing, though, was the panic. Muslims scrambled to leave India. Hindus scrambled to leave Pakistan. More than 15 million people moved. Of these, perhaps a half million died. Hindus and Muslims killed each other. It was a terrible time.

"After that, there were more problems. Did you know that there was a revolution in 1958? Well, the army took over and army Field Marshal Ayub Khan became president. There was some peace then. In 1962, we got a new constitution. Ayub Khan may have taken over by force, but he was a good leader. He set up a better government. It was based in the villages. He set up a plan for the economy to grow."

Aziz stopped to take a breath. Then he continued, "In 1965, Ayub Khan was elected to the presidency again. He faced more problems. The biggest, the worst, was the trouble between East Pakistan and West Pakistan."

"Those were bad times," Ali breaks in, shaking his head. "Much hatred. My people—the people in the east—felt we should have more say. There are more of us and we are poorer than the West Pakistanis. Then, too, the army was mostly in the west. We felt unprotected. There were riots in East Pakistan in the late 1960s. Ayub Khan was forced out in 1971. Then, there was martial law.

Bangladeshi soldiers ride atop a tank near Jessore, Pakistan, in 1971. Tensions ran high as East Pakistan declared independence from West Pakistan. In 1971, East Pakistan became Bangladesh and West Pakistan became Pakistan.

"Soldiers from West Pakistan were sent to East Pakistan to put down the riots. The army could not control things, so it began killing. Soldiers killed tens of thousands of East Pakistanis!" Ali says angrily. "Of course we revolted! There was war. India joined with us. They did it, probably, because millions of East Pakistanis fled to India. The Pakistanis did it to keep from getting killed. Anyway, we, the people of the east, won. And we no longer called ourselves Pakistani. In 1971, we became the new nation of Bangladesh. Pakistan now is what was once called West Pakistan."

Aziz is looking at Ali with a slight smile. "You can still get angry about all this, old friend. But now we are two nations. Surely we can be friends?"

Ali smiles a small smile. "You must forgive me. It is not so long ago, after all. I, like many, lost family and friends during that time. But you are right. And time does move on."

"Let us see," Aziz says. "Today Pakistan has a democracy. Since 1988, we have had free elections. And you, Ali? What do you see for Bangladesh?"

"We have had a hard time, as you know," Ali says. "We began life as a country with very little money. Things were in a shambles. Then, in 1974, we had the worst floods in two decades. There wasn't enough food. One leader, Major General Zia, was killed in 1981. In 1991, his widow, Begun Khalid Zia, became prime minister. A cyclone killed thousands in 1993. Then we had to take in Muslim refugees fleeing Burma. In Bangladesh, sometimes it seems we pick ourselves up just in time to be knocked down again. But we will get through this, too. We will make our nation."

Sri Lanka

Fringed palm trees rise from sandy shores. Sri Lanka is an island nation located southeast of India. It is a beautiful place. It looks like a tourist's paradise. But bitter fights between groups have scared away visitors.

Many people come to climb the Himalaya Mountains. Some come for adventure. Here, a group of Hindus makes a religious pilgrimage to the Amarnath Cave.

The first people to come to Sri Lanka were the Sinhalese from northern India. They came in the 500s B.C. On Sri Lanka, they met the Veddas and conquered them. The island was then called Sinhala. Two hundred years later, the Sinhalese converted to Buddhism.

In the A.D. 200s, Tamil kings from southern India came to the island. They made a Hindu kingdom in the north. The Portuguese, the Dutch, and the British came much later— in the 1500s. In 1796, the island became a British colony called Ceylon. It became famous for the tea that grew there on plantations.

After World War II, the people of Ceylon wanted independence from Britain. It happened at the same time India became a sta in 1947. Then, in 1972, the country changed its name to Sri Lanka. Since its founding, violence between the Hindu Tamils and the Sinhalese has marked its history. The Sinhalese had more power than the Tamils. The Tamils resented this, and fought for their own country on the island.

In the 1980s, terrorism and fighting became common. In February 1989, more than 1,000 people died in the violence. The 1990s have not brought peace. In May 1993, President Ranasinghe Premadasa was killed by a bomb. The following year, in a landslide victory, Chandrika Kumaratunga became Sri Lanka's first woman prime minister. In her campaign, she promised to end the "culture of assassination" that plagued her country.

Bhutan and Nepal

Set in the mountains, the countries of Bhutan and Nepal lie north of India, between India and China. Both countries are ruled by kings.

Nepal is larger than Bhutan. It is about 54,000 square miles (139,860 sq km) in size and has a population of more than 20 million people. Until recent times, the mountains isolated Nepal from the world. Its people lived a traditional lifestyle. The king even banned political parties. In 1990, though, he ended this ban. The first democratic election in 32 years was held in May 1991.

Nepal is a popular spot for tourists. They come to climb the highest mountain on earth, Mount Everest, and to enjoy the beauty of the country. They also come to see the ancient ways of the people.

The money that tourists bring is welcome. Nepal is a very poor country. Only 10 percent of its people can read and write. Some Nepalese make a living by joining the Indian army.

Bhutan is ruled by a king who has com-
control of his country's affairs.
Bhutan signed a treaty with India
nsult India about foreign
is about 18,000 square miles

(46,646 sq km) and contains about 1.4 million people. The people of Bhutan are related to the people of Tibet.

The leader of Bhutan is called the Dragon King. He is the grandson of the first Dragon King, who took power in 1907. The Dragon King holds power, but he has a group of advisers. India directs Bhutan's defense and foreign policy.

Bhutan's Dragon King has tried to keep the country isolated. In 1988, most tourists were banned. In 1990, a law was passed that forbids people from watching TV programs from other countries. Like the people of Nepal, most people in Bhutan cannot read or write.

Section 2 Review

1. Why did East Pakistan and West Pakistan separate into two countries?

2. **Comparing and Contrasting** What do Bhutan and Nepal have in common? How are they different?

SECTION 3

South Asia and the World

What role do India and Pakistan play in world politics?

After World War II, there emerged two major powers in the world: the United States and the Soviet Union (USSR). The two countries competed to win allies. Some countries adopted **communism** and allied themselves with the Soviet Union. Other countries

153

rejected communism and allied themselves with the United States. Still others decided to follow a different course. India was one of these nations.

Nehru, India's prime minister after the war, decided on a policy of **non-alignment**. In each individual foreign policy situation, India would decide how to act. Many countries that won their independence after the war agreed with India. They too adopted a policy of non-alignment. This policy, Nehru said, was different from **neutrality**. Neutral countries do not take sides in a conflict.

The policy of non-alignment made some people in the United States angry. The United States gave aid to India, people reasoned. How could India refuse to become its permanent ally? India, however, stuck to its position. Non-alignment meant that India voted to let China join the United Nations. The United States voted against it. India also refused to vote with the United States against the Soviet Union when it invaded Hungary.

India hoped that a policy of non-alignment would allow it to be on friendly terms with all nations. Based on this idea, the Soviet Union and India built strong ties. There were several reasons for this.

- The two countries were located close to each other in Asia.

- India admired the Soviet Union's attempts to get its economy moving.

- The leaders of the two countries were friendly.

- The two countries had some problems in common. Both were trying to build industry and farming.

- The Soviet Union gave India more than $1 billion in aid. This money was used to buy food and to build industry.

In 1954, the friendship between India and the United States cooled. In that year, Pakistan joined the United States in a **pact**, or agreement, against the Soviet Union. India saw that pact as a threat to its security.

The United States was also upset when India began to build nuclear weapons. The United States saw that as a danger. India said that having a nuclear bomb would help it keep the world peaceful.

In 1971, the United States supported Pakistan in the civil war that led to the creation of Bangladesh. This angered India. Since then, the United States and India have had an uneasy relationship.

Economic Challenges

In 1991, though, India announced a new policy. It decided to move away from a socialist economy, in which the government owned and controlled most big industries, to a capitalist economy, in which private individuals own and run most industries. India did this in hopes of attracting foreign investors. Foreign investors, India hoped, would pump money into its economy by building new businesses and creating new jobs.

Trouble With China

China and India became neighbors when China took over Tibet in 1950. Until 1959, the two countries were good neighbors. India supported China's admission to the United Nations. China was grateful for that.

In 1959, though, the people of Tibet rebelled against China. The Dalai Lama, the leader of Tibet, fled to India. Then Chinese troops took over some Indian land. India asked China to leave. China replied that India had encouraged Tibet to revolt.

The relationship between India and China remained uneasy. In 1962, China invaded India. Both Britain and the United States sent help to India. China stopped attacking, but it kept much of the land that it had taken. Today, China still holds that land.

Pakistan and the World

Pakistan has generally allied itself with the United States. In 1950, Liaquat Ali Khan, Pakistan's president, visited President Harry Truman. This angered the Soviet

In the late 1970s, millions of refugees from Afghanistan fled to Pakistan to escape the horrors of war in their country. Pakistanis did their best to help the refugees during their stay.

On Assignment...

Find at least three important dates in this section and write them on your list. Be sure to explain why these dates are important.

The United States joined the fight against the Soviets. It used Pakistan to give money to the Afghanis. More than 2.5 million Afghan refugees streamed into Pakistan. The Afghanis were poor, sick, disabled, and homeless. Many were taken in by individual Pakistanis. The Pakistani government also helped. In addition, the United States sent $3.2 billion to aid the refugees. With the collapse of the Soviet Union, however, there is no longer a need for the United States to send money to stop the spread of communism.

The war in Afghanistan upset the flow of life in Pakistan. Then the Persian Gulf War in 1990–1991 caused more problems. Thousands of Pakistanis who worked in the Middle East had to return home. That created a huge problem because the money these workers sent back to Pakistan had helped the country. Now, no money from the Middle East was coming to Pakistan.

Pakistan continues to face challenges. Natural disasters are a fact of life. So is overpopulation. Pakistan's need for outside aid is still strong. Its future role in the world is still to be determined.

Union. Then Pakistan accepted aid from the United States.

As you read earlier, in 1954, Pakistan signed a pact with the United States against the Soviet Union. The move made relations between Pakistan and India even more strained. It also soured the friendship between the United States and India.

In 1979, Pakistan began to build nuclear weapons. The United States became angry with its ally. Pakistan's leader, General Zia, refused to stop, however. President Jimmy Carter cut off U.S. aid to Pakistan. Then, in 1979, the Soviet Union invaded Afghanistan. The Soviets hoped that Afghanistan would remain a Communist state. Afghanistan and Pakistan share a border.

Section 3 Review

1. Why were both the United States and the Soviet Union dissatisfied with India's policy of non-alignment?
2. **Summarizing** Explain why India and the Soviet Union had close ties.

Benazir Bhutto:
The First Islamic Woman Leader

It was 1977. Benazir Bhutto, the beautiful daughter of Pakistan's leader, Ali Bhutto, was coming home. The time that she had spent in the West had been a triumph. Now, she was ready to join her country's foreign service.

Days after she arrived, her father was forced out in a military **coup**, or revolt, against the nation's government. Pakistan's new leader, General Zia, held her father in a tiny, dark, cold, jail cell. In 1979, he ordered Ali Bhutto hanged. Fearing that Ali's daughter Benazir would rally the people, Zia held her under house arrest for four years. Finally, in 1984, Zia allowed her to travel to England for treatment of an ear infection.

In 1986, Benazir Bhutto returned. In shock, she watched as three million people met her at the airport. "Jeevat Bhutto!" they shouted, throwing rose petals. "Long live Bhutto!"

For two years, Bhutto worked to rebuild her father's party. She married, and she was pregnant with her first child when Zia called an election for the post of prime minister. He may have reasoned that Bhutto, who was eight months pregnant, would not campaign.

He was wrong. Then, three months before the election, Zia died in a plane crash. In November, Bhutto's party won the most seats. Bhutto found herself the first Islamic woman leader in modern times.

Bhutto restored democracy. She released political prisoners and allowed a free press. She built close ties to other countries and started a bank that helped Pakistani business. But Bhutto's party had a slim margin in the National Assembly. It could not pass laws.

Then, in 1990, the president of Pakistan dismissed her. He was head of another political party. He charged her with corruption. Friends of Bhutto's husband may have made money from the government. However, the charges were not proven.

Bhutto became a leader of the opposition party. In 1993, she was again elected prime minister. In the Islamic world, where women are often not heard or seen, she blazed a trail.

Case Study Review

1. What changes did Benazir Bhutto make when she was elected prime minister of Pakistan?

2. **Drawing Conclusions** Why do you think Bhutto was able to become the first Islamic woman leader?

I. Reviewing Vocabulary

Match each word on the left with the correct definition on the right.

1. coup
2. non-alignment
3. neutrality
4. militant

a. a person who believes in using violence to win a cause
b. a policy of refusing to take sides in a conflict
c. a revolt, often by military leaders, against a nation's government
d. a policy of not being allied with other nations on a regular basis

II. Understanding the Chapter

Answer the questions below on a separate sheet of paper.

1. How do most Indians make a living?
2. Why did East Pakistan become Bangladesh?
3. What is the difference between non-alignment and neutrality?
4. Why was Benazir Bhutto forced from office in 1990?

III. Building Skills: Identifying Places

Name the country that is best described by each sentence.

1. This is the most crowded country in the world.
2. The Tamils and the Sinhalese still fight over this country.
3. This country is the home of the highest mountain in the world.
4. This is the largest democracy in the world.
5. This country was formed in 1971 from part of Pakistan.

IV. Working Together

In groups of four, choose a country in South Asia and write questions about that country on cards. Write the answers on the back of the cards. Each group should take turns asking its questions of the whole class.

On Assignment. . .

Creating an Illustrated Time Line: You should now have a list of at least ten key events. Arrange these events in chronological, or time, order. Now, choose two or three to illustrate. Create original drawings, or use photocopies or pictures from old newspapers and magazines. Present your time line to the class, explaining your reasons for choosing each event.

CHAPTER 12

The Heritage of Southeast Asia

What groups of people had the largest impact on Southeast Asia?

Hinduism is part of Southeast Asia's heritage. Traders from India brought the religion to the region. Today, Hinduism has large numbers of followers in several countries in Southeast Asia.

Looking at Key Terms

- **migrate** to move from one place to another
- **revolt** an uprising
- **canal** a ditch made by humans to carry water
- **animism** the belief that spirits live in the natural world in such things as rocks, trees, and streams
- **colony** a land that is controlled by another country
- **guerrilla warfare** hit-and-run attacks by small bands of fighters against a larger power

On Assignment...

Creating a Mini-History: Your assignment is to create a "mini-history" of Southeast Asia for students in the third grade. As you read this chapter, take notes, especially about events and people you think would interest third graders. Consider, too, how you would use illustrations to help students understand the history of Southeast Asia. Look for hint boxes to help you take notes. At the end of the chapter you will put your mini-history together.

Early Civilizations of Southeast Asia

What were the characteristics of early Southeast Asian civilizations?

The young prince stood up proudly. The shirt he wore was so dazzling that the maker hid when she wove it so she could keep her methods secret. "The clothes were so fine they rippled when the wind blew," the Philippine story reads. "They were woven from thread spun from the finest gold. This golden thread was mixed with the smoothest of silk threads." And the prince? "He looked so well in them, shining as bright as a star in the sky."

The Maranaos in the Philippines were one of many groups in ancient Southeast Asia. For their rulers, jewels, gold, and spices were part of life. This part of the world has many riches.

As you have read, these riches are one reason that so many outsiders came to Southeast Asia. Another reason is its location. Mainland Southeast Asia is close to China and India. Indian merchants came at first to trade. Some decided to stay and make the region their home. People from China **migrated**, or moved there, from the mainland. Some continued to migrate, spreading into the islands. Still others sailed to the islands from other regions.

Many small kingdoms in Southeast Asia rose and fell. Several great kingdoms held power for centuries.

The Kingdoms of Vietnam

China and Vietnam have shared a long history. The Chinese ruled the area from 100 B.C. to A.D. 900. The Vietnamese sometimes revolted against the Chinese. The most famous **revolt**, or uprising, was led by the two Trung sisters in A.D. 39. For two years,

they ruled. When the Chinese regained control, the sisters jumped to their deaths in the Day River.

During the 1,000 years of Chinese rule, the Vietnamese adopted some Chinese ways. The Vietnamese were influenced by Chinese religion, language, art, and poetry. In 939, the Vietnamese people broke away from China and formed the kingdom of Dai Viet. It lasted for nearly 1,000 years.

The Pagan Kingdom

People came to Myanmar (Burma) from India, Tibet, and China, building the Pagan (pah•GAHN) kingdom in the 800s. King Anawrahta and his son made the Pagan kingdom rich. The villagers paid taxes to the king.

Buddhism spread and became the kingdom's chief religion. The Pagan kingdom lasted until 1287. In that year, Mongol armies from China marched in and took over. It was not until the 1400s that the Burmese regained control of their country.

The Angkor Kingdom

A legend tells of an Indian prince who had a vision that he was to explore the South China Sea. When he reached Cambodia, a princess rowed out in a canoe to meet him. The prince shot an arrow through the boat. The legend says that the princess was thrilled with his daring. She promptly married him.

Although this story is only a legend, India did indeed influence Cambodia. Cambodia's system of writing is based on an Indian language. In its early history, Cambodians also adopted Hinduism, the religion that you read about in Chapter 9.

The glorious history of the Angkor kingdom began in 802. In that year, King Jayavarman stood on a mountain and declared himself a god king. He said that he would bring the rains and that he would bring happiness. For 250 years, the Angkor kings performed

Angkor Wat was originally built as a Hindu temple. Constructed from 1112 to 1152, it is the largest religious building in the world. Its highest point rises 200 feet (61 m) and it is surrounded by a moat that measures almost 2.5 miles (4 km) in circumference.

ceremonies to bring rain, riches, and happiness to their kingdom.

The kings wore silk clothing and gold jewelry. They were thought to be gods. Thousands of servants made their every wish come true. All the kings had to do was convince the spirits to bring good weather and to keep the earth spinning.

The Angkor kings built a series of Hindu temples. They are among the treasures of the world. One, Angkor Wat, is the largest religious building in the world. In 1860, hundreds of years after the decline of the Angkor kingdom, a Frenchman stumbled upon the temple of Angkor Wat. He was stunned by the temple's beauty. "It is grander than anything left us by Greece and Rome," he wrote.

The Angkor kings built and controlled Cambodia's water system. They constructed **canals** for farming. A canal is a ditch that is made to carry water. Cambodia's water system kept the area from flooding and stored water for the dry season. As a result, Cambodians grew much rice.

The golden time, however, did not last long. In the 1100s, the rulers began to ask too much of their people. Then the water system broke down. Malaria and plague struck. In 1431, Thailand fought for Angkor and won. The Cambodians left Angkor. Jungle grew over the wonders of Angkor and Angkor Wat. (See Case Study 13 on page 175 for more information about Angkor Wat.)

The Thai Kingdoms

There had always been small kingdoms in Thailand. The first unified Thai kingdom arose in 1350. One reason it did well was that the Mongols moved into Southeast Asia. Many of the other kingdoms in the area were destroyed. That gave the kingdom of Ayutthaya the chance to flourish and expand its territory. It existed for 400 years. During that time, as you learned, it conquered Cambodia.

The founder of Ayutthaya, Rama Tibodi, set laws for his people. The laws allowed slavery and they allowed men to have more than one wife. Officials in the government were severely punished if they stole money from the people.

This kingdom lasted until the Burmese attacked in 1767. Four years later, the Thais revolted. Their leader, General Pya Taksin, declared himself king. On his death, Pya Chakkri (CHAHK•kree) took the throne. To this day, the kings of Thailand are his descendants.

The Kingdoms of Indonesia

Indonesia's ancient kingdoms were based on trade. The first grand empire was the Sri Vijaya (shree vah•JIH•yah). From the 600s to the 1200s, it controlled trade in the region.

Sri Vijaya was located in Sumatra. When it was most powerful, in about A.D. 1000, it also held most of Java and Borneo. The clue to the kingdom's success was the Strait of Malacca. The strait was the shortest way between the Indian and Pacific oceans. (See the map on page 595.)

Through the strait, trading ships carried the treasures of the world. Gold, jewels, and spices were all carried on the ships. The wealth also attracted pirates, who were a constant threat. They hid in coves in the shadows of palm trees and attacked.

The kings of Sri Vijaya used many methods to stay in control of Indonesia. They maintained a huge fleet of ships to keep order. Sri Vijaya's kings also demanded high fees from the ships that sailed through their waters.

In the 1200s, the mighty Sri Vijaya kingdom faded. Other kingdoms took over trade. The most famous may be the Majapahit, which was based in Java. It lasted from about 1300 to the early 1500s. At its height, it controlled almost all of Indonesia and most of Malaysia.

The Role of Religion

The religions of outsiders had an impact on Southeast Asia. Probably the first was Hinduism, brought by traders from India. Buddhism, also from India, spread to Mainland Southeast Asia. (See the map on page 126.) Today it is the main religion of Myanmar, Cambodia, Thailand, Vietnam, and Laos.

Islam had a strong impact in the area. Arab traders brought this religion to Southeast Asia in about A.D. 900. Today Islam is the main religion in Indonesia, Brunei, and Malaysia. Indonesia is in fact the largest Islamic country in the world. It is an Islamic country unlike any other, though, because many Indonesian Muslims mix Islam with traditional island religions. The most popular traditional religion is **animism**. Animists believe that spirits live in trees, rocks, and streams. In Indonesia, it is not unusual to see a Muslim who both worships his ancestors and prays to the spirits in water.

On Assignment...

What facts about the ancient kingdoms of Southeast Asia would you include in your mini-history for third graders? Make sketches of drawings that you could include in your book.

Missionaries also came to Southeast Asia to convert people to Christianity. They had little impact, though. The only country in the region that is mostly Christian is the Philippines.

Section 1 Review

1. How did India and China influence the early kingdoms of Southeast Asia?
2. **Making Inferences** Why do you think the Angkor kingdom collapsed?

SECTION 2

Europeans Colonize the Region

How did Europeans gain control of most of Southeast Asia in the 1800s?

Spices! The seaman closed his eyes and breathed in the rich smells of clove, nutmeg, and cinnamon. This will make us all rich, he thought. The sailors had found a source for the spices that Europe needed. And they had an ocean route. No more paying Arab traders high prices for spices. This was a day to celebrate. Europe was hungry for spices. With them, food could be kept much longer. In the time before refrigerators, preserving food was very important.

The search for spices led to contacts between Europe and Southeast Asia. The

The Myths of Indonesia

It is an epic battle between good and evil. The two men playing the part of the Barong come out first. The mythical creature has a huge head. Its wide eyes and bared teeth gleam. Down its back spills tangled fur and hair. A gold headdress shines from its head. Rangda, the witch, faces the Barong. Rangda is evil. Her tongue is a flame. Her face is set in a terrible sneer. She wears a necklace of human body parts. The two face off in a dance of death. Men armed with daggers come under Rangda's spell. They fall into a trance. Then they stab themselves with their daggers. The Barong protects the men. As much as they stab, they cannot hurt themselves. In the end, the Barong always wins.

This Balinese myth is acted out in a dance. Like many Indonesian myths, this one has a moral. If people respect good and follow it, they will conquer evil.

Indonesian myths come from many sources. Some are taken from Hindu writings. Others are native to the islands. Even today, myths are an important part of life in Indonesia. Dances, plays, and stories all tell these tales of good and evil.

Case Study Review

1. How can a viewer tell that Rangda is evil?
2. **Drawing Conclusions** Why do you think myths in Indonesia come from many sources?

By the early 1700s, the Dutch had taken over most of what is today Indonesia. Other European nations soon established colonies in Southeast Asia. They wanted to control the spices and raw materials available in the region.

Portuguese explorer Vasco da Gama was the first European to find an ocean route. He came to Malacca on the Malay Peninsula in 1511. The Dutch were the next important visitors. By the early 1700s, the Dutch ruled most of Indonesia.

In the late 1700s, the British gained a toe-hold in Southeast Asia. They founded the port of Singapore. With its convenient location, it became the busiest port in the region. The British soon had most of Malaysia under their rule.

Then countries in Europe began to build factories. They needed more and more raw materials, such as cotton and tin. **Colonies**, or the territories these European countries controlled, became a good source of these raw materials. During the 1700s and 1800s, Europeans scrambled to win control of territories around the world. They competed in Africa, India, and Southeast Asia to gain the richest sources of raw materials. They then shipped these materials to their factories in Europe.

France took over Vietnam, Cambodia, and Laos during the 1800s. The United States won the Philippines from Spain in 1898.

Part of the reason for the success of the Western powers was sheer power. They had more weapons and trained soldiers, they were organized, and they used the fact that most of the Southeast Asian countries did not get along with one another.

The Effects of Western Rule

The Western powers set up plantations to grow crops, such as rubber and tea. They built roads, railroads, schools, and hospitals. They also often kept local leaders from fighting one another.

However, the Western nations took the best land and paid little or nothing for it. They paid local workers very little. The European nations took raw materials from the colonies back to Europe. With these raw materials, they manufactured finished products. Then they brought back the products they made and sold them in the colonies. European factory-made goods sold for less money than handcrafted local goods. Local makers of cloth and other products could not compete. Many stopped making the products that they had made for centuries.

Thailand was the one place in Southeast Asia that escaped foreign rule. It did this with the help of a clever ruler, King Mongkut. He wrote that "sense and wisdom" were the only true weapons he had. He was right.

The French were in Indochina, to Thailand's east. The British were in Burma, to the west. In the early 1900s, Mongkut made treaties with both Britain and France. Thailand gave land to both countries, but kept most of its land.

On Assignment. . .

What events in this section are most important to put in your mini-history? Make notes and draw sketches to illustrate the pages you will include.

Section 2 Review

1. What effects did colonization have on the local economies in Southeast Asia?

2. **Drawing Conclusions** Why do you think that European powers were so eager to colonize Southeast Asia?

SECTION 3

Southeast Asians Fight for Freedom

How did Southeast Asians win their independence?

It was 1905. The Japanese army had just defeated the Russian army. It was the first time that an Asian country had defeated a European country. It was an event that inspired the nations of Southeast Asia.

The Push for Independence

During the early 1900s, Europe's Southeast Asian colonies began to agitate for independence. As in India, the people who led the struggle were often those who had been educated in European-run schools, where they had learned about freedom and democracy. They became inspired to fight for their own independence.

The Europeans had no intention of letting go, though. The one colony that managed to gain its independence was the Philippines. In 1934, the United States agreed to let the Philippines become independent in ten

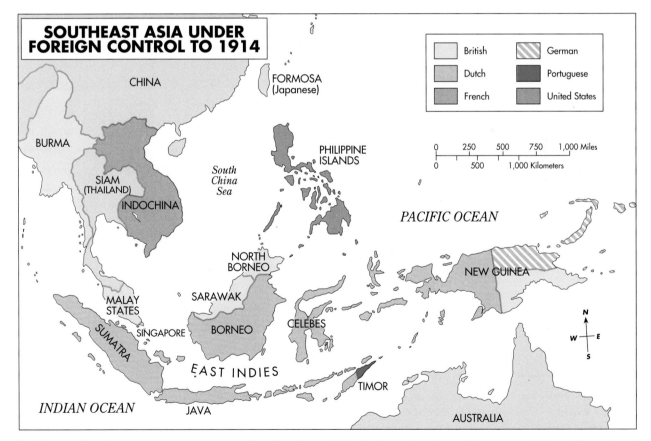

SOUTHEAST ASIA UNDER FOREIGN CONTROL TO 1914

British
Dutch
French
German
Portuguese
United States

CHINA
FORMOSA (Japanese)
BURMA
SIAM (THAILAND)
INDOCHINA
South China Sea
PHILIPPINE ISLANDS
PACIFIC OCEAN
NORTH BORNEO
SARAWAK
NEW GUINEA
MALAY STATES
SINGAPORE
BORNEO
CELEBES
SUMATRA
EAST INDIES
TIMOR
INDIAN OCEAN
JAVA
AUSTRALIA

0   250   500   750   1,000 Miles
0   500   1,000 Kilometers

Region At first, Europeans were attracted to Southeast Asia for its spices. Later, Europeans desired the region's raw materials. Which nations claimed land in Southeast Asia?

years. In 1946, it became the first colony in Asia to become a free country.

For the rest of the colonies, it took World War II to change things. During the war, Japan occupied most of Southeast Asia. At first, many in the region were pleased. The Japanese attack meant that the hated European powers would leave.

Then it became clear that Japanese rule was no better than European rule. The Japanese destroyed temples and killed people. They took food and supplies from Southast Asia to fight the war.

The people of the region soon began to organize against the Japanese. They received aid from the nations fighting Japan during World War II. With that money, they formed guerrilla groups to fight the Japanese. **Guerrilla warfare** is a tactic that uses hit-and-run attacks by small bands of fighters against a larger power.

After the defeat of the Japanese, the colonies pushed for their independence. The Europeans had been weakened by the wars. That helped the colonies succeed. Thus, the war helped the nations of Southeast Asia become independent.

Burma   The Burmese fought the Japanese and won in 1945. The British returned to Burma after the war and tried to convince the Burmese that they again needed British rule. The Burmese did not agree. They fiercely opposed the British. In 1948, Burma became a republic.

The next decades were rocky. There were fights among different groups in Burma. For almost 30 years, a military dictator, Ne Win, controlled the country. In 1990, free elections were held and the people voted Ne Win out. His response was to take control again. His opponents were forced to leave the country or be jailed. Ne Win changed Burma's name to Myanmar.

Malaysia   The push for Malaysian independence faced one big problem. The peoples who lived in Malaysia did not get along with each other. In the 1940s, only about half of the people were Malay. The Chinese population was 37 percent. The Chinese had come to Malaysia to work on plantations and to help the British build railroads. Another 12 percent of the population was Indian. In 1957, the agreement that was reached to make Malaysia a state tried to ensure that each group had power. The Malays, who were afraid that the Chinese and Indians would control the country's economy, were given a chance at more jobs.

Indonesia   The Dutch were determined to keep Indonesia after World War II. The Indonesians were just as determined to gain independence. Since the early 1900s, the Indonesians had been fighting for their independence. After World War II, Indonesia declared itself a state. The Dutch fought, but in 1949, they gave up. The Indonesian will for freedom was too strong.

Indonesia was ruled by President Sukarno, a Communist, until 1966. It was a time of unrest. As early as 1959, Sukarno declared martial law to quell disturbances. There were several attempts to take over the government. A half-million people may have died in anti-Communist riots in 1965. Finally, Sukarno left office. He was replaced by President Suharto, who rejected communism and set up a democracy.

Singapore   After World War II, Singapore kept its ties to Britain. Although the country became self-governing in 1959, it stayed close to Britain. In 1963, it joined with Malaya, North Borneo, and Sarawak to form Malaysia. That did not last, though. The Malays were suspicious of Singapore because of its large Chinese population. In 1965, Singapore became an independent nation.

Vietnam   French rule was never accepted by the Vietnamese. In the 1920s, many called for the French to leave. In 1930, Ho Chi Minh formed a Communist party. After World War II, Ho Chi Minh and his party saw their chance. For eight years, they

Made up of one main island and more than 50 small islets, Singapore is Southeast Asia's leading financial center. Its location at the tip of the Malay Peninsula has made the city of Singapore an important port.

fought the French. In 1954, the French withdrew, signing an agreement that left the Communists in control of the North. The Vietnamese who supported the French would retain control over South Vietnam.

Under the terms of the agreement, Vietnam was supposed to reunite in two years. Instead, the leader of the South refused. Ngo Dinh Diem (ngaw dihn dzee•EHM) was afraid that the Communists would win control of the entire country. Diem was not popular with his own people, though. His government was corrupt and he did not improve his people's lives.

The North saw a chance to make the whole country Communist and began to wage guerrilla warfare. Then Diem was killed in a coup in 1963. Chaos followed.

The United States feared that if the Communists won, the rest of Southeast Asia would become Communist, too. This was called the domino theory. The United States then entered the war.

For more than a decade, U.S. forces joined with the South Vietnamese to fight the North Vietnamese. More than two million Vietnamese died and 57,000 U.S. soldiers were killed. It was the longest war the United States had ever fought and one of the most bitter. Many in the United States protested U.S. involvement in this war.

In January 1973, the United States and North Vietnam signed a peace agreement that soon fell apart. In 1975, the Communists gathered their forces for one last effort. They overran South Vietnam and won the war. In 1976, the country reunited; it was a Communist state.

Cambodia Neighboring Cambodia had supported South Vietnam. Then, when South Vietnam fell to the Communists, a Communist group came to power in Cambodia. This group, led by Pol Pot, murdered anyone who disagreed with it. Two to three million people, out of a population of seven million, may have died.

Pol Pot's brutality led the Vietnamese to invade Cambodia. But Pol Pot's forces fought back. Finally, in 1991, the parties signed a peace treaty.

Section 3 Review

1. Why did the United States enter the Vietnam War?
2. **Analyzing Information** How did education help create the desire for independence in Southeast Asia?

On Assignment. . .

Decide on one or two events from this section to include in your mini-history. Choose events that are important as well as those that might interest third graders.

REVIEWING CHAPTER 12

I. Reviewing Vocabulary

Match each word on the left with the correct definition on the right.

1. animism
2. colony
3. migrate
4. guerrilla warfare

a. a land that is controlled by another country
b. the belief that spirits live in the natural world
c. hit-and-run attacks by small bands of fighters against a larger power
d. to move from one place to another

II. Understanding the Chapter

Answer the questions below on a separate sheet of paper.

1. List and describe two ancient civilizations in Southeast Asia.
2. Why were European powers able to control Southeast Asia?
3. Why did Southeast Asia want to throw off foreign rule in the 1900s?
4. Why did the Southeast Asians first welcome the Japanese in the 1930s and 1940s? Why did they change their minds?

III. Building Skills: Understanding Chronology

Put these events in chronological order, or the order in which they occurred.

1. The Japanese take over most of Southeast Asia.
2. The Angkor kingdom is formed.
3. The United States enters the Vietnam War.
4. Vasco da Gama sails to the Malay Peninsula.
5. The Dutch colonize Indonesia.

IV. Working Together

In a small group, choose one event from this chapter and create a newspaper that explains it. Include news stories and features that show the point of view of a person who was there. Design a page that includes headlines and pictures.

On Assignment...

Creating a Mini-History: Decide on three topics to present in your mini-history. Keep in mind that your audience is third graders. Collect your mini-histories into a 10- to 12-page booklet. Present your final product to your class and to any third graders that you know.

CHAPTER 13

Changing Patterns of Life in Southeast Asia

How do most people in Southeast Asia live?

Batik is the Southeast Asian art of cloth design. Artists, like this woman in Java, Indonesia, use wax to create intricate designs on cloth. The cloth is then dyed and the wax is removed. The result is a beautiful work of wearable art.

Looking at Key Terms

- **kampung** a village
- **consensus** an agreement reached by a group as a whole or by a majority
- **incense** material that makes a scent when burned
- **gong** a round musical instrument that is struck
- **percussion instrument** a musical instrument that is played by striking it
- **gilded** covered with a thin layer of gold

On Assignment...

Giving a Presentation: In this chapter, you will write a talk for people who want to travel to Southeast Asia. In each section, think about what visitors would like to know about the region. Think about pictures that you would show the travelers. At the end of the chapter, you will assemble your notes and write your talk.

SECTION 1

Patterns of Life in Southeast Asia

How are the cultures of the people of Southeast Asia changing?

Cik rubbed his eyes. The golden sunrise had just begun to fill the Malaysian sky. It was reflected in the still water in the rice paddies. It was time to get up. Around the **kampung**, or village, he could hear a voice, a laugh. Then silence.

The children were already in the kitchen, getting ready for the walk to school. Cik's children will probably go to school through sixth grade. Only about 30 percent of the village children will have further schooling.

Cik swung his feet off his sleeping mat and lit the kerosene lamp. Then he put on his sarong, a piece of cotton cloth that he wrapped around his waist.

His wife came in from the other room. She smiled. "Rice?" she asked, giving him a bowl. Cik ate the rice and vegetables quickly. Then he took his knife from a corner. It was sharp and long, the perfect tool for cutting the weeds from the rice paddies.

Outside, the sun had cleared the horizon. Others were already at work, bent over the water. They hacked at the weeds. Growing rice is an endless job. First, the paddies are plowed with a water buffalo. Then the rice is planted. Now it was the time when the shoots are young and weeds grow everywhere. Cik waded through the water, his sarong pulled up. He was barefooted. He knew that by the time he ended his work, there would be huge leeches, bloodsucking worms, to pull off his legs. The blood I lose to those leeches, he thought, and sighed.

Throughout the morning, Cik worked on. The sun rose. Sweat shone on his back as the day became hot. Cik squinted at the sun. Soon, it would be time for the main meal of the day. He rose and stretched. Around him, he saw that his neighbors were still bent over their work. Their wide, round hats reflected the sun. Beyond the rice paddies on which Cik worked, he could see terraces of rice paddies on the mountainside. Beyond that were the hazy greens and blues of the rain forest.

Cik heard a clicking noise and looked up. To his right, walking carefully on the edge of the paddy, was a young boy with a long stick. In front of him was a family of geese. With

A Cambodian farmer drives a water buffalo across a rice field. Most farmers in Southeast Asia work the land in much the same way as their ancestors have done for many generations.

Along the Mekong River, Cambodians take time to enjoy the Waters Feast. Part of the festivities include a boating competition. Teams paddle their canoes to compete in contests of speed and skill.

gentle clicks and swats of the stick, the boy moved the geese along. Soon, Cik thought, his children would be old enough to help him. But then there would be another problem. There was not enough land for all the children to make a living. At some point, they probably would have to leave.

Cik's life is one that millions of people in Southeast Asia understand. Two out of three people farm. Rice is the region's most important crop. Most families grow rice, and just enough vegetables to feed their family. On many of the islands of Indonesia, ash from volcanoes has left the soil rich. In some of the lowlands, rich soil washes down from the mountains during the rainy season. In much of Southeast Asia, farmers grow two or three crops of rice a year.

Village Government

Most of the kampungs in Southeast Asia are poor. Houses are made of bamboo or boards. In Malaysia, the custom is to build the houses on stilts, to protect them from flooding. In Indonesia and other countries, dirt floors are common. Many villages do not have electricity.

Government in these villages is often based on **consensus**, agreement by the group as a whole or by a majority. The people of the village choose a leader who makes decisions based on what everyone agrees to. The idea of consensus and cooperation may have come from the way in which Southeast Asians work in the rice paddies. Everyone in the village must cooperate to grow the village's rice. Perhaps that cooperation was the model for village government.

Rice is not the only crop in these rich lands. There also are rubber and tea plantations and pepper and spice farms. In villages on the coast, fishing is the main occupation.

Deep in the jungle, groups of people farm. They clear the forest, plant a crop, and when the land becomes less fertile, they move on to a new patch of land.

Festivals and Celebrations

Throughout Southeast Asia, festivals are important. In Singapore, every month brings a festival of some sort. In August, the Chinese there celebrate the Festival of the Hungry Ghosts. During that month, the dead are said to return to earth. The living entertain and feed them by putting food on their graves.

Bali, in Indonesia, is Hindu—with a twist. The Balinese have many festivals. Brightly colored flowers and food cover the temple altars. They are for the dead. But if the Balinese come back and the food is still there, they eat it. The dead must not have been hungry, they reason.

In Thailand, in April, the new year's festival of Songkran is celebrated. Children pour scented water into their parents' hands as a sign of respect. On the last day of the festival, the water pouring increases. People roam the streets, looking for people to throw water on. Luckily, it's often unbearably hot in April.

Malaysia's Chinese celebrate Chap Goh Mei in January. It's the end of the holiday season, the 15th day after the Chinese New Year. In the past, women who wished to marry went to the sea. There, they threw in oranges and wished for husbands. Often they got their wish. Waiting by the river were the young men of the village, dressed up and eager to marry.

These celebrations help to create a strong sense of community in the cultures of Southeast Asia. They remind people of their heritage and bring families together.

Family Life

For most Southeast Asians, the family is everything. In much of the Southeast Asian countryside, children live with their parents until they marry.

As part of this culture, most Southeast Asians would not think of doing things alone. The idea of moving to another part of the country for the sake of making one's own way is unknown. If people have to leave—to go to the city and make a living, for example—they are likely to live with relatives in the city. They are also likely to return home whenever they can.

Education

Today, most children in Southeast Asia go to elementary school. Some drop out to help their families farm. Others drop out because their families do not have the money for books. In some countries, schools are tied to religion. Islamic countries, such as Malaysia and Indonesia, have Muslim schools. Boys in

On Assignment...

What would travelers to Southeast Asia want to know about the region? Think what you have learned in this section that might be helpful to them. What pictures would you show?

Buddhist Vietnam often go to Buddhist schools. It is traditional in many countries for children to wear uniforms to school. Discipline tends to be strict. Students usually sit in rows and recite their lessons by heart.

Only a few fortunate students go on to high school and college. One exception is Vietnam. In the early 1990s, almost 40 percent of its people went on to high school. About 130,000 students attend college classes.

In many countries, competition for spots in high schools and colleges is intense. In some countries, such as Singapore, students who want to continue their education have to pass difficult tests.

Life for Women in Southeast Asia

Fewer girls than boys go to school. Some parents—especially those in rural areas—think that it is not important for girls to have a formal education. They believe that it is more important for a girl to learn the work of the house.

Life for women in Southeast Asia offers more freedom than life in other parts of Asia. In the Islamic countries of Malaysia and Indonesia, women have more choices than do women in other Islamic countries. In many Islamic countries, women remain veiled and in the house. In Southeast Asia, many Muslim women do not even wear a head covering. Although there are fewer chances for women to work than there are for men, many do work outside the home. In Singapore, women are expected to continue to work at paying jobs after they marry.

1. Explain how most villages are governed.
2. **Drawing Conclusions** Why do you think that education is more valued in the cities than it is in the country?

SECTION 2

Arts and Literature in Southeast Asia

What is unique about the arts and literature in Southeast Asia?

It is about 9 P.M. in the village. The people sit on folding chairs. In the front of the auditorium, a sheet hangs down. On a pole in one corner is a bull's skull. There is a burning stick of **incense** in the top of the skull. Beside the sheet is a group of men with **gongs** and other instruments. The light dims in the auditorium. The people grow quiet. A man dressed in white walks down the center aisle. He is carrying a lit torch and a handful of shadow puppets. The puppets are made of tooled leather. The man, called the *dalang*, takes his place behind the sheet. The torchlight flickers, throwing light on the sheet.

Soon, the dalang begins the *wayang kulit*, or shadow play. In a singsong voice, he tells the story. He plays the parts of all the characters. The puppets' lacy shadows dance across the sheet. The plays are usually ancient Hindu epics. For hundreds of years, Indonesians have enjoyed the retellings of these tales.

The dalang's voice chants on. For at least six hours, he will recite the story by heart, moving the puppets and saying their parts. The dalang is a scholar, a priest, and a holy man. The musicians play their instruments. The audience members come and go. The hypnotic voice of the dalang continues until dawn.

The elements of the wayang kulit show some of the reasons that the arts of Southeast Asia fascinate others. They are based on fantasy, religion, and mystery. They are colorful and almost otherworldly. Princes, demon monkeys, gods, and witches all play a part in the arts of Southeast Asia.

Vietnamese water puppets are another unique art form. These puppets appear to be floating on water. The puppeteers control the puppets from elsewhere.

In Southeast Asia, religion takes on a different feeling than it does in other places in the world. The people of Southeast Asia have taken the major religions of the world and fit them to their lives—and their arts. The wayang kulit is one example. Indonesia is 90 percent Muslim, but the popular wayang plays are based on Hindu stories. In the Philippines, the *cenaculo* is a play based on the life of Jesus Christ. This play, with its bright masks and fancy costumes, is a version that you would only see in the Philippines.

Shadow puppets are operated by a skilled dalang. The puppets retell the stories of ancient Hindu epics.

Many of Southeast Asia's arts were influenced by the cultures of India and China. Hindu and Buddhist epics and stories from India and China are the basis for many of the best-loved plays, poems, and stories in Southeast Asia.

Music The Indonesian gamelan orchestra is another strong tradition in Southeast Asia. The gamelan orchestra is at least 1,000 years old. It is made up of gongs and instruments like xylophones. Other **percussion instruments** round out the orchestra. The gamelan can sound like rippling water or like crashing waves. One thing is certain. It sounds quite different from Western music. Gamelan music is played for puppet shows and for religious rituals. It also accompanies dances.

Other Southeast Asian cultures have similar musical styles. For example, in the Philippines, the kulintang, a set of gongs, is popular. Like the music of the gamelan, music from the kulintang has a haunting quality.

Dance Most Westerners have seen photographs of the beautiful dances of Southeast Asia. The women often wear heavy **gilded** headdresses, which are covered with a thin layer of gold. Their clothes are made of silk and gold. They use tiny, graceful movements to tell a story. Often, the story is an ancient tale from Hindu legend. Sometimes it is a dance to help the rains come or to drive away evil spirits. In Thailand, the fingernail dance is popular. It was developed by wealthy women of ancient days who did not have to work. They could afford to allow their fingernails to grow very long. They then used these unusual fingernails as the basis for the dance.

Literature For many generations, the literature of Southeast Asia was an oral tradition that was handed down from parents

On Assignment. . .

What information from this section would a traveler want to know? What pictures could illustrate what you want to say?

to their children. Some stories were based on religious epics. Others were fantastic tales of heroism and love. In recent years, modern writers have begun to have these and other stories printed. In the early 1900s in the Philippines, José Rizal wrote about his country's wish for freedom.

Art and Architecture Southeast Asia's art and architecture is also unique. In Thailand, golden temples with tall spires reach the sky. The ancient Buddhas of Indonesia's Borobodur gaze silently at visitors.

Other ancient arts are still practiced. The art of batik was invented in Southeast Asia. Artists paint tiny areas of cloth with wax. Then they dye the cloth. The process is repeated many times. Some batiks can take six months or more to finish. In the old royal courts of Indonesia, certain patterns and colors were only for the king and his family. Today, anyone can buy the more than 1,000 designs.

Section 2 Review

1. How has religion influenced the arts in Southeast Asia?

2. **Identifying Relationships** How are the arts of different countries in Southeast Asia similar?

Preserving a Great Heritage: The Ancient Capital of Angkor

If you look at the Cambodian flag, you will find something very special—the towers of Angkor Wat, the largest religious structure in the world. To modern Cambodians, the great building symbolizes pride in their past. It represents the hope that they, like their ancestors, can build a strong nation.

From the 1100s to the 1400s, the ancient Khymer empire ruled over present-day Cambodia, as well as parts of Vietnam, Laos, and Thailand. Its capital Angkor bustled with soldiers, citizens, monks, and traders. Royal buildings covered more than three times the space covered by Manhattan Island.

The largest monument was Angkor Wat, or "temple of the capital." Its design represents the home of the Hindu gods. The five towers represent the peaks of sacred mountains. The outer walls symbolize the world's edge. The moat surrounding the temple stands for the sea. Carvings of demons, serpents, gods, and kings tell stories of heavenly and earthly history.

Although Angkor was abandoned in the 1400s, the Cambodian people have worked quietly to preserve their heritage. Today, citizens like Uong Von, a government official, volunteer to clear vines and to sweep the sacred sites. If you visited the ancient capital city, you would see little old women pulling weeds and young men cutting brush with huge knives. They are not paid, but they believe that it is the right thing to do.

The nations of the world have also recognized the value of preserving the ancient buildings. International help may mean that Angkor will be rebuilt. Until then, the Cambodian people will volunteer to clear rubble and restore statues. No matter what happens, Angkor will remain a lasting monument to the Khymer civilization. And the huge stone war elephants and ancient gods will stand watch for many more centuries.

Case Study Review

1. Explain what a visitor to ancient Angkor would find most amazing.
2. **Analyzing Information** Why do you think other nations are interested in preserving Angkor?

REVIEWING CHAPTER 13

I. Reviewing Vocabulary

Match each word on the left with the correct definition on the right.

1.	consensus	**a.**	a village
2.	gong	**b.**	an agreement reached by a group as a whole or by a majority
3.	kampung	**c.**	covered with a thin layer of gold
4.	gilded	**d.**	a round musical instrument that is struck

II. Understanding the Chapter

Answer the questions below on a separate sheet of paper.

1. How is village life changing in Southeast Asia?
2. Describe the role of the family in the life of Southeast Asians.
3. Describe what life is like for women in Southeast Asia.
4. How did China and India influence the arts of Southeast Asia?

III. Building Skills: Distinguishing Fact From Opinion

Look at the statements below. Decide which are facts and which are opinions. Explain your choices.

1. Many people in Southeast Asian villages grow rice.
2. Women have a better life in Southeast Asia than they do in the Middle East.
3. The festivals of Southeast Asia are exciting.
4. Only within the last century has there been much written literature in Southeast Asia.

IV. Working Together

Split up into six groups. Find five words from the chapter that are new to all of you. Write these words on separate pieces of paper. Put your pieces of paper into a box with the papers of the other groups. Take turns drawing pieces of paper and defining the words.

On Assignment. . .

Giving a Presentation: Review your notes from this chapter. Think about the audience who will listen to your talk. What will these people want to know about traveling to Southeast Asia? What pictures will illustrate your information? Write a three-minute talk. When you have finished, practice it with a friend. Have your friend make suggestions for improving your talk. Then revise it and present the travel talk to your class.

CHAPTER 14

Southeast Asia in the World Today

What forces are shaping Southeast Asia in the modern world?

Stores selling televisions, video recorders, computers, and other electronic items appear all over Southeast Asia. As the economy improves, more people are able to afford such luxuries.

Looking at Key Terms

- **capitalism** an economic system in which businesses are owned privately
- **market economy** a system in which prices are based on what people are willing to pay and companies make goods based on what people want to buy
- **insecticide** a chemical that kills insects
- **rigid** stiff; tightly controlled
- **investors** people who put money into businesses in hopes of making a profit

On Assignment. . .

Creating a Board Game: In this chapter, you will learn about Southeast Asia in today's world. You will then use this information to write questions for a game. In each section, you will write questions about what you learned. At the end of the chapter, you will design a board game that uses these questions. Then you can play the game.

The Economy of Southeast Asia

What are some recent economic trends in Southeast Asia?

The young woman bends to her task. The black glasses keep out the glare of the welding light. She holds the torch with ease. The glare of white light highlights the bicycle frame that she is welding.

There will always be a market for the bicycles Doan Nga is making. Behind her are piles of finished bicycles. The tools seem old. The workers have to cross the street to paint the bicycles.

"It is a state-owned factory," Doan says on her lunch break. "We have to make 16,000 bicycles a year." She shrugs. "If this factory were arranged better, we could make many more. But we have our goal. We meet it."

In Vietnam, as in some other Southeast Asian countries, Communist nations are struggling to incorporate **capitalism** to help their economies. Capitalism is an economic system in which businesses are owned privately. In Vietnam, people are now allowed to own businesses. Like this bicycle factory, though, many businesses are still owned by the state.

Challenges of Independence

When the colonies of Southeast Asia became independent after World War II, they faced a number of challenges. Before independence, Westerners owned and ran the businesses. The Western powers saw Southeast Asia as a place that supplied metals, lumber, and rice. Those products left the colonies. Finished goods were imported.

When the Western powers left, there was little industry in the former colonies. The newly independent nations needed to build new industries, but this was difficult. For one thing, there was little money for factories. Also, many of those who knew how to run factories were Westerners, and they were gone.

COUNTRIES OF SOUTHEAST ASIA

COUNTRY	CAPITAL CITY	AREA (square miles)	POPULATION (millions of people)	POPULATION DOUBLING TIME (years)
Brunei	Bandar Seri Begawan	2,030	0.3	27
Cambodia	Phnom Penh	68,150	9.0	27
Indonesia	Jakarta	705,190	187.6	42
Laos	Viangchan	89,110	4.6	24
Malaysia	Kuala Lumpur	126,850	18.4	30
Myanmar	Yangon	253,880	43.5	36
Philippines	Manila	115,120	64.6	28
Singapore	Singapore	240	2.8	55
Thailand	Bangkok	197,250	57.2	49
Vietnam	Hanoi	125,670	71.8	31

Source: World Population Data Sheet of the Population Reference Bureau, Inc.

The countries of Southeast Asia vary greatly in size and population. Which country is smallest in size? Which is largest? Which country has the most people? In how many years will this country's population double?

Southeast Asian countries dealt with these problems in different ways. Some adopted communism. Communist countries such as Cambodia, Laos, and Vietnam set up economies in which the state owned the factories. This helped countries to build new factories quickly. It also led to a system in which factories could make more of a product than people wanted to buy. Like the bicycle factory in which Doan Nga works, state-owned businesses did not need to use the most efficient methods of making products because they had no worries about profits—or losses.

States such as Thailand and the Philippines set up **market economies**. In a market economy, private companies own and run the businesses. Privately owned companies decide how much of a product to make based on the demand for that product.

In a market economy, business owners risk losing their money and their business if they do not pay careful attention to the needs of their customers and to their methods of manufacturing. A number of Southeast Asian countries blend communism and market economics. Indonesia is one of these. For instance, the government owns Pertamina, the country's oil company. Many smaller companies are owned and run by individual Indonesians, though.

In recent years, many Communist countries have been trying to change. Communism has proved to be an inefficient system for running industries.

Singapore: A Southeast Asian Jewel

Singapore is one of Southeast Asia's success stories. Led for almost four decades by Lee Kuan Yew, the country has prospered.

Singapore was also known as a place where people were fined for littering. Often, those who disagreed with Lee were jailed. But Singapore became a very good place to do business. Its people were well educated. It welcomed money from people in other countries who wanted to start companies. All this made Singapore's economy soar.

Southeast Asian governments include military dictatorships, Communist governments, constitutional monarchies, and democracies. Outside the royal palace in Phnom Penh, Cambodia, a crowd carries pictures of Prince Norodom Sihanouk.

This country, which is about the size of Chicago, has the second-highest living standard in Asia. That means its people live well. There is little unemployment. Many people work in factories. The country is also known for its busy port. Tourists are eager to visit because the country is known for being clean and safe. All this makes Singapore a jewel in the crown of Southeast Asia.

What Singapore doesn't have is land. That lack of farmland means that Singapore is very different from the rest of Southeast Asia, where more than 50 percent of the people make a living by farming.

Buses and motorcycles jockey for position on a crowded street in Bangkok, Thailand. Like other cities in Southeast Asia, Bangkok has experienced tremendous growth since the 1950s.

Agriculture

Farming is changing in Southeast Asia, too. In the 1950s and 1960s, farmers began to grow new kinds of rice. They began to use chemicals to help them farm. As a result, they were able to grow much more food. Countries had to import less rice. There was less hunger. All these changes created a phenomenon called the *Green Revolution.*

The Green Revolution also meant that many farmers had to borrow money for chemicals and equipment to increase their crop yield.

If farmers had a bad year and couldn't pay their loans, they lost their farms. Farmers began to grow crops other than rice. Coffee, rubber, and tobacco were grown on land that families once used only for rice.

The Green Revolution had environmental effects. The chemicals that farmers used began to show up in the water supply. Farmers no longer grew many kinds of rice. If a disease or pest attacked one kind of rice, the crop was in trouble across an entire country. In Java, an island in Indonesia, the brown planthopper, a bug that had not been a problem before, killed rice crops across the island. Planthoppers liked the new kind of rice.

Farmers began to realize that the **insecticides** that they had sprayed to get rid of pests could cause additional problems. These insecticides had killed the animals that ate the planthoppers. As a result, Indonesia banned some insecticides. It also tried to plant different kinds of rice.

Moving to the Cities

Even though most people in Southeast Asia still farm, more and more people are moving to the cities. In Bangkok, for example, there were one million people in 1950. By the mid-1990s, there were over seven million.

People come to the city because there is no more farmland and because they want better jobs. When they get to the cities, many live in shacks with no electricity, running water, or plumbing. Even so, these people can often make more money in cities than they can make at home. In the rural northeast of Thailand, almost half the income of the people comes from Bangkok. Why? Family members who live there send money home to relatives in the country.

Those who come to the city often live with friends and relatives who are already there. The result is a series of small cities-within-cities that contain people from the same area in the country. These people live together and often help one another find jobs.

There are other people, however, like many of those in Singapore, who live much better lives in the cities. They have good jobs and cars. They have money for movies and eating out. In some cities, such as Jakarta, a visitor can see many middle-class people.

But beyond their well-kept houses and apartments, there is another Jakarta. It is a land of dirt roads and families jammed together in shacks. It is a world of little work, of illness, and of dirty water.

Section 1 Review

1. How has farming in Southeast Asia changed as a result of the Green Revolution? What problems did the Green Revolution cause?

2. **Making a Chart** Make a chart that shows the differences between market economies and Communist economies.

SECTION 2

Political Trends in Southeast Asia

How are the governments of Southeast Asia changing?

Like Great Britain, Thailand is a constitutional monarchy. As you read in the Introduction, a constitutional monarchy allows the king and queen only limited power. In Vietnam, communism is still strong. In Singapore, leaders are elected—but there is only one real political party.

The countries of Southeast Asia have many different kinds of governments. Everyone from kings to Communists reigns. Nowhere is there a democracy as free as that of the United States, however.

Southeast Asia has faced many problems in its search for stable government. As you saw in Section 1, after World War II, newly independent countries had to build their own economies when the Western powers left. Then the war in Indochina dragged on for decades. The war unsettled many countries and made some armies too strong.

Vietnam and Laos are Communist countries. Communism as a form of government is becoming rarer in the world. The Soviet Union was once a huge Communist state. Its fall, in 1991, shook Communists around the world. Cambodia, which had been Communist, voted in 1993 to have a king rule. In Vietnam, more and more private businesses are allowed. Communist rule is

In Myanmar, Daw Aung San Suu Kyi speaks out against the military government. In 1991, she was awarded the Nobel Peace Prize.

becoming less common, as well as less **rigid**, or tightly controlled.

Military control has also been a factor in Southeast Asian governments. Some countries, such as Myanmar, or Burma, are still under army rule. Myanmar's people are not allowed to vote and military leaders are all-powerful.

In other countries, there is a strong military voice in government. One example is Indonesia. In Indonesia, there are elections with several political parties, but only one really counts. That party is supported by the army.

Challenge and Change in the Philippines

The story of power in the Philippines shows how progress can be made against a leader who rules with the support of the army. Ferdinand Marcos became president of the Philippines in 1965. He ruled with an iron hand. He gave his friends big jobs and he looted the country for himself.

The people of the Philippines showed their anger at this corruption in 1972. They began to protest. Marcos then declared martial law. He jailed many political enemies.

His biggest opponent was Benigno Aquino. Marcos put him in jail. In 1980, Marcos allowed Aquino to go to the United States. In 1983, Marcos's wife warned Aquino not to return to the Philippines. "You may be killed," she said.

She was right. When Aquino returned to the Philippines, he was shot and killed. The country was outraged. Many thought that Marcos had had Aquino killed. People across the country protested.

In 1986, Marcos called for elections. Aquino's widow, Corazon, decided to run against Marcos. After the election, Marcos declared victory. The election was clearly rigged, though. The people rose up. There were rallies everywhere for "people power" and for Corazon Aquino. The Catholic Church backed the movement. Even the army would not support Marcos.

On Assignment...

Write at least five questions about the information in this section for your board game. Write some questions about the political trends you studied.

Finally, Marcos fled to Hawaii. For the people of the Philippines, it was a moment of triumph. It showed that people power can be stronger than dictatorship.

Aquino took power and brought democracy to the Philippines. She faced big problems, though. Most Filipinos are poor. Aquino faced coups by Marcos supporters in the army. She won those fights. She also faced a movement by Muslims in the Philippines who wanted their own country. In 1992, she stepped down. The people elected Fidel Ramos, whom she supported. Corazon Aquino's story proved one thing to the people of the Philippines. They had the ability, and the right, to rid their country of a dictator.

Section 2 Review

1. What are the main types of governments in Southeast Asia?

2. **Analyzing Information** Why do you think that the Filipinos were able to force Marcos out?

SECTION 3

Southeast Asia and the World

How is Southeast Asia's role in the world changing?

Until World War II, many Westerners thought of Southeast Asia as a place to buy resources such as rice, tin, and rubber.

After World War II, however, colonies became countries. They wanted to be more than just a source for tin. They wanted to develop their own industries and to claim a place in the world economy.

Southeast Asia did have some advantages. People from other countries did not have to make big investments to start companies there. Southeast Asian workers were paid less than workers in other places. The presence of natural resources meant that the materials industries needed could be found nearby. Southeast Asia is also in a good geographic position. It links India and the Middle East with China.

Southeast Asia did have some difficulties in encouraging outside investment. World War II had left countries shattered. Many Westerners thought that their governments were not stable. In addition, until the 1980s, the Communist countries dealt mostly with other Communist countries.

In the 1970s, money began to flow into Southeast Asia. Big corporations built factories. Clothes sold in U.S. stores began to carry tags reading "Made in the Philippines" or "Made in Indonesia." But while these tags indicate that clothes are made in Southeast Asia, the company is often based in another country. The company's profits, then, do not go to Southeast Asia.

Japan is one country that is involved in the economy of Southeast Asia. Japan imports raw materials from the region. It owns plants in Southeast Asia that make goods that are sold in other parts of the world.

The Communist countries of Vietnam and Laos are beginning to welcome **investors**, or people who put money into businesses. For example, because Cambodia has become a kingdom and is no longer a Communist country, it expects more economic activity. Investors will be more willing to come to Cambodia because they can expect to make a profit.

In some ways, though, Southeast Asia is still tied to its colonial past. Other countries hold economic power there. At least now, though, Southeast Asia keeps some of that money at home.

Politics: Southeast Asia and the West

In 1967, five Southeast Asian countries united for the first time to form the Association of Southeast Asian Nations (ASEAN). This organization included Indonesia, Thailand, Malaysia, Singapore, and the Philippines. Brunei joined in 1984. ASEAN's goal is to increase trade among

Low start-up and labor costs have led many industrialized countries to build factories in Southeast Asia, like this one in Indonesia. If you check the labels on your clothing, chances are you'll find that at least one item was made in Southeast Asia.

During Pol Pot's reign of terror, hundreds of thousands of Cambodians were relocated, tortured, and murdered. Thousands fled and became refugees in Thailand and many other countries throughout Southeast Asia and the world.

On Assignment...

What information in this section could you add to your board game? Review the material and note details about Southeast Asia's economic growth. Write questions–and answers–about this information for your game.

member nations. It also encourages members to stand together against outsiders.

ASEAN was pro-Western. That is, it was friendly toward countries like the United States. It was against the Communist movements in Southeast Asia. The United States supported ASEAN, sending money to arm the ASEAN countries against communism.

Today communism has less power because of the fall of the Communist Soviet Union. Russia no longer needs to keep its influence strong by helping Communist countries. In July 1995, what was once unthinkable happened. Vietnam joined ASEAN. The same

year, Vietnam was finally recognized by the United States. Both of these events show how much the world has changed.

Since the Vietnam War—the only war the United States has ever lost—the United States has mostly stayed out of the region. For the first time in a century, there are no United States military bases in Southeast Asia. Its bases in the Philippines closed in 1992. One result of U.S. withdrawal is that Southeast Asia no longer has the nearby help of the United States.

Today, what interests the Southeast Asian countries most is China. This country of 1.2 billion people dominates Southeast Asia. The countries of Southeast Asia watch China carefully. There are still fights over some Southeast Asian islands. China says that it owns them. Other countries say that they do.

Southeast Asia, though, is developing into a worldwide economic force. It needs outside countries less. Many Southeast Asian countries have experienced strong economic growth. Southeast Asia has been a land of terrible war and of stunning beauty. Today Southeast Asia has a bright future.

Section 3 Review

1. What is ASEAN?

2. **Drawing Conclusions** Explain how the changes in Communist Southeast Asian countries may affect the region in the future.

Return to the Killing Fields

Sarat turned her dull eyes to the interviewer. "I watched my husband die. Then my son. Do you know of Pol Pot—the leader of the Cambodian Communists? His people rounded up the people. Some they killed. They killed my husband, right in front of me. They beat him to death with sticks. He was asking 'Why? Why?' He had the wrong ideas, they said. So they killed him."

These are the killing fields, the interviewer thought.

"One day, they came and said we were going to farm," Sarat said. "We marched for days. When we got there, we began working. From day to night, we worked. They would throw down a can of rice—oh, six inches high. That would be all 10 people got all day. We starved. People ate rats. They pulled up every piece of green and ate it. That was when I had to watch my son die in my arms. He was so weak and thin that he couldn't hold his head up. He just lay there, limp.

"That work went on for four years. Of the 150 who had come, 20 were still alive. Then the Vietnamese came. We had been told that they were even worse than Pol Pot's men. So I escaped. So many others were escaping that we went with them.

"Finally, we arrived at the border of Thailand. Someone saw us and said, 'Are you refugees? Do you want to go to the camp?' We have been there since. It is not as bad as Pol Pot, but still. . . .

"I wake in the night with dreams of my son dying in my arms. I have little to do here but think. That is something I do not want to do. Then, too, we are often hungry. People go to the woods to dig for roots to eat with the rice.

"Now you tell us we will go home. Where is home? It is 1992. My family is dead. What will I do?" Sarat buried her face in her hands.

The interviewer said, "Didn't you begin the school for the deaf children? Refugees are coming back now that Cambodia is a kingdom again. Many children are deaf from the war. Here," the man said. He scribbled some words on a piece of paper. "This is the name of a woman in Phnom Penh. She runs services for children. Good luck." It was a small hope. But it was all Sarat had.

Case Study Review

1. Describe Sarat's journey after Pol Pot took power in Cambodia.

2. **Making Inferences** Why do you think that Cambodia was called *the killing fields?*

REVIEWING CHAPTER 14

I. Reviewing Vocabulary

Match each word on the left with the correct definition on the right.

1. market economy
2. insecticide
3. capitalism
4. rigid

a. an economic system in which businesses are privately owned
b. a chemical that kills insects
c. a system in which prices are set by what people are willing to pay and companies make goods based on what people want to buy
d. stiff; tightly controlled

II. Understanding the Chapter

Answer the questions below on a separate sheet of paper.

1. Describe the different kinds of economic systems in Southeast Asia today.
2. Why do people in Southeast Asia move to the cities?
3. How did the downfall of the Soviet Union affect Vietnam?
4. Why did Cambodian refugees begin to return to their country in 1991?

III. Building Skills: Summarizing

Write a sentence that summarizes the important points about each topic below.

1. agriculture in Southeast Asia since the 1950s
2. forms of government in Southeast Asia since World War II
3. the importance of ASEAN to Southeast Asia

IV. Working Together

Work with a partner and choose one of the people you read about in this chapter. Write interview questions that you would ask this leader about his or her country and about Southeast Asia in general. Then answer your questions. Perform your interview for the class.

On Assignment...

Creating a Board Game: Organize the questions you wrote as you read this chapter. Choose the best of them to use for your game. Now create a board game based on these questions. You could create a game in which players move forward when they answer correctly. You could create a game in which falling on a certain square means that players have to answer a question. After you have designed your game, create the pieces. Now practice playing it to make sure that it works.

CHAPTER 15

Australia is a country of contrasts. Modern cities, such as Sydney, dot the coastline. In the center of the country, small towns and villages are scattered across a rugged land.

Australia, New Zealand, and Oceania

What do Australia, New Zealand, and Oceania have in common? How are they different?

Looking at Key Terms

- **outback** the dry lands of Australia where there are few settlers
- **geyser** a natural spring of hot water that shoots steam or hot water into the air from time to time
- **geothermal energy** energy produced from heat within the earth
- **penal colony** a colony for prisoners
- **squatter** someone who settles on land without the right to do so
- **atoll** a small coral island with a body of water at its center; most often found in the South Pacific

On Assignment. . .

Creating Posters: In this chapter, you will learn about Australia, New Zealand, and Oceania. Your assignment is to create two posters that will interest tourists in this part of the world. In each section, make notes about what tourists should know about this region. Look for hint boxes. They contain suggestions that will give you ideas for your notes.

SECTION 1

The Land and People of Australia and New Zealand

How has geography affected where and how people live in Australia and New Zealand?

Centuries ago, Europeans thought that Australia and New Zealand were located at the end of the world. On maps it was called *Terra Australis Incognita,* which means "the unknown land to the south." England thought so little of Australia that it sent its convicts there.

All that was long ago, however. Today, Australia and New Zealand are modern countries with thriving economies. Most people there are middle class. These countries are among the most popular tourist spots on earth. In this chapter, you will find out how Australia and New Zealand went from being "unknown lands to the south" to popular tourist spots. First, however, you will read about the region's geography.

The Land, Climate, and Natural Resources of Australia

Look at the map of Australia on page 189. Australia is the world's largest island. It is also the world's smallest continent. Australia is almost as big as mainland United States. Yet in 1994 only 17.8 million people lived there. More than 259 million people called the United States home in the same year.

Physical Regions Why does Australia have so few people? One reason is the huge desert in the island's interior. One third of the country is desert, called the **outback** by Australians. Another third is semi-desert. Australia is the driest continent in the world. It is also the world's flattest continent. Its highest point is Mt. Kosciusko, which is 7,316 feet (2,230 m) high.

This island has a group of animals found nowhere else in the world. Australia is the only natural home of the kangaroo and koala bear. In fact, Australia was so isolated that it developed many species of plants and animals that are unique.

Australia has three main areas. The Great Western Plateau takes up more than half of the country. It is a dry land. At its edge, in the middle of the country, is Ayers Rock. This reddish rock is 1,000 feet (305 m) high and six miles (9.75 km) around. It is the largest rock in the world.

To the east of the Great Western Plateau lie the east-central lowlands. On Australia's eastern edge is the Great Dividing Range. This is where Mt. Kosciusko is. The Great Dividing Range drops to the eastern coastal plains, which are only 248 miles (400 km) at their widest. Even so, the plains contain the country's largest cities and are home to almost all of Australia's population.

Climate and Resources Australia is a warm country. The coldest parts are the island of Tasmania and the highlands in the southeast. There, snow sometimes falls. During the winter months in the southern hemisphere—June, July, and August—people go skiing. In the southern hemisphere, the seasons are the opposite of the seasons in the northern hemisphere. January and February are the warmest months in Australia. In the far north, closest to the equator, it is hot throughout the year.

Rain is what makes the difference in Australia. The Great Dividing Range stops the moist air from the Pacific Ocean. It falls as rain on the coastal range, where most farming takes place. In most of the rest of the country, rain is not common. When rain does come, it floods the land. Then it dries, and the land is parched again.

This dryness means that farming is hard, except along the east coast. Australia's great river system, the Murray, helps to irrigate some land in the southeast.

Sugar cane and wheat are the main crops. In most of the interior, farmers raise cattle and sheep. Australia is the world's largest producer of wool.

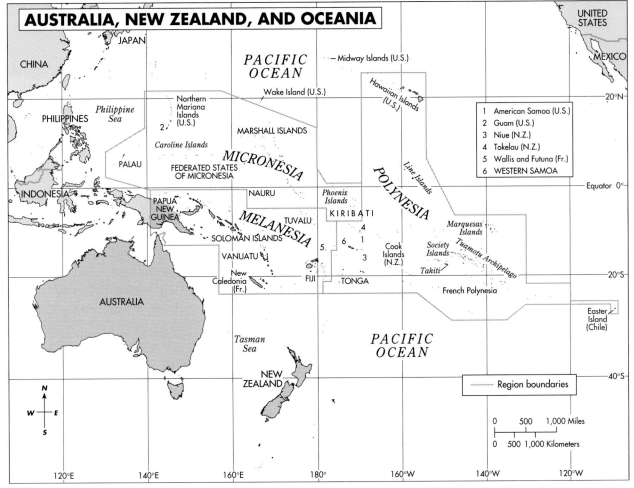

AUSTRALIA, NEW ZEALAND, AND OCEANIA

1	American Samoa (U.S.)
2	Guam (U.S.)
3	Niue (N.Z.)
4	Tokelau (N.Z.)
5	Wallis and Futuna (Fr.)
6	WESTERN SAMOA

Place and Region Thousands of islands dot the Pacific Ocean. Australia and New Zealand are the largest of these islands. Into what three main groups is Oceania divided? To which group does Fiji belong?

Australia also is rich in minerals. It contains deposits of iron ore, bauxite (to make aluminum), and uranium. Australia has coal, oil, and natural gas. In the 1850s and 1880s, news of gold brought many to Australia to try to strike it rich.

The Land, Climate, and Natural Resources of New Zealand

Australia and New Zealand look quite different from one another. New Zealand is green and mountainous. As you can see on the map above, New Zealand consists mainly of two islands: North Island and South Island.

South Island has high mountains that seem to dive into deep lakes. North Island is home to 70 percent of New Zealand's people. Most of the population lives there for several reasons. North Island is warmer and has a higher annual rainfall. Its mountains are gentler. It also has the country's best farmland. As in Australia, the centers of the islands are less populated. Most New Zealanders live in cities on the coasts. The center of North Island has two active volcanoes. It also has geysers and hot springs. **Geysers** are springs of hot water that gush into the air.

To some, New Zealand seems to have an ideal climate. It rains regularly. Summers are

SOME FACTS ABOUT AUSTRALIA, NEW ZEALAND, AND OCEANIA

COUNTRY	CAPITAL	AREA (square miles)	POPULATION (millions of people)	RESOURCES AND MAJOR INDUSTRIES
Australia	Canberra	2,941,290	17.8	wheat, barley, oats, coal, copper, iron, steel, textiles
Fiji	Suva	7,050	0.8	sugar, bananas, gold, timber, tourism
French Polynesia	Papette	1,410	0.2	coconuts, bananas, sugar, tourism
Marshall Islands	Majuro	70	0.05	agriculture, tourism
Micronesia	Palikir	271	0.1	tropical fruits, vegetables, coconuts
New Caledonia	Noumea	7,060	0.2	nickel, chrome, iron, cobalt, manganese, silver, gold, lead, copper
New Zealand	Wellington	103,470	3.4	grains, fruits, oil, gas, iron, coal, food processing, textiles, wool, timber
Papua New Guinea	Port Moresby	174,850	3.9	coffee, coconuts, cocoa, gold, copper, silver
Solomon Islands	Honiara	10,810	0.3	coconuts, rice, bananas, yams, fish canning
Vanuatu	Port-Vila	4,710	0.2	copra, cocoa, coffee, manganese, fish-freezing, meat canneries, tourism
Western Samoa	Apia	1,090	0.2	cocoa, copra, bananas, hardwoods, fish

Sources: *The World Almanac and Book of Facts 1995*, Funk and Wagnalls Corporation and World Population Data Sheet of the Population Reference Bureau, Inc.

The islands in this region are scattered across the Pacific Ocean. What resources and major industries do Australia and New Zealand have? What are the resources of the smaller islands of the region?

warm and winters are mild. Snow usually falls only in the mountains. South Island has a bit more variety. Rain clouds stop at the mountains in the west. The east can be dry.

As in Australia, the remoteness of New Zealand has led to the development of a variety of unusual wildlife. Before people came to the land, there were only a few large animals, two kinds of bats, and about 30 kinds of reptiles. One of these was the tuatara. The tuatara is the only remaining species left of an order of reptiles that died out 60 million years ago.

There are few large deposits of natural resources in New Zealand. However, New Zealand has developed hydroelectricity and **geothermal energy**. You'll remember from Chapter 8 that hydroelectricity is created by rushing water. Geothermal energy is created from steam trapped deep in the earth. Geysers release this steam naturally. The steam can also be used to drive a turbine to produce electricity.

New Zealand also is known around the world for its lamb and sheep products. New Zealand keeps most of what it grows, though. Because it is so far from other countries, it has had to learn to become self-sufficient.

The People of Australia and New Zealand

Australia's First People The first people known to have lived on these islands are called *Aborigines*. The Europeans gave them this name, which means "first people."

The Aborigines came to Australia at least 40,000 years ago from Southeast Asia. Traditionally, they are nomads who hunt and gather food. One tool that the Aborigines invented and used for hunting is the boomerang. A boomerang is a flat, curved object that is thrown at an animal. It is designed so that it returns to the thrower if it does not hit anything.

New Zealand's First People The Maoris are the first people known to live in New Zealand. They came from Polynesia, paddling to the islands in canoes. When they reached New Zealand in about A.D. 750, the Maoris named it *Aotearoa*—"the long white cloud." The Maoris lived in groups descended from common ancestors. They grew crops such as sweet potatoes.

Europeans Arrive In the 1600s, Europeans began to explore Australia and New Zealand. Once the Europeans arrived, the life of the people on these islands began to change.

One of the first Europeans to sail to New Zealand was a Dutchman. In 1642, Abel Tasman saw smoke and sent two boats ashore. Before they arrived, the Maoris set out from the beach to meet them. Wearing white feathers in their hair, the Maoris attacked Tasman's boats, killing four men. Tasman then fired on the Maoris. The boats returned to the ship. Tasman called the place "Murder's Bay." More than a century passed before the Europeans returned.

In 1768, James Cook set out from England on a three-year journey to explore the Pacific. He explored Australia as well and claimed it for Britain. Cook spent more than a year mapping Australia's east coast. He recorded the wildlife and plants he found there. He also tried to make contact with the Aborigines. According to Cook, the Aborigines

The Aborigines are the first people known to have lived in Australia. The man at the left is playing a didgeridoo, an instrument that is played by varying lip and tongue movements.

live in a warm and fine climate, and enjoy . . . wholesome air, so that they have very little need of clothing; . . . many to whom we gave cloth, etc., left it carelessly upon the sea beach and in the woods, as a thing they had no manner of use for; in short, they seemed to set no value upon anything we gave them. . . . This, in my opinion, argues that they think themselves provided with all the necessaries of life.

Australia as a Penal Colony "Thieves, robbers, and villains, they'll send them away to become a new people at Botany Bay," went a popular song in Britain in 1790. Three years earlier, in 1787, the first ship of convicts had sailed from Britain to Botany Bay, Australia. The country was to be a **penal colony**, or a colony for prisoners.

Of that first group of 759 convicts, 568 were men and 191 were women. More than half of the convicts who were sent to the colony had been charged with minor theft. Eleven-year-old James Grace had stolen ten yards of ribbon and a pair of silk stockings. Another teenager had taken a packet of tobacco. For these crimes they were sentenced to live in Australia—a barren land thousands of miles from home.

The eight-month voyage was the longest voyage ever attempted by such a large group of people. They slept in the lower decks without light or windows. When the sea was calm, they could walk on deck. When the sea was not calm, they stayed below the deck— for days and weeks at a time. The convicts were terrified of what lay before them. As it turned out, they had reason to be frightened. Forty-eight people died on board. Those who did not die faced other horrors when the ship landed.

When the convicts arrived in Botany Bay, it was soon clear that no colony could survive there. The land was dry. The Aborigines on shore shouted "Warra, warra!" at the newcomers. That meant "Go away!"

They did. Within days, the group sailed to Port Jackson, which was to become Sydney, Australia's largest city.

The convicts began to create a colony. For years, life was a nightmare. Their crops did poorly. Cattle were stolen by the Aborigines. There was not enough food.

Year after year, life improved. More people arrived. Some were convicts. Others were people who hoped for a better life in the new land.

Section 1 Review

1. How are the lands and climates of Australia and New Zealand similar?

2. **Analyzing a Primary Source** Review James Cook's description of the Aborigines on this page. What did the Aborigines do with the gifts that Cook gave them? What cultural differences does Cook describe between the Europeans and the Aborigines?

SECTION 2

Australia and New Zealand: From Colonies to Independent Nations

How did Australia and New Zealand become British colonies?

Australia's convicts and immigrants soon created colonies. In New Zealand, it was not

---

On Assignment...

What would visitors to Australia and New Zealand want to know? Make notes about these ideas for your poster. How would you show the geography and climate of the region on a poster? What words would you use to describe them?

until 1814 that European colonists came to stay. Samuel Marsden, who was a missionary, was the first colonist. He brought cattle and horses to New Zealand. The Maoris had never seen anything larger than a reptile. To them, the horses were huge.

Australia

By 1868, Britain had sent 160,000 convicts to Australia. As you read in Section 1, people other than convicts came as well. The British established six colonies in Australia. These colonies, however, did not get along with one another. People who belonged to one colony rarely visited people from the other colonies. This changed after 1851, however, when the Australian gold rush began. The population of Australia tripled in the 1850s as people from all over the world rushed to the island in hopes of making a fortune.

Some immigrants rejected life in the colonies. They set off into the outback. That rugged land was only for a hearty few, who were called **squatters**. The squatters did not have title to the land. They simply found an unclaimed piece of land and took it. Most tried to make a living by raising sheep.

Squatters' lives were difficult. They were often alone, poor, and in danger. Aborigines attacked the squatters. The Aborigines were angry because the squatters took their land and because they were no longer able to follow their nomadic way of life. The Aborigines stole sheep to eat and killed outback squatters and their families.

The squatters fought back, killing thousands of Aborigines. European diseases, though, took a heavier toll on the Aborigines. The Aborigines had no resistance to these diseases. Diseases that were relatively harmless to Europeans killed thousands of Aborigines. In the century after the first convicts came, the number of Aborigines fell from 300,000 to 80,000.

New Zealand

In New Zealand, the Maoris were angered and confused by many of the settlers' ways.

The Maoris are New Zealand's first people. When Europeans arrived, many Maoris died from disease. Others were killed in battles. About 320,000 Maoris live in New Zealand today.

Many settlers were farmers. The Maoris thought their plowing was killing the land. The Maoris owned land together. They had no idea of private ownership. Things worsened for the Maoris as more Europeans arrived and claimed the land.

Some of the Christian missionaries were unhappy at what was happening. They felt that the Maoris were being treated unfairly by the settlers. They asked the British to bring some order to the colony.

As a result, the Treaty of Waitangi was signed in 1840. The Maoris agreed to sell their land to the British government. In exchange, the British would bring government to New Zealand. They would also bring British protection.

Soon, wars broke out. The Maoris did not understand the treaty. The Maoris fought for the land that was sold out from under them. Other land was taken illegally. In the 1860s, the discovery of gold brought many more settlers.

The British burned Maori villages and many Maoris were killed. Like the Aborigines, the Maoris had no resistance to many European diseases. Nearly 200,000 Maoris were killed by war or disease.

Once peace was established, Europeans developed thriving settlements in New Zealand. New Zealand's economy improved when it began to export dairy products and meat. These products sold for better prices than farmers could get in New Zealand. New Zealand's settlers began to enjoy prosperity.

A New Century

Differences among the six British colonies of Australia kept them separate until the late 1890s. In 1898, the six colonies met to establish a constitution. The constitution created a parliamentary form of government that was similar to Great Britain's. In 1901, the British colonies in Australia joined to become the Commonwealth of Australia. The Commonwealth functioned as an independent nation within the British Empire.

New Zealand was granted some rights to self-government in 1865. In 1893, it became the first country to give women the vote. In 1907, New Zealand was granted dominion status within the British Empire. That meant that it, too, was an independent nation within the empire.

In the 1930s, a worldwide economic depression affected Australia and New Zealand. There were fewer buyers for their products and people rioted for food and jobs. During World War II, Australia and New Zealand fought on the side of the Allied Powers, which included Great Britain, France, and the United States.

After the war, Great Britain's relationship with Australia and New Zealand changed. In 1973, Britain joined the European Union (EU). The EU helps European countries trade among themselves. New Zealand and Australia were no longer favored trade partners. Both lost a good many of their markets. In the 1970s, New Zealand sold two thirds of its dairy products to Britain. In 1988, less than one fifth of New Zealand's dairy products went to Britain.

In New Zealand, sheep outnumber people by about 20 to 1. Sheep are an important part of the nation's economy. New Zealand ranks second only to Australia in wool production.

How might you show the history of Australia and New Zealand in a poster for tourists? What images would you show?

Australia and New Zealand looked to sell their wool and other products elsewhere. Now, Japan and other Asian markets are much more important. Japan is the biggest buyer of Australian goods today.

That connection with Asia is growing in other ways, too. Until the 1960s, Australia had a "white Australia" policy. Very few non-whites were allowed to settle in the country. That ended in 1973. Today almost a third of the immigrants to the country are Asian. The face of Australia is changing.

Section 2 Review

1. How did the EU change trading practices in Australia and New Zealand?

2. **Identifying Effects** What was the effect of European settlement on the Aborigines and Maoris?

SECTION 3

Oceania: A World of Pacific Islands

What is life like on the Pacific Islands?

I should like to rise and go
Where the golden apples grow;
Where below another sky
Parrot islands anchored lie.

Scotsman Robert Louis Stevenson wrote that as a young man. He later traveled to Oceania and found the world of his dreams:

white beaches with palm trees swaying, bright blue skies, calm green water. To someone who was used to the gray winters of Great Britain, this was paradise. Even today, when many people think of paradise, this is what they mean.

Three Main Groups

Oceania covers a huge area of the Pacific Ocean that extends from Japan to South America. Within this area lie about 25,000 islands. The islands are grouped into three areas, as you can see on the map on page 189.

Polynesia means "many islands." This area forms a rough triangle from Hawaii to New Zealand to Easter Island. It is a huge area of about 15 million square miles (39 billion sq km).

Micronesia means "tiny islands." This area stretches west from Polynesia and north of the equator. It includes the islands north of New Guinea.

Melanesia means "black islands." Melanesia includes the islands south of the equator and west of Polynesia. New Guinea is part of Melanesia.

Climate

All of the islands in Oceania are near the equator. Because the temperature of the Pacific Ocean in this region varies very little, there is little change in air temperature on the islands from one season to another. The average temperature is near 80°F (26°C). In addition, this part of the Pacific often has severe storms called *typhoons*. South Asia, as you read in Chapter 8, has severe storms called *cyclones*.

Low Islands and High Islands

The Pacific islands fall into two groups, the "high" islands and the "low" islands. The "high" islands are usually larger. They are the tops of underwater mountains or volcanoes that have been built up from the ocean floor. These islands contain more fertile land and support more people. The people who

Palm trees sway in the breeze on this beach in Tahiti, a popular tourist spot in Oceania. Look on the map on page 189. In which of the three main island groups is Tahiti located?

live on them have a higher standard of living than their "low"-island neighbors.

There are several reasons for this. First, "high" islands get more rainfall because their mountains catch the winds. The rainy hillsides are covered with forests that can be used to build boats and houses. Because of the rain and their fertile soil, a great variety of crops are grown: rice, yams, corn, coconuts, bananas, tobacco, and taro. Taro is a starchy root plant that is made into a pastelike food called poi. The people on the "high" islands live in the valleys. Each valley supports a village. The larger islands have cities. Many of the people also raise pigs or cattle to use for food along with the fish and fruit that are native to the region. The people grow what they need for themselves; there is little to be sold.

The "low" islands are usually coral reefs, or **atolls**. Many atolls barely reach above the surface of the water. The atolls are chains of small coral islands that have been formed by millions of tiny coral animals that live in the ocean. These animals produce a limy shell that hardens to form the atoll. In the center of the atoll is a lagoon, which is a shallow body of water like a lake or pond. The coral reefs protect the lagoons by breaking the heavy ocean waves.

Life on the "low" islands is much harder than on the "high" islands. There is little or no drinking water. The soil is thin, because much of it is washed away or broken up by wind and waves. Many people live on their own small farms. They use simple digging sticks to plant their crops. Their chief food crops are coconuts, taro, and yams. They also catch fish.

On both the "high" and "low" islands, the coconut palm is a chief resource. It provides food, clothing, and shelter. For the outside world, it is a source of *copra,* or dried coconut meat. Oil is pressed from the copra to make margarine, cooking and salad oils, fine soaps, and cosmetics.

The large continental islands have most of the minerals in Oceania. Oil, gold, nickel, and copper are some of the minerals that have been found in islands such as New Guinea. Today, Papua New Guinea (the country in the eastern part of the island) receives 80 percent of its export income from copper and gold. The volcanic and coral islands have few, if any, minerals.

Oceania: Land of Many Cultures

The first people to settle Oceania were probably nomads from Southeast Asia. They reached Australia about 40,000 years ago.

After thousands of years, some moved to other islands in Melanesia.

The other islanders seem to have come from a variety of places. Some may have come from Asia in huge canoes. There are tales of Pacific Islanders who can taste the sea water and tell if they are closer to Tonga than to Fiji.

Scientists who study the population of Oceania agree that the Melanesian islands were probably the first to be inhabited. Then people went north to Micronesia. Last, people settled Polynesia.

There are few ideas that all Oceanic peoples share. One is the idea that land should be owned in common. People take only what they need from the land.

There are many cultures in Oceania. There are hundreds of different groups in Melanesia. In New Guinea, between 600 and 700 languages are spoken. The groups in these islands often did not trust one another. That led to the development of separate cultures.

Another explanation of the many cultures in Oceania is that there are many islands. With few outside influences, these groups developed their own ways of looking at the world.

The first nonnatives to come to Oceania were explorers. They came as early as the 1500s and spread the word about the islands' stunning beauty. By the 1700s, the French and English claimed islands. Missionaries came to convert the islanders to Christianity. They made little progress—until traders and settlers appeared. Some Oceanic people converted to Christianity to gain missionary support to protect their islands.

Settlers came anyway, though. They formed plantations and set up governments. They established fueling stops for trading and for warships. The islanders did what they could to ignore these settlers.

By the 20th century, almost every island had been claimed by a major power. Sometimes, the islanders benefited. They received schooling and health care. More

On Assignment...

What kinds of images come to mind when you think of Oceania? Write those images and try to use them on your posters.

often, the Europeans simply took the land and offered nothing in return.

During World War II, the Japanese took over many Pacific islands. The Western powers fought bloody battles over these islands. Since the war, nine islands have become independent countries. Some are linked with other countries. One of these is Hawaii, which became the fiftieth U.S. state.

Today, the South Pacific Forum speaks for the nations in Oceania. The 15-nation group has protested and ended most nuclear testing in the region. The forum has also dealt with environmental issues. One issue has been global warming. Another has been fishing nets that trap and destroy everything they catch.

The islands of Oceania continue to lure tourists with their warm climate, beautiful beaches, and tropical breezes. In recent years, islanders have begun to grow new crops to make a living. There is more mining. More timber is being cut. Oceania continues to be one of the most beautiful places on earth. Its distance from other parts of the world may help it to stay that way for many years.

Section 3 Review

1. Why are there so many different cultures in Oceania?

2. **Comparing and Contrasting** Explain the similarities and differences between "high" and "low" islands.

The Aborigines:
Caught Between Two Worlds

This is a story from the Dreamtime. One night, women went to dig for yams. Those who did not find any yams felt ashamed. They flew to the sky. Then those who found yams decided to go, too. Today, all those women are stars. Those who found yams twinkle brightly. Those who did not are dim in the sky.

Life began in the Dreamtime, the Aboriginal people of Australia believe. It was a time when nature and people became one. Aboriginal peoples have been on the land for at least 40,000 years. The Dreamtime dates from that time.

During the thousands of years since, the number of Aborigines shrank. Today, Aborigines are about 1.5 percent of Australians.

Those who remain are caught between worlds. One is the world of the ancients. In that world, the land is mother and spirit. The people know the animals. They know every path and stream. Their art, which is drawn in caves, keeps the power of the Dreamtime alive.

About half of the Aborigines live in the other world. In this world of the city, Aborigines often live in very poor areas. The streets are dirt. Their houses are shacks. Today, an Aborigine in Australia can expect to live 56 years. Other Australians live an average of more than 70 years. The death rate for Aborigine babies is three times that of other Australian babies. Six times more Aborigines are out of work.

During Australia's bicentennial in 1988, 15,000 Aborigines marched on Sydney to protest. This was the anniversary of 200 years of ill treatment. Australians did more than just take land. The marchers said they treated Aborigines as subhuman.

That is changing. In 1993, the Australian High Court made an important ruling. Until then, Australia's law had said that until the Europeans came, no one lived in the country. The court ruled in 1993 that the Aborigines had been there first. The court also said that the Aborigines could claim unused land. That may mean that more Aborigines can claim land that belonged to their people thousands of years ago.

Case Study Review

1. What is the Dreamtime?
2. **Analyzing Information** How will the 1993 ruling affect Aborigines?

I. Reviewing Vocabulary

Match each word on the left with the correct definition on the right.

1. outback
2. atoll
3. geothermal energy
4. geyser

a. energy produced by the earth's heat
b. dry lands of Australia where there are few settlers
c. a small coral island
d. a natural spring of hot water

II. Understanding the Chapter

Answer the questions below on a separate sheet of paper.

1. What are the main physical regions of Australia?
2. What were two effects of European settlement on the Aborigines and Maoris?
3. What are the three main divisions of the Pacific islands?
4. Why did 15,000 Aborigines march on Sydney in 1988?

III. Building Skills: Reading a Map

Use the map of Australia, New Zealand, and Oceania on page 189 to answer these questions. Write your answers on another sheet of paper.

1. Where is Australia in relation to the equator?
2. Which of the three island groups takes up the most ocean area?
3. What sea lies between Australia and New Zealand?
4. About how many miles is it from Australia to the Samoas?

IV. Working Together

Work with a group of four classmates. Imagine that the year is 1853 and you are in Australia. You will each take one of the following roles: an Aborigine, a squatter who lives in the outback, a convict from Britain, and a gold seeker. Use library resources and your text to find out as much as you can about your person's life. Then prepare a dialogue for a talk show that features the four Australians.

On Assignment. . .

Creating Posters: Sketch a design and decide on the captions that you will use with each picture on your two posters. Now find pictures to use, or draw your own. Assemble your posters into a display that will attract tourists to Australia, New Zealand, and Oceania. Make sure that your display has headlines. Finally, put up your display. Be ready to answer questions about this region of the world.

I. Understanding the Unit

Answer the questions below on a separate sheet of paper.

1. (a) What are monsoons? (b) How do monsoons affect the climate and people of South and Southeast Asia?

2. (a) What is the caste system? (b) List one effect the caste system has on India today.

3. (a) Why did Europeans take an interest in South and Southeast Asia? (b) How did Europeans establish direct contact with the countries and kingdoms of Asia?

4. Identify and describe how three of the following are affecting India today: (a) overpopulation, (b) environmental issues, (c) rapid growth of cities, (d) lack of educational opportunities for villagers, (e) agricultural problems.

5. (a) Why did Pakistan separate from India after independence? (b) What is the main reason East and West Pakistan split into two separate nations?

6. Identify and briefly describe two of the following civilizations from South Asia and Southeast Asia: (a) the Maurya empire, (b) the Delhi Sultanate, (c) the Mogul empire, (d) the kingdoms of Vietnam, (e) the Pagan kingdom, (f) the Angkor kingdom, (g) the Thai kingdoms, (h) the kingdoms of Indonesia.

7. (a) Why did Britain send the first settlers to Australia? (b) What event in Australia in the 1850s triggered a large increase in the number of settlers?

II. Thinking Critically

Answer the questions below on a separate sheet of paper.

1. **Comparing and Contrasting** What three religions have the largest followings in South and Southeast Asia? What are the differences and similarities among them?

2. **Drawing Conclusions** During the Cold War, India maintained a foreign policy of non-alignment. What does non-alignment mean? Why do you think India used this policy? How did this policy affect India during the Cold War?

III. Writing to Learn

On a separate sheet of paper, write a three-paragraph essay about the following topic.

Think about the land and people of South and Southeast Asia. What current issues face both regions? What current issues are specific to either region?

IV. Practicing Skills: Interpreting Pie Charts

Read the pie charts below. On a separate sheet of paper, answer the questions that follow.

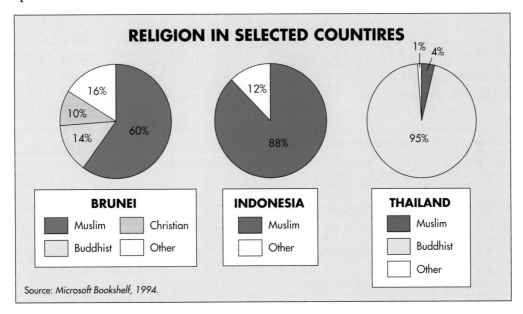

1. Which country has the greatest percentage of Muslims?
2. Which country has the greatest number of Buddhists?
3. The word *diverse* means "varied." Which country appears to be the most diverse? Explain.

V. Going Beyond the Unit

Work with two or three students to create a travel journal. Imagine you are given the opportunity to spend two months in South and Southeast Asia. First, decide which countries you will visit (choose at least three). Next, use library or classroom resources to gather photographs, drawings, maps and artwork from each place you plan to visit. Then write a description of what you would see and what the people would be like in each place. Copy or sketch pictures. Finally, assemble your pictures and descriptions into a travel journal. Present your journal to the class.

How Economic Systems Compare

Looking at Key Terms

command economies, market economy, capitalist system, free enterprise, supply and demand, competition, mixed economies

The scene is a busy stock market. A mob of clerks is buying and selling shares in privately owned companies. The wonder of this is that they are making these deals in China, the world's largest Communist country. In Communist systems, there is supposed to be no private property.

Under communism, governments are supposed to make all economic decisions. Yet, Vietnam, another Communist government, allows its farmers to plant what they want and sell their crops at whatever price they can get. As a result, Vietnam has gone from famine to the world's third largest exporter of rice.

Command Economies and Market Economies

There are basically two types of economies. **Command economies** are those in which the government decides what and how much to make. They decide when and where to sell and at what price. They decide where people will work and how much they will be paid. Command economic systems usually occur in dictatorships.

Communism is a type of command economy. Communist governments own and control everything of value in the country. They also try to provide benefits to all people in the society. The goal of communism is to ensure that no individual is too rich or too poor.

The opposite of a command economy is a **market economy**. A market economy is also called a **capitalist system** or **free enterprise**. In market economies, individual people make business decisions. They choose what to make, buy, or sell on the basis of their needs.

When buyers and sellers make economic decisions, the market determines which products will succeed or fail. This is the concept of **supply and demand**. If buyers demand a product, sellers supply the product. Supply and demand also helps to determine the price of a product. Sellers test how much buyers will pay for a product.

In many cases, there is more than one seller for a particular product. This situation produces **competition** among suppliers. Competition helps to set prices. Sellers have to compare their prices with other sellers to make sure their prices are not too high.

On the Shanghai stock market, in China, traders eagerly buy and sell shares in privately owned companies. Today, many communist countries use capitalist methods to boost their economies.

In our times, countries with market economies have been more prosperous than those with command economies. In the 1980s, communism failed in the world's largest country, the Soviet Union. This led to the breakup of the country. As we have seen, other Communist countries such as Vietnam and China have accepted some aspects of market economies. At the same time, countries with market economies, such as the United States and Japan have thrived.

Mixing Two Systems

No economy is purely market or purely command. These are examples of **mixed economies**. For instance, in Indonesia, the government owns the country's oil company, but private citizens own and run many of the smaller companies in the country. The government's ownership of the oil company is typical of a command economy. The private ownership of smaller companies, however, is characteristic of a market economy. In this type of economy, government and industry can work together to produce a strong economy.

Review

1. Why are Communist nations allowing individuals to make decisions usually made in a market economy?
2. **Making Inferences** Why do you think command economies occur most often in dictatorships?

Taking Action: Conducting an Interview

With a partner, conduct an interview with an imaginary leader of a Communist country. Write three questions that help explain why these countries have allowed mixed economies. Then write the answers that you think the official might give.

FOCUS ON

East Asia

	2500 B.C.	500 B.C.	A.D. 1000	1200	1400

History		**202 B.C.-A.D. 220** The Han dynasty rules China.	**676** The Silla kingdom unifies Korea.	**1215** Genghis Khan leads the Mogols in an attack against China.	**1392-1910** The Yi dynasty rules Korea.
Culture & Society		**551-479 B.C.** Chinese philosopher Confucius lives and teaches.	**552** Buddhism comes to Japan and is merged with Shinto.		**1368-1644** During the Ming dynasty, artists create fine porcelain jars and bowls.
Economics & Technology	**618-589 B.C.** The Grand Canal connects the Chang and Yellow rivers.			**1234** The Koreans invent movable type for printing.	

PREVIEWING THE UNIT

Study the time line. On a separate sheet of paper answer the questions below.

1. For how many years did the Han dynasty rule?
2. In what year did Genghis Khan attack China?
3. In what year was Japan's first constitution approved?
4. When was the Korean War?
5. When will China gain control of Hong Kong?

1600		1800	1900	2000

1603-1867
The Tokugawa shogunate rules Japan.

1889
Japan's first constitution is approved by the emperor.

1950-1953
The Korean War is fought.

1997
Hong Kong passes from British rule to Chinese rule.

1540s
Roman Catholic missionaries arrive in Japan.

1610
European traders bring tea from China to Europe.

1949
China adopts communism.

1990s
China's population reaches 1.2 billion.

1641
Japanese rulers ban foreign trade.

1839-1842
Modern weapons help Britain defeat China in the Opium War.

1990s
South Korea becomes one of the "four tigers" of Asia.

Population Density and Landforms of East Asia
Analyzing Maps

East Asia is the most populous region in the world. The rapidly growing population is an important issue for the region. Providing food and shelter becomes a challenge. However, the population is not evenly distributed. For example, almost all of Japan's population lives on only 16 percent of its land. Comparing a population density map with a landform map can show you why people live where they do. Below is a population density map and a landform map of East Asia. Study the maps. On a separate sheet of paper, answer the questions below.

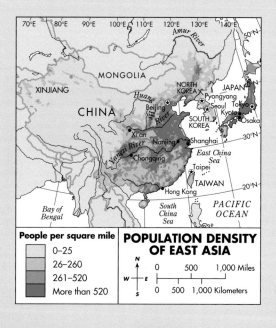

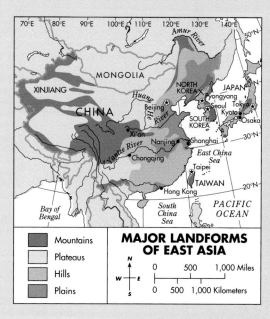

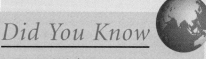

Did You Know

- East Asia is home to more than one fourth of the world's population. (See Chapter 16.)

- More people live in China than in any other nation in the world. (See Chapter 16.)

- Special pushers are hired to help squeeze people into subway and trains in Japan. (See Chapter 16.)

1. **Reading the Maps** (a) What do the shadings on the population density map represent? (b) According to the landform map, what are East Asia's major landforms?

2. **Thinking About the Maps** (a) Where is China's population least concentrated? (b) How do you think the landforms affect the population density in that region?

3. **Going Beyond the Maps: Proposing Solutions** (a) What might be some of the negative effects of living in a crowded area? (b) What might governments do to solve these problems?

More than 1.3 billion people live in the countries of East Asia, the world's most populous region. It is a land of ancient religions and traditions and modern industries.

CHAPTER 16

The Land and People of East Asia

How are the lives of East Asians influenced by the lands and climates of the region?

Looking at Key Terms

- **plateau** a large area of flat land that is higher than the surrounding land
- **tributary** a small river that flows into a larger river
- **delta** a broad area of soil deposits near the mouth of a river
- **hydroelectric power** electricity created by water
- **monsoon** a seasonal wind that brings wet or dry weather
- **typhoon** a fierce storm, like a hurricane
- **dialect** a way of speaking found in a particular region
- **exile** a person living outside his or her homeland for political reasons
- **nomad** a person who has no permanent home and moves from place to place

On Assignment. . .

Creating a Mural: A mural is a wall painting that shows a vivid variety of activities and people. Working in small groups, you will create a mural about East Asia after you have read this chapter. The mural should show the landforms, rivers, resources, climates, and people of the region. As you read this chapter, look for the On Assignment hint boxes. The boxes will contain ideas for your mural.

207

What and Where Is East Asia?

How have East Asia's landforms and waterways affected its people?

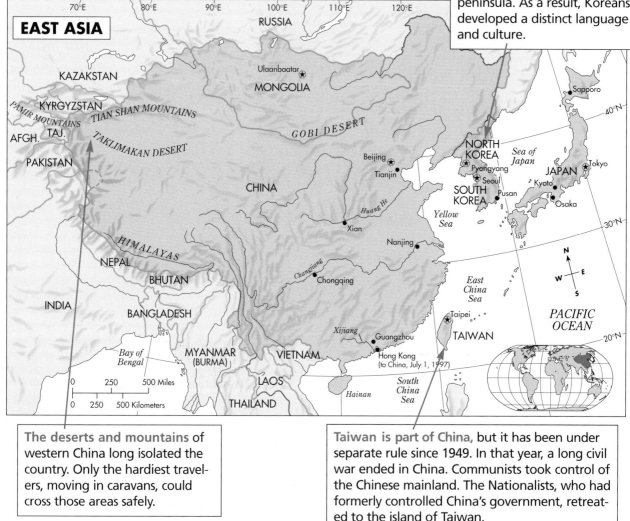

EAST ASIA

The Korean peninsula is cut off from the Asian mainland by high, rugged mountains. The mountains made it difficult for armies from China or Mongolia to conquer the peninsula. As a result, Koreans developed a distinct language and culture.

The deserts and mountains of western China long isolated the country. Only the hardiest travelers, moving in caravans, could cross those areas safely.

Taiwan is part of China, but it has been under separate rule since 1949. In that year, a long civil war ended in China. Communists took control of the Chinese mainland. The Nationalists, who had formerly controlled China's government, retreated to the island of Taiwan.

East Asia covers about as much land area as the United States and Mexico combined. It is home to more than one fourth of the world's people. China and Mongolia are the two largest countries in East Asia. Smaller lands of the region include Japan, North Korea, South Korea, and Taiwan. There are also two tiny territories, Hong Kong and Macao.

Much of East Asia's interior is made up of mountains and high flatlands called **plateaus** (pla•TOHZ). Tibet, which is part of China, lies on top of one very large plateau. Tibet's average altitude of 16,000 feet (4,900 meters) is higher than the tallest peak in the U.S. Rocky Mountains.

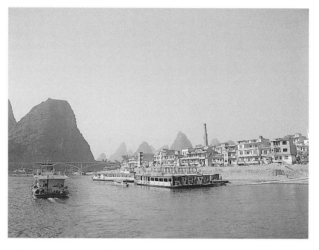

Japan is a small island nation with limited resources. In order to keep its industries going, it depends on international trade. Japan imports coal, iron, and oil. Japan also exports many manufactured products to other nations. It has the second largest economy in the world, after the United States.

China's rivers bring great benefits—and great dangers. Flowing from the mountains to the sea, the rivers bring water for drinking and for irrigating crops. The rivers also carry rich soil for farmers' fields. But because China's lowlands are flat, flooding often kills thousands of people at a time. Today, barriers, called dikes, hold back the water.

Mount Fuji's graceful shape has inspired Japanese poets and painters for centuries. Japan's mountains offer hiking in summer and skiing in winter. But the mountains take up so much space that people are squeezed into narrow lowlands near the coasts. Farmland is in short supply, and so is land for houses. One result is that the Japanese live in much smaller houses than do people in other industrial nations.

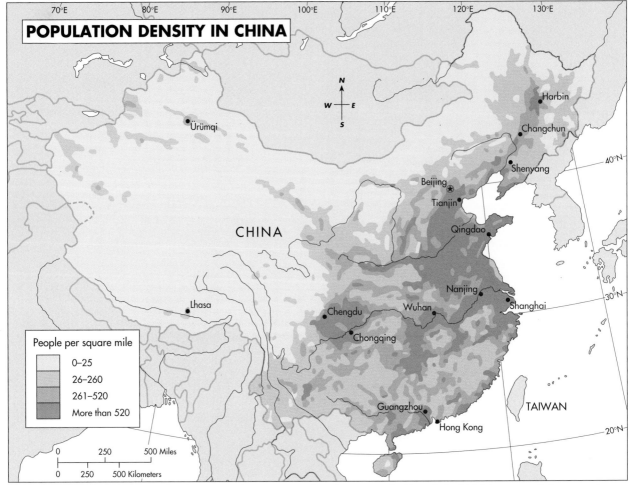

POPULATION DENSITY IN CHINA

People per square mile

- 0–25
- 26–260
- 261–520
- More than 520

Place and Region China is the the most densely populated country in East Asia. Which area of the country has the greatest population density? Why do you think that most of the people in China have settled in this region?

The Regions of East Asia

East Asia is a huge region with a rich variety of landscapes. It has desolate deserts and massive mountains. However, most of its people live in valleys and low-lying plains near oceans and seas. Farmers live where they can grow crops like rice and wheat. East Asia has vast numbers of people and needs lots of food.

The Geography of China

China covers a very large area. It is the world's third largest country. Only Russia and Canada are bigger.

You would have trouble crossing western China on foot. Its landforms do not make it a very practical place for a long walk. But if you could walk across China, you would see the amazing sights described below. You will find it helpful to follow this route on the map on pages 596–597.

Mountains and Plateaus

You might start walking at the border with Nepal, high in the Himalaya Mountains. Mount Everest, on the Tibet-Nepal border, is the world's highest mountain. It rises to 29,028 feet (8,848 meters) above sea level.

With many stops to catch your breath, you would wind your way north across steep slopes and towering peaks. After hundreds of miles, you would start to descend. You would find fewer trees and more grass. The grass would get shorter, and the air drier. Then you would be in the Taklimakan (tahk•luh•muh•KAHN) Desert. You'd better have plenty of water in your canteen.

If you went west, you would climb again, into the Pamir (pah•MEER) Mountains. If you kept going north, you would climb into the Tian Shan Mountains. Or, if your water held out, you could head northeast into the Gobi Desert and Mongolia. You might get lonely here. Not many people live in this area.

On China's Plains

The easiest walking is in China's plains, or level lowlands. Because they are level, plains are good places to raise crops. Most of China's plains lie in the east and northeast. You could walk for about 1,000 miles (1,600 km) across level ground in China.

China's Rivers

The Chinese sometimes describe their rivers as friendly dragons. Each dragon has arms and legs that are the river's **tributaries**, or small rivers, that flow into the main river. The dragon's mouth is where

On Assignment . . .

Make a large map of China as a background for your mural. Include mountains, hills, plains, and rivers. Show a route for a walking tour.

the river reaches the sea. That is where the river deposits the silt, or fertile soil, that has washed off the mountains and fields. The silt creates broad areas called **deltas** that yield rich crops. Because they bring water and precious soil to the nation's farmers, China's rivers are a source of life.

China's three main rivers flow from west to east. Which feature of China's landforms explains that fact?

The river that is farthest to the north is the Huang He (hwang huh), or the Yellow River. Its name comes from the yellow silt that the river carries. The Huang He empties into the Yellow Sea. At its entrance to the Yellow Sea, the Huang He carries so much silt that it creates huge sandbars. These sandbars keep large boats from sailing through the river.

In a land of many people and a rugged landscape, little usable land goes to waste. These terraced fields run up a hillside on the Tachai commune in central China.

The Chang (jang) River flows through the central part of China. It is 3,600 miles (5,760 km) long, making it China's longest river. Important cities like Shanghai, Nanjing, and Wuhan lie along the banks of this river.

The mighty Chang River cuts spectacular canyons through tall mountains. This river has been a tourist attraction in China. Recently, the Chinese have been building a dam in the river at a place called Three Gorges.

The Three Gorges dam will create a vast lake. As water from the lake flows over the dam, it will turn turbines to create electricity. (Electricity created by water is called **hydroelectric power**.)

Three Gorges is the world's largest construction project. More than a million people will have to move from their homes to make way for the water that will back up behind the dam. Work on the dam began in 1994. The project will not be finished until 2009.

The third major river is the Xi Jiang (shee kyang), or West River. It flows through southern China. The city of Guangzhou (gwang•joh), also known as Canton, developed at the river's delta. Tens of millions of Chinese live in the Xi Jiang delta. A favorable climate and good soil allow farmers to produce two, or even three, crops a year.

China's Climate

If heavy rain has ever forced you to stay inside day after day, then you can imagine what China is like during part of the summer.

The Monsoon System China has a long, wet period in the summer. It also has a long, dry period in the winter. The two periods are part of Asia's **monsoon** system. A monsoon is a seasonal wind.

When the monsoon blows inland from the sea, it brings rain. This monsoon occurs in the summer. When the wind blows over land and then out to sea, it brings a dry spell. This monsoon occurs in the winter.

A Land of Cold Winters, Hot Summers Southern China is as close to the equator as Puerto Rico is. Rain is abundant in the area. Guangzhou, near China's south coast, receives more than 60 inches (150 cm) of rain a year.

Northern China is as close to the North Pole as southern Alaska is. This area has cold winters and hot summers, much like the northeastern United States.

Rainfall in the central and eastern parts of northern China totals 30 to 40 inches (75 to 100 cm) a year. That is enough for growing most crops. But mountains block most ocean moisture from reaching the far north and northwest. That is why those areas have deserts.

The Geography of Japan

Have you ever felt the earth shake under your feet? That's what happens when an earthquake hits. Dishes rattle in the cupboards, windows break, and bricks fall. An earthquake can knock down bridges and even buildings.

Earthquakes are a part of life in East Asia. Japan sits on the boundary between two moving parts of the earth's surface. When these parts shift, earthquakes hit the surface.

Japan lies along what is called the Pacific Ring of Fire. In this area, earthquakes and volcanoes are common. Much of Japan was formed by violent earthquakes and volcanoes. Small and moderate shakes happen about 1,500 times a year.

The sea has played a large part in the history and development of Japan. The city of Nagasaki, shown here, is one of Japan's major port cities.

A String of Islands

Japan is made up of four main islands and hundreds of smaller ones. Almost all of its people live on the main islands. The largest island is Honshu (HAHN•shoo), which is where the cities of Tokyo and Osaka (OH•sah•kah) are located.

Japan is often compared to Britain because both are island nations that lie just off a major continent. The seas have protected both nations from attack, allowing them to develop their own cultures. Yet the seas have also provided a path for trade and other contacts with nearby cultures.

Mountains and Plains

The Japanese are proud of their mountains. The highest mountains run along the western side of Honshu. Some call them "the Japanese Alps." Mount Fuji, the tallest, is 12,385 feet (3,775 meters) high.

Mountains have helped to shape Japan's way of life. Until modern times, they have kept parts of the country isolated.

Most of Japan's people live in the one fourth of the country that is not mountainous. They live on narrow plains along the coasts. The largest lowland, which has the highest concentration of people, is the Kanto Plain. Japan's capital, Tokyo, and the port city of Yokohama are located on the Kanto Plain.

Japan's Climate

Because Japan is surrounded by water, it has a mild climate. Ocean winds keep Japan warm in winter and cool in summer. The weather is much like that along the southeast coast of the United States.

Japan's monsoons blow across water in both summer and winter. In summer, the monsoon blows over Japan from the southeast and brings rain. In winter, the monsoon blows from the northwest and brings snow. Most of the snow falls along the western slopes of the mountains. Japan is also exposed to fierce storms called **typhoons**. They are like the hurricanes that strike the coasts of the United States.

Japan's moderate climate provides a long growing season for crops. Most farms are in central and southern Japan. Farmers often plant two crops each year. That way they make good use of their limited space.

The Geography of Korea

Korea lies between China and Japan. It, too, is a mountainous land. In fact, the name *Korea* means "land of high mountains and sparkling streams."

Since 1948, Korea has been split into two nations. North Korea has been under Communist control. South Korea has been allied with the United States.

A mountain chain runs from north to south through eastern Korea. Most Koreans live in the nation's lowlands. Many live on plains along the western coast. South Korea's capital, Seoul (sohl), is on the western plains. Other people live on smaller plains near the southern coast. North Korea's capital, Pyongyang (p'yong•yang), lies on a plain in the northeast.

On Assignment...

Find the location of the Pacific Ring of Fire. Place it on your map. Draw pictures of volcanoes on your mural.

While Korea has mild summers, its winters are very cold. Farmers in the north can raise only one crop a year. But those in the south benefit from a longer growing season. The weather allows farmers to raise two crops a year.

North Korea has most of the peninsula's mineral resources. These include coal, iron, and copper. Both North and South Korea have powerful rivers that can be used to generate electricity.

Section 1 Review

1. How does the monsoon system affect the weather of East Asia?

2. **Hypothesizing** Why would winds that blow over land be dry?

SECTION 2

The People of East Asia

What are the differences among the peoples of East Asia?

The People of China

China has 1.2 billion people. More people live in China than in any other nation in the world. Although most of its people live in the countryside, China's cities are among the world's largest.

The Han Chinese Eleven out of twelve Chinese belong to the ethnic group known as the Han (hahn) Chinese. The name comes from one of China's first ruling families. The Han Chinese live mainly in the eastern and northern parts of China.

Ethnic Minorities China also recognizes 55 official minority groups. Many live deep in China's interior, in places like Tibet. They use their own languages in their homes and schools. The minority groups are allowed a certain amount of self-government.

The Chinese written language uses more than 40,000 characters. Calligraphy, the art of writing, is a valued art in China. Chinese communities often hold calligraphy contests.

The Chinese Language

Have you noticed that people in different parts of the United States speak English in a slightly different way? In China, speech differences are even greater. The Chinese language has many **dialects** (DEYE•uh•lehkts). A dialect is the way in which people in a particular region speak a language. Sometimes people who live in neighboring villages in China cannot understand one another's dialects.

Under Communist rule, China's government encouraged people to learn one standard Chinese dialect. It is called Mandarin. Today, about 70 percent of the people in China speak Mandarin Chinese.

People who speak different forms of Chinese have no trouble understanding each other's writings. That's because written Chinese is the same for all dialects.

The People of Japan

Like the Chinese, most Japanese come from the same culture. Koreans are the largest minority group in Japan. They make up less than 1 percent of the population.

An even smaller minority are the Ainu (EYE•noo). The Ainu lived in Japan before the Japanese people arrived centuries ago. Some 15,000 Ainu still live in Japan today.

The Japanese Language

Although the Japanese language is entirely different from Chinese, the Japanese borrowed the Chinese system of writing with symbols. However, the Japanese have adapted the symbols in various ways to fit their language.

Shinto and Buddhism

The ancient Japanese practiced a religion based on the worship of nature known as Shinto (SHIHN•toh). They believed that spirits lived in mountains and trees and rocks. They also believed that certain special people were gods.

On Assignment...

On your mural, draw people engaging in some of the activities discussed in this section.

About 14 centuries ago, the Buddhist religion reached Japan from China and Korea. Although large numbers of Japanese became Buddhists, they kept many of their earlier beliefs. Today both Shinto and Buddhism are important religions in Japan.

The People of Korea

Although fewer in number than the Chinese or Japanese, the Koreans have also created a unique culture. They have fought invaders, including the Chinese and Japanese, to keep their culture alive.

South Korea has 45 million people. North Korea has about half that many. People in North and South Korea speak the same language and share the same culture.

The Korean Language

Korean symbols resemble Chinese and Japanese symbols. The Koreans borrowed the Chinese system of writing long ago. Most educated Koreans know how to read and write Chinese symbols.

However, the Koreans also use an alphabet. If you were to pick up a Korean newspaper, it would use the 24 letters of this alphabet, called *han'gul* (hahn•gul). The Koreans have used han'gul for more than 500 years.

Section 2 Review

1. How are the writing systems used in China, Japan, and Korea similar?
2. **Making Generalizations** Write a generalization about one aspect of life in East Asia.

THE PEOPLE OF EAST ASIA

China's cities bustle with activity. Many people ride bicycles to work. Cars are far more common than they were a few years ago. However, most cars and trucks belong to government offices or businesses.

Fewer than one third of China's people live in cities. Yet many cities are quite large. Shanghai has more than 7 million people. The capital, Beijing, has about 6 million.

In rural areas, Chinese people live together in villages, rather than on isolated farms. In China's crowded countryside, there is little space to spare for individual farms. Most people own their own homes. However, they do not own the land on which the houses stand. That land belongs to the community as a whole.

Japanese workers push onto trains and subways to get to work. Special pushers are hired to help squeeze people into the cars. Crowds are a problem everywhere in Japan because space is limited. By U.S. standards, houses and apartments are tiny. Parking spaces are also hard to find. Before Japanese people buy a car, they must first produce a document showing they have a place to park it.

Buddhist ceremonies are a central part of life for many South Koreans, helping them link the past and the present. This temple is in South Korea, where the constitution guarantees religious freedom. In North Korea, however, religion is discouraged. People must worship in the privacy of their homes.

Tibetans Wait for a God-King

In the highlands of Tibet, Tibetan Buddhists wait for their god-king to return to earth. They have been waiting since 1959. The Buddhist god-king is called the Dalai Lama (dah•LEE LAH•muh). A lama is a Tibetan Buddhist monk. The Dalai Lama is Tibet's leading figure. He is a political as well as a religious leader.

Timeless Tibet

Over the centuries, Tibetians have often fought off invaders. Sometimes they came under outside control. But they have always kept their own rulers and their own form of the Buddhist religion.

In 1949, when China's civil war ended in a Communist victory, Tibet still had no roads, no schools, and no electricity. The Tibetan people were either nobles or commoners. Many country people were serfs, much like those found in medieval Europe. If their master ordered them to do a job, they had to do it.

Chinese Rule

China's new Communist rulers tried to impose communism throughout all of China. Like previous Chinese rulers, the Communists considered Tibet to be part of China. They called the land *Xizang* (she•ZHANG), meaning "Western Treasure."

In 1950, the Communist government formally took control of Tibet. Many of Tibet's Buddhists resisted the invasion. In 1959, a revolt broke out in the Tibetan capital, Lhasa (LAH•suh). Chinese soldiers crushed the uprising. The fourteenth Dalai Lama and 100,000 other Tibetans left Tibet to seek safety in nearby India. Since then they have been living in **exile**. People who live in exile live outside their homeland for political reasons.

Visit to a Nomad Camp

Most of the two million people in Tibet are herders or farmers. Many are **nomads** who have no permanent homes and move from place to place with their herds. In summer, the people follow their herds up into the mountains to find green pastures. In winter, they move back down to the valleys.

Many changes have come to Tibet in recent years. Large numbers of Han Chinese have arrived. Some are soldiers who patrol the countryside. Others work in the offices of the Chinese government.

Recently, some Tibetans have moved into modern houses with concrete block walls and electricity. However, most Tibetans still live in the countryside. The capital, Lhasa, has just 150,000 people.

Who Should Rule Tibet?

Chinese officials say that Tibet is a self-governing part of China. Tibetans who support the Dalai Lama say that Tibet is under foreign occupation. The United States and most other nations accept the Chinese claim that Tibet is part of China. However, the United States has criticized violations of human rights in Tibet.

Who Is the Dalai Lama?

The Dalai Lama travels widely. He speaks out on behalf of the Tibetan people. His goal, he says, is a democratic and self-governing Tibet that is loosely linked to China. He has called on Tibetans not to use violence against Chinese rule. In 1989, the Dalai Lama won the Nobel Peace Prize for his teaching of nonviolence.

The Dalai Lama is a man born into a simple family. His parents were peasants. His original name was Tenzin Gyatso. On the day Gyatso was born, the thirteenth Dalai Lama died. In Tibetan Buddhist belief, the spirit of the dead leader is immediately reborn into an infant. So Buddhist monks went all over Tibet looking for such an infant.

The monks found the infant Gyatso and gave him a test. They placed a collection of objects around him. The baby grabbed an object that had belonged to the Dalai Lama who had just died. The monks took that choice as a sign from heaven. In 1940, at the age of four, Tenzin Gyatso became the fourteenth Dalai Lama. He moved into the 1,000-room Potala Palace at Lhasa.

Will the Dalai Lama one day return to his mountain homeland? Many Tibetans pray that he will. Once someone asked him, "What do you miss most about Tibet?" "Yaks," he replied with a smile.

Case Study Review

1. Describe the role of the Dalai Lama in Tibetan religion.
2. **Drawing Conclusions** Why did the Dalai Lama go into exile?

REVIEWING CHAPTER 16

I. Reviewing Vocabulary

Match each word on the left with the correct definition on the right.

1. tributary
2. monsoon
3. plateau
4. nomad

a. a large area of flat land that is higher than the surrounding land
b. a small river that flows into a larger river
c. a seasonal wind that brings wet or dry weather
d. a person who has no permanent home and moves from place to place

II. Understanding the Chapter

Answer the questions below on a separate sheet of paper.

1. Why do most of China's people live in the eastern part of the country?
2. How does Japan's geography resemble that of Britain?
3. How do mountains affect the climates of East Asian nations?
4. Why does the Dalai Lama oppose China's control of Tibet?

III. Building Skills: Understanding Points of View

For each of the statements below, decide whether it represents the point of view of the Dalai Lama or of the Chinese government. Give a reason for your choice.

1. Tibet is an independent country that has a separate language and traditions from those of China.
2. The laws of China apply in Tibet because it is a part of China.
3. Tibet is an occupied country under the rule of another country.

IV. Working Together

With a small group, write a letter to students in an East Asian country. Tell them what you have learned about their country. Tell them how life here is similar to, and different from, life in their country. Display the letters on a classroom bulletin board.

On Assignment...

Creating a Mural: Add the final touches to your mural. Add scenes that you think show everyday life in East Asia. Be sure to include national borders, important landforms, rivers, and some information about the region's climates.

CHAPTER 17

China: The Longest History

In what ways is China's civilization unique?

During China's years of turmoil, Buddhist monasteries became places of calm in a violent world. These stone panels of Buddha teaching his followers date from the Tang dynasty.

Looking at Key Terms

- **dynasty** a family of rulers
- **oracle bones** bones that the ancient Chinese used to predict the future
- **mandate** permission to rule
- **bureaucracy** a group of officials who do the daily chores of government
- **tribute system** an arrangement by which China collected payments from nearby nations
- **kowtow** a ceremony in which a person bows down before a superior
- **republic** a government led by officials who are elected by the people they govern
- **warlord** a local ruler and military leader

Great Dynasties

How does the experience of ancient China affect the Chinese people today?

"Empires rise and fall. States break apart and come together."

Those words from a famous Chinese tale sum up the history of China. At times, China has been one powerful nation. At other times it has split into several warring states. Today China is one nation. In fact, it is one of the world's largest and most important nations.

China is unique. Its history stretches back at least 3,700 years. No other nation has had such a long, continuous existence.

China Before the Chinese

Ancestors of humans lived in China as long as 1.9 million years ago. They lived in caves and used primitive tools. In 1927, scientists discovered evidence of a human-like being they called "Peking man." This creature lived near present-day Beijing about 400,000 years ago.

By 5000 B.C., Stone Age people had developed a thriving culture in China. They farmed and made pottery. Their communities held up to 500 people.

Chinese legends tell of an early king named Yu who was known as "the Great Engineer." He and other kings like him were credited with great deeds. They are said to have taught people how to tame animals, how to tell the seasons, and how to write. It is not clear if these kings really existed.

Shang Dynasty

The first Chinese rulers in recorded history were the Shangs. The Shang **dynasty**, or family of rulers, began to rule about 1700 B.C. It lasted 700 years. By the time the Shang dynasty fell, China's civilization had begun to develop. The Shang was the first of many dynasties that ruled China until the year 1912.

"Dragon Bones"

For centuries, sick Chinese would ask for a special "dragon bone powder" to use as a medicine. Herb doctors made the powder by grinding up special bones. Some of the bones had lines scratched onto them.

About a hundred years ago, scientists examined those lines and found that they were Chinese writings from the Shang dynasty. The writings asked questions. The people who wrote the questions put the bones into fire. Then they looked at the cracks that resulted. The shapes of these cracks gave answers to their questions. Thus, the bones are called **oracle bones**. An oracle is a wise person who answers questions.

How People of the Shang Dynasty Lived

Oracle bones and other findings give us fascinating glimpses of life during the Shang dynasty. Besides having a written language, the people of the Shang dynasty knew how to use the wheel. This enabled them to transport heavy burdens over long distances. It also let soldiers fight from chariots.

Shang kings ruled a number of regions. They controlled an area of northern China along the Yellow River.

The Shang government directed the building of dikes to keep river water from flooding nearby fields. The officials also controlled the release of water for irrigating crops. The need to tame rivers and control irrigation led the Chinese to create a strong government. This government collected taxes to pay for its works.

The Shang kings led religious ceremonies. One of their jobs was to make offerings at the graves of Shang ancestors. This was a common practice because the Chinese have great respect for the founders of their families.

Zhou Dynasty

Shang rule came to an end in about 1027 B.C. A chief named Wu Wang attacked the Shang capital while the army was away at war. He killed the king and built a new capital. He then started a new ruling family, called the Zhou dynasty.

The Mandate of Heaven Imagine a strong ruler who can kill tigers with his bare hands. At first he is a good man. Then he abuses his power. He forgets to honor his ancestors. His people become unhappy. They rise up and overthrow him.

That is how the people of Zhou explained the end of the Shang dynasty. Later, this same story was repeated as each new dynasty fell. The Chinese said that rulers held power by "the Mandate of Heaven." **Mandate** means permission to rule. If the rulers were bad, Heaven removed their mandate.

To Confucius, the test of a person's life was not how long it was but how well it was lived. Confucius's ideas left a deep imprint on the Chinese people.

Zhou Accomplishments Under Zhou rule, Chinese civilization spread south to the Chang River. The Chinese learned to use iron to make deadlier weapons and stronger tools. Chinese farmers began to use iron plows pulled by oxen. Rice, a southern crop, became part of the Chinese diet.

At first, the Zhou rulers won many wars. They extended their rule to new areas. However, in time, civil wars broke out and parts of the kingdom broke away. The Zhou dynasty finally fell in 256 B.C.

Confucius

During times of war, life was hard. People asked some basic questions: How can family ties be made stronger? How can governments be fairer to all citizens?

A series of thinkers provided answers to these questions. A man named Confucius taught the need for order in both families and society. During his lifetime (551–479 B.C.), Confucius had little influence on China's rulers. They were more concerned with the civil wars that were tearing China apart. Later, when the fighting died down, the teachings of Confucius spread. His beliefs influence China to this day.

Great Empires

China's brutal civil wars lasted almost 200 years. Finally, the state of Qin (chihn) was victorious. As a Chinese historian wrote, Qin swallowed its neighbors "as the silk worm devours the mulberry leaves." The modern name *China* is derived from Qin.

The First Emperor

In 221 B.C., China became a unified empire for the first time. The Qin ruler took the title "First Emperor." Before this, Chinese rulers shared power with local chiefs or nobles. First Emperor stripped the nobles of their power. He set up a centralized state, dividing the empire into 36 counties. Each county had a governor who answered to the emperor alone.

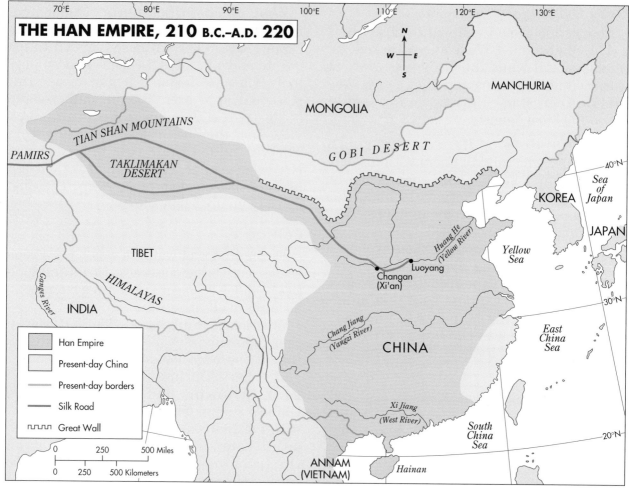

THE HAN EMPIRE, 210 B.C.–A.D. 220

Place and Location During the Han dynasty, military conquests extended the Chinese empire. What building project marked the northern border of the Han empire? Near which road was it built?

To ensure control, First Emperor built a network of roads. They reached out from his capital, Xi'an (shee•an). This allowed the emperor to send his troops to all portions of his empire. He set up a common system of weights and measures. He also established a common currency, or money. These actions helped unify the Chinese, so that they felt they were part of one nation.

In the north, several of the warring states had built walls. The walls were to keep out nomadic tribes that lived farther north. The First Emperor ordered that the walls be connected. This created the Great Wall of China. It stretches 1,400 miles (2,240 km) and is 15 to 50 feet (5 to 15 m) high. The top is so wide that soldiers could ride horses back and forth on patrol.

Building the wall was backbreaking work. China's people did the work, but they did not like it. After the First Emperor died in 210 B.C., revolts broke out. In 206, the Qin dynasty collapsed.

Han Dynasty

The Han (hahn) was the next family to rule China. The Han dynasty held power for more than four hundred years, from 210 B.C. to A.D. 220. The Chinese are proud of the Han dynasty. To this day they call themselves "the people of Han."

During the Han dynasty, China developed a strong **bureaucracy**, or group of government officials. Each official had to pass an examination that tested knowledge of classic Chinese learning—especially the teachings of Confucius.

One Chinese writer was 15 when he started to study for the exam. For 10 years, he continued his studies. "I had no time for sleep or rest, with the result that I developed sores in my mouth and my hands and wrists swelled," he said.

Passing the exam ensured a lifetime job in government. Chinese officials were so proud of their achievement that they let their fingernails grow long. This showed that they did not have to soil their hands with hard work.

During the Han period, China conquered northern Korea and part of Vietnam. Traders carried Chinese silks and other products as far as the Roman Empire. They used a trading route known as the Silk Road. In addition, the Chinese made many advances in technology. They invented water mills for grinding grain into flour. They made paper and published the first Chinese dictionary.

The religions of Daoism and Buddhism gained strength during Han times. Daoism had developed in China about the time of Confucius. Merchants and missionaries brought Buddhism from Nepal and India. You'll read more about these beliefs in Chapter 19.

Later Dynasties

When the Han dynasty fell from power in A.D. 220, a long period of war and disunity began. Many northern Chinese fled south to the Chang valley. From then on, the Chang valley would be the heartland of China.

More than 300 years after the fall of the Hans, China finally was reunited. A new dynasty—the Sui (swih)—ruled from 589 to 618. Its emperors widened and deepened existing canals. They constructed a system known as the Grand Canal to connect China's two big rivers, the Chang and the Yellow. Now, in times of famine, rice or wheat could be shipped easily to needy areas.

After a period of disorder, the Tang dynasty came to power. It ruled from 618 to 906. During this period there was a woman ruler, the Empress Wu (690–704). She was China's only female emperor.

Under Genghis Khan, Mongol forces swept across China and Central Asia. Their furious assaults kept China under Mongol rule for centuries. In this picture, Genghis Khan attacks a Chinese city.

The Tang emperors gained control of Tibet, extending China's western border into western Asia. Their capital, Changan, swelled to two million people. It was the world's largest city at that time. Chinese civilization under the Tang so impressed the Japanese and Koreans that they began to imitate it.

A new period of civil war followed the collapse of the Tang dynasty in 907. The Song (soong) dynasty (960–1279) managed to restore unity.

During the Tang and Song periods, China built large new irrigation works and improved crop yields. More and more people moved to cities. By 1100, China had at least ten urban areas with a million or more people. New inventions like the compass and the hydraulic clock came into use.

However, not all changes were for the better. A new practice of binding women's feet began. In childhood, girls' feet were wrapped tightly to keep the bones from growing normally. The process was painful and left women almost crippled. But their feet looked small and dainty, which men liked.

Mongols in China

The Great Wall could not protect China against the fierce cavalry from the northern plains. These nomads, called Mongols, attacked and conquered China. Then they swept west across Asia and into central Europe. Never in all of history has a single group conquered so much territory.

Genghis and Kublai Khan Led by a warrior named Genghis Khan (JEHNG•gihs KAHN), the Mongols sacked Beijing in 1215. They destroyed other

---

On Assignment. . .

Write a scene about a stranger who visits China during one of the dynasties. What things does the stranger notice? Why do they stand out?

---

cities, pushing deep into China. After Genghis Khan died, his sons became khans, or rulers.

Genghis's grandson Kublai Khan extended the Mongol conquests in China. By 1279, all of China was ruled by Kublai Khan from his capital in Beijing (bay•JIHNG). Kublai Khan founded the Yuan (yoo•AN) dynasty.

Now, all of China was under foreign rule. The Mongols brought in outsiders to run the government. However, in time they did adopt many of the ways of China.

Marco Polo With vast stretches of Asia under the strong control of the Mongols, travel became safer. Traders went back and forth along the Silk Road. A young man from Venice, in present-day Italy, arrived in Beijing. The man, Marco Polo, stayed for 17 years (1275–1292). When he returned to Europe, he told many strange and wonderful stories about China. China had all sorts of things that Europe did not have. It had paper money. It had a postal system. It had black rocks that could be burned for heat. These black rocks were chunks of coal.

After Kublai Khan's death, disorder spread. The Chinese were unhappy under the Mongols, whom they considered to be foreigners. Finally, rebels drove the Mongols out.

Ming Dynasty

With the downfall of the Mongols, China once again had a Chinese ruler. His name was Hong Wu. He had been the leader of the rebels that drove out the Mongols. He founded the Ming dynasty, which ruled China from 1368 to 1644.

After beating back the Mongols, the Ming emperors extended their control north of the Great Wall. One emperor, Yong Le, sent a fleet of ships across the Indian Ocean. The fleet visited India, Africa, and the Persian Gulf, trading with people throughout the region.

Today the Ming era is best remembered for its fine porcelain jars and bowls. Ming artisans strove for perfection, using precise skill and beautiful, detailed paintings to create priceless works of art.

Manchus in China

The decline of the Ming dynasty led to war, defeat, and a new period of foreign rule. Like the Mongols, the new rulers were from the north. This time they were Manchus, from Manchuria.

Unlike the Mongols, the Manchus adopted Chinese ways and used Chinese officials to help run the government. They started the Qing (chihng) dynasty, which ruled China from 1644 to 1912. During that time, Manchu rulers extended China's borders. Among the new territories was the island of Taiwan.

Section 1 Review

1. What did it mean for a ruler to lose "the Mandate of Heaven"?
2. **Summarizing** Summarize the rule of one of the dynasties you have read about in this section. Be sure to include at least two of the dynasty's accomplishments.

SECTION 2

Europeans in China

How did European control cause great resentment among the Chinese?

The Chinese believed that their civilization was superior to all others. They called China "Zhonghua," or Middle Kingdom, meaning it was at the center of the universe. But during the Qing dynasty, China's peace was disturbed.

China and Its Neighbors

Most of China's neighbors agreed that China was superior. Some neighboring lands had been defeated by China in war. Others agreed to trade only with China. They became part of China's **tribute system**. They made regular payments, called tribute, to China's emperors. The tribute was a kind of tax that kept the neighbors in good standing.

Imagine the scene in the court at Beijing when visitors arrived to pay tribute. A ceremony called the **kowtow** took place. The foreigners knelt down in a deep bow. Then they lay flat five times, touching their noses to the floor, without looking up. The purpose of the ceremony was to show humility before a superior. In fact, this ceremony was also performed by an emperor to *his* superiors—his parents and Heaven.

Europeans in China

The kowtow ceremony seemed strange to Europeans who visited China. They did not think like Confucius and did not see China as the center of the universe.

In 1514, Portuguese ships arrived at the southern port of Guangzhou. Soon the Portuguese had a settlement nearby, at Macao. Christian missionaries also came. Most were Roman Catholics of the Jesuit order. Matteo Ricci (REE•chee), for example, set up a mission in Beijing in 1601. Reports that the Jesuits sent home made Europeans curious to know more about China.

A Portuguese visitor to Guangzhou in 1556 reported, "It is customary to offer a visitor a kind of warm water which they call tea." In 1610, traders brought tea from China to Europe. It was immensely popular. The demand for tea spurred interest in China and its other products, including silk.

The Opium War To pay for China's tea and silk, British traders offered the Chinese opium. This habit-forming drug was produced from poppies grown in India.

During the first half of the 1800s, British ships carried opium to Guangzhou.

The drug turned many Chinese into opium addicts. So China's emperor tried to stop the importing of opium. In 1839, Chinese officials seized 20,000 chests of opium from the traders and dumped them into a river. To Britain, that—along with other incidents—became cause for war.

The Opium War lasted from 1839 to 1842. China's military power was no match for Britain's. In the distant past, Europe had lagged far behind China in technology. Beginning in the 1500s, however, European science had made great strides. Britain had modern weapons and easily won the war.

Unequal Treaties After 1842, Britain forced China to sign a series of treaties. Before the treaties, China had required all European trade to pass through Guangzhou. According to the treaties, China had to open more ports and give Britain special trading privileges. China gave Britain a lease on Hong Kong. This gave Britain complete control over China's most important port.

The United States, France, and other nations also exploited China's weakness. They, too, demanded and won special privileges. Some foreign nations gained control over areas of Chinese territory.

Rebellion and Reform

The Chinese people hated the unequal treaties. Some Chinese rebelled against their weak government. The Taiping Rebellion (1850–1864) almost succeeded. Rebels seized the city of Nanjing and demanded reforms such as land for every family.

Foreign nations were as surprised by the rebellion as the Manchu rulers were. Western soldiers helped the Manchus put down the uprising. Some 20 million people died, making it one of history's most brutal rebellions.

Chinese leaders saw that China would have to modernize to protect itself against the foreigners. They borrowed Western tech-nology. They built factories to make steel and constructed railroads. But China remained very weak.

Other nations began to carve up Chinese territory. Russia took part of Manchuria. Japan seized Taiwan and Korea. Japan and the European nations demanded special trading rights in certain areas of China. Each country had its own sphere of influence, an area in which it was dominant.

The United States had no sphere of influence, and it opposed the dominance of other nations. In 1899, the United States asked other nations to agree to equal trading rights within China for all. Rather than risk the anger of the United States, the nations reluctantly accepted this agreement, called the Open Door policy.

Boxer Rebellion

More unrest began in 1900, organized by a secret group called the Boxers. They were called the Boxers because one of the group's rituals involved shadow boxing, which was supposed to protect them against harm. The Boxers objected to the activities of Christian missionaries and other foreigners in China.

In 1900, the Boxers went on a rampage, killing 250 foreigners. In Beijing, they surrounded a building in which 1,000 foreigners and 3,000 Chinese Christians sought safety. For two months they kept the building under siege. Then a seven-nation military force crushed the rebellion.

China's rulers had secretly backed the Boxers. They were forced to pay large sums of money to foreign nations whose citizens had been killed.

On Assignment . . .

Write a scene in which Chinese people react to outsiders who have come to their country. The scene should explain why the Chinese feel as they do.

Between 1900 and 1910, China's rulers modernized the army. They allowed Chinese students to go abroad to study. But the reforms did not deal with China's problems. Time had run out for the Qing dynasty.

Section 2 Review

1. Why did the Boxers rebel?
2. **Determining Cause and Effect** What was the cause of the Opium War? What was its effect?

SECTION 3

Nationalists and Communists

How was China torn by civil war during the first half of the 20th century?

In 1912, Chinese opponents of the empire overthrew the Qing dynasty and established a **republic**, a government selected by the people. China entered a period of turmoil that would last almost 40 years as two main forces competed for power. They were the Nationalists and the Communists. In 1949, the Communists won, and China came under Communist rule.

Sun Yat-sen

The "Father of the Chinese Republic" was Sun Yat-sen (soon yaht•SEHN), the first leader of the Nationalists. As a young man, Sun had studied medicine. He had wanted China to become a modern, democratic nation. He started a secret society whose members wrote an oath with their own blood to work together to overthrow the Manchus.

Overthrowing the Empire

Sun's first plot against the Manchus failed in 1895, and he had to flee China. Sun trav-

Sun Yat-sen led the struggle to oust the Manchu emperors. In 1912, Sun became the first president of the Chinese republic.

eled to Japan and to many other countries. He collected money for the revolution from Chinese who lived abroad. In London, agents of the Chinese government kidnapped him, but he managed to escape to the United States.

One day in October 1911, Sun was in Denver, Colorado. He saw a surprising story in a newspaper. Revolution was sweeping China. Quickly, he returned home.

After ten failed attempts, the revolution in China had begun. In one province after another, uprisings led to the overthrow of the Manchus.

The revolutionaries chose Sun to be the first president of their new republic. However, he served for only a few weeks. Many officials shared Sun's desire to oust the Manchus. But they were suspicious of Sun's goal of democracy and social change. To help keep the nation united, Sun stepped aside. A leading general took his place as president.

On February 12, 1912, the Manchu emperor gave up control of China. The Qing dynasty had fallen.

The Nationalists

With elections scheduled for 1913, Sun and his supporters started a political party. They called it the Guomindang (GWOH•mihn•dahng), or Nationalist party.

The Guomindang won a majority of seats in the legislature. But the generals did not want to share power with the Nationalists. They had a leading Nationalist assassinated and banned the party. Once again, Sun had to flee.

By 1916, China faced civil war. Military leaders known as **warlords** took control. They ruled their regions without regard to the weak central government.

Chiang Kai-shek

The Nationalists organized an army to fight for power. One of its ablest leaders was a young officer named Chiang Kai-shek (chyang keye•SHEHK). Chiang rose rapidly within the Nationalist ranks.

Sun Yat-sen, who had returned, wanted to build the Nationalist army into a powerful fighting force. In 1923, he turned to Russia for money and weapons. Russia had had its own revolution in 1917. It was now part of a Communist nation, called the Soviet Union.

Chiang Kai-shek and other soldiers went to Russia for training. The Soviet Union also sent agents to China to support the Guomindang. Soon after Sun Yat-sen died in 1925, Chiang Kai-shek became the leader of the Nationalists.

Mao Zedong and the Communists

Chiang's leading rival among the people who wanted to modernize China was Mao Zedong (mow zuh•DOONG). Born into a family of peasants, Mao rebelled against the harsh ways of his father. He also rejected Confucianism and his mother's Buddhist faith. In 1911, at the age of 18, Mao joined China's revolutionaries.

Mao and Communism At this time, China was bubbling with political ideas. Eager young Chinese explored many different ways of thinking. One of them was Marxism, a political and economic theory based on the ideas of Karl Marx. Marxism was the basis of communism.

Marxism taught that mistreated people could take control of their own fates. Marx, who was German, had written mainly about industrial workers. However, China had few industries and few skilled workers. Most of its people were peasants. For Mao, organizing the peasants was the way to build a Marxist society in China.

United Front When a Chinese Communist party was formed at a meeting in 1921, Mao was there. Soviet advisers encouraged the Communists to form an alliance with the Nationalists against the warlords. Soon the Communists fought side by side with the Nationalist army.

But it was an uneasy alliance. The Nationalists and Communists were competing for power. In 1927, Chiang turned on the Communists. He sent his soldiers into Shanghai against the Communists. After bloody fighting, the Nationalists seized Shanghai. Chiang split with the Soviet Union and sent the Soviet advisers home.

Civil War

In 1928, the Nationalists captured Beijing and took control of China's government. They moved the capital to Nanjing. The Nationalists had beaten most of the warlords. Now they could concentrate their attacks on the Communists.

Mao and other leaders built a Communist army, which they called the Red Army. Most of their recruits were peasants from the countryside. Between 1930 and 1934, the Nationalists attacked the Communists' main base five times. Four times the Red Army defeated the attackers. Finally, however, the Red Army had to flee. In what became known as the Long March (page 232), Mao led the Red Army deep into China's interior.

Japanese Invasion

With China in turmoil, Japan saw an opportunity for invasion. It sent an army into Manchuria in 1931. Manchuria had been part of China, but Japan took it away and called it Manchukuo (man•JOH•kwoh). Then Japanese troops crossed into northern China.

Second United Front The Nationalists in China were alarmed. They believed that the Japanese were a more dangerous enemy than China's Communists. In December 1936, a band of soldiers kidnapped Chiang Kai-shek and refused to release him until he had agreed to form an alliance with the Communists against the Japanese. The Nationalists and Communists stopped fighting one another.

Resisting Japan In July 1937, the Japanese began a full-scale invasion of China. They seized Beijing, Shanghai, and Nanjing. They killed 100,000 people in Nanjing. Japan took control of much of China's coast and many of its industries.

But China's immense size helped the Chinese Nationalists. The Chinese

In the 1930s, the Japanese attacked China. In this picture, Chinese farmers, who were organized by the Communists, gather spears to defend against the Japanese in 1937.

On Assignment . . .

Write a scene for your skit in which Nationalists and Communists debate whether to join in a "united front" against the Japanese.

government withdrew to Chongqing (joong•CHIHNG), 1,200 miles (1,930 km) inland. To keep the economy going, people took factories apart and moved them to safer places in the interior.

World War II

Before World War II broke out in Europe in 1939, China received help from Britain and the other nations who made up the Allied forces. The war spurred the Allies to offer more help. Japan was an ally of Germany and Italy in the war.

In December 1941, the Japanese launched a surprise attack on the United States at Pearl Harbor in Hawaii. That brought U.S. forces into the war. Soon, Americans were transporting supplies across the mountains into western China. Later, U.S. fliers used bases in China to attack Japan.

Despite the urgency of the war, Nationalists and Communists jockeyed for power within China. U.S. diplomats tried to help the two sides settle their differences and concentrate on fighting the Japanese. It did not work.

World War II ended in 1945 with Japan's defeat. China was saved from the Japanese, but the war between the Nationalists and the Communists resumed almost at once.

Section 3 Review

1. Who were the Nationalists and who were the Communists?

2. **Making Inferences** Why do you think the Soviet Union and the Nationalists cooperated during the 1920s?

The Long March

The Communists' Red Army was trapped in October 1934. Nationalist troops surrounded the Communist base in Kiangsi (jang•see) province. Food and supplies were running out. Millions of civilians and tens of thousands of Communist soldiers had already died.

Breaking Out

In a last-ditch effort, 100,000 Red Army soldiers and their families broke through the Nationalist lines. But where could they find safety? With the Nationalists close on their heels, they began a desperate flight. Their journey lasted more than a year and covered 5,000 miles (8,000 km). This journey became known as the Long March. Only a small portion of those who started finished the Long March.

"As the days went by, there was less and less to eat," one of the survivors recalled. "After our grain was finished, we ate the horses, and then we lived on wild vegetables. When even the wild vegetables were finished, we ate our leather belts. After that we had to march on empty stomachs."

During the course of its march, the Red Army passed through 11 provinces. It crossed 18 mountain ranges and 24 rivers. Time and again, it fought battles against the Nationalists. How could the weary travelers keep on? "By keeping our two feet going," Mao said.

Crossing the Tatu River

When they came to the Tatu River, the fleeing army faced one of its greatest challenges. At this spot, 100,000 Taiping rebels had been cornered and killed in the 1860s. The river roared through a deep gorge, or canyon. The only way across was an old bridge suspended by 16 chains. Nationalist soldiers with machine guns guarded the bridge from a cliff on the far bank, while others removed half of the wooden planks in the 300-foot-long bridge.

Barefoot Red Army soldiers grabbed the chains and started to swing across. Machine gun fire raked the bridge. Some of the Red Army soldiers plunged to their deaths on the rocks below.

Chinese Communist leaders, including Mao Zedong, at center, review Communist troops during the Long March.

Flames roared up as the Nationalists set fire to the remaining floorboards. Somehow, a few soldiers made it through the flames. One soldier lobbed a grenade at the machine gunners, while others stormed the Nationalist positions.

The Red Army made it across, but there was no time to rest. The soldiers hurried on over a rugged mountain.

In October 1935, the Red Army reached a safe haven in northern China. From there, it carried on the fight against the Nationalists.

Future Leaders

During the Long March, Mao Zedong became the Communists' top leader. His comrades on the march included many of the men who later became China's leaders. They often told of the hardships of the Long March.

Case Study Review

1. Who went on the Long March and why?

2. **Predicting Consequences** How do you think the Long March affected Chinese Communist leaders as they struggled to gain control of the country?

REVIEWING CHAPTER 17

I. Reviewing Vocabulary

Match each word on the left with the correct definition on the right.

1. republic

2. bureaucracy

3. dynasty

4. warlord

a. a family of rulers

b. a local ruler and military leader

c. a government led by officials who are elected by the people they govern

d. a group of officials who do the daily chores of government

II. Understanding the Chapter

Answer the questions below on a separate sheet of paper.

1. Which aspects of ancient Chinese civilization still influence Chinese life today?

2. How was the rule of the Manchus different from that of the Mongols?

3. Explain the change in China's relations with Europe after the Opium War.

4. Why is Sun Yat-sen considered a key figure in 20th-century China?

III. Building Skills: Identifying Primary and Secondary Sources

Documents that are produced by people who were present at a historic event are called *primary sources*. An example would be a diary entry by a soldier about a battle he experienced. Writings by historians who depend on others for their information are called *secondary sources*. On a piece of paper, make two columns with the headings "Primary Source" and "Secondary Source." List each item below under the correct heading. Beside each item, give a brief explanation for your choice.

1. a description of the Long March written by Mao Zedong

2. an oracle bone with ancient writings scratched into it

3. notes by Sun Yat-sen describing his plans for a modern, democratic China

4. an encyclopedia article about the Long March

IV. Working Together

Work with a small group. Choose a Chinese dynasty and write a report that lists important facts about your chosen dynasty. Include people, events, and developments in Chinese life. Draw a picture to illustrate the dynasty you selected.

On Assignment. . .

Writing and Performing a Skit: Write a script that ties all of the scenes of your skit together. The script should explain important events in Chinese history. Review the scenes to make sure that you have your facts right. Ask other students to perform your skit for the class.

CHAPTER 18

The History of Japan and Korea

What significant events shaped the Japanese and Korean nations?

At the city of Heia, Japanese emperors ruled over a court where a new Japanese culture was created. Here, a noble is shown visiting the emperor.

Looking at Key Terms

- **clans** groups of related families
- **regent** someone who rules in the place of a child
- **feudalism** a social system based on ties of loyalty and service
- **vassal** under the feudal system, a person who served a more powerful lord
- **samurai** a member of Japan's traditional warrior class
- **shogun** a military leader who ruled in the name of the Japanese emperor
- **daimyo** a powerful local leader under the Japanese feudal system
- **truce** a halt to fighting in a war
- **demilitarized zone** an area of land in which armed troops are not permitted

On Assignment...

Writing a Journal: As you read this chapter, picture yourself as a participant in Japanese and Korean history. Keep a journal in which you write about the events that you witness. At the end of the chapter, you will combine your entries into one final journal entry.

235

SECTION 1

The Dawn of Japan

Why did Japan's early emperors have relatively little power?

In the year 1284, a great storm lashed the shores of Japan. The storm whipped the sea's waves into a frenzy. Boats sank, and with them tens of thousands of Mongol soldiers who were trying to invade and conquer Japan. The storm destroyed the Mongol fleet and allowed Japanese soldiers to defeat the invaders.

The storm saved Japan. It became known as the kamikaze (kah•mih•KAH•zee), or "wind from the gods."

Japanese students know that story well. It relates an event that happened more than 700 years ago, yet it seems fresh. To the Japanese, it is a reminder of how they have been protected by the seas.

The seas surround Japan and isolate it. Outside influences have affected Japan, to be sure. But the country's isolation has let it develop a unique way of life.

Japan's Beginnings

The first people reached present-day Japan from the Asian mainland as much as 150,000 years ago. By 8000 B.C., people in Japan were using clay to make pots and jars. Another group of people moved in from Asia about 250 B.C. They became the ancestors of today's Japanese. Family ties were strong among the early Japanese. Groups of related families, or **clans**, ran their own territories.

Japan's First Emperor In about A.D. 400, Japan's first emperor was installed. He was a ruler of a powerful clan that had joined with other clans to conquer their neighbors. Under him, Japan became more unified. The first emperor started a ruling

On Assignment...

From your village along the coast, you have seen the Mongol ships being battered and sunk by the kamikaze. Write about it in your journal.

dynasty. A member of that same dynasty heads Japan today.

From the first, the emperor was more than a political leader. He was also the leader of the Japanese religion, Shinto. The Japanese people believed that the emperor was descended from a sun goddess. However, emperors were not all-powerful. The clans controlled their own lands and could do as they pleased.

Chinese Influences In A.D. 552, monks from China introduced Buddhism to Japan. The Japanese continued to practice Shinto alongside Buddhism, merging elements of the two religions.

Other Chinese ideas and practices spread to Japan as well. The Japanese adapted Chinese characters to the Japanese language. Nobles wore Chinese robes. They admired Chinese paintings and music.

Japanese rulers tried to adopt the Chinese system of government, with its strong central power. Like the Chinese, they started a bureaucracy. They tried to bring local leaders under their control. But local leaders remained far more powerful in Japan than in China.

Powers Behind the Throne One of the major problems in the dynastic system is that rulers may die with no adult children. A ruler's young child cannot handle the affairs of state. So someone takes charge until the son or daughter grows up. That someone is called a **regent**. In 866, a member of the wealthy Fujiwara (foo•gee•WAH•rah) family became a regent in Japan and then seized power. Members of the Fujiwara family married members of the

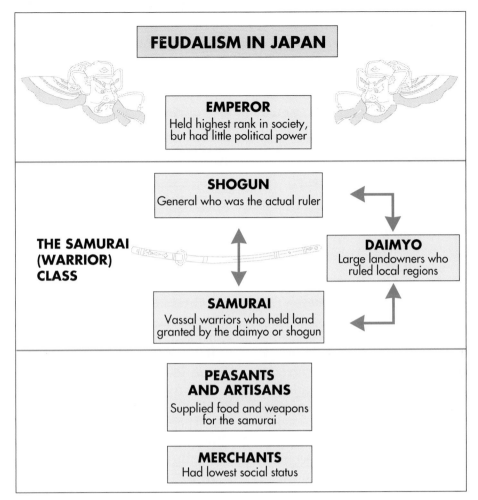

FEUDALISM IN JAPAN

EMPEROR
Held highest rank in society, but had little political power

THE SAMURAI (WARRIOR) CLASS

SHOGUN
General who was the actual ruler

DAIMYO
Large landowners who ruled local regions

SAMURAI
Vassal warriors who held land granted by the daimyo or shogun

PEASANTS AND ARTISANS
Supplied food and weapons for the samurai

MERCHANTS
Had lowest social status

In the 1600s, Japan's shoguns established a system of rule that kept order in Japan for three centuries. From the emperor to the peasants, everyone's role was carefully defined.

emperor's family. For 300 years, the Fujiwaras held the real power.

During that time, Japan gradually cut its ties with China. It encouraged its own writers and artists. One was a noblewoman named Lady Murasaki, who was one of the Fujiwaras. She wrote a famous novel, *The Tale of Genji* (GHEN•jee), about a Japanese prince. It is considered one of Japan's greatest novels.

Japanese Feudalism

Think of a medieval castle. Knights on horseback guard the gates. They wear heavy armor and long swords. The castle might be in Europe. Or it might be in Japan. For

Japan, like Europe, went through a period of **feudalism**.

Feudalism was a social system based on ties of loyalty and service. Powerful men, called lords, granted protection and favors to less powerful men, called **vassals**. In return, the vassals fought on behalf of the lords. Feudal society had no strong central government. Rival lords fought to keep the lands they had—and to get more land.

Samurai, Shoguns, and Daimyo

In Japan, the lords and vassals were descendants of the old clans. They included a new warrior class known as **samurai** (SAM•uh•reye). During the Fujiwara period

(858–1159), the Japanese government grew weak as the power of landowners grew. Landowners formed private armies to defend their estates.

A civil war broke out after the death of the emperor in 1156. Rival groups of lords fought for power until 1185. The leader of the winning group, Minamoto Yorimoto (yoh•ree•MOH•toh), became more powerful than the emperor, who appointed Yorimoto as military commander, or **shogun** (SHOH•gun). For the next 700 years, shoguns and the warrior class ran Japan.

Life for the common people was hard under the shoguns. Warring bands of samurai often raged across the countryside. This encouraged two Mongol invasions. They ended with the kamikaze of 1284.

A period of civil war in the 1400s weakened the shoguns. Powerful warrior groups took control of the provinces. The leaders of these groups were called **daimyo** (DEYEM•yoh), or "great names." They became the real rulers of Japan.

Despite all the fighting, Japan's economy was growing. Market towns became cities. Japanese goods were shipped to China. There they were sold for coins or for works of art.

Return to Unity

A new period of peace opened in the late 1500s. But it began with a war. One of Japan's leading daimyo captured the imperial capital, Kyoto. Then he was killed. One of his generals, Hideyoshi Toyotomi (hee•day•YOH•shee toh•yoh•TOH•mee), took control. He was Japan's first leader from a poor family. Hideyoshi forced all rivals to become his subjects.

Changing Japanese Society

Hideyoshi made it illegal for peasants to own swords. Before then, peasants had served as soldiers. Under Hideyoshi, only samurai could be armed.

Hideyoshi also helped to strengthen the central government. He minted new coins and made them Japan's only currency. He ordered a land reform that weakened the daimyo. Hideyoshi's changes made Japan a stronger and more unified nation.

When Hideyoshi died, powerful daimyo fought for power. The winner, Tokugawa Ieyasu (toh•koo•GAH•wah ee•ay•YAH•soo), became shogun in 1603. He and his successors ran Japan until 1867. The period of their rule is called the Tokugawa shogunate.

Japan and the Outside World

During the early Tokugawa years, Japan reached out to the world. Japanese merchants traded with many Asian nations. European merchants came to Japan.

Roman Catholic missionaries had reached Japan in the 1540s. By the early 1600s, they had converted to Christianity more than 200,000 Japanese, including some daimyo. The shogun became worried. He feared the Christians might help his enemies among the daimyo.

In a startling change, the shogun decided to close Japan off to foreign influences. In 1614, all missionaries were ordered to leave. Japanese Christians were killed. Then the shogun barred foreign travel. In 1641, he stopped foreign trade. Only a small Dutch trading post at Nagasaki was left. Japan entered a period of isolation that lasted for more than 200 years.

Turning its energies inward, Japan had an era of peace and stability. Many educated samurai became writers, artists, and painters.

Section 1 Review

1. How was Japan influenced by China?

2. **Identifying Relationships** How did the power of local leaders affect the imperial government of Japan?

Japan Takes a Leap

Why did Japan suddenly decide to modernize its society in the 1860s?

Under the late Tokugawa shoguns, it was a crime for any Japanese to leave the country. That did not stop a young man named Ito Hirobumi (ee•toh hih•roh•BOO•mee), however. Ito sneaked aboard a British ship at Nagasaki. He worked as a deckhand until he reached England. There, he studied science. When Ito returned home, he helped shape a new Japan whose isolation ended suddenly in the 1800s.

Commodore Perry's Visit

The Japanese called them the "black ships." They were iron warships of the U.S. Navy. In July 1853, four black ships sailed into a Japanese harbor. The leader of the Americans, Matthew C. Perry, had brought a list of demands. He told the shogun to open Japan's ports to outside trade. The United States wanted to benefit from trade with Japan.

The shogun had seen what had happened to China after the Opium War. He knew that he could not overcome Western arms. When Perry returned in 1854, the shogun agreed to allow trade with the United States.

European nations sent ships, too. Like China, Japan signed "unequal treaties" with the major powers.

On Assignment. . .

Imagine that you are Japanese. Write a journal entry telling your reaction to the entry of "black ships" and to Commodore Perry's demands.

Finely dressed women in the court during the Tokugawa shogunate were not allowed to deal with the serious issues that confronted the country.

Many Japanese opposed the changes. They thought that Japan had been shamed. Powerful daimyo joined with the emperor to overthrow the shogun in 1868. Then new leaders began to modernize Japan so that it could defend itself against other nations.

The Meiji Restoration

In 1868, a 15-year-old emperor, Mutsuhito (moo•tsoo•HEE•toh), took the throne. Today, he is known by the name Meiji (may•jee), which was applied after his death in 1912. Because the emperor's power was being restored, this period is called the Meiji Restoration.

Meiji moved the imperial capital to the city of Edo, where the shoguns had lived. Meiji gave the city a new name—Tokyo, which means "eastern capital."

The emperor was a strong supporter of reform. Change came to almost every aspect of Japanese life. The reformers borrowed ideas from many other countries. However, they changed those ideas to fit Japanese ways.

The first reform was reducing the power of the daimyo. The reformers put an end

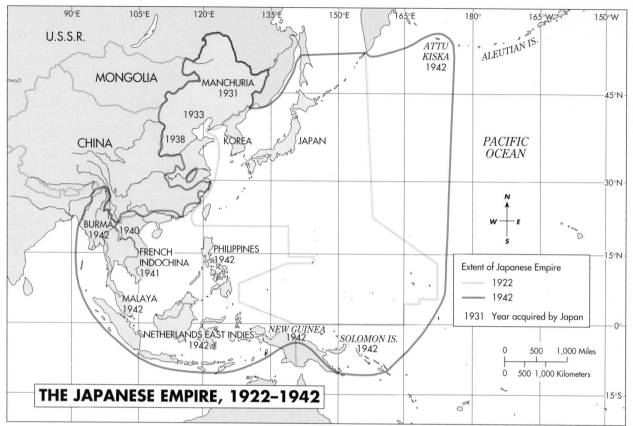

THE JAPANESE EMPIRE, 1922–1942

Extent of Japanese Empire
— 1922
— 1942
1931   Year acquired by Japan

Location and Place   In the 1920s, Japan began an aggressive policy that spread its control over East and Southeast Asia. How far south did the Japanese empire stretch in 1942?

to the feudal system. They started a modern army. They turned the samurai into professional soldiers who were paid by the government.

Another reform was strengthening the economy. New industries were started. Steel mills, textile factories, and railroads were built quickly. The reformers wanted a strong army and navy, and those required modern industries.

The reformers set up new schools that boys and girls had to attend. Although the schools followed a French model, the teaching was Japanese. Teachers taught such lessons as: "Honor your parents" and "Obey the emperor."

Ito, who had sneaked away to England as a young man (see page 239), achieved a position of importance in the new Japan. He headed a group that drew up Japan's first constitution. The emperor approved

it in 1889. Under the constitution, Japan became the first Asian nation to have a parliament.

Japanese Imperialism

Japan wanted colonies just as the European nations did. It had few natural resources. So it looked to nearby lands for supplies of coal, iron, and other needs.

Japan competed with China and Russia for influence in Korea. In 1895, Japan defeated China in a war. As a result, Japan gained special rights in Korea. It also took Taiwan from China.

Next, Japan fought Russia for control of Manchuria. Japan's victory in the Russo-Japanese War of 1904–1905 startled the Western nations. They were surprised that Japan had become so powerful. The victorious Japanese took over Russia's railroads and other interests in Manchuria.

In 1910, Japan made Korea part of the Japanese empire. Now Japan, like Britain, France, and the United States, controlled other nations and peoples.

New Military Adventures By the 1920s, Japan had become one of the world's major powers. A new emperor, Hirohito (heer•oh•HEE•toh), came to the throne in 1926. Japan's future seemed bright.

The Great Depression As it modernized, Japan had tied itself into the world economy. However, in 1929, that economy collapsed. A worldwide depression began. In a depression, economic activity slows down and people are thrown out of work.

Japan's sales to other nations dropped. Without income, the Japanese could not pay for the raw materials they needed.

On September 2, 1945, aboard the U.S. battleship *Missouri*, Japanese officers and diplomats signed the surrender document that ended World War II.

How could Japan save itself? Some of its military leaders had an answer. They wanted Japan to expand its colonial empire to gain more resources. They wanted to seize control of countries throughout East Asia.

War in Asia

In 1931, military leaders found an excuse to go to war. The Japanese army seized Manchuria from China. Japan's government opposed the seizure, but the army decided to act anyway.

In the years ahead, there was great turmoil in Japan. Assassins killed several leaders who opposed the military. Japan plunged into a full-scale war with China in 1937.

Other nations protested. The United States stopped the sale of military goods to Japan. But Japan continued its aggression. In 1940, it seized Indochina (see the map on page 240) from France. The United States then cut off shipments of oil to Japan.

World War II

Japanese leaders saw the actions of the United States as a threat to Japanese expansion. On December 7, 1941, Japan launched a surprise attack on Pearl Harbor, Hawaii, where the U.S. Pacific Fleet was anchored. Much of the fleet was sunk. Japanese forces also invaded the Philippine Islands and such British and Dutch colonies as Singapore, Malaya, and Indonesia.

Those attacks brought the United States into World War II. The war had started in 1939 when Nazi Germany attacked Poland, and Britain and France came to Poland's defense. In 1941, the United States joined Britain and France. The allies fought a two-part war. In Europe, they fought against Germany; in the Pacific, they fought against Japan.

The war in Europe ended with Germany's defeat in May 1945. Three months later, U.S. forces were massing for an invasion of Japan. U.S. leaders worried about how many Americans might die in the assault. In

August 1945, U.S. planes dropped atomic bombs on two Japanese cities: Hiroshima and Nagasaki. The bombs surprised the Japanese. They killed more than 200,000 people in two blinding flashes.

Knowing they had been beaten, Japanese leaders made the decision to surrender. On September 2, 1945, the war formally ended. From 1945 to 1951, U.S. troops occupied Japan.

Section 2 Review

1. How did the Meiji reforms change Japanese life?

2. **Analyzing Information** Describe Japanese foreign policy in the years from 1931 to 1941. What was Japan's goal?

SECTION 3

Korea's Beginnings

What was "the Hermit Kingdom"?

According to legend, Korea owes its existence to a god and a bear. The god turned the bear into a woman and married her. Her son, Tan-gun, became the father of the Korean people.

Early Kingdoms

The earliest recorded Korean kingdom began about 400 B.C. Called Choson, it was one of several small tribal kingdoms. China conquered Choson in 104 B.C. and set up colonies in Korea.

A Korean kingdom in northern Korea named Kogoryu (koh•goo•ryoh) destroyed the Chinese colonies about A.D. 100. Soon two other Korean kingdoms emerged in the south. The three kingdoms fought one another for hundreds of years.

During that time, Chinese culture was spreading through Korea. The ideas of Confucius were applied to government and family life. Many Koreans became Buddhists. The Korean kingdoms developed a small ruling class of people who owned tracts of land.

Korea Under One Rule

Finally, in 676, one kingdom, Silla, unified Korea. Its kings built great palaces and royal tombs. Like the Chinese, the Koreans created a strong bureaucracy to run the government. They adapted Chinese writing. The Koreans patterned their way of life on Chinese ways.

Two Dynasties

Another kingdom, Koryo, took over Silla in 935. The modern name *Korea* is derived from *Koryo*.

Koryo Dynasty Wang Kon, the first ruler of Koryo, founded the Koryo dynasty in 935. The Koryo rulers made Buddhism the state religion.

Mongols invaded Korea in 1231. For 100 years, Mongol armies controlled the country. Yet the Koreans continued to make cultural and industrial advances. In 1234, they invented movable metal type for printing.

Yi Dynasty By the late 1300s, the Mongols had been driven out of China. Korea's new king ordered his army to attack China. Instead, the army commander, Yi Song-gye (ee song•gee), seized power. The Yi dynasty that he started ruled Korea from 1392 to 1910.

The Hermit Kingdom

For hundreds of years, Korea had little to do with the outside world, except China. Outsiders called it "the Hermit Kingdom."

This Korean scholar has spent his life studying the works of Confucius in the village of Hahoe, which is famous for its celebration of old Korean traditions.

Within Korea, leaders interpreted Confucius's teachings in a rigid way. They refused to accept new ideas. Thus, Korea was not prepared to face new challenges from the outside world.

Challenges From Outside

Japan attacked Korea in 1592. Its army intended to sweep through Korea and move on to China. Japanese troops captured Seoul and much of the peninsula.

Then China sent troops to help the Koreans. Buddhist monks and peasants fought the invaders. A Korean fleet attacked the Japanese navy. As a result of the attack, the Japanese had to withdraw from Korea.

The Europeans Arrive

Korea was still isolated from the rest of the world when Europeans arrived in the 1800s. Korean kings ejected Catholic missionaries. They had Korean Catholics killed. They tried to block foreign trade.

The Koreans made some attempts to modernize. However, Korea remained weak.

Korea expected China to defend it, but China was not strong enough. Like Japan and China, Korea signed unequal treaties with many nations.

Korea in the Japanese Empire

In 1910, Korea became a Japanese colony. The Japanese built roads and railways. They opened mines and industries. Their goal was to send these resources to Japan to supply the growing industries there.

Koreans found themselves second-class citizens in their own country. Korean farmers, for example, could not keep the rice they grew. Their rice was shipped to Japan.

The Japanese tried to stamp out Korea's way of life. They forced Korean families to take new, Japanese names. Schools taught Japanese language and history.

Japanese rule did modernize the Korean economy and bring improved health care. But the Koreans resented the Japanese, and tried to resist them.

In 1919, the Korean ruler, King Kojong, died. His funeral became a protest against Japanese rule. Japanese police killed 2,000 people. The leaders of the protest fled to China and split into rival groups.

Section 3 Review

1. How did the Koreans react to the coming of Europeans?
2. **Identifying Relationships** How did Chinese civilization influence Korea?

On Assignment . . .

You are a Korean who attends the funeral of King Kojong in 1919. Write in your journal about your reaction. Do you support the demonstrations? How do you feel about the Japanese reaction to the demonstrations?

SECTION 4

Korea Divided

How do the two Koreas differ?

The end of World War II brought sweeping change to Korea. But the nation did not regain independence as a united country.

Postwar Split

Because Korea had been ruled by Japan, its fate after the war was in the hands of the nations that defeated Japan. The Soviet Union was part of the alliance against Germany. But it did not declare war on Japan until the last days of the war.

Occupation The Soviet Union attacked Japanese forces in Korea on August 10, 1945. The Soviets occupied the northern half of the country. U.S. troops arrived in September to occupy the southern half. The dividing line between Soviet and U.S. forces was the 38th parallel.

For three years, the Soviet Union and the United States quarreled over this division. They also quarreled over what to do about Germany and Eastern Europe. Their dispute began the Cold War.

Division In 1947, the United Nations urged free elections for all of Korea. The Soviets said no. So in 1948, North and South Korea held separate elections.

The result was two separate governments. South Korea had a Western-style constitution; North Korea had a Communist government. In the North, a harsh Communist dictatorship was in power. In the South, the constitution called for democracy, but the government ran things as it liked.

The Korean War

In June 1950, North Korean soldiers poured across the 38th parallel to attack South Korea.

Many Surprises North Korea expected an easy victory because it had a far larger army. Moreover, its leaders did not expect U.S. forces to step in.

But U.S. forces did step in. President Harry Truman saw the attack as an attempt to expand world communism. The United States then persuaded the United Nations to sponsor an army to defend South Korea.

First, North Korean troops swept deep into South Korea. Then U.N. troops pushed the Communists back, deep into North Korea. Then Chinese troops helped defend North Korea. By 1951, the war had reached a stalemate.

The Korean War Ends A **truce**, an agreement to stop fighting, brought the war to a halt in 1953. The line between the two sides ran near the 38th parallel. A strip of land on both sides of the line was declared a **demilitarized zone** (DMZ). No armed troops were permitted in this area. It served as a peaceful boundary between the two countries. Today, troops still patrol the edges of this DMZ.

Effects of the War The war settled nothing. Yet it caused immense destruction in both parts of Korea. One home out of every three was destroyed. Almost three million Koreans died. A half million North Koreans fled to South Korea. The war left bitter distrust between the two Korean governments. Contacts between families divided by the border became impossible.

Section 4 Review

1. Why was Korea divided in 1945?
2. **Formulating Questions** Write two questions about the Korean War that you would like to ask an expert. Answer the questions based on the information in this section.

What's in a Korean Name?

An old Korean saying declares, "If you throw a stone from the top of Namsan [a mountain near Seoul], it will hit a Kim or a Lee." This saying recognizes a basic fact: Many Koreans share the same family names.

Kim and Lee (in English, *Lee* is also written *Rhee*) are the two most common Korean names. Actually, many last names have several regional variations. For example, there are the Andong Kims (the Kims whose ancestors are from Andong) and the Kimhae Kims (the Kims from Kimhae).

The way Koreans use names reflects the dominant role of men in Korea. Until Korea became a Japanese colony in 1910, women did not even have given names (like Karen or Christine). All they had were nicknames, like "Small-baby." Today, Korean women now have names. When they marry, they keep their own family name.

In U.S. society, the given name comes first and the family name comes last. In contrast, Koreans place the family name first and the given name last. So the leader Americans called Syngman Rhee was known to Koreans as Rhee Syngman.

Case Study Review

1. How do U.S. and Korean naming traditions differ?

2. **Analyzing Information** What does the fact that they did not have given names say about the status of women in traditional Korea?

On Assignment . . .

You are a Korean with American friends. Write a journal entry explaining the difference in the placement of family names and given names in the two countries.

REVIEWING CHAPTER 18

I. Reviewing Vocabulary

Match each word on the left with the correct definition on the right.

1. vassal
2. samurai
3. shogun
4. truce

a. a military leader who ruled in the name of the Japanese emperor
b. under the feudal system, a person who served a more powerful lord
c. a halt to fighting in a war
d. a member of Japan's traditional warrior class

II. Understanding the Chapter

Answer the questions below on a separate sheet of paper.

1. How did the visit of the "black ships" help bring the downfall of the Tokugawas in Japan?
2. Why did Japan adopt a policy of imperialism?
3. Why was Korea unprepared to face challenges from the outside world in the 1800s?
4. Describe the differences between North Korea and South Korea.

III. Building Skills: Reading a Map

Study the map on pages 596–597. Then answer the following questions:

1. What is the capital of South Korea?
2. What is the capital of North Korea?
3. What river separates North Korea from China?
4. What body of water separates Korea from Japan?

IV. Working Together

With a small group, create a poster that shows one major event of either Japanese or Korean history. When you are finished, display the posters on a bulletin board. Arrange the posters in chronological order.

On Assignment. . .

Writing a Journal: Assemble the journal that you wrote as you read this chapter. Check your spelling and grammar, then exchange journals with a classmate. After you have read each other's journals, share suggestions about ways to improve them. Revise your work, taking into account your partner's ideas.

CHAPTER 19

Changing Patterns of Life in East Asia

How do traditions affect life in East Asia today?

The Great Wall, which is 1,400 miles (2,240 km) long and 15 to 50 feet (5 to 15 m) high, was built to protect China from invaders. This picture shows a part of the Great Wall that is near Beijing.

Looking at Key Terms

- **meditate** to think deeply
- **reincarnation** being reborn many times
- **cooperative farm** a farm in which families join their lands and work together, sharing the output
- **dissent** opposition to a government's policies
- **divine** godlike
- **martial arts** arts and skills related to warfare
- **sumo** a Japanese form of wrestling
- **shaman** a priest or priestess who conducts ceremonies involving the worship of nature

On Assignment...

Conducting an Interview: Choose a partner for this chapter. You will take turns interviewing each other. At various points in the chapter, you will receive suggestions for topics for the interview. The person being interviewed will pretend to be from one of the countries in East Asia. The interviewer will ask questions about life in that country. At the end of this chapter, you will turn your notes into a polished interview that you will conduct in front of the class.

Tradition and Change in China

What traditions influenced Chinese life and how did the Communists change those traditions?

Li Chen was a bride at the age of six. Following the age-old Chinese custom, her parents had chosen her husband. Mao Zedong reached the age of 14 before his parents chose a wife for him. His bride was 20—almost half again as old as he was. This was in the early 1900s.

Li Chen and Mao Zedong hated many of China's traditions. Mao became leader of the Chinese Communist party. Li Chen became a general in the Communist army. After the Communists came to power in 1949, one of their first acts was to ban child marriages. They also brought many other changes to Chinese life.

Traditional Beliefs

To understand China, we must look first at the traditional ways that the Communists rebelled against. Chinese life has been deeply influenced by three sets of ideas. They are Confucianism, Daoism, and Buddhism. These beliefs do not contradict one another. A person can follow more than one belief at a time.

Confucianism About 2,500 years ago, Confucius established a moral code. Its two key rules are to obey and to respect: *Obey* your father and your ruler and *respect* others.

Confucius assumed that fathers ran the family and kings ran the country. He taught people to obey authority, whether the authority was a father or a ruler. People in authority had duties, too. By their good conduct, they were to set an example for others.

The ideas of Confucius built on older Chinese ideas, such as honoring ancestors.

They became so much a part of Chinese life that they were accepted without question. In Confucius's words: "Let the ruler be a ruler and the subject a subject."

Daoism Another wise man, called Lao-Tzu, lived at about the same time as Confucius. One day he grew tired of the evils of the kingdom of Zhou, so he climbed into an ox cart and left. At the border, a guard saw that he was a wise man and asked him to write down his teachings. So Lao-Tzu wrote the basic book of Daoism.

Daoism teaches people to follow the ***dao***, which is the way, or path, to perfection. It says, "Be in tune with nature. Free yourself of all desire. Accept what exists. Don't struggle to change things." A famous Daoist statement is: "Dao does nothing and yet there is nothing that is not done."

Buddhism Unlike the first two beliefs, Buddhism began outside of China. In Nepal, a prince named Siddhartha Gautama (gow•TAH•muh) was upset by the suffering he saw. He began to **meditate**, or think deeply. For 49 days he sat under a fig tree. After meditating, he understood life and suffering. His followers called him Buddha, "the Enlightened One."

Buddha taught what he called the four noble truths: (1) Life is painful. (2) Pain comes from desire. (3) The way to end pain is to end desire. (4) To achieve this goal, one follows the Eightfold Path—a set of rules for proper living.

In Buddha's home, Nepal, people believed that souls are reborn many times. This is called **reincarnation**. Buddha said that one could release one's soul from the chain of rebirths by ending desire.

Traditional Society

Because Confucius stressed the importance of obedience, strict lines were preserved between social classes. Scholars and thinkers were the most valued group. "Those who are born with the possession of knowledge are the highest class of men,"

During the "Great Leap Forward," college students take a break from harvesting. Mao sent students to the countryside in an attempt to break the power of the educated class.

Confucius said. Scholars ran the government bureaucracy. Other groups—nobles, peasants, merchants, and soldiers—had their assigned places.

Family Life In the traditional Chinese family, a father's word was law. Sons and daughters had to respect the father in all things. The father, in turn, showed respect to his own father and to his father's father. He often performed ceremonies in honor of his ancestors.

Frequently, several generations of a family lived together. The head of the family might be a grandfather. His sons and grandsons and their wives and children would be part of his family.

Role of Women Traditionally, women in China had few rights. Here is one woman's experience of marriage in the early 1900s: "I was sold to Tuan Fu-yin. I was sold in the same way you sell a goat. But my parents got a lot for me. Tuan's father had to take out a loan. That made the family nasty to me. I was forced to work hard in order to make the loan worthwhile."

Chinese families preferred boy babies to girls because boys would carry on the family name and later take care of their parents. Sometimes, girl babies were put to death.

Setting up Communism

When the Communists came to power in 1949, they quickly set in motion major changes in Chinese society.

The main instrument for these changes was the Communist party. Communist leaders decided party policy. Lower-level party officials made sure that the policy was carried out. Millions of people joined the party because they were eager to build a new China. Others joined to advance their own careers.

Mao Zedong was chairman of the Communist party. He was also China's head of state. With those two powerful positions, he imposed his vision of a "new China."

Change on the Farm

"I cannot weed all the weeds in my fields by myself," the farmer said. "It takes too long. Cooperation is better. Cooperation will make us strong."

Hunger and famine had been common in China. However, farmers all over China saw great changes after the Communists came to power. The changes aimed to boost food production because China had so many people to feed.

The first change was to break the power of the old landlords. Their large estates were broken up. Families who had no land received plots of their own. Many landlords were put on trial. Between 500,000 and 2 million landlords were put to death.

In the early 1950s, party officials urged farmers to join together in small groups. That way they could share equipment and help each other with weeding and other work. Soon after, family farms were merged into larger farms, called **cooperative farms**. Each family received a share of the cooperative farm's output. Some families benefited from the new system and supported it. Others resented not being able to work for themselves.

Change in Industry

Years of warfare had left China's economy in poor condition. The new government repaired the railroads. It rebuilt damaged factories. It set controls on prices.

At the same time, it put in place a Communist economic system. That meant that the state took control of business and industry. Government planners decided what goods to produce and how much to charge for them. They drew up a series of five-year plans. The plans set goals and listed the steps to carry them out.

The government focused on building up heavy industries like steel and chemicals. It downplayed consumer goods like stoves and bicycles. They could come later, the government said.

"Let a Hundred Flowers Bloom"

In 1956, Mao Zedong decided to relax controls on freedom of speech. The life of most Chinese had been improving. Apparently, Mao thought people were happy with the new China. In a speech, he borrowed a slogan from China's history. "Let a hundred flowers bloom," he said. "Let a hundred schools of thought contend."

However, Mao was in for a surprise. During 1957, an outpouring of **dissent**, or opposition to government policies, shocked Mao and other leaders. People wrote their criticisms on large posters that they put up in public places. Some criticized party officials. Others took aim at the party itself and the basic goals of communism. By 1958, party officials had ordered an end to the dissent. Many protesters were punished.

Section 1 Review

1. How did Confucian ideas affect the Chinese family?

2. **Understanding Points of View** How might some farmers benefit from joining cooperative farms? Why might other farmers resent them?

SECTION 2

Japan: Old and New

How do ancient traditions affect present-day life in Japan?

Shinto priests pounded on drums. They rang bells. They waved a wand over a young girl's head and prayed to the God of Wisdom. This Shinto ceremony aimed

---

On Assignment. . .

What kinds of criticisms might Chinese citizens have had? Write down some ideas for your own wall poster.

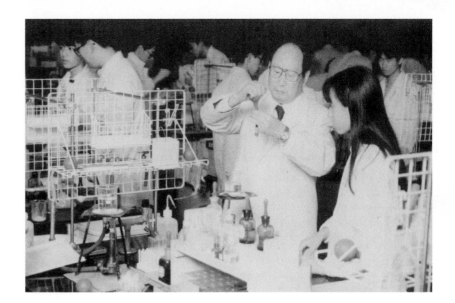

A high school student observes her chemistry teacher. Japan's emphasis on science and mathematics has led to the development of high-quality industrial products.

to assist the girl's preparations for a high school entrance exam. She was part of a thoroughly modern world. Yet she was drawing on Japan's ancient beliefs and practices for help. In Japan, as in China, old ways influence modern life.

Japanese Beliefs

Shinto is Japan's national religion. Its name means "the way of the gods." Shinto teaches that there are many gods or spirits. These spirits are part of nature. They live in trees and mountains, in the sun, the moon, and other natural places.

Shinto is often a part of official ceremonies. At one time, under the Shinto religion, the emperor was thought to be god-like. Since 1945, the government has said that the emperor is not **divine**.

Most Japanese homes contain a shrine to the Shinto spirits. People place offerings of things like rice and flowers there.

Most Japanese follow Buddhism as well as Shinto. Many homes have both Buddhist and Shinto shrines. It is common for a couple to be married by a Shinto priest and buried by a Buddhist priest.

For their ideas of right and wrong, the Japanese draw heavily on the ideas of Confucius. Like the Chinese, the Japanese

show great respect for older people. They honor those in authority. The Confucian belief that society should be well-ordered and that all people should know their place is very strong in Japan.

Influence of Feudalism

It is early morning. In clubs all over Japan, young men and women are practicing judo or karate. Some are doing judo kicks. Others are making the movements of *aikido* (eye•KIH•doh).

These **martial arts** are among the many traces of Japan's feudal past that survive into the present. Martial arts are related to war. They involve kicking, throwing, and other motions. They are viewed as a way of strengthening the soul as well the body. Many of the martial arts began among Japan's peasants who had no weapons to defend themselves.

The samurai code also influences present-day Japan. The code requires bravery, honor, and self-control. The duties of a warrior and his lord to one another live on. For example, workers show deep respect to superiors. People ask their bosses for advice, even about personal matters. In turn, bosses try to advance the interests of their workers through sponsoring sports teams and clubs.

Families and Women

In old Japan, as in old China, the father ruled the family. When a husband and wife walked in the street, the wife stayed a few paces behind. When the husband had friends to their home for a meal, the wife served quietly and ate later.

Since the end of World War II, the status of Japanese women has risen. Women can now vote. They can sue for divorce. One woman in two has a job outside the family.

Whether or not she has a job, the mother is in charge of raising the children. Middle-class fathers often spend the evening with business clients. They return home after the children are in bed.

Despite their progress, it is still hard for women to advance in Japanese firms. Women tend to have low-level jobs. Their pay is usually less than that of men. But movements for change are under way. Since the 1980s, Japan has had an "equal opportunity" law for women. Some women are becoming executives and managers.

Japanese Education

Do you like to sleep late on Saturday? Japanese students don't have that luxury. Schools are in session on Saturday morning. The six-day school week, with an eight-hour school day, is one of many signs that the Japanese take education very seriously.

Exams are difficult, and students study hard. Many high school students attend special "cram schools." Almost every day for four years, they put in extra hours of study. Only the students with the highest scores can enter the best universities.

Being admitted to one of the top-level colleges is the highest goal of most Japanese students. Competition for admission to these universities is fierce. A student who does not get into one of the chosen universities may be excluded from better jobs throughout his or her life. As a result, many Japanese students refer to this tense, strenuous period in their lives as "examination hell."

Japanese schools teach students to be loyal to a group. In many schools, Japanese students wear uniforms to build group feeling. The boys wear black military-style uniforms and the girls wear blue sailor outfits. If one member of a group excels, all members win praise. Group loyalty carries over into the workplace. Workers are expected to share ideas and cooperate. They may work overtime for no extra pay to help their group get its tasks done.

Literature and the Arts in Japan

Deeply rooted in Japanese culture is an appreciation of beauty and simplicity. Today, these traditions help to enrich Japanese life.

The tea ceremony is a good example. The simple motions of serving tea have become an art form. Participants carefully arrange their sleeves. Then they set out a delicate cup and pour the tea in a particular way. The tea ceremony is more than its motions. It is a vision of quiet in the midst of a busy life.

Many Japanese art forms focus on the details of natural objects. One example is the Japanese garden. In such gardens, there are only a few carefully chosen shrubs and rocks surrounded by borders of small pebbles that are raked each day to form a perfect landscape.

Classic Japanese paintings often consist of a few strokes of black ink with an occasional dab of brown or red. All around lies white space.

The *haiku* is a type of Japanese poem that has simple rules. Every *haiku* has only 17 syllables and three lines. Yet it can express very complex ideas.

On Assignment...

Pretend that your partner is a student in Japan. Interview him or her to compare the lives of Japanese and U.S. students.

In a type of play called *Noh*, Japanese actors wear blank expressions or masks. They use slow movements to create powerful emotions.

The Japanese have many popular entertainments as well. **Sumo** (SOO•moh) wrestling dates to the 600s. Baseball has been popular since the 1920s. Japan's two major leagues hold their own "world series" each fall.

Section 2 Review

1. What is Shinto?
2. **Drawing Conclusions** How are Japanese traditions and values expressed through the arts?

SECTION 3

Life in Korea

What traditional beliefs have influenced Korean life?

Korea is a divided land, and since the end of World War II, the two sides have not developed at the same pace. In the South, tradition and change blend smoothly. In the North, the government has attempted to stamp out Korea's traditions and replace them with the values of a Communist state. Under Kim Il Sung, North Korea outlawed religion. It has tried to replace Confucian values with Communist beliefs and practices. Because it is a closed state, we know little about North Korea. However, some visitors report that beneath the surface of the Communist state, traditional values survive.

South Korea has also seen major social changes. However, Confucian traditions still influence South Korean life. Confucian values, such as respect for elders, remain strong. Religions such as Buddhism and Christianity also play an important role in people's lives.

Both Confucianism and Buddhism have deep roots in Korea. Confucianism reached Korea from China about 2,000 years ago. Buddhism came some 400 years later.

Women in Korean Religion

It has been said that the Koreans tried to be "more Confucian than the Chinese." This was so in family life. In China, the father had the last word, but in Korea he became almost a dictator. He barely spoke

The Koreans maintain many of their age-old traditions. After a traditional Korean wedding ceremony, the bride is carried to the home of the groom's family in a litter, or hand-held carriage.

to his wife, except to give orders. He demanded strict obedience from his children. Korean men looked down on Chinese men as lacking true Confucian manners. Korean family life is much changed today, but Confucian ideas remain strong.

Although Korean women have low status under Confucianism, they rank highly in the native Korean religion. Like the Japanese, the early Koreans believed in nature gods or spirits. They performed certain prescribed tasks to please the spirits. Priests or priestesses who conduct such ceremonies are called **shamans** (SHAH•muhns). In Korea, shamans are usually women. Many South Koreans today consult shamans when they face a crisis, such as a death in the family.

Buddhism in Korea

Korea has many Buddhist temples and shrines. Each spring, crowds of South Koreans observe Buddha's birthday. The day ends with a festive lantern parade.

Christianity in Korea

Koreans living in China brought Christianity to Korea. Later, missionaries came from Western countries.

At one time, Christianity was banned as "un-Korean." Today, it is booming in South Korea.

Things Borrowed and Changed

The Koreans learned about agriculture from the Chinese. They probably imported their first rice plants from China thousands of years ago. But today's Korean diet is different from the Chinese diet. Most meals combine rice with the Korean national dish, *kim-chee*. This is a mixture of white radishes, Chinese cabbage, garlic, red

On Assignment...

Now switch roles and pretend that your partner is Korean. What have Koreans borrowed from China? How is Korean culture unique?

peppers, and other ingredients that is set aside to ferment.

Methods of education have also been borrowed from China and then changed. Korea used the Confucian method for centuries. Then, as a Japanese colony, it acquired more modern methods. Today, boys and girls attend schools together. They learn math, science, and technology, as well as Korean history and traditions. Korea has difficult entrance exams for college, like those in Japan.

Today's Korean Family

Korean women are no longer restricted to the home. Many hold jobs in offices and factories. Both North and South Korea have passed laws that promote the equality of the sexes. Korean men still dominate their families, but they do so more gently than in the past. It is rare nowadays for many generations of Koreans to live together. Young adults like to live on their own.

Section 3 Review

1. Why might Korean women have preferred shamanism to Confucianism?

2. **Interpreting a Quote** Explain the meaning of this statement: "Korean culture is distinctive, despite the tremendous influence of China."

The Year of the Animal

"I was the born in the Year of the Rat." That's how a traditional Chinese or Korean might describe coming into the world. Chinese and Koreans name their years after animals.

A Buddhist belief explains the 12-year cycle of names for the years. Buddha summoned all of the world's animals and offered to name a year for each one. But because only 12 animals agreed to obey and honor Buddha, they were the only ones chosen. In order, they are: rat, ox, tiger, hare, dragon, serpent, horse, ram, monkey, rooster, dog, and boar (or pig).

The Chinese give numbers as well as names to their years. For example, their 4700—the year of the horse—is the same as our 2002.

Chinese and Koreans celebrate the New Year according to the lunar calendar, which is based on the cycles of the moon. They wait for the start of winter. Then they count two new moons. That day is New Year's Day in their calendar. It usually falls between mid-January and mid-February.

On New Year's Eve, families gather to eat a special meal and honor their ancestors. Family members exchange gifts. Then come two weeks of festivities with nightly firecrackers. Finally it's time for the lantern festival. People parade through the streets carrying lanterns. Paper dragons and other objects dance in the crowd.

Case Study Review

1. Why did Buddha name years after animals?
2. **Identifying Alternatives** What would be three possible ways for a Chinese person to identify the year of his or her birth?

On Assignment. . .

Ask how your partner will celebrate the Chinese New Year.

REVIEWING CHAPTER 19

I. Reviewing Vocabulary

Match each word on the left with the correct definition on the right.

1. divine
2. dissent
3. reincarnation
4. meditate

a. opposition to a government's policies
b. to think deeply
c. being reborn many times
d. godlike

II. Understanding the Chapter

Answer the questions below on a separate sheet of paper.

1. How does the Communist value system differ from China's traditional value system?
2. How has the role of women changed in China, Japan, and Korea?
3. How has the role of the family changed in those countries?
4. Describe three of East Asia's distinctive performing arts or sports.

III. Building Skills: Classifying Information

Reread the chapter. Find five facts about the family, five facts about beliefs, and five facts about education. On your own paper, copy the chart below. Use the facts you found to fill in the chart.

	Family	Beliefs	Education
China			
Japan			
Korea			
All three countries			

IV. Working Together

Form small groups. Plan how the class might celebrate the next Chinese New Year. What events would you include? Whom would you invite? Find out which animal will represent the new year. Make drawings to illustrate your plans. Create a bulletin board display to interest others in your celebration.

On Assignment. . .

Conducting an Interview: Review the notes you took throughout the chapter. If you are the interviewer, write five questions that you will ask. Write the answers your partner gives. Next, review the answers together. Finally, using the notes you have prepared, conduct your interview in front of the class.

CHAPTER 20

As the Communist economy has stalled, China's government has allowed new private enterprises to open. Business people in private companies are a common sight in the big cities.

China Today

What recent developments have changed the lives of the Chinese people?

Looking at Key Terms

- **commune** a large farm, with all land and property jointly owned and operated by the farmers
- **Red Guards** students, workers, and soldiers who rampaged through China in support of Mao's Cultural Revolution
- **moderate** less extreme in ideas or behavior
- **radical** more extreme in ideas or behavior
- **incentive** a reward offered to encourage people to take a desired action
- **hunger strike** a refusal to eat; sometimes used as a tactic to pressure a government to meet a list of demands

On Assignment...

Creating a Poster: At key points in China's modern history, people have used large wall posters to spread their ideas. They have used large characters that are easily read. By putting the posters in public places, the creators can circulate their ideas to many others. In this chapter, you will find suggestions to help you make your own wall poster. At the end of the chapter, you will create the poster.

The Struggle to Reshape China

How has China changed since the 1960s?

"Everyone ought to take part in the revolution," a Chinese farmer said. "Revolution is not a thing you can let others do for you."

The farmer had fought for the Communist revolution. He spoke those words in the 1960s. Since then, China has expanded its revolution. Even today, China is struggling to shape its new society.

The Communists are now in power, but the path to the future contains many pitfalls. China experienced great turmoil as it struggled to find its way.

The "Great Leap Forward"

By the late 1950s, Communist leaders were seeking to push change even harder. Their second five-year plan set extremely high goals. It promised a "Great Leap Forward."

Working Harder To make this "leap," pressure was put on everyone in China. People worked longer hours in the factories and the fields. In the countryside, farm families were made to operate small steel mills in their spare time. Even poets were told to play a part. One poem began: "Labor is joy."

Still, the "leap" missed its mark. Planning was poor, and many things went wrong. The so-called "backyard furnaces" turned out only low-quality steel. Factories ran out of raw materials and had to wait for more.

On Assignment...

What kinds of criticisms might Chinese citizens have had about the Great Leap Forward? Note some ideas for your wall poster.

A New Type of Farm The Communists forced great changes during the Great Leap Forward. Large **communes** replaced collective farms. A commune combined all the farms of a village or district into one big unit. Some had 25,000 people or more.

Commune leaders told farm families where and when to work. In order to free both parents for work, small children were cared for in nurseries. Communes did away with private ownership of things like pots, pans, and tables. People ate together in dining halls. Families had no land of their own for growing food.

Communes had many problems. Central planning was less efficient than leaders had expected. Rains didn't come on time. Farm output went down rather than up.

After a year or two, the Communists had to pull back. Small work groups were allowed to make decisions about what the communes did. People went back to eating at home. They again were allowed to grow food for themselves.

The Cultural Revolution

The failure of the Great Leap Forward caused hunger and hardship throughout China. For a while, China's government changed its ways. It turned over major decisions about the economy to experts. Communist party leaders had less say than before. By 1965, the economy was improving.

Most party members supported the new policy. But the party chairman, Mao Zedong, opposed it. He decided to take drastic action. In 1966, he started a process that became known as the Cultural Revolution.

Revolutionaries, Not Experts What was Mao's goal? He said that he wanted to restore China's revolutionary enthusiasm. According to Mao, the Chinese were forgetting the Communist dream—a society in which all shared equally. Mao said that Communist leaders thought too much about making better tractors and not enough about

The Cultural Revolution of 1967 was a time of upheaval and terror. Here, people gather in Beijing to demonstrate under a portrait of Mao Zedong and banners that proclaim "Long Live Chairman Mao!"

making a better society. Mao believed that there were too many experts and not enough revolutionaries.

Mao gave stirring speeches. He urged young people to "learn revolution by making revolution." Students, workers, and soldiers formed groups known as **Red Guards**. Those groups sought people who had criticized Mao. They pulled victims from their homes and offices and hauled them through the streets as objects of ridicule. Sometimes the Red Guards killed these people.

A high party official named Deng Xiaoping (DENG shuow•PIHNG) was almost killed. Deng's son received even worse treatment. He was pushed from a window and suffered crippling injuries.

Drastic Results People spent so much time "making revolution" that production of food and factory goods fell. In some regions, China's army stepped in to stop the fighting. To try to halt the chaos, Mao ordered millions of students and workers from cities to go to the countryside to work on the farms.

By the end of 1969, life returned to normal. But the Communist party was more deeply divided than ever. Mao feared that top leaders were plotting to murder him.

Deng's Rise to Power "It does not matter whether a cat is black or white, so long as it catches mice." Those words of Deng Xiaoping are another way of saying, "If it works, let's try it." Deng was a leader of the so-called **moderate**, or less extreme, part of China's Communist party.

He differed sharply with Mao Zedong, who led the so-called **radical**, or more extreme, part of the party. Mao and the radicals wanted a pure Communist society. To them, building industry was less important than turning out eager Communist citizens.

The year 1976 brought great change to China. In that year, Mao Zedong died and a new generation of Communist leaders came to power.

A month after Mao's death, moderates in the government ordered the arrest of four top radical leaders. Among them was Mao's wife. Moderate leaders said this "gang of four" had plotted to seize power. They put the four in jail and stripped them of their official posts.

The moderates were now in charge. In 1977, Deng was named vice premier.

Although that was not China's highest position, Deng became the most powerful leader in China.

Reforming the Economy

Deng set China on a new course. He wanted economic growth above all else. Deng began a campaign called "the four modernizations."

The overall goal was to make China into a major industrial and military power. Deng abandoned parts of the Communist system. He allowed people to start private businesses. He encouraged **incentives**, such as bonuses for people who worked hard. He let local leaders make decisions that previously had been made at the national level.

Communist critics called Deng a "capitalist." But Deng said he was a good Communist. "What's wrong with increasing the wealth of the country and the people?" he asked.

The changes affected both country and city dwellers. In the country, the communes were closed. Farmers could now lease land from the government and farm on their own. The government took a part of their crops. However, farmers could sell the rest and keep the money.

Incentives like this led to a boom in farm output. Chinese farmers eagerly took the opportunity to profit from their work. The result was more food grown and more money for the farmers.

In the cities, people started businesses of their own. Some made products like brooms or clothing. Others offered services, such as repairing radios and cutting hair.

During the 1980s, China's economy boomed. People lived better than they ever had before. It seemed that capitalism and communism could indeed be mixed.

What About Political Freedom?

Some Chinese were not content with economic reform. They wanted more political freedom. Deng and other leaders could not decide how much freedom to allow. At times, they allowed protests. At other times, they cracked down—hard.

During 1978, people began putting up posters on a brick wall at a busy spot in Beijing. At first the posters criticized Mao and the Cultural Revolution. That was all right to Communist leaders. Party leaders, too, were criticizing Mao in public. But soon people began to put up wall posters that called for more democracy. That was too much. The government ordered all but official posters to be removed from "Democracy Wall."

A major new round of protests came in 1989. Massive demonstrations in Beijing's Tienanmen Square drew worldwide attention. The army crushed the protests in a brutal attack. (See Case Study 20 on page 263.)

During the 1990s, criticism of the government went underground. The government continued its policies of economic reform and tight political control. The world waited to see what the next steps in China's revolution would be.

Section 1 Review

1. What was the difference between radicals and moderates at the time of Mao's death?

2. **Predicting Consequences** Imagine that Deng had allowed greater political freedom in China. What consequences might have followed?

SECTION 2

A Communist Value System

How did the Communists attempt to change education, the arts, and family life?

The Chinese Communists criticized religion and many of the old values. They said the old ways oppressed the people, keeping them down by cruel or unjust uses of power. When the Communists came to power, they launched a campaign against the "four olds"—old ideas, old habits, old customs, and old culture. Party members went from village to village explaining the Communists' new ways.

The Communists worked to undercut traditional Chinese respect for authority. Or, rather, they tried to substitute a new authority—the Communist party.

Changes in Family Life

After gaining power, the Communists launched a campaign against the traditional family structure. Leaders urged sons and daughters to show "backward" parents the "errors" of the old ways. They encouraged young couples to live on their own.

The Communists said that women and men were equal. They banned child marriages. They said that women had the right to decide whom to marry.

China's leaders attempted to deal with China's age-old problem of overpopulation. The Communists set a limit of one child per couple. Couples who had more than one child would be fined and face other penalties. As a result of these strict policies, China is one of the few countries that has been able to bring down its rate of population increase.

Abandoning Children One unhappy result of the population control campaign has been a rise in the number of abandoned children. Most of these children are girls, abandoned by parents who want healthy boys and are afraid to challenge the one-child policy. Hundreds of thousands of children are deserted every year, to be put into overcrowded orphanages. Conditions in the nurseries are dismal.

At one Beijing nursery, several orphans asked a nanny, "When are we going to get cake again?" The nanny's reply was,

Concerned with its huge population, the Chinese government has used economic and social pressure to force married couples to limit their families to one child.

"Orphans in China eat cakes only once a year, on Children's Day, June 1."

Attacking the Landowners

China's Communists destroyed the landowners and gave their land to the poor. Many landlords were executed. In the new China, peasants and workers were honored. However, Communist party members received special privileges.

The Communist party has about 40 million members. That is about 4 percent of the nation's people. Party members hold the most important jobs in the government, in the factories, and also on the farms.

Education

One of the Communists' goals was to modernize China. Like the Meiji reformers in

Japan 100 years earlier, the Chinese reformers stressed education. Both boys and girls now go to school for at least nine years. Leaders said that it was important for everyone to know how to read and write. This would enable poorer Chinese to take jobs in management and technology. To promote literacy, many of the characters in Chinese writing were made simpler. Special classes were started to teach adults how to read.

One of the main functions of education in China is to teach loyalty to the Communist state. Instead of working for the family, generations of students were taught that they must work for the state.

The Communists also built modern industries. They put the government in charge of running businesses. This led to advances in industry and technology. But it also brought mistakes and new problems.

One of the most famous performing arts companies in China is the Beijing Opera. Artists tell their stories through the use of elaborate costumes and exaggerated gestures.

On Assignment...

List some of the effects of modernization on Chinese life. You can use these notes when you make your wall poster.

Chinese goods were expensive and often poorly made. Even today, Chinese industries lag behind those of other nations.

The Arts and Literature

The Communist government says that culture should serve the Communist state. It should not just reflect personal interests.

Performing Arts The Chinese love going to movies. In villages, films may be projected onto bedsheets in an outdoor park.

Billions of movie tickets are sold every month, making China the world's largest market for films. In a Chinese movie, it's easy to tell who's the bad guy. Films present lessons that reflect Communist teachings.

For live entertainment, the Chinese have concerts, dances, and ballets. The Beijing Opera is very popular. It uses songs and dances to tell tales from China's past.

Literature Most books tend to follow the Communist line. Many plots feature a farmer or laborer who works tirelessly to help build a better future for China. A few Chinese writers have tried more daring topics. But the government keeps a close watch on dissent, or opposition to its policies.

Section 2 Review

1. What changes did the Communists attempt to make in the relationship between parents and children?
2. **Evaluating Policies** With which of the policies of the Chinese Communists do you agree? With which do you disagree?

Death in Tienanmen Square

The country is our country.
The people are our people.
The government is our government.
If we do not cry out, who will?
If we do not take action, who will?

With those words, some 3,000 Chinese students began a **hunger strike** in Tienanmen Square in Beijing. It was May 13, 1989. The students said they were ready to die if necessary to achieve greater democracy.

The hunger strikers were part of a democracy movement that was sweeping China. The original 3,000 protesters attracted more than a million people who marched through Tienanmen Square in late May. Large crowds demonstrated in other Chinese cities, too. The marchers were students and other citizens. For them, China's economic reforms were not enough.

The protesters wanted an end to dishonesty among party officials. They wanted to debate political issues freely. They wanted a free press. They wanted rival parties to compete with the Communists for the right to rule. In short, they wanted democracy.

Although officials held talks with the hunger strikers, the government did not meet their demands. Instead, on the night of June 3, it sent soldiers and tanks into Tienanmen Square to crush the democracy movement. The students held their ground.

Soldiers and riot police charged the students, striking them with clubs and other weapons. Then soldiers began shooting machine guns. Armored vehicles roared forward, crushing some of the protesters beneath their treads. The student described what happened next. "I was running and crying. Many people fell down. When we reached the edge of the square, soldiers rushed us. They carried large clubs and hit us fiercely." The student escaped when some of the protesters stopped to fight back.

The assault in Tienanmen Square killed hundreds, perhaps thousands, of protesters. Thousands more were injured, arrested, or both. Supporters of democracy went underground, but their demands did not go away. Sooner or later, they will be heard again.

Case Study Review

1. How did the Chinese government respond to the protest?
2. **Determining Cause and Effect** What were the causes of the 1989 democracy movement? What were its effects?

The world watched in June 1989 as a brave student stood in front of Chinese tanks. Bystanders pulled the student away and the tanks continued on their mission: to break up the protests in Tienanmen Square.

SECTION 3

The "Other" China

Why is Taiwan called the "other" China?

One hundred miles off the coast of China lies the island of Taiwan. In 1949, Nationalist forces fleeing the Communists

On Assignment...

Add the democracy movement's goals to your poster.

moved their government to Taiwan's capital, Taipei (teye•BAY). They quickly established control over the entire island. U.S. armed forces kept the island from being invaded by the Chinese Communists.

Since then, Taiwan has claimed to be the legal government of all of China. Officially, Taiwan's government calls itself the Republic of China.

Like mainland China, Taiwan has been through many changes. At first the Nationalist government was little more than a dictatorship. After the death of Nationalist leader Chiang Kai-shek in 1975, however, a slow shift to democracy began. Today Taiwan is a lively democracy. People are free to speak their minds.

A Prosperous Economy

One of the most striking things about Taiwan is its successful free enterprise economy. Taiwan's annual economic output topped $12,000 a person in the mid-1990s. That was four or five times as much as in mainland China. (However, China's total output is larger. The mainland has more than 50 times as many people as Taiwan.)

Many of Taiwan's people work in factories built since the 1950s. A rapid buildup of industry made Taiwan one of the world's top 15 exporting nations. Its industries produce products that range from computers and chemicals to automobiles.

The Nationalists reformed Taiwan's system of land ownership. They took land from wealthy families and distributed it to peasants. This reform helped to boost farm production. Today, nine out of ten Taiwanese farmers own their own land.

Taiwan's Status

If you had visited the United Nations in the 1950s and 1960s, you would have seen a delegate from Taiwan sitting in China's seat. Strong backing from the United States helped Taiwan hold onto the seat. In the 1970s, President Richard Nixon adopted a friendlier stance toward mainland China. He wanted China's help in ending the Vietnam War.

In 1971, the UN voted to let the Communist government in Beijing have China's seat. In 1979, the United States opened diplomatic relations with Beijing—which meant downgrading U.S. relations with Taiwan.

Much has changed since the 1950s, when the United States and Taiwan were close military allies. In 1958, China bombarded two small islands under the control of the Nationalists. In response, U.S. leaders said they would go to war if necessary to protect Taiwan. Tensions later cooled, and Beijing said it would not use force to take over Taiwan. However, occasional flurries of military activity on one side or the other keep soldiers on the alert.

In recent years, Taiwanese leaders have softened their hard-line stance against the mainland government. Taiwanese businesses have found eager customers in China. Each year a million or more Taiwanese citizens visit China as tourists. What they find often surprises them. Said one visitor from Taiwan, "When we go back to China, it's another culture. I'm a foreigner in that country."

One issue is whether Taiwan should officially claim independence. That would mean abandoning the idea—supported by both sides—that Taiwan is still part of China. The Beijing government has said it would not accept Taiwanese independence. But with growing democracy in Taiwan, some Taiwanese have set up political parties that are pro-independence.

What other future might Taiwan have? China has proposed a "one country, two systems" plan. In that scheme, Taiwan would recognize the authority of the government in Beijing. But Beijing would guarantee that Taiwan could keep its separate economic and political ways. That idea has little appeal to most of Taiwan's people.

Section 3 Review

1. Why does Taiwan no longer hold China's seat in the United Nations?

2. **Comparing and Contrasting** How is Taiwan similar to mainland China? How is it different?

REVIEWING CHAPTER 20

I. Reviewing Vocabulary

Match each word on the left with the correct definition on the right.

1. commune
2. moderate
3. radical
4. incentive

a. more extreme in ideas or behavior

b. less extreme in ideas or behavior

c. a reward offered as encouragement for people to take a desired action

d. a large farm, with all land and property jointly owned and operated by the farmers

II. Understanding the Chapter

Answer the questions below on a separate sheet of paper.

1. How did China change after its civil war?
2. Describe a major turning point in China's history since 1949 and tell why you consider it to be important.
3. What role did Mao Zedong play in China's history after 1949?
4. Why does the government of Taiwan call itself the Republic of China?

III. Building Skills: Distinguishing Fact From Opinion

Tell which of the statements below are statements of fact and which are statements of opinion. Explain why you made each decision.

1. China's people should oppose the Communist revolution.
2. Mao Zedong was long the dominant figure in China.
3. Deng Xiaoping's reforms brought improvements to China's economy.
4. Deng Xiaoping was a great leader.

IV. Working Together

Form a small group. Imagine that you are Chinese citizens. Draw up a petition that asks the Chinese government to make at least three changes in its policies. Work together to phrase your petition so that you have the best chance of achieving your goals. Choose a member of the group to read your petition aloud to the class and explain your choices.

On Assignment. . .

Creating a Poster: To create your wall poster, select one set of notes that you made while reading. Make statements that show your opinions about developments in China. Your poster will serve as an editorial on your "newspaper wall." Illustrate your poster with a picture portraying one of the events or people you mention. Display your poster on a bulletin board.

No Way Out

Harry Wu

*In 1960, a young geology student in Beijing named Harry Wu
was arrested. His crime: criticizing the Communist party. The
young man had no trial. For the next 19 years, Wu was a political
prisoner in China's brutal prison system. During these years, he
suffered torture, physical abuse, and near starvation. When he was
finally released, Harry Wu (Wu Hongda in Chinese) became a leading critic of China's Communist government. He moved to the
United States and published an autobiography,* Bitter Winds.
Below is a chapter from Bitter Winds *titled "No Way Out." It
describes how, after he secretly planned to escape from China, the
author was called to a Communist party meeting.*

. . . Over the past two years, I had been summoned often to
group criticism sessions. Out of habit I took a seat in the back row
of the classroom, hoping that this morning would bring merely a
repetition of previous proceedings. Then I looked up. On the black-
board, beneath the colored portrait of chairman Mao, the chalked
characters "Meeting to Criticize Rightist Wu Hongda" stared back
at me. My stomach tightened. Then Wang Jian strode to the front
of the room. Normally Kong and his fellows from the Youth League
branch office chaired these criticism meetings themselves. Some
people sat stiffly, while others turned awkwardly to look at
me. Wang's opening words broke the silence: "Today we meet to
criticize the rightist Wu Hongda." A chorus of allegations[1] sprang
from the audience.

"Wu Hongda still refuses to reform himself!"

"He opposes the Party. He must be expelled!"

"Down with Wu Hongda, he must now show us his true face!"

For perhaps 20 minutes the accusations continued. I stared
straight ahead until Wang Jian signaled for me to stand.
"According to the request of the masses and with the full authority
of the school," he intoned, "I now denounce, separate, and expel the
rightist Wu Hongda, who has consistently refused to mold himself
into a good socialist student and has chosen to remain an enemy
of the revolution."

Precisely at that moment a uniformed Public Security officer
appeared at the doorway. "Representing the people's government of
Beijing," he declared as he stepped to the front desk, "I sentence

---

[1]**allegations** (al-uh-GAY-shuhnz) *n. pl.* accusations without proof

Detained in Chinese prisons for 19 years on suspician of spying, Harry Wu was finally released in 1979. Here, he speaks to the press in Beijing following his release.

the counterrevolutionary[2] rightist Wu Hongda to reeducation through labor." He motioned me forward and pulled a piece of paper from his jacket pocket. My eyes fixed on the blood-red badge beside his lapel. How could this be happening, I wondered.

"Sign here," the officer commanded, pointing to the bottom of the form. His hand seemed purposely to cover the body of the document, preventing me from seeing the charges for my arrest.

"I wish to see the accusation against me," I replied, guessing that my year-old plan to escape had been discovered.

"Just sign your name," he repeated.

"It is my right," I asserted, suddenly feeling bold, "to be informed of my crimes."

"The people's government has placed you under arrest," he countered impatiently. "Whether you sign or not doesn't matter."

I knew that signing the warrant meant agreeing with the decision for my arrest, and I tried to stall, hoping that someone in the room would support my request to know the charges against me. Anger and fear rose in my throat. No one spoke. With no other choice, I bent to scrawl my name. I knew that anyone arrested for trying, even just planning, to escape was usually shot. . . .

---

[2]**counterrevolutionary** *n.* a person who does not support the reform movement, or revolution

The only concrete evidence of our escape plans lay in my dormitory room. Under the sheets of newspaper that served as a liner for my desk drawer, I had hidden a map of the Burmese border taken from the library. The school's security personnel would certainly collect all my belongings after I left. If they found the map, my life would be worthless.

We walked into my building, North Dormitory Number Five, then up three flights of concrete steps to my room. Six double bunks flanked the walls and six desks clustered in the middle, each with two drawers. Leaning against the bunks, two security cadres watched us enter. Their eyes never left me. Fortunately the far corner of my top bunk lay outside their line of sight.

Acting as if frantic to collect my possessions, I slid out my lower drawer and reached over to dump its contents onto my bunk. A bottle of blue ink spilled across the quilt, and I threw up my hands in dismay. I had formulated a plan. "No need to hurry," one of the cadres said. "Take your time." By then I had found the map. I perched on the bunk and twisted my body toward the wall, slipping the folded page into my pocket.

Jumping down, I told the Public Security officer I had washed a length of cotton cloth and left it hanging in the basement to dry. "Take only what you need for tonight," he ordered. "The rest will be sent later." Ignoring his words, I darted past him into the corridor. I was agile and strong after my years of athletic training, and I flew down the stairs, hearing his footsteps not far behind me. Just inside the door to the basement, I pulled open the heavy furnace door and stuffed the map inside. By the time the angry officer reached my side, I was calmly folding the cloth beside the drying line. My heart pounded, but I said quietly, "You see? I wanted to have it made into trousers, and I was afraid if I left it here, it would disappear."

I finished tying a few belongings inside my quilt, and the angry officer guided me to a waiting school jeep. At the district police station, a duty officer took my fingerprints and removed my keys and watch, my shoelaces and belt, even my library card.

"This can't be happening," I thought to myself again. "There must be some way out."

Outside they motioned me back to the jeep, where I sat alone for perhaps two hours. I thought about trying to escape, but many police walked around inside the Public Security compound. Finally the driver appeared, then a guard leading a second prisoner, who climbed in beside me on the hard rear seat. He looked dirty and disheveled. I felt insulted to be thrust alongside a common criminal, no doubt a vagrant[3] from the countryside picked up for stealing food from a Beijing market during this time of famine. We rode in silence for more than an hour. I could see nothing outside the olive green canvas roof. The screech of brakes signaled

---

[3]**vagrant** (VAY-gruhnt) *n.* a person who wanders from place to place

While Harry Wu remained in jail, Mao Zedong formed the Red Guards. These troops led rallies that supported Mao's policies and attacked his critics.

our arrival at the Beiyuan Detention Center, which I soon learned was a holding facility for prisoners awaiting relocation to the labor camps.

Inside the first gate, a sentry inspected the documents of arrest. A ten-foot-high brick wall stretched as far as I could see across the flat, green expanse of the North China plain. I stared at the second gate. When a duty prisoner motioned me forward, I hoisted my bedroll awkwardly to one shoulder, grabbing my beltless pants with my free hand. Then I waited, squatting awkwardly just inside the yard, seemingly forgotten. . . .

Making Connections

1. Why is this selection entitled "No Way Out"?
2. **Making Inferences** How does Harry Wu's experience reflect the problems of modern-day China?

CHAPTER 21

Japan and Korea Today

What recent developments have changed the lives of the Japanese and Korean people?

Between 1950 and 1990, Japan had the fastest growing economy in world history. By 1990, Japan's economy was the second largest in the world, after the United States.

Looking at Key Terms

- **Diet** Japan's two-house parliament
- **Cold War** a conflict between the Soviet Union and the United States in which each side made threats against the other and built up its military forces and weapons
- **parliamentary rule** a system of government in which a nation's legislature chooses the country's leader
- **coalition** a combination of two or more parties that act together to form a government
- **zaibatsu** giant family businesses in Japan, which supposedly were broken up during the U.S. occupation
- **work ethic** the belief in the benefits of hard work
- **quality circles** groups of workers that look for better ways to get jobs done
- **self-sufficiency** making do with one's own resources

On Assignment...

Writing a Letter:
Imagine that you are visiting Japan and Korea. Write a letter to a friend at home telling about things that you have seen or learned. As you read this chapter, look for hints to help you plan your letter. Take notes on what you might say. You will do the actual writing at the end of the chapter.

271

SECTION 1

Government in Japan

How does Japan's democracy work?

Take one war-torn nation—defeated, humiliated, and impoverished. Kick out the old leaders. Put them on trial for crimes against humanity. Send in an occupying army. Set up a short-term dictatorship under an American general. And don't forget to provide lessons in democracy.

That describes the policies that the United States followed in Japan at the end of World War II. Surprisingly, they worked. Japan turned away from the military adventures of its past. It built a world-class economy and a thriving democracy.

The American Occupation

After Japan's surrender in September 1945, U.S. soldiers moved in to take over the country. At their head was General Douglas MacArthur. For the next few years, MacArthur set the rules for Japan. His goal: to make sure that Japan would be a peaceful country. This period of U.S. control is known as "the American Occupation."

A New Constitution The Americans drew up a new constitution for Japan. They wanted Japan to have a truly democratic system. The emperor remained, but he had no real power. Full power lay in the hands of the two-house parliament, or **Diet**, which was elected by the people. "The people" now meant men *and* women. Before the war, women did not have the vote.

Under the new constitution, the Diet elected the prime minister. The prime minister chose a cabinet to direct the departments of government.

The new constitution spelled out a series of rights. Like the U.S. Bill of Rights, the document guaranteed freedom of speech, religion, and the press. It recognized the equality of women and men. It also established the right of workers to join unions.

After approval by the Diet, the new constitution went into effect in 1947.

Enemy or Ally? After World War II, Japan was a defeated enemy. Many Americans wanted to strip the nation of its military power so that it could never again attack the United States. Therefore, they wrote Article Nine into Japan's new constitution. It said, "The Japanese people forever renounce [give up] war as a . . . right of the nation." The new Japan would have no army, navy, or air force with which it could threaten other nations.

Some Japanese resented Article Nine because it limited Japan's role in international affairs. But many others welcomed it. Japan lay in ruins because of the past military adventures of the armed forces. Many Japanese wanted no such burdens in the future.

Within a few years, however, the United States began to have second thoughts. Tensions grew between the United States and the Soviet Union. People spoke of a **Cold War**. This was a conflict between the two countries in which each side made threats against the other and built up its military forces and weapons.

The Communists took control of China in 1949. An actual war began in Korea the next year with an attack by Communist North Korea on South Korea. The United States rushed soldiers to South Korea from bases in Japan. General MacArthur became head of a United Nations force that pushed back the Communists in Korea.

Americans took a new look at Japan. Could this former bitter enemy become an ally in the Cold War? In 1951, the United States signed a peace treaty with Japan. The two nations also signed a defense treaty that made the United States and Japan allies. Today, some 45,000 U.S. troops are stationed in Japan.

Although most Japanese accept the need to share the burden of peacekeeping, they have resisted taking an active role. Japan's Self-Defense Forces are shown here on parade in 1989.

With Japan as an ally, the United States gave its blessing to the creation of a Japanese military force. Because of Article Nine, the 75,000-strong organization is called the Self-Defense Forces.

Today, Japan has the second largest military budget in the world. However, its self-defense forces are small—only about 200,000 men and women. Japan has no foreign bases. However, it is considering participating in international peacekeeping actions.

With the end of the American occupation, Japan once again became master of its own affairs. Under the new constitution, Japanese political parties competed for power.

Parliamentary Democracy

Like many countries in the world, Japan has a parliamentary system of government. **Parliamentary rule** is a system of government in which a nation's legislature chooses the country's leader.

Voters elect the members of the parliament. Parliament then chooses the nation's leader. If no one party has a majority of seats, then two or more parties must join forces in a **coalition**. These parties then act together to form a government.

One Party in Control

From 1955 until 1993, one strong party ruled Japan year after year, with no need to form coalitions. It was the Liberal Democratic Party. The LDP was formed by the merger of two parties with U.S. backing.

Under LDP rule, Japan had a strong, stable government. This drew the support of people in many parts of Japanese society. Business leaders gave the LDP large sums of money. Farmers, rural people, and many members of the middle class gave it their votes. At election time, the party received nearly as many votes as all other parties combined.

Losing Its Grip

The LDP's tight grip on power ended in the 1990s. A series of scandals tarnished the party's reputation. Top leaders had taken

---

On Assignment. . .

In a letter to a friend, explain how the American Occupation changed Japan.

Japan has taken the lead in the new field of high-definition television. In 1991, Japan became the world's first country to broadcast daily programs in this new format.

secret gifts from big businesses. Some had made deals with gangsters.

Reform-minded politicians broke away from the LDP and formed new parties. In 1993, for the first time in 38 years, the LDP lost its majority in parliament. However, it remained the biggest party. A reform party, along with several partners, took control of the government. Japan entered an era of shaky coalition governments. Although the LDP again formed a government in 1996, it needed the help of partners with whom it had many disagreements.

The LDP was not the only party that lost ground. The Socialist party had long been the main opposition group. It weakened in the 1990s. Voters began to divide their support among many rival parties. Some observers believe that Japan may move toward a new political lineup, with two major parties or alliances of parties.

Section 1 Review

1. How does Japan's constitution limit the country's military forces?

2. **Comparing and Contrasting** How are the United States and Japanese political systems similar? How are they different?

SECTION 2

Japan's Economic Miracle

How has Japan's economy changed since World War II?

The Japanese sports fan sits down to watch a big game. The TV picture is crystal clear. It is much sharper than any American TV picture. The secret is high definition television, or HDTV. HDTV displays twice as many lines as an American television screen. Only a small number of Japanese homes have HDTV sets, however, because they are expensive.

Japan has much more than HDTV. It has one of the world's most modern economies. Citizens enjoy the latest high-tech devices, from consumer electronics to high-speed "bullet" trains. Japan's recovery from the devastation of World War II has been truly remarkable. It is known as "Japan's economic miracle."

The Japanese Way of Business

When the United States occupied Japan after World War II, the Americans insisted on many changes in Japan's economy. They wanted to prevent control of Japan from falling into the hands of a small group of powerful business people.

General MacArthur ordered the breakup of giant family businesses known as **zaibatsu** (zeye•baht•SOO). During the Meiji period of the late 1800s, the *zaibatsu* had become very powerful.

Despite the breakup, some big companies remained very strong. They were among Japan's leading business firms in the post-war years. Other important firms, like Sony, Honda, and Toyota, also grew fast.

Japanese businesses work closely with the government to plan for the future. In the United States, the government takes a much more hands-off attitude. In Japan, there is a close link between business and government. It's as if government and big business were one giant corporation. Yet Japanese businesses are owned by private stockholders, just like U.S. corporations.

Starting Over

By 1945, bombs and fires had ruined many of Japan's factories. The factory owners had to start over. They borrowed money and built new factories with the latest equipment. That gave them an advantage because they could turn out products with fewer workers and less waste. Soon, Japanese firms were selling their goods all over the world.

At first, Japanese products tended to be low in price and low in quality. Western business firms did not take Japanese competition seriously. But Japan began making high quality goods at the lowest possible cost. Before long, many Japanese goods were of better quality than other nations' goods.

Taking Up High Tech

Throughout the 1950s and 1960s, Japan concentrated on "traditional" industries. It had some of the world's most advanced steel mills. It was a leading builder of ships, trucks, and cars. Japan's industries were heavy users of energy—mostly oil that was imported from the Middle East. (Remember that Japan has few energy resources of its own. See Chapter 18.)

In 1973 came an "oil shock." War broke out between Israel and its Arab neighbors. To punish nations that supported Israel, Arab oil producers cut off oil shipments. When shipments resumed, the price of oil shot up.

In response, the Japanese cut back on oil use. Industries tried new technologies that conserved energy. Even more important, Japan decided to concentrate on products that used less energy and fewer imported raw materials. Japan's businesses focused on such high-tech fields as computer chips, VCRs, and electronic cameras. In the 1970s and 1980s, Japan became a world leader in high-tech products.

Reasons for Success

Since the 1980s, Japan has had the world's second largest economy. Only the United States turns out more goods and services than Japan does. What are the ingredients of Japan's success?

One is a strong **work ethic**. The Japanese do not avoid hard work. Many white-collar workers extend their business day into the evening. Some work six days a week.

A second ingredient is careful planning. The close links between business and government help companies to foresee new developments and prepare for them.

A third ingredient is extensive teamwork on the job. Teams often work together to complete a task. This is part of the Japanese focus on groups. A common practice in Japanese factories is to organize workers into **quality circles**. In these groups, workers look for better ways to do their jobs.

A fourth ingredient is strong worker loyalty. Japan's largest corporations operate almost like big families. Workers usually stay with the same company until they retire. The company offers extensive benefits, such as paid health care and bonuses. Workers play on company sports

In many Japanese companies, workers exercise before starting work. Such activity strengthens workers' sense of belonging to a group and their dedication to their company.

teams. They may even live in company-built apartment complexes with other company employees.

However, large companies employ only about 40 percent of the Japanese work force. Small companies employ the rest. Small companies offer fewer benefits. They quickly lay off workers when times are tough. These small companies are an important part of

Japan's success story. Many small companies work for larger companies. Competition is stiff, so the small companies keep their prices low. Thus, large companies save money.

Finally, Japan benefits from a high savings rate. Most Japanese "save for a rainy day." They don't spend money as fast as they earn it. They don't use their credit cards to the limit. Most people put money into savings accounts. Banks then lend the money to businesses for expansion, research, or other purposes.

Challenges for the Future

Despite its economic success, Japan still faces a wide range of challenges. Many other

On Assignment. . .

Describe the life of a worker in Japan. What would seem unusual to your reader back home?

Japanese cities are as crowded as Tokyo. Workers spend long hours commuting by car or railroad. City air is often polluted. At times, people wear masks to protect themselves against the bad air. Fortunately, pollution controls have made the air cleaner in recent years.

Social relations pose a different type of challenge. Some Japanese young people have rebelled against strict families and the stresses of school life. Cities are plagued by motorcycle gangs and rising crime. However, Japanese crime rates are far lower than those in the United States.

Yet another challenge is Japan's slumping economy. Japan's economic miracle began to fade in the early 1990s. The economy slowed. Unemployment rose to the highest levels since the late 1940s. Some banks that had made bad loans were forced out of business and many Japanese worried that their savings might not be safe. Property values, which had soared during the 1980s, began to plunge. Japanese business people began searching for ways to rebuild the economic miracle.

Section 2 Review

1. What was Japan's "economic miracle"?

2. **Predicting Consequences** How might Japan's economy be different today if its factories had not been destroyed during World War II?

While their apartment in the city of Nara is modern, it is small, like most Japanese apartments. See Case Study 21 on page 278 for more information on family life in Japan.

A Tokyo Family

It's Saturday morning, and Tomoko Matsuko (TOH•moh•koh mah•SOO•koh) is late for school. She quickly rolls up her *tatami* (tah•TUH•mee), or sleeping mat. Grabbing her books, she's out the door and into the elevator.

Like most residents of the Tokyo area, Tomoko and her family live in an apartment building. Their apartment has barely half the space of a modest American home. Living space is scarce in Japan, especially around the capital. Thirty million people live in the Tokyo-Yokohama metropolitan region.

When she's ready to go to sleep, Tomoko spreads her *tatami* on the floor. She has no bed, but she does have a desk at which she studies.

Her family's home looks bare by U.S. standards. The family does not need chairs for its dining table. Everyone sits on the floor around a low table, which practically fills the small living room. The small kitchen is but a step away.

Back and Forth by Train

Tomoko's family lives in a suburb of Tokyo. Her father commutes to a job in the city center. He rides an hour and a half morning and night, standing all the way.

Tomoko's father is a manager at one of Japan's large companies. He earns a good salary, but he cannot afford such luxuries as a large house. Prices are at least twice as high in Japan as in the United States. Most of the family's income goes for rent, groceries, and train fare.

Tomoko's mother must shop every day or two because the family's refrigerator is tiny. She buys rice in 10-kilogram (22-pound) bags. Almost every meal is built around rice. Small bits of fish and vegetables are combined in tasty dishes to accompany the rice.

Tomoko and her brother Hiroshi (HEE•roh•shee) have some of the same tastes as U.S. teens. Tomoko collects CDs of Japanese rock music. She does gymnastics after school. Hiroshi has a collection of Japanese comic books. On Saturday afternoons, both attend cram schools to prepare for college entrance exams.

Case Study Review

1. How do Japanese homes compare to U.S. homes?
2. **Formulating Questions** Write a question you would like to ask Tomoko or Hiroshi about daily life in Japan. Then try to answer the question.

Korea Today

How do the lives of South Koreans differ from those of North Koreans?

Sometimes, Yang wonders what has happened to her relatives in North Korea. Kim Yang-ok lives in Seoul, the capital of South Korea. Although her relatives live scarcely 50 miles away, she has not seen them in years. The border that divides the two Koreas is kept tightly shut.

In many ways, the two Koreas are a study in contrasts. South Korea is an emerging democracy. It has become a modern industrial nation with a rising standard of living. North Korea is a Communist dictatorship. At times, its people experience hunger.

The two Koreas share a history and a culture. But they have grown apart since the division in 1945, when Japanese rule ended.

South Korea

South Korea has changed dramatically since 1945. Then it was a poor country. It had never experienced democracy. Today its industries turn out everything from athletic shoes to ships. Military rulers have given way to elected presidents.

The Slow Coming of Democracy In its early years, South Korea experienced harsh rule by strict leaders. An election in 1948 brought Syngman Rhee to power. Rhee imposed strict discipline, especially after 1950. That's when a North Korean attack touched off the Korean War. Rhee's opponents went to jail. The government put pressure on newspapers to report only favorable news.

In 1960, student riots forced Rhee to resign after he rigged an election. A new election was held. Soon, however, military leaders seized power from the elected government. From 1961 to 1993, a series of military officers ruled South Korea.

Modern Seoul houses the factories, banks, and other businesses that spark South Korea's industrial economy. It also contains many buildings from its centuries-old past.

Park Chung Hee ruled the longest—from 1961 until 1979. Then he was assassinated. Chun Doo Hwan ruled from 1979 to 1988. Protests against him were brutally crushed. In 1980, soldiers killed hundreds of demonstrators in the city of Kwangju (gwahng•JOO). Later, more protests broke out. Finally, Chun agreed to hold an election and step down.

Supporters of democracy split their votes between two candidates. A third candidate, Roh Tae Woo (no tie woo), was one of Chun's military colleagues. Roh won with 37 percent of the vote. He ruled from 1988 to 1993, allowing a slow transition to democracy. He gave the press more freedom and he allowed workers to form labor unions.

In 1993, voters elected Kim Young Sam, the first civilian president in 32 years. Under Kim, South Korea began to strengthen democracy. Chun and Roh were arrested for the Kwangju shootings of 1980. In addition, they faced charges of taking bribes from businesses.

South Korea's "Economic Miracle"
Like Japan, South Korea allows businesses to be privately owned. Also like Japan, it experienced an "economic miracle." Through the years of military rule, the nation's economy grew rapidly.

The government drew up a series of five-year plans. It promoted Korean industries that made products for export to other countries. Old industries grew. New industries blossomed. South Korea exported shirts, designer sneakers, and other articles of clothing. It produced steel and ships. It made computers, autos, and many other consumer goods.

As sales abroad rose, Koreans began to enjoy a higher standard of living. By the mid-1990s, the average South Korean citizen earned about four times as much as the average Chinese citizen. Because of its success, South Korea became known as one of the "four tigers of Asia." The other fast-growing "tigers" were Taiwan, Singapore, and Hong Kong.

Becoming Modern
For people like Yang, the many changes since 1945 have been breathtaking. For centuries, Yang's people had been farmers. But as industry grew, the family moved to the city. Yang found a job in an office. She became a member of the middle class.

Today's South Koreans manage to blend ancient Confucian traditions with modern attitudes. When Yang goes to the office, she wears a modest dress, not the traditional Korean wraparound skirt. On weekends, she might go skiing or dancing. But she still shows the utmost respect to her husband and to her father, in the Confucian tradition.

North Korea

While South Korea has zoomed ahead, North Korea seems to be in a time warp. It has been a Communist dictatorship for more than 50 years. It is one of the world's most secretive nations, with closed borders and few personal freedoms.

"The Great Leader"
For almost 50 years, North Koreans were ruled by "the Great Leader," Kim Il Sung. Kim had led a guerrilla army that fought against Japanese rule in Korea. After 1945, he became head of Korea's Communist party. He was the only ruler North Korea had had up to the day of his death in July 1994.

Under Kim Il Sung, a secret police force stamped out all opposition to the government. North Korea's media portrayed Kim as an almost superhuman figure—"the sun of the country." Thirty thousand statues of "the sun of the country" graced the squares of the capital, Pyongyang. Kim's birthday was celebrated as a national holiday. On that day each year, great crowds turned out for special sports events. In schools, children memorized Kim's sayings.

Seeking to Be Self-Sufficient
North Korea took its own approach to economic growth. It shunned South Korea's method of building up trade with other nations. Instead, it worked for **self-sufficiency**.

Kim Il Sung did not want to depend on non-Communist nations, either as suppliers or as customers, so he tried to make Korea do with its own resources. He did, however, accept aid from the Soviet Union and China.

North Korea's economy is tightly controlled by the state. The government owns all factories. It even owns all farms. North Korea has large industries like steel and armament plants. However, it produces few modern consumer goods. The average income of North Koreans is about one eighth the income of South Koreans. In recent years, the economy has been shrinking. Food has been scarce.

A Closed Society Even after Kim Il Sung died, North Korea's government maintained tight control over the people. Power passed to Kim's son, Kim Jong Il (kihm djahn ihl). He had been commander of the North Korean army. He showed the same devotion to communism as did his father.

For its size, North Korea maintains unusually large military forces. It has an army of more than one million. Many of the soldiers are stationed along the border with South Korea. North Korea says the large army is necessary to defend against a possible attack from South Korea. (South Korea has an army of about 500,000. Also, 37,000 U.S. soldiers are stationed in South Korea.)

In the 1990s, tensions flared. U.S. leaders charged North Korea with using its nuclear power program as a cover for building nuclear weapons. The two sides finally reached an agreement. North Korea said it would let international inspectors see what it was doing. In return, South Korea and Japan promised to help North Korea boost its power production.

On Assignment. . .

Will North Korea and South Korea reunite in the next few years? Tell your readers back home what you think, and why.

Together Again?

Are there any prospects that South Korea and North Korea could reunite as a single state? Some days, the answer seems to be yes. Other days, it's a blunt no.

At the time Kim Il Sung died, a first-ever summit meeting was in the works. The North Korean and South Korean presidents were to meet a few weeks later to talk about reunifying the Koreas. After the death of Kim, the summit was canceled.

North Korea and South Korea have moved carefully toward more cooperation in recent years. In 1985, dozens of members of families separated by the North-South border were reunited. In 1991, both Koreas gained admission to the United Nations. Still, serious tensions remain. Both sides keep their armies ready.

Section 3 Review

1. How do ideas about the role of government in the economy differ from North Korea to South Korea?

2. **Analyzing Information** What details in this section show that North Korea is a closed society?

REVIEWING CHAPTER 21

I. Reviewing Vocabulary

Match each word on the left with the correct definition on the right.

1. quality circles   **a.** the belief in the benefits of hard work
2. work ethic   **b.** groups of workers that look for better ways to get jobs done
3. coalition   **c.** making do with one's own resources
4. self-sufficiency   **d.** a combination of two or more parties that act together to form a government

II. Understanding the Chapter

Answer the questions below on a separate sheet of paper.

1. How did the U.S. occupation after World War II change Japan?
2. What happened to Japan's military after World War II?
3. How do the relations between business and government differ in Japan and the United States?
4. What elements contributed to Japan's "economic miracle"?

III. Building Skills: Proposing Solutions

At the end of Section 2, some of the challenges facing Japanese society are discussed. Three of those challenges are listed below. Write a brief paragraph for each challenge, suggesting steps the Japanese might take to address the issue.

1. Tokyo is dirty, noisy, and crowded.
2. Japanese workers spend long hours commuting by car or railroad.
3. Crime rates have been rising in Japan.

IV. Working Together

Form a small group. Make a mural about life in one of the three countries discussed in this chapter: Japan, South Korea, or North Korea. The mural should show a wide variety of scenes that should represent everyday activities, political events, work life, family life, common problems, and so on. First decide which country to show. Then discuss which activities or events you will include. Finally, on a large sheet of paper, draw your mural. Share in the drawing so that everyone contributes.

On Assignment. . .

Writing a Letter: Review the notes you took as you read this chapter. Imagine that you are completing a visit to Japan and Korea. Write a letter to a friend at home. What did you see that interested you? Tell what it must be like to be a citizen of Japan or Korea. Be sure to review your letter, looking for ways to draw a clear picture of what you observed.

CHAPTER 22

East Asia and the World Today

What is East Asia's role in the world today?

Despite its small size, Hong Kong plays an important role in world trade. Each year, billions of dollars in goods are shipped from Hong Kong to Europe and the United States.

Looking at Key Terms

- **coexist**   to live peacefully side by side with others
- **non-aligned nation**   a nation that claimed not to prefer one side over the other in the Cold War
- **trade surplus**   the result when a nation sells more to other nations than it buys from other nations
- **trade deficit**   the result when a nation buys more from other nations than it sells to other nations
- **nuclear umbrella**   the military protection provided to a nation by another nation that possesses nuclear weapons

On Assignment. . .

Writing a Newspaper Editorial: Newspaper editorials express an opinion or offer advice about an issue of current importance. As you read this chapter, look for issues that make you want to speak out. At the end of the chapter, you will be asked to write an editorial that deals with an issue involving China, Japan, or Hong Kong. Scattered throughout the chapter you will find suggestions to help you write your editorial.

China Becomes a World Power

How have China and other nations gotten along since 1949?

Forget the creaking sounds of camel caravans trudging along the Silk Route to China. Listen now to the roar of sleek silver airplanes. Catch the sound of the foghorns of oil tankers. Hear the clang of cargo containers dropping into the holds of big ships.

As in centuries past, China carries on a brisk trade with the outside world. But gems and spices have largely given way to more everyday goods. At almost any U.S. department store, you can buy cotton shirts, wicker baskets, or inexpensive radios from China.

China has become a major trading partner of the United States and other industrial nations. But this has happened only since the late 1970s. During the early years of Communist rule, a wall of suspicion kept China largely isolated from Western nations. China's recent "opening" to the industrial world has brought new opportunities—and new challenges—for East Asia and the world at large.

The Cold War and China

The Cold War had already begun when Mao Zedong and the Communists came to power in China in 1949. Communist China quickly lined up with the Communist Soviet Union. For years, the Cold War provided the background for China's relations with the world.

China in U.S. Politics

In 1949, many Americans were fearful. How had the Communists gained control of China? Why was communism spreading? How could it be stopped?

Politicians rushed forward with answers. Republicans said the Democrats had "lost China." They blamed bumbling diplomats or Communist sympathizers in the administration of President Harry Truman, a Democrat. Democrats had other answers. They said China became Communist because the Nationalist forces of Chiang Kai-shek were corrupt.

The Nationalist government of Taiwan wanted U.S. support for an attack on the mainland. U.S. leaders did not want that. They moved ships of the U.S. Seventh Fleet into the narrow waterway between China and Taiwan. The fleet would protect Taiwan from any Chinese attack. But it would also keep Chiang from attacking China.

Isolation From the West

Through the 1950s and 1960s, U.S. support allowed the Nationalists to keep China's seat in the United Nations General Assembly. Nationalists held China's permanent seat on the U.N. Security Council.

U.S. laws barred American companies from trading with China. Americans could not visit the Chinese mainland. Other Western nations, including Britain and France, did allow dealings with China. Because of U.S. policies, China remained largely isolated from the industrial world.

China and the Soviet Union

Soon after the Communists came to power in China, Mao Zedong went to the Soviet Union. Early in 1950, Mao signed a treaty of friendship and alliance with the Soviet Union. The treaty was supposed to last for 30 years.

At first, China and the Soviet Union seemed like natural allies. Both were under Communist rule. Both were eager to see communism spread. But the friendship soon fell on rocky days. The two nations became rivals for the leadership of world communism.

As Stalin and Mao, standing center, watch, Soviet and Chinese officials sign a treaty of friendship in 1950. By the 1960s, the alliance between the Soviet Union and China was dissolving.

A key issue was whether or not communism and the Western free enterprise system could **coexist**, or live peacefully side by side. By the late 1950s, the Soviet Union was supporting the idea of coexistence. Soviet leaders attended summit conferences with Western leaders to talk about ways to lessen the threat of nuclear war.

This angered China's radical leaders. Mao Zedong accused Soviet leader Nikita Khrushchev of weakening in his commitment to communism. Mao announced that China was developing its own nuclear weapons. He said that he was not afraid of a nuclear war because it would put an end to capitalism.

This frightened the Soviets. Khrushchev decided to break a Soviet promise to share important nuclear technology with China. In 1960, Soviet nuclear experts in China went home. Soviet aid to China fell to a trickle.

"Paper Tiger" Other issues also divided the two Communist giants. In 1962, the Soviet Union moved nuclear missiles into Cuba. Then it withdrew them under the threat of U.S. attack. After this Cuban missile crisis, the Chinese accused the Soviets of being weak. Mao said that capitalism was a "paper tiger." In other words, nations like the United States were not as powerful as they seemed to be.

China and the Third World

Mao wanted to spread communism wherever he could. The Chinese called for "people's wars" against the colonial powers in Africa and Asia. China supported many revolutionary movements with arms and funds.

Under Mao Zedong, China tried to set an example for the developing nations. Follow us, the Chinese said. We were an oppressed nation, too, but we rose up and rid ourselves of our colonial oppressors. We showed how a peasant army could fight a revolution and win.

During the 1950s and 1960s, nations in Asia and Africa that had been under colonial rule were gaining their independence. In some cases, independence came peacefully. In others, the colonial powers resisted and wars of independence broke out.

China encouraged such people's wars. But China did not send soldiers to fight against colonialism. Instead, it preached self-reliance, while sending arms and money. China urged Third World countries to win their own wars.

China associated itself with the movement of nations that called themselves **non-aligned**. Those nations said that they would not take sides in the Cold War.

They claimed not to be on side of either the United States or the Soviet Union.

China claimed to fit into this "Third World." But few people in the West could accept this claim.

Border Problems

Finally, China quarreled with the Soviets over the long Soviet-Chinese border. Certain areas had been taken from China by Russia in the mid-1800s. When the Communists came to power, they refused to give these areas back. In 1969, soldiers of the two nations fought along the border. It was clear to the world that the era of Soviet-Chinese friendship had ended.

U.S. President Richard Nixon's historic 1972 trip to China opened a new era of friendly relations between the two one-time enemies. Here, President Nixon visits China's Great Wall with high-ranking Chinese officials.

Renewed Ties to the West

China's Communist leaders were eager to increase ties with the West. In the fall of 1971, the United States did not object when the United Nations gave China's seat to the Beijing government.

An invitation in 1971 surprised almost everyone. Chinese officials asked a U.S. table tennis team to play in a tournament. In the world of diplomacy, this was a clear sign of something new. It indicated that China was ready to repair its relationship with the United States. It was even ready to accept coexistence.

Henry Kissinger, President Richard Nixon's assistant for international affairs, made a secret trip to China. In February 1972, Nixon flew to Beijing for a formal state visit. The United States and China were opening a new era.

The Cold War, however, was still raging. President Nixon wanted to widen the split between China and the Soviets. He wanted China's help in bringing the Vietnam War to a close. (U.S. soldiers had been fighting in Vietnam since the early 1960s.) He also wanted to begin trade between the United States and China.

At the end of Nixon's visit to China, he and Mao Zedong signed a document. It said that China was a single country, of which Taiwan was a part. It also said that differences between the Beijing government and the Nationalists on Taiwan must be settled peacefully.

The United States was not yet ready to cut off diplomatic relations with the government of Taiwan. That step did not come until 1979. It was the price Beijing required before it would open full relations with the United States. Even after 1979, the United States maintained close trade relations with Taiwan.

By 1979, both Mao Zedong (in China) and Chiang Kai-shek (in Taiwan) had died. New leaders were in power. In China, Deng Xiaoping's reforms gave China new spirit.

The new China had many products to sell. It had customers eager to try the wares of foreign merchants. In the 1980s, trade boomed between China and such industrial nations as the United States and Japan.

An End to the Cold War

As Chinese students and workers staged pro-democracy protests in 1989, Soviet leader Mikhail Gorbachev (GAWR•buh•chef) arrived in Beijing. He, too, was ready to repair relations with the Chinese. After more than 20 years, the Soviet-Chinese split was healing.

Two and a half years later, the Soviet Union broke apart. The Cold War was at an end. A lively trade sprang up between Russia and China.

Border problems remained, but the two nations solved most of them. In 1994, the president of China became the first Chinese leader to visit Moscow in 37 years. China and Russia pledged not to use force against one another. They promised not to target one another with nuclear missiles.

China and Its Asian Neighbors

Above the sparkling waters of the South China Sea, a small shack was perched above the water on stilts. Nearby stood a larger complex of three shacks. Laundry fluttered from a line. With the tide in, the structures seemed much bigger than the rocks on which they were built. The blue waters stretched as far as the eye could see.

Why build shacks on these lonely rocks? To stake a claim. For beneath the waters may lie oil—lots of it! And six nations are claiming ownership.

The shacks were built by China in the mid-1990s. They sit in the midst of the Spratly Islands—a sprawling collection of islands and reefs in the South China Sea.

Six governments have claims in the Spratlys. They base their claims on a number of conflicting facts. For example, each nation says it was the first to claim certain islands. Each nation has taken actions—like patrolling the islands, or building on them—to show possession. Besides China, the nations with claims are Vietnam, Taiwan, the Philippines, Malaysia, and Brunei.

All six say that they want to settle their claims peacefully. However, many have military forces in the Spratlys. In a 1988 clash, China sank two Vietnamese boats, with a loss of 70 lives.

Because of its huge size and its military power, China's intentions are of great concern to its immediate neighbors. In the early 1990s, China cut back its army. But it increased its navy and modernized its weapons. China's relations with its neighbors have had many such ups and downs.

Relations With Japan

Japan followed the U.S. lead in the "opening to China" of the 1970s. China and Japan signed a treaty of peace and friendship. Japanese firms invested in Chinese industries. Japan granted foreign aid as well. In 1980, China's premier went to Japan. It was the first visit by a Chinese leader in Japan's 2,000 years of existence. Japan became China's number two trading partner, after Hong Kong.

Still, the Chinese view Japan with great suspicion. They have not forgotten that Japan brutally attacked China in the 1930s

Life in Hong Kong

In steel towers, business leaders wheel and deal. On bustling streets below, noodle-sellers peddle their wares. On busy construction sites, workers in hard hats hurry to finish another tall building. In rice fields, women kneel to insert the green shoots of new rice plants into the muddy ground. In miserable huts, poor people close their eyes and try to get through another night. Hong Kong is sharply divided between rich and poor. About 1.4 million of Hong Kong's 5.8 million people live in temporary huts and other poor dwellings.

These are the sights of Hong Kong—a collection of islands, hills, and mountains on the south coast of China. Hong Kong is less than half the size of the smallest U.S. state, Rhode Island. It is peopled largely by Chinese. But a long era of British rule shaped it into something unique.

Hong Kong island fell under British control during the Opium War of the 1840s. (See Chapter 17.) In 1898, Britain took a 99-year lease on a patch of the Chinese mainland nearby. The resulting Hong Kong colony remained a part of the British Empire long after most of the rest of the empire had melted away. But in 1984, as the 99-year lease entered its last 13 years, Britain reached an agreement with China. Britain would withdraw when the lease expired.

All calendars were marked for the big day: June 30, 1997. At midnight that night, Britain's flag, the Union Jack, would come down. The red flag of Communist China would take its place. Hong Kong would enter a new era—changed, but still unique.

With six million people, Hong Kong is a major population center. Under British rule, it became a center of free enterprise. Hong Kong businesses built factories in the colony and across the border in China. They did a brisk business importing goods from other countries and passing them on to buyers in China.

Hong Kong's red-letter day is June 30, 1997. On that date, Communist China will take control of the bustling city. The six million people of Hong Kong will then enter a new era.

The Rise of MTV

The colony gave rise to world-class business leaders. In 1991, a Hong Kong resident named Richard Li started a satellite television service called StarTV. By 1993, viewers in more than 42 million homes from Taiwan to Turkey could see its programs. They could watch rock videos on MTV. They could see news programs from British TV stations. They could even see reruns of U.S. soap operas.

Hong Kong also is home to old-line British business firms. One of them is Jardine Matheson. That company was trading opium to China before the Opium War. By the 1990s, it was Hong Kong's largest employer, except for the Hong Kong government. Of course, it no longer trades in opium.

Many business people became worried when they learned that China would take over the colony. Some sought British citizenship. That way they could move elsewhere if life in the new Hong Kong became difficult. But Britain tightened its immigration rules, so few Hong Kong residents were able to move there.

Waiting for Changes

Under British rule, local democracy was not allowed in Hong Kong until recently. Only in 1995 did Britain allow an elected legislature in Hong Kong. China's government voiced strong objections to the last-minute British reforms. It claimed the changes were intended to hamper China's plans to reform Hong Kong's government in 1997.

In its agreement with Britain, China promised to allow the territory to keep its way of life "essentially" unchanged until at least 2047. Chinese leaders promised that Hong Kong could keep its economic, political, and social systems. But changes were inevitable. And Hong Kong residents anxiously wondered how those changes would affect their lives.

On Assignment...

What advice would you give the people of Hong Kong about what to expect when China takes over? You may decide to choose Hong Kong's merger into China as the topic for your editorial.

Case Study Review

1. Why did people in Hong Kong mark their calendars for June 30, 1997?

2. **Making Generalizations** Using Hong Kong as an example, what generalizations can you make about colonial rule?

The visit of Japan's emperor and empress to China in 1992 showed how much these two East Asian nations need each other. Japan is China's number two trading partner, after Hong Kong.

and 1940s. In recent years, Japanese leaders have apologized to China. But public statements by prominent Japanese have sometimes undercut the apologies. For example, in 1994, a Japanese official declared that Japan had not massacred many Chinese at Nanjing in 1937. Another Japanese leader said, "During the wars waged by this country, it never happened that the military committed atrocities." These statements have made many Chinese very angry.

Relations With Vietnam

Early Chinese dynasties extended their influence into Vietnam as early as 111 B.C. Since that time, the relationship between the Chinese and the Vietnamese has been a touchy one.

During the Vietnam War of the 1960s and early 1970s, China assisted North Vietnamese forces that fought against the United States and its South Vietnamese allies. But then relations soured.

China resented the fact that Vietnamese Communists had sided with the Soviet Union in the Soviet-Chinese split. They complained that Chinese people in Vietnam were being mistreated. They objected to Vietnamese soldiers' occupying Cambodia during that country's civil wars. In 1979, China and Vietnam fought a brief border war.

In recent years, the two nations have settled their differences. Like the United States and Russia, Vietnam has restored relations with China. But the dispute over the Spratlys remains.

Relations With Taiwan

Taiwan is one of the most difficult issues on the world scene. So long as Taiwan did not claim outright independence, China was willing to let it remain independent. But a growing movement in Taiwan for full independence brought threats of military action from the Chinese.

During the 1980s, China and Taiwan seemed to be close to solving their differences. China's economic reforms and Taiwan's trend toward democracy led to a new relationship. Taiwanese business people began to invest in mainland companies. Tourists from Taiwan made visits to their old homes on the mainland.

In the 1990s, however, the Chinese began conducting tests of missiles in the narrow passage between Taiwan and the mainland. Chinese missiles fired from the mainland crashed into the water not far from a number of major Taiwanese ports.

The tests were a reminder of the differences that still existed between China and the Taiwan government. The Taiwanese insisted that they would rejoin China only if they could keep their democratic institutions. In the wake of the missile firings, Taiwan upgraded its air force. The United States reminded Chinese leaders that they had promised not to settle the Taiwan issue by force. China reminded U.S. leaders that Taiwan has always been considered a part of China.

Section 1 Review

1. What did Mao Zedong mean when he said the United States was a "paper tiger"?

2. **Summarizing** Summarize the main issues in China's relations with the other nations of East Asia since 1949. Include issues on which Americans disagreed among themselves.

SECTION 2

Japan: A World Leader

What new problems have resulted from Japan's economic success?

Travel almost anywhere in the world and you'll see Japanese products in use. Count the automobiles passing a street corner in Thailand's capital, Bangkok. Nine out of ten will be made by Japanese corporations. Look at the motorcycles in the crowded streets of Indonesia, or the portable tape players worn by American joggers, or the VCRs in homes throughout the world. They probably are made by Japanese companies such as Toyota, Honda, Kawasaki, Sony, Aiwa, and Pioneer.

Japan is an economic powerhouse. In total output, it ranks second only to the United States. The secret to Japan's economic success is foreign trade. But trade also creates problems. Japan's trade relations with the rest of the world have frequently been rocky.

Trade: A One-way Street?

First it was President Ronald Reagan. Then President George Bush. Then President Bill Clinton. All pressured Japan to buy more U.S. goods. Usually, talks were held and agreements were reached. Japan

said yes, it would try to do better. But United States complaints continued.

Selling More, Buying Less Since the mid-1970s, Japan has built up an enormous **trade surplus** with the United States. That means that Japan sells much more to the United States than it buys from the United States. From the U.S. point of view, this situation is called a **trade deficit**. It causes a drain of money from the United States. (The United States also has a large trade deficit with China.)

Japan also has trade surpluses with other developed nations. On the other hand, it buys more than it sells from some Asian nations, such as China and Singapore. Thus, Japan has a trade deficit with those nations.

In part, Japan's success in selling its products is due to the skill of its business people. Japanese products are high in quality. Japanese production methods keep costs low. Thus, Japan's goods sell briskly.

Many U.S. families began buying Japanese cars in the 1970s. They were impressed by the cars' low price, high fuel mileage, and solid construction. To remain competitive, U.S. automakers had to hold down their prices and improve the quality of their cars.

But U.S. leaders see a second reason for Japan's large trade surpluses. They say that some Japanese laws and customs prevent U.S. firms from having a fair shot at the Japanese market. They claim that the Japanese have put limits on how many U.S. exports can enter the country. For example, for many years, the Japanese government limited the amount of U.S. beef that could enter Japan. Japan still limits the amount of rice that can be imported from the United States. This is done to help Japanese rice farmers.

Changing Japanese Ways?

In recent years, the United States has sought changes in the way the Japanese do business. The United States wants Japan's

On Assignment. . .

Why does the United States have a trade deficit with Japan? What should be done about it? Use the information in this section to gather facts for your editorial. You may choose this topic for your editorial.

companies to stop buying mainly from other Japanese companies. It wants the Japanese government to open government contracts to U.S. as well as Japanese bidders. It wants an end to laws that favor Japanese food products over imported ones.

The Japanese have given in on many points. But they have resisted on others, such as food. Japan is a small nation, the Japanese say. It needs to be able to produce its own basic products, like rice, rather than depend on outsiders. Thus, protecting rice farmers is a matter of national security, not just of trade policy, according to the Japanese.

Security and Defense

Since 1952, Japan and the United States have been close military partners. Japan has been protected by the U.S. **nuclear umbrella**. That is, the United States promises to use its nuclear weapons, if necessary, to protect Japan. In exchange, Japan serves the United States as its "unsinkable aircraft carrier in the Pacific." The United States maintains 45,000 troops and actual aircraft carriers at bases in Japan.

The presence of U.S. troops on Japanese soil has become an issue in Japanese politics. Many Japanese resent these troops. Hostile feelings are particularly strong on the island of Okinawa in the East China Sea. Okinawa was occupied by the United States from the end of World War II until 1972, when it was returned to Japan. However, about 29,000 U.S. troops are stationed on Okinawa. Some troops have committed crimes, provoking anti-American protests. Some local leaders demanded that U.S. bases be closed. Most Japanese, however, resist these demands. They want to continue the benefits of protection under the U.S. nuclear umbrella.

Change Article Nine?

In recent years, some Japanese have been pushing for a change in Article Nine of their constitution. As you read in Chapter 21, that article is supposed to block Japan from maintaining its own military forces.

Some Japanese want a constitutional change to allow Japanese forces to serve outside Japan. Because of Article Nine, Japan has not sent soldiers to serve as members of United Nations peacekeeping forces. Japan is seeking a place on the U.N. Security Council. In the view of some Japanese, such a position would require Japan to play a role in peacekeeping and other operations.

Other Japanese are strongly against even talking about such a constitutional change. They fear a return to the military aggression of the 1930s. Such fears have lessened in recent years.

In 1994, Japan's Socialist party changed its long-standing policy against Japan's having any military force at all. The Socialists for the first time accepted Japan's alliance with the United States. However, they did not agree to change the constitution.

Low Defense Budgets

Japan saves money by depending on the United States for defense. Only about 1 percent of its national output goes for its own self-defense forces. In contrast, the United States devotes more than 4 percent of its output to the military. During the Cold War, the percentage was even higher.

A "Free Ride"? Some Americans say that Japan gets a "free ride" by depending on the United States to maintain peace in East Asia. On the other hand, the Japanese point out that they make a large contribution toward the expense of keeping U.S. troops in

MAJOR JAPANESE EXPORTS AND IMPORTS

PRODUCT EXPORTED	EXPORTS (in thousands of U.S. dollars)	PERCENT OF TOTAL EXPORTS
Machinery	$125,108,690	37.7%
Electrical Equipment	56,217,640	18.0
Passenger Cars	44,712,595	14.2
Transport Equipment	31,310,506	10.0
Industrial Chemicals	17,195,281	5.5
Toys and Musical Instruments	16,243,823	5.2

PRODUCT IMPORTED	IMPORTS (in thousands of U.S. dollars)	PERCENT OF TOTAL IMPORTS
Mineral Fuels	$54,756,348	23.1%
Food and Other Consumable Goods	34,698,137	14.7
Machinery	27,419,324	11.6
Crude Materials	24,644,751	10.4
Industrial Chemicals	16,909,947	7.1
Metals	15,078,356	6.4

Data covers the year 1991. Source: U.S. Dept. of Commerce; "Summary of Trade," Japan Tariff Association, January 1992.

Japan depends on trade with other nations to export its manufactured goods and to provide raw materials. In terms of dollars, what are Japan's top two import categories?

Japan. Also, Japan contributed almost $10 billion toward the cost of the war that the United States led against Iraq in 1991.

Japan's Role in Asia

Japanese tourists pour into Bangkok, Thailand, and other cities on daily flights. Japanese business people run factories in countries like Malaysia and Taiwan. Japanese cars crowd the streets of Singapore and other Asian cities. Japanese electronic goods fill shop windows in Manila. As a matter of fact, Japan sells more to East Asia than it does to the United States.

In World War II, Japan tried to conquer a large part of Asia. It failed. But in today's business world, Japan is the dominant influence over a broad stretch of the continent.

Many Asians are uneasy about Japan's new role. They resent Japan's past actions.

They wonder if Japan could one day return to its aggressive policies.

Relations With the Koreas

Koreans still resent the long years of Japanese colonial rule over their country. They admit that the colonial period, from 1910 to 1945, brought economic advances. But at what cost?

In the mid-1990s, a Japanese cabinet member talked about "some good things" that Japan had done in Korea. He said, "Japan built schools in every town in Korea and also constructed railroads and ports."

Koreans expressed shock and anger at these comments. They thought that the official was making light of the brutalities the Koreans suffered under Japanese rule. In the end, the cabinet member apologized and resigned.

On the whole, however, Japan and Korea have close ties. Japan is South Korea's number two trading partner (after the United States). It is one of North Korea's top three trading partners (along with Russia and China). Japanese banks have large investments in Korea. Japanese companies have set up factories there.

Relations With Russia

Japan and Russia are close neighbors. Only a 25-mile-wide water passage separates the major Japanese island of Hokkaido from the Russian island of Sakhalin (SAHK•uh•leen).

When Russia opened its doors to foreign investments at the end of the Cold War, the Japanese showed interest. Japanese companies increased exports to Russia. But Japan's trade with Russia has lagged behind its trade with other neighbors.

Still at War Japan and Russia have never signed a peace treaty to end World War II. The stumbling block is a dispute over the ownership of a chain of 56 islands called the Kuriles (KOOR•ihlz). The Soviet Union took the Kuriles from Japan in the closing days of the war. Japan insists on getting back at least four of the islands, which it calls its "northern territories."

In the 1990s, Japan offered financial aid for Russia's economic reforms—but only if Russia gave back the islands. The two countries held talks, but reached no agreement.

Relations With Southeast Asia

Southeast Asia has been a major area for Japanese investment. It includes countries on the Asian mainland such as Thailand and Vietnam. It also includes island countries such as Indonesia and the Philippines. Before World War II, Vietnam and Indonesia were European colonies, and the Philippines was under the control of the United States. Japan's conquest of those colonies during World War II helped lead to their independence after the war.

Japan has provided large-scale foreign aid to Southeast Asia. In fact, Japan gives more foreign aid than any other country in the world. Its aid helped Southeast Asian nations to recover after World War II. The region became a profitable market for Japanese products. Japanese banks and companies have made major investments in the region.

Section 2 Review

1. Why has the issue of trade caused friction between Japan and the United States?

2. **Identifying Alternatives** What other defense policies might Japan choose?

I. Reviewing Vocabulary

Match each word on the left with the correct definition on the right.

1. coexist
2. nuclear umbrella
3. trade deficit
4. trade surplus

a. the military protection provided to a nation by another nation that possesses nuclear weapons

b. the result when a nation sells more to other nations than it buys from other nations

c. to live peacefully side by side with others

d. the result when a nation buys more from other nations than it sells to other nations

II. Understanding the Chapter

Answer the questions below on a separate sheet of paper.

1. Why did U.S. and Chinese leaders want to improve relations in the 1970s?
2. What changes in Japan's business policies do U.S. leaders seek? Why?
3. Why have Japan and Russia never signed a formal peace treaty to end World War II?
4. What will happen to Hong Kong after 1997?

III. Building Skills: Understanding Points of View

For each of the following issues, write one paragraph giving China's point of view and another paragraph giving a neighbor's point of view.

1. Should Taiwan again come under the rule of the Chinese government?
2. Should the Spratly Islands be a part of China?

IV. Working Together

Form a small debating society. Consider adopting new defense policies for Japan. Decide what changes might be made and select some members of your group to speak in favor of these changes. The rest of the group can criticize the proposed changes. Try to guess what the other side will say and figure out how you will respond. Then hold the debate. Take turns speaking until all students on each side have spoken. Then, have the class vote on the best defense policies for Japan.

On Assignment . . .

Writing a Newspaper Editorial: Review the suggestions in the chapter that offer ideas about topics for an editorial. Then decide on one topic. First tell your readers the background of the issue: How did it arise? Why is it a problem? Then offer your own advice or opinion: How should the issue be resolved? Who should do what, and why? When you have finished your first draft, review what you have written. Make revisions. Use direct, clear language. Remember that you want your readers to *do* something about this issue.

I. Understanding the Unit

Answer the questions below on a separate sheet of paper.

1. (a) Describe the major physical features of Japan. (b) How have these features affected Japanese history and culture?
2. (a) Who built the Great Wall of China? (b) Why was it built?
3. (a) Describe Japanese feudalism. (b) What role did the warrior class play in the leadership of Japan?
4. (a) What were Japan's foreign policy goals in the first half of the 1900s? (b) How did Japan become involved in World War II?
5. (a) What happened to Korea at the end of World War II? (b) What was the fate of Korea during the Cold War?
6. Identify and describe the three religions or sets of beliefs that are practiced throughout East Asia.
7. (a) In what industries has Japan become a leading producer and exporter? (b) List three reasons Japan has become so successful.
8. (a) What is the major source of conflict between Japan and the United States today? (b) What kinds of changes has the United States asked for in Japanese policy?

II. Thinking Critically

Answer the questions below on a separate sheet of paper.

1. **Determining Cause and Effect** Mao Zedong and the Communist party took control of China in 1949. What effects did this have on China's people and culture? What changes did the Communist government make in traditional Chinese life?
2. **Comparing and Contrasting** Describe the differences and similarities in the lifestyle, economy, and politics of North Korea and South Korea.

III. Writing to Learn

On a separate sheet of paper, write a three-paragraph essay about the following topic.

Imagine you are interviewing a Taiwanese man or woman who witnessed the Chinese Revolution in 1949. What might this witness tell you about the revolution? How did the Communists come to power? What changes did the Communists make in Chinese life? What has the relationship between Communist China and Taiwan been like since the revolution?

IV. Practicing Skills: Interpreting a Table

Read the table below. On a separate sheet of paper, answer the questions that follow.

WORLD POPULATION, 1996

	Number of People	Land Area (square miles)	Population Density (per square mile)
WORLD	5.7 billion	58,433,000	97.5
ASIA (excludes former USSR)	3.4 billion	10,644,000	319.4
AFRICA	721.5 million	11,707,000	61.6
NORTH AMERICA	454.2 million	9,360,000	48.5
SOUTH AMERICA	319.6 million	6,883,000	46.4
EUROPE	509.3 million	1,905,000	267.3
OCEANIA	28.7 million	3,284,000	8.7
FORMER USSR	297.5 million	8,647,000	34.4

Source: *1996 Information Please Almanac.*

1. (a) What is the population of the world? (b) On average, how many people per square mile live in the world?
2. (a) Which region of the world has the greatest number of people? (b) Which region of the world has the smallest number of people?
3. Why might some regions have higher population densities than others?

V. Going Beyond the Unit

Work with two or three students to create an illustrated time line of Chinese, Japanese, and Korean history from 1700 B.C. to the present. First, make a list of all the significant events and dates from each country. Then put this list in chronological, or time, order. Next, place these events on a time line in the order in which they occurred. Color code your time line to distinguish among Chinese, Japanese, and Korean events. Finally, gather photographs, drawings, or other artwork to illustrate your time line. Present your completed time line to the class.

The Information Age

Looking at Key Terms

Internet, lasers, communication satellites, website

How can students from Moscow University hold debates about global issues with U.S. college students? They can use the **Internet**, a network of computers around the world. The Internet carries messages, pictures, and other data to people all over the world.

A new Internet program, called "Mirage," links young people in urban areas around the world. These young people capture their lives through words and drawings. Says Margaret Burr, who runs the program, "Electronic mail is an inexpensive way to break down barriers."

College students at Russia's Moscow University use e-mail to discuss issues with students at Tufts University in Massachusetts. "I didn't think Americans cared at all about the environment," says Marina Federova, a Russian student.

The Wired and the Wireless

Communication between societies has come a long way since all messages were carried by hand. In those days, ordinary messages between two nations might take months to deliver. The invention of the telephone and the telegraph in the 19th century allowed societies to exchange large amounts of information very quickly. However, these means required wires and poles.

Today, information can be sent without wires, in the form of radio waves or special light waves called **lasers**. **Communication satellites** have vastly improved the ability of people in different nations to communicate with one another. These human-made objects orbit the earth, sending information vast distances.

Communications Break Down Barriers

Although the information superhighway may sound like science fiction, it is already affecting life in major ways around the globe. The island of Sumatra has a thick rain forest. Until recently, this made it difficult for Sumatrans to communicate with one another. They often waited in line for a half-day to make a phone call. Now with wireless communication, Sumatrans just pick up a phone and dial a number.

Modern communications have also made it possible for people to make their views known to their government much more quickly. Fifty years ago, if citizens wanted to express their opinions to the President of the United States, how could they do it? They could

The Internet has opened a world of instant communication between people on different continents. Students around the world can send messages and pictures to one another in a matter of seconds.

telephone, but long-distance calls were very expensive at that time. Most people used a well-known means of communication: the postal service.

Today, you can type this address into a computer: "http:/www. whitehouse.gov." This is the White House **website**, or the Internet home address of the President. You will see a menu of choices—from tours of the building to guides for finding specific information. With one click, you can send a message to the President, the First Lady, or the Vice President. If you sign the White House electronic Guest Book, you will receive a signed "Thank You" from the President!

In the not-too-distant future, it actually may be possible to use the Internet to make government decisions. Americans may be able to discuss their ideas and even vote by home computer. In that way, our elected representatives would be able to represent everyone's views.

Review

1. How have the ways of sending and receiving information changed in the past 100 years?
2. **Predicting Consequences** How do you think modern communications will change your life?

Taking Action: Expressing a Political Opinion

Do you have strong opinions about the environment, the minimum wage, or another issue? Think of an issue about which you feel strongly. Compose a short message stating your views and send it to the President through his e-mail address or through the postal service. Be sure to include an address so that the President can respond to your message.

FOCUS ON

Latin America & Canada

	A.D. 900	1300	1400	1600
History		**1325** The Aztecs begin to build the city of Tenochtitlán.		**1521** Spanish conqueror Hernán Cortés defeats the Aztecs. **1533** Spanish conqueror Francisco Pizarro destroys the Incas.
Culture & Society	**300-900** Mayan civilization reaches its height.			**1500s** Enslaved Africans begin to arrive in Latin America.
Economics & Technology		**1300s** The Aztecs build causeways and aqueducts.	**1200s-1400s** The Incas construct large temples.	**1500s** Superior weapons help the Spanish defeat Native American empires in the Americas.

Study the time line. On a separate sheet of paper answer the questions below.

1. In what year did the Aztecs begin building Tenochtitlán? How many years later did Hernán Cortés defeat the Aztecs?

2. What was one reason the Spanish were able to defeat Native Americans in the Americas?

3. Who led enslaved Africans in Haiti in a revolt against the French?

4. What was the effect of the Great Depression?

5. How will NAFTA increase trade among the United States, Canada, and Mexico?

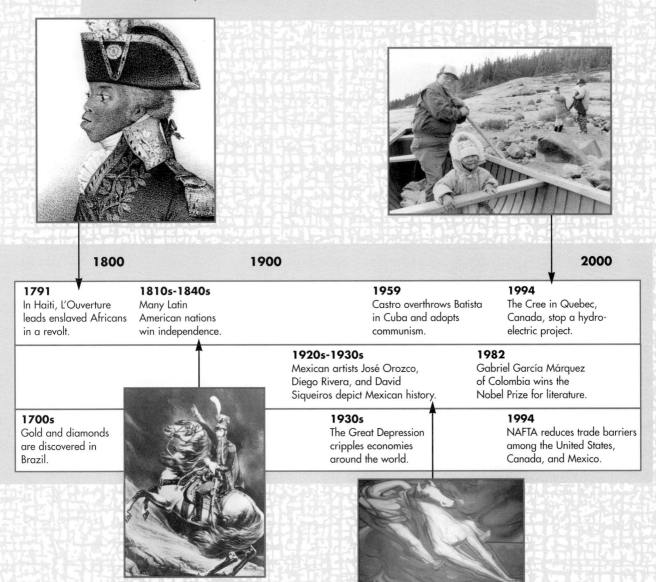

1800 **1900** **2000**

1791
In Haiti, L'Ouverture leads enslaved Africans in a revolt.

1810s-1840s
Many Latin American nations win independence.

1959
Castro overthrows Batista in Cuba and adopts communism.

1994
The Cree in Quebec, Canada, stop a hydro-electric project.

1920s-1930s
Mexican artists José Orozco, Diego Rivera, and David Siqueiros depict Mexican history.

1982
Gabriel García Márquez of Colombia wins the Nobel Prize for literature.

1700s
Gold and diamonds are discovered in Brazil.

1930s
The Great Depression cripples economies around the world.

1994
NAFTA reduces trade barriers among the United States, Canada, and Mexico.

301

Urbanization in Latin America
Reading a Line Graph

Since the 1960s, many Latin Americans have moved to the region's cities. Most people hope to find jobs there. But the cities strain to provide housing, electricity, water, health care, and other services to a growing number of people. The line graph below shows the percentage of the population living in five major Latin American cities. Study the graph. On a separate sheet of paper, answer the questions below.

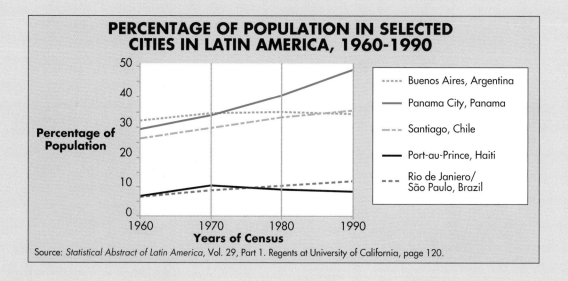

PERCENTAGE OF POPULATION IN SELECTED CITIES IN LATIN AMERICA, 1960-1990

Percentage of Population

Years of Census

Buenos Aires, Argentina
Panama City, Panama
Santiago, Chile
Port-au-Prince, Haiti
Rio de Janiero/ São Paulo, Brazil

Source: *Statistical Abstract of Latin America*, Vol. 29, Part 1. Regents at University of California, page 120.

Did You Know

- Rio de Janeiro, one of Brazil's largest cities, has a population of more than 12 million. (See Chapter 23.)

- About three out of every four Latin Americans live in cities. One in three Latin Americans live in cities with populations of more than one million. (See Chapter 26.)

- Some Latin American governments have tried to carry out land reform programs in hopes of slowing the flow of people to the cities. (See Chapter 27.)

1. **Reading the Line Graph** (a) What do the numbers on the left side of the graph represent? (b) What do the numbers at the bottom represent?

2. **Thinking About the Line Graph** (a) What percentage of Chile's population lived in Santiago in 1970? (b) How did the percentage of Port-au-Prince's population change in each decade from 1960 to 1990?

3. **Going Beyond the Line Graph: Making Predictions** (a) What do you think will happen to the populations of Rio/São Paulo, Brazil, and Santiago, Chile, by the year 2000? (b) What problems might occur in the countryside when large numbers of people move to the city?

Using a canoe carved from a huge tree of the Panamanian rain forest, a woman sets out from the mainland to her home on an island in the Atlantic Ocean.

The Land and People of Latin America

What is unique about the land and the people of Latin America?

Looking at Key Terms

- **peninsula** a body of land that is surrounded on three sides by water
- **volcano** a mountain with an opening near the top from which hot melted rocks, ash, and gases sometimes flow
- **tropics** lands that are near the equator
- **moderate** mild
- **mestizos** people who are part Native American and part European

On Assignment. . .

Creating Posters: This chapter covers the land and the people of Latin America. Imagine that you are working for a travel agency to promote tourism in Latin America. Your assignment is to design a poster for an advertising campaign. The theme of the campaign is "Visit Latin America — A Place of Beauty and Diversity." As you read this chapter, look for On Assignment hint boxes. They contain suggestions to help you think of ideas for your poster.

What and Where is Latin America?

What are Latin America's key landforms?

LATIN AMERICA'S PHYSICAL FEATURES

The West Indies separate the Caribbean Sea from the Atlantic Ocean. These islands are actually the tops of an underwater mountain chain.

The Amazon is the second longest river in the world. It runs 3,900 miles (6,275 km). It starts in the Andes Mountains and flows across South America to the Atlantic Ocean.

The Andes is the world's longest mountain range. It stretches more than 4,500 miles (7,240 km) along the entire west coast of South America.

Rio de Janeiro, Brazil, is one of the largest cities in the world. More than 12 million people live there. Cities throughout Latin America are growing at an extremely fast rate.

Latin America is the vast region located south and southeast of the United States. It extends from the northern border of Mexico to the tip of South America, a distance of 7,000 miles (11,200 km). Latin America also includes the islands of the Caribbean Sea.

The climate of Latin America varies greatly. The equator runs through the northern part of South America. That means that Latin America lies partly in the Northern Hemisphere and partly in the Southern Hemisphere. Areas of Latin America around the equator have a hot and steamy climate. Areas near the southern tip of South America are cold throughout the year.

Mountains are one of Latin America's most important landforms. This picture shows Mount Illimani (ee•yah•MAHN•ee), one of the highest mountains in the Andes. The mountain towers over the city of La Paz, Bolivia's largest city. Mount Illimani is part of the Andean mountain range. The Andes is the longest mountain range in the world. It is known as the "backbone" of South America.

The *pampas* are the rich grassy plains of eastern Argentina. The plains of Venezuela and Colombia are called the *llanos* (YAHN•ohs). Ranchers raise huge herds of cattle on the pampas. Farmers grow grains such as wheat and corn. Meat, wool, hides, and grain are the region's most important products. Most of these are exported to other countries through the port of Buenos Aires, capital of Argentina.

The Amazon River, the second longest river on earth, flows for more than 3,900 miles (6,275 km). It sends more water into the Atlantic Ocean than any other river in the world. It rushes through the hot, thick tropical rain forest like a mighty inland sea. The river and its branches are so vast that they drain nearly half of South America.

The Regions of Latin America

Geographers divide Latin America into four regions. These regions are Mexico, Central America, the Caribbean, and South America.

Mexico Of all Latin American countries, Mexico is the furthest north. It is very mountainous, with the mountains running down the middle of the country. On either side of the mountains lie narrow plains. Jutting out on the east coast is the Yucatán (yoo•kuh•TAN) **peninsula**. A peninsula is a body of land surrounded on three sides by water.

Central America Central America is a long ribbon of land that connects Mexico with South America. Mountain chains that begin in Mexico continue through Central America. Many of the mountains in the region are volcanoes. A **volcano** is a mountain with an opening near the top. When a volcano erupts, hot melted rocks, ash, and gases flow from the opening.

A highland area runs through the middle of Central America. Ranchers and farmers in the highland raise cattle and grow coffee and bananas. On either side of the highlands are narrow coastal plains.

The Caribbean The islands of the Caribbean Sea are sometimes known as the West Indies. These islands stretch between North and South America in the shape of a half moon. The largest Caribbean island is Cuba. The smaller islands, such as Bermuda and Anguilla, are only a few square miles in size.

South America South America is by far the largest land area in Latin America. South America contains almost every type of known landform. Its landscape is similar to North America's. Both continents have a high mountain range near their west coast. Both have lower mountain ranges along their east coast. Huge plains with mighty rivers lie in the middle of both continents.

On Assignment. . .

For your poster you may wish to feature one of the four regions of Latin America. Highlight the natural beauty of the region you choose. Think of words and phrases to describe the region that might appeal to travelers.

Barriers to Movement

The landscape of Latin America has had an important impact on its people. In the past, vast mountains and dense tropical forests isolated people from one another. These natural barriers were very difficult to cross. In recent years, however, modern technology has helped Latin Americans gain a sense of unity. New roads, airplane travel, radio, and television have brought Latin Americans closer together.

Section 1 Review

1. What are the four regions of Latin America?

2. **Analyzing Information** How has Latin America's geography been a barrier to people in different parts of the region?

SECTION 2

The Many Climates of Latin America

What are the climate regions of Latin America?

If you were planning a trip to Latin America, what type of clothing would you take with you? It would not be easy to decide. Here are some of the reasons why:

- From north to south, Latin America stretches over a great distance. This means that some parts of Latin America are near the equator and others are very far away. Most places near the equator are hot.

- Latin America is a mountainous region. A valley close to sea level may be very warm. Meanwhile, only a few miles away, a place in the mountains may be very cold.

- Like any region, Latin America has places where winds blow in different directions. Places where winds blow in from the sea are rainy. Lands near the Amazon River are among the wettest on earth.

- South of the equator, the seasons are opposite to those in North America. Most of South America is located south of the equator. In June, July, and August, when it is summer in the United States, it is winter in most of South America. In December, January, and February, South America has its summer season.

Refer to the map on page 308 as you are reading this section. It will help you understand Latin America's climate regions.

Tropical Climates

About three fourths of Latin America lies in the **tropics**. The tropics are lands that are near the equator. These areas have two types of climates.

In tropical wet climate areas, temperatures are warm, and there is rain throughout the year. Rain falls almost every day, making the air moist and uncomfortable. Look at the climate regions on the map on page 308. What parts of Latin America have tropical wet climates?

The second tropical climate zone in Latin America is called the tropical wet-and-dry climate. This climate is warm throughout the year. However, some months are rainy and some months are dry. Look at the map on page 308. What parts of Latin America have tropical wet-and-dry climates?

Moderate Climates

North and south of the tropical areas lie areas that have **moderate** climates. The word *moderate* means "mild."

The most widespread of these moderate climates is the humid-subtropical climate. Many Latin Americans live in areas with this climate. Here winters are mild and summers are warm. The pampas of Uruguay lie in the humid subtropics.

The Impact of Rain and Wind

Winds and ocean currents also affect climate. In much of the Southern Hemisphere, winds blow from east to west. Winds from the Atlantic Ocean are warm and moist. As these winds move westward, they bring rain to the West Indies and to the northern part of South America.

The winds continue across South America until they reach the east side of the Andes Mountains. There the winds are forced upward. The air is cooled and the rain falls on the eastern side of the mountains. When the air passes to the western side of the mountains, it is dry. Therefore, the area on the west coast has little rain. Here lies the Atacama Desert of southern Peru and northern Chile. In some parts of the Atacama, rainfall has never been recorded.

Vertical Climate

The main influence on climate in Latin America is altitude, or distance above sea level. Within a single country, the climate can vary enormously, depending on whether you are in the lowlands or the highlands. This effect is known as a vertical climate. *Vertical* means "up and down."

At sea level, the climate is tropical, or hot. As you climb into the mountains, the climate becomes somewhat cooler. Near the peaks of the mountains, it is very cold.

LATIN AMERICA'S CLIMATES

N
W — E
S

PACIFIC OCEAN

ATLANTIC OCEAN

Gulf of Mexico

Caribbean Sea

Tropic of Cancer
20°N
Equator 0°
20°S
Tropic of Capricorn
40°S
60°S

Havana
Mexico City ★
Managua
Caracas
Bogotá ★
Quito ★
Lima
La Paz
Recife
Brasília
Rio de Janeiro
São Paulo
Santiago
Buenos Aires

▨	Tropical wet (rain forest)	hot, humid, rainy
▨	Tropical wet-and-dry (savanna)	hot, wet summers; warm, dry winters
▨	Steppe	hot summers; mild to cold winters
☐	Desert	hot and dry
▨	Mediterranean	hot, dry summers; mild, moist winters
▨	Humid subtropical	hot, humid summers; mild, moist winters
☐	Marine	warm summers; cool winters
▨	Vertical	temperature and rainfall depend on altitude

0   500   1,000 Miles
0 500 1,000 Kilometers

160°W 140°W 120°W 100°W 80°W 60°W 40°W 20°W 0°

Location and Region Latin America is a land of many climate zones. Is the tropical wet climate zone located near the equator or further away? Why is the vertical climate zone found on the western coast of South America and not on the eastern coast?

On Assignment. . .

A second idea for your poster is to highlight the climates of Latin America. To attract tourists from the Northern Hemisphere, you might point out that during the Northern Hemisphere's winter, it is summer in the Southern Hemisphere.

Section 2 Review

1. Describe two climates found in Latin America.

2. **Making Inferences** Why might someone from Chicago want to travel to the Southern Hemisphere in January?

Winds lose their moisture by the time they reach Salta in western Argentina. The result is a semi-desert similar to the southwestern United States.

SECTION 3

The People of Latin America

What types of people live in Latin America?

Who is an American? When we use that term in the United States, we usually mean people who are citizens of our country. But the people of Latin America are just as American as we are. They live on the continents of North or South America or on islands nearby.

Where Latin Americans Live

More than 460 million people live in Latin America today. Latin America has almost twice as many people as the United States.

It is also more than twice the size of the United States.

Most Latin Americans live in two general areas. One area is the coastal plains. The plains lie on the east and west coasts of the continent. The second area is the highlands. More than 150 million people live in this strip of land that stretches from the Amazon River to the grasslands of Argentina.

The population of Latin America is growing quickly in certain places. Countries such as Mexico, Jamaica, and Guatemala have fast-growing populations. Sudden population increases put a great strain on the economies of these countries. You will read more about the effect of population growth on Latin America's economy in Chapter 27.

A Blending of People

Latin America has a rich mix of people. The people of Latin America fall into four main groups. These are Native Americans, people with African backgrounds, people with European ancestors, and people whose background is a mix of Native American, African, and European cultures. This last group is the fastest growing group.

New Immigrants

Other immigrant groups have also come to Latin America. During the late 1800s, many Asians settled in Latin America. Today, many Japanese make their homes in southern Brazil. Chinese live in Mexico, Peru, and Cuba. On some Caribbean islands, Indians from Asia make up about half the population.

Section 3 Review

1. What are the four main groups of Latin American people?
2. **Understanding Points of View** Explain why Latin Americans might object to the use of the word "American" to refer only to U.S. citizens.

THE PEOPLE OF LATIN AMERICA

Native Americans were the first people to live in Latin America. Today there are about 30 million Native Americans in the region. They make up the largest group in Bolivia and Peru. Many Native Americans also live in Mexico, Central America, the Andes highlands, and the Amazon valley.

Africans first arrived in Latin America in the 1500s. They came as enslaved people, torn from their homes and forced to work on plantations under brutal conditions. Today, people of African descent live in most areas of Latin America. The largest numbers are in Brazil, Haiti, Cuba, Jamaica, and Venezuela.

Europeans first came to Latin America during the late 1400s. Millions have come since. Early settlers were from Spain and Portugal.

In the late 1800s and early 1900s, many people came to Latin America from Italy and Germany. About a third of all the people in Argentina and Uruguay have Italian backgrounds. Large numbers of people with German backgrounds live in Argentina, Brazil, and Chile.

Mestizos are part Native American and part European. In Mexico and many countries of Central and South America, mestizos make up the largest group. Mulattos have African and European backgrounds. Many of the people in the Dominican Republic, Cuba, Brazil, and other countries are mulattos. Other people are of mixed Native American and African descent.

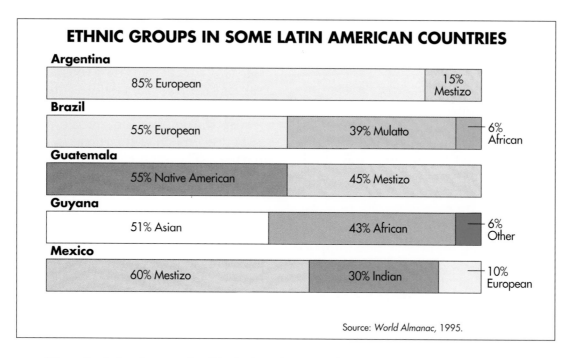

ETHNIC GROUPS IN SOME LATIN AMERICAN COUNTRIES

Argentina
85% European | 15% Mestizo

Brazil
55% European | 39% Mulatto | 6% African

Guatemala
55% Native American | 45% Mestizo

Guyana
51% Asian | 43% African | 6% Other

Mexico
60% Mestizo | 30% Indian | 10% European

Source: *World Almanac*, 1995.

The ethnic backgrounds of Latin Americans are diverse. The chart above shows how the population makeup varies from one Latin American country to another. Because of this diversity, the people in some of Latin America have not been greatly concerned with a person's skin color. In general, education, wealth, and jobs are more important than skin color. However, prejudice based on skin color does exist. Prejudice based on ethnic background is also found. For example, in countries with large Native American populations, the Native Americans are the poorest and least educated.

Millions of square miles of Amazon rain forest is covered by tropical trees. Heavy rain and constant heat encourages rapid plant growth.

SECTION 4

Living in Different Environments

How do the people of Latin America interact with their environments?

Only a small portion of the land of Latin America can be used for farming and building. Much of the land is covered by mountains and deserts. The Andes Mountains are too high and too cold for large-scale farming. The soils of the rain forest and dry grasslands are poor. The deserts cannot support much life.

Yet for thousands of years, the people of Latin America have made their living from the land. They have done this by adapting their ways of life to the challenges presented by the land.

Rain Forests

A large part of Latin America is tropical rain forest. The largest rain forest is located around the Amazon River. The rain forests have many products that are useful to people in other parts of the world. Wood is one of the most important of these products. Another important product of the rain forest is chicle. It is used to make chewing gum.

In the forest, small groups of Native Americans live in villages near rivers. Growing food is a problem for these people because the soil is poor. Yet the people manage to grow much of their food in small forest clearings. The men clear the land by chopping down trees or burning away the thick brush. Once the land has been cleared, the women plant. The men go into the forest to get more food by hunting and fishing.

The people who live in the rain forest make almost everything they use from the products of the forest. They make their houses from thatch, straw, grass, and leaves. The women weave clothing, mats, and baskets out of grasses and leaves.

World interest in rain forest products and the desire for more land to farm are having a dramatic effect on the rain forests. They are being destroyed at a record rate. The destruction threatens the wildlife and plant life that need the forest to survive. You will read more about this in Chapter 28.

Farming in a Vertical Climate

As you have learned, the vertical climate zone is widespread throughout Latin America. In this zone, the climate changes with the altitude.

Vertical climate affects the crops a farmer grows. In the hot and damp lowlands of Central America, there are plantations of bananas and cacao (kuh•KOW) beans. Cacao is the bean from which chocolate is made. These crops need the wet, rainy weather and long growing season of the tropics.

In the cool climate of the highlands, the most common crop is coffee. Coffee is grown in the highlands of Brazil and Colombia. Most of the coffee is grown on large estates. Brazil is the world's leading coffee grower. Colombia is the second largest.

Life on the Savanna

The grassland, or savanna, north and south of the Amazon rain forest stretches over parts of Brazil, Venezuela, and Colombia. This area has only two seasons: rainy and dry.

In the grassland, cattle are raised on huge ranches, called haciendas (ah•see•EHN•dahs). The cattle are always on the move. In the dry season, the rivers become little more than streams. Cattle graze near the streams where the grass is still moist and green. In the rainy season, the rivers flood their banks. Then the cowboys drive the cattle to higher land, or mesas, between the swollen rivers.

Life in an Oil Economy

The developed world depends on oil. Some of the richest oil reserves in the world are found in Mexico, Venezuela, and the plains of Ecuador and Peru. Mexico is one of the world's leading producers of oil. Most of its oil is shipped to the United States.

Oil is also a major product of Venezuela. The sale of oil has brought the country much wealth. As a result, the average income of Venezuelans is one of the highest of any people in Latin America. As you will read in Chapter 26, however, that wealth is not spread evenly. There is still much poverty and misery in the cities and villages of Venezuela.

Section 4 Review

1. What products come from the rain forests of Latin America?

2. **Determining Cause and Effect** What is one effect of oil production in Latin America?

The Aymará people live in a barren land in the *altiplano*, or the high plains, of Peru and Bolivia. Few food crops grow on the altiplano. One crop that does grow in this environment is potatoes. The Aymarás eat potatoes at every meal.

The Aymarás: People of the Andes

High in the Andes of South America, the mountains divide into two ranges. Between the ranges, great plains stretch for more than 2,000 miles (3,220 km). The highest part of this plain lies in Peru and Bolivia. In certain places, the plain rises to more than 13,000 feet (3,960 m). One such place is along the border of Peru and Bolivia.

The High Plains

The land along the border is bleak and barren. The winds blow constantly. In winter, the cold wind roars fiercely over the land. In summer, the wind blows up a fine stream of dust. The dust gets on everything — including the lungs of the people who live here. The soil is poor and the grass is thin. Rainfall is light.

In this harsh land live the Aymará (ay•mah•RAH) people. About 100 Aymará villages dot the *altiplano*, or high plain. One of the villages is Chapito, which lies at the end of an ancient Native American trail. Chapito is cut off from other villages by steep hills and deep gorges. It lies in Peru, but in this remote area few people care whether they are in Peru or Bolivia. The people have so little to do with the politics, economy, or culture of either of these countries.

Chapito is a poor village. Almost all the villagers scrape out a living from the dusty land. Some raise *llamas* (YAH•mahz) to carry supplies. These camel-like animals also provide people with wool to make blankets and coats. The llamas survive by eating a brown straw-like grass. Not much else grows in this land.

For hundreds of years, Aymará men have been leaving the villages to work in the mines. At first, they were forced to work in the silver mines of the Spanish. About 100 years ago, as the supply of silver ran low, the Aymarás went to work in the tin mines. Here, they worked under very harsh conditions. Few miners lived to celebrate their thirtieth birthdays. Thousands died in mining accidents.

Farmers and Herders

Today, most Aymarás survive by farming and herding. They grow crops on the poor soil of the plains. Fish from nearby Lake Titicaca adds to their diet.

Potatoes are one of the few foods that grow well at this altitude. The Aymarás eat potatoes at almost every meal. They dry and preserve them for winter. They prepare them every way they know how — roasted, fried, stewed, and steamed.

The Aymarás have their own way of "freeze drying" potatoes. They spread the potatoes out on the ground to freeze at night. When the

sun comes up, the pota-
toes thaw. The next
night, they freeze
again. Finally, the
Aymarás tramp on the
potatoes with their bare
feet to squeeze
out the last drops of

On Assignment. . .

The Aymarás might make a good subject for your poster. Focus on their unique way of life as a point of interest on a trip to the Andes.

moisture. This leaves a mush called *chuño* (CHOON•yoh), which is used in stews and soups.

Family Life

If you had visited an Aymará village 500 years ago, you would have found houses not very different from those in Aymará villages today. These houses are built of a mud-dried brick called adobe. Each house has one room — and no windows! The only opening is a small door. This keeps as much heat as possible inside the house.

Family life is important to the Aymarás. Children learn to perform tasks early in life. At age five, children are sent out to herd a few llamas or lambs.

At age 12, boys are sent to work in the fields. By 16 or 17, many boys leave the village to work in the mines.

Life is hard on the altiplano. The cold and the lack of oxygen take their toll on the body. The average baby born on the altiplano can expect to live only about 32 years.

To find an easier life, whole families have moved from the villages to the cities of Lima and La Paz. Lima is the largest city in Peru. La Paz is the largest city in Bolivia. About half the people of La Paz are Native American. Many are Aymarás.

A Proud History — An Independent Future

Though their life is harsh, the Aymarás have a strong sense of pride. They take satisfaction in their history. Aymará stories tell of people who were independent until they were conquered by the Spanish in 1542. Spanish rule was harsh. The Aymarás were forced to work in mines and to send bribes to the Spanish.

In 1780, the Aymarás rebelled. Forty years of bloody war followed. Finally, in 1821, the Spanish gave up the war. The Aymarás became independent again. When the countries of Bolivia and Peru were formed, their border cut across Aymará land. But lines on a map mean little to the Aymarás. Out on the altiplano, they scratch a living out of a barren land regardless of what country they live in.

Case Study Review

1. What is the altiplano?
2. **Comparing and Contrasting** How are the lives of young Aymarás different from your life?

I. Reviewing Vocabulary

Match each word on the left with the correct definition on the right.

1. volcano
2. peninsula
3. tropics
4. mestizos

a. land that is surrounded on three sides by water
b. a mountain from which hot melted rocks, ash, and gases sometimes flow
c. people who are part Native American and part European
d. lands that are near the equator

II. Understanding the Chapter

Answer the questions below on a separate sheet of paper.

1. What are the major geographic features of each of Latin America's four regions?
2. What is a vertical climate? Describe how a vertical climate affects how people live on the land.
3. In what two general areas do most of the people of Latin America live? Why?
4. Why are many Aymarás leaving their traditional villages for the city?

III. Building Skills: Studying Maps

Study the maps on pages 598 and 599. Then answer the following questions.

1. Which countries of South America are north of the equator? Which are south?
2. What is the largest country in Latin America in terms of size?
3. What are the chief bodies of water that border Latin America?
4. Name three Latin American nations that are on islands.

IV. Working Together

With a small group, write a television script about a Latin American culture. For example, you may choose to write about the life of the Aymarás on the altiplano of Peru. Before you begin writing, brainstorm and outline ideas for the show. Be sure to include information about Aymará traditions and history.

On Assignment. . .

Creating Posters: Review the notes you took as you read the chapter. Sketch out your ideas for travel posters on sheets of paper. Create messages to appear on your posters. Choose the best sketch and message and transfer your idea to a large piece of paper. Present your work to your teacher or to the class. Include a paragraph or two explaining how your poster will attract tourists to Latin America.

CHAPTER 24

The Early Civilizations of Latin America

Which civilizations existed in Latin America before the European conquest?

People from early Mexican cultures are shown crafting gold and feather works in this colorful mural by the modern Mexican painter, Diego Rivera.

Looking at Key Terms

- **glacier** a huge sheet of ice
- **nomads** people who have no permanent home and move from place to place in search of food and water
- **irrigation** a system of human-made ditches that carry water
- **pyramid** a building that is rectangular at its base with four triangular sides that meet at the top in a point
- **drought** a long period without rain
- **causeway** a raised road across water or marshland
- **aqueduct** a system of pipes that carry water to where it is needed
- **immune** protected against a specific disease

On Assignment. . .

Keeping a Journal: The chapter you are about to read describes three major empires that existed in Latin America hundreds of years ago. Imagine that you have the opportunity to travel through these empires. On your journey, you will keep a journal to record your impressions of these three civilizations. As you read the chapter, take notes for your journal entries. Look for several hints placed throughout the chapter that will help you gather your notes. At the end of the chapter, you will organize your notes and put together your journal entries.

The First Americans

Who were the first Americans and where did they come from?

Have you ever thought about what your town or city was like hundreds or even thousands of years ago? Perhaps you've wondered what kind of people lived there and what those people did for a living.

Scientists have thought about those very same things. In this chapter, you will learn some of what they have found. You will also learn about the major civilizations of early Latin America.

Settling a Continent

About 30,000 years ago, nearly one third of the world was covered with huge sheets of ice. These ice sheets are called **glaciers** (GLAY•shuhrz). It was a time known as the ice age. During this time, a narrow strip of land connected Asia and North America across what is now called the Bering Sea.

Herds of Asian moose and other animals began to cross this strip of land. Hunters followed the animals. Scientists believe that these hunters were the first people to live in the Americas.

This movement of people from Asia to America did not take place all at once. It occurred over thousands of years. It ended when the glaciers finally melted. Then the sea once more covered the land between the two continents.

The first Americans lived as **nomads.** They moved from place to place in search of animals to hunt. Many traveled through parts of what is now called North America. Others drifted southward, settling in Mexico and Central America. In the years to come, some people continued on into South America.

Farming Develops

Over thousands of years, the hunters learned new ways of life. People living around lakes and rivers began to fish. Others ground seeds to make flour, or gathered berries, nuts, and bulbs.

Then people in the area of Mexico made a key discovery. They learned that when the seeds of wild plants are placed in the ground, new plants will grow. This was the discovery of farming. Farming changed the way many Native Americans lived. With food from crops, many groups stopped being nomads. Over many years, Native American farming villages were established all over North and South America.

Another major development was **irrigation**. This is a system of human-made ditches that carried water from streams to the fields. Irrigation was important because it allowed farmers to water their crops during the dry season.

Civilizations Emerge

The discovery of farming led to other developments. Farming made food supplies more predictable. Fewer people died of hunger. Populations increased. Also, as the size of farms grew, not everyone in the village had to farm in order to eat. Therefore, some people farmed while others focused on other work, such as pottery or toolmaking.

After a time, small villages grew into larger communities. Governments were formed to organize these communities. Religion became more complex as people looked for explanations of the mysteries of life. Priests and other religious officials took charge of rituals and ceremonies that marked the seasons of the year and the passage of people through time.

Over the years, powerful city-states and empires appeared. Three of the greatest empires in Latin America were the Mayan, the Aztec, and the Incan empires.

1. Why did people first come to the Americas?

2. **Understanding Cause and Effect** How did the development of farming lead to the creation of large communities?

SECTION 2

The Mysterious Mayas

Who were the Mayas and where did they live?

Deep in the rain forests of Guatemala, the city of Tikal (tee•KAHL) lay hidden. For a thousand years, the city sat empty. Trees and vines grew around and over the buildings.

The Glory of Tikal

There was a time when Tikal was a thriving city. Around A.D. 600, more than 40,000 people lived there. At the center of Tikal, huge pyramids soared to the skies. A **pyramid** is a building that has a rectangular base and triangular sides that usually rise to a point. Mayan pyramids, however, were flat on top.

Near the pyramids was a huge market. At the market, people traded goods such as food, pottery, leather hides, and jewelry.

Around Tikal's pyramids were the palaces of rulers and wealthy people. These palaces had many rooms built around courtyards. At the outskirts of town were canals to bring the water to farmland during the dry season.

For about 200 years, Tikal was the largest city of the people known as the Mayas. But by A.D. 800, Tikal had begun to decline. About 100 years later, Tikal lay abandoned.

What caused Tikal's decline? Experts don't know for sure. But they have many theories

Huge pyramids lay buried in the rain forests of Mexico and Guatemala for a thousand years. They testify to the glories of Mayan civilization.

about what happened to the mysterious city of the Mayas. Some of these theories will unfold in this section.

Mayan Cities

Mayan civilization developed in the rain forests of Guatemala. By about 300 B.C., the Mayas were building cities. The Mayas built about 40 cities with more than 20,000 people in each. Tikal was the greatest Mayan city.

The Mayan cities served as religious centers. These religious centers had many steep flat-topped pyramids. Graceful stone temples stood atop these pyramids.

Religion was a very important part of Mayan life. The Mayas believed that the earth had been created and destroyed four or five times. They believed that it would be destroyed again. To persuade the gods to delay destruction, Mayan rulers prayed and sacrificed prisoners. *Sacrifice* means "to kill as a way of pleasing the gods."

Seers of the Stars

The Mayas were experts at mathematics. They also carefully studied the heavens and the movements of the stars and planets. They used their knowledge to develop an accurate calendar of 365 days. The calendar helped the Mayas predict solar eclipses. A solar eclipse occurs when the light of the sun is blocked by the moon.

The Decline of the Mayas

Mayan civilization was at its height between A.D. 300 and 900. Around the year 800, the Mayas suddenly abandoned their great cities in Guatemala and moved northward into the Yucatán peninsula. The reasons for this move are unknown. Experts have suggested a number of possibilities. Among them are a sudden change in climate, a civil war, or a foreign invasion.

During the years in Yucatán, the Mayas began to rebuild. Their new empire reached great heights. Beginning around 1100, however, the Mayas were weakened by **drought**, a long period without rain. The Mayas also faced attacks from other Native Americans.

Mayan civilization continued to decline for a few hundred years. Finally, it came to an end when the Mayas were conquered by the Spanish in 1546.

Today, the great cities of the Mayas are only beautiful ruins. However, several million people who are descendants of the Mayas live in Guatemala and Mexico.

Section 2 Review

1. What theories have scientists used to explain the decline of Mayan civilization?

2. **Formulating Questions** Imagine that you could speak to an ancient Maya. What one question would you most like to ask that person? Explain why you would ask this question.

SECTION 3

The Golden Empire of the Aztecs

How did the Aztecs build a great empire in the valley of Mexico?

For weeks, the emperor Montezuma (mahn•tuh•ZOO•mah) had shut himself off from the world. He remained in his palace. He spoke to no one but his closest advisers. Day after day, he sat silently by a window looking out over his great city.

Montezuma was the ruler of the powerful Aztec empire. He was the most powerful person on earth — or so he thought. Yet he was frightened by a small band of light-skinned strangers. Were they enemies? Did they mean to destroy him? Or were they the light-skinned gods of Aztec legend that had come to reward the Aztec people?

Finally, Montezuma reached a decision. He summoned the great lords of the land. They were suspicious of the strangers and were eager to destroy them. They needed only a word from Montezuma.

But the word, when it came, was disappointing. The leader of these strangers may be the light-skinned god of legend, Montezuma said. The Aztecs would treat the strangers with respect and invite them to come to the Aztec capital. So began the downfall of the mighty Aztec empire.

The Eagle and the Snake

More than 300 years before Montezuma's rule, the Aztecs were a wandering band of poor warriors. They were so poor that they traveled from place to place, fighting for anyone who would pay them. Around A.D. 1200, they entered the Central Valley of Mexico. The valley runs down the center of the modern-day nation of Mexico.

According to legend, an Aztec god told them to wander until they came to a place where an eagle was eating a snake. After many years of wandering, the Aztecs saw

Montezuma, emperor of the Aztecs, one night saw a blazing comet. It was an omen of death both for the emperor and for his powerful empire.

On Assignment...

For your journal, imagine that you traveled through the city of Tenochtitlán at its height. What do you find most impressive about the city? What similarities and differences does it have to the place where you live?

their sign on an island in a shallow lake. In about 1325, they began to build a settlement there.

As their power grew, the Aztecs needed more land. They increased the size of their islands by pouring land into the lake until the islands almost touched. They built **causeways**, or raised roadways, to connect the islands. The Aztecs called their city Tenochtitlán (teh•nahch•tee•TLAHN).

As time passed, Tenochtitlán grew into a large and beautiful city. It had great pyramids, broad avenues, and handsome buildings. The Aztecs built a system of **aqueducts**, pipes that carry water to where it is needed. Tenochtitlán had large parks and even a zoo. At the height of its power, over 300,000 people lived in Tenochtitlán.

The Aztecs Build an Empire

As the years passed, the Aztecs extended their rule over their neighbors. The conquered peoples were forced to work for the Aztecs. They also had to pay heavy taxes. Defeated cities were forced to send gold, jewels, animal skins, and food to the Aztecs. Worse, they had to send men and women.

Many of these men and women were sacrificed to Aztec gods. Prisoners taken in battle were also sacrificed.

As more territory was conquered, the Aztec empire became wealthy. By 1519, Montezuma ruled a land of 35 provinces. In it lived about 25 million people. Montezuma commanded an army of as many as 200,000 soldiers.

Then, one day in March 1519, messengers raced to the city with startling news. A small group of light-skinned strangers had landed on the east coast. The pale-skinned men rode strange animals that looked like deer but made noises like dragons. These animals were horses, which the Aztecs had never seen before. The messengers also reported that the men had weapons that fired iron balls.

The light-skinned strangers were Europeans. The Aztecs did not know it then, but the end of their empire was close at hand.

Section 3 Review

1. Why did the news of strangers in the east frighten Montezuma?

2. **Making Inferences** Do you think that the people the Aztecs conquered felt any loyalty toward Montezuma or the Aztec empire? Why or why not?

The Incas: People of the Sun

How did the Incas use science to build an empire?

While the Aztecs were building their empire in Mexico, another group was creating a great civilization in South America. This group was the Incas.

The Incas were scientific farmers. They farmed the dry areas along the Pacific coast by building irrigation systems. These brought water to the fields from more than 100 miles (166 km) away. They learned to use fertilizers and crop rotation. They cut terraces on the mountain slopes to increase the amount of land they could farm. The terraces kept the soil from washing away. Incan rulers ordered farmers to put part of their crops in public storehouses. In drought years, when the farming was bad, crops from the storehouses were given to the needy.

The religion of the Incas was based on sun worship. The Incas believed that their emperor, called the Lord Inca, was descended from the sun. Eventually, all people of the empire were called Incas, or "children of the sun."

The Incas lived in the Andes highlands. In about A.D. 1200, they spread their rule over other groups in the area. By the late 1400s, they had conquered many of the peoples of South America. Their empire covered much of present-day Peru, Ecuador, Bolivia, and Chile. At its height, the Incan empire had a population of about 12 million people.

The Master Builders

The capital of the empire was Cuzco (KOOS•koh). Incan rulers worked hard to unify the people of their vast empire. Conquered people had to learn the Incan language, Quechua (KECH•wah). Incan nobles were sent to live among newly conquered people to teach them Incan customs and

Machu Picchu, an ancient city of the Incas, was built high up in the Andes Mountains. The city lay hidden for many years until it was rediscovered in the 1800s.

laws. They established schools that taught the Incan religion. Unlike groups conquered by the Aztecs, groups conquered by the Incas tended to be loyal.

The Incas were great builders. They built a vast system of roads connecting all parts of the empire. Ten thousand miles of roads and bridges stretched from the Pacific Ocean across the Andes to the Amazon River. Some of these roads are still in use today. Besides roads and bridges, the Incas built great temples and palaces. Their builders were so skilled that they fitted stone blocks together without cement.

Decline of the Incan Empire

In the early 1500s, the Incan empire was divided by civil war. In 1525, the Incan ruler died, and his two sons fought for control of the empire. Although one son eventually won, the fighting took its toll. When the light-skinned strangers arrived in 1533, they found the Incan empire greatly weakened.

Imagine that you were visiting a group of the people that the Incas conquered. In your journal, record how these conquered people felt about the Incas. How did the Incas try to make these people a part of their society? What do you think about the way in which the Incas treated the people they conquered?

Section 4 Review

1. What advances did the Incas bring to farming?

2. **Comparing and Contrasting** How did Incan rulers differ from the Aztecs in the way they treated the people they conquered?

SECTION 5

The European Conquest

Why did Europeans come to the Americas?

While the Aztec and Incan civilizations were reaching new heights, the people of Europe were beginning to sail the seas on a grand scale. In the 1400s, Spain and Portugal competed fiercely with one another to find all-sea trade routes to Asia. Asia was the source of rich trade goods such as silks and spices.

In the late 1400s, Portugal established a water route to Asia around the coast of Africa. Spain had put its faith in an Italian sea captain named Christopher Columbus. Columbus had convinced the Spanish queen, Isabella, to support a wild idea. He wanted to reach Asia by sailing west across the Atlantic. Most people thought the idea was foolish, but the queen backed him anyway.

Instead of Asia, of course, Columbus reached the Americas. No one in Europe knew these huge lands existed. Between 1492 and 1504, Columbus made four voyages to the Americas. During his second voyage, he began the first European settlement there. Other explorers working for Spain extended the conquests.

Conquest of the Mainland

By 1500, there were a number of Spanish settlements on the islands of the West Indies. Once the Spanish began settling down, they brought all sorts of European goods to the Americas. These goods included horses, cattle, sheep, citrus fruits, and sugar cane—none of which existed in the Americas. The Spanish also brought goods from the Americas back to Europe. These included potatoes, corn, tobacco, tomatoes, green peppers, and chocolate.

From their island forts, soldiers were sent to explore the nearby coasts in search of riches.

The Fall of the Aztecs and the Incas
In 1519, Hernán Cortés (kor•TEHZ) landed with a small force on the coast of Mexico. It was Cortés's landing that so worried Montezuma, the leader of the Aztecs. On the coast, Cortés learned of the Aztec belief that a light-skinned god would come to save them.

Making certain to approach from the east, as the god was supposed to do, Cortés and his forces arrived in the Aztec capital in November. They captured and imprisoned Montezuma. For a while, Cortés tried to rule through the emperor. He thought that this would be the easiest way to control the Aztecs. However, by 1520, many Aztecs began to reject the idea that the Spanish were gods. They saw them simply as greedy men who could not seem to get enough gold. The Aztecs launched an attack on the Spanish, killing half of them. In the struggle,

The Spanish, left, were heavily out-numbered by the Aztecs, right. But the Spanish had modern weapons, which devastated the Aztecs who used old-fashioned weapons.

Montezuma died. Cortés escaped at night with the rest of his forces.

In 1521, Cortés returned, leading a force of about 1,000 Spanish soldiers and many Native American allies. These Native Americans had been conquered by the Aztecs and were eager to fight against them. They believed that once the Spanish defeated the Aztecs, they would be free.

After a three-month siege, the Aztecs surrendered. The city of Tenochtitlán was destroyed, and Cortés began to ship Aztec treasures back to Spain.

In 1532, Francisco Pizarro sailed southward along the west coast of South America and arrived at the Incan empire. Pizarro captured the Incan chief and killed him. The Incas were soon defeated. The Spanish were now masters of two treasure houses in Latin America — Mexico and Peru. Other conquerors pushed Spanish control throughout Latin America.

Spain's Rivalry With Portugal

Before long, both Spain and Portugal claimed lands in the Americas. These countries asked the Pope — the head of the Roman Catholic Church — to divide the Americas between them. In 1493, the Pope drew an imaginary line running north and south on the map. All lands west of this line would belong to Spain. All lands east of this line would belong to Portugal. Because of this agreement, Portugal later claimed the land that is now Brazil.

Section 5 Review

1. How did Christopher Columbus propose to get to Asia?

2. **Understanding Points of View** Why do you suppose that Spain was more interested than Portugal in sailing west to reach Asia?

Why the Aztec Empire Fell:
The Real Story

As you read on pages 323–324, the Aztecs crushed a Spanish force led by Hernán Cortés in July 1520. After that the Aztecs thought they were safe.

Yet little over a year later, the Aztec empire was in ruins. The Spanish were in total control. How did this happen?

Aztec Enemies

Cortés knew that many of the people that the Aztecs had conquered hated them. Cortés played on this anger. He promised to help free the conquered people from Aztec rule. He soon won many allies.

When Cortés first marched into Tenochtitlán in 1519, thousands of Native American soldiers marched with him. They thought that once the Aztecs were defeated, the Spanish would leave.

The Power of Disease

Unknowingly, Spain had an even more destructive weapon than its forces. That weapon was disease. The Spanish carried to the Americas diseases that were common in Europe. Among them were measles, mumps, and smallpox. These diseases were unknown in the Americas. No one there was **immune** to them. The word *immune* means "protected against disease."

Spanish soldiers who marched with Cortés in 1520 carried one of these European diseases, smallpox. Soon smallpox raged through the Native American population in Mexico. The disease killed nobles and slaves, soldiers and farmers, adults and children. The Aztec government and army were badly weakened.

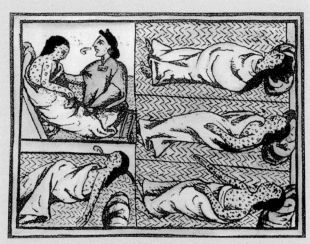

Smallpox destroyed the Aztec people. One Aztec said, "The illness was so dreadful that no one could walk or move. So they simply starved to death in their beds."

The Last Battle

After the death of Montezuma, an Aztec noble ruled briefly. He, however, died of smallpox. Then a 22-year-old noble named Cuauhtémoc (kwow•TEH•mohk) became emperor. Cuauhtémoc was a cousin of Montezuma. He would be the last Aztec ruler.

Cuauhtémoc tried to rally his people to defeat the Spanish. He asked a nearby city for help. The neighboring people were not moved by his plea. The leader of the city told Cuauhtémoc, "How would I gain by sending men to you, for we are always at war. Let the strangers kill the Aztec."

In May 1521, the Spanish attacked again. There were 900 Spanish soldiers and 100,000 Native American allies. Soon, Tenochtitlán was sealed off. No food or supplies could enter.

Still, the Aztecs fought on. The Spanish had to take the city house by house. For 93 days the Aztecs resisted.

Finally, on August 13, 1521, the battle was over. There was no longer a city to fight for. Tenochtitlán lay in ruins.

The Last Aztec Emperor

Cuauhtémoc survived the battle. He was taken prisoner and brought to Cortés. The Aztec prisoner spoke to his conqueror.

> *I have done everything in my power to defend myself and my people, and everything that it was my duty to do. You may do with me whatever you wish. So kill me, for that will be best.*

Cortés did not kill Cuauhtémoc then. The Spanish kept Cuauhtémoc as a prisoner. They tortured him, hoping that he would reveal where to find more Aztec gold.

Cortés feared that if Cuauhtémoc escaped, he might lead an uprising of the Aztecs. In 1525, Cortés led a campaign into Central America. On the way, Cortés charged that Cuauhtémoc had tried to start a rebellion. Far from his home, Cuauhtémoc was hanged by the Spanish.

Cuauhtémoc's courage made him a hero to Mexico's people. Today, a statue of him stands in Mexico City, not far from where his palace once stood. It is a monument to the last emperor of the Aztec nation.

Case Study Review

1. Who was Cuauhtémoc?
2. **Understanding Points of View** Why do you suppose that Spanish histories of the conquest emphasize the heroic role of Spanish soldiers, rather than the spread of disease?

I. Reviewing Vocabulary

Match each word on the left with the correct definition on the right.

1. causeway   **a.** a long period without rain
2. aqueduct   **b.** a system of pipes that carry water to where it is needed
3. drought   **c.** system of human-made ditches that carry water
4. irrigation **d.** a raised road across water or marshland

II. Understanding the Chapter

Answer the questions below on a separate sheet of paper.

1. In Section 2 of this chapter, Mayan culture is described as being very advanced. Give two examples of this advanced culture.
2. Why did the Aztecs decide to settle and build the city of Tenochtitlán?
3. Describe Incan accomplishments in building and farming.
4. What foods did the Spanish bring to the Americas and take back to Europe?

III. Building Skills: Making a Chart

Copy the chart below into your notebook. Fill in the approximate dates and major accomplishments of each of the three civilizations discussed in this chapter.

Civilization	Approximate Dates	Major Accomplishments
Maya		
Aztec		
Inca		

IV. Working Together

Form a small group with three or four of your classmates. With the group, think of an important event or accomplishment described in this chapter. Create a cartoon book about the event or accomplishment. Be sure to give full details about whatever you show.

On Assignment. . .

Keeping a Journal: Review the notes that you took as you read this chapter. Then create several journal entries that describe your thoughts and feelings about the early civilizations of Latin America. Read your journal entries to a classmate. Then discuss any similarities and differences in your impressions of these early civilizations.

CHAPTER 25

Breaking the Grip of the Crown

Why did Latin American nations seek independence?

Built on the foundations of an Aztec temple, Mexico City's Cathedral symbolized a new city. "Mexico City," Cortés said, "will soon be the most noble in the known world."

On Assignment. . .

Creating a Mini-History: Work with two or three classmates to create an illustrated mini-history for third grade students. Your mini-histories will contain three chapters about life in Latin America and the struggle for independence. As you read this chapter, note topics that you think would make interesting chapters for third graders. Consider featuring action-packed events, interesting characters, and good stories. Also, look for hint boxes providing suggestions to complete your assignment. At the end of the chapter, you will be given further instructions on how to complete your project.

Looking at Key Terms

- **Middle Passage** the journey across the Atlantic Ocean from West Africa to the Americas that was the route of the African American slave trade
- **mission** a religious settlement devoted to spreading Christianity
- **Creole** a person in Spanish Latin America whose parents or ancestors were from Spain
- **peon** a poor person who works all his or her life for rich landowners
- **viceroy** a person who governs a colony as a representative of the king or queen

SECTION 1

Building a Great Empire

How was Spain's empire in the Americas organized?

Sugar cane was harvested by enslaved Africans. Why was the labor of enslaved people from West Africa so important to the Spanish colonies?

One summer day in 1566, the people of Mexico City watched as wagon after wagon passed them in the street. Each wagon was loaded with a fortune in silver. Armed guards rode beside the wagons. The wagons were headed east — to the port of Veracruz.

In Veracruz, merchants waited for the first sight of the Spanish fleet. News that the ships were near meant that it was time for the great silver fair to begin. For 20 days, merchants of New Spain would trade their silver for furniture, glassware, and the latest fashions from Spain.

When the fair was over, the silver would be loaded onto the Spanish boats. Within weeks, much of the silver would be safely locked in the vaults of the king of Spain. The flow of silver and gold from its Latin American colonies made Spain the richest country in Europe. It also made Mexico City a wealthy city.

Slavery in the Spanish Empire

Spain's empire in the Americas grew over a number of years. Much of its growth was due to the labor of the people it ruled.

Native Americans made up much of the work force. They were forced to work on Spanish plantations and in mines. Disease and too much hard labor killed thousands of Native Americans.

The Spanish began to look for other ways to fill their need for free or cheap labor. Soon enslaved Africans were being shipped to the Americas under brutal conditions for this purpose. Millions made the forced journey.

The slave trade left memories of misery from Africa to the Caribbean. Countless Africans died in the horrible journey across the Atlantic known as the **Middle Passage**.

On the trip, chained Africans were packed together in cargo holds swarming with rats. One enslaved African later reported that the white men tore babies from their mothers' arms and threw them overboard. Two mothers leaped into the water after their children. One drowned. The other threw herself overboard one night.

By the mid-1500s, there were more enslaved Africans than Europeans on some Caribbean islands. To control the enslaved Africans, the Spanish used cruel means of punishment. Yet Africans endured the heartless treatment and managed to keep some of their traditions alive. Over time, African and

On Assignment...

One chapter of your mini-history could describe the Middle Passage. What images and words came to mind as you read about the journey of enslaved Africans? Use those thoughts in your mini-history.

Spanish ways mixed with those of Native Americans. This produced the unique cultures of the Caribbean region.

Organizing the Colonies

As the colonies prospered, Spanish settlers established new towns. By royal order, these new towns were all built in the same pattern.

The heart of every Spanish town was the main square, or plaza. In the plaza, people met for business or pleasure. The plaza still serves the same purposes in many Latin American and Spanish towns today.

The most important building in the Spanish town was the church. Sometimes the church faced the plaza. Other times, it was built on higher ground and could be seen for miles around. On the other sides of the plaza were the town hall and other public buildings.

The Role of the Church

One of the goals of the Roman Catholic Church was to get Native Americans and African Americans to become Christians. The church established **missions**, religious settlements devoted to spreading Christianity. The church tried to teach the Spanish language and customs. Some church leaders also tried to protect Native Americans from cruel treatment.

The Catholics of the Jesuit order set up missions along the Paraná River. For more than 150 years, Jesuits worked with the Guaraní (gwah•rah•NEE), Native Americans in Paraguay, Argentina, Uruguay, and Brazil.

In time, the Jesuits founded more than 30 missions devoted to converting Guaraní. They taught Guaraní to read and write. They also helped set up a Guaraní army to fight slave-hunting bands. Before this army formed, thousands of Guaraní were captured and taken to slave markets in Brazil.

On the other hand, the missions put Native Americans to work for the benefit of the religious orders. Native Americans provided the labor to build churches and raise food. The missions added a great deal of wealth to the Roman Catholic Church. This helped make the church the largest landowner in the Americas.

Social Order in Spanish America

The Spanish American colonies had a rigid social order. In Spanish America, a person was born into a class and remained there for life. There was almost no chance to move from one class to another.

At the top were people who had been born in Spain. They controlled most of the power and wealth. They held the highest offices in the church and the government. These people looked down on other people in the colonies.

Slightly lower on the scale were the **Creoles**. They were people born of Spanish parents in the Americas. The Creoles could not hold important positions in the government. But many were very

The conquered people of Mexico were put to work creating cities for the Spanish. Here, the city of Vera Cruz is being built.

wealthy. Some owned silver mines or huge country estates.

Many Creoles resented the power of the Spanish. Tensions between the classes would lead to revolutions during the 1800s.

Mestizos were people of mixed Spanish and Native American ancestry. They had no voice in the colonial government. However, they did many of the skilled jobs in Spanish colonies. They tended small farms and stores. Many also sold handmade goods.

Mulattos made up another group. These were people who had one parent of European descent and one of African descent. Some mulattos were accepted by mestizos or Africans as social equals. They were not accepted by the Spanish or by Creoles.

At the bottom of society were Native Americans and enslaved Africans. These groups lived in extreme poverty. Many toiled from sunrise to sundown. They lived in small huts with few pieces of furniture.

Destroying Native American Life

The Native Americans who survived conquest and disease were an important part of the labor force. Native peoples built mansions and churches for Spanish officials. They tilled the soil and mined for silver. They performed most of the basic tasks of colonial life.

Many Native Americans received wages for their work. But the wages were so low that workers had to borrow heavily from landowners to buy seed, farming equipment, and other necessities. In order to repay the debt, they were forced to become **peons**. Most Native Americans worked all their lives for landowners and were never able to pay off the debt.

The Spanish attempted to wipe out Native American culture. In missions, priests taught Native Americans to speak Spanish and to follow the Roman Catholic faith. Native Americans who worked on farms for Spanish landowners were forced to wear European-style clothing.

As they tried to change Native American culture, the Spanish found that their own culture in the Americas had also changed. The Spanish added such Native American foods as potatoes and corn to their diets. They also added Native American words to their language. Slowly, Spanish and Native American cultures blended. This blending produced the mestizo culture that is widespread in modern-day Mexico.

The Portuguese in Brazil

As you read in Chapter 24, Portugal controlled the region now known as Brazil. Brazil was a rich source of brazilwood — a wood from which red dyes could be made — and sugar cane.

Because of its favorable soil and climate, northeastern Brazil soon became the site of enormous sugar plantations. Enslaved Africans worked the sugar fields under harsh conditions.

In the 1700s, gold and diamonds were discovered inland. This led to a rush of settlement. Thousands of people left the coast hoping to get rich. Thousands more came from Portugal. New towns sprang up almost overnight.

Section 1 Review

1. Describe the way in which towns in Spanish America were built.

2. **Evaluating Information** Consider the following: Today in Paraguay, most people claim some Guaraní ancestry, and the Guaraní language is spoken by 90 percent of the population. Ninety-five percent of Paraguay's population is Roman Catholic. What role do you think the Jesuits played in preserving Guaraní heritage? What aspects of Guaraní heritage did the Jesuits change?

Sor Juana: A Woman in Latin America

In the 1600s, Mexico City was a center of the Spanish empire. In the city, carriages trimmed in gold clattered down stone streets. Bells rang in cathedrals. Students attended classes at the University of Mexico.

During this period, people in Latin America and in Europe admired the author of these words:

*Costliness and wealth bring me
no pleasure; the only happiness I
    care to find
derives from setting treasure in
    my mind,
and not from mind that's set on
    treasure.*

The author was a lonely nun who cared little for the splendor of Mexico City. She wanted only to study and to write poetry. She was known as Sor, or Sister, Juana.

According to legend, Juana Inés de la Cruz (HWAH•nah ee•NEHS deh•lah•kroos) began to read at age three. As a teenager, she wanted to go to the university, but women were not allowed to attend. She begged her mother to let her dress as a man so that she could attend the university anyway. Horrified, her mother refused. That left Juana with two choices. She could marry, or she could become a nun.

When she was 17, Juana chose to become a nun. She thought that life at the convent would give her time to study and write. Because she was a nun, her poetry came to the attention of church officials. Many of them thought it was wrong for a woman to have such intellectual interests as writing poetry. When she criticized a sermon, one church official demanded that she stop writing.

The anger of church officials finally broke Juana's spirit. She gave up writing poetry and sent officials a letter using her blood as ink. In the letter, she renewed her vows as a nun. In 1695, at age 43, Sor Juana died.

Case Study Review

1. Why couldn't Sor Juana attend the university?
2. **Analyzing Poetry** What does the poem above say about Sor Juana's beliefs and interests?

Struggle for Independence

How did the nations of Latin America gain independence?

Spain and Portugal were not the only European countries with colonies in Latin America. France, Britain, and the Netherlands also won territories in the region. (See the map below.) These European powers tried to keep tight control over their colonies. But the people who lived in the colonies grew more and more independent. One by one, the colonies began to fight for freedom.

Toussaint L'Ouverture was a self-educated former slave. He took charge of Haiti's independence struggle and defeated the French in a number of battles.

Haiti's Fight for Freedom

The first Latin American war for independence was fought against France. In 1791, enslaved Africans who worked on Haiti's sugar plantations revolted against colonial rule. They were led by a former slave named Toussaint L'Ouverture (loo•ver•TOOR). L'Ouverture had escaped slavery and educated himself. He was one of the main leaders in the fight against French rule. In 1802, he was captured. He died that year in a French prison.

However, the struggle for independence continued. By 1804, the Haitians had driven out the French, and Haiti became the first independent Latin American country.

Resentment in Spain's Colonies

Independence for Spain's colonies came later and not all at once. Colonists fought for freedom for a number of reasons. The system of colonial government was one of those reasons.

LATIN AMERICA UNDER EUROPEAN CONTROL ABOUT 1790

Legend:
- Spanish
- Portuguese
- British
- Dutch
- French

Place By the 1790s, Spain and Portugal had built large empires in the Americas. Who controlled Guiana in 1790? What name was used for Mexico in 1790?

Colonial government in Spanish America was very rigid. Spanish America was ruled by **viceroys**. Viceroys were appointed by the Spanish king or queen to rule in his or her place. The viceroy's job was to carry out the orders of the king or queen. A court appointed by the king and queen made sure the viceroy did his job.

The Spanish king and queen and a group of advisers in Spain made all the laws for their American colonies. Because all the decision making took place in Spain, it took a long time to bring about even small changes in the Americas. Also, colonial governments were often corrupt. Wealthy landowners often bribed officials to look the other way when they broke the law.

Another problem was hostility between classes. This was a serious problem by the 1800s. People who had been born in Spain continued to hold the highest positions. Creoles resented this power. Although they were often wealthy landowners, the Creoles were not permitted to hold high positions in government.

First Steps Toward Independence

One event that sparked revolution in Latin America was the American Revolution. The fact that British colonists in North America had won independence from Britain inspired Latin American revolutionaries to get rid of the Spanish.

In Spain's colonies, the movement for independence began on September 16, 1810, in the tiny Mexican village of Dolores. On that day, a local priest called for revolt against Spanish rule. His name was Father Miguel Hidalgo (ee•DAHL•goh).

Hidalgo led an army of thousands of mestizos and Native Americans against Spanish rule. Within a year, the Spanish captured Hidalgo. He was executed in 1811. But other leaders kept up the fight. After ten years of fighting, the rebels ended Spanish rule in Mexico.

Across the Andes

Most Latin American nations had to fight long and hard to break away from European rulers. Like the struggle in Mexico, the fight for independence in Central and South America would take years.

One such fight began in June 1819, when an army of more than 2,000 soldiers struggled to cross the Andes Mountains. They had set out from Venezuela and were marching toward the city of Bogotá in Colombia. There they hoped to surprise the Spanish army.

The leader of the army was Simón Bolívar (boh•LEE•vahr). Bolívar was a wealthy Creole. He had been educated in Europe. There he was inspired by the ideals of the French Revolution and vowed to free South America from Spanish rule.

Bolívar marched his army over the Andes. The soldiers climbed higher and higher into

Simón Bolívar was given the name "The Liberator." Bolívar led Latin Americans to freedom in the northern part of South America.

the snowy mountains. They suffered terribly from the bitter mountain cold.

Despite many hardships, the rebel army made it across. On August 7, 1819, the small army faced 3,000 veteran Spanish troops. A fierce battle followed. In it, the Spanish lost more than 1,000 soldiers. The rebels had won a key battle in Latin America's struggle for independence.

Soon after his victory, Bolívar established the republic of Gran Colombia. It was made up of the present-day countries of Venezuela, Ecuador, Colombia, and Panama.

While Bolívar led the struggle for independence in the northern part of South America, José de San Martín (sahn mahr•TEEN) led it in the southern part. For years, the struggle went back and forth. The rebels made some gains. Then they were defeated by the Spanish. Over time, San Martín continued the struggle and finally won. First, he freed his native land, Argentina. Then he led his army over the Andes into Chile. In 1818, Chile won its independence.

From Chile, San Martín's forces sailed north to Peru. San Martín captured the Spanish stronghold of Lima, but he could not drive the Spanish out of the nearby mountains. San Martín then joined forces with Bolívar. In 1824, they finally drove the Spanish out of Peru. By 1844, all that remained of Spain's once huge empire in the Americas was Cuba and Puerto Rico.

After Independence

Simón Bolívar and other leaders had dreamed of organizing Latin America into one large federal republic like the United States. However, the end of the Spanish empire did not unify Latin America. Vast distances, towering mountains, and thick rain forests separated different parts of South America. Also, the regions had no history of working together. Under Spanish rule, each region had been ruled by its own viceroy. In 1830, Bolívar died bitter that he could not unite South America.

After Bolívar's death, Gran Colombia split into three nations. Central America, which had joined Mexico in 1821, divided into five republics.

The revolutions in Latin America did not change the class system much. The Creoles became the new ruling class. Mestizos and Native Americans had also fought for independence. However, they remained as oppressed as before, being barred from holding high positions in the government, church, and private industry.

The wars of independence caused much damage. Cities filled with poor people who had been thrown off the land by the fighting.

Creole leaders drew up constitutions modeled on the U.S. Constitution. But with no experience in self-government, they had

Region The map of Latin America in 1828 was far different from the map today. In what way was Mexico in 1828 different from Mexico today?

trouble getting their plans to work. Latin America now faced the challenge of building new governments and new economies.

Brazil

In Brazil, independence was won without bloodshed. In 1807, Emperor Napoleon of France invaded Spain and attacked Portugal. The royal family of Portugal fled to Brazil. Once there, the king declared Brazil a kingdom. The king returned to Portugal after Napoleon was defeated. His son Pedro stayed in Brazil to rule. When Brazilian patriots demanded independence from Portugal, Pedro used it as an opportunity to further his own power. In 1822, Pedro declared Brazil an independent country and proclaimed himself emperor.

In 1889, a military revolt forced the Brazilian king to give up his throne. Brazil then became a republic. In the republic, citizens vote for their leaders in elections.

Section 2 Review

1. Why did Bolívar's dream of a unified South American nation fail to come true?

2. **Comparing and Contrasting** How was Mexico's struggle for independence different from Brazil's?

SECTION 3

Pain and Progress

What challenges did newly independent Latin American nations face?

Now that most Latin Americans were independent, they had to find ways to build their nations. In many nations, like Mexico, the army took charge of the governments.

A New Republic

After independence, Mexico struggled to form an effective government. This was a difficult task. After 11 years of war with Spain, Mexico was torn by power struggles.

Mexico also faced troubles in its territory of Texas. In the 1820s and 1830s, many people from the United States had settled in Texas. In 1835, fighting broke out between the Texans and the Mexican government. The Texans won the war. In 1836, Texas became independent.

When Texas became a part of the United States in 1845, tensions rose between the United States and Mexico. In 1846, the United States declared war on Mexico. In the war, the United States won a stunning victory. Mexico lost almost half its territory. The war also left Mexico with bitter feelings toward the United States.

Reform in Mexico

After the war with the United States, opposing groups in Mexico struggled to gain control of the government. By 1860, a group of reformers led by Benito Juárez (HWAH•rehs) won the power struggle.

Juárez became the first Native American to gain control of a country since the Spanish conquest. In 1861, Juárez was elected president of Mexico. The reformers passed laws that curbed the power of the military and of the Roman Catholic Church. They ended the special privileges of the church and seized church lands.

Juárez soon faced serious problems, however. France quickly invaded Mexico and installed an emperor. Juárez and his followers did not give up. They ousted the French and regained control of Mexico in 1867. Juárez ruled until his death in 1872.

Dictatorship and Revolution in Mexico

One of the Mexicans who led the fight against the French was the mestizo Porfirio Díaz (DEE•ahs). Díaz rose to power and ruled Mexico as a dictator from 1876 to 1911.

Two leaders of the Mexican Revolution were Pancho Villa, left, and Emiliano Zapata. Each man fought to overturn the old order in Mexico.

One day in January 1910, a short, quiet man approached Díaz. He identified himself as Francisco Madero. He told Díaz that the man Díaz had chosen for vice-president would be a very poor leader if anything should happen to Díaz.

Then the man astonished the dictator by offering himself as Díaz's next vice-president. Díaz ignored that suggestion. About a year later, Madero and a group of rebels overthrew Díaz and sent him into exile. In the first phase of the Mexican Revolution, Madero became Mexico's new president.

Madero proved unable to lead the country into bold reform. Many Mexicans wanted major changes in their country. They wanted the big estates to be broken up and the land given to villagers or small farmers.

In 1913, Madero was ousted from office and killed. General Victoriano Huerta (HWER•tah) seized power. Revolts soon broke out all over the country. Different rebel bands struggled for power. More than ten years of violence and troubles followed.

Many revolutionaries believed that the key to Mexico's future lay in economic reforms. One of the leading reformers was Emiliano Zapata (sah•PAH•tah). Zapata wanted to take land away from the wealthy. He saw the Revolution as a way to give land to poverty stricken farmers. Zapata continued to fight for change until 1919, when he was murdered by a rival.

By the time of Zapata's death, important changes were underway. There was a new constitution which included plans for land reform. Schools were set up in poor areas of Mexico and labor unions were recognized. But there would be more upheavals before the revolution was over. The Mexican Revolution did not end until the mid-1920s. Even then the promises of the revolution were left largely unfulfilled.

The changes brought about by the Mexican Revolution eventually improved the lives of Mexicans. However, the changes came at a fearful price. In the long struggle, about one million Mexicans died. This was one out of every 15 people in the country. Thousands of Mexicans fled north to the United States to escape the violence and famine.

Elsewhere in Latin America

Other Latin American countries also faced periods of trouble after they gained independence. In Argentina, for example, there was conflict between the people of Buenos Aires and the gauchos (GOW•chohs), or cowboys, of the pampas. After about 20 years of dictatorship, a democratic government gained control.

Stability and Poverty

The second half of the 1800s saw important changes taking place in Latin America. Larger countries such as Mexico, Argentina, and Chile began to make progress. Stable governments helped bring better economic times.

Latin American governments tried to attract foreign countries to invest. Latin America had tremendous natural resources. Yet, it lacked the money to develop them. Foreign countries could provide this money.

Changes in Argentina

Starting in the late 1850s, the British put a lot of money into Argentina. They built thousands of miles of railroad tracks across the grasslands. They built docks in Buenos Aires. They brought in British cattle to be raised on huge ranches.

Argentina also needed workers and began to encourage immigration. By 1914, foreigners made up about 30 percent of Argentina's population. Most immigrants came from Spain and Italy.

Foreign investment caused new problems for Latin American countries. They now depended on the industrial nations. Hard times abroad could mean economic disaster in Latin America as well.

Furthermore, the new wealth did not benefit most Latin Americans. A huge gap remained between the few wealthy people and the masses of poor people.

The End of Spanish Rule

Cuba and Puerto Rico were Spain's last colonies in the Americas. During the 1800s, they struggled to free themselves from Spain's control. The Spanish put down the rebellions with great brutality. Angered by such brutality, the United States entered the fight in 1898.

After a brief war, Spain lost its colonies. But Cuba and Puerto Rico did not gain full independence. The United States took over

On Assignment...

What struggles and challenges did Latin American countries face as they fought for and won independence? Choose some of the most action-packed events to include in your mini-history.

Puerto Rico. It also played a major role in the affairs of Cuba.

Other Latin Americans watched these developments with alarm. They worried about how far the United States might go in trying to control Latin America.

Central America

The people of Central America were especially worried. Central America was largely agricultural. Its economy depended on the export of coffee and bananas. Foreign companies, especially from the United States, were attracted by the profits to be made from these crops.

Large U.S. companies dominated Central America for many years. One company, the United Fruit Company, dominated the banana trade. It also controlled some Central American governments.

Workers resented the power of the foreign-owned companies. They believed that the United States used its influence to protect U.S.-owned businesses. In the future, these feelings would lead to unrest and revolution. You will read more about those events in Chapter 27.

Section 3 Review

1. What reforms did Benito Juárez undertake?

2. **Identifying Cause and Effect** Name one effect of foreign investment in Latin America.

I. Reviewing Vocabulary

Match each word on the left with the correct definition on the right.

1. mission
2. viceroy
3. Creole
4. peon

a. a person who governs in place of the king or queen
b. a poor person who works all his or her life for rich landowners
c. a person in Spanish Latin America whose parents or ancestors were Spanish
d. a religious settlement devoted to spreading Christianity

II. Understanding the Chapter

Answer the questions below on a separate sheet of paper.

1. How did Spain's American colonies make Spain the wealthiest nation in Europe during the 1500s?
2. What was the role of Roman Catholic missionaries among the Native Americans?
3. How did Haiti gain its independence?
4. What impact did foreign investment have on the countries of Latin America?

III. Building Skills: Summarizing

On a separate sheet of paper, write a few sentences that summarize each topic below.

1. Summarize the role of one class of people in New Spain: Africans, Creoles, mestizos, mulattos, or Native Americans.
2. Summarize Simón Bolívar's and José San Martín's roles in the struggle for Latin American independence.
3. Summarize the Mexican Revolution and how it changed Mexico.

IV. Working Together

Form a small group. With your group, create an illustrated time line showing the main events in Latin America's struggle to gain independence from Spain.

On Assignment...

Creating a Mini-History: Review the notes you and your group members took while you were reading the chapter. Together, decide on three topics to present in your mini-history. Brainstorm ideas on how to present the topics in pictures and words. Keep in mind that the audience is third graders. Plan a 10- to 12-page booklet in which to present your mini-history. Ask your classmates for feedback before preparing the final draft of your mini-history.

CHAPTER 26

Changing Patterns of Life in Latin America

How has life in Latin America changed in recent times?

The soaring lines of the new stock exchange building in Mexico City symbolize how Latin America is becoming a modernized urban society.

On Assignment...

Creating a Storyboard: A storyboard is a plan of action in pictures. It is made up of a series of cartoons or sketches that show key scenes in a movie or television show. Filmmakers use storyboards to plan the scenes of a movie. Imagine that you have been asked to create a storyboard for a film about the people of Latin America. At three points in the chapter, there are hints to help you sketch storyboard panels for the film. At the end of the chapter, you will put your panels together and present your storyboard to the class.

Looking at Key Terms

- **dialect** a form of a language that belongs to a certain region
- **urban** characteristic of a city or city life
- **liberation theology** a belief that the Roman Catholic Church should take an active role in ending poverty in Latin America
- **chaperon** an older person who accompanies a boy and girl on a date to assure proper behavior
- **squatter** person who settles on land he or she doesn't own

SECTION 1

A Land of Many Cultures

What are the cultural roots of Latin Americans?

A newspaper writer in Ecuador goes to a party. There she meets a woman with a Native American background. She also meets a woman with Spanish ancestors. She meets a woman who speaks Quechua (kehch•WAH), a Native American language. She meets a woman who is a devout Roman Catholic. Finally, she meets a woman who observes a Native American religion.

Question: How many women has she met?

Answer: In Latin America, the writer could have met just one person!

A Blend of Cultures

As you have read, the people of Latin America have their roots in many parts of the world. Some have Native American backgrounds. Others have African, European, or Asian backgrounds.

Some Latin Americans have a background that blends two of the cultures. Some have roots in three or four cultures. The word used to describe this mix of cultures is diversity. Diversity means "differences."

Latin America is a very diverse region. However, some countries are more diverse than others. The greatest diversity is in countries such as Mexico and Brazil. Here Native American, African, and European influences have mixed since the 1500s. The least diverse countries are Argentina and Uruguay where the European influence has been strongest. Few Native Americans live in these countries. Disease and fighting nearly wiped them out during the Spanish takeover. (See Chapter 24.)

Despite the diversity, some generalizations can be made about the people of Latin America. For example, most Latin

On Assignment. . .

The first scene of your film could be about the cultural diversity of Latin America. Sketch out ideas for your first storyboard panel. The sketches could show the person the writer met at the party in Ecuador. One sketch might show the person explaining her traditions. Another could show her explaining her religion. Use cartoon "bubbles" to write the words.

Americans speak Spanish and most are Roman Catholic.

The Role of Culture

Culture is the way of life of a group of people. Everyone has a culture. We grow up with it. The language we speak is part of our culture, as are our religious beliefs and the foods we eat.

A culture also includes the governments that people set up and the ways in which people make a living. Culture includes music, art, and literature. In short, culture is all the things that make up a people's way of life.

Culture affects many aspects of our life. It affects what we consider right and wrong. It influences what we consider beautiful. It helps determine our goals for the future.

Section 1 Review

1. (a) What is diversity? (b) Give an example of diversity in Latin America.

2. **Applying Information** (a) What historical events account for the diversity within many Latin American nations? (b) What accounts for the lack of diversity within some others?

Daily Life in Latin America

What cultural traditions do Latin Americans have in common?

We talk of Latin America's many cultures because there is no single Latin American culture. Like the people, the cultures of Latin America blend many heritages. These blends differ from one nation to another. Daily life in Latin America reflects the mix of cultures, offering a variety of experiences.

Latin America's Many Languages Spanish is the language most Latin Americans speak. However, Brazilians speak Portuguese. In Haiti, the official language is French. In Suriname, it is Dutch. English is the official language on many Caribbean islands such as Trinidad and Tobago and Jamaica.

In addition, millions of people speak a Native American language such as Quechua or Guaraní. Some speak only a Native American language. Others speak both their Native American language and Spanish. In fact, Peru and Paraguay have two official languages. One is Spanish. In Peru the other is Quechua and in Paraguay it is Guaraní.

Across the Language Divide Language is one of the most important links for people across Latin America. For example, because most people speak Spanish, someone from Colombia could communicate with someone from Peru. Although Brazilians speak Portuguese, some can understand Spanish-speaking people.

Over the years, differences in the Spanish language have developed. In some countries, Native American words have been added to the Spanish language. Each Latin American region also has its own Spanish **dialect**, or form of the language.

The meaning of some words may differ from place to place. For example, in Cuba, "bus" is *guagua*. In Chile, it is *micro*. In Mexico, it is *camión*. Ask for a *torta* in Mexico and you will receive a sandwich. Ask for the same thing in Chile and you will be served a slice of layer cake.

Despite the minor differences in dialect, the language is the same. Therefore, most Latin Americans who speak Spanish can understand one another.

Life in Latin America is strongly affected by religious ties to the Roman Catholic Church. Here, a parade in Cuzco, Peru, blends Catholic and Native American practices.

Religion in Latin American Life

Most Latin Americans share the same religion. More than 90 percent of the people are Roman Catholic. The church continues to be an important force in Latin American life.

Everyday life is strongly affected by religion, particularly in rural areas. In tiny villages in the mountains, churches are the center of the community. Almost every home has a table decorated with statues of saints.

In general, religious ties have weakened among people who have moved to the cities from villages. In recent years, however, poor city people have strengthened their religious ties. You will read more about this trend below.

Sometimes, the people of Latin America have mixed their traditional practices with the Roman Catholic religion. Native Americans and people of African heritage who have converted to the Roman Catholic religion often blend traditional practices into their new faith.

Protestant churches have attracted large numbers of Latin Americans in recent years. Many people in **urban** areas, or cities, have converted to Protestant religions.

There are Jews, Muslims, and Hindus in Latin America. However, their numbers are small.

The Changing Role of the Catholic Church As you read in Chapter 25, the Spanish and Portuguese settlers brought the Roman Catholic religion to Latin America. In the early years, many church leaders and clergy worked to defend the rights of the weak and poor. Over time, the church grew in power and wealth. It eventually became the largest landowner in Latin America. As its wealth grew, the church more often supported the wealthy classes.

Latin Americans felt that the church was tied too closely with Latin America's rich people. Many thought the church opposed reforms that might threaten its own wealth. Such reforms included redistributing land to the poor.

In the 1960s, support grew to strip the church of some of its power. More and more, the role of the church came under attack.

In response, some Catholic leaders called for change. They demanded efforts to help the poor. They helped build clinics in the cities. They worked to provide education for the young. These actions increased the loyalty of many poor city dwellers to the church.

Liberation Theology Many priests and nuns thought these actions did not go far enough. They argued that the church had to take a more active role in ending Latin American poverty. They proposed a new idea. It came to be known as **liberation theology**. *Liberation* means "freedom." *Theology* is the study of religious belief.

Liberation theology held that poverty was created by the people who had power in society. The Catholic Church had to do more than just help the poor. It had to help change the society that created such poverty.

Thousands of priests and nuns took up liberation theology. They moved into poor urban neighborhoods. There they helped the poor organize groups to fight for change. They also formed movements to force governments to make changes in society.

Many church members opposed liberation theology. Some argued that a church should only deal with religious matters and stay out of politics. Leaders in the church ordered priests not to become political leaders. Thus, not everyone who worked for change accepted liberation theology.

Cultural Life

Another institution that plays a large role in Latin American life is the family. Most Latin Americans have a strong sense of family loyalty. Most people are supported by an extended family. This includes cousins, aunts, uncles, and other relatives. Often, several generations of a family live in one home.

"Mi Casa Es Su Casa." Most social events involve the family and the home.

Family ties are especially strong in Latin America. Here, a family in Buenos Aires, Argentina, gathers for one of the most important family ceremonies—a baptism.

Most of a child's early life is spent with members of the family. Families mark birthdays, weddings, and saints' days with major celebrations. Sometimes the parties will last all night. Guests are welcomed with the greeting *"Mi casa es su casa."* This means "My house is your house."

Family ties are especially strong in rural areas. Cousins, uncles, and aunts usually live nearby. If someone is ill, other family members are there to help.

Family ties are not as great in the cities. Newcomers often feel alone. If they have an accident or lose their jobs, there is often no one to help them.

Godparents An important Latin American tradition is that of godparents. It is considered an honor to be asked to serve as *padrino* (godfather) or *madrina* (godmother) to a child. Godparents provide young people with support as they are growing up. If a child's parents die, the godparents take on the responsibility of raising the child.

Dating In the past, young people could date only with a parent's permission. They were accompanied by a **chaperon**, an older person who ensured proper behavior. Today, however, the traditional patterns are changing. Young people now meet on their own.

Most young people live at home until they get married. When a Latin American woman marries, she does not give up her family name. If Maria García marries Eduardo Martínez, she becomes Maria García de Martínez.

All children bear a given name, the father's family name, and the mother's family name, in that order. Thus, if Maria García and Eduardo Martínez have a son whom they name Gabriel, the child's full name will be Gabriel Martínez García.

Changing Role of Women In the traditional family, the father heads the household. He is expected to support the family. The mother is responsible for raising the children and for maintaining religious ties.

In rural areas, the tradition of *machismo* remains strong. *Machismo* means "male dominance." A woman is expected to accept whatever her husband decides. Many families believe that girls do not need an education. Therefore, many girls in rural areas cannot read or write.

In rural areas, women carry the main burdens of the family. They do most of the farming. They buy and sell goods at market.

In the cities, however, many women have jobs outside the home. The money they earn often keeps the family going and at the same time gives women a sense of independence.

More women are earning university degrees and entering professions. Many women have become lawyers and doctors in recent years. Yet they often have a hard time finding jobs. This is due in part to traditional discrimination against working women.

Foods of Latin America

It is not surprising that foods in Latin America are different from place to place. However, some foods can be found in almost all countries. These include tomatoes, beans, rice, potatoes, corn, and chicken. A wide variety of fresh fruits is also available. Latin American foods usually blend Spanish and Native American or African ingredients.

For your second storyboard panel, you might draw a sketch that describes family life in Latin America. Look back at this section for an explanation of the roles of different family members.

Each country has its own food specialty. One of the most popular dishes in Mexico is *guacamole* (gwah•kuh•MOH•lee). It consists of avocados seasoned with hot peppers and tomatoes. In Argentina and Uruguay, the specialty is the *asado* (ah•SAH•doh), an outdoor barbecue of roasted meats. The national dish of Brazil is *feijoada* (fay•ZWAH•dah), black beans cooked with sausages, beef, and pork.

Most Latin Americans eat their main meal at midday. This meal consists of several courses. It includes soup, rice and beans, and meat or fish. Dinner is usually a simple dish or snack. It is not served until 8 or 9 p.m.

Section 2 Review

1. How does language help link the people of Latin America?
2. **Defending a Point of View** Do you think it is a good idea for young people to be accompanied by a chaperon on dates? Why or why not?

SECTION 3

A Region of Cities

What are the characteristics of Latin American cities?

La Paz is Bolivia's most important city. La Paz lies in a deep canyon on the Bolivian plains. At the base of the canyon are the large houses of the wealthy. These houses are often surrounded by high walls. Many houses have a half dozen or more bedrooms, large spaces for entertaining, and apartments for live-in servants. Nearby are high-rise buildings, shops, and offices. Climbing toward the top of the canyon are the shacks of the poor people. Many of these shacks perch on the edge of the canyon.

Until recently, there were only two classes of people in La Paz: a rich minority and a poor majority. There are still few rich and many poor in La Paz. In recent years, however, the city has changed in two major ways.

- There are many more middle class people in La Paz. Middle class neighborhoods have grown up in downtown La Paz. Government workers, merchants, and office workers all have come to live in the city. They occupy the apartment houses that are being built all over the downtown. Middle class suburbs have spread out along the canyon floor. Now they are beginning to creep up the canyon. One such middle class suburb is Villa Fatima. It is built on a steep canyon wall overlooking downtown La Paz. Here, a family may sit on a patio that is little more than a ledge in the canyon side.

- Poor people have flooded into La Paz from all over Bolivia. They have crowded into whatever free space they can find. As the poor people have entered the city, the search for living space grows harder. Many people have built homes on the steepest slopes of the canyon. Some people live in places not meant to support humans. Heavy rains cause landslides that sweep homes down into the canyons. Stone walls help keep small children from tumbling down the cliff.

Despite the hardships, people still flow into La Paz. As you will read on the following page, the city offers more opportunity than the countryside. People who move to La Paz dream of making a better life for themselves and their children.

Booming Cities

What's happening in La Paz is happening all over Latin America. Until the 1950s, most Latin Americans were farmers. Since the 1960s, huge numbers of Latin Americans have moved from rural areas to cities. Today, Latin American cities are growing by about 14 million persons a year.

People come to the cities to escape poverty. They hope to find better jobs, education for their children, and better living conditions.

About three out of every four Latin Americans now live in cities. This is one of the highest rates in the world. In Asia and Africa, about one in three people live in the cities. One in three Latin Americans lives in a city with more than a million people.

The Great Cities Latin America is the land of the "mega-city." Mega-cities are places where a large portion of the people of a country live. For example, there are 32 million people in Argentina. About 12 million, or 37.5 percent, of them live in Buenos Aires. Santiago has 5 million of Chile's 12 million people. Mexico City is home to 20 million of the 90 million people who live in Mexico.

Latin America has some of the world's fastest-growing mega-cities. For example, by the year 2000, Mexico City may have a population of more than 30 million!

More than 20 Latin American cities have populations larger than one million. Four Latin American cities are among the world's ten largest urban areas. They are Mexico City in Mexico, Rio de Janeiro and São Paulo in Brazil, and Buenos Aires in Argentina.

Many of Latin America's cities are very modern. They have towering skyscrapers and busy highways. They have mass transit rail lines and busy airports.

Parts of these cities are very attractive. There are wide streets, tall buildings, and beautiful shops and homes. They also have restaurants, theaters, and universities. Latin America's growing middle class lives in the cities. Here, children have the best chance for an education.

The Darker Side of City Life Rapid growth has made urban living difficult. Many of the largest Latin American cities have high levels of air pollution. There are few rules restricting how and where buildings may be constructed. Factories are often built close to housing areas and spew smoke into these areas.

Barrios and Slums Most cities are divided into neighborhoods called barrios. Most workers commute from their barrios to work. To get there, many workers spend two or three hours a day riding a bus. Urban highways are often jammed with traffic. During rush hours, the traffic often comes to a stop.

The poorest city people live in terrible slums. These people are usually **squatters**. Squatters are people who settle on land they do not own. Many of these squatters have low paying jobs. Others are recent arrivals from rural areas and are therefore unemployed. When they move, they do so in the middle of the night. They quickly build shacks on public land. The squatters use sheet metal, aluminum, and scraps of lumber to build their shacks.

Lima In recent years, the people of Peru have been fleeing the countryside for Lima and other cities. More than a thousand Peruvians a day come to live in Lima. "The city has grown like a wild animal," one expert has said.

In one case, 600 families took over land that had once been a garbage dump in Lima. Overnight, they built straw huts. The police moved in the next day. They threw out the families and tore down the huts. But the

On Assignment...

For your third storyboard, show life in urban Latin America. Based on the information in this section, sketch pictures that capture life in a Latin American city.

In the mountains of Bolivia, farmers prepare the land for potato planting. High up in the Andes, potatoes are one of the few crops that grow well.

settlers came back the next day. Within six months, 10,000 people were living in the former garbage dump. It had become a shantytown — a place filled with tumble-down shacks and poor people.

Crime is widespread in the shantytown. Pollution there makes people's eyes water. These days, the police rarely come to the shantytown. The people of the town have organized their own patrols. Water is brought in with barrels. No one collects trash. Residents just dump it by the side of the road.

Village Life

For Latin American peasants, life continues much as it has for centuries. Most villages have fewer than 400 people. The pace of life is slow. In warm climate regions, when the sun is hottest at midday, no one is to be seen. People stay indoors to escape the brutal heat. There may be no school in the village. If there is, children must often walk miles to get to it. Very few people can read or write. They learn about the outside world by listening to the radio or attending movies.

Landowners and Peasants Most of Latin America's cash crops are grown on large farms. These farms are usually owned by a single family. The family does not work the land. Instead, peasants pay rent to farm the owners' land.

The landowners make large profits by demanding high rents from the peasants. These rich landowners live most of the year in large cities. A manager runs the plantation for them. This system of land ownership has caused serious problems in Latin America.

Some small farmers do own land. Most often, the soil is very poor. The small farmer is too poor to buy fertilizer and good seed. In remote areas, some farmers use the same methods their ancestors used centuries ago. Other farmers survive by raising animals on hillsides. Poverty in rural areas is the main reason farmers move to cities. For many poor farmers, the city is the only hope for a better life.

Section 3 Review

1. How have Latin American cities changed in recent years?
2. **Proposing Solutions** The cities of Latin America face huge problems. Identify two of these problems and propose a possible solution to each of them.

Inside a Shantytown in Caracas

At night, when the sun goes down, the city of Caracas (kah•RAH•kahs), Venezuela, provides a show of light and sounds. The high-rise buildings sparkle. Automobile headlights glow like fireflies as they move slowly down the broad avenues. Fine shops stay open late, catering to wealthy shoppers. Outdoor cafes are filled with young people. The subway, called the Metro, glides through the city.

During the 1970s, Venezuela had an oil boom. Money from the sale of oil poured into Caracas. High-rise buildings and highways sprouted across the city. This created what city residents proudly called "Miami with mountains."

From Town to Shanty

From his shack on a hillside overlooking the city, Marcos Lopez Crespo can watch the city's light and sound show. Four months ago, he first came to the hillside from the village of Maturín (mah•toor•REEN) in the east. Then, he was awed by the lights. He could stand for hours watching the movement, hearing the noises.

After a while, he stopped noticing. There were too many other things to do. His cousin Hector helped Marcos. Hector had come to Caracas six years before. He knew his way around the city.

Hector and Marcos collected pieces of metal and wood from an abandoned construction site. With these, they built a one-room shack. Then, with Hector's help, Marcos got a job at a car wash.

Three weeks after coming to the hillside, Marcos was able to send for Juana (HWAH•nah), his wife of two years. Together they expanded their shack with flattened tin cans and scraps of wood. They put in a slab of paperboard they found on the hillside. The shack now has two rooms.

Hector showed Marcos how to tap into the city's power lines. This gave him light and electricity to run his most prized possession, his television set.

There is still no running water in the shack. A pipe at the bottom of the hill is the main source of water. Juana spends several hours each day carrying cans of water up the hill.

The slums of Caracas have been called some of the worst in the world. But Marcos doesn't think of the neighborhood as a slum. In fact, he doesn't think it's such a bad place.

Like Marcos and Juana, most of the people in the slum are recent arrivals to the city. Most have come from rural areas of Venezuela. There, living conditions are even worse than they are in the Caracas slum. Many were drawn to the city by the dream of high-paying jobs. When they reached the city, they found they lacked the skills to do any more than the lowest-paying work.

Are times hard in the slum on the hillside? Sure, Marcos says. But they are better than in Maturín. At least in Caracas, there are jobs.

Loss of Faith in Government

If he is going to improve himself, Marcos believes, he will have to do it on his own. Marcos doubts that he will get help from the government. "They are a bunch of rich old men," he says. "All they want to do is make themselves richer."

To survive, Marcos will have to get a better paying job. When he first got the car wash job, he thought he was earning enough money to live well. Now he is not sure. Prices continue to rise. "Medicines, flour, milk are always going up. My salary remains the same."

Marcos hasn't lost hope. He knows that his shack doesn't always have to remain a shack. "Look at Hector," he says. "Hector also began by washing cars. Now he has opened a little hardware shop at the base of the hill."

Six years ago, Hector put up a shack much like Marcos's. Since he paid no rent, he put the money into improving his house. Six years ago, Hector's house was made of cardboard. Now he lives in a two-story brick house.

Case Study Review

1. Why did Marcos come to Caracas?
2. **Understanding Points of View** Why doesn't Marcos think of his neighborhood as a bad place to live?

I. Reviewing Vocabulary

Match each word on the left with the correct definition on the right.

1. squatter
2. urban
3. dialect
4. chaperon

a. person who accompanies a boy and girl on a date
b. person who settles on land he or she doesn't own
c. characteristic of a city or city life
d. a form of a language that belongs to a certain region

II. Understanding the Chapter

Answer the questions below on a separate sheet of paper.

1. Which Latin American countries mentioned in the chapter have very diverse cultures? Which ones mentioned in the chapter do not have diverse cultures?
2. How has the role of the Roman Catholic Church in Latin America changed in recent years?
3. What is a "mega-city"? Describe why mega-cities are important to Latin America.
4. How has the city of Caracas changed in recent years?

III. Building Skills: Recognizing Cause and Effect

In each of the pairs of sentences, tell which is the cause and which is the effect.

1. a. Rural poverty is extreme.   b. Millions of Latin Americans flood into cities.
2. a. Many Catholic clergy follow "liberation theology."   b. The Roman Catholic Church has been criticized for not solving Latin American poverty.
3. a. Latin American cities grow.   b. Extended family ties weaken.

IV. Working Together

Form a small group. With the group, write dramatic newspaper headlines about key facts you have learned in this chapter about Latin America. With other members of your class, make a bulletin board display of your headlines.

On Assignment...

Creating a Storyboard: Imagine that you are a filmmaker who is planning a film about Latin America. A storyboard will help you lay out your ideas for scenes in the film. To create your storyboard, put together the sketches you made as you read this chapter. Then write a brief narrative that links the three scenes in the storyboard together. Present your storyboard to the class, while you read your narrative to them.

The Changing Face of Latin America

How have the governments and the economies of Latin American nations changed since independence?

Brazil's rapidly growing economy has made it one of the world's leading industrial nations. Above, cranes load goods for export on the docks of Rio de Janeiro.

Looking at Key Terms

- **land reform** a government policy that involves breaking up large estates and giving the land to peasants
- **exile** a person who lives in another country because of political disagreements
- **caudillo** a Spanish term for a military strongman
- **civilian** a citizen who does not belong to the military
- **illiterate** unable to read or write

On Assignment . . .

Creating a Map: After you have read this chapter, you will be asked to create a classroom resource map that shows a portion of Latin America. To prepare for your assignment, take notes about the countries, cities, and other locations that are discussed in the chapter. Look for countries that seem especially interesting to you. Pay attention to political events and economic programs in the countries of your choice. Hint boxes are located throughout the chapter to help you take notes.

Divisions Over Land

Why has the issue of land reform caused conflict in Latin America?

Most of Latin America's wealth is based on its land. However, most of the region's problems also arise from the land. For most of its history, the people of Latin America have fought over control of the land. In many cases, heated battles between those who controlled the land and those who did not threw Latin American countries into conflict and disorder.

The Gap Between the Rich and the Poor

In Latin America, there were usually two major classes of people. One class was made up of a few very wealthy people. They owned much of the land, mineral deposits, and factories.

The poor people made up the second class. In Latin America the poor people were the majority. Most poor people farmed small plots of land. Others lived in urban shantytowns. There were few people in the middle class.

By the middle of the 1900s, the gap between the very wealthy and the very poor was wide. Farm workers had little hope of improving their lives. Their anger led to frequent violence. When this happened, the military stepped in.

In the 1900s, many workers began to join labor unions. Unionized workers fought for better wages and working conditions. The workers also pushed for a greater voice in the government.

Hard Economic Times

Just as some workers began to make gains, the world was hit with a major crisis. In the 1930s, the Great Depression crippled the economies of countries around the world.

For Latin America, worldwide depression meant disaster. Most of the countries of Latin America relied on exports to support their economies. If countries around the world could no longer afford to buy Latin American goods, Latin Americans would suffer terribly.

Economic problems caused political problems. Governments rose and fell quickly in many Latin American nations. To combat this, nations tried to gain control over their economies. Argentina, Mexico, and Brazil tried to build industries. By doing so, they hoped to depend less on money from exports.

Struggles for Land Reform

In the 1900s, **land reform** became a major issue. Land reform is a government policy that involves the breakup of large estates. Usually, the small pieces of land are given to peasants.

Those who supported land reform said that Latin America was poor because most peasants farmed land owned by the wealthy. They pointed in particular to Central America. In Guatemala, two thirds of the land was in the hands of just 2 percent of the people. In Honduras, 5 percent of the people owned two thirds of the farmland.

The landowners of Honduras and Guatemala were powerful. They fought any effort to change the system. They were supported by the United Fruit Company, which also owned huge amounts of land. (See Chapter 25.) The U.S. government backed the United Fruit Company.

In the early 1950s, a reform government came to power in Guatemala. It proposed breaking up the estates. Owners of United Fruit panicked. They asked the U.S. government to help them. The United States responded by supporting an invasion of Guatemala by Guatemalan exiles in 1954. An **exile** is someone who leaves (or is thrown out of) his or her native country — usually for political reasons. The U.S.-backed

On the barren altiplano, or high plain, a Bolivian farmer uses a wooden plow and the muscle power of oxen. Land reform requires money to help farmers buy modern tools.

invasion toppled Guatemala's reform government. Land reform efforts came to an end.

First Steps Toward Land Reform

In other parts of Latin America, land reform was more successful. The first Latin American nation to carry out land reform was Mexico. Beginning in 1917, huge estates were broken up. The land was given to Mexican peasants.

During the 1950s, Bolivia gave land to thousands of peasant families. Venezuela broke up land estates in the 1960s.

In Cuba, land reform was different. In the 1960s, Cuban leader Fidel Castro broke up large estates. However, the land did not go to individual peasants. Rather, the land was taken over by the state. Today, most Cuban farm workers work on farms for the Cuban government. You will read more about Cuba in Case Study 27 on pages 360–361.

Land Reform Today

Land ownership is still an issue in Latin America today. Most governments have passed reform programs. But they have not always been able to enforce them.

Land reform is one of the most bitterly contested issues in Latin America. The people who own large amounts of land strongly resist reform. They say that large estates are more efficient than a lot of small farms. Supporters of land reform believe that people who own their own land will farm it better. They also believe that it will help give poor farmers a stake in society.

Governments that carry out land reform programs hope to slow the flood of people into Latin America's cities. As you read in Chapter 26, cities are crowded with people from the countryside who are looking for work.

An effective land reform program is expensive. It requires a great deal of money to pay the people whose land is being taken away. It also requires training to teach peasants better ways of farming.

Latin American countries are facing the need for more land in other ways. Brazil has a huge undeveloped interior. The government of Brazil has supported the opening of new land. During the 1950s, the government decided to move its capital from Rio de Janeiro to the interior. The government hoped to attract people and businesses to this region. Brazil sponsored the construction of an entirely new capital city called Brasília. After a slow start, Brasília succeeded in bringing people to the interior.

A growing population has increased the need for land and resources. Logging companies have stripped trees away from large areas of Latin America's rain forests.

However, developing new land creates other problems. Many people worry that valuable natural resources will be destroyed. Each year, an area of forest larger than the state of Massachusetts is stripped of lumber in Brazil. As the forest is cut down, an army of landless peasants follows. These peasants occupy the free land.

The global community is concerned about the destruction of the world's forests for many reasons. One reason is that many species of animals and plants live in these forests. Destroying the forests puts species in danger of extinction. Another reason for concern is that Brazil's forests produce vast amounts of oxygen. Cutting down the Brazilian forests or any other forests may endanger the earth's oxygen supply.

Section 1 Review

1. Why was the city of Brasília built?
2. **Supporting Generalizations** Find three facts to support this generalization: Most of Latin America's wealth is based on its land. However, most of the region's problems also arise from the land.

SECTION 2

Fighting Poverty

What factors have contributed to poverty in Latin America?

Poverty is Latin America's biggest problem. Thousands of farmers live on tiny plots of poor land. They are barely able to grow enough food for their families. Many cannot read and write.

All over Latin America, poor farmers have the same needs. They need more and better land, pure water, better roads, electricity, public schools, and health services.

Moving to the Urban Slums

As you read in Chapter 26, Latin Americans are becoming an urban people. Sadly, about one out of every three Latin American city dwellers lives in an urban slum. Many of these are people who have recently arrived from rural areas.

You have also read about the squatter villages. These shantytowns have different names in different countries. In Argentina, they are called *villas miserias*. In Brazil, they are known as *favelas*. In Venezuela, they are called *ranchos*. No Latin American nation has escaped them.

On Assignment...

Make a list of the countries and cities mentioned in this section. Which countries are of particular interest to you? Why? How would you indicate these interesting facts on a map? For example, what kinds of things might you show on a map of Guatemala, Mexico, Cuba, or Brazil?

One way to escape from poverty is to get an education. However, getting an education is not easy. All Latin American countries require young people to attend school. But Latin American governments lack the funds to enforce this law. There are not enough schools and teachers for all the students. Even where there are schools, many young people do not attend. They must work instead to help support their families.

Population Increase

Another factor that contributes to poverty is Latin America's growing population. The population is growing so fast that it may double in 30 years. Rapid population growth makes it even harder for Latin Americans to feed, educate, and employ themselves.

Depending on One Crop

Latin America has sometimes been called a region of one-crop countries. For example, Colombia has long depended on one crop for most of its income. That crop is coffee. The countries of Central America depend upon selling bananas. Cuba depends upon sugar. If the crop is a poor one, the whole country suffers greatly.

Some Latin American countries are dependent on one natural resource such as tin, iron, or oil for most of their income. Copper makes up two thirds of Chile's exports. Tin accounts for three quarters of Bolivia's foreign sales. Venezuela relies on oil sales. Again, a sudden drop in world prices can badly hurt a country that depends on one natural resource.

Lacking a school building, these Bolivian children go to an outdoor school. Rapid population growth has put a strain on public services in Latin America.

In the last half century, many countries have made progress in building new industries. For example, Argentina, Brazil, Venezuela, and Mexico have become major industrial powers.

However, most Latin American countries find it very difficult to build new industries. These nations lack good transportation systems. They have little fuel to power machines. They also lack the trained workers to run the industries. Therefore, industry has been limited to a few small factories in the largest cities.

Natural Wealth, Hidden Resources

Latin America has enormous potential for wealth. It has a great deal of rich farmland. After the Middle East, Latin America has the world's largest oil reserves. Mexico and Venezuela have huge stores of oil.

Latin America also has large mineral reserves. Brazil and Chile have just begun to scratch the surface of their copper, iron ore, and tin supplies. Although Latin America still has huge debts and domestic problems, it may some day develop its exports and become economically powerful.

On Assignment...

Add to the list of countries and cities you began in Section 1. Which countries depend on one crop or one natural resource? Think of symbols that could be used to show these resources on a map. For example, what symbol could you use for coffee? For copper?

COUNTRIES OF LATIN AMERICA

COUNTRY	CAPITAL	AREA (Square miles)	POPULATION	AGRICULTURE AND INDUSTRIES
Anguilla (U.K.)	The Valley	35	8,800	salt, boat building, tourism
Argentina	Buenos Aires	1,065,189	33,900,000	oil, lead, zinc
Bahamas	Nassau	5,380	300,000	salt, tourism, rum
Barbados	Bridgetown	166	300,000	sugar, tourism, cotton, lime
Belize	Belmopan	8,867	200,000	sugar
Bolivia	La Paz/Sucre	424,165	8,200,000	tin, antimony, textiles, potatoes
Brazil	Brasília	3,286,470	155,300,000	coffee, cotton, sugar, steel
Chile	Santiago	292,257	14,000,000	copper, iodine, fish processing
Colombia	Bogotá	439,735	35,600,000	coffee, textiles, oil, gas, emeralds
Costa Rica	San José	19,575	3,200,000	coffee, bananas, gold
Cuba	Havana	44,218	11,100,000	sugar, tobacco, cobalt
Dominica	Roseau	290	100,000	bananas, tourism
Dominican Republic	Santo Domingo	18,816	7,800,000	sugar, cocoa, coffee, nickel, gold
Ecuador	Quito	109,483	10,600,000	bananas, coffee, oil
El Salvador	San Salvador	8,124	5,400,000	coffee, cotton, rubber
Falkland Islands (U.K.)	Stanley	4,700	1,900	sheep raising
French Guiana (Fr.)	Cayenne	43,740	133,376	gold, shrimp, timber
Grenada	St. George's	133	100,000	bananas, rum, nutmeg
Guadeloupe (Fr.)	Basse-Terre	660	400,000	tourism, sugar, rum, bananas
Guatemala	Guatemala City	42,042	10,300,000	coffee, oil, sugar, bananas
Guyana	Georgetown	83,000	800,000	sugar, bauxite, diamonds
Haiti	Port-au-Prince	10,579	7,000,000	coffee, sugar, bauxite
Honduras	Tegucigalpa	43,277	5,300,000	bananas, coffee, gold, silver
Jamaica	Kingston	4,232	2,500,000	sugar, coffee, rum, tourism
Mexico	Mexico City	761,604	91,800,000	cotton, oil, steel, silver, natural gas
Netherland Antilles (Neth.)	Willemstad	385	200,000	tourism, oil refining, offshore banking
Nicaragua	Managua	50,193	4,300,000	bananas, oil refining, gold
Panama	Panama City	29,208	2,500,000	bananas, oil refining, copper
Paraguay	Asunción	157,047	4,800,000	corn, cotton, iron
Peru	Lima	496,222	22,900,000	cotton, sugar, copper, lead
Puerto Rico (U.S.)	San Juan	3,435	3,522,037	coffee, plantains, manufacturing
Saint Lucia	Castries	238	100,000	bananas, tourism
Saint Vincent and the Grenadines	Kingstown	150	100,000	bananas, tourism
Suriname	Paramaribo	63,037	400,000	aluminum, rice
Trinidad and Tobago	Port of Spain	1,980	1,300,000	sugar, cocoa, oil
Uruguay	Montevideo	68,037	3,200,000	corn, wheat, meat packing
Venezuela	Caracas	352,143	21,300,000	steel, coffee, oil, iron
Virgin Islands (U.S.)	Charlotte Amalie	133	101,809	tourism, rum

Sources: *Microsoft Bookshelf '94*, Microsoft Corp.; *Information Please Almanac, 1995*, Houghton Mifflin, Boston

Latin America's oil reserves are an important part of its hidden wealth. It has the world's second largest oil reserves. Shown here is a drilling rig in the Mexican state of Chiapas.

Section 2 Review

1. Why are many Latin Americans moving from the country to the city?

2. **Analyzing** How does dependence on one crop or natural resource affect the economies of Latin American countries?

SECTION 3

Democracy's New Age

How did the trend toward democracy affect economic growth in Latin America?

Until recently, democracy had not taken hold in much of Latin America. In the 1800s, when most Latin American nations won independence, many people expected democratic rule. However, Latin Americans did not have experience with democracy. It would take time for Latin American nations to build democratic governments.

A Rocky Road to Democracy

The constitutions of most Latin American countries promised democracy. In many countries, however, democracy was not practiced. Power was in the hands of *caudillos* (kaw•DEE•yohz). **Caudillo** is a Spanish term for a military strongman. Caudillos came to power by the use of force. They ruled as dictators, often harshly. Yet they usually had widespread support. People valued the order that caudillos brought.

In recent years, rule by the military has become less popular. Economies have expanded. A new middle class has developed. In bigger countries, a large class of skilled workers has emerged. These people have protested against military rule.

In many countries, the military has been persuaded to give up power. New **civilian** governments have been formed. Civilians are ordinary citizens of a country. Democratic elections have strengthened civilian governments.

Democracy on the Rise Democracy is on the rise in Latin America. In Argentina, Uruguay, and Peru, elected governments replaced military dictatorships. Democratic governments in Venezuela and Colombia date back to the 1960s.

Democracy also took a step forward in Mexico. Since 1929, Mexico's elected government had been controlled by one party. In the 1980s, however, several opposition parties began to challenge the party in control.

Bringing Peace to Central America

Since independence, the region of Central America has been in conflict. In many countries, civil war has caused loss of lives and great destruction. Nicaragua is one of these countries. By the 1980s, it was torn by a

Democracy has recently been on the rise in Latin America. Above, a celebration is held to honor the first democratically elected president of Haiti, Jean-Bertrand Aristide.

struggle between two forces: the Sandinistas (sahn•dih•NEES•ahs) and the contras.

The Sandinistas came to power in the late 1970s after ousting a dictator of the long-ruling Somoza family. The Sandinistas were supported by the majority of Nicaraguans. However, more than 30,000 Nicaraguans had lost their lives in the fight to overthrow the Somozas. In addition, the nation's economy was almost destroyed.

At first, the United States supported the Sandinistas. In the early 1980s, however, the U.S. government accused the Sandinistas of helping Communist rebels in the nearby country of El Salvador. In late 1981, the United States approved a secret plan to support military actions against the Sandinista government. The U.S.-backed group was made up of former Somoza supporters and Sandinista leaders who no longer supported

the government. The U.S.-backed group was called the contras.

The struggle continued throughout the 1980s. Then, in February 1987, the president of neighboring Costa Rica took a bold step. Oscar Arias (AH•ree•ahs) put forward a peace plan.

It seemed fitting that Costa Rica should begin the peace process. Costa Rica is a successful democracy. It has a strong economy and a stable government. Arias's plan reflected the belief that peace should come from within the region.

Early in 1988, Daniel Ortega, the president of Nicaragua, agreed to peace talks. In February 1990, the Sandinista government held a national election. The Sandinistas were voted out of office. Violeta Barrios de Chamorro (chah•MOHR•oh), who represented an anti-Sandinista party, was elected

Civil war in Central America in the 1980s involved the United States. Above, U.S.-backed contra forces set up a roadblock in Nicaragua.

president. Both sides agreed to stop fighting and work to rebuild the nation.

Chamorro launched programs to reduce the size of the national army and to stop rebel contra forces. Programs to improve the economy were put into place. Nicaragua is making a slow recovery, but it remains one of the poorest countries in Latin America.

Promoting Economic Growth

In the 1990s, Latin American governments continued to promote growth. They built factories, turning out products such as automobiles. To widen the market for these goods, the governments lowered import taxes and other trade barriers with neighboring countries.

This development came at a high cost, however. Many Latin American governments borrowed heavily from banks in the United States and Europe. By the early 1980s, they had some of the world's biggest debts. They were also having trouble repaying their debts.

Mexico, for example, had counted on the sale of oil to pay its debts. Mexico was the world's fourth largest oil producer. But a slump in world oil prices sent Mexico into a crisis. To make matters worse, terrible earthquakes struck Mexico in 1985. They caused thousands of deaths and billions of dollars worth of damage.

Changing Times

Yet by the middle of the 1990s, many Latin American countries were on the road to recovery. They were paying off their huge debts. In Mexico, in particular, industry was booming.

Many U.S. companies had set up factories in Mexico, where labor costs were cheaper than in the United States. In addition, Mexicans benefited from an agreement with the United States and Canada. This agreement was called the North American Free Trade Agreement, or NAFTA.

Under NAFTA, taxes and laws limiting trade were reduced. Goods could move freely among the three countries. Mexicans hoped the agreement would open up new markets in the United States and Canada.

The Promise of the Future

Latin America will face tremendous challenges and problems in the future. However, Latin Americans can point with pride to all they have accomplished over the years. One accomplishment is the creation of new cultures that blend European, Native American, and African traditions. In addition, Latin American nations have a wealth of untapped natural resources. The wise development of these resources makes the chances for change and growth great indeed.

Section 3 Review

1. What effect has a skilled working class had on military dictatorships in Latin America?

2. **Analyzing** Why did some of the nations of Latin America have a debt crisis in the 1980s?

Forty Years of Castro's Cuba

On January 1, 1959, Havana, the capital of Cuba, exploded in celebration. Thousands of people poured into the streets singing and chanting. Everywhere people dressed in black and red — the colors of revolution.

The Cuban people had often seen their dreams of good government go sour. Many Cuban presidents had promised reform. Most promises had never come to pass. Reform presidents often became corrupt dictators.

In 1933, a young army sergeant named Fulgencio Batista brought a new president into power. Off and on between 1933 and 1959, Batista was the real power in Cuba. At first, he held power mostly through presidents who owed their positions to him. But in 1952, Batista took power for himself. He then ruled as a dictator.

Batista had the support of the United States for most of his rule. He gained the support of U.S.-owned businesses in Cuba. These business owners knew that Batista would protect their interests. In turn, Batista helped himself to a share of the prosperity. He built up a huge fortune. However, most of the Cuban people still lived in poverty.

Batista's rule began to crumble in 1956. In that year, a young lawyer named Fidel Castro took a group of rebels into the mountains to fight Batista. Castro had tried to bring down the Batista government several years earlier. That attempt had failed and Castro had been jailed. Upon his release from jail, he went into exile, spending time in the United States and Mexico. In 1956, Castro had returned to lead the rebels to victory. His group began attacking army posts.

Castro won the support of many students, business people, and church officials. These groups believed that he would bring justice to the island. By the end of 1958, Batista had lost most of his support and decided to flee. He left the country with a large share of the national treasury.

Into Havana

Castro now left his base in the mountains. He led his forces on a march to Havana. Millions of Cubans turned out to cheer the rebels.

On January 8, 1959, Castro and his army entered Havana. The fight to get rid of Batista was over. But a new struggle had just begun. Castro set out to revolutionize the country. He promised to eliminate poverty in Cuba.

Castro accepted communism and began tightening his control over the nation. He looked to the Soviet Union to support his government. Castro put Cuba's economy under state control. He favored state ownership of land and businesses and seized plantations, factories, and other privately owned businesses. The government took hundreds of millions of dollars worth of property. Castro also raised taxes on foreign investors.

U.S. sugar companies controlled almost 75 percent of Cuba's farmland. They were angered when Castro raised taxes.

First Worries

By the middle of 1959, some Cubans were having second thoughts about Castro. They did not support Castro's move to communism. In the 1960s, thousands of Cubans left the islands. Most went to Miami, Florida. They hoped one day to reclaim their homeland from Castro.

Between 1959 and 1973, nearly 10 percent of Cuba's six million people left the island. In 1973, Castro limited the number of people who could leave. However, by that time, the Cuban-born population of Miami was almost 300,000.

Cuba Today

Cuba in the 1960s and Cuba today are very different countries. In the 1960s, about half the people lived in the countryside. By the 1990s, about 70 percent lived in cities. In 1965, about one of every three Cuban workers worked in agriculture. Today, that figure is closer to one in five.

Cuba has made great strides in providing housing, medical care, and education for its citizens. For example, better health care has resulted in a dramatic decline in the rate of infant mortality. This is the rate at which babies die in their first year of life.

Before the revolution, about half of Cuban children did not attend school. Today, many more children attend school. Only 3 percent of the population is **illiterate**. Illiterate people cannot read or write. Cuba has one of the lowest illiteracy rates in Latin America.

Yet the changes have come at a great cost. Castro rules as a dictator. With a small handful of supporters, he makes all major decisions. The Communist party is the only legal political party. There is no right to a free press. Many political prisoners are held in jail without trial.

Despite Castro's programs, Cuba is a very poor country. When the Soviet Union collapsed in 1991, Castro lost the aid that kept his economy working. Yet Castro vowed that communism would stay in place in Cuba. Whether he will be able to keep that promise remains a major question.

Case Study Review

1. Who was Fulgencio Batista? What happened to him in 1958?
2. **Drawing Conclusions** Why did many Cubans leave their country in the 1960s and 1970s?

I. Reviewing Vocabulary

Match each word on the left with the correct definition on the right.

1. exile
2. illiterate
3. civilian
4. caudillo

a. unable to read or write
b. citizen who does not belong to the military
c. Spanish term for a military strongman
d. person who leaves his or her homeland because of political disagreements

II. Understanding the Chapter

Answer the questions below on a separate sheet of paper.

1. Why did land reform efforts proceed so slowly in Latin America?
2. What was the attitude of the U.S. government toward land reform in Guatemala in the 1950s?
3. How does dependence on one crop or resource affect the economy of some Latin American countries?
4. How did the collapse of the Soviet Union in 1991 affect Cuba?

III. Building Skills: Comparing Map Projections

Our view of the world depends on the kind of map projection we use to show that world. A map projection is a way of showing the curved earth on a flat surface. On the left is a Mercator projection of the world. On the right is a Peters projection. Study the two maps and then answer the questions on page 363.

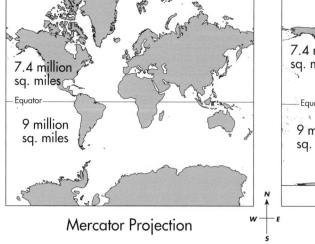

Mercator Projection

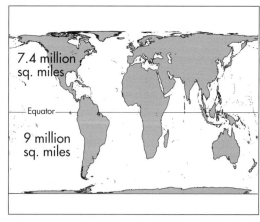

Peters Projection

1. Which map shows the Southern Hemisphere as larger, the Mercator projection or the Peters projection?

2. North America is 7.4 million square miles in area. South America is 9 million square miles in area. Which map projection shows South America as larger than North America?

3. How do you think these two maps affect the way we think of North and South America?

IV. Working Together

Form a small group. Together, write an editorial for a newspaper that supports or opposes land reform in Latin America. Find as many facts as you can in the chapter to support your point of view.

On Assignment. . .

Creating a Map: Review the notes you have taken as you read this chapter. Now prepare a resource map of one country that you found interesting. A resource map shows the natural resources and industries found in a particular area. First make a rough map of your country. Then mark the map with the information you collected as you read the chapter. Create a key to show natural resources and other information. Use the chart on page 356 to help you. Present your finished map to your classmates.

CHAPTER 28

Latin America and the World

What role does Latin America play in the world today?

The flags of the United States and the Commonwealth of Puerto Rico fly over the fortress of El Morro in San Juan. Puerto Rico became a commonwealth of the United States on July 25, 1952.

On Assignment. . .

Creating an Illustrated Time Line: After you have read this chapter, you will create an illustrated time line of the events covered in the chapter. You will list at least ten events from the chapter in chronological order. *Chronological* means "in the order that events happened." Then you will draw pictures to illustrate at least three of those events. Take notes as you read to help you remember and organize the events.

Looking at Key Terms

- **commonwealth** a self-governing state with close ties to another more powerful state
- **gunboat diplomacy** a foreign policy that calls for threatening the use of military force to achieve a country's goals
- **tariff** a tax on goods entering or leaving a country
- **extract** to remove or take from
- **mural** a very large painting or photograph that is applied to a wall or ceiling

SECTION 1

Latin America and the United States

Why has the relationship between Latin America and the United States often been strained?

In 1898, a fleet of U.S. ships approached San Juan Bay in Puerto Rico. Three months earlier, the United States had declared war on Spain. After a quick victory in Cuba, U.S. forces wanted to take over Puerto Rico. As the ships drew closer, the great fortress El Morro came into view. Rising 140 feet (43 meters) above the ocean, El Morro stood strong against U.S. gunfire.

This was not the first time that El Morro had been attacked. During the 1500s, British ships had tried to take the fort. In the 1600s, Dutch ships attacked it. Both forces were driven back. For nearly 400 years, Spain's flag had flown over El Morro.

As you read in Chapter 25, Spain's rule over Puerto Rico ended as a result of the Spanish-American War. On July 25, 1898, the Spanish flag was removed from El Morro. But the Puerto Rican flag did not go up. Instead, the U.S. flag was raised. Puerto Rico had become a colony of the United States.

Becoming a Commonwealth

Exactly 54 years later to the day, on July 25, 1952, another turning point in Puerto Rican history occurred at El Morro. Governor Luis Muñoz Marín (MUN•yoz mah•REEN) raised the Puerto Rican flag next to the U.S. flag at El Morro. Puerto Rico had become a **commonwealth** of the United States. A commonwealth is a self-governing state with close ties to another more powerful state. Puerto Rico now governed itself. Yet it had close ties to the United States. (See Case Study 28.)

The struggles at El Morro remind us that Latin America is not an isolated region. It is a region with strong ties to the rest of the world. In particular, Latin America has had to deal with the United States. Often, these dealings have led to anger, distrust, and even bloodshed.

Latin America and the United States have a special relationship. They share a common past as European colonies. However, most Latin Americans see the relationship as unequal. They believe that the United States has long had the upper hand in the relationship.

According to the Mexican poet Octavio Paz, the people of the United States

> *are always among us even when they ignore us or turn their back on us. Their shadow covers the whole hemisphere. It is the shadow of a giant.*

The Monroe Doctrine

Like most giants, the United States has often demanded that it get its own way. In the early 1800s, Spain lost most of its American colonies. The U.S. government worried that Spain or other European countries might try to regain control of the newly independent nations. U.S. President James Monroe feared that this would put the United States in danger.

With this in mind, Monroe issued a warning in 1823. He warned the European powers not to meddle in the Americas. Monroe stated that the United States would defend the new countries of Latin America. This statement became known as the Monroe Doctrine.

The Mexican War

In 1836, Texas won its independence from Mexico. For the next nine years, Texas remained independent. However, in 1845, it joined the United States. The Mexican people were outraged. The next year the United States and Mexico went to war over the boundary between Texas and Mexico.

Although the Mexicans fought hard, victory went to the United States. As a result of the war, the United States gained a huge area. (See Chapter 25.) Many Latin Americans thought that the United States had picked on its smaller neighbor. The bad feelings caused by the war lasted for many years.

The Spanish-American War

As you read in Chapter 25, by the mid-1800s, Spain's only colonies in Latin America were Cuba and Puerto Rico. For years, Cuba and Puerto Rico had struggled to free themselves from Spanish control. People in the United States were disturbed by newspaper stories of Spanish cruelty and sided with the colonies.

In 1898, the United States went to war with Spain. After the Spanish-American War, Spain lost its colonies. But Cuba and Puerto Rico did not gain full independence. The United States took over Puerto Rico. It dominated Cuba. These actions angered people on both islands. Other Latin Americans watched these developments with alarm. They worried about how much further the United States would go.

"Policing" the Americas

The United States was determined to show its muscle in Latin America. In 1902, U.S. President Theodore Roosevelt sent warships to Venezuela. Venezuela owed money to a number of European countries. Roosevelt did not want the Europeans to send troops to Latin America. He announced that the United States would act as a police force in the Americas. It would step in if Latin American countries could not pay their debts to other nations.

In 1905, Roosevelt sent troops to the Dominican Republic to make sure that the nation paid its debts. Later, U.S. Marines were sent to other Latin American countries. In each of these countries, the United States trained special armies. The commanders of these armies often seized power as military dictators.

The Panama Canal

As the United States became a world trading power, it looked for a quicker way for ships to travel between the Atlantic and Pacific oceans. The only route was a long trip around the southern tip of South America. A canal across narrow Panama would cut the Atlantic-to-Pacific voyage in half.

At that time, Panama was a territory of the country of Colombia. President Theodore Roosevelt offered to pay Colombia for the right to build a canal through this territory. When Colombia turned down the offer, Roosevelt took action to get the canal built.

In 1903, the United States encouraged Panama to stage a revolution. A U.S. warship was stationed nearby. When the revolution broke out, the warship was available to keep Colombian troops from ending the revolt.

Panama became a free country. A few weeks later, it signed a treaty with the United States. The United States won control of a strip of land called the Canal Zone.

President Theodore Roosevelt had said that when dealing with Latin America, the United States should "speak softly and carry a big stick." This cartoon reflects U.S. policy of acting as a police force in the Americas.

Building the Panama Canal in the early years of this century was a major feat. More than 35,000 workers toiled for years, cutting through mountains and clearing swamps.

Critics charged that the United States had used **gunboat diplomacy**, or military action, to gain access to the Canal Zone. This drew strong protests from Latin American countries.

The Good Neighbor Policy

In 1913, the Argentine author Manuel Ugarte (oo•GAHR•teh) wrote a critical letter to U.S. President Woodrow Wilson. Ugarte asked that "the stars and stripes cease to be a symbol of oppression in the New World." *Oppression* means "unjust use of power." Still, Wilson sent U.S. Marines to Haiti and the Dominican Republic. He also ordered two invasions of Mexico.

Twenty years later, U.S. President Franklin Roosevelt helped to better relations between Latin America and the United States. In 1933, he announced a new policy toward Latin America known as the "Good Neighbor Policy." The United States promised to respect the rights of Latin Americans. The United States agreed not to interfere in the affairs of other countries.

During World War II, a spirit of cooperation grew. The nations of the Americas worked together to defeat their enemies. By the end of the war, the United States had become the most powerful nation in the world. Latin Americans hoped that the United States would use its power and wealth to help them solve their problems.

Section 1 Review

1. What was the Monroe Doctrine?
2. **Understanding Points of View** Why did the United States send troops into Latin American countries during the early years of the 1900s?

SECTION 2

A Changing World

In what ways is Latin America's role in the world changing?

In 1959, relations between the United States and Latin America entered a new phase. In that year, Fidel Castro took power in Cuba. (See Chapter 27.) Castro denied that the United States had special privileges in the Western Hemisphere. He built up close relations with the Soviet Union and other Communist countries. He supported groups in Latin America that were trying to overthrow U.S.-backed governments.

The United States responded in different ways. One way was to support an invasion of Cuba in 1961 by anti-Castro Cubans. The United States sponsored an invasion force of

On Assignment. . .

Make a list of the events covered so far for which dates have been given. Decide which ones are the most important. Include these on your time line.

1,800 Cuban rebels that landed in Cuba at a place called the Bay of Pigs. In a matter of days, Castro's forces captured or killed most of the rebels. The failed invasion embarrassed the United States.

Since then, the United States sought other ways to oust Castro. But Castro remained in tight control of Cuba.

In the 1990s, the Soviet Union crumbled. Its economic aid to Cuba ended. This hurt the Cuban economy. It put pressure on Castro to ease Communist rule. However, Castro vowed never to accept capitalism.

Alliance for Progress

Fidel Castro was very popular in many parts of Latin America. Part of the reason was that Latin America continued to distrust the United States.

One of U.S. President John F. Kennedy's main goals was to build greater trust. In 1961, he announced a new policy known as the Alliance for Progress. The United States promised to give money to improve conditions in Latin America.

The Alliance started many useful programs. Teams carved roads out of the mountains. Banks made loans to poor farmers to buy seed. Medical teams traveled to isolated villages to care for sick people.

Still, the Alliance did not do all that Latin Americans hoped it would. The money was not always used to help the poor. Some of the money was used to keep unpopular governments in power.

Support With a Price Tag

Democracy faced a rocky road in Latin America. The United States often made choices that hurt democracy. Would it support governments with socialist or communist leanings? Or would it support military rulers who promised to protect U.S. interests? The United States often chose those who would protect U.S. interests.

In 1970, the people of Chile elected Salvador Allende (ah•YEN•deh) as president. Allende seized many businesses. He maintained warm relations with Cuba.

In 1973, the Chilean military moved against Allende. He was killed. A military dictatorship took control of Chile. It soon became clear that the United States had helped in Allende's overthrow. Many Latin Americans protested. To them, it was another example of U.S. interference in their affairs.

Opposing the Sandinistas in Nicaragua

The United States has long exercised great power in Central America. We have seen in Chapter 5 how the United States helped oust a leftist government in Guatemala in the 1950s. In 1979, leftist rebels in Nicaragua overthrew a brutal dictatorship. These rebels called themselves Sandinistas.

The Sandinistas soon showed their dislike for the United States. Then fighting broke out in Nicaragua. The United States sent aid to groups fighting the Sandinistas. It also banned all trade between Nicaragua and the United States. These events brought Nicaragua close to collapse. To end the war, the Sandinistas had to allow a free election. To their surprise, they lost the election. In early 1990, Violeta Barrios de Chamorro, an anti-Sandinista candidate, was elected president. (See Chapter 27.)

Panama Canal Update

In 1978, the United States took a major step in solving one of the big issues that angered people in Latin America. It agreed to give up control of the Panama Canal. The people of Panama were pleased. They believed strongly that a foreign nation should not control territory within their country.

Supporting Democracy in Haiti

In September 1991, the first democratically elected president of Haiti, Jean-Bertrand Aristide, was overthrown by the Haitian military. Aristide was a Roman Catholic priest who was popular with Haiti's poor. The United States reacted angrily. It banned all trade with Haiti. Haiti's economy was hurt. But the generals refused to surrender. It took the threat of invasion to force the military to give up power. In October 1994, President Aristide returned to power.

In February 1996, Haiti held elections for president. Aristide was prevented by Haitian law to run for a consecutive term. He supported candidate Rene Preval, a well-known champion of democracy. Preval won the election and became president. This marked the first peaceful transfer of power in Haiti since it declared independence in 1804.

Section 2 Review

1. How did the United States react to Fidel Castro's policies?
2. **Summarizing** Summarize how the role of the United States has changed in Latin America in the last century.

SECTION 3

Working Together

How have Latin American nations tried to build unity in the region?

For many years, Latin Americans talked about forming a union that would include all the countries of the Americas. They felt that such a union would allow them to do some things together that no one country could do alone.

Latin American liberator Símon Bolívar had dreamed of a united Spanish America. He wanted to unite all the new Latin American nations under one government. But the nations could not agree. Rivalries blocked all attempts at cooperation. Before his death in 1830, Bolívar wrote bitterly: "America is ungovernable. Those who have served the revolution have plowed the sea."

Bolívar's dream of bringing Latin American nations together did not die. In 1889, the nations of the Americas formed the Pan-American Union. *Pan* is a Greek word meaning "all." This group was set up to deal with common problems of the region.

In 1948, this Union grew into the Organization of American States (OAS). Member nations have worked for the peaceful settlement of disputes in the Americas.

The OAS has handled many conflicts in the Americas. It cannot force any nation to do as it says. But it can try to be a peacemaker when there is trouble.

Many Latin Americans are not satisfied with the OAS. They feel that the United States uses the organization to protect its own interests. Over the years, there have been attempts to set up another group that does not include the United States. However, none of these efforts has been successful.

In Search of Unity

Despite their differences, the nations of Latin America have reached agreement on a number of important issues. For example, they have agreed to use peaceful means to solve disputes. They have also agreed not to get involved in the internal, or national, affairs of other countries.

Encouraging Trade

Latin American countries have worked among themselves to improve their economies. One problem was the high **tariffs**, or taxes, on goods traded among Latin American countries. In 1960, Mexico

The huge Apui trees of the Amazonian rain forest are just one of the treasures that concerned people around the world are working to preserve.

and many South American countries set up an organization to reduce tariffs. In 1963, several Central American nations set up the Central American Common Market. Both these groups have helped increase trade between countries. This has helped the growth of industries within Latin America.

Saving the Rain Forest

Scientists know that effective medicines can be **extracted**, or taken, from plants in the rain forests. Yet rain forests around the world are rapidly disappearing.

Much of the battle over the disappearing rain forests centers on the Amazon basin. The Amazonian rain forest covers an area about half the size of the United States. About 90 percent of it is located in Brazil. In the 1970s, Brazil's leaders began a program to bring settlers to the Amazon region. (See Chapter 27.) The Brazilians saw forest clearing as a quick way to provide more land and a better life for their people.

The rain forest of the Amazon contains thousands of different types of plants. It has thousands of different types of animals. Some of the plants and animals found in the rain forest are valuable to humans. Curare (kyoo•RAH•ray) is an important medicine that comes from trees in the rain forest. Rubber is another useful product. It is collected from trees in the rain forest.

Efforts to save the rain forest must balance different interests. On the one hand are the people who live in the region. On the other hand are the interests of the world as a whole. Many Latin Americans believe that their economies cannot expand unless they use their untapped resources. Environmentalists, however, point out that the destruction of the rain forests affects the health and well-being of the earth.

Section 3 Review

1. What does the Organization of American States do?

2. **Understanding Points of View** Write a paragraph defending the point of view of environmentalists who wish to preserve the rain forests. Then write a paragraph defending people who wish to use the resources of the rain forests to boost their country's economy.

SECTION 4

Latin America's Cultural Contributions

What forces have influenced some of Latin America's writers and artists?

We can learn much about Latin America from its writers and artists. Many Latin American artists portray a world where nothing is secure. In this world, force rules.

Civil war happens all the time. Natural disasters disturb life. There is a vast gap between rich and poor.

García Márquez, Giant of Literature

In the past 25 years, many Latin American writers have become popular throughout the world. Perhaps the most popular author is Gabriel García Márquez. He was born in Colombia in 1928. García Márquez was one of the 16 children of a poor telegraph operator. He grew up listening to tales of civil war and ghosts. He wrote about this in his great novel *One Hundred Years of Solitude.* It traces the lives of a fictional Colombian family over a period of 100 years.

The work of García Márquez mixes dreams with reality. Dead husbands return as ghosts to frighten their wives. People fly off into the darkness. Women live on a diet of dirt. It rains for four years!

García Márquez has won worldwide fame. In 1982, he received the Nobel Prize for literature.

The "Big Three" of Mexican Art

Trains back from the battlefield unloaded their cargoes. The wounded soldiers suffered on their stretchers. In the world of politics, it was the same. It was war without quarter [mercy].

This quote from the Mexican artist José Orozco (oh•ROHS•koh) helps explain how the Mexican Revolution influenced his art. Orozco was an artist during the revolution. Two other great artists of the period were Diego Rivera and David Siqueiros (see•keh•EE•rohs). The three became Mexico's most famous artists.

They developed a truly Mexican style of art. They used the **mural**, an art form that dates back to Aztec times. A mural is a large

Mexican artists created large murals to show dramatic scenes from the history of Mexico. This mural by David Siqueiros shows a soldier during the Mexican Revolution.

picture painted on a wall. The murals of these artists used powerful images to show the history of Mexico. The murals supported the causes of the poor.

After the revolution, the three painted murals on a number of public buildings. These murals can be seen in Mexico today. Through the murals, the ideas of these artists still reach the people of Mexico.

Frida Kahlo Frida Kahlo is another well-known Mexican artist. Like those of the "big three," her paintings were infused with elements of her Mexican heritage. She worked during the 1930s and 1940s to create a number of highly personal self-portraits among other works. Kahlo was married to Diego Rivera.

Section 4 Review

1. Who is Gabriel García Márquez and what does he write about?

2. **Analyzing** How did the paintings of Mexico's "big three" artists reflect the history of their country?

Puerto Rico: An Island Commonwealth

In the autumn of 1949, Verania Gonzáles boarded a plane bound for New York. As the plane cut through the clouds, the 17-year-old from San Juan, Puerto Rico, wondered what her new life would be like. She spoke only Spanish. Her sister lived in the South Bronx, a section of New York City. Here Verania would live.

After landing, Verania caught her first glimpse of the South Bronx. She spotted Spanish signs in the windows of bodegas, small grocery stores. She heard the sounds of Spanish in the streets. Then she met Luis Cancel (kahn•SEHL). He was also 17 years old and of Puerto Rican descent. Unlike Verania, he had been born in New York.

In 1952, the couple married and took up life in the South Bronx. There the Puerto Rican population was booming. As both Puerto Ricans and New Yorkers, Luis and Verania lived through a time of many changes in their native land.

A month after the Cancels married, Puerto Rico became a commonwealth of the United States. Under the law, Puerto Ricans could elect their own officials. Puerto Ricans remained U.S. citizens. They could be drafted into the military. However, they did not have to pay federal income taxes if they lived in Puerto Rico.

The person most responsible for commonwealth status was Luis Muñoz Marín. Governor Muñoz Marín hoped to build a sense of pride among the people of his island. He created a program known as Operation Bootstrap. It was designed to improve the economy and the standard of living of Puerto Ricans. Puerto Ricans were asked to "pull themselves up by their own bootstraps."

A Drive to Modernize

To provide jobs, Muñoz Marín invited U.S. companies to build factories in Puerto Rico. Through foreign investment, Muñoz Marín hoped to change Puerto Rico into a modern industrial society.

Operation Bootstrap brought great changes to the island. In 1952, there were only 82 factories in all of Puerto Rico. By 1970, the island had more than 1,000 factories. Thousands of new jobs were created.

Workers moved into new public housing. New paved roads crisscrossed the island. The literacy rate soared.

Despite these advances, there is growing debate over Puerto Rico's status. An independence movement has formed. Independistas call for an end to all political ties with the United States. They believe that independence is best for the future of Puerto Rico.

On the other side are people who want Puerto Rico to become a state of the United States. They especially want the right to be represented in the U.S. Congress.

For most Puerto Ricans, the island's

On Assignment...

Conclude your list of the events in this chapter for which dates have been given. Which dates are most important? Why? Think of images to accompany the important dates.

political status remains a very important issue. Few Puerto Ricans support independence. Most favor ties with the United States. But just what will these ties be? Will Puerto Rico continue to be a commonwealth? Or will it become a state?

Case Study Review

1. What is Puerto Rico's relationship with the United States today?

2. **Determining Cause and Effect** Identify one short-term and one long-term effect of Puerto Rico's commonwealth status.

Under Operation Bootstrap, Governor Luis Muñoz Marín invited U.S. companies to build factories and plants in Puerto Rico. This electronics factory was built during the 1970s.

REVIEWING CHAPTER 28

I. Reviewing Vocabulary

Match each word on the left with the correct definition on the right.

1. gunboat diplomacy
2. extract
3. commonwealth
4. tariff

a. a self-governing state with close ties to another more powerful state
b. threatened use of force to achieve foreign policy goals
c. tax on goods entering or leaving a country
d. to remove or take from

II. Understanding the Chapter

Answer the questions below on a separate sheet of paper.

1. How did the "Good Neighbor Policy" attempt to change U.S. policy toward Latin America?
2. How did the U.S. policy supporting Haiti's president Aristide differ from its policy toward Chile's president Allende in the 1970s?
3. What goals did the Alliance for Progress have?
4. What was "Operation Bootstrap"?

III. Building Skills: Reading a Chart

Read the chart and answer the questions on page 375.

U.S. Investment in Latin America, 1897–1914 (in millions of dollars)

	Caribbean	Mexico and Central America	South America	Total
1897	4.5	221.4	37.9	263.8
1908	220.2	713.0	129.7	1,062.9
1914	329.0	946.7	365.7	1,641.4

1. What happened to U.S. investments in Latin America during the period of 1897–1914?

2. Did U.S. investments in Latin America grow faster in 1897–1908 or in 1908–1914?

IV. Working Together

Latin America is a diverse place. Its countries have many different types of governments. With a small group of classmates, pick one country of Latin America. Find out what kind of government that country has today. Find out about its experience with democracy. In addition, find out about U.S. relations with that country. Report your findings to the class.

On Assignment...

Creating an Illustrated Time Line: Put together the list of events you have collected for your time line. Pick out the ten events that you think are the most important. Then create a time line that shows these events in the order in which they happened. Pick three of the events from your time line and draw pictures of each of them.

Chile is a land of great physical beauty with rain forests and deserts, volcanoes and glaciers. Chile is also a land that has been torn by political and social troubles. Poet Gabriela Mistral wrote of these troubles. She also wrote of Chile's great potential.

In 1945, Gabriela Mistral became the first Latin American writer to win the Nobel Prize for literature. Mistral grew up in northern Chile. There she was influenced by the beautiful farmlands, the hard-working people, and her grandmother's love of the Bible. While still a teenager, Mistral became a teacher. For the rest of her life—no matter where she traveled or what honor she received— Mistral encouraged people to think of her as a humble rural schoolteacher.

Mistral used her poems to offer vivid images of her homeland. She frequently spoke for Chilean women, children, and others who had little chance to speak publicly for themselves. She wrote with a style that was simple, yet powerful.

"What the soul does for the body so does the poet for her people." That was Mistral's view of her work, and it became the inscription on her tomb.

Mexican artist Diego Rivera showed his respect for the land and the people who worked on it. His simple paintings celebrate the labor of Latin American peasants.

Chilean Earth

Gabriela Mistral

We dance on Chilean earth
more beautiful than Lia and Raquel:
the earth that kneads[1] men,
their lips and hearts without bitterness.

The land most green with orchards,
the land most blond with grain,
the land most red with grapevines,
how sweetly it brushes our feet!

Its dust molded our cheeks,
its rivers, our laughter,
and it kisses our feet with a melody
that makes any mother sigh.

For the sake of its beauty,
we want to light up fields with song.
It is free,
and for freedom we want
to bathe its face in music.

Tomorrow we will open its rocks;
we will create vineyards and orchards;
tomorrow we will exalt its people.
Today we need only to dance!

---

[1] **kneads** (needz) v. massages or presses with the hands

Making Connections

1. What feelings about Chile does "Chilean Earth" show?
2. **Making Inferences** What do you learn about the geography of Chile from this poem?

Canada: Building the Mosaic

What challenges does Canada face as a culturally diverse nation?

Founded in 1608, the city of Quebec has a distinct French Canadian flavor. French Canadians have a strong sense of identity that sets them apart from other Canadians.

On Assignment...

Making a Presentation: Imagine that you work for the Canadian Department of Tourism. You have been given the job of preparing a three-minute talk about Canada to tourists. In your presentation, you are to describe Canada's geography and people. As you read this chapter, look for On Assignment hint boxes to help you make notes for your talk. At the end of the chapter, you will write your talk and present it.

Looking at Key Terms

- **mosaic** a design made up of many small pieces of materials
- **province** a territory governed as an administrative or political unit of a country
- **hydroelectricity** the power that comes from the force of rushing water
- **bilingualism** the policy of recognizing two official languages
- **Commonwealth of Nations** the group of nations that were once colonies of Great Britain
- **federal system** a system in which power is divided between a central government and local governments

The Land of Canada

How does geography make it hard for Canada to be a united nation?

"Let Canada be free!"

Those stirring words were uttered in 1774. In those days, the British Empire had just taken over France's empire in North America. French-speaking people made their feelings clear. They did not want to be part of Britain's 13 colonies to the south. They wanted to maintain their language, laws, and culture.

More than 200 years later, a similar cry is being heard in Canada. It has raised concerns that this huge country to the north of the United States may break up.

By sheer size alone, Canada demands attention. From coast to coast, it stretches out over 4,500 miles (7,200 km). Canada is the world's second largest country, ranking just after Russia.

Canada possesses vast wealth in natural resources. These natural resources fuel several large industries that contribute to the country's strong economy. Canadians enjoy one of the highest standards of living in the world.

Unfortunately, Canada's huge size divides Canadians. Canadians tend to live in pockets of settlements scattered across the country. Each pocket is separated from the others by geographic barriers. The people around Ontario, for example, are separated from the people of the prairies by hundreds of miles of forests and lakes. The Rocky Mountains separate the people of British Columbia from the prairies. (See the map on page 381.)

Although railroads and airplanes have helped break down these barriers, Canadians still tend to have a strong sense of loyalty to the region in which they live. Sometimes this regional loyalty is stronger than national loyalty.

Canadians often speak of their nation as a **mosaic**. A mosaic is a design made up of many small pieces of materials. From a distance, those pieces blend into one picture. But as you move closer, you become aware of the role each of the separate pieces plays in the overall design.

Canada's Provinces

Take a look at the map on page 381. As you can see, Canada is divided into provinces and territories. A **province** is an area or region that is part of a larger country. The powers of government are divided between the provincial governments and Canada's national government.

Canada is made up of ten provinces. From east to west, the provinces are Newfoundland, Prince Edward Island, Nova Scotia, New Brunswick, Quebec (kuh•BEHC), Ontario, Manitoba, Saskatchewan (seh•SKACH•eh•wahn), Alberta, and British Columbia. There are also two territories—the Yukon and the Northwest Territories.

Nunavut At the beginning of the 21st century, a third territory will be carved from the central and eastern portions of the Northwest Territories. This territory will be called Nunavut, which means "Our Land" in the Inuit (IN•yoo•it) language. The Inuit are a culture group who live in the cold Arctic north.

The territory of Nunavut is about 772,000 square miles (2 million sq. km) — about one fifth of Canada's territory. It includes Baffin and Ellesmere islands. Baffin Island is Canada's largest island. Most of the 21,000 people in Nunavut are Inuit. An agreement made with the Canadian government in 1992 allows the Inuit to gain control over the territorial government and to control hunting and fishing rights by 1999.

Canada's Geographic Regions

Canada can be organized into six major geographic regions: the Maritime Provinces, the St. Lawrence and southern Ontario lowlands, the Canadian Shield, the Central

Canada's Maritime Provinces have a close connection with the sea. Most people make their living through fishing or seafaring. Here, a lighthouse towers over the rocky Atlantic coast of Nova Scotia.

Plains, the Western Mountain region, and the Arctic North. The history, geography, and people combine to give each region a distinct character.

Maritime Provinces East of the St. Lawrence River lie the Maritime provinces. The Maritimes are sometimes called the Atlantic provinces. The provinces that make up this region are Newfoundland, Nova Scotia, New Brunswick, and Prince Edward Island.

The Maritimes have a close connection with the sea. Many people of the Maritimes earn their living through fishing and seafaring. In recent times, however, the waters have been overfished and stocks of fish have been declining. This has thrown the fishing industry of the Maritimes into crisis. The people of the Maritimes hope that recent discoveries of offshore oil and natural gas will boost the region's economy.

The Lowlands The St. Lawrence and southern Ontario lowlands lie further south and west along the St. Lawrence River and the Great Lakes. This region falls across the southern portion of Quebec and Ontario. A moderate climate, fertile farmland, and access to good water routes attracted many settlers to the region in the 1700s and 1800s. Today the lowlands contain 60 percent of Canada's entire population, making it the most populated area of the country.

The St. Lawrence Seaway has much to do with the economic success of the lowlands. Opened in 1959, this joint Canadian and U.S. project built a series of locks along the St. Lawrence River. The locks allow large ocean liners to sail from the Atlantic Ocean, along the St. Lawrence River, and into Lake Ontario. Every year several million tons of goods are transported through the seaway.

Canada's largest cities are located in the lowlands. These cities include Toronto, Montreal, and Quebec. Ottawa, the federal capital of Canada, is also located in the lowlands.

Canadian Shield North and west of the lowlands is a massive rock formation. It is known as the Canadian Shield. The Shield is a treasure house of minerals. It has hundreds of thousands of square miles of forests. It also has thousands of lakes. The lakes were formed by giant sheets of ice called glaciers that melted thousands of years ago.

In fact, Canada has more lakes than all the rest of the world combined. There are so many lakes that some of them do not even have names.

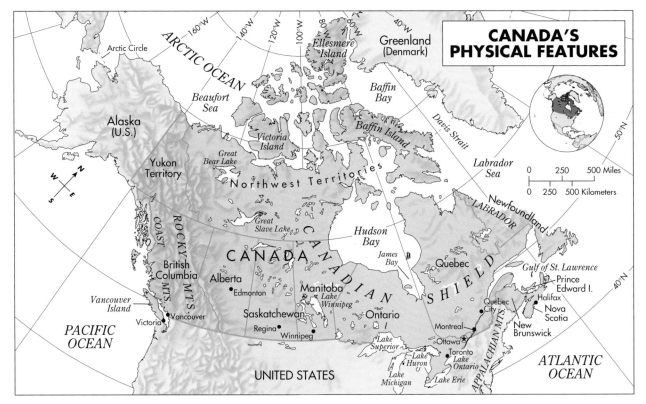

CANADA'S PHYSICAL FEATURES

Location From Newfoundland in the east to the Yukon Territory in the west, Canada presents a remarkable array of physical wonders. What island lies furthest east? What island is its northernmost point?

Central Plains The Central Plains are located west of the Canadian Shield and east of the Rocky Mountains. These rolling plains stretch across North America from the Gulf of Mexico to the Arctic Ocean. This region contains some of the world's richest farmland. Because massive amounts of wheat grow here, it is known as the "breadbasket" of Canada.

Western Mountains Western Canada is marked by great mountain ranges. Before the days of air travel, the Rocky Mountains formed a huge barrier between eastern and western Canada. Few mountain passes make the Canadian Rockies difficult to cross.

West of the Rockies lie the Coastal Ranges. These mountains are lower, but still difficult to cross. Most people in this region live in a small flat coastal area in the Fraser valley. Vancouver, the region's chief city, is located at the mouth of the Fraser River.

Arctic North The region of Canada that lies farthest to the north is the Arctic. This is a region of ice and snow. The Yukon, Northwest, and soon-to-be-formed Nunavut territories are located in the Arctic North. Few people live in this vast, cold region. The Inuit have survived in the Arctic by hunting and fishing. Other culture groups in the territories include the Dene and the Métis. You will read more about the Métis in Section 3.

On Assignment...

What would you tell visitors to Canada about its physical regions? To which regions would you recommend tourists go? Why?

Thousands of years ago, giant glaciers gouged huge chunks of rocks and earth out of the landscape. The result: lakes, thousands of them, such as beautiful Lake Moraine in the Canadian Rockies.

Canada's Climates

Any country as large as Canada is bound to have a variety of climates. Canada reaches north almost to the North Pole. However, the southern tip of Ontario province is almost the same latitude as northern California. Latitude is a measure of distance north or south of the equator.

Despite the variety, a few generalizations may be made about Canada's climate. Generally, winters are long and cold. Cold winds blow south from the Arctic. They bring frigid weather for much of winter. Sometimes the temperature gets as low as 80 degrees below zero. Further south, in the prairies, it is not as cold. However, it is cold enough so that winter blizzards are a familiar part of life. Summers are short.

On the west coast, the climate is far different. Warm, moist air blows in from the Pacific. This gives coastal regions a mild climate year round.

Resources

Canada's supply of natural resources is huge. Vast forests support a thriving lumber industry. Canada is the world's leading producer of paper. The rich soil of the prairies makes Canada one of the world's leading growers of wheat. Canada also has valuable stores of oil and iron ore. Canada's rushing rivers are a source of electric power.

Section 1 Review

1. How has Canada's size kept its people divided?

2. **Expressing an Opinion** The people of Canada often feel more loyal to their region than to the nation as a whole. In your opinion, what are some of the things that unify a nation? What are some of the things that divide a nation?

Canada's Native Americans

Who were the first Canadians?

Scientists believe that the first people to arrive in North America came from Asia. About 30,000 years ago, people traveled over a land bridge that connected North America and Asia. As you read in Chapter 24, this land bridge was exposed during the last ice age. The people who crossed the bridge fanned out in all directions. Some people went south, while others went east. Those who went east became the first humans to live in what today is Canada. These people are often called Native Americans.

Groups of Native Americans traveled across the continent. Each group developed its own distinct culture. However, one thing all the groups had in common was respect for the earth. Native Americans viewed the earth as a provider of food and shelter for all living creatures. Each group of Native Americans developed rituals and ceremonies to honor the environment. Each generation taught the rituals to the next generation. Native Americans today carry on many of those ancient traditions.

Today, there are over 600 groups of Native Americans in Canada. Like other cultures around the world, the cultures of Native Americans were shaped by the forces of the environments in which they lived. In this section you will read about the major culture groups in Canada.

Culture Regions

Scientists have organized the Native Americans of Canada into six major culture regions. These regions are the Arctic, Subarctic, Eastern Woodlands, Great Plains, Plateau, and Northwest Pacific Coast.

Arctic As you read earlier, the Arctic is a harsh region inhabited by the Inuit. You may know the Inuit by another name—Eskimo. The Inuit were given the name Eskimo by the Cree. Eskimo means "eaters of raw meat." However, the Inuit do not eat raw meat. Inuit is the name this group calls itself. Inuit means simply "the people."

As you have read, the Inuit of the Northwest Territories signed an agreement with the Canadian government giving the Inuit control over a new territory called Nunavut. The Inuit tried for over 15 years to reach this agreement. The agreement is one of the largest peaceful land transfer deals in history. In return for gaining Nunavut, however, the Inuit had to give up their claim to another 640,000 square miles (1.7 million sq. km) of traditional lands. These lands may contain gas and oil fields.

Subarctic The Subarctic region is located just south of the Arctic. It is the largest region of Canada, stretching from the Atlantic coast in the east to the mountain ranges in the west. Major groups in the eastern portion of the region include the Cree and the Naskapi. In the west, live the Kutchin, Carrier, Dogrib, and Chipewyan, among other groups.

Traditionally, the people of the Subarctic were nomads. They moved from place to place following herds of animals. The subarctic people also relied on fish from the lakes and rivers of the region. The poor soil and harsh climate of the Subarctic made farming impossible. Today, many subarctic people live in settled villages. A number, however, still hunt and fish for a living.

Eastern Woodlands The people of the Eastern Woodlands lived in the lowlands of the St. Lawrence–Great Lakes region and the southern Maritimes. The woodlands were home to many groups including the Huron, Iroquois, Ojibwa, and Micmac. Because of the mild climate and good soil, many of the groups in this region lived in settled villages and farmed the land.

Great Plains Years ago, great herds of bison, sometimes called buffalo, roamed the plains of North America. In the southern portions of Manitoba, Saskatchewan, and Alberta, the Blackfoot and the Plains Cree followed the buffalo. They ate the meat of the animal, used the hide for clothing, and the bones for tools. When white settlers came to the Great Plains, they nearly drove the buffalo to extinction, or total destruction. The decline of the buffalo drastically changed the Plains Native American way of life.

Plateau The Plateau is a small region in the southeast portion of British Columbia. In the grassy valleys, such groups as the Okanogan, Colville, and Lake fished, hunted, and traded with the Native Americans who lived on the plains and Pacific coast.

Pacific Northwest The mild climate of the Pacific coast of Canada allowed such peoples as the Bellacolla, Wakashan, and Mootka to live in settled villages year round. They caught salmon in the rivers and hunted whale in the ocean waters.

Europeans Arrive

The first contact between Native Americans and Europeans occurred about the year 1000. Vikings from Scandinavia sailed west from Greenland and landed on the coast of Newfoundland. The Vikings tried to establish a settlement, but Native Americans drove them away.

About five hundred years later, Europeans again sailed into the North Atlantic waters. They made contact with Native Americans living along the coast. This time, the Native Americans were friendly. The Europeans began to fish the waters and to trade beaver skins with the Native Americans.

The Fur Trade The trade in beaver skins had a huge impact on Native American life. Felt hats made from beaver skin were in fashion among European men during the 1500s. European traders could make fortunes in the fur trade. Native Americans were eager to trade the fur for metal tools, guns, and other goods from Europe.

Canada's diverse Native Americans are determined to preserve their individual ways. Above, at a gathering of Cayuga Iroquois, old ways are celebrated.

Over the next hundred years, Native Americans trapped beaver in greater and greater numbers. At the same time, French settlers began to establish permanent colonies along the St. Lawrence River. The French founded Quebec in 1608 and Montreal in 1642.

Eager to profit from the fur trade, the English set up trading posts around the Hudson Bay area. The French and English competed for control of the fur trade. Native Americans were able to take advantage of the conflict between the French and English to strike good deals for their fur. The Native American traders would get the English and French to bid against one another for the furs.

Eventually, competition between the French and English led to war. In 1763, the British defeated the French and took control of Canada. Many French, however, remained.

Missionaries Soon after the Europeans arrived in Canada, missionaries came to convert Native Americans to Christianity. French and English missionaries worked in much the same way as the Spanish missionaries you read about in Chapter 25.

Many Native Americans converted to Christianity. However, a number of those that did convert continued to practice the traditional ceremonies of their own cultures. They did not see a reason to choose between their traditional religions and their new religion — Christianity.

The missionaries, however, felt otherwise. As the number of Europeans in Canada increased, missionaries did all they could to force Native Americans to give up their cul-

Each spring, Native Americans brought fur pelts to French trading posts. The trade brought wealth to Native Americans, but it changed their lives forever.

tures. Children were sent to missionary schools where they were punished for speaking their native languages. They learned French or English and dressed in European styles. Made to give up their native cultures, the children were taught to think and act like Europeans.

Disease: A Fatal Blow Perhaps the worst blow to Native Americans in Canada came in the form of disease. In much the same way as the Spanish and Portuguese exposed Native Americans in Latin America to disease, so did the French and English in Canada. Tens of thousands of Native Americans fell to diseases such as smallpox and measles. Native Americans had no immunity against these diseases. Whole communities disappeared in a matter of years.

Conflict Over Land The fur trade, missionaries, and disease took a terrible toll on Native American culture. As more Europeans arrived in the 1700s and 1800s, yet another threat to Native Americans emerged. Land-hungry settlers pushed Native Americans out of areas the settlers wished to own. Sometimes Native Americans were forced to sign treaties giving up their lands. In other cases, Native Americans fought openly to keep the land. However, whether they willingly signed treaties or went to war, the result was always the same — Native Americans were driven off their lands.

During the 1830s, the British began what they called a "civilization" program. They forced Native Americans to live on large tracts of land, called reserves. A similar program was being carried out in the United States, where the lands were called reservations.

Most often, the land on the reserve was divided among the Native Americans who were to live there. Each family received a plot of land to farm. But many Native American groups were nomads or hunters and gatherers. Farming was not part of their

Mohawks in Quebec march to protest the expansion of a golf course onto traditional land and to voice other grievances. The sign says "No to Racism."

In 1990, a group of Mohawk in Quebec protested the expansion of a golf course into traditional Mohawk territory. The Canadian government agreed to purchase the land for the Mohawk nation. The Mohawks, however, decided to use the incident to stage protests. They wanted to bring to the public's attention other grievances they held, such as Native Americans' right to self-government.

When the government ignored their protests, the Mohawks blocked a main bridge connecting Montreal with the shores of the St. Lawrence River. Other Native American groups throughout Canada staged protests in sympathy with the Mohawks. The situation turned increasingly violent. The Quebec government had to ask the federal government to send troops in to help stop the protests.

After 78 days of protest and negotiation, the Native Americans surrendered. Although the issue of self-government had not been resolved, the Mohawk nation had succeeded in bringing the issue to the forefront.

culture. In addition, the lands they were given were often worthless.

Despite the hardships, many Native Americans managed to preserve their traditional cultures. Today there are about 555,000 Native Americans and Inuit in Canada. They make up about 2 percent of the total population. Many groups are locked in battle with the Canadian government over land and cultural issues.

Fighting for Rights

As you read earlier, the Inuit managed to gain the territory of Nunavut from the Canadian government in the early 1990s. Other groups have waged similar fights.

Section 2 Review

1. List the six cultural regions scientists use to divide Canada's Native Americans. Choose two of the regions and describe how geography affects the Native American groups that live there.

2. **Expressing an Opinion** Why did the Mohawks continue their protests after the Canadian government agreed to stop the expansion of the golf course? What is your opinion of their actions?

The Power to Win:
The Cree of James Bay

It was 1972. Sixteen-year-old Matthew Coon Come was graduating from high school when he read something that changed the course of his life. Coon Come remembers

> *I picked up a Montreal newspaper that had a map of what was then the new James Bay power project. I was stunned to see that my home, the place where I had played as a child, was going to be submerged [placed under water] under a gigantic lake.*

The Cree

Matthew Coon Come, a Cree Native American, lives in the James Bay region. The Cree have lived on lands around James Bay in northern Quebec for about 6,000 years. When Europeans arrived in Canada, the Cree were one of many Native American groups that took part in the fur trade. The Cree felt the effects of contact with the Europeans in the same ways that other Native American groups felt them. Cree children attended missionary schools and a number of Cree converted to Christianity. Many Cree died from European diseases.

The Cree, however, lived in an isolated area of Quebec. Once the fur trade declined, the people of Canada left the Cree pretty much on their own. The Canadian government did insist upon sending Cree children to distant boarding schools. Coon Come remembers the day when he was six years old and a Canadian official arrived by floatplane. The official was the first white person the boy had ever seen. He had come to remind Coon Come's father that it was time to send his son to boarding school.

James Bay I

In 1971, Coon Come was away from home finishing high school. That year, the Canadian government announced that the national utility company, Hydro-Quebec, would start "the project of the century." The project, known as James Bay I, aimed to harness the power of the rivers in the James Bay region. To do this, Hydro-Quebec would construct a huge dam across the La Grand River. Hydro-Quebec would then build hydroelectric generating stations along the river's rapids. **Hydroelectricity** is power that is produced by flowing water. The electricity created by the power plants would be transmitted hundreds of miles south to Montreal and to cities in the

A Cree father and son prepare for a journey on the La Grand River in northern Quebec. The James Bay dam has endangered the traditional Cree way of life.

United States. It was an ambitious project that would create jobs and income for the province of Quebec.

Yet, damming the La Grand would flood thousands of acres of ancient Cree hunting and burial grounds. The government of Quebec did not even bother to tell the Cree and Inuit who lived in the area about the project. They heard about it through radio reports. The Cree and Inuit banded together to fight the project, but their efforts failed. Hydro-Quebec was allowed to build the dam and power stations.

After the dam was built, about 4,425 square miles (11,400 sq. km) of Cree and Inuit territory lay under water. The area under water is as large as the state of Connecticut. The flooding created terrible problems for the Cree. Fish, a main part of the Cree diet, became contaminated as a result of mercury poisoning. Caribou, beavers, and many birds lost their feeding grounds and homes. The flow of rivers and the cycle of floods changed. The environment of the James Bay region was thrown out of balance.

In addition, Hydro-Quebec built roads to bring supplies and equipment to construct the dam and electric plants. This opened a once-isolated region to sport hunters, loggers, mining companies, and others. Outsiders brought rapid change to Cree villages. Not all the changes were good. For example, before the influx of outsiders, Cree society was practically free from drug and alcohol abuse, divorce, and suicide. Suddenly the Cree faced these and other problems.

After James Bay I was well underway, the Cree and Inuit signed the James Bay and Northern Quebec Agreement (1975) with Canada. The pact granted the Cree approximately $135 million to compensate for lost land, exclusive hunting and fishing rights to 29,000 square miles (75,000 sq. km) of land, and the right to have a say in future projects.

Broken Promises: James Bay II

After signing the James Bay and Northern Quebec Agreement, the Cree felt safe from further threats to their land. But then in the late 1980s, Hydro-Quebec announced plans to build roads into Cree lands and construct additional dams and power plants. The Cree were outraged. By this time Matthew Coon Come had risen to become Grand Chief of the Quebec Cree. He and others led the fight against Hydro-Quebec.

First, the Cree and Inuit took Hydro-Quebec to court to block them from building roads. Then, in April 1990, a group of Cree and Inuit paddled a boat from Hudson Bay south. They traveled on the Hudson River all the way to New York City. They hoped to make their case public by bringing it to the attention of the people of the United States, especially New Yorkers. New York was thinking about buying power from Hydro-Quebec's James Bay project. In 1992, New York State canceled its plans to buy power. In addition, many in Quebec began to believe that the energy project was too costly. Considering the damage to the environment, they wondered whether the project was really worthwhile after all. Two years later, in November 1994, Hydro-Quebec put James Bay II on "indefinite hold." For the time being, the project was stopped.

Coon Come and the Cree vow never to stop fighting plans to destroy their land. "Everything flows from the land," says Coon Come. "As long as we have it, the Cree will survive."

Case Study Review

1. What is James Bay I and how did it affect life for the Cree and Inuit in the region?

2. **Analyzing Cause and Effect** How did the building of roads and dams cause the life of the Cree to change?

The People of Canada Today

Why is Canada called "a small nation in a big country"?

Though Canada is a land of great wealth, there is one natural resource in short supply — people. Canada is far larger in area than the United States. Yet it has only about one tenth the people. This has led some people to describe Canada as "a small nation in a big country."

Canada's people are not spread out evenly over its vast territory. If they were, they would be very isolated from one another. About 85 percent of all Canadians live within 200 miles (334 km) of the U.S. border. Most of Canada's large cities are located close to the U.S. border.

Divided by Language

Canada has two official languages, English and French. If you travel in Canada, you will see road signs in both languages.

One of Canada's biggest challenges is the disagreement between English-speaking Canadians and French Canadians. Almost one third of Canada's people speak French as a first language. The province of Quebec is about 85 percent French Canadian. Many of the people of Quebec consider themselves citizens of Quebec first and of Canada second.

People of British background make up about 40 percent of Canada's population. Many are descended from people who came from Ireland, England, and Scotland. Others are descendants of people who left the United States after the American Revolution. Descendants are people who can trace their heritage back to an individual or a group.

The rivalry between English speakers and French speakers is well known. This causes people to think that these are the only two culture groups in Canada. Actually, Canada has a great variety of people. As you have read, the first Canadians were Native Americans and Inuit.

In the past 100 years, people from all over Europe have come to settle in Canada. Many Canadians in western Canada have their roots in Asia. One way to understand Canadian culture is to look at its different provinces.

The Maritime Provinces

The eastern part of Canada has a long and rich history. The French were the first Europeans to settle in this region. They cleared the forests and worked the land in a colony called Acadia. France lost Acadia to Britain as a result of a war in 1713. However, few British came to settle there at first. People from Germany did come. Their descendants still live today in Nova Scotia.

In 1753, the British threw French settlers out of Acadia. British troops burned farms and arrested the Acadians. Then the Acadians were loaded on ships and sent to various British colonies.

Many of the French eventually came back to Acadia. But the best land had been taken. Today, there is a growing French Canadian population in the Maritime provinces.

The next wave of settlers to the Maritimes came from Scotland in the mid-1700s. Scots settlements grew in New Brunswick and Nova Scotia (which means "New Scotland" in Latin). Today, many people here have an accent like that of the Scots people.

A new wave of settlers arrived in the Maritime provinces with the beginning of the American Revolution. Colonists who had been loyal to the British left the American colonies. Many of them settled in the Maritimes.

Quebec

West of the Maritime provinces is the large province of Quebec. More than 85 percent of Quebec's people speak French. About

PROVINCES AND TERRITORIES OF CANADA

Facts About Canada

Capital City: Ottawa

Size (sq. mi.): 3,844,907

Population: 27,351,000

Population Density: 7.2 persons per square mile

Ethnic Groups: 40% British, 27% French, 20% Other Europeans, 2% Native Americans, 11% other (includes Americans, Russians, Ukrainians, Chinese, and Japanese)

The Provinces	Size (sq. mi.)	Population
Alberta	255,287	2,545,553
British Columbia	365,947	3,282,061
Manitoba	250,947	1,091,942
New Brunswick	28,355	723,900
Newfoundland	156,949	568,474
Nova Scotia	21,425	899,942
Ontario	412,581	10,084,885
Prince Edward Island	2,185	129,765
Quebec	594,860	6,895,963
Saskatchewan	251,866	988,928
The Territories		
Northwest Territories*	1,322,909	57,649
Yukon	186,661	27,797

Sources: *The World Almanac and Book of Facts 1994*; "Canada" *Microsoft Encarta '95.*

*In 1992, voters in the Northwest Territories approved the creation of Nunavut, a self-governing territory to be carved from the Northwest Territories. Nunavut will cover an area of about 772,000 square miles and have a population of 21,000 (mostly Inuit people). It is scheduled to begin in 1999.

Spread out over ten provinces and two territories, Canada is the world's second largest country. How many Canadian provinces have more than three million people?

two million French-speaking people of Quebec have moved to the United States. There they live mainly in New England and in New York State.

Quebec is a Native American word for "the place where the river narrows." At such a place along the St. Lawrence River, Samuel de Champlain (sham•PLAYN) established a French post in 1608. There French settlers cut down trees and built small buildings. The colonists cleared fields and planted wheat and other crops.

Quebec remained a colony of France until 1763. In that year, the French signed a treaty ending a long and bitter war with Britain. The British took over Canada.

However, British rule did not change the way the people of Quebec lived. They continued to speak French. They also practiced their Roman Catholic religion.

Until recently, Quebec was very much a rural province. Tidy farms sat along riverbanks. Many of these farms were owned by the same family for many generations.

This part of Quebec still exists. In the rural areas, life revolves around the farm and the close-knit family. However, many of the people of Quebec have moved to cities to seek work.

Montreal is the largest city of Quebec. It has many English-speaking residents. But Montreal is a French Canadian city. Its major churches attract thousands of pilgrims each year.

Montreal is an important banking, shipping, and industrial city. The main portion of the city runs up the slip of an extinct volcano.

Quebec City, the province's other major city, is the heart of French Canada. Quebec is a historic city. The "lower town" is tucked under the shadow of a high cliff. This is the site of the original French settlement of 1608.

To the north lies a vast treasure house of resources. Until recently, few people lived in northern Quebec. Mainly Cree, Inuit, and other native groups lived there in isolated villages. However, great mineral wealth has been discovered underneath the rocky Canadian Shield. As you have read in Case Study 29, huge hydroelectric plants have been built along Quebec's rushing rivers.

Ontario

Ontario is almost as big as Quebec. In many other ways, it is similar. Both Ontario and Quebec border on the United States. Both reach far up to the north. Both are heavily populated in the south and lightly populated in the north.

Yet Ontario and Quebec are different in one important way. Quebec is the center of French Canada. Ontario is British in language and culture.

English-speaking settlers in the late 1700s found the St. Lawrence valley already settled by French Canadians. Thus they traveled further west. Here they found a rich triangle of land that cut down to the Great Lakes. Many of these settlers were fleeing during the American Revolution.

Today, Ontario is one of Canada's fastest growing regions. It is also the most ethnically diverse province. Ontario's capital city, Toronto, boasts many ethnic neighborhoods. It also has radio and television stations that broadcast in over 20 foreign languages.

The Prairie Provinces

West from Ontario, the green eastern landscapes give way to the rolling "prairie provinces." These three provinces grow most of the wheat that makes Canada the fourth-largest wheat producer in the world.

Here in the prairies, it is clear that Canadians are not all of French and British origins. These provinces are almost as ethnically diverse as Ontario. Slightly less than half of the people of the prairies claim

In the provinces of Manitoba, Saskatchewan, and Alberta, the fertile land, summer rains, and dry harvest season make the prairies ideal for growing wheat. Canada is one of the world's largest producers of wheat.

Vancouver is one of the world's most beautiful cities. Locate the city on the map on page 381. How do you think Vancouver's location encourages trade with Asia?

British ancestry. Ethnic groups in the prairies include the descendants of eastern European immigrants who came to Canada around 1875.

The Métis are another group that live in the prairies. They are descendants of French trappers and Native American women who settled here more than 100 years ago. They settled in a cold, dry land that was supposed to be bad for farming. Through years of struggle, they created some of Canada's most successful farms.

The Pacific Coast

Look at the map of Canada on page 381. You will see that cities such as Vancouver and Victoria are quite far north. In fact, they are located north of Montreal, Minnesota, or Maine. Yet the climate is so gentle that flowers begin to bloom as early as February or March. That's because the Pacific coast benefits from warm ocean currents.

This mild climate is partly responsible for the rapid growth in population of Canada's Pacific coast region. Many people have moved there to find work in the new industries of the Pacific coast.

Vancouver is one of Canada's fastest-growing cities. Its harbor teems with activity. From the docks of Vancouver, Canadian products are shipped to Australia, Asia, and other parts of the world.

British Columbia has drawn people from all over the world. Asians are an important part of the population. The first Chinese Canadians came to the area more than 100 years ago. Many came to build the Canadian Pacific Railroad. This railroad was cut through the Rockies to connect western Canada with the prairies.

People from Japan and India followed. In recent years, a large number of people have come from parts of East and Southeast Asia. A large number of Chinese have come from Hong Kong. These new immigrants are usually well educated and wealthy.

Section 3 Review

1. How have French Canadians maintained their culture?

2. **Drawing Conclusions** Do you think calling Canada "a small nation in a big country" is accurate? Why or why not?

Changing Patterns of Life

Why do many French Canadians want to declare Quebec independent from Canada?

Though Canadians live in thousands of scattered villages, Canada is an urban country. At the beginning of the 1900s, less than 40 percent of all Canadians lived in cities. Now, close to 80 percent do. One main reason for this shift is the growth of industry in the cities.

About three out of ten Canadians live in Canada's three largest cities, Toronto, Montreal, and Vancouver. Toronto is now the nation's center for industry and finance. Montreal is the world's second largest French-speaking city. Vancouver handles most of Canada's exports to the nations of Asia.

The Changing Face of Canada

Most Canadians are either of British or French origin. However, about one third are neither. Canada has brought together a variety of people. In Toronto, Canadians from Jamaica play cricket on Sundays. Chinese Canadians in Vancouver celebrate the Chinese New Year with dragon dances. Ukrainian Canadians decorate brightly colored Easter eggs. German Canadians on the prairies celebrate the harvest with an "Oktoberfest."

In many ways, Canadians are still trying to complete their mosaic. They have all the

Canadians take great pride in their country and its ethnic heritage. They celebrate their diversity at festivals such as this summertime meeting in Quebec.

independent pieces. However, they are trying to fit these pieces into an overall picture of Canada.

The French Canadian Challenge

Almost all of the "new Canadians" have adopted the English language. This has helped make French Canadians feel isolated. In all provinces but Quebec, they feel shut out of the mainstream. This has led them to resent other Canadians.

The reasons for this resentment can be traced far back into Canada's history. As you have read, the British and French fought for control of Canada in the 1700s. After the British won control, the government, society, and culture of Canada took on a British character. In recent years, Canadians have tried to narrow the differences between English- and French-speaking Canadians. Language is one issue. Many of the French speakers resent the dominance of English. Economic control is another issue. The French speakers resent that the English speakers often hold the best-paying jobs.

The Canadian government has tried to protect the French language. One result is **bilingualism**, the use of two languages.

On Assignment...

What would you tell visitors to Canada about its many cultures? Which cities would you recommend that tourists visit? Why?

French and English are both official languages of Canada. Signs and government papers are printed in English and French. At official ceremonies, Canada's national anthem is always sung in English and in French.

Separatism

Since 1960, French speakers have taken over much of the economic life in Quebec. Yet many French Canadians are not satisfied by these changes. They are concerned that their culture will be overshadowed by the culture of English-speaking Canada.

"Long live free Quebec!" is the slogan of the French Canadian separatists. Separatists want Quebec to be independent from the rest of Canada. In 1995, the voters of Quebec came within a hair of voting to leave Canada. By a margin of less than 1 percent, voters in Quebec chose to remain a province of Canada. However, the debate over Quebec remains. Some people think it is only a matter of time until Quebec wins its independence.

Many Canadians worry about the problems that an independent Quebec would create. It would split the country in two. Quebec separates the four Maritime provinces from the rest of Canada. Trade, transportation, and communications among those provinces would be difficult if Quebec were independent.

Canada and the United States

Armed with its rich resources, Canada has taken its place among the world's leaders. Canada belongs to several international organizations. Canadian troops have served in United Nations peace-keeping operations.

However, Canada's closest ties are with the United States. The two countries have long been friendly. More than two thirds of Canada's trade is with the United States. The United States is the main buyer of Canadian resources. American investors control a large portion of Canadian industry.

However, many Canadians are concerned about the strong influence of U.S. business and culture. Most popular magazines in Canada are U.S. magazines. U.S. television programs are shown over all of Canada. Popular music and fast foods also reflect the U.S. influence.

Despite these concerns, the United States and Canada are close allies for the most part. Sometimes the neighbors squabble. But the peace arch at the border between Washington State and British Columbia is a symbol of the friendship that exists between the two countries.

Canada and the World

Canada, like the United States, is a democracy. While it is an independent country, it has close ties with Britain.

Canada is a member of the **Commonwealth of Nations**. The commonwealth is made up of independent countries that were once part of the British Empire. Members of the commonwealth have agreements with one another. There are 47 members in all. Queen Elizabeth II of Britain heads the commonwealth. However, she does not govern any of the member countries.

The government of Canada is a **federal system**. The power to make laws is divided between the federal government in Ottawa and the governments of the ten provinces.

There has often been a tug-of-war between the federal and the provincial governments. Disputes have arisen over who controls natural resources. The powers of the provincial governments are another source of conflict.

Section 4 Review

1. Why have Canada's cities grown so large in recent years?

2. **Understanding Points of View** Why do many Canadians resent the influence of U.S. culture? What might they do to preserve their own culture?

I. Reviewing Vocabulary

Match each word on the left with the correct definition on the right.

1. mosaic
2. bilingualism
3. hydroelectric
4. federal system

a. design made up of many small pieces
b. a system in which government power is divided between a central government and local governments
c. power that comes from the force of rushing water
d. the policy of recognizing two official languages

II. Understanding the Chapter

Answer the questions below on a separate sheet of paper.

1. In what region of Canada are most of its lakes?
2. How are the provinces of Quebec and Ontario similar? Different?
3. What three provinces make up the region known as "Canada's breadbasket"? How did these provinces earn that name?
4. Why do French Canadians resent the culture of English Canada?

III. Building Skills: Studying a Map

Study the map on page 381. Answer the following questions on another sheet of paper.

1. Which province or territory of Canada is located farthest east? Which is located farthest west?
2. Which city is the capital of Canada?
3. What oceans border Canada?

IV. Working Together

Work with several classmates to construct a debate about independence for Quebec. Half your group will argue for independence and half will argue against it. Use information in this chapter to build your arguments. Hold your debate in class.

On Assignment. . .

Making a Presentation: Review the notes you took while reading the chapter. Remember that your audience is people who will be visiting Canada. You may choose one of the following topics or come up with one of your own. One possible topic is how the landscape has prevented Canadian unity. The other topic is what a visitor to Toronto should know about the city. After you have made your choice, create an outline for your presentation. Then, write a narrative based on your outline and present it to the class.

I. Understanding the Unit

Answer the questions below on a separate sheet of paper.

1. (a) What are the main physical features and climates of Latin America? (b) How have they affected patterns of settlement?
2. What are the major ethnic groups in Latin America?
3. (a) What were the three major ancient civilizations in Latin America? (b) How were Europeans able to conquer these civilizations?
4. (a) What were the immediate effects of independence in Latin America? (b) What effect did foreign investments have on the newly independent nations?
5. (a) How did Christianity come to Latin America? (b) What is the role of the Catholic Church in Latin American life today?
6. (a) Why are Latin Americans moving to cities? (b) What are the advantages and disadvantages of life in Latin American cities?
7. (a) In your opinion, what is the biggest problem facing Latin America today? (b) Give at least two causes and two effects of this problem.
8. The United States has a history of interfering in Latin American affairs. What effect has this had on the relationship between Latin American nations and the United States?
9. (a) What are the two official languages in Canada? (b) What is the relationship between people who speak these languages?

II. Thinking Critically

Answer the questions below on a separate sheet of paper.

1. **Interpreting a Quote** President Theodore Roosevelt said that when dealing with Latin America, the United States should "speak softly and carry a big stick." What did President Roosevelt mean by this? Give two examples of this policy toward Latin American nations.
2. **Understanding Points of View** In both Latin America and Canada, Europeans took land that once belonged to Native Americans. What arguments might each side use to suggest that they have rights to the land? Give two examples of Native American groups that are claiming their traditional homelands and the results of these claims.

III. Writing to Learn

On a separate sheet of paper, write a three-paragraph essay about the following topic.

Imagine you are a time traveler who is able to travel to Latin America in the following years: 1500 B.C., A.D. 1000, and 1996. Describe what you would see in each of these years. What issues face Latin Americans in each time period?

IV. Practicing Skills: Interpreting Bar Graphs

Read the bar graphs below. On a separate sheet of paper, answer the questions that follow.

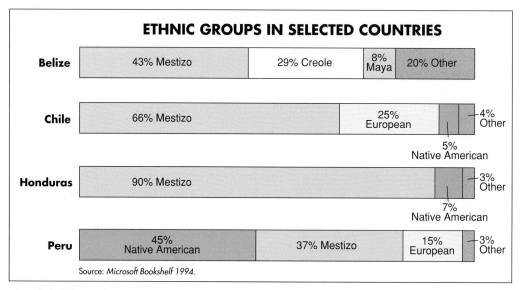

ETHNIC GROUPS IN SELECTED COUNTRIES

Belize: 43% Mestizo | 29% Creole | 8% Maya | 20% Other

Chile: 66% Mestizo | 25% European | 5% Native American | 4% Other

Honduras: 90% Mestizo | 7% Native American | 3% Other

Peru: 45% Native American | 37% Mestizo | 15% European | 3% Other

Source: *Microsoft Bookshelf 1994.*

1. (a) What percentage of Belize's population is Mestizo? (b) What percentage of Chile's population is Native American?
2. (a) Which nation has the largest percentage of Native Americans? Which has the smallest percentage of Native Americans?
3. A generalization is a broad statement supported by facts. Make a generalization about the ethnic diversity of Latin America based on the information in this bar graph.

V. Going Beyond the Unit

Work with two or three students to create a four-page feature news story about Latin America for a magazine that focuses on geography. Your article should include a summary of the following topics: the geography of Latin America, the history of Latin America, the people and culture of Latin America, the economy and politics of Latin America, current problems facing Latin America, and Latin America in the global society. Your article should contain several pictures, drawings, photographs, and other artwork. Present the summary of your news story to the class.

Rain Forests Around the World

Looking at Key Terms

tropical rain forests, temperate rain forests, species, extinct, bio-prospecting, sustainable development, strip-logging

Tropical rain forests are dense woods that receive at least 80 inches (205 cm) of rain a year and have an average temperature of 80° F (27° C). Because they require constant moisture and temperature, most rain forests are found near the equator, between the tropics of Cancer and Capricorn. There are tropical rain forests in North and South America, Africa, and Southeast Asia. The largest single stretch of rain forest is in South America. It is nearly 3 million square miles (8 million sq km) of land drained by the Amazon River.

Some rain forests, called **temperate rain forests**, are found in cooler places. The Hoh Rain Forest in Washington State and the Tongass National Forest in Southeast Alaska, are examples. Often, such rain forests are found on coasts and receive part of their moisture in the form of fog.

Occupying about 5 to 6 percent of the earth's surface, tropical rain forests contain more than half of all the planet's **species**, or separate kinds of animals and plants. In a tropical rain forest in Borneo, one scientist found 1,000 different kinds of trees in an area the size of a suburban mall. By comparison, there are only 700 kinds of trees in all of the United States and Canada combined.

Perhaps 40 percent of all medicines today come from plants or animals native to the rain forests. For example, a drug that fights cancer in young people comes from a flower that grows in the rain forest on the African island of Madagascar. However, no miracle medicines can come from living things that are destroyed before they are known to science.

Rain Forests Are Dying

Every *second* of every hour of every day, an area of rain forest the size of a football field is destroyed somewhere in the world. Every year, the rain forest loses an area the size of the state of Florida. In the southern reaches of the Pacific Northwest, 95 percent of the rain forest has been destroyed. At this rate of destruction, 27,000 species *a year* will become **extinct**—will perish forever from the Earth.

Most tropical rain forests are located in poor countries. Desperate for money, these countries cut down rain forest trees to sell or clear

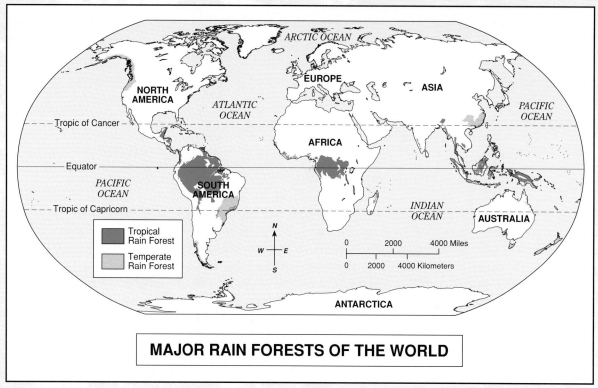

MAJOR RAIN FORESTS OF THE WORLD

Location There are rain forests on nearly every continent in the world. Where are temperate rain forests located? Where are tropical rain forests located?

the forest to raise cattle and create farmland. Rain forests are also cleared to dig up valuable minerals that lie hidden under the earth.

All this activity disturbs the people native to rain forests. Groups such as the Yanamamo of Brazil, the Mbuti of the African Congo, and the Dayak of Borneo are generally not able to defend their land against modern societies. However, these people may be able to contribute greatly to our future. Having occupied the forests for many thousands of years, rain forest peoples know what the plants and animals of their world can be used for. Their experts can guide our experts.

Saving the Rain Forests

With rain forests disappearing at a rapid rate, scientists around the world have formed groups to study the rain forests as quickly as possible. These groups swoop in and take a quick look at rain forest areas scheduled for destruction. These groups then store and coordinate the information in central computer libraries.

Rain forest destruction is driven by economic need. Wealthier countries and industries are getting involved in identifying the resources of the forest. They are **bio-prospecting**. This means they pay countries for the right to search for animals and plants that have medicinal or industrial value. A very large drug company recently paid a million dollars to Costa Rica to search among that country's estimated 12,000 plants and 300,000 insects. Just one drug—something that cures acne, obesity, or cancer—could be worth billions. Costa Rica would share in the profits from such a drug, and use these profits to protect its rain forests and to find other billion-dollar drugs.

Another push is for **sustainable development**. That means taking some resources constantly from the rain forest, but never taking enough to destroy the whole forest. For example, rain forests have many valuable woods like teak, ebony, and mahogany. Often, loggers cut down everything, take out the valuable lumber, and burn the rest. However, **strip-logging**, or taking out narrow roadlike strips of the forest, may be a better solution. This method preserves enough living forest nearby to reseed the strip, so the forest will heal itself and never die.

As a last resort, scientists and others are trying to save what they can, in whatever way they can. They propose putting some animals in zoos, or putting plants in seed banks. They suggest freezing some living matter so that it will be available hundreds of years from now. They try to buy land in the rain forests and set up parks and national refuges. Above all, they educate others. The West African conservationist Baba Dioum has said it best: "In the end, we will conserve only what we love, we will love only what we understand, we will understand only what we are taught."

Review

1. Why are rain forests important to the global community?

2. **Making Inferences** What method of saving the rain forests seems to have the greatest chance of success? Why?

Taking Action: Researching a Topic

The largest group of native rain forest dwellers in Brazil is the Yanamamo tribe. The tribe has about 16,000 people. Scientists estimate that in order to live the kind of life they are accustomed to, the Yanamamo need about 16 million acres of land to live in. Find out about the Yanamamo. Find out how many people live in Brazil, how much land in Brazil 16 million acres covers, and estimate the Yanamamo's chances of getting their preserve.

FOCUS ON

The Middle East

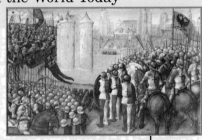

	3500 B.C.		A.D. 1000	1200	1400
History	**3500s B.C.** Sumerian civilization emerges in the Tigris-Euphrates valley.			**1095-1291** Crusaders from Europe invade the Holy Land.	
Culture & Society	**2000 B.C.** Judaism emerges in the Middle East.	**30** Christianity is established in the Middle East.	**622** Islam is founded by Muhammad on the Arabian peninsula.		
Economics & Technology	**3500s B.C.** Sumerians develop writing and methods for keeping time.				

Study the time line. On a separate sheet of paper answer the questions below.

1. What three religions were founded in the Middle East?

2. When did European Crusaders invade the Holy Land?

3. How many years after Christianity was established did the religion of Islam emerge in the Middle East?

4. What water-based project was constructed in Egypt?

5. How many years after oil was discovered in the Middle East was OPEC formed?

1600		1800	1900	2000

1481-1683
The Ottoman empire controls lands around the Mediterranean and Black seas.

1800s
European powers begin to control lands in the Middle East.

1948
The State of Israel is founded.

1979
Ayatollah Ruhollah Khomeini seizes power in Iran.

1520-1566
Suleiman, emperor of the Ottomans, expands trade and increases public services.

1700s-1800s
Nationalism becomes a strong force among the ethnic groups controlled by the Ottoman Empire.

1970s-1990s
Religious fundamentalism increases in the Middle East.

1869
The Suez Canal is built in Egypt.

1920s
Oil is discovered in the Middle East.

1960
Oil-rich countries establish OPEC to control the price of oil.

Oil Production and Consumption in the Middle East
Comparing Circle Graphs

Oil production is a critical issue for the Middle East. Many Middle Eastern countries are major producers of oil. Oil is an important source of energy for countries around the world. The two circle graphs below show production and consumption of oil by world region. Study the circle graphs. On a separate sheet of paper, answer the questions below.

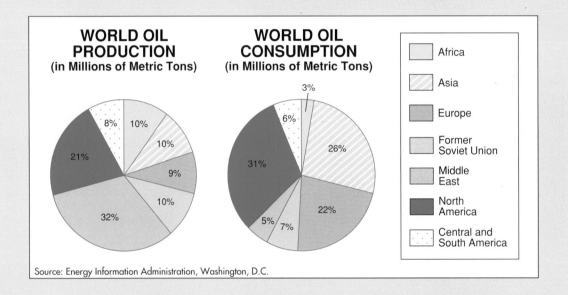

WORLD OIL PRODUCTION (in Millions of Metric Tons)

WORLD OIL CONSUMPTION (in Millions of Metric Tons)

Africa
Asia
Europe
Former Soviet Union
Middle East
North America
Central and South America

Source: Energy Information Administration, Washington, D.C.

Did You Know

- Some countries in the Middle East, like Israel and Turkey, have little or no oil. (See Chapter 30.)

- Due to oil wealth, no one in Bahrain pays income tax. Medical care and schooling are free for all citizens. (See Chapter 34.)

- About a quarter of all the known oil in the world lies in Saudi Arabia. (See Chapter 34.)

1. **Reading the Circle Graphs** (a) What percentage of world oil does the Middle East produce? (b) What percentage does the Middle East consume?

2. **Thinking About the Circle Graphs** (a) Which region of the world consumes the most oil? (b) Does it consume more or less than it produces? (c) How much more or less?

3. **Going Beyond the Circle Graphs: Drawing Conclusions** (a) What advantages might abundant oil reserves bring to a region such as the Middle East? (b) What are some potential problems for nations that cannot produce their own energy?

The Land and People of the Middle East

How have the land and climate of the Middle East affected the people who live there?

Mountains are very important to the people of the Middle East. Most of the rain the region gets falls in the mountains. Here, the snow-capped mountains of Iran tower over Tehran, the capital city.

Looking at Key Terms

- **oasis**   a place in the desert where water comes to the surface
- **civilization**   a highly organized group of people with their own culture
- **nomads**   people who have no permanent home and travel from place to place in search of food and water
- **mosque**   an Islamic house of worship
- **kibbutz**   a farm where the land is owned by everyone who farms it
- **migrate**   to move from one place to another
- **urbanization**   movement of people from the countryside to the cities
- **refugee**   a person who is forced to leave his or her country

On Assignment. . .

Giving a Talk: Prepare a 10-minute background talk about the Middle East. The talk will be given to people who will be traveling there. As you read this chapter, you will be asked to make notes for your talk. At the end of the chapter, you will write your talk and present it.

The Land of the Middle East

Why is the Middle East a crossroads of many cultures?

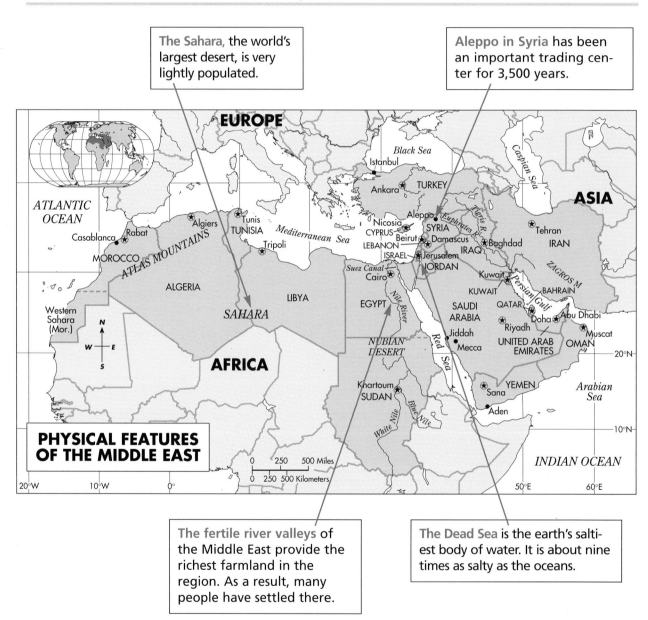

The Sahara, the world's largest desert, is very lightly populated.

Aleppo in Syria has been an important trading center for 3,500 years.

The fertile river valleys of the Middle East provide the richest farmland in the region. As a result, many people have settled there.

The Dead Sea is the earth's saltiest body of water. It is about nine times as salty as the oceans.

PHYSICAL FEATURES OF THE MIDDLE EAST

The Middle East includes land on three continents: Asia, Africa, and a tiny bit of Europe. It is a place of busy cities, high mountains, vast deserts, and fertile river valleys. Note from the map how the Middle East connects Europe, Asia, and Africa. For centuries, the Middle East has linked major trade routes. People from the Middle East have used these routes to spread their ideas and achievements across the three continents.

Some of the vast deserts of the Arabian peninsula are so large that they are called "sand seas." Here, in the desert of Dubhai, sand flows endlessly in every direction.

The world's longest river, the Nile, is more than 4,000 miles (6,437 km) long. A fertile valley spreads from the banks of this river. Most of Egypt's people have always lived along the banks of the Nile. Today, about 99 percent of Egyptians live in the Nile valley.

The discovery of oil has shaped the recent history of the Middle East. Many Middle Eastern countries were once very poor lands. Those that have oil underground have found a new source of wealth.

A Land in Search of Water

The region known as the Middle East stretches more than 3,400 miles (5,440 km) from the Atlantic Ocean to the heart of Central Asia. It includes land in North Africa, Asia, and Europe. Much of the Middle East has a hot and dry climate. Much of the land of the Middle East is desert. Much of the rest is mountainous. Thus, vast stretches of the Middle East are not suitable for farming. Few people live in these dry regions.

That does not mean that there is no good farming land in the Middle East. Some areas are better watered. Thus, most people live along the coasts, in river valleys, and around oases. An **oasis** (oh•AY•sihs) is a place in the desert where water comes to the surface.

Ribbons of Green

Oil has made some Middle Eastern countries wealthy. However, the most valuable resource in the Middle East is not oil, but water. Cutting through the world's driest region are the miraculous rivers of the Middle East. The rivers bring life to the region. Green fields spread out from their banks. These fields spring from soil made rich every year by floods.

The Nile River flows more than 4,000 miles (6,437 km) from central Africa to the Mediterranean Sea. It has always been the source of life for the people of Egypt. It was along the Nile that the ancient Egyptians developed their **civilization** thousands of years ago. Historians say that civilizations, or highly developed societies, arose when people began settling in towns and cities.

Almost all of Egypt's agriculture takes place around the Nile. In fact, almost all industrial and economic activity in Egypt takes place near the Nile.

Another river system has made life possible in a region known as the Fertile Crescent. The Euphrates (yoo•FRAY•teez) and Tigris (TY•gris) rivers flow through Turkey and northern Iraq. The two rivers run parallel until they merge in Iraq. Like the Nile valley, the valley of the Euphrates and Tigris rivers was home to ancient civilizations.

Floods on the two rivers allowed people to settle down and farm there. In the spring, melting snows cause the rivers to flood. The flood waters spread fertile soil over the land.

The floods in the Tigris and the Euphrates can be dangerous, however. They often come without warning, bringing disaster and death.

Land Without Water

Deserts stretch for hundreds of miles across the landscape of the Middle East. The Sahara is the largest desert in the world. The Sahara stretches over a third of Africa. Large parts of Iran, Jordan, and southern Israel are desert. The Arabian Peninsula is also mostly desert. Here lies the Rub' al Khali, one of the hottest, driest places on earth. The high plateaus of central Iran are also deserts. They are cold, barren places, with freezing winters. These areas share a common lack of water. Fewer than 10 inches (25.4 cm) of rain fall in the desert in an average year. There are places where rain has not been measured for hundreds of years.

Mountains of the Middle East

The snowy mountains of Turkey and Iran are about as different from desert as can be. Much of Turkey is mountainous. These mountains skim the edge of northern Iraq and cover most of Iran, as well. The Atlas Mountains run across Morocco and Tunisia.

The mountains are very important to the people of the Middle East. Most of the rain the Middle East gets falls in the mountains. As it rushes down the mountains, it brings soil with it. Streams filled with rich topsoil run into swollen rivers. The result is flooding that adds rich soil to the river valleys.

Climate

If you were taking a trip to the Middle East, you would want to pack for warm

Some of the Middle East's richest farm-land is located in the mountain valleys where melting snow provides water and topsoil each spring. Pictured here are the Atlas Mountains in Morocco.

weather. Summers tend to be long and hot. Temperatures often reach above 100°F (37.8° C). In most of the region, winters are mild. Go to the mountains of Iran and Turkey, though, and you may run into freezing weather in the winter.

Don't worry too much about bringing an umbrella on your trip. As you have just read, much of the Middle East gets less than 10 inches (25.4 cm) of rain annually. That is about what a state in the eastern United States gets in two or three months. The areas of the Middle East that get the most rain stretch around the coasts of the Mediterranean Sea and across northern Turkey, Iraq, and Iran. These are some of the best farming areas of the Middle East.

Resources

Next to water, oil is the most important resource of the Middle East. In some places, there are vast amounts of oil, but there is very little drinking water. Here, oil pays for costly factories that remove the salt from sea water.

Oil Brings Wealth to the Middle East

Millions of years ago, the remains of animals and plants were trapped in mud. These remains were pressed by tons of rocks for millions of years. The result was huge underground pools of oil.

In the early part of this century, engineers found these oil reserves. Large international companies began drilling deep underground to bring the oil to the surface. Huge supertankers plied the oceans to bring the oil to the industrial world.

Suddenly, other countries in the world began to pay attention to the Middle East. The people of the industrial world needed oil to make their houses warm. They needed it to run their cars and power their factories. Within a few decades, the Middle East became one of the most closely watched areas of the world. People in other parts of the world discovered that events in the Middle East could affect them.

Middle Eastern countries have more than 50 percent of the world's known oil and gas. However, Middle Eastern countries do not

Oil has transformed much of the Middle East, bringing vast wealth to some countries. It has also begun to destroy ancient ways, such as the dependence on camels of the desert-bound Bedouins.

benefit equally from oil. Some countries, such as Saudi Arabia and Kuwait, have vast amounts of oil. Other countries, like Egypt, Israel, and Turkey, have almost none.

Other Resources There are not many other natural resources in the region. Egypt, Algeria, Iran, and Turkey mine coal, iron ore, copper, and other minerals. Several countries mine phosphate, which is used to make fertilizer. Because there are few raw materials, little industry has developed. Oil is by far the major industry of the Middle East.

Agriculture and Industry

The lack of farmland is one of the Middle East's major problems. Less than 10 percent of the land area can be farmed. Because there is so little good farmland, the land can easily be overworked. This can turn it back into desert.

The main food crop grown throughout the area is wheat. It is also the food eaten most often by the people of the Middle East.

Cotton is the main industrial crop. Most of it is exported to countries such as Britain that have large textile industries.

Herds of cattle are rare in the Middle East. Instead, people raise animals that need less grass, such as sheep, goats, and camels.

Along the Mediterranean coast, where rain is plentiful, farmers plant vegetables and groves of citrus trees. Farmers also grow barley, dates, figs, olives, and tobacco.

On Assignment...

What are the most important facts that a visitor to the Middle East should know about the region's land and climate? Make notes about the land and climate to use in your talk.

Section 1 Review

1. How have rivers affected life in the Middle East?

2. **Summarizing** In one sentence, summarize the impact of mountains on the lives of the people of the Middle East.

SECTION 2

The People of the Middle East

What cultural bonds tie together the people of the Middle East?

About 346 million people live in the Middle East. There are vast differences among these people. Many live in communities that have existed for thousands of years. However, some are **nomads**, people who have no permanent homes. A few are wealthy from oil. Many more are very poor. Most Middle Easterners are farmers. Yet the region contains some of the world's largest cities.

What do the people of the Middle East have in common? Above all, they are linked by two factors: language and religion. Most Middle Easterners speak the Arabic language. And most Middle Easterners are Muslims, people who practice the religion of Islam. Muslims believe that Allah is the supreme deity whose thoughts are contained in the holy book, the Koran.

Muslim and Arab: The Differences

There is an important difference between the terms Muslim and Arab. People who speak the Arabic language are known as Arabs. Most, but not all, are Muslims. There are Arabs who are Christian and Arabs who are Jewish.

Throughout the world, there are millions of Muslims who speak a language other than Arabic. People in some Middle Eastern countries such as Turkey and Iran are predominantly Muslim. Yet they speak languages that are very different from Arabic.

The Arabic Language

Middle Easterners who speak the Arabic language share a strong bond. A person from Iraq who speaks Arabic has a common tie with an Arabic-speaking person from far-off Algeria. An Iraqi person is likely to feel less close to a person from nearby Iran who speaks Farsi, the Persian language.

A Language All Arabs Can Read When it is printed or written, Arabic is very similar throughout the Middle East. A person in Iraq can read the same newspaper as a person in Algeria.

While written Arabic is similar all over the Middle East, the language is spoken and pronounced differently in different parts of the Middle East. An Algerian may have difficulty understanding what an Iraqi says.

The Role of Hebrew Another important language in the Middle East is Hebrew, the official language of Israel. Hebrew and Arabic are related languages. Both languages grew from the ancient language of the Semites. The Semites were a nomadic people who lived in the Arabian Peninsula in ancient times. Some words in Arabic and Hebrew are the same or similar. For example, "hello," "good-bye," and "peace" are similar in both languages. The Arabic word is *salaam*. The Hebrew word is *shalom*.

Other Languages There are two other main languages in the Middle East. About 30 million people in Iran speak Farsi, or Persian. In Turkey, about 30 million people speak Turkish. European languages are frequently spoken in the Middle East. Quite often, the use of these languages reflects past European rule over a country. For example, many people in the countries of North Africa that were once ruled by France speak French as well as Arabic.

The Dome of the Rock in Jerusalem is one of the holiest sites in Islam. Muslims believe that Muhammad, the founder of the religion, rose to heaven from this spot. The Dome of the Rock is a **mosque**, an Islamic house of worship. Many Muslims go there to pray.

Kibbutz life is important to Israelis. Although only about 10 percent of Israelis farm, many of those who do live on a **kibbutz**. A kibbutz is a farm where the land is owned by everyone who farms it. People who live on the kibbutz work together and share the profits. Life on a kibbutz can mean long hours and hard work. Ties among people of the kibbutz are strong. Those who live there take pride in what they produce.

In many of the region's largest cities, people dressed in Western-style clothes mix with traditionally dressed people. In the center of most of these cities are marketplaces. In the markets, shoppers can find anything from Persian rugs to bicycles.

Many Middle Easterners still farm as their parents did. Though new ways are spreading, most farmers still work the fields with wooden plows. Less than 10 percent of the land in the Middle East supports farming. The lack of rainfall is the most critical problem. As a result, irrigation is an ancient practice in the Middle East. Irrigation is the practice of bringing water from another source to use in growing crops.

The Role of Islam

In every country in the region except Israel, most of the people are Muslims. In countries such as Algeria, Libya, Saudi Arabia, and Turkey more than 95 percent of the people are Muslims. Cities such as Mecca, Medina, and Jerusalem are important Islamic religious centers. Mecca and Medina are located in Saudi Arabia. They are holy to Muslims because of their role in the founding of Islam. Jerusalem is holy to Muslims, Jews, and Christians. Other cities such as Baghdad and Cairo have important Islamic educational centers. (You will learn more about Islam later in this book.)

TEN LARGEST CITIES IN THE MIDDLE EAST

CITY	COUNTRY	POPULATION
Cairo	Egypt	6,600,000
Tehran	Iran	6,100,000
Istanbul	Turkey	5,500,000
Baghdad	Iraq	4,700,000
Alexandria	Egypt	3,000,000
Ankara	Turkey	2,300,000
Casablanca	Morocco	2,200,000
al–Jizah (Giza)	Egypt	1,700,000
Beirut	Lebanon	1,600,000
Algiers	Algeria	1,600,000

Source: Encyclopædia Britannica

In recent years, the cities of the Middle East have grown rapidly as people have moved to them from villages. What country has three cities among the Middle East's largest ten?

Millions of people in the Middle East practice other religions. In Israel, most of the people are Jewish. Many Christians also live in the Middle East. For example, Syria, Lebanon, and Egypt have large Christian populations.

Where People Live

Some parts of the Middle East have almost no people. Others have many. Where there is water, there are people. Many millions of Middle Easterners live along the banks of the great rivers. Nearly all of Egypt's 59 million people are crowded on two narrow strips on either side of the Nile River. Millions of other Middle Easterners live along the coasts or at the base of mountain ranges.

Old and New in the Cities

Towns and cities have always played an important role in Islamic life. Ancient cities such as Damascus, Cairo, and Istanbul have long been great centers of trade.

Middle Eastern cities are a fascinating mix of the old and new. There are new buildings and broad avenues. There are modern schools and office buildings. There are also old quarters with narrow streets. In these old quarters, houses seem to be piled one on top of another.

Fewer than half of all Middle Easterners live in towns and cities. Those who do include factory workers, government officials, doctors, and merchants.

Many city dwellers wear modern Western-style clothes. Some wear long, flowing cotton robes of traditional dress. Many women follow the traditional Muslim practice of wearing veils to cover their faces.

Population Shifts

There are three important facts you should know about the population of the Middle East.

1. It is growing very quickly.
2. Many people **migrate.** They move from one place to another within the region.

3. There is a great deal of **urbanization** in the Middle East. People are moving from the countryside to the cities.

Rapid Growth

Fifty years ago, the Middle East had about 52 million people. Today, more than 350 million people live there. This increase is due largely to better health care. The people of the Middle East are living longer than they did 50 years ago. Many more babies survive their first year of life.

Of course, these new children must be fed. Finding food is a huge problem for the people of the Middle East. The region does not grow enough food to feed all its people. Food must be imported from other places, such as Russia and Africa.

Migration

Fifty years ago, people who lived in the Middle East could expect to live out their lives in the town or village where they were born. That is no longer true. People in the Middle East are moving from one part of the region to another.

There are many reasons for this migration. People leave some areas of the Middle East because they are **refugees** who are forced to leave their country. Many Middle Easterners are refugees because their native countries have become battlefields. In Palestine, Iraq, and Lebanon, people have fled their homelands to find lives without fear of war.

Others move because they are looking for work. Some leave to take jobs in oil-rich countries or at high-paying oilfields. Others travel to Western Europe to find work. Often, these migrants are men who send home to their families some of the money they earn.

On Assignment...

Think about what would be most useful for a visitor to the Middle East to know about the people of this area. To prepare for your talk, make notes about what you have learned about the people of the Middle East.

Urbanization

Fifty years ago, no city in the Middle East had more than a million people. Today, more than 6 million people live in Cairo, Egypt. Tehran in Iran, Istanbul in Turkey, and Baghdad in Iraq are not far behind in size.

Why do people leave the country for the city? Usually, it is to find a better job. Most move because of the difficulty of making a living from farming. However, the flood of migrants to the cities has put a strain on the cities. There are not enough jobs to go around. Often, there is not enough housing for the newcomers.

Section 2 Review

1. What cultural ties do Arabs of the region share?

2. **Analyzing Information** Which of the following people would find an Algerian newspaper easiest to read: an Israeli, an Iranian, or an Egyptian? Explain your answer.

The Bedouins of the Desert

The camels move slowly across the desert. On their heavily-loaded backs are men wearing long headdresses. The sand whirls around their caravan.

This is the image that most people have of the Middle East. As we have seen, it is a limited image. The Middle East is a region of farmers on small plots of land. It is a region of bustling cities that combine old traditions and new ways of life.

However, one small group of people live in the desert. The Bedouins (BEHD•oo•inz) of North Africa live an extremely hard life. That is one reason why more and more Bedouins give up their traditional life each year.

Fewer and fewer Bedouins use camels as transportation. Now, it is more common to see a Bedouin come into town in a pickup truck. Still, the Bedouins live as nomads.

Braving the Desert

The Bedouins live where few others will. Bedouins have been herding camels in Egypt and Syria since 1000 B.C. In the centuries since, some moved through the Arabian Peninsula. Others moved into North Africa where they lived for many centuries. Their way of life was largely unchanged.

In the 1800s, parts of North Africa were taken over by Europeans. The Bedouins were pushed out of many of their traditional places. Today, fewer than 5 percent of the Bedouins choose to live the

A veiled Bedouin woman engages in the ancient art of spinning wool in the Saudi Arabian desert. She sits in a tent that she has worked months to weave.

hard nomadic life in the desert. The rest have settled down in villages and cities.

For those who live in the desert, many parts of life remain the same. The Bedouin diet remains mostly meat, milk, and other dairy products. These are the products of the sheep, goats, and camels the Bedouins herd.

Bedouins call their tents "houses of hair." These tents are long strips of goat or camel hair. Inside, the family's tent is divided into a women's section and a men's section. In the men's section are the fire, the supplies for making coffee, a light, and often a gun. On the women's side are clothing, bedding, food, and often a loom for weaving.

Bedouin women are highly skilled weavers. Those who live in towns have looms that are easy to use and hard to carry. Bedouin weavers who still live as nomads use simple, light looms. They weave cloth for the tent, rugs, and other items the family needs. Wool may be brought from town or sheared from the livestock the family owns.

On the Move

For nomadic herders, life is dominated by the needs of their livestock. For camel herders, that means traveling when a pasture is used up. Camel-herding Bedouins can move more than 25 miles (40 km) a day. At night, they set up enough of the tent to cover the children. Everyone eats flour mixed with milk. The next morning, they may be on the move again. A camel-herding group will move about 800 miles (1,280 km) a year from pasture to pasture.

These days, nomads often herd sheep and goats instead of camels. With more pickup trucks traveling the desert, and more roads, camels are less prized. Unlike camels, however, sheep and goats cannot spend long days without water. Thus, the Bedouins must stay closer to water and grass. They travel into the desert only during the spring when there is grass.

Oil has changed the Bedouins' way of life, as it has changed life for many other Middle Easterners. Many Bedouins have moved to towns. There, they work for oil companies. Others work for local governments. Still others may join the army. Some Bedouins, however, refuse to give up their hard life in the desert. For them, the rewards of an easier life in town are nothing compared to the sense of freedom in the desert.

Case Study Review

1. Why do Bedouins call their tents "houses of hair"?
2. **Formulating Questions** If you could ask one question to a Bedouin, what would it be? Explain your choice.

REVIEWING CHAPTER 30

I. Reviewing Vocabulary

Match each word on the left with the correct definition on the right.

1. oasis
2. civilization
3. refugee
4. migrate

a. a highly organized group of people with their own culture
b. a person who is forced to flee his or her country
c. to move from one place to another
d. place in the desert where water comes to the surface

II. Understanding the Chapter

Answer the questions below on a separate sheet of paper.

1. Why are the rivers of the Middle East so important?
2. How does language connect people of different countries in the Middle East?
3. Why are the cities of the Middle East growing so quickly?
4. Why are some Bedouins choosing to end their nomadic life?

III. Building Skills: Determining Cause and Effect

For each item below, provide either the cause or the effect.

1. **Cause:**
   Effect: In recent years, some Middle Eastern countries have gained great wealth.
2. **Cause:** People in the Middle East are living longer than they once did.
   Effect:
3. **Cause:**
   Effect: A person from Syria will feel closer to a distant Algerian than to a nearby Turk.

IV. Working Together

Divide the class into two groups. Have each group create quiz questions about the land and people of the Middle East. Groups should take turns asking and answering the questions. See which group knows more about the subject. The first group to answer five questions correctly wins.

On Assignment. . .

Giving a Talk: Look at your notes about the land and the people of the Middle East. Arrange the information you wrote so it creates an informative talk for people who will be visiting this region. Practice your talk at home. Then give your talk to a partner in your class. Ask your partner for advice about how to improve your talk. Then switch places. Comment on your partner's talk. Finally, give your talk to the entire class.

CHAPTER 31

The Rich Heritage of the Middle East

An ancient carving shows King Hammurabi at left receiving the law from a sun god. The goal of Hammurabi's laws was to prevent the powerful from destroying the weak.

Why was the Middle East home to so many important early civilizations?

Looking at Key Terms

- **city-state** a large community that has its own government and controls the land around it
- **cuneiform** form of writing in ancient Sumer that had wedge-shaped characters
- **pharaoh** a ruler of ancient Egypt
- **pyramid** a large stone building with a square base and sides like triangles that rise to a point
- **hieroglyphics** form of writing in ancient Egypt that used characters that look like pictures
- **papyrus** reeds that the ancient Egyptians pounded flat to make paper for writing
- **mummy** dead body that has been preserve
- **covenant** an agreement or contract
- **pilgrimage** a journey that a believer makes to a religious site

On Assignment...

Creating a Time Line: The ancient peoples of the Middle East had a number of important civilizations. Charting these civilizations on a time line will help you understand when and how they grew. Draw a time line for each section of the chapter. At the end of the chapter, you will put your work together. This larger time line will give you a picture of the rise and fall of the many ancient civilizations in the region.

Civilization Between the Rivers

Why did civilizations grow in Mesopotamia?

The farmer looked out over the green fields. He beamed. This land between the Tigris and Euphrates rivers seemed perfect. It was flat. It was fertile. There were no stones or trees. This was land to plant in. This was land to rejoice in.

That farmer looked out over his fields in the year 5000 B.C. He was part of one of the world's oldest civilizations. Later, the Greeks named the land in which the farmer lived Mesopotamia. Mesopotamia means "land between rivers." Today this region is part of Iraq.

How did civilizations begin in the river valleys of the Middle East? First, people learned that when wild seeds were planted they grew into food that could be eaten. People began settling down and planting crops. A regular food supply allowed people to live longer. Thus, the population began to grow.

When people settled down to farm, they needed water to grow their crops. Over hundreds of years, these people learned how to build canals to bring water to their fields. They built dams to prevent floods. Soon, the farmers of Mesopotamia were growing plenty of food.

In fact, they grew enough food to feed more than their families. This meant that not everyone in the community had to be a farmer. Some could be weavers. Others could work in metal. Still others could become traders.

Traders helped the ideas of a civilization to spread. Traders traveled from place to place buying and selling goods. They brought the wealth of the river valleys to other groups. Gradually, the knowledge of farming spread.

There were other great advantages to settling down in communities. By banding together, people could better protect themselves. Some people could devote all their time to being soldiers. Others could be builders.

Over the centuries, settlements grew into towns and towns grew into cities. **City-states** formed. Each city-state included a city and the land around it. Each was ruled by its own king.

The city-states were well organized. A ruling council made laws. People paid taxes. They stored grain in case of hard times. They built public buildings. Many of the public buildings were temples to their gods. These temples were usually the most important buildings in a town. Often the temples were decorated with paintings of flowers, bushes, and trees.

The first civilization in the Tigris-Euphrates valley is known as Sumer (SOO•mer). By about 3500 B.C., a number of farming settlements had grown into powerful city-states in Sumer. The people who lived there are called Sumerians. As Sumerian civilization grew, it became more complex. People developed writing skills. This allowed the Sumerians to record important information. Records of sales and purchases, contracts, and laws could be written down. So could ideas about life.

The written Sumerian language looks like a series of wedges. It is called **cuneiform** (kyoo•NAY•uh•form). It was written on soft clay with a sharpened reed. When the clay hardened, the Sumerians had a permanent record.

Only in recent years have people learned to read these ancient tablets. As they read them, they began to understand the richness of Sumerian society. They learned of other Sumerian contributions. The Sumerians gave us our understanding of time. Because of the Sumerians, we divide a minute into 60 seconds and an hour into 60 minutes. We believe the Sumerians were the first people to use the wheel. They also invented the sail and developed the plow. They even knew how to perform surgery.

The early civilizations of the Middle East made many advances in mathematics, the sciences, and medicine. This picture from the 1200s, shows an Arab pharmacy where medicine is being made from honey.

Sumerian Culture Spreads

Over hundreds of years, the Sumerians grew powerful. The city-states began to control land beyond the rivers. This led to battles over land and water. These rivalries over land and water weakened the city-states.

Stories of the wealth and power of Sumer attracted invaders. The most powerful were the Akkadians, who came from the north. Around 2500 B.C., their king, Sargon I, captured city after city in Sumer. Sargon created the world's first known empire.

The Sumerians gained control of their lands again 300 years later. Then, other invading groups came in from the north. In about 1750 B.C., Hammurabi, (hah•moo•RAH•bee), king of Babylon, created a large empire. To provide justice throughout his empire, Hammurabi issued a set of new laws. These laws replaced many of the earlier laws of the Sumerians.

Hammurabi's laws were written on stone slabs. Perhaps the most famous is his "eye for an eye" law. For example, a man who blinded another was punished by losing an eye.

New Conquerors

About 200 years after Hammurabi's death, it was the Babylonians' turn to be conquered. The Hittites, from what is today the country of Turkey, were fierce warriors. They had a secret weapon. They had discovered that by heating iron ore, they could make iron. Their iron weapons were much stronger than any their enemies had.

The Hittites managed to keep the secret of their weapons for centuries. Finally, though, the use of iron spread. When it did, the Hittites lost their great advantage.

To the west, the Phoenicians (fuh•NEE•shuns) gained control of the eastern shore of the Mediterranean Sea. They built a number of city-states. The Phoenicians were master sailors. They earned their living through trade with other nations. From their ports, they traded glass, metals, and ivory. Hardy Phoenician sailors built cities along the shores of the Mediterranean. There were Phoenician cities in Greece, Italy, Spain, and North Africa.

Probably the greatest gift of the Phoenicians was their alphabet. It had 22 letters. The Greeks added other letters. The Romans later adapted it. The Phoenician alphabet is the source of the alphabet we use today in the Western world.

The Persian Empire

Persia is the old name for Iran. The Persians were nomads for hundreds of years. Then, in about 550 B.C., the Persian emperor Cyrus the Great began expanding Persia's territory. Under Cyrus and other

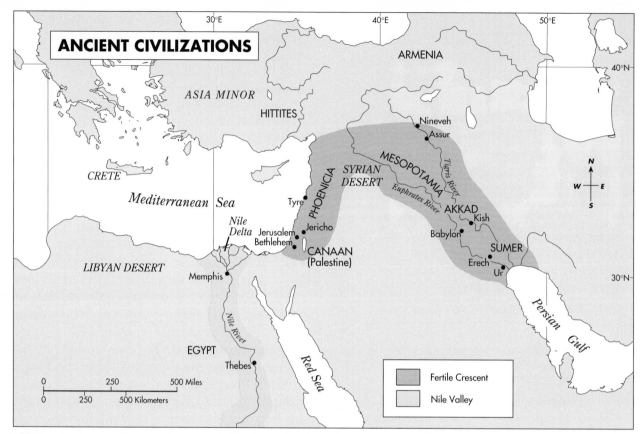

ANCIENT CIVILIZATIONS

Location In ancient times, advanced civilizations developed along the Mediterranean's eastern shore. Along what rivers in the Middle East and North Africa did civilizations also develop in ancient times?

kings, the empire stretched from India to Egypt.

Darius I created a government to hold this huge empire together. He divided the empire into provinces. Each province had a governor who collected taxes and kept order. Darius built miles of roads that linked the provinces of the empire. Those roads were used for trade.

Alexander the Great conquered the Persian Empire around 334 B.C. Alexander was a brilliant soldier from Macedonia, just north of Greece. He lured some Persians into fighting against their own people. His combined armies then overran the Persians. After the conquest, Alexander made his soldiers take Persian wives. This helped unite his new empire. Greek culture and customs spread during Alexander's empire. Even after his empire was gone, Greek ways of life remained.

On Assignment. . .

Your time line should start at the beginning of civilization in Mesopotamia. Include the important events that are covered in this section.

Section 1 Review

1. How did civilizations begin in Mesopotamia?

2. **Drawing Conclusions** Why do you think the lands of the Middle East were invaded so often?

SECTION 2

Civilization in Egypt

What strengths allowed Egyptian civilization to last for 3,000 years?

"At first I could see nothing. The hot air escaping from the chamber caused the candle to flicker. But my eyes became used to the light. Then details of the room emerged slowly from the mist. There were strange figures of animals, statues, and gold. Everywhere there was the glint of gold!"

With these words, an Englishman named Howard Carter described his first glimpse of the tomb of the Egyptian king, Tutankhamun (toot•ank•AH•muhn). Carter discovered the tomb in 1922. It had been closed for 2,300 years.

Carter gasped as he entered the small room. He could see vast riches all around him. Containers of jewels were piled on the floor. Carter picked up a handful of jewels and gazed at them with wonder. Nearby was a priceless golden mask. Then at the far wall, he saw the king's coffin. The lid had a golden statue carved on it. It was decorated with precious jewels. Carter realized that he was looking at one of the largest treasures ever gathered in one room.

The Giver of Life

The treasure that Howard Carter discovered came from Egypt, one of the world's first civilizations. Just as Mesopotamia developed around the Tigris and Euphrates rivers, the Egyptians owed their civilization to the gifts of the Nile River.

"Hail to you, O Nile. You flow from the earth and come to keep Egypt alive." This ancient Egyptian song reveals an important truth: without the waters of the Nile, civilization would never have developed in Egypt.

The Nile's yearly floods gave Egypt its rich farmland. The floods spread over the valley in summer. They brought with them rich soil from the mountains. By October, the ground was covered with a thick layer of black soil. The land was so fertile that it was possible to grow two crops a year.

Small towns developed in the Nile Valley of North Africa beginning around 5000 B.C. These gradually grew into cities. Egypt developed into two kingdoms. Around 3100 B.C., Menes (MEE•neez), the king of the southern kingdom, conquered the north. Menes became Egypt's first **pharaoh** (FAIR•oh). This word for king comes from the Egyptian term for "great house."

The Old Kingdom

Menes began what is known as the Old Kingdom of Egypt. It lasted from about 3100 B.C. to about 2200 B.C. During this time, the Egyptians built their first **pyramids**. A pyramid is a huge stone building with a square base. It has sides shaped like triangles that rise to a point at the top. The pyramids were massive tombs for Egypt's pharaohs. They took years to build. Thousands of workers labored to put up the pyramids. The cost in lives and suffering was enormous.

The Egyptians believed that pharaohs were gods. Thus they needed great buildings to house their spirits after death. Kings were buried with what they might need after death. In the pyramids were jewels, furniture, and gold.

From treasures found in the pyramids and other tombs, we have learned what life in Egypt was like. We also learned about daily life from wall paintings inside the pyramids. These paintings show everything from baking bread to making war.

People have long puzzled over how the pyramids were built. How could such giant buildings be put up without the aid of the wheel? How did the Egyptians get the huge stones to the top?

Scientists today think that workers built winding ramps around the pyramids. They loaded blocks on sleds and then pulled them up to the top. Each of the blocks weighed more than 4,000 pounds (1,800 kg).

Picture Writing

Developing a written language allowed the Egyptians to record the property of the pharaohs. The Egyptian form of writing was called **hieroglyphics** (heye•uhr•oh•GLIHF•ihks). It was made of pictures that stood for words and sounds.

At first, these hieroglyphics were carved on stone. Later, Egyptians discovered that the plant called **papyrus** (puh•PY•rus) could be pounded flat to make a writing surface, similar to paper. For the first time, written information could be transported easily.

Egyptian Contributions

The Egyptians developed many ideas that help us today. The Egyptians were skilled at measuring time. They developed one of the most accurate calendars in the ancient world. The Egyptians used this calendar to tell them when the Nile would flood. This let them know when to plant their crops. The Egyptians also studied medicine and science. They studied the human body and learned how to mend broken bones and per-

On Assignment...

Your time line for Egypt should include events in all three kingdoms. Put in the dates the kingdoms began and ended. Include the important events that happened in each period of time.

form brain surgery. They also discovered how to treat certain illnesses by using herbs.

The Middle Kingdom

The cost of building the pyramids was enormous. It weakened the Egyptian government and led officials in the provinces to seize control of their territories. By 2200 B.C., civil wars disrupted trade. The Old Kingdom ended in disorder.

By 2050 B.C., a new series of rulers from the south restored order to Egypt. The second great period of Egypt's history was about to begin. This period is known as the Middle Kingdom. It lasted until about 1800 B.C. During this time, art and literature flourished. The pharaohs also undertook a number of important projects. One project was

Massive tombs for Egypt's pharaohs, the pyramids took many years to build and involved thousands of workers. They are among the largest buildings on earth.

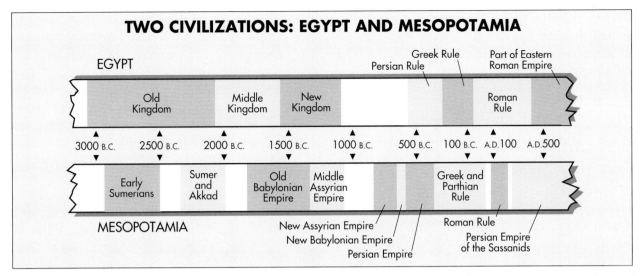

TWO CIVILIZATIONS: EGYPT AND MESOPOTAMIA

Egypt and the kingdoms of Mesopotamia grew up along separate river valleys about 5,000 years ago. Around what time period did the Greeks gain control of both Egypt and Mesopotamia?

the draining of swampland in the delta of the Nile River. This created thousands of acres of new farmland.

By 1800 B.C., however, Egypt was divided by civil war. This allowed foreign invaders to conquer Egypt. About 150 years later, the Egyptians took back their country. They vowed that they would not be conquered again. They took over more land beyond the Nile Valley to protect themselves. This period is known as the New Kingdom.

The New Kingdom

The New Kingdom was the final period of ancient Egypt's glory. It lasted from 1570 B.C. to 1090 B.C. Its pharaohs kept Egypt strong. Trade with foreign lands increased. This made Egypt a wealthy and powerful land once again.

During the New Kingdom, pharaohs were buried in secret underground tombs. Over the years, robbers broke into most of the great tombs of Egypt. They stole the gold and other treasures. But one tomb was well hidden. This was the tomb of the pharaoh Tutankhamun. People today often call him "King Tut." Howard Carter searched for King Tut's tomb for many years. In 1922, he finally found it. It had not been robbed. The tomb was still full of gold and other precious items.

Egyptians thought that a life force remained in the body after death. To make sure that a person would have life after death, the Egyptians learned to preserve bodies. They treated the bodies with spices and herbs and wrapped them in cloth. These wrapped bodies are called **mummies.** Today, we still can see mummies from Egypt.

Section 2 Review

1. Name one accomplishment of the ancient Egyptians that helps us today.

2. **Comparing** How was the Nile River similar to the Tigris and Euphrates in helping civilization to begin?

SECTION 3

Judaism and Christianity

In what ways are Judaism and Christianity linked together?

Three great religions of the world began in a small area of the Middle East. These three religions—Judaism, Christianity, and Islam—all propose the same idea. All believe in one God. These religions have spread around the world. Yet worshipers in all three religions look to the Middle East as the source of their beliefs.

The Kingdom of Israel

In Mesopotamia about 2000 B.C., a group of people called the Hebrews moved across the Jordan River into the land of Canaan. The religion of the Hebrews is known as Judaism (JOO•day•ihz•um). Although Judaism developed over many years, its central belief remained the same. This was the belief in one God. The first Hebrews believed that God would take care of them if they remained faithful to Him as His chosen people.

About 1700 B.C., some Hebrew tribes left Canaan to settle in Egypt. These tribes lived in Egypt for about 400 years. Then the Egyptian pharaoh made them slaves. One of the most dramatic events in the history of the Hebrews grew out of their slavery. In about 1300 B.C., the leader Moses led the Hebrews from slavery in Egypt to freedom.

To return to Canaan, the Hebrews had to travel through the desert. After many years, they finally reached Canaan. They fought the people who were there. Of these people, the most powerful were the Philistines.

These bitter struggles for control of the land along the Jordan River lasted for more than 100 years. At last the Hebrews were victorious. In 1025 B.C., the 12 Hebrew tribes set up the kingdom of Israel.

This kingdom became powerful. About 1000 B.C., King David captured the city of Jerusalem and made it the capital of Israel. Later, his son Solomon became king and further strengthened Israel. Solomon developed trade with Egypt and with the Phoenicians. He also built a magnificent temple in Jerusalem.

After Solomon died, disagreements caused the kingdom to split in two parts. The Assyrians then conquered the northern kingdom of Israel in 722 B.C. In 586 B.C., Babylon overran the southern kingdom of Judea. The Babylonians destroyed the temple there and sent many Hebrews to Babylon. They stayed there for about 50 years. When Babylon was captured by Cyrus the Great, some of the Hebrews returned to Jerusalem and rebuilt their temple.

Carvings on a Roman building built by the emperor Titus celebrate his conquest of Jerusalem. The Romans looted the candlesticks and other sacred objects from the Jewish temple.

Ruled, but Not Conquered

The people who remained in the land were called Jews, after the name of their kingdom, Judea. Judea was conquered by the Romans in 63 B.C.

The Jews revolted against Roman rule in A.D. 66, but the revolt was not successful. In A.D. 70, the Romans destroyed the temple. All that remained was the Western Wall, which is now a Jewish holy place.

Through these hardships, the Jews kept their beliefs. They continued to worship God no matter where they lived. They continued to believe in God's **covenant,** or contract. The covenant says that if the Jews obey God's laws, God will recognize them as his special people.

Since ancient times, Jews have had books of laws that help them follow the covenant. These books teach Jews to think of everyone as equal. They teach that all people have rights. Jews are taught to be fair and do good in the world. Their reward is knowing they are doing God's will.

The Rise of Christianity

During the wars between the Jews and the Romans, Jesus was born in Judea. Jesus preached to everyone, especially the poor. Jesus stressed love for God and good will toward other people. A person's chief duties, he said, were to "love the Lord thy God with all thy heart" and to "love thy neighbor as thyself."

Jesus traveled around his homeland teaching about the kingdom of God. He preached that God loved sinners as well as the good. Jesus taught that wealth was unimportant. He said that there was a better life to come after death. People who were humble and unselfish would be rewarded with eternal life.

What was the appeal of Christianity? Jesus made a point of including everyone, even poor people, in his message. It was a message that said God forgives people for their mistakes. If Christians tried to live a life of goodness, Jesus promised them life after death. That promise has led Christianity to become one of the world's leading religions.

The Roman rulers were worried by Jesus' popularity. Seeing Jesus as a threat to their power, they killed him. Christians believe that Jesus rose from the dead on the third day after his death. Christians believe that God sacrificed his only son in order to show all people that there is life after death.

If the Romans hoped to stop Jesus' teachings by killing him, they made a mistake. His death made the religion grow. Followers of Jesus kept telling people about his teachings. They drew huge crowds. Many eagerly accepted Jesus' promise of life after death.

The Romans were concerned by the growth of this new religion. Christians stubbornly refused to worship the Roman emperor. Roman authorities saw the Christians as troublemakers who were winning converts throughout the empire. The Romans harshly punished people who became Christians. Some were burned to death. Some were thrown into an arena to be eaten by lions.

None of these attacks stopped the new religion. By A.D. 300, Christianity had become popular in the Roman Empire. In A.D. 313, Emperor Constantine made Christianity equal to other religions in the empire. In 395, it became the official religion of the empire.

Section 3 Review

1. What is one major similarity between Judaism and Christianity?

2. **Making Inferences** Why did rulers in the Middle East find Judaism and Christianity so threatening?

On Assignment...

Make a time line that includes the major events in the history of Judaism and Christianity.

The Growth of Islam

How did the teachings of the prophet Muhammad start a new religion?

Islam is the third of the world's great religions born in the Middle East. Today, there are more than 900 million Muslims. It is one of the world's fastest-growing religions.

Islam grew out of the teachings of a man named Muhammad who was born about 570 in Mecca. It was a city where traders often came. Today, Mecca is in Saudi Arabia.

Early Days Muhammad's father died before Muhammad was born. His mother died when he was six. Muhammad grew up with his uncle, who was a trader. He came to know the religions of the traders. Some believed in the many gods of the Arabs. Others were Jews or Christians.

Muhammad was about 40 years old when he had a vision of the angel Gabriel. This was the first of many dreams that would change his life. During this dream, a voice told Muhammad to preach the word of God.

Muhammad taught that there was one God. He preached against worshiping many gods. He promised that all people were equal before Allah. *Allah* is the Arabic word for God. Muhammad said that for Muslims to gain Allah's grace, they must give in to Allah's will. In fact, the word *Islam* means "submission to Allah."

Hejira When Muhammad began to attract followers, local officials became alarmed. In 622, Muhammad discovered that some officials were plotting to kill him. Muhammad and a handful of followers escaped to Medina, a city about 200 miles (320 km) away. Muslims call the journey from Mecca to Medina the hejira (HUH•jeye•ruh), or departure. The year 622 is the first year of the Muslim calendar.

The hejira marked a turning point in Muhammad's life. In Medina, he gained power as a religious leader. In 630, Muhammad returned with an army to Mecca. He captured the city. Before Muhammad's death in 632, he had united Arabs on the Arabian Peninsula.

Teachings of Islam

Muhammad knew many Jews and Christians. He accepted the teachings of the Jewish and Christian scriptures as God's word. Like Judaism and Christianity, Islam sets moral standards.

These standards are presented in the Koran, the sacred book of Islam. Muslims believe that the Koran contains the word of God. The Koran is the basis for law all over the Muslim world.

For Muslims, there are five main duties. They are known as the Five Pillars of Islam. The most important pillar is belief in one God. The second is prayer. Muslims must pray five times a day. While they pray, they face Mecca, the birthplace of Muhammad.

Islam teaches concern for the poor. Giving charity is the third pillar. The fourth duty is fasting. During the holy month of Ramadan, Muslims fast during the day. At night, they feast. The fifth pillar is the **pilgrimage** to Mecca. Once in every Muslim's life, he or she is expected to go to Mecca.

Section 4 Review

1. What was the hejira?

2. **Making Inferences** Why are the five duties of Muslims known as the "Five Pillars"?

A Pilgrimage to Mecca

The scene was filled with color. Camels were decorated with gold and silver bracelets. People who had come hundreds of miles to Mecca wore silk trimmed with gold. The richness and color of the camel caravans stunned the traveler Ibn Batuta. He had never seen such wealth. And the number of people! They spoke languages Ibn Batuta had never heard.

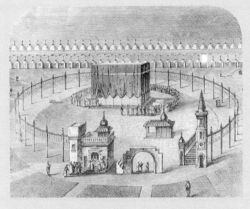

The Ka'aba in Mecca is the holiest shrine in Islam. Muslims who visit Mecca on pilgrimage circle the Ka'aba seven times while reciting prayers.

The year was 1325. Ibn Batuta was 21 years old. He had endured many hardships on the pilgrimage from his home in Tangier, on the northern coast of Africa. Late in his life, he would write about his emotional journey in a book.

Ibn Batuta neared the Ka'aba (KAH•bah), a small building shaped like a cube. It is the most sacred place of Islam. Inside the Ka'aba is a black rock believed to have come from God. It is edged with silver. Muslims believe that Abraham put the stone there centuries ago. All Muslims are supposed to visit the Ka'aba at least once in their lives.

Like the people around him, Ibn Batuta put on a simple white garment. Like an ocean, the white robed mass of people kneeled and prayed. Some people had begun to walk around the Ka'aba. Ibn Batuta, too, walked around the holy place, praying. Seven times Ibn Batuta circled the Ka'aba, as Islamic law calls for. Seven times he kissed the stone. He was moved to tears as he said the prayers.

Ibn Batuta would live many years after his pilgrimage. Before he died in 1369, he would visit many far-off places. He would travel to China, Russia, and Spain. But for all his life, he would remember his pilgrimage to Mecca as the high point of his travels.

Case Study Review

1. Why were so many people at Mecca?
2. **Drawing Conclusions** Why do you think his pilgrimage to Mecca was the high point of Ibn Batuta's travels?

Islam and the World

Why did Islam spread so quickly from Arabia to much of the world?

After Muhammad's death in 632, his followers kept spreading the faith. Islamic armies had stunning success. By 750 the Islamic empire ran from India to Spain. It controlled North Africa south to the Sahara.

The march of Islam was successful for several reasons. First, the soldiers of Islam were skillful warriors. They were fortunate to invade empires that were weak. But perhaps most important, Islam spread because people were attracted to it.

On Assignment...

Plot the major developments in the rise of Islam on a time line. Remember that these events happened in the period known as A.D.

After Muhammad's death, though, there was a split in Islam. Muhammad had a daughter, Fatima, but no sons. Some Muslims, called Shiites (SHEE•eyets), thought her family should rule. Others called Sunnites (SOON•eyets) thought any Muslim should be able to become the ruler. Today, these two main branches of Islam reflect this early split.

The golden age of Islam began to fade by the year 1000. Many forces invaded and waged war on the Islamic empire. Here, the Crusaders surround Damascus, an important Islamic city.

The Golden Age of Islamic Civilization

Over the years, the Islamic empire grew strong. Trade increased, bringing new goods to the empire. Muslim traders brought silk from China. Long lines of camel caravans brought furs from Russia. Other caravans brought gold and jewels from Asia.

Through their travels, traders exchanged ideas as well as goods. By 700, the Muslims had built great universities. Their cities became great centers of learning.

The Muslims blended together the ideas of many civilizations. From India, they learned to use zero as a number. Muslim advances in mathematics led to the development of algebra. Muslim scientists also pioneered in chemistry. Their interest in medicine led to books widely used in Europe.

Centuries of Turmoil

No golden age lasts forever. In the Islamic empire, the first problems came from within. Groups of Muslims with different beliefs clashed with the ruling Muslims. These battles weakened the empire. When attacks came from outside, the leaders were in trouble.

Seljuk Turks were nomads from Central Asia. They invaded beginning about the year 1000. In the 1100s, the Seljuks brought Iraq, Egypt, and Syria under their control.

In the meantime, the Crusaders galloped in. The Crusaders were Christians from Europe. Their goal was to return the Holy Land to Christianity. From 1095 to 1291, the Crusaders waged war on Islam. They conquered parts of the Holy Land and set up kingdoms. However, they were driven out by 1300.

On Assignment...

Add to your time line for this section the important events that led to the decline of the Islamic empire. Show the invasions by the Seljuk Turks, the Crusaders, and the Mongols.

From Central Asia came the Mongols in the 1200s. Their leader, Ghengis Khan, (GEHN•gus•kahn) remains one of history's most successful military leaders. The Mongols caused much destruction. In 1258, they captured the city of Baghdad and left it in flames. Many of the Mongols finally became Muslims. Before they did, they helped weaken the Islamic empire.

The next great conquerors, the Ottomans, built an empire that would stretch across three continents. It would last many centuries. Indeed, there are people alive today who grew up in the Ottoman Empire. As you will read in the next chapter, when the Ottoman Empire crumbled, it led to a war that involved people all over the world.

Section 5 Review

1. Who were the Seljuk Turks?
2. **Identifying Relationships** What was the relationship between problems within the Islamic empire and outside invaders?

I. Reviewing Vocabulary

Match each word on the left with the correct definition on the right.

1. covenant
2. pyramid
3. pharaoh
4. cuneiform

   a. a form of writing using wedge-shaped characters
   b. an agreement or contract
   c. a ruler of ancient Egypt
   d. a large building with a square base and sides like triangles that rise to a point

II. Understanding the Chapter

Answer the questions below on a separate sheet of paper.

1. Why did so many civilizations begin in the river valleys of the Middle East?
2. Why did Egyptians turn their rulers' bodies into mummies after they died?
3. What belief do Judaism, Christianity, and Islam share?
4. What is the Koran and why is it important to Muslims?

III. Building Skills: Inferring Information

Match each statement on the left with the person who might have had that opinion.

1. Only the sons of Fatima, the daughter of the prophet, should rule.
2. If I am to live after death, my body must be kept safe.
3. Ever since Babylon destroyed our temple, our people have been captives.
4. My leader Jesus rose from the dead on the third day after His death.

   a. a Shiite Muslim
   b. a Jew
   c. a Christian
   d. an Egyptian pharaoh

IV. Working Together

Divide into groups of three. With your group, create a script for a 15-minute interview with "experts" on the following religions: Judaism, Christianity, and Islam. Have each person choose one of these religions and write five questions to ask that religion's "expert." Each person should also prepare the answers to the questions. Then perform the script for the class.

On Assignment...

Creating a Time Line: Look at the time line entries you have made. Put all the information together on one time line. Keep the time line in your notebook to use as a study tool on Middle Eastern history.

CHAPTER 32

Under Suleiman the Magnificent, the Ottoman Empire became a world power. Here, foreign ambassadors pay their respects to the emperor.

From Empire to Independence

Why do the nations of the Middle East have a history of hostility to rule by outsiders?

Looking at Key Terms

- **Industrial Revolution**   time of change from making goods by hand to making goods by machine
- **nationalism**   the belief that a people should have its own government; a feeling of loyalty to a nation
- **ethnic group**   a large group of people with the same cultural background
- **mandate**   an area or country put under the protection of another
- **protectorate**   a country that is actually under the control of another country, although it is officially independent
- **corrupt**   dishonest
- **Holocaust**   the systematic slaughter of millions of Jews by the Nazis during World War II
- **anti-Semitism**   prejudice against Jews

On Assignment...

Creating a Mural: In this chapter, you will make a mural of changes in the Middle East. Your mural should start at the end of the 1700s. It should end with World War II. When you finish your mural, you will have a good idea of what happened in the Middle East during this period.

SECTION 1

The Ottoman Empire

What events led to the rise—and the decline—of the Ottoman Empire?

"I know of no state which is happier than this one," reported a traveler in 1525. "It is furnished with all God's gifts. No state can compare with it."

The land praised so highly was the Ottoman Empire. At the time, it was ruled by a powerful Muslim leader named Suleiman (SOO•lay•mahn). He was so powerful a ruler that he is known as "Suleiman the Magnificent."

Rise of the Ottomans

The Ottomans were Turks. They were Muslims who wanted to rid Asia of Christian rule. By A.D. 1300, they had succeeded. In 1453, they captured the city of Constantinople. This was a huge victory because Constantinople had been one of the greatest cities of the Christian world. The Ottomans renamed the city Istanbul. They made Istanbul the capital of their growing empire.

In the next 200 years, the Ottomans spread their empire as far west as Hungary. They took control of North Africa from Algeria to Egypt. They ruled over most of the Middle East except the Arabian Peninsula. At its height under Sultan (or prince) Suleiman, the empire reached almost to the gates of the city of Vienna.

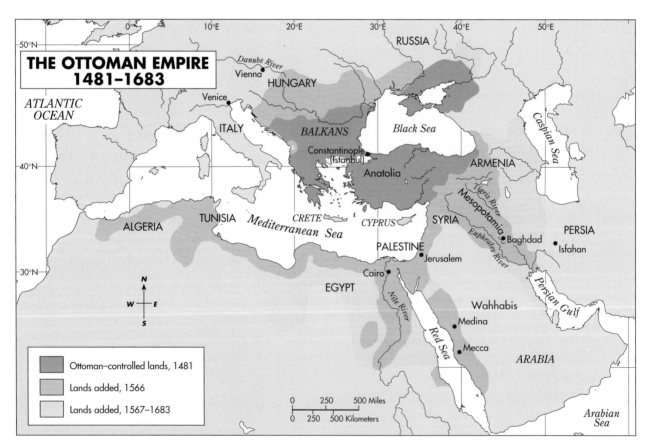

THE OTTOMAN EMPIRE 1481–1683

Legend:
- Ottoman-controlled lands, 1481
- Lands added, 1566
- Lands added, 1567–1683

Movement The Ottomans expanded their empire over large stretches of Europe, Asia, and North Africa. In what time period did the empire reach the Caspian Sea?

Suleiman ruled from 1520 to 1566. He expanded trade and built hospitals, mosques, schools, and bridges. He ordered laws rewritten to make them fairer. He encouraged the work of artists, writers, and craftspeople.

Markets in Istanbul sold silks, ivory, spices, and other goods from all over the world. Great deposits of silver were found and traded with other nations.

The time of glory for the huge Ottoman Empire did not last. By the 1600s, pieces began breaking off. The Ottomans faced enemies everywhere. Both Christian Europeans and other Muslims tried to take over parts of the empire.

Over the years, the power of the sultans declined. By the 1600s, the sultans had little power. Local officials taxed their people more and more. They became rich, but the empire suffered.

Just as important, the world around the Ottoman Empire changed. Europeans began building better weapons. This allowed them to fight the Muslims more effectively. Also, Europeans created new trade routes to Asia. This meant they did not need the Ottomans to trade with. The Ottomans lost their trading profit. All these factors caused the empire to fade.

The Empire Weakens

Two factors in Europe caused the empire to lose even more power. One was the **Industrial Revolution**. It changed the way goods were made. By using machines, Europeans could make things more cheaply and quickly than by hand. They needed raw materials to keep their factories running. Europeans looked to the Middle East as a source of cheap raw materials.

The second factor was the rise of **nationalism**. Nationalism is the belief that **ethnic groups** should have their own borders and governments. People of many different ethnic backgrounds lived in the Ottoman Empire. Muslims, Orthodox Christians, and Roman Catholics lived uneasily side by side. People within the empire spoke dozens of different languages. Around 1800, many of these ethnic groups began demanding their own governments.

The sultans who ruled the empire saw the empire falling apart. They tried to reform it. However, it was too late. People no longer wanted to live in the Ottoman Empire. They wanted to rule their own countries. The Ottoman Empire would never regain the glory it once had.

Egypt Breaks Away

Egypt had never been closely ruled by the Ottomans. Egyptians had a strong sense of their nationhood. In the early 1800s, an Albanian officer in the Ottoman army gradually gained power in Egypt. This officer's name was Muhammad Ali. Eventually, he seized control of Egypt and slaughtered his opponents.

Muhammad Ali helped make Egypt more modern. He invited French officers to Egypt to train his army. He built a modern fleet. By 1822 he had captured the Sudan.

The nations of Europe saw the Ottoman Empire getting weaker with each passing year. One European leader described the empire this way: "We have a sick man on our hands. This man is gravely ill."

Wars Over the Empire

The Crimean (cry•MEE•un) War (1853–56) showed just how ill the "sick man" was. The reason that countries gave for going to war was the issue of who should control holy places in Palestine. However, the real reason was that each European country wanted to control Ottoman territory. Each was eager to gain control of it before another European country could do so.

In the war, Britain, France, and the Ottomans fought the Russians. The war was fought over land that belonged to the Ottomans. However, the other countries involved cared little about the Ottomans. When the combined forces defeated the Russians, Britain and France gained some new rights to land. The Ottomans gained little.

Twenty years later, the Russians again went to war against the Ottomans. This time they defeated the Ottomans and seized territory. Two more wars called the Balkan Wars broke out in 1912–13. The Balkan Peninsula is an area in southeastern Europe that was under the control of the Ottoman Empire for centuries. In the Balkan Wars, different Balkan ethnic groups fought the empire to gain their own countries. In these wars, the empire lost almost all its remaining land on the continent of Europe.

Europe Seizes North Africa

As they fought over the Ottoman Empire, the European powers were becoming very interested in North Africa. In 1827, a French diplomat got into an argument with the Ottoman governor of Algiers. The argument ended with the governor slapping the French diplomat in the face. The French used this as a reason to take Algiers and remove the governor from office. By 1848, France controlled all of Algeria. In 1881, France took control of Tunisia.

In 1869, a French company finished building the Suez Canal. This canal allowed ships to travel from the Mediterranean Sea to the Red Sea. It greatly shortened the sea route between Europe and Asia. French investors owned one half the stock in the company. The Egyptian government owned the other half.

The British were alarmed by the growth of French power. They quietly made a deal with the Egyptian government, buying the government share in the company that ran the canal. Then in 1882, Britain took control of Egypt. From Egypt, the British army moved south into the Sudan. After a long struggle, the British defeated the Sudanese army in the 1890s.

Europe's seizure of North Africa went on into the 1900s. France seized Morocco in 1909. Italy took Libya. Italy had earlier tried to win control of Ethiopia but was defeated by the Ethiopians.

Soldiers of the Young Turks revolutionary society are shown entering Istanbul in 1908. The Young Turks were reformers within the army who wanted to modernize Turkey.

The Young Turks

Many Turkish people were angered by the way Europe carved up the Ottoman Empire. Among them was a group of army officers who called themselves the Young Turks. In 1908, they rebelled against the sultan, Abdul Hamid, and overthrew him. A new sultan more favorable to their views took power. The Young Turks hoped to restore the glory of the Ottoman Empire.

Once they were in charge, the Young Turks faced big problems. One of the biggest was nationalism. The Balkan Wars occupied their army. Other groups, such as the Armenians, also demanded their own countries. So did different Arab groups. The Young Turks fought these rebels and often lost.

The Ottomans had become allies of Germany before World War I. Russia had long been the empire's main enemy. Wars between Russia and the empire had been going on for centuries. When Russia sided against Germany, the empire's ties with Germany grew closer.

With the beginning of World War I in 1914, the nations of Europe split into camps. The Ottomans sided with Germany. That decision would lead to the end of the Ottoman Empire.

Section 1 Review

1. Who were the "Young Turks"?

2. **Analyzing Information** What do you think was the most important reason for the end of the Ottoman Empire?

SECTION 2

New Political Directions

How did independent nations rise out of the ruin of the Ottoman Empire?

It was 1916. World War I was still raging. Officials from the leading Allied Powers— Britain, France, and Russia—met to decide what the fate of the Ottoman Empire would be after the war was over.

The men met in secret. They quickly decided that the empire would be carved up. France would take a large piece of the empire. Britain would take an even larger piece. The sick man would finally die.

This agreement had to be kept secret for one simple reason. The British had already promised the Arabs of the Ottoman Empire their own nations after the war. The Arabs were promised this because they had helped fight against the Ottomans during the war. If the Arabs had known that Britain was going back on its promise, they would have stopped fighting.

Arab Hopes Dashed

So it was that after World War I, the Arab people found out that they would not have their independence. The hopes of many Arabs were crushed. Once again, they found themselves governed by foreign powers.

After the war, the League of Nations was formed. The League gave the Arab lands to the Allies. These territories were called **mandates.** The Allies were supposed to govern these territories until the Arabs were "ready" for self-government.

The mandates created countries that had not existed before. There had never been a country called Iraq, for example. This region had been three areas under the Ottomans.

Arab groups revolted. They tried to form their own countries. These efforts failed. The only country the Arabs were able to form was Saudi Arabia. Even there, the British had a strong hand in what happened.

The fact that much of their land was controlled by the Western powers made many Arabs furious. This dislike of foreign control stayed with Arab peoples for many years. It still influences their attitude toward Europe and the United States today.

The Oil Factor

European countries had no intention of leaving the Middle East. In fact, the Middle East grew in value to them. In the 1920s, the United States discovered massive pools of oil underground. Soon the Arabian Peninsula became a major source of the fuel that provided energy for Western industry.

Then, a major oil discovery was made in Iraq in 1927. The next year, British, French, and U.S. companies formed one large company to sell that oil.

Other parts of the Middle East became important to the nations of the West. Most of the Persian Gulf was under British control. Oil became the most important cargo shipped through the Suez Canal. Protection of the canal was a major reason the British continued to control Egypt. French oil companies began looking for oil in Libya and Algeria.

France and Britain built dams, railroads, and schools in the lands they held. Despite these advances, the Arab peoples desperately wanted to control their own governments. "After all," they might say, "you Europeans talk so much about self-government. Why can't we have the right to govern ourselves?"

Turkey Is Born

What was left of the Ottoman Empire became the modern nation of Turkey. The spirit of nationalism grew in Turkey. In 1919, the Greek army seized some territory from Turkey. When the sultan of Turkey did not oppose this, the Young Turks overthrew this sultan. They were led by an army officer whose name was Mustafa Kemal (MOOS•tah•fah kuh•MAHL). In October 1923, Turkey became a republic with Mustafa Kemal as its new leader.

Kemal was a strong leader. Under his leadership, Turkey became a modern nation. New industries were started. Railroads were built. Schools were opened to educate Turkey's people.

However, Kemal could be ruthless. He got rid of opponents by claiming they wanted to kill him. He ruled more like a king than the head of a republic.

One issue Kemal faced was the hatred among ethnic groups in Turkey. Before World War I, the Turks had tried to rid their country of every Armenian. They forced hundreds of thousands to leave. Many Armenians died of starvation. Many others were killed.

When the Turkish republic was formed, Kemal and the Turks tried to expel every-one who was not Turkish. They forced about 1.4 million Greeks to leave.

Kemal longed to make Turkey modern. For the first time in an Islamic country, government was no longer influenced by religious authorities. Previously in the Ottoman Empire, laws were based on the teachings of the Koran. Under Kemal's rule, laws were based on laws in Europe. People were allowed to practice any religion.

Kemal began a long campaign to make Turkey more like the West. He forbade Turkish men from having more than one wife. He told women to throw away their veils. According to the Koran, women had to wear veils that almost completely covered their faces.

Kemal ordered the Turks to take family names, like Europeans. He took the name Ataturk. That means "Father of the Turks." Kemal also ordered his people to use the Western alphabet.

Religious Turks hated Kemal. They wanted the country to be governed according to Islamic religious law. The tension between these two opposing views still divides people in the Middle East today.

Iran in the 20th Century

Early in the 1900s, both Britain and Russia controlled parts of Iran. During World War I, Iran was a battlefield. After the war, many Iranians were starving. The government of Iran was weak and unable to feed its people.

In 1919, the Iranian government agreed to a treaty with Britain. The treaty provided some British aid to the country. However, many Iranians hated the treaty. They thought it gave too much control to Britain.

Nationalists found a leader in an army officer named Reza Khan. In 1925, Reza Khan seized power. He took the name Reza Shah Pahlavi (PAH•lah•vee). (*Shah* means "king" in Persian.)

Reza Shah wanted to free the country from foreigners. He also wanted to make Iran a more modern country. His government introduced Western reforms. It built new schools. It reduced the power of religious leaders. These and other reforms caused great problems between the "traditionalists" and the "reformers." In the 1970s, these two groups would fight bloody battles for control of Iran.

Egypt on the World Stage

Egypt in the early 1900s faced the same forces that were shaping the rest of the Middle East. Egypt had been controlled by Britain since the British had bought control of the Suez Canal in 1875. In 1914, the British army made Egypt a **protectorate.** A protectorate is a country that has its own government but is controlled by an outside power.

The protectorate ended in 1922. Egypt became independent and was ruled by a king. However, the British were determined to defend their interests in the Suez Canal and continued to control Egypt. As a result, Egyptians protested British control. In 1936, the British left Egypt except for a zone around the Suez Canal.

Egypt's government was extremely **corrupt**, or dishonest. It granted favors to British interests when the price was right. In 1952, a group of Egyptian army officers seized control of the Egyptian government. The man who became the new leader was Colonel Gamal Nasser (guh•MAHL NAH•sur). Nasser's goal was to end British control of business in Egypt.

Nasser had the government take over major industries. He divided large estates among the poor. Although he crushed any opposition, he was popular with the Egyptian people.

Nasser's most important project was the building of a huge dam at Aswan. The purpose of the dam was to improve farming along the Nile. The United States and Britain had agreed to finance the dam.

On Assignment...

How could you show the events of the 20th century in a mural? Write down the most important events. Then make sketches of them. Keep your ideas and sketches for the mural.

However, Nasser wanted to limit Western influence in Egypt, so he turned to the Soviet Union for help. The dam was finished in 1970. It provided electric power and water for irrigation. However, the dam also ended the annual flooding of the Nile that had fertilized land along the river. As a result, farmers have to buy expensive fertilizers.

Nasser as an Arab Leader

Nasser's leadership soon inspired other Middle Eastern peoples. For example, in 1958, Iraqi soldiers overthrew the king and made Iraq a republic.

Nasser dreamed of a united Arab state. In 1958, Egypt and Syria combined. However, the union lasted only three years. The Syrians came to resent Nasser's power. In 1961, they left the union. Nasser continued to serve as the leader of Egypt until his death in 1970.

Section 2 Review

1. What promises did the British break after World War I?

2. **Summarizing** In three sentences, summarize the role of nationalism in the Middle East after World War I.

The Founding of Israel

Rachel looked at the picture and sighed. It was a grainy, old photograph that showed her as a child with her parents. She traced the image with her finger. Her parents were smiling. More than anything, Rachel wished her parents were here. They had long dreamed of coming to the Jewish homeland.

Rachel had grown up in Poland, but was now in Israel. Her parents would never see Israel. They had died in the **Holocaust.** The Holocaust was the systematic slaughter of more than six million Jews by the Nazis during World War II. Rachel had survived because her parents made sure that she was hidden on a farm. After the war, she came to the new State of Israel. She thought losing her family was a very high price to pay for a homeland.

Rachel well knew that **anti-Semitism** had gotten worse in the 1800s. Anti-Semitism is prejudice against Jews. In the 1880s, thousands of Jews had been killed in Russia. Many Jews then formed groups to establish a Jewish nation in Palestine. For years, leaders of these groups tried to get the British to agree to a Jewish nation. Then, in 1917, the British issued a statement called the Balfour Declaration. It said the British would support "a national home for the Jewish people" in Palestine.

Arabs were bitter when they heard of the statement. They believed Palestine belonged to them alone. Arabs in Palestine fought to keep Jews out. The struggle between Jews and Arabs became more violent.

In the 1930s, the world changed for Europe's Jews. The Nazis came to power in Germany. The Nazis set out to destroy all the Jews of Europe. As German armies swept over Europe, Jews were herded into concentration camps and death camps. Of the nine million Jews that had lived in Europe, more than six million were murdered by the Nazis.

Some Jews from Europe were able to flee to Palestine. By 1945, they made up about 30 percent of the people there.

Struggle Over Palestine

After World War II ended, a shocked world learned about the atrocities of the Holocaust. This crime against the Jewish people changed many minds about the need for a Jewish nation. In 1947, the United Nations voted to divide Palestine so that part would become the country of Israel. Another part would become an Arab country. A third zone would be controlled by a small international police force. That zone would include Jerusalem, which contained holy sites for three religions: Judaism, Christianity, and Islam. The plan was not acceptable to either Arabs or Israelis.

Jewish immigrants to Palestine are shown as they leave a boat in 1947. After the Holocaust, the British rulers of Palestine tried to prevent Jewish refugees from reaching Palestine.

On May 14, 1948, Israel declared its independence. Within hours, Israel was attacked by Egypt, Syria, Iraq, Lebanon, and Jordan. The fighting was fierce. Hundreds of thousands of Arabs fled Palestine. In 1949, the Arab nations gave up the attack. Israel had taken 50 percent more land than it had been given under the United Nations agreement.

Fighting was something Rachel knew well. She had lived through the war in Europe. She had lived through the fear of being unmasked as a Jew. She had lived through the grief of learning her parents had been killed. She was ready to fight for this new land.

Rachel remembered the ship that took her from Amsterdam to Israel in 1947. She stood on deck with thousands of other Jews from Europe. They looked at the shoreline of their new country. "I'm going to do it for you," she whispered, gazing at her parents' picture.

Case Study Review

1. What was the Balfour Declaration?
2. **Understanding Points of View** An Israeli and an Arab are arguing over the new land of Israel. The Israeli believes that Jews deserve their own homeland in Palestine. The Arab believes that Palestine belongs only to Arabs. What facts will each person use to support his or her argument?

REVIEWING CHAPTER 32

I. Reviewing Vocabulary

Match each word on the left with the correct definition on the right.

1. nationalism
2. ethnic group
3. anti-Semitism
4. protectorate

   a. prejudice against Jews
   b. loyalty to a nation
   c. a large group of people with the same cultural background
   d. a country that is under the control of another country

II. Understanding the Chapter

Answer the questions below on a separate sheet of paper.

1. What two factors in Europe led to the weakening of the Ottoman Empire?
2. How did World War I bring about the end of the Ottoman Empire?
3. How did Mustafa Kemal try to make Turkey more modern?
4. Why was there fighting in Israel after it became an independent state?

III. Building Skills: Reading a Map

Study the map of the Ottoman Empire on page 434 and then answer the questions that follow.

1. What major area of Europe did the Ottoman Empire control in 1481?
2. To what European river shown on the map did the Ottoman Empire reach by 1566?
3. Was most of the North African coast added to the Ottoman Empire before or after 1566?
4. Which of the following cities became part of the Ottoman Empire earliest: Vienna, Constantinople, or Cairo? Which became part of the empire latest? Which never became a part of the empire?

IV. Working Together

Divide the class into groups. Each group should create a series of cards that list important events. The events should have happened in the Middle East between 1700 and 1950 and should be covered in this chapter. Do not put the dates on the cards. When you have finished, swap cards with another group. See if you can put the cards in correct chronological order.

On Assignment. . .

Creating a Mural: Look at your notes and sketches for a mural. Make a rough sketch of everything your mural should include. Next, use a pencil to draw an outline of your mural on butcher paper. Fill in the outline with markers or paint. Next to the picture of each event, write a short description of the event.

The House
on the Border

Aziz Nesin

Aziz Nesin is one of the most popular contemporary Turkish writers. Nesin's stories show his sense of humor. Many of his characters find themselves trapped in strange circumstances. They laugh and give a sort of shrug that says, "Oh, well, what's a person to do?" This acceptance creates a mood that Islamic book reviewers have called a total surrender to kismet, *the Muslim belief in fate.*

We can see this acceptance of fate in "The House on the Border." This humorous story begins when a husband and wife rent a house for a year. The first night they surprise a burglar in the house. The burglar is perfectly friendly and invites them to call the police. To show his good faith, the burglar agrees to be tied up while the couple visits the police. The police tell the couple that the house lies outside their jurisdiction, or area of responsibility. They visit another police station and are told that the house also lies outside that jurisdiction. At a third station, they get the same message. Apparently, the house lies on a border. No one police station has jurisdiction over it. No one can arrest the burglars.

. . . This time we went to the gendarmerie.[1] After listening to our story, the commandant asked for our address.

"Aha," he said, "That house."

Apparently, we had rented a famous place.

The commandant shook his head. "This is not a case for the gendarmerie. You should call the police."

"Now look," I cried. "We went to the police. They sent us here. Now you say we must call the cops. Is this a runaround? Isn't there anybody to look into the case?"

The commandant pulled out a map.

"I hope you know how to read a map," he said. "Here, it gives the height. See? One hundred and forty feet. This is the water tower—116 feet—and here is the hill. Now, this area is under the jurisdiction of the gendarmerie. If your house were built further up, say about two yards toward the northwest, you would have been in our area."

"All this for two lousy yards," I said. "Do something, man! What would happen if you helped us now?"

---

[1] **gendarmerie** (jahn-DAHRM-uh-ree) *n.* police force

In "The House on the Border," living on a border causes major problems. This painting by Marc Chagall suggests what it is like to live in a house on a border.

The commandant pursed his lips. "What would happen?" he repeated. Then he nodded his head sagely. "Only we know what would happen. . . . Only we know." Again he put his finger on a spot on the map. "Look, this is your house. Right on the line that separates our area from the police's. See? Of course, a part of your garden is under our jurisdiction, but the robbery didn't take place there, did it?"

There was nothing we could do but go to the police again.

"Let's first see how the thief is doing," my wife suggested. "God help us if something should happen to him."

So we went home.

I almost clasped the thief to my bosom. "How are you?" I panted.

"Water! Quick!" he cried out. "I'm thirsty!"

After drinking the water, he looked at us sternly.

"Listen," he said. "Don't say that I didn't warn you. You have no right to hold me here. You are restricting the freedom of a citizen. I have a good mind to sue you."

"But what can we do?" I cried. "We don't know who is supposed to look after us. Apparently, we are in the middle of nowhere. Why they built this house right on the border line is beyond me."

"Didn't I tell you? . . . Now, let me go. Otherwise I'll drag you through the courts for restricting my freedom."

"Give me time," I begged. "Give me till tonight. I want to go to the police again."

"By all means, he replied affably.[2] "Go and see anyone you wish. But it's futile.[3] I've been aware of the situation for a long time now. They have to decide whether to include your house in one of the areas or change the borders. Till then. . ."

Again, we went to the precinct. This time the chief brought out a map too.

"Look," he sighed, "this area is under the jurisdiction of the gendarmerie. Your garden and a small part of the house are within their area. Only a fraction of the house is under our jurisdiction."

"The bedroom is in your area," I pointed out. "And the robbery took place there."

He looked at me owlishly. "Quite. First this must be definitely established. Then there is another problem: the thief didn't fly in through the window, did he? He crossed the garden and then entered your house. Right? And the garden is under the jurisdiction of the gendarmerie. Yours is not a new problem. It is already under discussion. First they have to reach a decision; then they have to inform us of their decision concerning the area your house is supposed to be in. Then we can act accordingly."

We returned home. Our elderly next-door neighbor was at the window, as usual.

"So they broke into the house again," he cackled.

"Yes," I nodded.

"No one stays there long," he said cheerfully. "That's why the rent is low. Neither the owner nor the tenants could live there. The owner decided to pull down the house and rebuild it two yards further up. But then he found you fools—I mean he found you and rented the place."

His wife was looking at us sadly. "It's not your fault," she informed us. "It's the owner's. When they build a house they think of water, gas, electricity, and the view. But do they think of the jurisdiction? No! What sort of a fool would build a house right on the border?"

I couldn't answer that question even if I wanted to.

Since we had paid the whole year's rent in advance, to move away was out of the question. So we went home and untied the thief. Then we settled down comfortably in the study and discussed

---

[2]**affably** (AF-eh-blee) *adv.* in a friendly manner
[3]**futile** (FYOO-tihl) *adj.* useless

Turks often approach life with a sense of humor. Realizing that no one will protect their house on the border, the residents shrug their shoulders and say, "Isn't this absurd?"

the world situation for a while. The thief dined with us that evening.

"So long," he said after the meal. "I'll be back tonight."

Now we have five or six resident thieves. All our neighbors are familiar with them. We collaborate[4] with the thieves too. That is to say, we help them to defend our home against other, unfriendly thieves, who are, after all, strangers to us.

I don't know what will happen eventually. Either all eight of us, my wife and I and the six thieves, will spend the remainder of the year here, or they will include the house in one of the areas, thus enabling me to complain to the authorities. But we are now used to our friends, the thieves. And to report them would be rather embarrassing—after all, they share the household expenses now.

---

[4]**collaborate** (kuh-LAB-uh-rayt) *v.* cooperate; work together

---

Making Connections

1. What is humorous about the thief's comment: "Now let me go. Otherwise I'll drag you through the courts for restricting my freedom"?

2. **Making Inferences** What statement is the author making about how government affects people's lives?

CHAPTER 33

Traditional Patterns of Life

What are the traditional patterns of life in the Middle East?

Covered by long robes and veils, these Tunisian women visit the suq, the traditional Middle Eastern marketplace.

Looking at Key Terms

- **tradition** behavior handed down from generation to generation
- **headman** the leader of a village
- **suq** a large market in the Middle East
- **hospitality** generous treatment of guests
- **polygamy** the practice of having more than one spouse
- **custody** control over another person
- **purdah** the practice of keeping women from public view
- **Ramadan** the holiest month in the Islamic calendar

On Assignment...

Writing Letters From the Middle East: This chapter shows different ways people live in the Middle East. Imagine that you have a chance to stay with people of different cultures in the Middle East. In each section of the chapter, you will write a letter home to the United States describing life in this culture. At the end of the chapter, you will have letters that show what traditional life is like in several Middle Eastern cultures.

447

Village, City, and Desert Life

How does life in the Middle East reflect the traditional values of the region?

In the Middle East, **tradition** is important. Tradition is behavior that is handed down from generation to generation. No matter where they live, people practice tradition. For example, people who live in cities continue to follow traditional ways of life. After all, cities were built in the region as early as 3000 B.C.

Village life in the Middle East is also governed by tradition. Villages began in the Middle East even earlier than cities did. Today, many people in villages live in ways similar to those of centuries ago.

Nomads who live in the deserts of the Middle East may be the most traditional people of all. Some nomads still follow ways of life that are hundreds of years old. Many have resisted changes that might make their lives easier.

Of course, some people who live in the Middle East have been eager to adopt new ways. But there are still many who prefer the old traditions.

Village Life

In the Middle East, the number of people who live in traditional villages is declining. About 50 years ago, approximately 80 percent of the region's people lived in villages. Today, less than 50 percent of the people in the Middle East live in villages.

Villagers in the Middle East have some things in common. Most are farmers and most are also poor. In villages, the family is very important. Villagers often believe in the old ways and work hard to preserve their traditions.

Most villages in the Middle East are still run by a **headman**. He may be chosen by

While Middle Eastern cities are growing, many Middle Easterners are still traditional farmers living in poor villages. The village shown here is near the ancient city of Jericho.

men in the village. He may be appointed by the government. He is usually a member of an important family in the village.

Of course, change has come to the villages, too. One change is that some farmers now own the land they farm. In the past, many farmers worked the land and paid the owner a share of the harvest. Often, this left the farmers with little food for themselves. In recent years, some governments have helped farmers buy their own land. In 1961, Egypt passed a law that limited how much land one person could own.

Although villages differ from area to area in the Middle East, it is in the villages that visitors can see the traditional customs that people in the city no longer practice. Imagine that you were visiting a village in Turkey. Here are some of the things you might find.

As you come up a dirt road, the village comes into view. In one field, women are doing the hard work of clearing the land of rocks. It is a dry, gray landscape.

The houses are made of mud bricks. They are a little hard to spot. Often, houses in the villages are hidden. This gives them extra protection. For many centuries, Turkey was frequently invaded. By building houses behind rocks, Turkish villagers hoped to be concealed from their enemies.

As you get closer, you can see that something is piled on top of the houses. "What's that?" you ask.

"Ah," says Abdullah, your guide for the day. "That is dung drying. This winter, it will be used as fuel."

Abdullah stops the car in the village. You notice that there is a mosque. There is also a coffeehouse. Outside the coffeehouse are four men. They are sitting and talking, with glasses of coffee before them.

As you get out of the car, children watch you. They are shy. Their hands are firmly in their mothers' hands. Abdullah walks with you to a friend's house. "Be prepared for a long visit," he tells you, smiling. "Talking is a way of life here."

Abdullah's friend greets him outside the house with a wide smile and a handshake. He invites you in. Inside the mud walls, there is little furniture. A wood-burning stove sits in one corner. Near the stove is an older woman wearing a full skirt and a head covering. She is cleaning beans. "Grandmother," Abdullah says quietly, nodding at the woman.

Aside from the grandmother, there are kitchen tools, bedding, and clothing. On the floor is a burst of rich color. In this home, as in most Turkish homes, the floors are covered with the colorful rugs that some Turkish villagers have woven.

Abdullah's friend's wife brings a meal of sheep cheese, fried lamb, olives, bread, and tea. During lunch, Abdullah's friend talks about the hard life in the village. "We have little water. There is a stream. Most people live by selling the little extra potatoes and wheat they grow."

Abdullah looks outside at the dusty street. A sheep wanders by. His friend continues:

> *The government wants to keep us in this village. They have begun a school for girls to learn how to weave Turkish rugs. The tourists want the rugs. It is hard to keep people in the villages, though. Many want to leave. They say there is a better life in the city.*

City Life

Those villagers who do move to the city go with high hopes of getting good jobs. They are often shocked by what they find. The cities are extremely crowded. The large number of people makes it hard to find places to live and work.

Over hundreds of years, Middle Eastern cities grew. As cities grew, walls went up. Within the walls of the city were neighborhoods where people from different towns had settled. These neighborhoods were also walled off from other neighborhoods. At night, the gates were closed and locked.

Today, people of a particular ethnic or religious group still tend to live together in neighborhoods. When people move from villages, they find friends and family who came to the cities before them. Then they live with or near them. In days past, most people lived with their extended family. That is still true today, though some would rather live with just their husband or wife and children.

One of the most important parts of the traditional city in the Middle East is the **suq** (sook), or market. In some ways, the suq has changed very little over the centuries. If you were to visit a suq in Iran, here is what you might see.

A man gestures to you as you stand at the entrance to the suq. You are too dazzled to pay attention. You are looking at the scene before you. The suq is amazing. It is a huge, moving mass of people. The noise makes you want to cover your ears. There are odors you have never smelled before.

As you stand there, the man comes over. "Ah!" he says, smiling. "You are new to our suq. I can see that. Allow me to give you a tour. It will help me practice my English. My name is Ahmed." Still dazed, you follow him.

The babble of voices rises as you enter the market. Every tiny stall has a person in front, calling to those passing by. You can't understand what each one is saying, but that does not matter. The message is clear: "Buy here."

"Pay no attention," Ahmed says, taking your arm to pull you away. "First, I will explain how this came to be." He finds a small stall selling coffee. It is quieter in here. You sit down, and he orders coffee. It comes in a small glass on a plate with a spoon. Ahmed stirs the coffee with enthusiasm. You take a drink. The hot, sweet liquid slides down your throat.

"Let me tell you," Ahmed says, settling in, "knowing the suq is knowing the Middle East. Ever since the beginning, the suq has been important. Back then, everything had to be in its place." He points. "Over there, carpets. Over there, gold and jewelry. There, copper and brass. There, perfume. And way in the back, so the smell won't bother people, the leather. That is the way it was in the beginning. That is the way it is now." He finishes his coffee and gets up.

"Now, you will try your hand at buying something. A rug, perhaps? Some lovely jewelry? In the suq , we have everything."

You walk among the stalls. Finally, you see one with beautiful shirts. You stop there and find a shirt you want to buy. You take it to the shopkeeper, who smiles and offers his hand. Ahmed looks horrified. "No, no, no!" he hisses, taking you by the arm. He whispers, "You must bargain. Here. I will show you."

Ahmed takes the shirt from you. In Arabic, he talks to the shopkeeper. It is clear he is pointing out all the problems with the shirt. The shopkeeper shakes his head. As this goes on, a small boy comes in silently, and puts down a tray with three cups of coffee on it. Still talking, the shopkeeper hands you one. The talking continues. Then Ahmed looks angry and heads for the door. The shopkeeper hurries after him. After more talking, Ahmed smiles. He and the shopkeeper

The suq, or marketplace, in a Middle Eastern city is a busy place. Here, artisans at a suq in Cairo display their wares in the streets outside their shops.

exchange money and the shirt. You follow Ahmed out of the store.

"That is how we do things," Ahmed says, handing you the shirt. "I tell him what is wrong with the shirt. I offer him very little money. He tells me the shirt is the best shirt ever made. He refuses my offer and suggests another price. I refuse that. And so on. But now, you have your shirt. And for a good price, too." Ahmed smiles broadly. Thanking him, you look at the beautiful shirt. You are impressed by Ahmed's bargaining and wonder if you can do it, too.

Nomadic Life

There are fewer and fewer nomads in the Middle East each year. Even so, the ways of the nomads are the basis for many customs and beliefs in the Middle East. Those who have survived in the desert have had to be tough. They also have had to stick together.

Hospitality is very important to the desert dwellers. In the harsh desert, people never know when their survival will depend on someone else. Therefore, they treat guests with hospitality, or kindness. There is one story of a Saudi Arabian prince and the wolves of the desert. It is said that this prince would order his servants to give a sheep to the wolves when he heard them howling. He told his people that no guest should be left hungry, including the wolves.

Honor is another deeply held value among the nomads of the desert. In part, the prince gave gifts to the wolves because he considered it an honorable thing to do. He had to be hospitable or risk losing his honor.

Another important value to the nomads is loyalty to family. For centuries, the family has always come first. In the desert, nomads have to rely on their families. They also need each other for companionship. That love of family remains today throughout the Middle East.

Most nomads in the Middle East are devout Muslims. Devotion to Islam continues in those people who have long since left the nomadic life.

Middle Easterners often admire the nomads' freedom in the way that people in the United States admire cowboys. Like cowboys, nomads have the image of being brave and free. As with cowboys in the United States, the nomads of the Middle East set values others live by. A Middle Easterner may never know anyone who lives in the desert but still shares the nomads' values of hospitality, family loyalty, and a sense of honor.

Some nomads in the Middle East do not live in the desert. One such group is the Bakhtiari (bak•tee•AH•ree) in Iran. In the summer, the Bakhtiari ride horses, donkeys, and mules to the mountains. There is more rain and grass there for their herds of sheep and goats. When the mountains turn cold and snowy in the winter, the Bakhtiari leave for their pastures on the coast.

No matter where they live, nomads are becoming more scarce. The life of a nomad may seem romantic to others. However, it is a very hard way to live. More and more, nomads have moved to the city to seek higher-paying jobs. Many work in the oil fields.

"Bedouin life is disappearing," says a Saudi Arabian Bedouin now living in the city. "I prefer to be here, with people around me, than to be alone, the last person in the desert. But I still have my sheep. And I have a shepherd who tends them. When I miss the desert, I get into my pickup truck and go out for a visit. But I have a permanent home now. I am no longer a nomad."

On Assignment...

Imagine that you have been staying with someone in a place you just read about. What would you want to tell people at home about that place? Write a letter that describes what you learned.

1. Why are nomadic people and people from the villages moving to the cities?

2. **Making Inferences** How would you feel if your life changed as dramatically as the nomads' lives are changing?

SECTION 2

Family Life

How does family life reflect traditional values?

The extended family is still very important in the Middle East. In one house, you might see a mother and father plus their unmar-

The extended family provides support for Middle Easterners who must live in a harsh and isolated environment. Above, a family travels across the vast landscape of northern Turkey.

ried children, married sons and their wives and children. You might also see the father's widowed mother. Wealthy families add on another few rooms to their homes when a son marries and starts a family.

Living in extended families is a strong tradition in the Middle East. In nomadic days, extended families helped ensure that there were enough people to do all the work. Members of an extended family could also take care of one another. It was a matter of pride that if someone in the family had problems, the entire family would deal with it.

If the father of the family dies, the sons may stay together in the house. In that case, the oldest son becomes the head of the family.

However, the family may decide to split up when the father dies. That often happens because each son wants to be the head of his own household.

Family leadership explains why more value is put on sons than on daughters. A daughter will keep her family's name, but she will marry and leave her family. Sons are expected to stay with their families. Their earnings go toward the family. Sons also become fathers. The father of the house has the last word. He makes the decisions, and the family obeys.

Even when women marry, they often live close to their families. When family members have extra time, they are likely to spend it with one another.

Marriage

Traditional marriage in the Middle East is much different from marriage in the United States. Many young people in the Middle East think it's natural that their spouses will be someone their family chooses. In villages, young people may well have had their spouses selected when they were children. In the cities, it is likely that friends or relatives will play matchmaker. In Saudi Arabia, it is thought to be good for first cousins to marry. That keeps their wealth in the family.

In some Middle Eastern countries, a couple may not meet before their wedding. In others, the couple is introduced to one another by their families. They may then go out, but never alone.

The idea of love does not play a big role in most marriages in the Middle East. The most important concern is that the marriage be good for the two families. If love does occur, however, it is expected to grow from marriage.

Before the wedding, there is a contract. This sets out the rights of each partner. The groom and his family promise things such as money, sheep, goats, and jewelry to the bride's family. This is called the "bride price." As part of the contract, a woman has the right to these gifts in case of a divorce. She will also get some money if there is a divorce. Most of the money from the divorce settlement will go to the husband. In Islamic countries, men are expected to protect women and provide for them. Men get more money in a divorce because it is thought that they will have other women to provide for.

According to Islamic law, a man may marry up to four women. The practice of having more than one spouse is known as **polygamy**. The Prophet Muhammad saw polygamy as a way of making sure that all women would be taken care of. Today, polygamy is rare. That's because a man with more than one wife has to support them all equally well.

Divorce

In much of the Middle East, getting a divorce is easier for men than for women. In some parts of the Middle East, the man has only to say "I divorce you" three times. Then he gives the woman whatever they agreed on in the marriage contract. A woman may also divorce her husband, but under strict conditions. Under Islamic law, if the husband stays away from home a long time or marries another woman, his wife may divorce him. However, she needs approval from a religious leader. After the children reach a certain age, it is the father who gets **custody**, or control, of them.

In some parts of the Middle East, new ways are replacing the traditional. This photo shows a Western-style wedding in Egypt. In the past, couples might not even have met before their wedding day.

The Lives of Women

Most Middle Eastern women live a life very different from that of women in the United States. In traditional Middle Eastern societies, women are expected to wear veils over their faces when they are in public. Some women's veils cover their entire heads.

The reasons for this date from before Muhammad's time. A family's honor was very important. That honor was bound up in the modesty of the women in a man's family. The best way to guard women was to hide them. From this came **purdah**, or keeping women from public view. Connected to purdah was the view that women should stay at home as much as possible. There, they would not be seen and would not lose their honor.

On Assignment...

Imagine that you have just visited a traditional Muslim family in the Middle East. In a letter to friends at home, describe what you saw.

Once severely limited in what they could accomplish outside the home, women are finding new opportunities in the Middle East. Shown here is a class of medical students in Cairo.

Women at Home Women rule the home in traditional Middle Eastern families. They are expected to be good mothers and wives. Inside their homes, women are free to dress as they wish. In traditional societies, women form close friendships and rely on each other.

In many countries, these roles would be hard for women to accept. However, traditional women in the Middle East believe that the system has some good points. For one, women in the Middle East often feel secure about their lives. For another, families in the Middle East are very strong. Women who grow up in this life have few complaints. "It is my life," says one Middle Eastern woman. "I like my veil."

Section 2 Review

1. Describe traditional marriage customs and practices in the Middle East.

2. **Comparing and Contrasting** Think of what you learned about traditional Muslim women in the Middle East. How do their lives compare and contrast with the lives of women you know?

SECTION 3

Everyday Life

What are the most important values and practices that affect everyday life?

Every culture expresses itself through daily life. People in the Middle East are no exception. They express the variety and richness of their cultures in many ways, such as in the foods they eat and the clothes they wear.

Food

If there is an important visit or a holiday, Middle Easterners will sit down to a special meal. In Saudi Arabia, this is how a celebration goes. First, a sheep is killed and cooked. (You would never be served pork. Muslims are not allowed to eat it.) Then, the women cook rice or barley. The rice is placed on a plate with the meat on top. On top of that, the cook sprinkles spices or dried fruits. The plate is big enough to hold the whole sheep. Two men carry it out and place it on a large mat on the floor.

Next to the platter of lamb and rice are smaller dishes. In one is a scramble of eggs and cheese. In another, there is eggplant. In a third is a salad made with apples, dates, walnuts, lettuce, and yogurt. A pile of round flat bread is on one side. For dessert, there is fruit or a custard.

Everyone sits on the floor or on cushions to eat. The men and women eat in different rooms. Each person chooses what he or she wants from the large plates.

Everyone eats with his or her fingers, using the right hand only. Most Middle Easterners will make a small ball of rice and meat each time they take a bite.

Because Muslims do not drink alcohol, fruit juice is often served. Another drink is tea made from soaking raisins in hot water.

Offering Coffee

The ritual of offering coffee is one of the most interesting in the Middle East. The custom began with the nomads. If you were to visit a traditional home, here is what might happen.

Rashid smiles and invites you into his home. Without asking, he begins to prepare the coffee. First, he pours some green coffee beans into a small, highly decorated round pan with a long handle. The rich smell of roasting coffee soon fills the air. Rashid sniffs deeply. "Ready," he tells you.

Rashid pours the roasted beans into a small dish to cool. As he waits, he puts a brass pot on the fire. Then he gets out his mortar and pestle, which he uses to grind the coffee. The mortar is like a small bowl. Sticking out from the top is the pestle, a handle with a heavy bottom.

Rashid pours the beans into the mortar and begins pounding them. "Do you notice I am grinding these beans in a certain way? That rhythm tells everyone that I have a visitor," he tells you.

Next, Rashid adds the coffee to the boiling water. After a bit, he pours the boiling coffee into a smaller pot. He adds a pinch of spice to this pot. Then he carefully pours the coffee into tiny cups. You drink the bitter, spicy coffee. "Good," you tell him. He pours you another cup, and then another.

"You are not from here," Rashid tells you. "To be polite, you should now tilt the cup from side to side. That tells the host you have had enough. To have more than three cups of coffee is very bad manners." You tilt the cup, hand it to him, and smile.

Hospitality towards strangers and a fierce loyalty to family members are important values based on Bedouin traditions. Shown here are a Bedouin father and sons in Jordan.

Dress

Western dress is a common sight in most parts of the Middle East. However, there are styles of clothing the region is known for. The hot climate has much to do with the way people traditionally dress in the Middle East. The traditional dress of both men and women is a full-length, long-sleeved gown. It is loose and comfortable. Both men and women traditionally wear head coverings. These clothes keep out the sand and the wind of the desert. They also provide protection from the fierce sun. Around men's head coverings is a woven rope that helps keep the cloth in place in the wind.

Traditional women's clothing varies in the Middle East. Almost all traditional women wear some kind of head covering. Most wear some sort of long dress or skirt. Other than that, the traditional dress may be the dark robes Islamic women wear in Egypt. It may be the colorful dress of women from Yemen. It may be the decorated costume of the Kurds, a separate group of Muslims.

Religion

In the Islamic countries of the Middle East, religion is a key part of everyday life. In traditional Islamic countries, laws are based on the Koran. In Islam, God is believed to direct everything that happens. The word Islam means "submission to the will of God." This is a good way to describe the way religious Muslims look at the world. Often, a visitor to the Middle East will hear someone say *"Insha'allah."* This means "if God wills it." Religious Muslims often feel that God decides what happens to them.

Muslims are expected to pray five times a day. If you are in a Muslim country, you will likely hear the call to prayer from a nearby mosque. The first time will be an hour before sunrise. The next will be at noon. There is another call mid-afternoon. There is one at sunset. The final call comes about 90 minutes after sunset.

When Muslims pray, they sit on the floor and face the holy city of Mecca. As they pray, they lower their hands and upper body to the ground. The holy day of the week for Muslims is Friday. That day, they go to the mosque to pray.

Ramadan is the holiest time of the year for Muslims. During the month of Ramadan, Muslims do not eat or drink between sunrise and sunset. Instead, the family gathers for a big meal after sunset. Special foods are served that help give Muslims enough nourishment to last through the next day.

The day after the end of Ramadan begins a three-day holiday. During these days, children get gifts, people give money to the poor, and everyone wears new clothes.

Here is how a family in a village in Oman might celebrate. First, Mahmoud would buy a goat on the last day of Ramadan. After he has killed it, he will save the skin to be made into leather.

The goat is roasted in a large hole in the ground. At the bottom of the hole, Mahmoud makes a fire. While he is waiting for the fire to burn down, he wraps the goat meat in leaves and places them in the pit. He covers the pit with dirt. A day later, when Ramadan is over, the meat will be delicious.

Mahmoud's wife will fix the rice, dates, and fruit that will go with the goat. After the meal, everyone will drink coffee and eat a dessert made of sesame seeds and honey.

On Assignment. . .

Write a letter home that explains one of the unique aspects of traditional life in the Middle East that is discussed in this section. Make sure your letter has details that bring the customs of the Middle East to life.

Section 3 Review

1. What is Ramadan and how is it different from other months?

2. **Making Inferences** How does the coffee ritual described in this section express the importance Middle Easterners place on hospitality?

Mind Your Manners

Imagine you are planning to visit people in the Middle East. Before you go, you need to learn a new set of rules. If you say or do some of the things you are used to, you could find yourself misunderstood and could deeply offend someone. Here are a few examples:

- Arabs are used to much less space between them when they talk. People from the United States stand much farther apart. Don't be offended. It's a cultural difference.
- Don't compliment anything particular in an Arab's house. The Arab sense of hospitality will mean that the host must offer it to you as a gift. Instead, give compliments in a general way.
- Shake hands with less force than you would in the United States. Also remember that people in the Middle East are likely to hold your hand longer than people in the United States do.
- Privacy is different in the Arab world than in the West. Do not be surprised if an Arab host asks you questions you would consider personal. Arabs may ask why you are not married. They may ask how much money you make. They may want to know how much your clothes cost. They are not being rude. It is the way friends talk to one another in their culture.
- If you want to show "no," here are three ways to do it: You can move your head back and raise your eyebrows. You can move your head back and raise your chin. You can move your head back and click your tongue.
- To show "come here," hold your right hand out. Put the palm up. Open and close the hand.
- To mean "never," put your right index finger up. Move it from right to left quickly.
- Homes are sacred to people in the Middle East. If you are lucky enough to be invited, know that your hosts really like you. Remember that in much of the Middle East, dinner is not served until 10 P.M. You might want to have a snack before you go.

Case Study Review

1. How are ideas of privacy different in Western and Middle Eastern cultures?

2. **Predicting Consequences** Imagine that you are a business-person who has come to the Middle East without knowing its customs. What could be the results of your lack of knowledge?

I. Reviewing Vocabulary

Match each word on the left with the correct definition on the right.

1. tradition
2. purdah
3. custody
4. suq

a. a large market in the Middle East
b. control over another person
c. behavior handed down from generation to generation
d. the practice of keeping women from public view

II. Understanding the Chapter

Answer the questions below on a separate sheet of paper.

1. What do most villages in the Middle East have in common?
2. What values from the nomadic way of life are still important to many people in the Middle East?
3. Explain how a man and a woman can get a divorce in much of the Middle East.
4. You go into a home in the Middle East and see a painting on the wall that you like. Should you tell your host how much you like it? Explain.

III. Building Skills: Comparing and Contrasting

In two or three sentences, compare and contrast each of the pairs below.

1. nomads and village dwellers
2. the rights and responsibilities of men and of women
3. traditional dress of men and of women
4. marriage in the United States and traditional marriage in the Middle East
5. Middle Eastern manners and manners of someone from the United States

IV. Working Together

Divide the class into groups. Each group should select one scene from this chapter to re-create in a one-act play. Write a script in which a person from the Middle East is explaining a tradition from his or her culture to a group of visitors from the United States. When you have finished writing your play, rehearse with your group. Then act it out for the rest of the class.

On Assignment. . .

Writing Letters From the Middle East: Reread all the letters you wrote. Now imagine that you are sending the letters to someone who is interested in learning more about the area. Write an introduction to the letters that gives an overview of traditional life in the Middle East. Your introduction should help explain how all the letters tie together. Share your letters with a classmate.

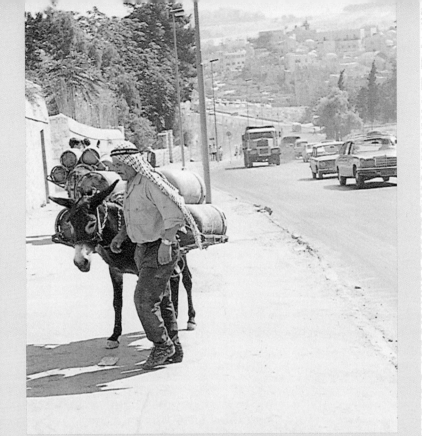

CHAPTER 34

Two ways of life mix on this street in southern Israel. In recent years, traditional patterns of life have been replaced by new ones that have diffused from Western lands.

Changing Patterns of Life

How have traditional patterns of life in the Middle East changed in recent years?

Looking at Key Terms

- **natural gas**   underground reserves of gas that can be used as a fuel
- **public works**   projects done for the good of everyone, such as constructing roads and public buildings
- **emir**   an Arab ruler
- **fundamentalists**   people who oppose modern ideas and favor a return to strict religious values of the past
- **morality**   rules of proper conduct
- **literacy**   the ability to read and write

On Assignment. . .

Creating a Radio Report: In this chapter, you will learn how life in the Middle East has changed in recent years. Use what you find out to create a 10-minute radio report. The report will give listeners an overview of tradition and change in the Middle East.

Changes Brought by Oil

How has oil wealth changed life in parts of the Middle East?

The plane banks over the island country of Bahrain (bah•RAIN). You touch down in a city that looks as modern as any in the United States. Ali is there to greet you as you land.

"Ah, my friend. I am so pleased to show you Bahrain," he says, shaking your hand.

Soon, you are in his brand new car. He drives you past new department stores. Office buildings soar to the sky. You stop at a supermarket. There Ali takes you down aisles filled with taco shells, maple syrup, canned fruit, and other familiar products.

"What are these doing in the Persian Gulf?" you wonder to yourself.

It's almost as if Ali can read your mind.

"All of this is imported from the West," Ali says. "Oil made it possible. Oil was the gift of Allah."

The people of this tiny island country know that before the end of the century, most of their oil will be gone. However, there is some natural gas. **Natural gas** comes from natural underground reserves. It can be used as a fuel. The Bahrainis will sell natural gas, too.

Bahrain is counting on more than oil and natural gas to keep its good fortune going. These resources have allowed Bahrain to build itself into a banking center for the Middle East.

The ways of the past are still here in Bahrain. Most of its people are religious. Most dress in the traditional way and pray five times a day.

Oil wealth has changed the nation. No one in Bahrain pays income taxes. Medical care and schooling are free for all citizens. Luxury cars are common. So are televisions and boats. **Public works** projects, such as building roads and hospitals, are underway everywhere in the city. It seems that anyone who wants a job can find one.

Bahrain is more westernized than most Middle Eastern countries. Many women are not veiled. They can drive, and they can even choose their own husbands.

With the proceeds from rich oil and gas deposits, the tiny nation of Bahrain has built a thriving, modern economy. Here men conduct business in a Bahraini bank.

Most Bahraini people do not need to take low-paying jobs. This is true in other oil-rich countries in the area, too. The countries with oil import hundreds of thousands of workers to fill low-paying jobs. Many workers are from other countries in the Middle East. Others come from countries farther east in Asia, such as Pakistan, the Philippines, and India. They are paid less than citizens are, and they are treated poorly. They must return to their homelands as soon as they stop working.

Depending on Foreign Workers

For the foreign workers, though, leaving home is worth it. They make much more money than they would make at home. For many poor Middle Eastern countries, the money their citizens earn in oil-rich countries is critical. In the early 1980s, more than three million Egyptians were working outside their country. They provided more money for Egypt than did any product Egypt sold. In the country of Qatar, there were four foreign workers for every citizen.

When these foreign workers return home, they bring change to their own countries. In Egypt, for example, workers came home and bought televisions. Then they stayed up so late that they didn't begin farming until mid-morning the next day. The government ordered the state-run television stations to stop broadcasting an hour earlier in the evening.

For the most part, the newly-rich countries have used their wealth wisely. They have built roads and schools. They have invested in hospitals and housing projects.

Some people who grew up with oil wealth may have lost something, though. Everything has been very easy. They no longer need the courage of their ancestors. Families have become less important because people do not depend on them for life.

Stories about the oil-rich countries of the Middle East may give a false picture. Their

On Assignment. . .

Make notes about what you have learned in this section that you can use in your radio report. What would most help a listener understand the changes that oil has brought to the Middle East.

wealth may conceal the fact that most of the Middle East is very poor. Millions of Middle Easterners live from day to day. For them, the world of banks and shopping centers in Bahrain does not exist at all.

Section 1 Review

1. What changes has oil brought to the country of Bahrain?

2. **Determining Cause and Effect** Decide which of the following is the cause and which is the effect: Oil-rich countries have imported foreign workers. Countries not rich in oil receive money from these wealthy lands.

SECTION 2

Urban Growth

How have Middle Eastern cities changed in recent years?

Cities in the Middle East have exploded in size since the middle of the 20th century. The new growth has made Middle Eastern cities very exciting places. The growth has also made these cities some of the most crowded places in the world. Cars choke the streets. Large families often live in very small rooms.

Here is a description of two cities and how they have grown. The first is the ancient city

In Bahrain's Gold Suq, Bahrainis can buy traditional goods. But they also can buy expensive consumer items and luxuries imported at great cost from Europe and the United States.

of Damascus, Syria's largest urban center. Damascus is suffering from too many people in too little space. The second city is Kuwait City. Its story shows how oil has brought dramatic improvements to the lives of some city dwellers.

Damascus: A City Trying to Catch Up

"Damascus? Last stop on the way to the desert," grins Afif. You are walking with him on the crowded streets of the old part of the city. "The rich came here to trade. The poor came here because the rich were here. Thousands of years ago, it was so. Today, it is still so."

The roads you are walking on are narrow and winding. The old streets present solid walls to the outside world. Inside many of these thick walls is a quiet oasis. Many of the homes are built with inside courtyards. Often, these courtyards have bubbling fountains and vine-covered walls. All is peaceful.

On the streets, there is little quiet. People are everywhere. "See, over there?" Afif is pointing at a yellow machine. "Another bulldozer. They want to tear down the old city. True, it is crowded. But these machines rip the heart out of our city."

You walk by the suq, or market, and hear the sellers calling. The scene might have been the same hundreds of years ago. But in another part of town, sleek new apartment buildings rise to the sky. "Only the rich will be able to afford to live there. Once, Damascus was said to be the Garden of Eden," Afif says, looking at them. "For some, it still is. Have you seen the Umayyad (OO•may•ad) Mosque? The beauty! The carvings! Damascus is a rich place."

"What about the other people? What about those who are not rich?" you ask. Afif shrugs and says, "Life for them is not the Garden of Eden. Some live where the rich once lived. In these dwellings, many people live in a single room. The buildings are crumbling. There are also high-rise apartment buildings outside of town. Some people live there. Not everyone in this city is rich or poor. Many are in the middle."

The city is trying to catch up with all the newcomers, Afif explains. New buildings are always rising on the outside of town. But in the meantime, the new people need water. They need places to bathe. They need places to sleep. The city is having trouble giving them what they need.

Kuwait City: What Oil Built

Many hundreds of miles away is the small country of Kuwait. Its capital, Kuwait City, is the city that oil built. At one time, most of the people in this small country were nomads. In the 1950s, Kuwait City was not much more than one street. Then oil was discovered in Kuwait.

"It is hard to believe, isn't it?" your cab driver Aman asks you. He speaks English, as do many people in Kuwait. He is not a Kuwaiti native, though. Only about 40 percent of the people in Kuwait were born there. The others are foreigners who work at jobs the Kuwaitis create. They also do the jobs the Kuwaitis do not want to do.

Kuwait has the highest per-person income of any country in the world. Most Kuwaitis would not want the cab driver's job.

When Aman talks of Kuwait City being hard to believe, you know what he means. For someone who has just come from Damascus, Kuwait seems brand new. In fact, it is. When Kuwait became rich, the **emirs** who ruled the country tore down the mud huts. They ripped up the dirt roads and the old market. In their places, they built fine houses, office buildings, and hospitals.

The suq was torn down, and a modern shopping mall with a huge number of shops was put up. Kuwait was rebuilt from the ground up.

In the early 1990s, neighboring Iraq invaded Kuwait in the Gulf War. (See Chapter 36.) Kuwait City was heavily damaged. Many cities would have found it difficult to recover. Not Kuwait! The city has been rebuilt, better than before.

As Aman drives, he points out the sights. "See those towers over there? There's a restaurant up there. And there—a new hospital. For Kuwaitis, medical care is free. Not for us foreigners, though. And there are only some places we can live. Even so, it is better here than in Jordan. Here, I will never be a citizen. But I can support my family back home."

Aman sighs. "Yes, it would be good to be from Kuwait. Everything is free. School, college, medicine. Everything. When you get married here, the government gives you $7,000! A beautiful city, a beautiful life. If you are Kuwaiti, that is."

On Assignment...

Think about how you could explain the differences between Damascus and Kuwait City in a radio report. Make rough notes on the differences between the two cities.

Section 2 Review

1. How have the growth of Damascus and Kuwait City been similar? How have they been different?

2. **Predicting Consequences** What do you think the consequences will be of many more people moving to Damascus?

SECTION 3

The Changing Role of Women

How does the role of women in the Middle East change from place to place—and person to person?

What is the proper role for women? In the Middle East, everyone has an opinion. In some ways, how women are treated is a battle-ground for beliefs. People hold strong views, and often they do not agree. Sometimes, women in the same family do not agree. In the Middle East, you may see a woman wearing a black veil from head to toe walking with a woman who has only a scarf covering her head. A third woman might be wearing a suit from New York. Yet, the three women could be sisters.

Several forces tug at the women of the Middle East. One force is that of tradition. Another force is Islam. Another is the impact

Life for Middle Eastern women varies greatly. In some countries, women are expected to stay at home. In Iraq, however, many women–like this engineer—pursue careers outside the home.

of the West on the Middle East. Yet another is the influence of education.

The lives that women lead vary a good deal among different Middle Eastern nations. In Israel, women are on equal footing with men. In Iran, women live a sheltered life. Their faces are never seen in public.

Early in this century, there were attempts to change the traditional role of women. In the 1920s, Turkey's Kemal Ataturk rewrote the laws of his country. (See Chapter 32.) For the first time, laws were not based on the Koran. Polygamy was outlawed. Ataturk told women they should stop wearing veils. Turkish women got the right to vote in 1934.

Today in Turkey, 20 percent of the lawyers are women. Turkey has had a woman prime minister. There are as many women as men in schools. Yet in Turkey you might still find traditional women veiled from head to foot.

The Fundamentalists

As in other places in the Middle East, Islamic **fundamentalists** in Turkey believe women should dress traditionally. Islamic fundamentalists believe in a return to the values taught in the Koran. They believe women belong at home, taking care of the children and the household.

Since the 1970s, Islamic fundamentalism has grown in the Middle East. Since then, more women have been veiled. They have returned to what their leaders believe is Islam's role for them.

Some Islamic women have returned to the veil because of their own religious beliefs. Many people in the Middle East think the West does not have enough **morality**, or proper conduct. Many Middle Eastern women think wearing the veil and being modest help stop the influence of the West.

Others wear the veil because they would be punished if they did not. In some countries, a woman who is not veiled may be arrested.

Iran is a fundamentalist country. Iranian women live in a world of other women and children. They wear the veil whenever they are in public. Girls go to school, but they are separated from boys. Women and girls cannot play sports in public. They cannot use public buses. Most women teachers have been banned from teaching in Iran.

Neighboring Iraq is also Islamic. Law in Iraq is not based on the Koran alone, though. In the cities, life is freer for women. Women do not have to wear the veil. Fewer and fewer do. More women are going to college. Iraqi women become lawyers, doctors, and business owners. They can hold political office. Some of the old ways remain, though. Men rule the family. In most places in Iraq, women and men spend much of their time with people of their own gender.

The Role of Women in Israel

In Israel, women have rights much like those of women in the West. Israel is a land where Jews from around the world have gathered. Many come from the West. As a result, Israeli women have a great deal of freedom. Like men, Israeli women are expected to serve in the military. Many are highly educated and play leading roles in Israeli science and engineering. Other Israeli women are active in the political life of the nation. Israel's views of the rights of women are best seen in the rise of a woman named Golda Meir (my•EER). She served as prime minister of Israel.

However, some religious groups in Israel do not believe in all Western ideas. Women in such groups accept the views of their religious community.

Education and Women

Some women in the Middle East think outsiders place too much importance on the question of the veil. They believe education is far more important and will give women real freedom.

Rates of **literacy** among women in the Middle East are rising. Literacy is the ability to read and write. Today in every Middle Eastern country, elementary school education is available to girls. In many countries, all children must go to elementary school.

In fundamentalist Islamic states, boys and girls go to different schools. In Saudi Arabia, men are not allowed to look at unveiled women. What happens when women go to college? Saudi Arabia deals with this problem by closed-circuit television. Women see the professor on the TV screen and can ask questions over the phone. He answers the questions from behind the television camera.

One of the problems with this arrangement is that women have trouble using their education. Women are not allowed to drive. They are not allowed to work with men outside their families. Therefore, women find it hard to apply what they have learned in school to their real lives.

On Assignment...

For your radio report, what would you want someone to know about the lives of women in the Middle East? How could you best explain it? Write some notes to help you tell the story in a radio broadcast.

You might wonder why all Middle Eastern women do not demand more freedom. Many women like the life they lead. They may like it because they are religious. They may like it because they are protected. They may like it because it is what they are comfortable with. Many people in the Middle East are not sure that they want to trade their traditional ways of life for more freedom.

Some Middle Eastern women are trying to gain more freedom, though. They want to be allowed to work at different types of jobs. They want to be able to make more decisions. In some of the oil-rich countries, oil money has meant more contact with the outside world. That has led some women to ask for more freedom. Sometimes, they have gained it, as in Bahrain.

Section 3 Review

1. Why do many Middle Eastern women wear veils in public places today?

2. **Comparing and Contrasting** Compare and contrast the attitudes of women in Iran to those of women in Iraq toward wearing veils.

Life in Saudi Arabia

To an outsider, everything in Saudi Arabia may seem extreme. The country is very wealthy. Under its sands lies about a quarter of the known oil in the world. Its princes have been known to spend millions on airplanes and then leave them on runways when they tire of them. Saudi Arabia is also a strict Islamic country. Its law is based on the Koran. Women are kept at home. They must wear black veils when they go out. They cannot drive. They cannot talk to a man who is not a member of the family.

Sudden Wealth

Their sudden wealth was a shock to many Saudi Arabians. Fifty years ago, Saudi Arabia was a poor country. Its people were mostly from the nomadic tribes that traveled the fringes of the desert.

Saudi Arabia's wealth started to grow after World War II. It exploded in the 1970s. Before the 1970s, Saudi Arabia's largest income came from Muslims from other countries making pilgrimages to Mecca.

Then, in the 1970s, the price of oil rose rapidly. Vast amounts of money flowed into Saudi Arabia. The Saudis became rich enough to buy almost anything they wanted.

The country began big projects. It built hospitals, schools, universities, roads, airports. The city of Jubail is one example. It is the biggest public works project in the world's history. Before it was finished, 50,000 men had worked to build it.

Saudi leaders spent much of the country's wealth wisely. They built schools and roads. If the royal family also spent money on palaces and planes, it may have been because the money seemed endless.

Like any resource, though, oil has its ups and downs. In the 1980s, Saudi Arabia and its rich neighbors hit hard times. There was less demand for oil. Oil prices dropped. In 1990, Saudi Arabia's income was about one quarter of what it had been in 1980. Today, the Saudis still have money, but the lavish days are over.

Demands for Reform

One result of the large number of newly educated people is that they have begun to demand changes in the government. Saudi Arabia is ruled by the Saud (sah•OOD) family. Until recently, the kings of Saudi Arabia had almost total power. In 1992, King Fahd bowed to pressure for reform. He set up a council of citizens to advise the royal

Fifty years ago, Saudi Arabia was a desperately poor land. Today, Saudi Arabia is one of the world's richest nations. Above, wealthy Saudis attend an agricultural show in the capital city of Riyadh.

family. He also gave citizens a bill of rights. Before that, Islamic religious police patrolled the streets. They punished women they thought were not properly dressed. They made sure stores were closed at prayer time. Those caught drinking alcohol could be lashed.

Saudi society has taken the recent changes in stride. The family is still the first concern. Religion is still of great importance. Saudis are interested in the West. But most Saudis are determined to preserve their customs. As one Saudi woman says:

> *You know, we go to the United States and see playgrounds. We say, "Oh, we need playgrounds, too." So we build swings for $5,000 and our children don't use them. Swings aren't part of our culture. We would rather spend our time with our families than be on a playground with strangers.*

Case Study Review

1. How did Saudi Arabia use its oil wealth?
2. **Drawing Conclusions** Why do you think King Fahd decided to make reforms in the government?

REVIEWING CHAPTER 34

I. Reviewing Vocabulary

Match each word on the left with the correct definition on the right.

1. emir
2. public works
3. morality
4. literacy

   a. an Arab ruler
   b. rules of proper conduct
   c. the ability to read and write
   d. projects done for the good of everyone

II. Understanding the Chapter

Answer the questions below on a separate sheet of paper.

1. How did oil change the lives of people who live in oil-rich countries?
2. What effect did workers returning from oil-rich countries have on their home countries?
3. How is education changing life for women in the Middle East?
4. What changes has the Saudi Arabian government made since 1992? How have these changes affected the lives of Saudi Arabians?

III. Building Skills: Making Inferences

Read the quote from the Saudi woman on page 467. Then answer these questions.

1. The speaker says, "Swings aren't a part of our culture." What does she mean?
2. What do you think is the speaker's attitude toward the United States? What words does she use to reveal her attitude?
3. What is the speaker saying about the difference between Western culture and Saudi Arabian culture?

IV. Working Together

Divide the class into four groups. Hold a press conference on how tradition and change mix in the Middle East. Each group should take one section of the chapter. (Include the Case Study as a section of the chapter.) Imagine that you are experts on that section. Each group should take a turn sitting at the front of the room. The rest of your classmates are reporters. Answer their questions about your section of the chapter.

On Assignment. . .

Creating a Radio Report: Reread your notes for each section. Think about how you want to organize your radio report. You want to tell people how life in the Middle East has been changing. Use your notes to help you write an outline of what you want to say. Then write your script. After you have finished, read it out loud and time how long it takes. Try to keep your talk between eight and ten minutes long. Change your report if you need to make it shorter or longer. Now present your report to your classmates.

CHAPTER 35

Economic and Political Trends

What major economic and political trends have shaped the Middle East since World War II?

Ayatollah Khomeini, Iran's spiritual and revolutionary leader, led the fight to transform Iran into a fundamentalist Islamic nation.

Looking at Key Terms

- **Knesset**   the governing body of Israel
- **immigration**   coming to one country from another country
- **Cold War**   the period of time when relations between the United States and the Soviet Union were very tense
- **peninsula**   a body of land surrounded on three sides by water
- **embargo**   a restriction on trade with another country
- **exported**   sent to other countries for sale
- **diverse**   varied
- **sabras**   Jewish people who were born in Israel
- **secular**   not related to religion
- **hydroelectric power**   power created by the force of rushing water

On Assignment. . .

Creating a Picture Book for Young Children: In this chapter, you will learn more about how economics and politics have shaped the Middle East. You will take notes so you can create a picture book for children. The book will help them understand more about the forces that shaped the Middle East. At a number of points, you will be asked to take notes and make sketches of what you think is most important. At the end of the chapter, you will put your book together.

Israel in the Middle East

Why has it been difficult to resolve the Arab-Israeli dispute?

Here is a strange place to begin a story of the Arab-Israeli dispute: a mountain ridge in Maryland sparkling with the red and gold colors of autumn. But on a crisp September day in 1978, history was made at a lodge in the Blue Ridge Mountains in Maryland. The place was Camp David, a weekend retreat of U.S. Presidents. There, the leaders of the Arab nation of Egypt and the Jewish nation of Israel met to hammer out their disagreements.

Three men led the discussions. One was Anwar Sadat, President of Egypt. The second was Menachim Begin (meh•NAH•kehm BAY•gihn), Prime Minister of Israel. The third was Jimmy Carter, President of the United States. He had invited the other two leaders to the United States to try to make peace.

For two weeks the three leaders held secret talks at the lodge. They often argued late into the night. At first, it seemed the talks would fail. The two sides were very far apart.

Finally, however, there was a breakthrough. The Israelis agreed to withdraw their troops from Egyptian land in the Sinai peninsula that they had occupied since 1967. In return, Egypt agreed to recognize Israel's right to exist.

Later, a large crowd gathered in the White House to hear what had happened at Camp David. Carter, Begin, and Sadat entered the room. They smiled, but they looked very tired. Carter announced the good news. The Camp David talks had been a success. Begin and Sadat, who had once been bitter enemies, now rose to hug each other. Israel and one of its Arab neighbors had taken the first steps on the difficult road to peace.

Israel: Creating the Dream

Since it was founded in 1948, Israel has been in the center of a storm. Israelis believed deeply that they had a right to a homeland in the Middle East. Arabs believed just as strongly that the land belonged to them.

The Arabs soon learned that the Israelis were determined to remain. By early 1949, fighting had forced thousands of Palestinian Arabs to flee their homeland. (See Chapter 32.) The refugees became a source of conflict between Israel and the Arab world.

The government of the newly founded Israel was a democracy. Its legislature was known as the **Knesset** (KNEHS•eht). The Knesset passed the Law of Return, which gave every Jew the right to come to Israel. Within 20 years, Israel's Jewish population tripled. Much of this increase was due to **immigration**, or people coming to one country from another. Jews came to Israel from all over the world.

Israel did not allow most of the Arabs who had left the country in 1948 to return. Thus, the Arab population remained small. The Israeli government gave the Arabs in Israel the same rights as Jews. For example, Israel gave the vote to female Arab citizens before any Arab country allowed its women to vote.

Even though it won the war in 1948, Israel knew it was at a disadvantage. It had few people compared to the millions of Arabs around it. It also had few natural resources. Its economy was weak, too.

However, Israel quickly built a strong defense force. At the age of 18, every teenager was trained as a soldier. Then he or she returned home until called upon to fight.

During the 1950s, Israel got aid in the form of money. Some was from Jews around the world. Germany also gave money to Jews who had been victims during World War II. Finally, the United States began to support Israel.

The 1950s was the height of the **Cold War**. This was a period of time when relations between the United States and the Soviet Union were very bad. The United States wanted an ally in the Middle East. As a democracy, Israel became that ally.

The Arab states had never recognized Israel's right to exist. In the late 1960s, the threat to Israel changed. Palestinians made attacks on Israel from bases in Lebanon and Jordan. Then, in 1967, President Gamal Abdel Nasser of Egypt brought together several Arab states. His goal was to force Israel to give up land it had won in previous wars.

Place After the 1967 War, Israel seized control of territory that was larger than its original size. In what three areas did Israel assume control after the 1967 War?

In May of 1967, Egyptian soldiers moved into the Sinai **Peninsula**. A peninsula is a body of land surrounded on three sides by water. Jordan joined Egypt in attacking Israel. On June 5, Israel struck back. Within a few hours, Israeli planes destroyed almost all of Egypt's air force. Israeli soldiers marched into the Sinai. They trapped Egypt's army. By June 9, the Israelis had reached the Suez Canal. Within days, Israel had taken the whole Sinai Peninsula. It had taken land from Syria called the Golan Heights. Jordan lost land west of the Jordan River known as the West Bank. Within six days, the war was over.

The Arab world was shocked by Israel's victory. The Six-Day War was a major blow to Arab pride. Power shifted in the Arab world. Countries that had taken a major part in the war, such as Egypt, Jordan, and Syria, lost prestige. Oil-rich countries that had taken no major part in the fighting became more important. The Six-Day War had changed the face of the Middle East.

Years of Change

Israel was joyful after the war. It had much land. It had captured places sacred to Jews. It had proved that Israel was the strongest military power in the Middle East. However, the victory left Israel with problems. About 1.5 million Arabs lived in the new lands gained by Israel.

In the years that followed, small groups of Israelis began moving onto this land. They believed Israel should keep the land it had won in the Six-Day War. The settlers belonged to the Likud (lee•KOOD) party. In 1977, the Likud party won an election and took control of the government. The losing party, the Labor party, had been in power since 1948. The Labor party had been more willing to talk to the Arabs. The Likud party was determined to keep land that had religious importance to the Jewish people.

The Palestinian Arabs were also changing. They came to believe that they could not depend on other Arabs to win back their country. Many of these Palestinians were young. They had grown up in refugee camps. They were angry and ready to fight. Many of these young people joined the PLO. PLO stands for the Palestine Liberation Organization.

The PLO's leader was Yasir Arafat (YAH•sur AH•ruh•fat). He led the group in raids against Israel. The PLO believed that constant raids would force Israel to leave the occupied territory. To show their anger at the West's support of Israel, the PLO began hijacking Western airplanes. The PLO also attacked unarmed Israeli athletes at the Olympic Games in 1972. Eleven Israelis were killed. A concerned world watched as the terror increased. Another war was looming.

In 1973, it happened. After Egypt's Nasser died, Anwar Sadat became president. He decided to wage war to regain land Israel had taken. On October 6, 1973, Egypt and Syria attacked. The day was Yom Kippur, the holiest day in the Jewish religion. The war came to be called the Yom Kippur War.

At first, the surprise attack worked. Egypt seized land it had lost in 1967. Then the Israelis attacked, at the cost of many lives. They defeated the Egyptians and had just about surrounded the Egyptian army. To the disgust of the Israelis, the United States and the Soviet Union stepped in and helped arrange peace talks.

During the war, the Arab nations had begun an oil **embargo**. An embargo is an order not to trade with another country. Oil-producing countries would not sell oil to nations on Israel's side. Oil prices in the United States rose steeply.

Moves Toward Peace

Egypt's Sadat had come to realize that peace with Israel would benefit Egypt. It might mean the return of most of the Egyptian land Israel had occupied since 1967. Sadat first journeyed to Israel, saying the two nations needed to live in peace. The next year, he and Menachim Begin worked out a peace agreement at Camp David.

In the West, Sadat was seen as a wise leader. In the Arab world, though, many believed that Sadat was a traitor to the Arab cause. In 1981, he was killed by Islamic fundamentalists.

Section 1 Review

1. What happened at Camp David in 1978?

2. **Analyzing Information** What was the main reason for the wars between Israel and its neighbors?

Israel: Building a Nation

Imagine this situation. It is 1948. Poor refugees are pouring into your country. It is a country with few natural resources. Much of it is desert. You have very little industry. You have even fewer people who can start an industry. To make matters worse, your neighbors have just told you they will do everything they can to destroy you.

Sound bad? To an Israeli in 1948, it might have seemed hopeless. But with hard work and faith, the people of Israel created a thriving nation. The barren deserts of 1948 are blooming today. Israel's cities are as busy and modern as those anywhere. Today, an Israeli is likely to live as well as anyone in the West.

To see how far Israel has come, you need to start at its beginning. In 1948, the new country faced a war. There was no time to think about industry. The main thought on people's minds was survival.

After the first war was over, Israel began the work of building a nation. By 1952, the population had doubled. The new Israelis needed food and shelter. Often, they needed help getting on their feet. Sometimes this help was not available since almost all of Israel's efforts were going for defense.

Some help came from the United States and from Jews around the world. The German government also paid money to survivors of the Holocaust.

Getting to Work

With some financial help from others, Israelis rolled up their sleeves and got to work. From the late 1940s to the mid-1970s, Israel's production of goods went up 10 percent a year. That beat any country in the Western world.

One of Israel's worst problems was the lack of housing for all the newcomers. Israel did a massive job building homes in cities.

Israel is not an easy place to be a farmer. Much of the land is desert. There isn't much water. One way Israelis dealt with the problem of farming the desert was to work together. The Israelis created kibbutzim, farms on which a number of people live and work the land together. The kibbutzim have a long history in Israel. The first kibbutz was begun in 1909. Today there are about 250 kibbutzim. However, only about 3 percent of the people of Israel live on kibbutzim.

After gaining their independence, Israelis set to work building a nation. Through hard work and determination, the people of Israel created thriving cities and successful farms. Today, cities, such as Haifa above, continue to prosper.

Farming in a Dry Land

Hard work and bright ideas have led Israeli farmers to some creative ways of farming. Israelis began to grow dates. But there wasn't much water. The Israelis invented the drip system of irrigation. Thin hoses with tiny holes allow a trickle of water to escape. That water goes right to the roots.

In the Negev desert, the only supply of water is salty. How did Israeli farmers solve the problem? They found and grew plants that do not soak up the salt. That led to the Negev tomato. Israelis sell masses of these tomatoes to Europeans, who love their taste.

Today, Israel grows most of its own food. Citrus growers produce more than a million tons of fruit every year. About a third of that is **exported,** or sold to other countries.

A Blend of Cultures

The people of Israel are not all Jewish. In fact, there is a rich mix of people in Israel. About one in five is Arab. There are also Christians and members of other religions. Even though close to four out of five Israelis are Jewish, the Jewish population is very **diverse,** or varied. Israeli Jews come from more than 100 countries. They speak 85 different languages or dialects. Then there are the **sabras**. These are Jews who were born in Israel. They get their name, people say, from the sabra cactus. The sabra fruit is prickly on the outside, but sweet within.

Hebrew: The Unifying Force

How can one small country possibly bring all these people together? One way is through a common language. The ancient Hebrew language is the national language of Israel. For more than a thousand years, very few people spoke Hebrew. Then, Jews the world over began learning it. Hebrew is the only language in history that had been "dead" and returned to life.

Much of the credit for bringing Hebrew back to life goes to a man named Eleazar Ben Yehuda, who moved to Israel in 1881. Ben Yehuda published a Hebrew newspaper and dictionary. He gathered a group of scholars to develop modern words for the language. For example, there was no Hebrew word for *babysitter*. To create a word, the scholars combined the Hebrew words for "young child" and "guard." One hundred years ago, Hebrew had a vocabulary of only 7,500 words. Today, Hebrew consists of more than 100,000 words.

Since its creation, Israel has insisted that newcomers share in all aspects of Israeli life. The government set up hundreds of centers where immigrants could learn Hebrew. There, Russian Jews learned to communicate with Ethiopian Jews, South African Jews, and Jews from the United States.

Case Study Review

1. How did farmers solve the problems of farming in Israel's desert?

2. **Drawing Conclusions** Why is it important for a country to have a national language?

SECTION 2

Changing Political Patterns

Why have fundamentalists gained power in the Middle East?

After World War II, Europe's colonial empires in the Middle East began to collapse. Country after country gained independence. Here are the stories of these new countries.

Syria

In Syria and in most of the Middle East, there was a great gulf between the rich and the poor. The rich lived in luxury. Others worked for the rich and remained very poor. Vast differences in wealth often lead to unrest. In Syria, trouble happened when the French gave Syria independence in 1944. After the French left, the government was controlled by wealthy landowners and merchants. They proved to be poor rulers. Middle-class Syrians soon challenged their rule. In two years, Syria suffered four military takeovers. In the next two decades, the takeovers continued.

Algeria

Algeria revolted against the French in 1954. More than 250,000 people were killed in fighting that lasted eight years. In 1962, the French finally left. The new Algerian government took control of many industries. Arabic replaced French as the official language. In the new Islamic nation, women lost much of the independence they had won under French rule.

Lebanon

France had created Lebanon from part of Syria in the 1920s. Lebanon's problems lay in its religious differences. It had large Christian and Muslim populations, and the two groups did not get along very well. At first, the Christians controlled the government. During a rebellion by Muslims in 1958, the Lebanese president requested help from the United States. Thousands of U.S. Marines landed in Lebanon. They did restore peace, but they created a great deal of bitterness among Muslims.

Tensions grew after the PLO moved its headquarters to Lebanon in 1970. Most Muslims supported the PLO. Most Christians did not. The country split along religious lines.

Beginning in 1975, Lebanon suffered a bloody civil war. Tens of thousands of Lebanese were killed in the fighting. Once-beautiful cities such as Beirut were reduced to ruins. The Lebanese economy collapsed.

In 1976, the Israelis invaded Lebanon. They aimed to destroy PLO bases where attacks on Israel were staged. Israel invaded Lebanon twice more, in 1978 and 1982. Each invasion was successful in military terms.

A long and bloody civil war engulfed Lebanon after 1975. Above, a Muslim militiaman takes a bleeding boy from the scene of a car bombing that had killed more than 40 people in a neighborhood of Beirut.

Islamic fundamentalism has grown quickly in the Middle East. The fundamentalists want to move religion back to its central role in Islamic life. Shown here is a Muslim prayer meeting in Tehran in 1980.

However, each attack raised anti-Israeli feelings in the Muslim world.

The civil war ended in 1991. However, the peace was not very firm. It seemed as if the war might erupt again at any time. By 1992, a Syrian-controlled government ran Lebanon. Syrian troops helped keep the civil war from breaking out again.

Islamic Fundamentalism

As you have read, religion has always been an important force in the Middle East. In recent years, many groups in the region have called for a return to traditional Islamic values. Westerners call these groups "fundamentalists." (See Chapter 34.) It is not a term that people in the Middle East use. Middle Eastern fundamentalists see themselves as restoring religion to its proper place.

The fundamentalists want to move religion back to its central role in Islamic life. That means creating governments based on the Koran. It also means cracking down hard on disorder, reducing the influence of Western countries in the Middle East, and returning all of Palestine to Arab rule.

Iran

One way to understand the fundamentalist movement is to look at Iran. In recent years, Iran has become the center of Islamic fundamentalism.

As you read in Chapter 32, Iran had been ruled by the Pahlavi family since 1925. The shahs, or kings, tried to make Iran a modern state. Women were given more rights. The country obeyed **secular** laws, rather than Islamic laws. *Secular* means "not related to religion."

Iran did well during the oil boom. But this wealth from oil did not reach everyone. There was a big gap between rich and poor. That caused unrest among the Iranian people.

There were many signs that a religious movement was building. However, the shah paid little attention. He rejected demands by the fundamentalists for a return to strict religious rule. The shah's secret police used brutal means to keep the country under control. The shah also maintained close relations with the United States. He did not understand that many Iranians thought the West was an evil place.

In 1978, serious protests against the government began. Many people were killed in antigovernment riots.

The main opposition to the shah came from religious leaders of Iran's Shiite Muslims. (For the differences between Shiite and Sunni Muslims, see Chapter 31.) More than 90 percent of all Iranians are Shiites.

The leader of the religious protests was Ruhollah Khomeini (koh•MAY•nee). He was called "ayatollah" (ay•ah•TOHL•uh), which means "reflection of God." He had been living in exile in France. From France he directed the uprisings in Iran.

In January 1979, the shah left Iran for medical treatment. A month after the shah left, Khomeini returned to Iran. Ten days later, he took power. The shah never returned to Iran. He died in Egypt in 1980.

Khomeini set about changing Iran. Women had to wear veils in public. School courses were changed to agree with Islamic law. Western-style culture was attacked. The government made attempts to ban aspects of Western culture such as music. The country was shaped into a nation based on Islam. Opponents of the government were arrested and put to death.

On Assignment...

How has the rise of fundamentalists affected the Middle East since the 1970s? Think about how you would present the issue to children. How would you explain this in a few pages of a picture book? Make sketches of your ideas.

Attacks on the United States

To the fundamentalists, the United States was the major enemy. The ayatollah's supporters believed that the United States had helped keep the shah in power. In November 1979, Khomeini's supporters took control of the United States embassy in Tehran. They took 52 Americans hostage. The hostages were imprisoned for more than a year. They were finally freed in January 1981.

Section 2 Review

1. Explain what led to the Lebanese civil war from 1975–76.

2. **Making Generalizations** Explain the factors that led to the rise of fundamentalism in the Middle East after World War II.

SECTION 3

Changing Economic Patterns

What are the barriers to growth in the Middle East?

For most of its history, the Middle East was an important economic center in the world. From the time of the Sumerians, traders from the Middle East spread their influence throughout the Eastern Hemisphere. (See Chapter 31.) At the height of the Ottoman Empire, the Middle East was a center of economic strength.

The influence of the Middle East declined in the 1600s. At the same time, Europe became more important. By the 20th century, the economies of Middle Eastern lands were under the control of Europe.

Then oil was discovered in the 1900s. The Middle East once again assumed great economic importance. However, the really big

COUNTRIES OF THE MIDDLE EAST

COUNTRY	CAPITAL	AREA (Square miles)	POPULATION (Millions of people)	AGRICULTURE AND INDUSTRY
Afghanistan	Kabul	250,000	16.6	wheat, textiles
Algeria	Algiers	919,590	26.0	grains, grapes, oil
Bahrain	Manama	240	0.5	oil, banking
Egypt	Cairo	386,660	54.5	cotton, rice, sugar
Iran	Tehran	636,290	46.6	grains, oil, natural gas, carpets
Iraq	Baghdad	167,975	19.9	grains, rice, oil, textiles
Israel	Jerusalem	8,020	4.9	citrus fruits, diamond cutting, electronics
Jordan	Amman	35,480	3.4	grains, olives, phosphates
Kuwait	Kuwait City	6,880	1.4	oil, natural gas
Lebanon	Beirut	4,020	3.4	citrus fruits, olives, tobacco
Libya	Tripoli	679,360	4.4	wheat, barley, oil, natural gas
Morocco	Rabat	172,410	26.2	grains, fruits, leather goods, tourism
Oman	Muscat	82,030	1.6	dates, fruits, oil
Qatar	Doha	4,250	0.5	oil, natural gas
Saudi Arabia	Riyadh	830,000	15.5	wheat, oil, natural gas
Sudan	Khartoum	967,490	25.9	cotton, peanuts, dates
Syria	Damascus	71,500	12.8	cotton, grains, olives
Tunisia	Tunis	63,170	8.4	grains, olives, citrus fruits, phosphates
Turkey	Ankara	301,380	58.5	cotton, tobacco, machinery, food processing
United Arab Emirates	Adu Dhabi	32,280	2.4	vegetables, dates, oil
Yemen	Sana	203,850	49	wheat, sorghum, cotton, oil refining

Source: Population Reference Bureau, Inc., World Almanac

The nations of the Middle East range from huge desert territories to tiny countries along the Persian Gulf. What Middle Eastern country ranks among the top five in size and the top three in population?

changes did not take place until after World War II. You have read about these changes in Chapter 34.

In recent years, Middle Eastern nations have tried to use economic strength to build national strength. After gaining independence, many countries nationalized, or took over, large industries. Middle Eastern governments hoped to bring benefits directly to the people.

In many cases, just the opposite happened. The nationalized industries were poorly run. In order to keep the industries running, the government often raised prices.

In recent years, there has been little nationalization. Now, governments are relying more and more on private companies. They are making deals with foreign companies to develop resources.

On Assignment. . .

How can you explain the major economic issues in a picture book? Outline the major issues. Then plan how you will describe these issues to young people.

Barriers to Growth

Several major problems face all Middle Eastern nations. One is the quickly growing population. It is hard to grow enough food for so many people. Another problem is the amount of money Middle Eastern states spend for defense. That money cannot be used for things their people need.

Several other barriers stand in the way. For one thing, there is a lack of skilled managers and workers. Many adults in the region are illiterate. It is only since the 1970s that anyone who wished to go to elementary school could do so. Even today, many young people do not have a chance to go on to high school.

New Ways of Farming

Except for farmers in Israel and Turkey, most Middle Eastern farmers are poor. There are many reasons why this is so. Most farmers do not own their own land, although Egypt, Iran, Syria, and Iraq have made some land reforms. Many large landowners live in the cities and have no real interest in farming.

Although farmers work hard, their crop yields — the amount of crops they grow in an acre of land — are small. This is because the same crops are grown year after year. The soil wears out unless fertilizers are used. There is little money to buy fertilizers.

Furthermore, plots of farmland are often small and scattered. Thus modern equipment cannot easily be used.

Besides these problems, the farmer must always worry about the water supply. The future of the Middle East depends on the full use of its scarce water resources.

In times past, people used clever ways to get water. Systems of ditches are thousands of years old. Today, some wealthier farmers use costly irrigation methods. They also buy expensive fertilizers. That means that they often cannot afford to grow grain crops. Those grain crops are what most people in the Middle East depend on for food. Instead, Middle Eastern farmers grow products to sell elsewhere. Middle Eastern countries still must import much of their basic food.

The oil-rich countries have been able to spend their money on developing water supplies. They are tapping water that is far underground. Underground water has helped to increase Saudi Arabia's crop yield greatly. The oil-rich countries have also built plants to take the salt out of sea water.

The Aswan High Dam in Egypt (see Chapter 32) was built to stop the yearly flooding of the Nile. That way, crops could be grown all year. The dam provides Egypt with billions of tons of water each year. It also gives Egypt one-third of its power through **hydroelectric power.** Hydroelectric power is created by the force of rushing water.

Section 3 Review

1. How are oil-rich countries trying to expand their economies?

2. **Comparing and Contrasting** What problems do the oil-rich and oil-poor countries of the Middle East have in common?

I. Reviewing Vocabulary

Match each word on the left with the correct definition on the right.

1. sabras   a. the governing body of Israel
2. Knesset   b. a restriction on trade with another country
3. embargo   c. Jewish people who were born in Israel
4. secular   d. not related to religion

II. Understanding the Chapter

Answer the questions below on a separate sheet of paper.

1. How did the founding of Israel affect Arabs in the Middle East?
2. What was the reason for the Lebanese civil war?
3. What were the causes of the shah's fall in Iran?
4. How have countries in the Middle East tried to deal with the lack of water in modern times?

III. Building Skills: Distinguishing Fact From Opinion

The following quotes could have come from people in the Middle East. Decide which is a fact and which is an opinion. Explain your answers.

1. "Every Jew is welcome in Israel."
2. "If the shah of Iran had been a good leader, the revolution would not have happened."
3. "Arab countries were wrong to nationalize oil companies."
4. "Most people in Israel live in the cities."

IV. Working Together

Divide the class into three groups. Each group should take one section of the chapter. Each group should think of a new way to explain the section to others. For example, you might want to create a board game that has players moving around the board when they answer questions correctly. After you have done your work, present it to the class.

On Assignment. . .

Creating a Picture Book for Young Children: Reread your notes and outlines for each section. Look at the sketches you made. How can you best put these together to make a picture book? The book should show the important issues that have shaped the Middle East since World War II. Plan your book. Now write and illustrate it. You may use your own drawings. You could also trace photos or cut them out. Create a front cover for your picture book. Invite a class of younger students in for a story hour. Share your picture books with them.

CHAPTER 36

The Middle East in the World Today

What major issues does the Middle East face today?

Oil wealth has allowed some Middle Eastern countries to dream of dominating the region. Above, Iraqi revolutionary guards pursued a costly war against Iran in the 1980s.

On Assignment...

Writing a Feature Story: In this chapter, you will take the role of reporter and write a feature story on current issues in the Middle East. Work with a partner. For each section in the chapter, you will write the questions a reporter would ask about the subject. At the end of the chapter, you will answer the questions in your feature story. Remember, a good story answers the questions *who? what? where? when? how?* and *why?*

Looking at Key Terms

- **consumers**   people who buy and use products
- **sanction**   the decision to cut off trade with a country until it changes its policies
- **intifada**   protests and attacks that began in 1987 by the Palestinians against Israeli rule in the West Bank and Gaza
- **environment**   the surroundings in which people live
- **satellite**   a spacecraft that orbits the earth
- **oral history**   history that is passed down verbally, rather than in writing
- **calligraphy**   the art of beautiful handwriting
- **minaret**   a large tower near a mosque from which Muslims are called to prayer

The Middle East and the World

How have the nations of the Middle East adjusted to worldwide changes?

In recent times there have been dramatic changes in the world. First, the empire of the Soviet Union crumbled. With the collapse of the Soviet Union, the Cold War came to an end. Then, worldwide demand for oil dropped sharply. This put economic pressure on oil-producing countries.

People in the Middle East had to adjust to these new issues. Middle Eastern nations took a hard look at their alliances. Nations that had depended on the Soviet Union for money and supplies found themselves without a source of aid. They began to see how cooperation between Middle Eastern nations could replace the past support they had received from the Soviet Union or the United States. They also began to explore possible solutions to the Arab-Israeli dispute.

One alliance that faced a big change was OPEC. OPEC stands for the Organization of Petroleum Exporting Countries. The members of OPEC work together to limit competition and keep oil prices high.

The Rise of OPEC

OPEC was founded in 1960. However, it gained world attention during the 1973 war between Israel and the Arab nations. An Arab oil embargo caused oil prices to rise sharply in the United States, Japan, and Europe.

Through OPEC, the Arabs were able to use oil as a political weapon. They stopped oil shipments to nations that supported Israel. Though the embargo was lifted in 1974, the price of oil did not come down. OPEC discovered that by reducing oil production, it could keep the price high. Oil that had been selling for around $2 a barrel suddenly skyrocketed in price. In the 1980s, a barrel of oil cost as much as $44.

Does Middle Eastern oil have an impact on the United States? During the oil embargo of 1974, Americans had to wait in long lines to fill up at those service stations that had gasoline.

Shock Waves

Rising oil prices sent shock waves through the world. Countries that bought oil were badly hurt. Prices rose as companies passed along the high costs to **consumers**, or users of oil products. Hardest hit were poor countries in Africa, Asia, and Latin America. They needed oil to run their new industries. The leap in oil prices took money away from other projects.

On the other hand, vast riches poured into the already rich oil states. In 1970, for example, Saudi Arabia earned $1.2 billion from its sale of oil. In 1981, it earned $101 billion. This new wealth brought great power to the oil-rich nations.

In the long run, the rise in oil prices caused some unexpected results. Countries that imported oil began using it more wisely. They created new fuels. They found new oil fields. OPEC once had two-thirds of the world oil market. By the 1990s, it produced only about one third of the world's oil.

These changes reduced OPEC's power. In the mid-1980s, the price of oil dropped. OPEC tried to get its members to reduce the amount of oil they sold. They hoped that smaller supplies would make prices rise.

However, OPEC was unable to control its members. Some OPEC members refused to reduce production. They were more interested in immediate profits than in following the advice of OPEC. They sold what they could.

The world does not depend as much on Middle Eastern oil as it once did. However, the region is still the world's single largest source of oil. As long as that is true, other parts of the world will depend on the Middle East. Oil has made the Middle East important in world affairs. That will not change for a long time.

Libya's New Role

Libya used oil to make its own bid for importance. It had stayed out of the Six-Day War in 1967. Then, in 1969, a group of Libyan army officers overthrew the king and

Muammar al-Qaddafi came to power in Libya in 1969. Since then, relations between the United States and Libya have been hostile. Qaddafi has supported terrorist attacks against Israel and the United States.

created a new government. The government was headed by Colonel Muammar al-Qaddafi (MOO•ah•mar al kuh•DAH•fee). He changed the face of Libya.

Qaddafi had big plans to develop his country. He first nationalized the banks. Then, in the early 1970s, he nationalized oil companies. With the money from oil, Qaddafi built roads, airports, schools, and low-cost housing.

Qaddafi was not content simply to improve Libya. He wanted to be a leader of all Arabs. He gave vast amounts of money to the PLO. He also supported Arab terrorist attacks against Israel.

Qaddafi had scores to settle with other Muslim leaders. He gave money to groups trying to overthrow governments in Turkey, Jordan, and Egypt. Qaddafi was brutal in dealing with Libyan opponents as well. In the early 1980s, Qaddafi was tied to killings of Libyans abroad.

Since Qaddafi took power, relations between the United States and Libya have been hostile. In the 1980s, Libya paid for a number of terrorist attacks against U.S. army facilities. In response, the United States attacked two Libyan cities. Libyan agents were then linked to the 1988 bombing of a U.S. airplane over Scotland. Hundreds of innocent people were killed in that attack. Qaddafi refused to turn these agents over to the West. As a result, the United Nations banned shipments of arms to Libya. Qaddafi, however, remained firmly in power.

Iran and Iraq Go to War

In 1980, Iraq invaded its oil-rich neighbor, Iran. Iraq was taking advantage of the troubles in Iran during the ayatollah's revolution. (See Chapter 35.) Iraq believed it could make quick gains at its neighbor's expense.

Iran suffered huge losses. But Iran's army proved tougher than Iraq's leader, Saddam

The loss of life was devastating in the Iran-Iraq war of the 1980s. About one million people were killed. Here, women mourn for their sons and husbands at Martyr's Cemetery in Tehran.

Hussein, expected. Iran's government appealed to people's religious feelings. It recruited many volunteers, including young teenagers, into the army. Boys were told that a beautiful afterlife was theirs if they died for their country. By 1981, Iran had regained much of the lost ground.

The fighting continued for years. Both sides were badly hurt. The fighting cut off Iraqi oil shipments through the Persian Gulf. Saddam Hussein asked other Arab states for money. Many of these states feared the spread of Iran's revolution to their countries. As a result, Saddam Hussein got about $60 billion from these nations.

In 1988, the war finally ended. Neither side had gained or lost much land. However, the loss of life was terrible. Almost one million people had been killed. The economies of both countries were in ruins.

The war had exposed Saddam Hussein as a dangerous leader. Many wondered what he might do to restore Iraq's fortunes.

War in the Persian Gulf

In 1990, Iraq saw another chance for gain. Despite its oil wealth, Iraq was poor after the Iran-Iraq war. Neighboring Kuwait was rich. Also, Iraq still owed Kuwait $8 billion from the Iran-Iraq war. If Iraq controlled Kuwait, its money problems would be over.

Saddam announced that Iraq had the right to Kuwait. He claimed that Kuwait had been stolen from Iraq by colonial powers. He also charged that Kuwait was stealing Iraqi oil. He said that the Kuwaitis were drilling under Iraqi land.

On August 2, 1990, the Iraqi army attacked. Iraq was the strongest military power in the area. It sent tens of thousands of soldiers over the border. Tiny Kuwait was overwhelmed.

Saddam Hussein thought no one would oppose him. He thought the United States would not try to stop him because it did not want to get involved in a faraway dispute. He believed the other Gulf states would not

You are a reporter preparing a feature article on the two wars in the Persian Gulf. Write five questions relating to the two wars. With your partner, formulate the answers you think an expert would give to the questions you wrote.

move because they resented Kuwait's vast wealth.

Saddam figured wrong. For the first time in modern history, one Arab nation had invaded another. The nations of the Persian Gulf took an unusual step. They asked for help from the United States. This request was historic because it came from many nations that had condemned the United States for years.

The world reacted quickly. The United Nations demanded that Iraq get out of Kuwait. People throughout the world feared that an Iraqi victory would give Saddam control of the Persian Gulf oil fields.

The United Nations placed economic **sanctions** on Iraq on August 6. That meant that U.N. members would not trade with Iraq. Two days later, the first U.S. soldiers arrived in Saudi Arabia. Their mission was to defend that country in case Iraq attacked there. Before long, troops from 28 countries were in Saudi Arabia.

Saddam was trapped. He could not leave Kuwait without giving in to his enemies. This would hurt his image as a leader in the Middle East. He hoped that if he just held on to Kuwait, world attention would fade.

Instead, the world turned up the pressure to force Iraq to leave Kuwait. Saddam was desperate. He took U.S. and British hostages. When the two countries threatened to attack if the hostages were not let go, Saddam released them.

U.S. President George Bush was not sure that the U.S. public would support a war over Kuwait. War could mean the loss of many Americans' lives. On the other hand, the stories of Iraqi violence in Kuwait were terrible. The United States and other nations began a military buildup of forces to force Saddam out of Kuwait.

By January 1991, there were 460,000 soldiers from 28 Allied countries in Saudi Arabia. Iraq had about 350,000 troops. The United Nations had given Iraq a deadline to get out by January 15, 1991. If not, Iraq should expect military action.

January 15 came and went. There was no movement from Saddam. On January 16, Allied forces launched their attack. It was called Operation Desert Storm.

For 40 days, bombs lit up the skies over Iraq and Kuwait. The Iraqi capital, Baghdad, and other Iraqi cities were hit. Iraqi targets suffered heavy damage. As the Allies prepared for a ground war, they gave Iraq one more chance to pull out of Kuwait. There was no reply. On February 24, 1991, the ground attack began.

The sweeping action quickly flushed Iraqi forces out of Kuwait. Just 100 hours later, the war was over. Kuwait was once again independent.

Allied casualties were much lower than Iraqi casualties. The Allies counted 177 dead and 597 wounded. The Iraqis counted 50,000 dead and the same number wounded.

One of the most important goals of the Allies was not met, however. That was to remove Saddam Hussein from power. He remained in power in 1996.

The Persian Gulf War marked a change in world relations. The United States and Russia worked together to stop an invader. Also, the United Nations proved it could play an important military role.

Section 1 Review

1. Why did Iraq invade Kuwait?

2. **Determining Cause and Effect** What effect did the end of the Cold War have on the Middle East?

In the uprising known as the intifada, Palestinians in Israeli-held territory staged attacks and held protests. Here, young Palestinians display the Palestine Liberation Organization flag during a demonstration.

SECTION 2

Arabs and Israelis Seek Peace

How have Arab-Israeli peace efforts advanced in recent years?

On December 8, 1987, an Israeli truck driver accidentally ran over four Palestinians in the Gaza Strip. The Gaza Strip is an area of Palestine that was occupied by Israel. The truck driver's carelessness changed Israel's history.

The deaths made Palestinians furious. Within a day, rioting had spread to other Arab areas occupied by Israel. This series of stone-throwing attacks by Palestinians began what is known as the **intifada** (ihn•tuh• FAH•duh), or "the shaking." Palestinians attacked Israeli soldiers and civilians. They organized strikes against Israeli businesses.

The intifada was the result of 20 years of strict rule by Israel. Year by year, there were more Israeli settlements in occupied areas.

The Palestinians were increasingly angry over their poor living conditions.

PLO leaders quickly realized that the intifada was their strongest weapon against Israel. It kept the Palestinian problem on the front pages. More important, it might force Israel to seek a settlement.

The PLO was also under pressure now. It had fought for a Palestinian homeland for years. Its efforts had been unsuccessful. Palestinian leaders saw that their best hope of success was to do what they had refused to do for 40 years. That was to recognize Israel as a nation.

In 1991, Israeli and Arab leaders met in Spain. Just the fact that they met was important. Little was settled at this first meeting. However, other peace talks soon followed.

In September 1993, Israeli Prime Minister Yitzak Rabin signed a peace treaty with the PLO leader Yasir Arafat. The PLO recognized Israel. In return, Israel promised to turn over some territory to the PLO.

Some Israelis, such as members of the Likud party, were against this treaty. They did not believe that certain lands should be given back to the Palestinians. They argued that this land was sacred.

The Likud did not support violent actions. However, some extremists in Israel were ready to use violence. In November 1995, Rabin was killed by an extremist who was trying to stop the peace process.

The killing was a huge shock to Israel. Israelis had always taken pride in their commitment to democracy. They were stunned that political differences would lead one Israeli to kill another. The murder made Israelis aware of just how difficult reaching peace in the Middle East would be.

Section 2 Review

1. Explain the reasons for the intifada.
2. **Drawing Conclusions** How did Israelis and Palestinians both suffer from the murder of Yitzak Rabin?

SECTION 3

Winds of Change

How is cooperation between Middle Eastern nations helping to change the region?

As the search for peace in the Middle East went on, some countries began to focus less on the issues that divided them. They began to try to solve common problems. The nations of the Middle East are linked in many ways. Some of those ties are ties of language and religion. Other ties are based on the **environment,** the surroundings in which people live. When the Iraqis set fire to Kuwaiti oil fields during the Persian Gulf War, the damage to the environment affected every country along the Persian Gulf.

Sharing Resources

Almost every resource in the Middle East is shared. Kuwait's oil and Iraq's oil come from the same underground oil fields. Israel and Jordan pump water from the same underground water sources. In fact, every country in the region shares water supplies with several other nations.

Resources may be the one thing that brings the Middle East together. In the Middle East, water is more important than oil. Oil can make a country rich. But "water is our life," as one Israeli official says. Water costs twice as much in the Middle East as it does in North America. As a result, even traditional enemies have found ways to cooperate. For example, Jordan and Israel have cooperated over water. Yet, the two nations were officially at war for more than 40 years.

There is still a long way to go. Almost every country in the region has a plan to expand its water resources if peace ever comes to the Middle East. Turkey would like to build what it calls a "peace pipeline." It would pump water from rivers in northern Turkey to drier lands farther south.

King Hussein of Jordan would like to build a dam on the Yarmuk River. It would provide badly needed water for the Jordan valley. However, Jordan cannot build the dam without Israeli approval, because bankers will not lend the money without the approval of all sides affected by it. Israel is not willing to approve the project without the promise that it will get a fair share of the water.

The links that unite the Middle East offer chances for peace in the region. Sharing natural resources such as water, and communication links such as phone lines, connect Middle Easterners to each other.

Communication Links

People throughout the Middle East can listen to the same music and see the same movies. They can also watch the same TV shows. Since 1985, 22 Arab nations have been linked by two **satellites.** A satellite is a spacecraft that circles the earth. These satellites are controlled from a ground station in Saudi Arabia. They are known as "Arabsat." Arabsat allows international telephone calls, television shows, and other electronic signals to be sent from one nation to another.

By 1987, Arabsat was relaying local television programs to countries throughout the Arab world. The network also broadcasts live events, including prayers at the grand mosques at Mecca and soccer matches between nations.

The links that unite the Middle East offer opportunities for peace. Many people believe that with those links, the Middle East has a chance to end the conflicts that have divided the region for so long.

Section 3 Review

1. What is "Arabsat"?
2. **Understanding Points of View** What is Jordan's point of view about the Yarmuk River dam? What is Israel's point of view?

SECTION 4

The Arts in the Middle East

What can we learn about the Middle East from its writers and artists?

The Middle East has a rich heritage of arts and literature. As far back as the ancient Sumerians, the Middle East has produced brilliant artists. It still does so today.

What questions might a reporter ask an expert on Middle Eastern art and literature? Make a list of your questions. Be sure to write the answers as well.

The Middle East has a rich tradition of **oral history**. Oral history is history that is passed down verbally. Before there was a written language, there were Middle Eastern poets. Among the tribes of the Middle East, it was a high honor to be thought of as a great poet. Poets recorded brave deeds. Poets spoke about history around late-night campfires. The most famous work from this tradition is "A Thousand and One Nights." It is the story of Sheherazade (shuh•heh•ruh•ZAHD). Her nightly stories to the king kept her from death.

The Persian poet Omar Khayyam (KY•yam) is perhaps the most famous Middle Eastern poet. He died about 1123. In the Muslim world, Khayyam is known as a scientist and mathematician. His poem "Rubaiyat" is one of the most famous poems of all time. It is a series of thoughts about human life. For example, he writes,

Ah, make the most of what we yet may spend,
Before we too into the dust descend.

In recent years, an Egyptian novelist has won worldwide praise for his work. Naguib Mahfouz (NAH•geeb mah•FOOZ) won the Nobel Prize for literature in 1988. He writes of changes in Egyptian life during this century. Mahfouz creates strong characters that readers want to know more about.

Israel has also made important contributions to literature. Israeli writers have explored such themes as the Holocaust and the Arab-Israeli dispute.

Middle Eastern Art

Islamic artists and architects have produced some of the world's finest works of art. Yet many Muslim societies ban art that shows human or animal life. They argue that Muhammad said that only God can create life.

As a result, much Islamic art is based on symbols or on **calligraphy**. Calligraphy is the art of producing fine handwriting. Skilled calligraphers can create an entire picture using the Arabic words from the Koran.

The use of symbols is also seen in one of the most famous of Middle Eastern arts. Carpet weaving has been done in the area for thousands of years. Today, the fine work of Middle Eastern weavers draws high prices around the world.

In Iran, birds, flowers, and even people are shown in carpets. Shiite Muslims in that country allow artists to depict living things. Iranian carpets are also called Persian rugs. One way to tell the quality of a Persian rug is to turn the rug over and look at the number of knots per inch. The more knots, the better the rug.

Fine Architecture

Like Arabic calligraphy, Arabic architecture also uses sweeping curves. Islamic architects built splendid mosques and palaces that glittered with colorful tiles. Large domes often crowned the mosques. A **minaret,** or tower, is a familiar feature of mosques. From those towers, Islamic religious leaders call the faithful to prayer.

Section 4 Review

1. Who is Naguib Mahfouz and why is he important?

2. **Determining Cause and Effect** How did the beliefs of Islam affect the art of the Middle East?

The Kurds Seek a Home

"There are 25 million of us Kurds," says Jahan Ahmed. "We need a home." She is sitting by a fire warming her hands. "Can you name another people, so many, with no home?" The fire blazes bright as the snow falls. Jahan is huddled with her family in a camp near Kirkuk, Iraq. She sighs. "For us, until we have our own land, there is only this." Her arm sweeps the barren ground, with its few tents. "The Iraqis destroyed our village."

"We are the forgotten ones."

She fixes her blue eyes on the reporter. "What do you know of us?" The reporter opens her mouth. Jahan waves her hand. "So few know. So I will tell you. We are the forgotten ones. But we will make the world remember."

She settles herself on the ground. "We are an ancient people. We were always independent. That is what may have caused our problems. We would not give in."

She chuckles. "And sometimes, we would not give in even to one another. But there are some things all Kurds share. We speak the Kurdish language. We have our ancient stories. Most of us are Muslims. There are Jewish Kurds, though. And there are some Christian Kurds.

"We want a home."

"So why will we not blend in with the Turks and Iraqis? Because we are different. We come from the mountains. We have our own traditions. We are a people.

"The land we Kurds come from is called Kurdistan. It contains parts of several countries. Iran, Iraq, Turkey all have Kurdish people. Most Kurds are in Turkey. But we are not Turks. We are not Iranians. We are not Iraqis. We are Kurds. And we want a home."

Since the 1800s, Jahan says, the Kurds have tried to carve out a homeland. Many times the Kurds revolted against their rulers. Every time, the Kurds were crushed.

One of the most recent revolts was against Iraq's Saddam Hussein. It began after the Gulf War in 1991. Four million Kurds live in Iraq. They make up almost a quarter of Iraq's people. At first, the Kurds did well. They captured the city of Kirkuk, which they consider a major Kurd city. Before long though, Iraq had crushed the revolt. Thousands of Kurds were killed. Some tried to get into Turkey. But Turkey let few in. Others fled to Iran.

One of the Kurds' major disappointments was that the rest of the world did nothing during the fighting. United Nations forces watched the army of Saddam Hussein murder Kurds. Finally, the United Nations told Iraq it could not fly over much of Iraqi Kurdistan. That at least stopped the Iraqi attack. Still, from time to time, the Kurds are attacked by forces from Turkey, Iraq, or Iran.

"We will never give up," says Jahan, her eyes blazing as bright as the fire. The flames flicker on her colorful clothes. They flicker on the faces of the men and children around the fire. "We will have our country."

Case Study Review

1. Who are the Kurds?
2. **Proposing Solutions** What do you think the United Nations should do if the Kurds are attacked again in northern Iraq? Explain your answer.

I. Reviewing Vocabulary

Match each word on the left with the correct definition on the right.

1. intifada
2. sanction
3. calligraphy
4. satellite

a. decision to cut off trade with a country until it changes its policies
b. the art of beautiful handwriting
c. protests and attacks by the Palestinians against Israeli rule
d. a spacecraft that orbits the earth

II. Understanding the Chapter

Answer the questions below on a separate sheet of paper.

1. How did OPEC's actions in the 1970s affect oil use in the West?
2. What was the cause of the Iran-Iraq war?
3. What role does calligraphy play in Middle Eastern art?
4. Explain the relationship between the Kurds and Iraq.

III. Building Skills: Predicting Consequences

Based on what you have learned in this chapter, predict the consequences, or results, of each of the hypothetical events below.

1. OPEC breaks up.
2. Qaddafi is overthrown by a pro-Western group of Libyans.
3. Israel changes direction and decides to break off the peace process with the Arabs.
4. Saddam Hussein launches a major attack to wipe out the Kurds.

IV. Working Together

Form small groups with your classmates. Each group should choose one of the conflicts or events described in this chapter. Create a short poem or rap song to explain the event or conflict. When you finish, present the poem or song to the class.

On Assignment. . .

Writing a Feature Story: Look at the questions and answers you wrote for each section. Check the answers for accuracy. Work with your partner to choose the information you will use in a feature story about a current issue in the Middle East. Make sure that you have answered the questions: *who? what? where? when? how?* and *why?* Next, write a headline for the story. You might also want to supply some pictures. Post your feature story on the classroom bulletin board.

UNIT 5 REVIEW

I. Understanding the Unit

Answer the questions below on a separate sheet of paper.

1. (a) What is the most important natural resource in the Middle East? (b) What role have rivers played in the history of the region?

2. (a) What are two cultural characteristics that most people in the Middle East share? (b) What are some other common cultural characteristics in the region?

3. Identify three ideas or contributions ancient Egyptians made to society that are still in use today.

4. (a) What modern nation arose from the remains of the Ottoman Empire in the 1920s? (b) What European nations took control over the rest of the Middle East? (c) Why did European interest in the Middle East grow in the 1920s and 1930s?

5. (a) Compare and contrast the following three Middle Eastern lifestyles: village life, nomadic life, and city life.

6. (a) Describe traditional life for the women in the Middle East. (b) How are women's lives changing in the Middle East?

7. (a) What is the source of the conflict between Israelis and Arabs? (b) What have been the results of the wars fought between them?

8. (a) What is OPEC and what is its goal? (b) How successful has OPEC been in meeting its goal?

II. Thinking Critically

Answer the questions below on a separate sheet of paper.

1. **Making Inferences** After Muhammad's death, the Islamic religion spread through much of North Africa and Asia. Why do you think so many people converted to Islam?

2. **Comparing and Contrasting** The discovery of oil in the Middle East has helped the economies of some countries more than others. Describe two cities or countries in the region: one that has benefited from oil and one that has not. How is life in these two places different? How is it similar?

3. **Predicting Consequences** Many Western nations participated in the Persian Gulf War in 1991 to liberate Kuwait from Iraqi occupation. Why do you think so many nations in the world got involved in the Persian Gulf War? What do you think might have happened to the world economy if Iraq had remained in control of Kuwait?

III. Writing to Learn

On a separate sheet of paper, write a three-paragraph essay about the following topic.

Imagine you are a reporter writing a story about life in the Middle East in the 20th century. Write an article describing how life has changed in the past 90 years. What was life like at the beginning of the century? How has the discovery of oil changed life? How has the creation of the nation of Israel changed the balance of power in the region? What do you think life in the Middle East would be like if these two events had not occurred?

IV. Practicing Skills: Interpreting a Bar Graph

Read the bar graph below. On a separate sheet of paper, answer the questions that follow.

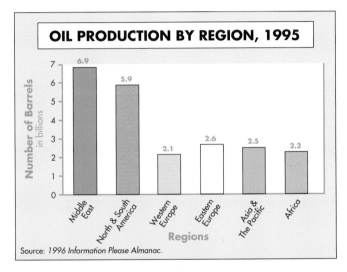

1. (a) How many barrels of oil did Western Europe produce in 1995?
   (b) How much more did Eastern Europe produce?
2. Which two regions of the world produced the most oil?
3. A generalization is a broad statement supported by facts. Make a generalization about oil production based on this bar graph.

V. Going Beyond the Unit

Work with four or five students to stage a debate on the Palestinian-Israeli conflict. Divide into two groups and assign sides for the debate. Each side should answer the following questions: (1) What is your historic claim to the land? (2) Why do you feel you deserve this land now? (3) What ideas do you have for bringing about a peaceful solution to the dispute? Each side should prepare the following: a five-minute presentation arguing its side, three questions it would like to ask the other side, and answers to possible questions from the other side. Perform your debate for the class.

The Growth of World Cities

Looking at Key Terms

service occupations, population density

In this book, you have seen how urbanization, the rapid growth of cities, has caused problems all over the world. A look at Istanbul, Turkey, today shows some of these problems. Istanbul is a crowded city. In some parts of the city, hundreds of thousands of people have no plumbing or running water.

However, there is another side to city life. Cities allow millions of people to live, work, and play in a space that may be no larger than a big cattle ranch in Argentina. The cities of the world support culture in all its forms, from museums and opera to TV studios, comedy clubs, and sports. In the city, a person can find a place to repair a violin, a television, or a torn ligament.

Istanbul is a good example of this other side to the city. Istanbul straddles two continents, Europe and Asia. Between the two parts of the city runs the body of water known as the Bosporus. Spanning the water is the world's busiest bridge. Above the bustle of traffic rises the magnificent dome of the Hagia Sophia mosque, built more than 1,400 years ago.

Where the Jobs Are

The main reason for urbanization is simple. Cities are where the jobs are. Most cities are centers of industry and business.

In addition to jobs in industries, there are jobs in **service occupations**. Service occupations are jobs that provide services to people. For every person who works in a factory, there are two others in service occupations. Grocers, teachers, doctors, and police are all service professionals.

Cheaper and Better Services

Why do people in cities have public transportation systems that are not available to people in rural areas? These services make sense only when **population density** is high. Population density is the number of people per square mile. If population density is low in an area, train or bus service would be too expensive to provide.

Almost all services, including education, health care, and police protection, can be provided more effectively in a city. For example, it is cheaper to provide power, water, and phone service to 100 families

Spanning two continents, Istanbul is more than a link between Asia and Europe. For thousands of years, it has served to bridge the cultures of Eastern Europe with those of West Asia.

living in one building than to the same number of people living on 100 separate farms.

More Chances in Life

Many world cities have large numbers of poor people. Nevertheless, as UN reports have pointed out, poor people in the city have more chances in life and live longer than poor people in rural areas. Newcomers to Istanbul are no exception. They look with awe at the concrete buildings on the outskirts of the city. Compared to the mud-baked homes they left behind in the country, these apartments look like mansions.

Review

1. Why is it cheaper to provide services to people in the city than to people in the country?
2. **Drawing Conclusions** What changes do you think a farmer would find between living in the country and living in the city?

Taking Action: Creating a Model

How will the city of the future look? How will buildings look? How will people move from one place to another? Make a drawing of a city in the year 2025.

UNIT 6

FOCUS ON

Europe & Eurasia

	500 B.C.	A.D. 1000	1200	1400
History	**500s B.C.** The citizens of Athens, Greece, create a democracy.	**476** The Roman Empire collapses.	**1215** King John of England signs the Magna Carta, limiting the king's power.	**1400s** Ivan III expands Russia's borders.
Culture & Society		**988** Christianity becomes the official religion of Kievan Russia.	**1095-1291** European Crusaders fight for the Holy Land.	**1350-1600** The Renaissance encourages new learning in Europe.
Economics & Technology		**1000** Better farming methods in Europe increase the food supply.		

498

PREVIEWING THE UNIT

Study the time line. On a separate sheet of paper answer the questions below.

1. How long did the European crusaders fight for the Holy Land?

2. When did the Reformation take place?

3. Which Russian leader tried to modernize the country?

4. Which war followed the Great Depression?

5. During which world war did the Holocaust occur?

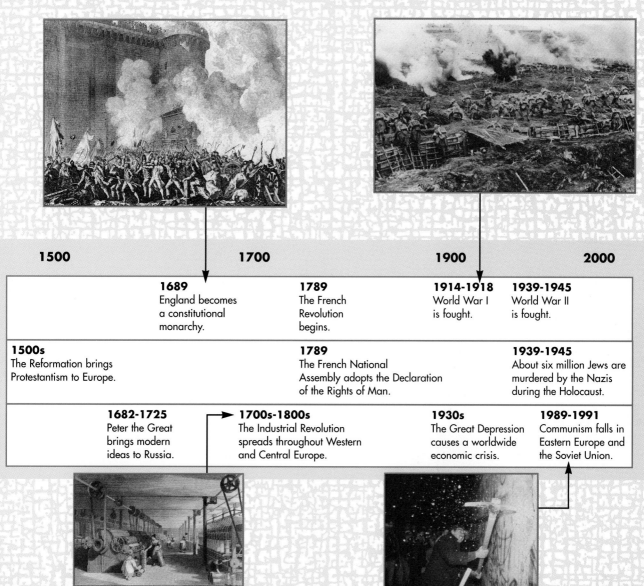

1500	1700	1900	2000

1689
England becomes a constitutional monarchy.

1789
The French Revolution begins.

1914-1918
World War I is fought.

1939-1945
World War II is fought.

1500s
The Reformation brings Protestantism to Europe.

1789
The French National Assembly adopts the Declaration of the Rights of Man.

1939-1945
About six million Jews are murdered by the Nazis during the Holocaust.

1682-1725
Peter the Great brings modern ideas to Russia.

1700s-1800s
The Industrial Revolution spreads throughout Western and Central Europe.

1930s
The Great Depression causes a worldwide economic crisis.

1989-1991
Communism falls in Eastern Europe and the Soviet Union.

Per Capita Income in Europe and Eurasia
Interpreting a Bar Graph

One way to look at Europe's economy is to study each country's per capita income. *Per capita income* means the average amount of money each person in a country makes in a year. Per capita income is usually a good indication of the strength of a country's economy or its standard of living. The higher the per capita income is, the higher the standard of living is. Below is a bar graph of the per capita income of selected European and Eurasian countries. Study the graph. On a separate sheet of paper, answer the questions below.

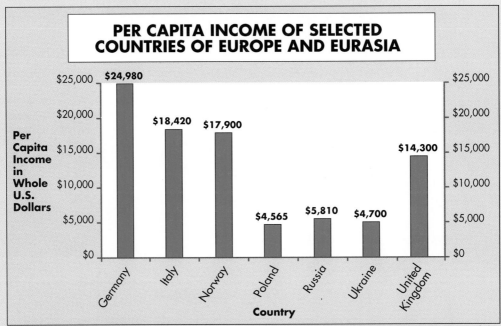

PER CAPITA INCOME OF SELECTED COUNTRIES OF EUROPE AND EURASIA

Per Capita Income in Whole U.S. Dollars

Germany $24,980
Italy $18,420
Norway $17,900
Poland $4,565
Russia $5,810
Ukraine $4,700
United Kingdom $14,300

Country

Source: *Information Please Almanac, World Almanac and Book Of Facts,* World Population Data Sheet of the Population Reference Bureau, *Time*

Did You Know

- Europe and Eurasia are rich in natural resources. (See Chapter 37.)

- Even the poorest country in Western Europe ranks among the top 30 countries in the world in income per person. (See Chapter 40.)

- The Soviet Union spent a great deal of money building up its military strength. (See Chapters 43 and 44.)

1. **Reading a Bar Graph** (a) What do the numbers on the left side of the bar graph represent? (b) What is the per capita income in the United Kingdom?

2. **Thinking About the Bar Graph** How much higher or lower is Poland's per capita income than that of the United Kingdom?

3. **Going Beyond the Bar Graph: Analyzing Information** Russia and Ukraine have had difficulties rebuilding their economies since the breakup of the Soviet Union. How is this reflected in the chart?

CHAPTER 37

The Land and People of Europe and Eurasia

What is unique about the land and people of Europe and the Eurasian Heartland?

Europe's cultural contributions are symbolized by the soaring spires of Mont-St.-Michel in France. Parts of this beautiful building were built as a monastery in the 1200s.

Looking at Key Terms

- **peninsula** a body of land that is surrounded on three sides by water
- **diverse** different or varied
- **warm-water port** a port that is ice-free all year
- **strait** a narrow body of water that connects two larger bodies of water
- **plateau** a flat area that is higher than the land that surrounds it
- **tundra** a level, treeless region with long winters
- **taiga** a large forest of the Eurasian Heartland
- **steppe** a large, treeless plain in the Eurasian Heartland that is very fertile
- **minority** less than half
- **democracy** government by all citizens
- **multilingual** able to speak more than one language

On Assignment...

Creating Posters: This chapter describes the land and people of Europe and the Eurasian Heartland. Imagine that you are working for a travel agency to promote tourism in the region. Your assignment is to design two posters for an advertising campaign. The theme of the campaign is "Visit a Beautiful and Diverse Region." As you read this chapter, look for the On Assignment boxes. These boxes contain ideas that will help you design your posters.

501

The Land of Europe and Eurasia

What geographic features influence life in Europe and the Eurasian Heartland?

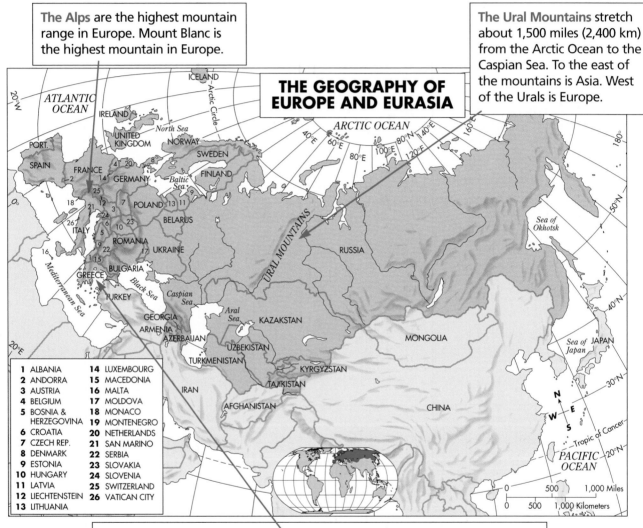

The Alps are the highest mountain range in Europe. Mount Blanc is the highest mountain in Europe.

The Ural Mountains stretch about 1,500 miles (2,400 km) from the Arctic Ocean to the Caspian Sea. To the east of the mountains is Asia. West of the Urals is Europe.

THE GEOGRAPHY OF EUROPE AND EURASIA

1 ALBANIA	**14** LUXEMBOURG
2 ANDORRA	**15** MACEDONIA
3 AUSTRIA	**16** MALTA
4 BELGIUM	**17** MOLDOVA
5 BOSNIA & HERZEGOVINA	**18** MONACO
6 CROATIA	**19** MONTENEGRO
7 CZECH REP.	**20** NETHERLANDS
8 DENMARK	**21** SAN MARINO
9 ESTONIA	**22** SERBIA
10 HUNGARY	**23** SLOVAKIA
11 LATVIA	**24** SLOVENIA
12 LIECHTENSTEIN	**25** SWITZERLAND
13 LITHUANIA	**26** VATICAN CITY

The Olympic Games began in Greece about 2,700 years ago. The games drew athletes from all over Greece and the Greek colonies. The games were held every four years at the temple of Zeus at Olympia.

Europe and the Heartland Most continents are land masses surrounded by water. Europe does not fit this pattern. Though Europe is a continent, it is not surrounded by water. You can see from the map above that Europe is a huge **peninsula** attached to an even larger land mass, the continent of Asia. A peninsula is a body of land that is surrounded on three sides by water.

The other part of the region discussed in this book is known as the Eurasian Heartland. The Eurasian Heartland is a term that has been given to the area that was once called the Soviet Union. This land stretches from the eastern border of Poland to the Pacific Ocean.

Rivers have played an important role in Europe's history. Europe's rivers are important because many are deep and wide enough for ships to sail on them. The Thames (temz) River in England is only about 200 miles (325 km) long. However, the Thames is one of the world's most important rivers because oceangoing ships can use it to reach London, one of the world's busiest ports.

The sunny fields of ripening grapes and the bleak cold of Siberia show how varied Europe's climate is. These grape fields are in the Bordeaux (bawr•DOH) region of France. Some of the best wines in the world come from Bordeaux. On the other hand, Siberia, a region in Russia, has some of the coldest and longest winters in the world. In many areas, winter begins in October and lasts until May. In winter, temperatures in Moscow drop to 45° F below zero (43° C below zero). Farther east, in northern Asia, it is even colder.

A Region With Few Borders

The geography of a region shapes the lives of its people. Look carefully at the map of the region on pages 602–603. Note that there are few natural borders across the north from the Atlantic Ocean deep into Siberia.

This lack of natural borders has left Europe and the Heartland open to invaders. Most of the region's countries have been attacked many times by people from Europe and Asia. Russia and its neighbors to the west have fought many wars over territory on the North European Plain. Germany and France have also fought wars over territory on the plain.

Small Places, Huge Spaces

Europe is a very **diverse**, or varied, place. It has many countries within a small land area. Europe's landforms also are diverse. Within a small area, there are plains, hills, and mountains.

The Eurasian Heartland is very different from Western and Central Europe. In the Eurasian Heartland, huge forests and plains stretch for thousands of miles. The Heartland also contains several huge countries. Ukraine is larger than any country in Western Europe. Kazakstan (KAH•zak•stan) is four times larger than Ukraine. Russia is more than six times larger than Kazakstan. It is the largest country in the world.

River Highways

Mighty rivers flow in all directions through Europe and the Heartland. Many of Europe's rivers have served as highways for centuries. They have made trade possible over large areas. They also serve as routes for moving raw materials to factories. The Seine (sehn) flows through Paris, the capital of France, on its journey to the Atlantic Ocean. Rouen (roo•EHN), one of France's most important ports, is on the Seine near the Atlantic.

Rotterdam, in southwestern Netherlands, is one of the world's major seaports. From its busy docks, the products of Germany's Ruhr valley are shipped to the rest of the world.

The Rhine (reyen) is Germany's most important river. Ships have traveled the Rhine for centuries. For more on the place of the Rhine in European history, see Case Study 37.

Europe's longest river is Russia's mighty Volga. The Volga flows for 2,194 miles (3,531 km) from Russia's northern woodlands to the Caspian Sea in the south. Like other rivers in Russia, the Volga is frozen during the winter months.

Many Ports, Few Ports

Most countries in Europe have some territory along the coast. A jagged coastline and Western Europe's mild climate have given it many excellent **warm-water ports**. A warm-water port can be used all year because the sea around it never freezes.

Rotterdam, in the Netherlands, is the busiest port in the world. Many products from Belgium, Germany, Switzerland, and France are shipped along the Rhine to Rotterdam. There they are put on ships and sent to other continents. Germany also uses its ports of Hamburg and Bremen for shipping. France's most important port is Marseilles (mahr•SAY) on the Mediterranean Sea. Find these ports on the map on pages 602–603.

On the other hand, Eastern Europe and the Heartland have fewer good ports. To the south, there are few outlets to the open seas or oceans. To the north, the ports are blocked much of the year by mountains of ice. For example, St. Petersburg in Russia is blocked by so much ice during winter that it is possible to walk from the shore to islands miles from shore.

Ukraine's largest port, Odessa, is on the Black Sea, a large inland sea. Ships leaving Odessa pass through two narrow **straits** in Turkey to reach the Mediterranean Sea. A strait is a narrow body of water that connects two larger bodies of water.

Western Europe's ports have helped create a lively exchange of goods and ideas. Areas further east have depended far less on seagoing trade.

The Regions of Europe

Geographers divide Europe into four major regions. One of these regions, the North European Plain, stretches far into the Eurasian Heartland. The three other regions are the Northwest Mountain region, the Central Uplands, and the Alpine Mountains.

The Northwest Mountain Region The Northwest Mountain region includes Ireland and northern Great Britain. It also includes northwest France, Norway, northern Finland, and the northwest corner of Russia. The mountains of northwestern Europe have been worn down by wind and rain over hundreds of thousands of years. For the most part, the region's soil is thin and not fertile.

The North European Plain The North European Plain is narrow in the west and widens as it stretches eastward. Most of the land is flat or has gently rolling hills. It contains some of the world's most fertile farmland. The Ural Mountains cut through the plain in a north-south direction.

The Alps, which stretch from southern France to Croatia, are sometimes called "Europe's backbone." Here, the Clausen Pass cuts through majestic peaks in Switzerland.

One of your posters should describe one of the four geographic regions of Europe. You might highlight the natural beauty of the Alps. Write words and phrases that would attract travelers to Europe. Make a sketch of the picture you might use.

The Central Uplands The Central Uplands lie south of the North European Plain. They are made up of hills, low mountains, and small **plateaus**. A plateau is a flat area that is higher than the land that surrounds it. The Central Uplands include land in Spain, Portugal, France, Germany, and the Czech (chehk) Republic. The Uplands have fertile soil and large deposits of coal.

The Alpine Mountains The Alpine Mountains run throughout Europe. They have been called Europe's "backbone and ribs." The "backbone" is the Alps, which stretch through eight countries. Vacationers swim in the clear mountain lakes in summer and ski the glistening white slopes in winter.

The "ribs" are mountain ranges that extend in every direction from the Alps. One "rib" is the Pyrenees (PEER•uh•neez) range. It forms the border between France and Spain. Other "ribs" are in Italy and the Balkans.

Section 1 Review

1. What are Europe's four major geographic areas?

2. **Drawing Conclusions** Why are ports in Eastern Europe and the Heartland less busy than ports in Western Europe?

SECTION 2

Resources

How do the resources of Europe and the Heartland influence life in the region?

The greatest natural resource of Europe and the Heartland is its land. In the west, the European plain has some of the world's most fertile farmland.

Three great belts of plant life cover the Heartland. In the far north is the **tundra**. Here the winters are so long and cold that only mosses and small plants can grow. South of the tundra is a huge belt of evergreen forest called the **taiga**, stretching in every direction to the horizon. The Heartland has one fourth of the world's forests.

South of the taiga is a grassland called the **steppe**. The steppe has some of the world's most fertile soil. However, long winters leave farmers with a short growing season. Farmers also must worry about getting enough rain for their crops. Still, the land is so fertile that the steppe is one of the world's best wheat-producing areas.

Europe's Wealth

Some of the best soils in Western Europe are in its river valleys. Farmers in the Po River valley in Italy grow fruits, olives, grapes, and other crops. Another rich farming area is in the Netherlands. Even in the cooler northern regions, the soil is so rich that farmers can grow many crops.

The rivers of Europe and the Heartland are another valuable resource. Many of the rivers have dams that produce electric power. Some of the world's largest electricity-producing dams are in Norway and Russia.

Europe has large underground supplies of fuels such as coal, oil, and natural gas. There are large coal fields in Poland, Germany, France, and Britain. Large deposits of oil and natural gas lie under the North Sea off the coasts of Britain, Norway, and Denmark.

It is not easy to get this oil and natural gas out of the ground. Workers must live and work on huge platforms called oil rigs that are set out in the North Sea. They work 12-hour shifts, 24 hours a day.

Section 2 Review

1. Which is a better farming area: the taiga or the steppe?
2. **Comparing and Contasting** Compare Europe and the Heartland for the following: length of growing season, forest resources, and use of water power.

SECTION 3

People of Europe and Eurasia

What are the major ethnic differences in Europe and the Eurasian Heartland?

About 500 million people live in the area between the Atlantic Ocean and the Ural Mountains. That is about nine percent of the world's population. About 290 million people live in Russia and the Heartland.

Patterns of Settlement

The land between the Netherlands and the city of Munich is one of the most densely populated regions on earth. The southern part of the British Isles and parts of France, Italy, and Spain also are densely populated.

Other parts of Western Europe are less densely populated. The Alps, the highlands of Spain, and the northern parts of Scandinavia have few people.

In general, the Heartland is not heavily populated. However, there are large centers of population around St. Petersburg, Moscow, and Kiev (kee•EHF).

An Urban Region

Western Europe is a region of great cities. Its largest cities are Paris (8.7 million people) and London (9.1 million). The largest city in Europe and the Heartland is Moscow, capital of Russia (10.5 million people).

The Role of Democracy

Europe is the birthplace of democracy. The world's first democracies were cities in ancient Greece. Today most of the countries of Western Europe are democracies.

Most Eastern European countries are trying to build democratic governments. They suffer from economic hardship and division among their people. Economic problems have also made it especially difficult to build democracy in Russia.

Western European Ethnic Groups

In Europe, people from many different ethnic groups live in a very small region. Some, like the French, have their own nation. There are many small ethnic groups, though, that do not have their own nation. They are a **minority**, or less than half, of the people in these countries.

People in the East

Further east, more than 80 percent of Russia's 149 million people belong to the Russian ethnic group. Another 25 million Russians live in other countries in the region.

About 30 million of the people in Russia belong to more than 100 different ethnic groups. There are many small ethnic groups, too. Only a few of these have their own homeland.

Section 3 Review

1. Which part of Europe is the most densely populated?
2. **Hypothesizing** Why do you think that the Soviet Union did not stay together?

Today's Greeks are proud heirs to a civilization that is thousands of years old. The Greeks were the first people to develop the idea of **democracy**, or government by all citizens. Greek civilization lasted for hundreds of years. Then, the Greeks were conquered by the Romans. For more than a thousand years, the Greeks lived under foreign rule. Yet the Greeks preserved their culture over many centuries. The Greeks did not regain their independence until the 1820s. Today in Greece, old customs live side by side with those of the 1990s.

The ancestors of today's Irish people arrived in Ireland well over 2,000 years ago. The sport of hurling, shown at right, dates from those ancient times. The Irish first became Christians about 1,500 years ago. Today most Irish people are Roman Catholic. The original Irish language is called Irish Gaelic. Today it is spoken in only small parts of the country. Most of the people in Ireland speak English. In fact, some of the greatest writers in the English language have been Irish.

The people in Europe speak many languages. In Switzerland, you might need to speak three languages: German, French, and Italian. The native language of the largest percentage of Swiss is German. In the western part of the country, the native language is French. In the southeast, it is Italian. Of course, most Swiss citizens are **multilingual**. *Multilingual* means "able to speak more than one language." Although Switzerland is made up of three different ethnic groups, its people get along very well. Ethnic groups are people who share a culture. Switzerland is a stable, democratic country.

Europe's Balkan Peninsula has long seen violence between ethnic groups. In 1992, the country of Yugoslavia split apart. Violence immediately broke out in an area called Bosnia between Muslim, Serb, and Croat groups. One of the differences between these groups is religion. The Serbs are Orthodox Christian. The Croats are Roman Catholic. Violence in Bosnia has claimed thousands of lives and caused great destruction.

The Rhine in European Life

The historic castles that perch on the cliffs over the Rhine River are reminders of a day when the Rhine was a major highway for invading armies traveling through Europe.

When people think of the Rhine, they think of great German castles on cliffs high above the river's waters. They picture small German villages along its shores that look as though they have not changed in hundreds of years.

It makes sense to think of Germany when we think of the Rhine. It is Germany's most important river.

However, the Rhine is also a European river. It begins as a crystal-clear stream high in the Swiss Alps. On its 820-mile (1,300 km) journey to the North Sea, it passes through the heart of Western Europe. The Rhine's waters touch six countries. Then it ends its journey at Rotterdam in the Netherlands.

History and Legend

The Rhine is connected to centuries of history and legends. Traveling downstream near the German town of Speyer, travelers see a huge cathedral. It towers over the river and the town. Here, during the early 1500s, the followers of Martin Luther first took the name Protestants. (See Chapter 38.)

An industrial zone begins just beyond Speyer. For miles, the riverbanks are covered by factories, power stations, and docks. Heavy trucks move up and down the shore. On the river, long barges move slowly past each other.

Further downstream, the beautiful Rhine gorge begins. Castles that were built in the Middle Ages top many of the hills and cliffs. Over the centuries, most of the castles were damaged or destroyed. Today, many have been rebuilt. Some once again are homes of the wealthy. Others are hotels that welcome tourists.

The Rhine gorge ends at the city of Cologne (kuh•LOHN). Cologne's great cathedral has two steeples that are more than 500 feet (150 m) high. That is higher than the highest cliff in the gorge.

The Rhine plays a major part in the economy of Europe. It carries more cargo than any river in the world. The leading port of Europe, Rotterdam, is located near its mouth. Today the Rhine's network of rivers and canals stretches from the North Sea to the Black and Mediterranean seas. The Rhine River truly plays a central role in European life.

Case Study Review

1. What historic places are located along the Rhine River?
2. **Analyzing Information** Why is the Rhine River important to the people of Germany?

I. Reviewing Vocabulary

Match each word on the left with the correct definition on the right.

1. plateau   **a.** a narrow body of water that connects two larger bodies of water
2. peninsula   **b.** a flat area that is higher than the land that surrounds it
3. diverse   **c.** a body of land that is surrounded on three sides by water
4. strait   **d.** different or varied

II. Understanding the Chapter

Answer the questions below on a separate sheet of paper.

1. Why are rivers important to the economies of the people of Europe and the Eurasian Heartland?
2. What are Europe's "backbone and ribs"?
3. Which is more densely populated, Western Europe or the Eurasian Heartland?
4. Why is the steppe better farmland than the taiga?

III. Building Skills: Identifying Cause and Effect

In each of the pairs below, tell which is the cause and which is the effect.

1. **a.** extremely cold winters
   b. unusable ports
2. **a.** mild weather
   b. grape-growing region
3. **a.** ethnic violence in Bosnia
   b. differences between Serbs, Croats, and Muslims

IV. Working Together

Form a small group. With the group, write dramatic headlines for a newspaper or a travel magazine about key facts you have learned in this chapter about the land and people of Europe and the Eurasian Heartland. Each headline should use colorful words that will make the reader want to read the story. On the other hand, the headline should be brief—not more than six or seven words. With other members of your class, make a bulletin board display of your headlines.

On Assignment...

Creating Posters: Put together the two poster sketches you created as you read this chapter. Choose one of the two sketches and finish it. The words you choose and the ideas you have should interest tourists in the beauty of this region.

CHAPTER 38

The Roots of European Civilization

How have the traditions and values of European civilization helped shape our world today?

While a few nobles held fabulous wealth in medieval Europe, many peasants led hard lives. In this painting from the 1400s, the French Duke of Berry feasts and exchanges gifts with his friends.

Looking At Key Terms

- **city-state**   a political unit made up of a town and the area around it
- **republic**   a form of government in which citizens elect their leaders
- **feudalism**   a system in which a person gave loyalty to a lord in return for protection
- **serf**   a peasant during the Middle Ages who lived and worked on a manor
- **anti-Semitism**   hatred of Jews
- **nation-state**   a unified country
- **absolute monarchy**   a system in which one person has total rule
- **constitutional monarchy**   a system in which a monarch's power is limited by law
- **capitalism**   a system in which people, not government, make economic decisions

On Assignment. . . .

Creating a Storyboard: A storyboard is a plan of action in pictures. It is made up of cartoons or sketches. Filmmakers use storyboards to plan the scenes of a movie. At three points in this chapter, there are boxes to help you sketch storyboard panels about European history. Each box will deal with an important period or event in European history. At the end of the chapter, you will put the storyboard together.

513

The World of Ancient Europe

What importance does the ancient world have for us today?

High on the Acropolis (uh•KRAH•puh•luhs), a hill over the city of Athens, stands an ancient temple called the Parthenon. Although today the Parthenon is in ruins, it is still possible to see its beauty. The Parthenon and other fine buildings were built by the ancient Greeks. They founded the first great European civilization.

The Greek City-States

The Greeks learned from earlier civilizations in the Mediterranean region. Around 800 B.C., the Greeks made some great advances. One of those advances was a new way to govern **city-states**. A city-state consisted of a town and the area around it.

On Assignment...

Draw a sketch of a public meeting in ancient Athens that was called to decide important matters. You might show Pericles making a speech to his fellow citizens.

The Dawn of Democracy

At first, kings and wealthy nobles ruled the Greek city-states. Then some city-states created a new form of government called democracy. Democracy got its start in the city-state of Athens in the 500s B.C. The citizens of Athens had freedoms and rights that had never been seen in the ancient world. They could take part in public meetings that decided important matters for their city. Their greatest leader, Pericles, (PEHR•uh•kleez) described democracy as government "not in the hands of the few but of the many."

Athens was one of the wonders of the ancient world. Towering above the city is the Acropolis, the hill that was the city's central meeting point. On the Acropolis stands the Parthenon, an ancient temple.

Not all Athenians were citizens. Women, slaves, and foreigners had no political rights. Still, Greek democracy was the first giant step toward the goal of self-government.

The Questioning Spirit

Greek culture was based on two attitudes not found in other ancient cultures. First, the Greeks believed in thinking based on logic. Second, they believed that each individual person had worth.

The Greeks were the first people to believe that it is possible to understand the world. They believed they could use logic to understand the laws of nature.

Greece Is Unified

In the 300s B.C., King Philip of Macedonia took control of the Greek city-states. Macedonia is just north of Greece. Later, Philip's son, Alexander the Great, conquered a huge empire. Although the empire fell apart after Alexander's death, his conquests spread Greek culture to many parts of the ancient world.

Growth of the Roman Empire

In 500 B.C., the city-state of Rome, in Italy, won its independence. The Romans then established a **republic**. A republic is a form of government in which citizens elect leaders to represent them.

During the 400s B.C., the Romans established a code of laws. Roman law had two important principles of justice. The first was equality before the law. This meant that all citizens should be treated equally. The second was that all citizens accused of a crime were considered innocent until proven guilty.

By the middle of the 200s B.C., Rome had conquered most of Italy. In the next 200 years, Rome conquered most of the land along the shores of the Mediterranean Sea. However, about this time, the republic was replaced by a monarchy. Rome became the Roman Empire.

The Roman Empire built thousands of miles of paved roads. Its army and navy made the roads and the seas safe for travelers. This allowed trade to grow throughout the empire. The Romans were excellent engineers who built long aqueducts to carry water to their cities.

The Romans set up a government that could run a vast empire. Centuries later their methods were copied by other European powers.

Christianity and Rome

Shortly after Rome became an empire, a teacher named Jesus of Nazareth began preaching in the province of Judea (joo•DEE•uh), in Palestine. Judea was the homeland of the Jewish people. The Jews were the first people to believe in one God. Their religion required that each person have the strength to choose good over evil and live a moral life.

Jesus told people to love God and their fellow human beings. He also spoke of a new age of love and justice under God's rule.

A new religion called Christianity, which was based on Jesus's teachings, began to spread. At first the Romans did not interfere with Christianity. Then they worried that it was becoming too strong. The Romans began persecuting Christians. Many Christians were murdered. Yet the new religion won new followers all across the empire.

Decline in the West

After A.D. 180, the Roman Empire weakened. In 286, the emperor split the Roman Empire in half. The western half of the empire was governed from Rome. The eastern half was governed from the city of Byzantium (bih•ZAN•tee•uhm), in what is today the country of Turkey. Later, the city was renamed Constantinople.

The western part of the empire continued to weaken. It was attacked by waves of tribes from the north. In A.D. 476, the emperor in

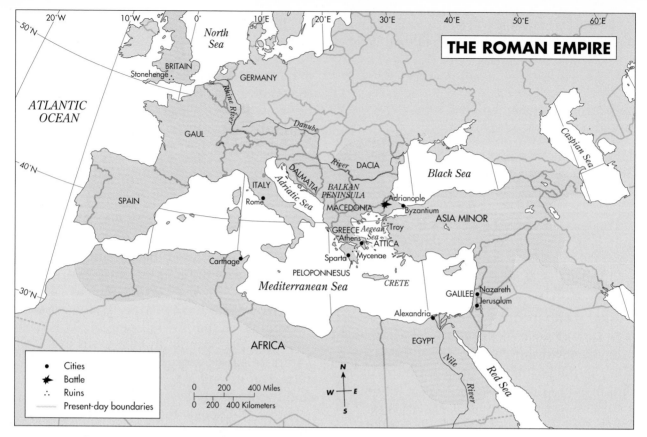

THE ROMAN EMPIRE

Interaction The Roman Empire expanded mostly through war. At its height in the A.D. 100s, Rome was prosperous and stable. On which continents did the Romans control land?

Rome was overthrown. The years that followed saw unrest and violence. This unrest had a great cost. Much of the ancient learning of the Romans was lost.

In the east, the Byzantine Empire survived for another 1,000 years. The Byzantine Empire was based on Greek culture, Roman law and government, and the Greek Orthodox religion. It preserved much of the learning of the Greek and Roman worlds.

Section 1 Review

1. What was unique about government in ancient Greece?

2. **Making Inferences** How did the government of Greece differ from the governments of other ancient peoples?

SECTION 2

The Beginnings of Modern Europe

How did a modern Europe emerge from the Middle Ages?

The period from the fall of Rome to the mid-1400s is called the Middle Ages. During that period, three traditions came together to produce a great civilization. They were Christianity, the learning of the Greek and Roman world, and the customs of the Germanic tribes.

In the 800s, there was a brief attempt to reunite the west. A king named Charlemagne (SHAHR•luh•mayn) conquered a large part of Europe. However, shortly after his death in 814, his empire fell apart.

Feudalism

After Charlemagne's empire collapsed, governments throughout Europe were weak. Invaders swept over much of the countryside. People had to put themselves under the protection of powerful landowners.

The need for protection led to a system called **feudalism**. Under feudalism, nobles gave loyalty to more powerful lords. In return, the nobles received land and protection. The nobles in turn protected the peasants who lived on their land. Many peasants called **serfs** worked the land of nobles. The serfs were bound to the land.

There was little trade or contact with the outside world. Most peasants never traveled more then ten miles from their homes.

The Church in the Middle Ages

The most important organization in Europe during the Middle Ages was the Catholic Church. The center of the Church was Rome. However, Catholic churches and priests were in towns and villages all over Europe. The Church taught reading and writing to boys who planned to become priests or monks. It also helped preserve Greek and Roman learning.

In the Middle Ages, the idea of religious freedom was unknown. A religious group that suffered because of this were Jews. **Anti-Semitism**, which is hatred of Jews, became common.

Europe Starts to Modernize

After about A.D. 1000, conditions in Europe improved. Better farming methods increased the food supply. Towns expanded. Farmers sold their surplus food to people in the towns. The townspeople in turn sold goods they made to local farmers.

As the roads became safer, trade increased. Merchants sent goods to distant customers. Shopkeepers and craftspeople in towns prospered.

The Crusades

The Crusades were military campaigns to free Jerusalem and the Holy Land from Muslim control. The Holy Land was the part of the Middle East where Jesus had taught. The Crusades were possible because of Europe's new strength and wealth. The first Crusade, from 1096 to 1099, was successful. It ended with the capture of Jerusalem.

However, the Muslims mounted their own campaigns. In the 1100s, Muslim forces recaptured Jerusalem and the Holy Land. New Crusades failed to defeat them. The contacts Crusaders made, though, led to increased trade with Asia. This led to more

As trade expanded, European cities began to grow and prosper. Cities such as Seville, which had been small in medieval times, became busy centers of trade and culture.

economic growth in Europe. Through contacts with the Arab world, Europeans learned of advances in mathematics and science.

The Renaissance

By 1300, cities in Italy that controlled the trade routes to the east were prospering. Many merchant families grew wealthy in cities such as Florence and Venice. These people were interested in art, literature, and music. They hired artists to create statues and paintings. They built beautiful buildings. This period came to be known as the Renaissance (REH•nuh•sanhs). The word *renaissance* means "rebirth" in French. The Renaissance began in Italy and spread throughout Western Europe. It lasted from about 1350 to 1600.

During the Renaissance, Europeans gained a new outlook on the world. This outlook was based on the learning of the ancient Greeks and Romans. Renaissance thinkers believed that human beings could achieve great things. Giovanni Pico della Mirandola, a thinker of the Renaissance, summed up the ideas of the times when he said, "Men can do all things if they will."

The Renaissance produced some of the greatest artists in history. They included Michelangelo (mih•kuhl•AN•juh•loh) and Leonardo da Vinci (lay•uh•NAHR•doh dah VIHN•chee). Few works of art can match Michelangelo's statue *Pietà* or da Vinci's painting Mona Lisa.

Religious Changes

The changes that were sweeping Europe by 1500 led to an event called the Reformation. The Reformation began as a protest against corruption in the Catholic Church. It ended by splitting the Western Christian world. Some parts of Europe remained Roman Catholic. Other areas, protesting against corruption, adopted new forms of Christianity called Protestantism.

On Assignment. . .

Find a picture of one of the works of da Vinci or Michelangelo. Use it to sketch a storyboard of the artist at work. Write a caption that tells how the Renaissance differed from earlier times.

The Reformation began in 1517 in Germany. That year, a monk named Martin Luther attacked the Church for being corrupt. Luther's protest spread, and kings and princes started taking sides. Wars broke out between Catholics and Protestants.

As the struggle raged, the Roman Catholic Church began a reform movement. It was called the Counter-Reformation. Its goals were to reform the Church and to roll back Protestantism. However, Europe remained divided between the Catholic and Protestant churches.

Section 2 Review

1. What were the Crusades?
2. **Drawing Conclusions** Why did feudalism develop?

SECTION 3

Expanding Europe

How did Europe leave its mark on the rest of the world?

For the most part, Europe was cut off from the rest of the world during much of the Middle Ages. This changed in the late 1400s when Europeans began to travel the earth.

The Age of Exploration

The reasons for travel were mainly economic. Europeans wanted to trade with Asia for spices, silks, and other products. However, in 1453 the Turks conquered Constantinople. This closed the main trade route from Europe to Asia. The search for a new route to the east began.

The Europeans found new routes because they developed better ships and better methods of sailing. By the late 1400s, their ships had sails instead of oars. They had tools such as compasses to show direction when they were sailing. These and other advances let European ships sail far from the coastline into the open sea.

Portuguese sailors found one route to Asia by sailing around Africa. They reached India in 1498. By then, Spanish explorers led by Christopher Columbus had crossed the Atlantic Ocean in search of an all-water route to Asia. Of course, they did not reach Asia. Instead, they began Europe's settlement of North and South America.

A wave of European expansion followed during the 1500s and 1600s. The Spanish and Portuguese conquered most of South America. The French, British, and Spanish built colonial empires in North America.

At the same time, Europeans sailed to Asia to trade in India, China, and elsewhere. European exploration created the world's first global trading network. European nations also fought wars as they competed for colonies.

The Rise of Nation-States

One reason that Europe could expand was that several European countries had become very powerful. By the 1600s, England, France, and Spain had strong central governments. This type of unified country is called a **nation-state**.

Kings were largely responsible for creating these nation-states. Kings increased their power at the expense of the nobles. When kings were successful in doing this, the governments were called **absolute monarchies**. In an absolute monarchy, one person rules the country.

A good example of an absolute monarch was Louis XIV (say: LOO•ee the Fourteenth)

In the late 1400s, Europe entered an "Age of Discovery." From ports such as Lisbon, shown here, European ships set out on voyages of exploration across the oceans.

of France. He ruled from 1643 to 1715. Louis set out to reduce the power of the nobility by increasing the power of the middle class. He appointed middle-class men to high office. Louis never missed a chance to show his power. He is supposed to have said, "I am the state."

Limits to Absolute Power in England

Other European kings tried to rule as absolute monarchs. One country in which they did not succeed was England. In England, there were laws and traditions that guaranteed people certain rights. In 1215, English nobles forced King John to sign a document known as the Magna Carta. It placed limits on the king's power.

Over the centuries, a body called Parliament gained power. Parliament had two houses. Its lower house, or House of Commons, was elected by "commoners." These were men who were not nobles but who owned some property. Only men who owned property were allowed to vote.

During the 1600s, England's king and Parliament struggled for power. Civil war broke out. Parliament won and, in 1649, the leaders of Parliament voted to execute the king, Charles I. For a time, Parliament governed without a king. After a new king regained power, the struggle continued. Parliament again removed the king.

In 1689, William and Mary, England's new king and queen, accepted the Bill of Rights. It gave Parliament certain powers, including the right to control taxes. It also granted the people rights, such as the right to trial by jury. Thus, England became a **constitutional monarchy**. Under this system, a monarch shares power with an elected legislature. That power is limited by law.

The Commercial Revolution

Along with political change, Europe saw important economic changes after 1500. New discoveries led to increased trade. The population grew, as did cities and towns.

More farmers raised crops for market. Industries such as cloth making and printing grew quickly. They produced more and more goods for a growing market.

Out of this, the modern economic system of **capitalism** began to emerge. Under capitalism, private individuals decide what to produce and what price to charge. They risk their own money to make a profit. We call these people capitalists.

Section 3 Review

1. Which European country developed a constitutional monarchy?
2. **Identifying Relationships**   How did increased travel and trade change the nations of Europe?

SECTION 4

Developments in the East

What different paths to modern times did Central Europe take?

While Western Europe progressed, Central Europe faced many problems. Germany, the Balkans, and Poland went through hard times. Germany's greatest problem was that it did not have a strong central government. It was divided into more than 300 different states. At the head of these states was a person with the title of emperor. However, the emperor had little power over the states. In addition, Germany was split about equally between Catholics and Protestants. They fought a war between 1546 and 1555 that did not resolve their differences.

In 1618, another war, called the Thirty Years' War, broke out. It began as a struggle between Protestants and Catholics. Then foreign countries entered the war. The war finally ended in 1648 with little settled. However, Germany lay in ruins.

In the Balkan Peninsula, a foreign conqueror was the biggest problem. During the second half of the 1300s, the Turkish empire overran the region. The Turks were a Muslim people from Asia. The people of the Balkans were Christians. By the 1520s, the Turks held all of the Balkans and most of Hungary. It took almost 400 years for some Balkan nations to recover their independence.

In the 1500s, Poland controlled a huge chunk of Eastern Europe. However, Polish power gradually declined. Polish nobles could not work together. Poland lost its strong government. In the 1660s, Poland lost some of its territory. Between the 1760s and 1790s, its neighbors divided the country among themselves. By 1795, the country of Poland no longer existed.

Section 4 Review

1. Why did Germany remain a divided country in the 1500s and 1600s?

2. **Comparing and Contrasting** What problems did Germany and Poland have in common? How were their problems different?

SECTION 5

The Rise of Modern Europe

How did the Europe of 200 years ago shape events in Europe today?

Between the mid-1500s and 1700, Europe made great progress in science. Such scientists as Galileo (gal•uh•LAY•oh) and Sir Isaac Newton forever changed how we look at the universe.

The Enlightenment

The work of scientists like Galileo and Newton set the stage for the period known as the Enlightenment. Enlightenment thinkers believed that they could learn about human society in the same way as scientists learned about nature. They also believed that they could use that knowledge to improve the world.

The Enlightenment lasted from the 1690s to the late 1700s. The first great Enlightenment thinker was an Englishman named John Locke. He wrote that all people had certain natural rights, which he called life, liberty, and property.

One of the greatest Enlightenment thinkers was a Swiss named Jean-Jacques Rousseau (ZHAN ZHAHK roo•SOH). Rousseau mistrusted any government. He believed that people became free by working for the good of the whole community.

The French Revolution

The Enlightenment helped to weaken the idea of absolute monarchy. France's nobles and middle class began to demand a share of power.

Revolution in France began in June 1789, when a body called the National Assembly first met. It was controlled by members of the middle class. On July 14 of that year, about 900 working people in Paris stormed a prison called the Bastille. In the countryside, peasants attacked nobles.

In August 1789, the assembly adopted the Declaration of the Rights of Man. It says, "Men are born and remain free and equal in rights." The slogan of the revolution soon became "Liberty, Equality, Fraternity (Brotherhood)."

Power in the assembly soon shifted to its more extreme members. Wealthy French people began fleeing the country. They asked Europe's kings to invade France and end the revolution.

War between France and Britain and a number of its allies broke out in 1792. The

The Bastille, the symbol of the power of the French kings, was attacked by an angry mob on July 14, 1789. Its fall marked the beginning of the French Revolution.

extreme members who were in control of the revolution then removed King Louis XVI from the throne. France became a republic. In 1793, the extremists executed the king and queen.

The disorder caused disagreements among the extremists. The most extreme group decided to use force to keep power. They began the Reign of Terror, during which thousands of people were arrested and executed. The rights of the people were ignored. Anyone criticizing the government risked arrest.

By mid-1794, France had defeated its foreign enemies in battle. At home, the people turned against the extremists. Their leaders were arrested and executed. Moderates took over the government.

The extreme part of the French Revolution was over. However, the revolution's ideals of equality and liberty were already spreading across Europe.

The Age of Napoleon

In 1799, a young army general seized power in France. A few years later he made himself emperor of France. His name was Napoleon Bonaparte. Napoleon restored order to France. He also began a campaign of conquest. Napoleon was a brilliant general. Within a few years, France controlled much of Western Europe.

Although Napoleon was a dictator, he believed in some of the ideals of the revolution. He introduced a code of laws that guaranteed all people equality. Napoleon's conquests carried the ideas of the revolution beyond France to other European countries.

Eventually Napoleon was defeated. France returned to its old borders. However, the ideals of the French Revolution continued to influence both European and world history.

The Industrial Revolution

A second revolution, which began in the late 1700s, changed Europe forever. It is known as the "Industrial Revolution." The Industrial Revolution changed the way people worked and made the things society needs.

The Industrial Revolution made it possible to increase by an enormous amount what workers could produce. Goods also could be produced much more cheaply.

The Factory System

The Industrial Revolution began in England. There, machines were invented to do work that had been done by hand. The most important machine was the steam engine, which used steam to power machines that made items. The new machines were expensive and only wealthy people could afford them. This led to the growth of large factories where the machines were located.

In the early days of the Industrial Revolution, working conditions in the factories were poor. Men, women, and children worked long hours for low wages. Working conditions were unsafe and unhealthy.

Factories led to the growth of cities. Because cities grew so fast, living conditions were bad. Tens of thousands of people squeezed into overcrowded slums.

The Reform Movement

Over the years, the English government slowly made reforms. A law in 1833 limited the workday of children in factories. It also made young children attend school two hours a day. A law in 1842 said that women, girls, and young boys could not work underground in mines. In 1847, Parliament said that women and children could not work more than 10 hours a day in factories. Slowly, living and working conditions improved.

On Assignment...

For the final panel of your storyboard, draw a picture that shows a few scenes from the Industrial Revolution. Try to show both the achievements and problems of the Industrial Revolution.

The Industrial Revolution Spreads

From England, the Industrial Revolution spread to Western Europe and the United States. Everywhere there were problems similar to those in England. However, the Industrial Revolution also increased the wealth of countries. For the first time, ordinary people could have a decent standard of living and most people's lives improved.

Section 5 Review

1. How did the Industrial Revolution change the way people worked?
2. **Making Inferences** Why do violent times, such as the Reign of Terror, sometimes occur during revolutions?

In textile mills like this one in England, many of the tasks that were formerly done by hand in the home were now done by machines. In this picture, women, who worked long hours for low pay, tended the machines.

Women in the Industrial Revolution

I first saw the coal pits at night. As I rode over a hill, I suddenly saw before me strange lights in every direction. They only seemed to make the darkness deeper. Out of the darkness came groans and other sad sounds.

As I got closer, I saw a wild landscape. It was the coal pits. There were fires everywhere. The groans I had heard were the sounds of machines drawing up the coal. Nearby, there were steam engines clearing the pits of water. Everywhere there were young people climbing into the pits. From head to toe, they were covered by black dust.

This is the way that Penny Clarke remembered her first day at work in the coal mines of England. Penny went to work at the mines when she was nine years old. She worked there, six days a week, twelve hours a day, until she was seventeen.

Although these conditions were harsh, Penny was happy to have the job. It was either work or starve. Some of her friends starved.

The Industrial Revolution changed the lives and roles of women. At first many women and children worked in factories and mines. One reason owners hired them was that they could pay women and children less than they paid men.

Before reforms began, women worked twelve to sixteen hours a day in factories. This work added to women's burdens. After work, married women cared for their homes. One woman remembered how tired she was after a day in the coal mines. She came home to a house with "no fire lit, nothing cooked, no water fetched, the house dirty, and nothing comfortable for my husband."

Work in the factories was little better. Owners often demanded twelve or thirteen hours of work, six days a week. The women were at their machines by 5:00 A.M. At 7:30, workers were allowed to eat breakfast. At noon, there was a thirty-minute lunch break. Finally, at 7:30 P.M., a bell released the women workers to go home. Sometimes, they were needed to work late.

Case Study Review

1. What were the "groans and other sad sounds" that Penny Clarke heard on her first visit to the coal mines?
2. **Summarizing** Summarize in two sentences what life was like for a woman in a British textile mill in the early days of the Industrial Revolution.

I. Reviewing Vocabulary

Match each word on the left with the correct definition on the right.

1. republic
2. anti-Semitism
3. capitalism
4. city-state

a. a political unit made up of a town and the area around it
b. a form of government in which citizens elect their leaders
c. hatred of Jews
d. a system in which people, not goverment, make economic decisions

II. Understanding the Chapter

Answer the questions below on a separate sheet of paper.

1. How was Greek government different from the governments of other ancient peoples?
2. What important principle of justice did the Romans contribute?
3. Why did Europeans seek a new route to Asia?
4. How was English government different from French government by the end of the 1600s?
5. How did the Industrial Revolution make it possible for ordinary people to enjoy a better standard of living?

III. Building Skills: Interpreting Quotes

1. What did Pericles mean when he said that democracy is a government "not in the hands of the few but of the many"?
2. Explain what Pico della Mirandola meant when he said, "Men can do all things if they will."
3. When the woman coal miner came home, she found "no fire lit, nothing cooked, no water fetched, the house dirty, and nothing comfortable for my husband." What does this quotation tell you about her life?

IV. Working Together

Form a small group. Make a time line that shows seven of the most important events discussed in this chapter. Make a bulletin board display of your time line.

On Assignment. . .

Creating a Storyboard: Assemble the three storyboard panels you created as you read this chapter. Use them to create a presentation on Europe's history. Write an introduction that links the three panels. Tell what you find interesting about European history. Present your storyboards to the class while you read your narration aloud.

CHAPTER 39

Europe in the 20th Century

How have two world wars and the Cold War changed Europe?

In this French cartoon from the 1860s, the world is balanced dangerously on the bayonets of soldiers. What is the point of view of the cartoonist?

On Assignment...

Writing Newspaper Articles: This chapter covers many dramatic events that hundreds of millions of people read about in newspapers. Imagine that you are a newspaper reporter. Think about how you might try to capture some of these events in a newspaper article. Remember that in a newspaper article you must answer the questions "who," "what," "when," "where," and "why." As you read this chapter, look for suggestions for articles in the On Assignment boxes.

Looking at Key Terms

- **alliance** an agreement between two or more countries to help each other
- **crisis** a tense period or turning point
- **trench** a long, deep ditch
- **dictatorship** rule by a person who has total power
- **fascism** a system of dictatorship that stresses extreme nationalism
- **concentration camps** large prisons built by Germans to hold people they were going to kill
- **Holocaust** the Nazi attempt to wipe out the Jews and other people in Europe
- **Cold War** the long period of hostility between Western and Communist countries that began after World War II
- **satellite** a country controlled by another country

World War I

How did World War I change Europe?

In 1900, the mood in Europe was positive. During the 1800s, Europe had made great strides in science. The standard of living of Europeans rose as the Industrial Revolution advanced. Democracy continued to spread.

In the early 1900s, most people expected the good times to continue. Europeans thought that the world would remain at peace. It turned out that the 1900s would bring very little peace. As 1914 began, World War I was just seven months away.

The Causes of World War I

By the early 1900s, tension began to grow between the European powers. Germany and Britain were rivals for world trade. France and Germany disagreed about where part of their border should be. Austria-Hungary and Russia competed for influence in the Balkans.

By themselves, these tensions might not have led to war. However, **alliances** made war more likely. An alliance is an agreement between two or more countries to help each other. By 1914, Britain, France, and Russia were in one alliance. Germany and Austria-Hungary belonged to a rival alliance.

Added to this dangerous mix were tensions in the Balkans. A **crisis** in the Balkans began in June 1914. A crisis is a tense period or turning point. At first it involved Austria-Hungary and Serbia. In late July and early August, that crisis drew most of Europe into war.

Many people in Europe believed that war would solve their problems. Leaders spoke to cheering crowds as soldiers marched off to war. Some people knew better. As the war began, a British leader named Edward Grey said, "The lamps have gone out all over Europe. We shall not see them lit again in our lifetime."

New Ways of Fighting War

When the fighting began, both sides expected the war to be short. Instead, it became long, costly, and deadly.

During World War I, both sides used new weapons, such as machine guns and modern cannons. The new weapons changed how battles were fought. Machine guns and other

Allied troops go "over the top" and into a World War I battle. Battles were bloody and produced little gain. Many of these troops would be dead by the time night fell.

new weapons made it impossible for soldiers to charge at each other. The attackers would almost always be slaughtered.

Because they could not advance, both sides dug **trenches**. These networks of long, deep ditches soon stretched across northern France. The worst fighting of World War I took place in the land between the trenches.

Some battles lasted for many months. Both sides used poison gas. Millions of people died on both sides. Yet neither side could break through the other's lines.

The worst fighting of the war was at Verdun (vehr•DUN) and at the battle of the Somme (sahm). Together these battles lasted from February to November 1916. On the first day of the battle of the Somme, 60,000 British servicemen were killed or wounded. More than one million men were killed or wounded in the horrible battles. Yet neither side advanced more than a few miles.

The Slaughter Ends

In April 1917, the United States entered the war on the British-French side. That tipped the scales. By November 1918, Germany and its allies were defeated. World War I was over.

The cost of the war was enormous. More than 10 million soldiers were killed and more than 20 million were wounded. More than one million civilians also died.

The war did more than kill and wound millions. It brought down governments throughout Europe. During the fighting, a revolution took place in Russia. Austria-Hungary fell apart as the war ended. The German emperor was driven from his throne. All of Europe had suffered from the worst war it had ever seen.

Results of the War

In 1919, the victors met in Paris to draw up peace treaties. President Woodrow Wilson of the United States played a central role at the meeting. He hoped the treaty would be fair to the defeated powers.

On Assignment. . .

Write an article about the horrors of trench warfare. Imagine that you are a reporter at the battle of the Somme. Use the real facts to create imaginary characters fighting trench warfare.

Wilson also wanted to form an organization called the League of Nations. Its job would be to bring the nations of the world together to preserve peace.

At the meeting, Wilson ran into trouble. The leaders of Britain and France did not share Wilson's vision. The treaty that ended the war set harsh terms for Germany. The treaty blamed the war entirely on Germany. Germany was forced to pay billions of dollars to repair the damage to other countries.

Wilson did gain one of his goals. The League of Nations was set up. However, in the United States many people opposed it. Americans were tired of war and wanted to have nothing to do with Europe.

Wilson tried to convince Americans that the League was necessary for world peace. However, the United States refused to join. This crippled the League from the beginning.

Section 1 Review

1. Where did the crisis begin that drew Europe into World War I?

2. **Interpreting Primary Sources** What did Edward Grey mean when he said, "The lamps have gone out all over Europe"?

An Age of Dictators

Why did the rise of dictators lead to the slaughter of millions of people in World War II?

During the 1920s, Europeans tried to return to normal lives. However, their hopes were never achieved. In the early 1920s, economic hard times hit. Factories closed. People went hungry.

Conditions began to improve in the mid-1920s. Yet serious problems remained. Many soldiers who survived the war could not find a place in civilian life. In 1929, an economic crisis called the Great Depression began. It forced millions out of work. Millions more lost faith in the future.

These problems undermined democratic governments. During the 1920s and 1930s, democratic governments failed in many European countries. **Dictatorships** of various kinds took control of governments in Europe. A dictatorship is rule by a person who has total power.

Fascism in Italy

Italy was on the winning side in World War I. However, after the war, it remained poor. At the time, Italy was ruled by a king who was unable to deal with the country's problems. Italy's troubles opened the door for Benito Mussolini and his Fascist party. **Fascism** is a system of dictatorship that stresses extreme nationalism. In October 1922, Mussolini and his followers staged a "March on Rome." The king did not act. Instead, he backed down and appointed Mussolini prime minister.

Over the next several years Mussolini used fear, threats, and violence against his opponents. He destroyed Italy's constitutional government. In its place, he built a fascist dictatorship.

A master at staging ceremonies and spreading his message of hatred to a German people dealing with an economic depression, Adolf Hitler won a large following in the 1930s.

Germany Faces the Great Depression

After World War I, Germany became a democratic country. During the mid-1920s, the new government tried to deal with some of Germany's problems. However, the Great Depression caused hardship in Germany. It made the German people lose faith in democracy. That created the opportunity for Adolf Hitler and the Nazi party.

Nazi Racism

The Nazis were fascists whose program was based on Hitler's ideas. Hitler said that the German people were superior to all others. He called them the "master race." Hitler also was a violent anti-Semite. He blamed the Jews for all of Germany's troubles.

The Nazi Rise to Power

Until the Great Depression, the Nazis remained a small party. But after 1929, Nazi strength began to grow. Hitler used German anger over the depression to get votes. He promised to restore Germany's past power and glory.

Hitler also attacked the Jews, who were a tiny minority in Germany. By attacking the Jews, Hitler gave the Germans an easy target for their anger.

By 1933, the Nazis were the largest party in Germany. In January, Hitler became prime minister legally. The Nazis then used their new power to attack Germany's democracy. Within a year, Germany was a Nazi dictatorship.

The Nazis moved quickly. They ignored treaties and built up the German military. They created a dictatorship. No one seriously challenged their power.

New race laws took all rights away from Jews. Jews could no longer be German citizens. They could not hold government jobs or even go to public parks. The Nazis also built large prisons called **concentration camps**. They put Jews and others they hated, including gypsies and Jehovah's Witnesses, into these camps.

World War II

One of Hitler's goals was to expand Germany's territory. That goal led directly to World War II. On September 1, 1939, Nazi forces attacked Poland. France and Britain came to Poland's defense. World War II had begun.

At first the Germans won victory after victory. They conquered Poland and took over France. In the west, only Britain held out. The British defeated the German attempt to cross the English Channel in the Battle of Britain in 1940. In June of 1941, Germany attacked the Soviet Union. Now the Soviet Union was drawn into the fight against Germany.

In December 1941, Japan, Germany's ally, bombed the American port of Pearl Harbor in Hawaii. The United States responded by declaring war on Japan. A few days later, Germany declared war on the United States. The United States joined the Allies, the countries fighting Germany.

It took a more than a year to turn the tide of battle. The first important victories for the Allies came in late 1942 and early 1943. On June 6, 1944, U.S., British, and Canadian troops landed on the coast of France. The soldiers faced deadly machine guns and cannon fire as they hit the beaches. Many men were killed as they fought their way through barbed wire and minefields. Yet they took and held the beaches and fought their way inland.

The struggle to free Western and Central Europe lasted into 1945. In April, Soviet troops fought their way into Germany's capital, Berlin. As the Soviets closed in, Hitler committed suicide. On May 7, Germany surrendered. World War II in Europe was over.

The Holocaust

The Nazis committed many horrible crimes during World War II. They murdered millions of people in the countries they conquered. However, one crime shocked the world more than any other. During World War II, the Nazis tried to wipe out the entire Jewish population of Europe.

The Nazi attempt to wipe out the Jewish people is called the **Holocaust**. Never before had there been such a carefully planned effort to murder a group of people.

The Nazis built death camps especially to murder Jews. They brought Jews from all over Europe to the camps. Jews were then murdered in gas chambers and their bodies burned in huge ovens. The Nazis continued the murders even when the war was lost. Nothing was more important to Hitler than wiping out the Jews.

The Nazis murdered more than 6 million European Jews. About 1.5 million of them were children. After the war, some Nazi leaders were tried for their crimes and sent to prison or hanged. However, most escaped justice. They lived on in Germany or fled to other countries.

The Global Impact of the War

World War II took many more lives than World War I. At least 35 million people died. Most were civilians. From deep inside the Soviet Union to the Atlantic Ocean, large parts of Europe lay in ruins. Tens of millions of people were homeless and hungry.

As a result of the war, the world power balance shifted. Before the war, Britain, France, and Germany had been major military powers. After 1945, the world's most powerful countries were the Soviet Union and the United States. Europe's fate lay in the hands of these two nations.

Section 2 Review

1. What were the causes of World War II?

2. **Determining Cause and Effect** How did the depression help the Nazis gain power?

SECTION 3

Europe in the Cold War

How did the Cold War divide Europe?

Even before World War II was over, the Allies were showing signs of disagreement. Early in 1945, the Allies agreed to divide Germany into four zones. The United States, Soviet Union, Britain, and France each controlled a zone.

Shortly after the fighting ended, the alliance fell apart. The reason was tension over the fate of Poland and other countries in Eastern Europe. In 1945, the Soviet Union controlled these countries. The main concern of the Soviets was Poland. The Soviets said that they should control Poland because it was a route that invaders often took into their country. They also showed that they intended to keep their Soviet armies in other countries in Eastern Europe.

The United States and the countries of Western Europe opposed Soviet control of Eastern Europe. They thought that the Soviet Union was a threat to Western Europe.

These tensions led to the **Cold War**. The Cold War was a period of hostility that lasted over 40 years. The United States and its allies in Western Europe were on one side. The Soviet Union and the countries it controlled were on the other side. It was called the Cold War because the two sides never fought a shooting, or hot, war with each other.

In 1946, Winston Churchill of Britain said that an "iron curtain" had come down on the continent. Behind that curtain were countries under Soviet domination. They were cut off from the free nations of Western Europe. The iron curtain divided Europe for more than 40 years.

Between 1945 and 1948, the Soviet Union set up Communist governments in the countries behind the iron curtain. These countries were called **satellites** because they were under the control of another country.

The Marshall Plan

Western Europe was slow to recover from the war. The destruction was too great. People were hungry and did not have the strength or money to rebuild. Leaders in Western Europe and the United States were worried. They feared that people might turn to communism.

These leaders convinced President Harry Truman of the United States to help its friends in Europe. The man he appointed to work out a plan was General George Marshall. Under the Marshall Plan, Western Europe received $12 billion in aid from the United States. The plan was successful. By

Defiant Czechs carry their nation's flag past a burning Soviet tank in Prague in 1968. The defiance did not last long. Within a few days, Soviet tanks had put down the revolt.

the early 1950s, Western Europe had recovered. Today, Western Europe has a thriving economy.

Two Germanies

The division of Germany in 1945 was supposed to be temporary. However, the Cold War kept Germany divided. Each side feared that the other might win control of a united Germany. The Soviet zone became East Germany. The American, British, and French zones became West Germany.

Two Alliances

As tensions grew in Europe, so did the fear of the Soviet army. As a result, the United States took the lead in forming a new alliance. It was called the North Atlantic Treaty Organization, or NATO. Its purpose was to defend its members against the Soviet Union. In 1955, the Soviets formed their own alliance called the Warsaw Pact. NATO and the Warsaw Pact faced each other in Europe with modern armies and atomic weapons.

Rebellion Against Soviet Rule

Many of the people of Eastern Europe never accepted Soviet control of their countries. In 1953, people in East Germany protested against the Soviet Union. The protests were put down by Soviet tanks. The Soviet army crushed a rebellion in Hungary in 1956. More than 20,000 people died in the fighting.

In 1968, the Communist government of Czechoslovakia (chek•oh•sloh•VAHK •ee•uh) introduced democratic reforms. These efforts went too far for the Soviet leaders. They sent thousands of soldiers to invade Czechoslovakia and end the reforms.

In Poland, the people never stopped struggling against communism and Soviet control. In 1989, Poland became the first Soviet satellite to end Communist rule and Soviet control.

By the end of 1989, every Communist government in Central and Eastern Europe had fallen. The end of Soviet control in the region led to the end of the Cold War. We will examine this process in Chapters 41 and 43.

Section 3 Review

1. What was the "iron curtain"?
2. **Making Inferences** How do you think prosperity in Western Europe might have led to the downfall of communism in Eastern Europe?

The Berlin Airlift

When the Allies divided Germany in 1945, they also divided its capital, Berlin, into four sectors. Berlin was located in the Soviet zone. The Americans, British, and French had to travel through Soviet-controlled territory to reach Berlin.

In 1948, the Soviets tried to force the three other powers out of Berlin. They said that the Americans, British, and French no longer could travel through the Soviet zone. In June 1948, the Soviets blocked all traffic into Berlin. The Western powers had to find a way to supply the people of Berlin.

They decided to supply Berlin by air. The job seemed impossible. How could the United States supply a city of 2.5 million people by air? Everything the people needed had to be flown in.

Yet the job was done. For almost a year, the sound of airplane motors in the sky of Berlin never stopped. The planes came on bright days and on foggy days. They came loaded with coal, dried milk, medicine, clothing, and many other products.

As soon as the planes were unloaded they took off for West Germany, 110 miles away. When they landed in West Germany, they immediately were reloaded and sent out again.

In June 1949, the Soviets gave in. They reopened the roads to Berlin. The Berlin Airlift had defeated the blockade.

Case Study Review

1. Which country controlled the territory around Berlin after World War II?
2. **Determining Cause and Effect** How are the Cold War and the Berlin Airlift linked?

On Assignment. . .

You are a reporter on the airfield in Berlin during the Airlift. Write a news story based on the details in this chapter and your imagination.

I. Reviewing Vocabulary

Match each word on the left with the correct definition on the right.

1. trench   **a.** a country controlled by another country
2. crisis   **b.** a long, deep ditch
3. alliance   **c.** a tense period or turning point
4. satellite   **d.** an agreement between two or more countries to help each other

II. Understanding the Chapter

Answer the questions below on a separate sheet of paper.

1. What factors contributed to the outbreak of World War I?
2. How did the winners treat Germany at the end of World War I?
3. What actions did the Nazis take soon after they gained power?
4. How did World War II shift the world power balance?
5. What did Winston Churchill mean when he said that an "iron curtain" had come down on Europe?

III. Building Skills: Identifying Cause and Effect

In each of the pairs below, tell which is the cause and which is the effect.

1. a. the Great Depression
   b. despairing Germans turn to Hitler
2. a. Germany's democracy is destroyed
   b. the Nazis take power
3. a. Germany is divided after World War II
   b. the Soviets blockade Berlin

IV. Working Together

Form a small group. Select what you consider the five most important events you have read about in this chapter. Arrange the list in order of importance. Share your list with the rest of the class and see how all of your lists compare. Be prepared to explain why you consider these events to be important.

On Assignment. . .

Writing Newspaper Articles: Review the two newspaper articles you wrote. Create headlines for each article that summarize the ideas in the articles. Make sure the headlines give important information about the story in no more than six or seven words.

CHAPTER 40

Patterns of Life in Europe

How do people live in the different parts of Europe?

Change can be seen everywhere in Europe's cities. Here, in Berlin, a modern office tower soars next to a church that is hundreds of years old. Traditional and modern influences are both felt in the cultures of Europe.

Looking at Key Terms

- **emigrate** to leave one country permanently and settle in another
- **industrialize** to develop industries
- **welfare state** a government that assumes responsibility for the welfare of its citizens
- **pension** a regular payment to retired people
- **bilingual** speaking two languages
- **hereditary** passed from one generation to another
- **efficient** well run, without extra expenses
- **exporting** selling a country's products abroad
- **Bundestag** the lower house of the German parliament
- **Romance languages** languages such as Italian and Spanish that developed from Latin

On Assignment. . .

Writing a Letter: Imagine that you are touring Europe and writing letters to your family and friends describing what you see. You see different things as you go from region to region. As part of your work in this unit, you will be asked to write several letters. You might describe the people, the culture, or something else that interests you about a particular region. Look for suggestions in the On Assignment boxes.

Northern Europe

What is life like in Northern Europe?

Northern Europe is a region of long winters and short summers. It stretches about 1,500 miles (2,400 km) across the northern border of Europe. Almost all of Northern Europe is located near the seas. This makes its climate milder than that of most of Alaska.

At the western end of Northern Europe is the island of Iceland. At the eastern end is Finland, which borders Russia. Between are Norway, Denmark, and Sweden. Together these three nations are called Scandinavia. Along the eastern coast of the Baltic Sea are Estonia, Latvia, and Lithuania.

People and Culture

Northern Europe is an urban region. Most of the people live in cities near the sea. The people of Northern Europe have some of the highest standards of living in the world.

Scandinavians speak languages that are related to one another. The exception is Finland, which is sometimes considered part of Scandinavia. The Finnish language is distantly related to the Hungarian language.

In all but Finland and Lithuania in Northern Europe, the majority of people are Lutheran. The Lutheran church is one of the many branches of Protestantism. The only country in which most people are Catholic is Lithuania, but there are small Catholic communities in other Northern European countries.

In rural areas, many people still follow traditional ways of life as farmers, herders, and foresters. Many of the Lapp people of the far north herd reindeer for a living and move around with their herds.

Most nations of Northern Europe have a long history of democracy. Iceland set up the world's first parliament in A.D. 930. Sweden, Norway, Denmark, and Finland also have strong democratic traditions.

Estonia, Latvia, and Lithuania are struggling to build democratic governments. They were part of the Soviet Union for half a century, regaining their independence in 1991.

Sweden: Living in a Welfare State

Thousands of years ago, all of Sweden lay under giant glaciers. As the glaciers melted, they scraped gashes in the land. The gashes filled with water and became the more than 90,000 lakes that dot Sweden today. Swedes

Scenes of spectacular beauty abound in Norway. The city of Alesund, shown here, is built on a number of islands around a broad bay in western Norway.

COUNTRIES OF NORTHERN EUROPE

COUNTRY	CAPITAL CITY	POPULATION (in millions)	AREA (square miles)	INCOME PER PERSON
Denmark	Copenhagen	5.1	16,631	$24,500
Estonia	Tallinn	1.5	18,370	6,240
Finland	Helsinki	5.0	130,119	15,000
Iceland	Reykjavik	0.3	39,709	24,031
Latvia	Riga	2.7	25,400	not available
Lithuania	Vilnius	3.6	25,174	3,000
Norway	Oslo	4.3	125,049	17,900
Sweden	Stockholm	8.6	173,800	15,700

take great pride in their lakes. They also take pride in their standard of living. It is as high as any in the world.

A century ago, Sweden was one of the poorest countries in Europe. With its cold northern climate and small amount of good farmland, growing enough food was difficult. Between 1850 and 1930, about one out of every five Swedes **emigrated**. Many of these Swedes moved permanently to the United States.

As late as 1900, about nine out of ten Swedes still lived on farms. Today, four out of five Swedes live in cities.

Sweden began to **industrialize** after 1900. To *industrialize* means "to build modern industries." Sweden's new industries were based on iron and other natural resources. They also included wood products. Today, Sweden's factories turn out cars, products made from high-quality steel, and machinery.

Sweden's Welfare State

Sweden is one of the most modern countries in the world. In the last 70 years, Sweden and its Scandinavian neighbors all built **welfare states**. In a welfare state, the government assumes responsibility for the welfare of its citizens.

On Assignment. . .

In your letter home, describe what the Swedish welfare state provides and why it is having trouble.

Sweden's welfare state provides many benefits to its people. However, Swedes pay high taxes for these benefits. Government insurance pays a large part of workers' salaries if they lose their jobs. A government program pays a large part of people's medical and dental bills. Swedes also receive generous **pensions** when they retire. A pension is a regular payment to retired people.

In the 1990s, Sweden's economy slowed. Factories closed and unemployment rose. Government tax receipts fell. As a result, Sweden had to make cuts in its programs. Swedes must now decide how much of their welfare state they can still afford.

Section 1 Review

1. What is a welfare state?
2. **Understanding Points of View** What is one reason to support a welfare state? What is one reason to oppose it?

Western Europe

What is life like in Western Europe?

Modern democratic government began in Western Europe. The United States drew many of its ideas about democratic government from Britain. The French Revolution helped spread democratic ideas around the world.

The two largest countries in Western Europe are Great Britain and France. Ireland shares the British Isles with Britain. Belgium and the Netherlands are two small countries on the coast of the North Sea. Tiny Luxembourg is wedged between France, Belgium, and Germany.

People and Culture

The main languages of Western Europe are English, French, and Dutch. In some parts of the region, people speak what are called Celtic (KEHL•tihc) languages. Irish, Scottish, and Welsh are Celtic languages spoken in the British Isles. In Ireland, Irish is the official language and English is the second official language.

One country that is sharply divided along language lines is Belgium. In the southern part of Belgium, called Wallonia, the people speak French. In the northern part, called Flanders, the language is Dutch.

Both French and Dutch are official languages in Belgium. The nation's capital Brussels is officially **bilingual**. *Bilingual* means "speaking two languages."

Today all of the countries of Western Europe are modern industrial societies. Their people enjoy high standards of living. Even the poorest country in the region, Ireland, ranks among the top 30 countries in the world in income per person.

A Rich Heritage

Each year, millions of tourists visit Western Europe. They visit cultural attractions that are an important part of Western Europe's history. They visit museums, palaces, historic battlefields, and much more.

Paris has been one of the great cultural centers of Western Europe for centuries. Paris's first settlers arrived more than 2,000 years ago. They built a village on an island in the middle of the Seine River. Today that village is a city of more than two million people.

Paris is home to the Louvre (LOOV•ruh) museum, one of the finest museums in the world. In its collection are the Mona Lisa and many other treasures of Western culture. The beautiful building that holds all of these treasures was once a royal palace.

COUNTRIES OF WESTERN EUROPE

COUNTRY	CAPITAL CITY	POPULATION (in millions)	AREA (square miles)	INCOME PER PERSON
Belgium	Brussels	9.9	11,781	$17,000
France	Paris	56.7	211,208	14,600
United Kingdom	London	57.5	94,247	14,300
Ireland	Dublin	3.6	27,136	8,900
Luxembourg	Luxembourg	0.4	999	17,200
Netherlands	Amsterdam	15.0	16,041	18,000

Europe's cultural treasures fill its many museums. Here, at the Louvre museum in Paris, a student learns to paint by copying the work of a master.

The Cathedral of Notre Dame in Paris was begun in the 1100s on the same island on which Paris was founded. It was not finished until the 1300s.

Notre Dame has been a central part of French life for centuries. Around 1200, it established a religious school that became the University of Paris. This university was one of the first in Europe.

Britain: A Constitutional Monarchy

Britain was the center of a great empire for several centuries. A popular expression in the 1800s was, "The sun never sets on the British Empire." At the time, when it was nighttime in London, it was daytime in some British colony.

Today Britain no longer has the political and military power it once had. Other nations also have passed Britain in economic strength. It ranks only fifth in income per person among the six nations of Western Europe.

The full name for Britain is the United Kingdom of Great Britain and Northern Ireland. The original core of the kingdom was England. Today the United Kingdom is made up of four parts. England, Scotland, and Wales are on the island of Great Britain. Northern Ireland is the northeast corner of the island of Ireland.

British Government

Britain is a constitutional monarchy. The power of the ruling king or queen has been limited for many centuries. Today the real political power in Britain is in Parliament. Parliament is divided into a House of Commons and a House of Lords.

Of the two houses, the House of Commons is more powerful. The House of Commons is democratically elected and has most of the lawmaking power.

The leader of the majority political party in the House of Commons becomes the head of government, or prime minister. He or she forms a government by appointing other

---

On Assignment . . .

Take notes about what you would see if you visited Paris. Then write a letter about the attractions of the city. You should point out the historical importance of these attractions.

Britain's Parliament stretches majestically along the Thames River in London. The United States drew many of its democratic ideas from Britain's parliamentary form of government.

ministers. All of the ministers are members of the House of Commons.

Membership in the House of Lords is not earned by election. Most of its members hold **hereditary** titles, or titles that have been passed from one generation to another. A few members are "life peers." These are people who have been honored for their achievements.

Britain's Changing Economy

Beginning in the late 1940s, Britain built its own welfare state. However, in the 1960s and 1970s, the British economy suffered. Many factories went out of business because they could not compete with foreign goods.

The Conservative party argued that Britain's welfare state was too expensive. Led by Prime Minister Margaret Thatcher, the Conservatives trimmed the welfare state during the 1980s. They cut government programs and reduced taxes. They also sold government-owned industries to private buyers.

The Conservatives said that these measures made Britain's economy more **efficient**. Efficient industries are able to compete in world markets. Opponents complained that Thatcher's measures hurt Britain's poor people.

Ties With Europe

Another debate in Britain is how closely it should tie its economy with the economies of other European countries. Since World War II, Britain has drawn much closer to its neighbors on the European mainland. (See Chapter 41.) However, many British people fear that this process has gone too far. They worry that Britain may be giving up some of its independence.

1. What is the Louvre?
2. **Comparing and Contrasting**
   How is the British system of government different from the U.S. system? How is it the same?

SECTION 3

Central Europe

What is life like in Central Europe?

The borders of Central Europe have changed many times in this century. Before World War I, much of Central Europe belonged to a large empire called Austria-Hungary. Austria-Hungary contained 30 million people, including people of many different ethnic groups.

At the end of World War I, Austria-Hungary collapsed. (See Chapter 39.) Several smaller countries took its place. At the same time, Poland emerged from former Austrian, Russian, and German territories.

Germany's borders changed after World War I and World War II. Each time Germany lost territory. After World War II, the country was split into two separate nations. In 1990, Germany again became one country. In recent years, the countries of Yugoslavia and Czechoslovakia have broken apart, and new countries were formed from the old.

People and Cultures

The people of Central Europe belong to three main groups. The two largest groups are German speakers and people who speak a Slavic language. The third main group is the Magyars of Hungary.

German speakers trace their roots to tribes that lived in Northern Europe in ancient times. Today most German-speaking people of the region live in Germany and Austria. Two thirds of the people who live in Switzerland also speak German. Small German communities are scattered in several other countries.

The Slavic people, or Slavs, speak different, but related, languages. They include the Polish, Czech, and Slovak languages. The Magyars live in Hungary. Their language is related to Finnish and Estonian.

COUNTRIES OF CENTRAL EUROPE

COUNTRY	CAPITAL CITY	POPULATION (in millions)	AREA (square miles)	INCOME PER PERSON
Austria	Vienna	7.7	32,275	$13,600
Croatia	Zagreb	4.8	35,132	not available
Czech Republic	Prague	10.4	30,584	14,300
Germany	Berlin	78.7	137,838	24,980
Hungary	Budapest	10.4	35,919	6,108
Liechtenstein	Vaduz	0.03	61	15,000
Poland	Warsaw	38.2	120,727	4,565
Slovakia	Bratislava	5.2	18,917	12,800
Slovenia	Ljubljana	2.0	12,584	not available
Switzerland	Bern	6.8	15,941	17,800

Religion

Most of the people in Central Europe are Roman Catholic. Only in Germany and Switzerland are the number of Protestants and Catholics about equal.

Before World War II, Central Europe had a large Jewish population. However, most of Central Europe's Jews were murdered by the Nazis during World War II. (See Chapter 39.) Today few Jews live in Central Europe.

A Region of Industries

Germany built many industries during the 1800s. By the end of the century, Germany was Europe's economic leader. Its factories turned out many of the most advanced machines in the world. Today Germany again is Europe's leading economic power.

It took longer to build industries in most other parts of Central Europe. The Czech Republic is the most industrialized country in the region east of Germany. By the 1930s, it had many modern industries. In some countries, such as Poland and Hungary, industrial development did not begin until after World War II.

Economy and Environment

The Communist regimes that built industries in East Central Europe paid no attention to the environment. As a result, the region suffers from some of the worst industrial pollution in the world.

People who visit Warsaw, Poland's capital, sometimes notice a brown haze over the city. It comes from the smokestacks of factories. Rivers are polluted and forests have died. Polluted air and water have caused serious heath problems to the people in the area.

The Czech town of Ostrava has several steel mills. The air in Ostrava is so bad that Ostrava's schools have had to limit children's outdoor play. A resident says, "We keep windows closed, even in summer. Otherwise soot blackens walls and curtains."

Some Communist governments paid little attention to their impact on the environment. In this picture, a coke plant in Sverdlovsk, Russia, ejects tons of pollutants into the atmosphere every day.

Germany: From Two Countries to One

Between 1945 and 1990, there were two Germanies. The symbol of Germany's division was the Berlin Wall. Communists in East Germany put up the Wall to keep people from escaping to the West.

Only in 1989 did the Wall come down. By that time, Communist East Germany was on the verge of collapse. Less than a year later, Germany became one country again.

The new united Germany began with great hope. However, it has not been as easy as many hoped to fit the two parts of Germany together. In Communist East Germany, people worked under government control. East German factories, farms, and shops did not have to compete in the marketplace. The government bought whatever they produced.

Most East German factories were outdated. Few East Germans knew how to compete in a free-market world. Today, the united Germany is spending billions of dollars to rebuild the East.

Economic Powerhouse

Despite these problems, Germany remains the economic powerhouse of Europe. The value of the goods it produces each year is almost double the value of goods produced in France. Germany ranks with the United States and Japan as one of the world's three top **exporting** nations. Germany sells far more of its products abroad than it buys.

Germany's factories produce huge amounts of manufactured goods. German cars, electronics, and other high technology products are popular throughout the world.

Germany's Government

The democratic government set up in 1918 in Germany collapsed in the early 1930s. This led to the Nazi era and terrible disasters for Germany, Europe, and the world.

Today Germany is a democracy once again. The German parliament has two houses. The lower house is called the **Bundestag** (BOON•deh•stahg). This house is the more powerful part of parliament and elects the country's leader, or chancellor.

Section 3 Review

1. What environmental problems do the people of Central Europe face?
2. **Making Inferences** Why was the Berlin Wall an important symbol for all Germans?

SECTION 4

Southern Europe

What is life like in Southern Europe?

Americans look to ancient Greece for the first example of democracy. They look to Rome for ideas about the rule of law.

However, Southern Europe is much more than Greece and Rome. The region stretches

On Assignment...

In a letter to your family, describe the different cultural influences you see in Southern Europe.

from the Atlantic to the Black Sea. It includes ten nations and five "mini-states." The Mediterranean Sea is the "highway" that ties the region together.

People and Culture

Southern Europe is made up of three major peninsulas. From west to east, they are the Iberian Peninsula (Portugal and Spain), the Italian peninsula (which is shaped like a boot), and the Balkan Peninsula (which contains several countries). Most of the land is mountainous. Flatlands occur in river valleys or on high plateaus.

Many cultures have left their mark on Southern Europe. At its height, Rome ruled the entire region. Later, a Muslim people called the Moors conquered most of Spain and Portugal. The Moors left their influence on the architecture, food, and music of Spain and Portugal.

The Balkan Peninsula is a mixture of many cultural influences. The people of Bulgaria, Croatia, and Serbia speak Slavic languages. The Romanians trace their language to Rome.

In ancient times, Greece had colonies throughout much of Southern Europe. Its influence also reached western Asia and northern Africa. Today, Greeks live mainly in Greece, on the southern tip of the Balkan Peninsula.

The Italian language developed from the Latin language that was spoken by the ancient Romans. So did languages like Spanish, French, Portuguese, and Romanian. Together these languages are called **Romance languages**.

COUNTRIES OF SOUTHERN EUROPE

COUNTRY	CAPITAL CITY	POPULATION (in millions)	AREA (square miles)	INCOME PER PERSON
Albania	Tirana	3.3	11,100	$1,200
Andorra	Andorra la Vella	0.5	175	not available
Bosnia and Herzegovina	Sarajevo	4.1	19,741	not available
Bulgaria	Sofia	9.0	42,823	5,710
Greece	Athens	10.0	50,961	5,605
Italy	Rome	57.7	116,500	18,420
Macedonia	Skopje	1.9	9,928	not available
Malta	Valetta	0.4	122	5,645
Monaco	Monaco-Ville	0.03	1	not available
Portugal	Lisbon	10.4	35,550	6,900
Romania	Bucharest	23.4	91,700	3,445
San Marino	San Marino	0.02	24	not available
Spain	Madrid	39.0	194,884	10,100
Vatican City	Vatican City	0.001	0.2	not available
Yugoslavia	Belgrade	10.3	39,450	not available

Religion

Most people in Italy, Spain, and Portugal are Roman Catholic. The Eastern Orthodox branch of Christianity is as old as Roman Catholicism. Large areas of the Balkan Peninsula are Orthodox.

The Muslim Turks conquered most of the Balkan Peninsula beginning in the 1300s. In some places, their rule lasted until the 1920s. During Turkish rule, some people in the Balkans became Muslims.

The Economy

Southern Europe is the poorest of all Europe's regions. It has the fewest industries. However, many of Southern Europe's countries have been able to build their economies in recent years. Spain, Portugal, Italy, and Greece have all experienced economic surges since the 1980s. They have found markets for their minerals, farm products, and fishing industries. All four countries have also begun developing industries that sell to other countries of the European Union.

Section 4 Review

1. How has the Mediterranean Sea influenced life in Southern Europe?

2. **Comparing and Contrasting** Which country in the chart above has the largest population? Which has the largest area?

Italy: Between North and South

If you visit southern Italy you might think you have gone back in time. Many villages in southern Italy are little changed from the way they were 100 years ago. Villagers often get water from a pump. Farmers plow with horses instead of tractors.

Northern Italy is different. It has modern industrial cities like Milan, Turin, and Genoa. Another important city in the north is Venice. The valley of the Po River in the north is Italy's richest farming region. Its farmers use modern machinery to raise their crops.

Central Italy has Rome, Italy's capital and largest city. It is also the world center of the Roman Catholic Church. Vatican City in Rome is the home of the Pope, the spiritual leader of the Roman Catholic Church. Vatican City includes beautiful gardens, libraries, museums, church offices, and places of worship.

St. Peter's Cathedral is the most famous building in the Vatican, the center of the Roman Catholic religion. The Vatican is an independent nation tucked within the city of Rome.

545

Progress and the Good Life

Italy has made much economic progress since World War II. During the 1980s, its economy grew faster than that of any other country in Europe. Modern industries helped create that growth.

Italian products are sold all over the world. Italian cars, tires, business machines, and clothing have excellent reputations. The city of Milan is one of the world's fashion centers.

North and South

One of Italy's most serious problems is the difference between the north and south. The north is much more prosperous than the south. In the south, unemployment is higher. Workers in southern industries produce only half as much as northern workers.

The Italian government has tried to ease differences between the two regions. It has spent money on building industries in the south. However, few industries have prospered.

Case Study Review

1. How has Italy's economy changed since World War II?
2. **Comparing and Contrasting** How are northern and southern Italy similar? How are they different?

I. Reviewing Vocabulary

Match each word on the left with the correct definition on the right.

1. emigrate   **a.** to sell a country's products abroad
2. bilingual   **b.** passed from one generation to another
3. export   **c.** to leave one country permanently and settle in another
4. hereditary   **d.** speaking two languages

II. Understanding the Chapter

Answer the questions below on a separate sheet of paper.

1. Why do Swedes debate what their welfare state can provide today?
2. Why is Paris a good place to learn about the culture of Western Europe?
3. What is the House of Commons and what is its position in the British government?
4. What is Eastern Europe's most serious environmental problem? What caused this problem?

III. Building Skills: Summarizing

In each of the items below, summarize the idea in three sentences or less.

1. Summarize the role of the monarch in Britain's government.
2. Summarize the role of the Berlin Wall as a symbol of the Cold War.
3. Summarize the reasons tourists are attracted to Italy.

IV. Working Together

Form a small group. Choose one country from each of the four charts presented in this chapter. Compare each of these countries for the following features: type of government, major industries, and main points of interest for tourists.

On Assignment. . .

Writing a Letter: Take the letters you have written and write a one-page summary of your impressions of Europe. Collect the summaries in a portfolio so that class members can use them for review.

Facing Hatred During Kristallnacht

Frederic Zeller

On November 9, 1938, the beautiful German city of Leipzig became a place of terror. Mobs of Nazi storm troopers attacked Jews and anyone who dared challenge the Nazi government. Mobs of civilians soon joined the storm troopers. They smashed the property of Jews, throwing furniture and valuables into the street. The mobs smashed store widows and looted the stores. They fire-bombed Leipzig's synagogues. They viciously attacked any Jews they saw, including women and children. One boy was thrown from a three-story window. Both his legs were broken in the fall.

Similar attacks against Jews took place all over Germany and Austria on the night of November 9. This destruction is known as Kristallnacht. *In English the name means "Crystal Night," or "the night of the broken glass." The Nazis chose that name to describe this period of terror because of the enormous amount of shattered glass that littered the streets after the riots.*

Frederic Zeller was a Jewish boy in Berlin during the 1930s. He faced a great deal of persecution during those years. He and his sister were sent to England before World War II began. In 1957, Zeller moved to the United States. Below is an excerpt from his autobiography, When Time Ran Out: Coming of Age in the Third Reich. *In this excerpt, Zeller describes his experiences on Kristallnacht.*

. . . Mother was relieved to see me back, but tears were running down her cheeks.

"They're looting the Hochmann store. They have no shame. The poor woman will have nothing left. . . ."

"Yes, I just saw them. I'll empty her [store] window and take the stuff to the back, if there's anything left. . . ."

I ran down, crossed the street, interrupted a woman in the process of putting her hand into the window and saying "Please" climbed over the glass . . . into the narrow window space. The woman pulled her arm back hastily, looked embarrassed, then huffed, then ran. . . .

People stopped and watched me curiously. It must have seemed strange: a thin, gangling[1] kid clearing the window all on his own. Some people looked sulky, others sad or shocked. And then there

---

[1]**gangling** (GAN-glihng) *adj.* tall, thin, and awkward

Hatred and fear, the same emotions that sparked Kristallnacht, led the Germans to invade this Warsaw neighborhood and send the Jews who lived there to Nazi death camps. More than 6 million European Jews died in these camps.

were those who gloated.[2] What hateful faces. Suddenly I became aware of a thin, tall, gray-haired man. . . . He was screaming at me, and in such a rage, I could hardly understand a word. What had I done, I wondered. Had I dropped some glass on him? A few words stood out:

"Jewpigs . . . murderers . . . filthy cowards . . . killed . . . good German!"

And all the while he was holding, with both hands, a shabby, leather briefcase, folded in two—threatening to smash it into the large jagged glass spikes next to and above my head. . . . I knew that if I showed fear, flinched, or jumped back, he would strike. I knew this for sure. . . .

I saw the hate-distorted face of the man . . . [and] the person next to him, intercepting him in slow motion. And I heard the words. . . .

"Stop it, he's only a child." I felt my face freeze into non-expression. I emptied myself of fear. Turning . . . turning my back to the threat. Turning my back to him. . . . Starting to work again, emptying the window. Numb. I felt nothing.

---

[2]**gloated** (GLOHT-uhd) *v.* enjoyed someone else's pain or misfortune

---

Making Connections

1. Why did Frederic run to the store?
2. **Identifying Relationships** How did the curses of the gray-haired man reflect later German actions toward Jews?

Europe in the World Today

How has Europe's position in the world changed in recent years?

A prosperous Europe has the means and the time for recreation. At the Olympic Stadium in Rome, hundreds of thousands of Italians may attend a soccer match or other sporting event.

On Assignment. . .

Conducting an Interview: After finishing this chapter, you will be asked to conduct a mock interview about how the nations of Europe interact with the rest of the world. The person being interviewed will be an "expert" on European affairs. Look for the suggestion about what kinds of questions to ask in the On Assignment box.

Looking at Key Terms

- **civil disobedience** a form of protest that involves disobeying laws
- **stalemate** a situation in which two sides oppose each other but neither can win
- **tariff** a tax on a product one country sells to another
- **privatize** to end government control of factories, farms, and businesses and turn them over to individuals

The End of European Empires

How did Europe's own values lead to the end of European colonial empires?

On April 18, 1980, Britain gave up its last colony in Africa. With Zimbabwe's independence, the once mighty British Empire shrank to a tiny size.

All of Europe's colonial powers faced the same fate. They did not long survive the ruin of World War II. Within a few years after the end of the war, the once powerful empires began to collapse. All over Asia, Africa, and the Middle East, nations won their independence. At the same time, the spirit of nationalism was growing in Europe. People who did not have their own governments began demanding independence.

The Road to Independence

Even the victors of World War II were far weaker after the war than before it. World War II also challenged the idea that countries could own colonies. After all, the nations of Europe had fought World War II to save their freedom. How could they now deny this freedom to the people of the colonies?

The British Leave India

India was the first colony of a European power to win its freedom after the war. It was also Britain's most important colony.

The struggle for independence in India was led by Mohandas K. Gandhi (GAHN•dee). Gandhi used **civil disobedience** and other nonviolent tactics against the British. His followers peacefully disobeyed the law as a form of protest.

In 1947, after a bitter struggle, India won its independence. However, the independence struggle had brought to the surface ancient hatreds between Hindus and Muslims. Before independence, fighting broke out between Hindus and Muslims. To end the fighting, India was divided into two countries—a Hindu India and a Muslim Pakistan.

The French Are Driven From Indochina

Unlike the British, the French fought to keep several of their colonies. The first struggle took place in Indochina. Today this part of Southeast Asia includes the countries of Vietnam, Cambodia, and Laos.

The French had first taken over part of Indochina in the 1860s. During World War II, the Japanese drove them from the region. After the war, the French tried to regain control of Indochina. However, a group called the Viet Minh (vee•eht MIHN) opposed them in Vietnam. The Viet Minh were led by a Communist named Ho Chi Minh.

War between the French and the Viet Minh broke out in 1946. The French were soon defeated. In 1954, Vietnam became independent. It was divided into Communist North Vietnam and non-Communist South Vietnam. Laos and Cambodia also became independent.

New Relationships

Despite the breakup of the colonial empires, European influence often remained strong in the new nations. In India and Pakistan, for example, educated people continued to speak English. The same was true in many African nations. Young people often were educated at European universities.

Between 1958 and 1960, France granted independence to its colonies in west Africa. It also sent valuable economic help to the new countries. France, therefore, kept a good deal of influence in the region.

The Irish Troubles

The Irish call the political violence that has torn their country since 1969 "the Troubles." If you asked people to explain the causes of the Troubles, you would hear many answers.

With the fall of the French in Indochina, the days of Europe's vast colonial empires were at an end. Here, Vietnamese forces parade into a city in 1955 after the French defeat.

The roots of the problems go back hundreds of years. In the 1100s, the English conquered Ireland, ruling it until the early 1900s. The Irish people resisted English rule and fought English attempts to make them Protestant. The government seized land and gave it to Protestant settlers from England and Scotland.

In 1921, the southern part of Ireland won its independence and became the Republic of Ireland. The northern part remained under British control. Friction grew in Northern Ireland between Protestants and Catholics.

The Troubles began in 1969, after Roman Catholics demanded greater civil rights and economic opportunities. Soon, extremists in both Catholic and Protestant communities turned to violence. An organization called the Irish Republican Army (IRA) launched a campaign of terror. Its goal was to break Northern Ireland's ties with Britain and to unite it with the Republic of Ireland. Most members of the IRA were Catholic. Protestant groups also used terror tactics.

The IRA set off bombs in Northern Ireland and in England. Often the bombs killed innocent people. Shootings and murders multiplied on both sides. By the 1990s, the Troubles had taken some 3,000 lives.

In 1994, all sides declared a truce and started talks toward a settlement. However, by 1996, violence had broken out again.

Section 1 Review

1. Why did India become independent as two nations, India and Pakistan?

2. **Analyzing Information** Why did force fail to preserve Europe's colonial empires?

SECTION 2

The Fall of Communism

What forces led to the fall of communism in Europe?

As the Cold War deepened, Europe found itself deeply divided. Communist governments ruled the East. In the West, governments were based on democratic principles.

Before World War II, European nations controlled the fates of millions of people outside Europe. When Europe was divided, its fate was in the hands of outsiders.

The outsiders were the United States and the Soviet Union. The Soviet Union dominated Eastern Europe. Its huge army and its atomic weapons guaranteed control. The people of Western Europe feared the Soviet Union. They depended on the United States for protection. The United States kept soldiers and atomic weapons in Europe.

By the 1980s, however, it was clear that the Soviet Union's hold on Eastern Europe was weakening. Under communism, the economy was not providing for the needs of the people. Soviet citizens demanded more rights. National groups within the Soviet Union began to call for independence.

The Soviet Union Crumbles

In 1985, Mikhail Gorbachev (mihk•HAIL GAWR•buh•chof) became the leader of the Soviet Union. He saw that if communism were to survive, it would have to change. He said that the Soviet Union could not help Communist governments that did not reform.

Gorbachev expected that reforms would strengthen the Communist governments in Eastern Europe. Instead, the opposite happened. Gorbachev did not understand how much the people of the region hated Soviet control and communism.

Once reforms began, they became impossible to control. This was true in both the Soviet Union and the countries of Eastern Europe.

1989: The Year of the People

In 1989, a series of events began that destroyed the Communist governments of Eastern Europe. By 1991, the Soviet Union lay in ruins.

Poland Leads the Way

The end of empire began in Poland. There, the people and the government were locked in a **stalemate**. A stalemate occurs when two sides oppose each other but neither can win.

This stalemate had existed since 1981. The Communist government controlled the army and the police. However, the Polish people refused to cooperate with the government.

The stalemate finally broke in mid-1989, when Poland's Communist government decided to allow free elections for the first time. The Communists thought that they would win the elections. They controlled the government and the press. They also were far better organized than any other party.

The Communists suffered a complete defeat in the elections. In some places they received less than 5 percent of the vote.

In August 1989, Poland's first non-Communist government since World War II took control. It was a turning point in the history of Eastern Europe.

The Berlin Wall Comes Down

The most dramatic events of 1989 took place in East Germany. The Communists there tried very hard to hold onto power.

In the late summer, large crowds gathered to demand more freedom. Communist party leaders wanted to use force and crush the demonstrations. However, other leaders disagreed. A new Communist government took power.

The new government made a last effort to save communism in East Germany. It promised free elections. But that was not enough to satisfy the people. They wanted the Berlin Wall to come down. Since 1961, the Berlin Wall had been a place of sadness, fear, and death. Guards in watchtowers armed with machine guns kept East Germans from escaping.

During the years the Wall stood, about 5,000 people escaped. However, more than 3,000 people were caught and arrested. Another 75 were shot to death at the Wall. Often the killings took place while people in West Berlin watched in horror.

Suddenly, on November 9, 1989, the Berlin Wall became a place to celebrate. On

Taking an ax to the Berlin Wall, Berlin residents celebrate the unification of the city. After 50 years of division, East and West Germany had become one country.

that day, the East German government announced that the Wall would be opened.

First a few people came. By 1 A.M. on November 10, thousands of people were at the opened Wall. They came from East and West Berlin. People danced on top of the Wall.

In East Berlin, cars lined up for a mile to pass into West Berlin. Some people left their cars and walked through the opened Wall. Many had close relatives on the other side whom they had not seen for almost 30 years.

Not even opening the Wall could save communism in East Germany. East Germany held elections and chose the country's first democratic government. Then, leaders announced that East Germany would unite with West Germany. On October 3, 1990, Germany was reunited.

Peaceful and Violent Change

The day after the Berlin Wall was opened, change came to Bulgaria. The Communist leader, Todor Zhivkov (TOH•dohr ZIHF•kof) was removed from power.

In Hungary, the Communist system fell apart bit by bit. The first reforms took place in January 1989. In May, the government removed the barbed-wire fence that had separated Hungary from non-Communist Austria. A small part of the Iron Curtain was gone. Before the year was over, Hungary's Communist party fell apart.

Change also came quickly to Czechoslovakia. At first, the Communist government there took a hard line against the people. In mid-November, police attacked student protesters, but the people refused to back down. On November 20, more than 200,000 people demonstrated for democracy in the capital city of Prague (prahg).

The people had found a leader in a writer named Vaclav Havel (VAHTZ•lahv HAH•vehl). In December, the Communists caved in. Havel became the country's new president. (For more on Havel, see Case Study 41 at the end of this chapter.)

Only in Romania was there widespread violence. In mid-December, the secret police fired on a crowd that was calling for freedom, killing several hundred people.

Less than a week later, a rebellion began. After bloody fighting, Romania's Communist dictator was killed and his government overthrown.

During 1989, the people of Poland, East Germany, and Romania regained their freedom. They destroyed the Iron Curtain and ended the division of Europe. That is why 1989 is called the "Year of the People."

Section 2 Review

1. Why did East Germany and West Germany reunite?

2. **Compare and Contrast** In 1989, how were events in East Germany different from those in Romania?

SECTION 3

Europe and the World Economy

How are the nations of Europe trying to lower trade barriers?

How long should it take to travel 270 miles (430 km) by train? On the line from Paris to Lyon in France, special trains speed along as fast as 186 miles (295 km) per hour. Such speeds are becoming more common as Europe plans for a modern rail network linking many of its major cities.

Train travel in Europe has seen many improvements since the 1940s. Europeans have torn down barriers and found new ways to unite people from different countries.

The Chunnel

Perhaps the boldest sign of a united Europe was the construction of a tunnel under the English Channel connecting Britain and the mainland of Europe. The Channel Tunnel, nicknamed the Chunnel, was officially opened in 1994.

The Chunnel allows passengers to travel by train between London and Paris in about three hours. By the year 2003, the Chunnel is expected to carry more than 120,000 people between England and France each day.

The European Union

Since the end of World War II, countries in Western Europe have taken steps toward greater economic cooperation. The first

On Assignment. . .

Take notes on the events that ended communism in Eastern Europe. In your interview, you may want to ask questions about how the fall of communism took place in different countries. You may also want to ask how communism was toppled without widespread violence.

breakthrough occurred in 1957. In that year, six countries formed an organization that is now called the European Union (EU). The goal of the EU was to remove **tariffs** and other barriers to trade. A tariff is a tax on a product one country sells to another. The first members of the EU were France, West Germany, Italy, the Netherlands, Belgium, and Luxembourg.

Over the years, the EU grew. By 1996, it had 15 members. The most important new member was Britain. By the 1990s, the EU was a trading market of 380 million people. The EU has more people than the United States and Japan combined.

The EU is a big step forward for Europe. Taken alone, no European country except Germany has an economy large enough to make it a world economic power. Taken together, the EU is one of the world's three strongest economic powers. It is in a position to challenge Japan or the United States for economic leadership.

Section 3 Review

1. How have some European countries torn down barriers in recent years?

2. **Analyzing Information** How does the European Union help build prosperity in its member countries?

Creating the Czech Republic

When Vaclav Havel was a struggling writer living under Communist rule, he wrote an essay called "The Power of the Powerless." In it, he said that ordinary people can overcome dictatorships. What they need is the courage to speak up and tell the truth. Havel himself was arrested because he spoke out.

On January 1, 1990, Havel became president of Czechoslovakia. Havel believed that people had to learn to tell the truth as they saw it. He called that "living in truth." All citizens had to start caring for each other again.

Under Havel's leadership, the government passed laws that guarantee basic rights and liberties. In 1991, it began to reform the economy. The goal was to **privatize** the economy. The government's goal was to turn over ownership of factories, farms, and businesses to individual owners.

One man who helped Havel rebuild the country was Jaroslav Koran (YAR•oh•slahv koh•RAHN). Like Havel, Koran was a writer. When the Communists controlled the country, they put him in prison for speaking out. Later Koran could not find work as a writer and had to work maintaining Prague's sewers.

After communism's defeat, Koran was elected mayor of Prague. He said that working underground in the sewers taught him how to run a city "from the bottom up."

A Historic Treasure

Prague is a city with centuries of history. It has one of the oldest universities in Europe and beautiful historic buildings. Yet, Prague suffered during more than 40 years of

Prague suffered during 40 years of Communist rule. Recently, the city has enjoyed a burst of energy and redevelopment in the new Czech Republic.

Communist rule. The old buildings were not maintained. The transportation system was not modernized.

Since the fall of communism, Prague has come to life. The city's historic Old Town is typical of what has been going on. Old Town Square has been a marketplace for almost a thousand years. It has seen many dramatic events in Czech history. Czech kings, German soldiers, and Soviet soldiers have all marched through it. Today it is once again a crossroads of Central Europe.

Each morning, blacksmiths, carpenters, and potters fill the square. Merchants fill small shops with wooden toys, breads, and shining crystal. The music of a jazz band comes from a coffeehouse.

In other parts of the city, people have opened pizza shops, laundries, copy centers, and much more. Large foreign companies also have added to Prague's new life.

Most of the people of Czechoslovakia came from two closely related ethnic groups: the Czechs and the Slovaks. The two groups have similar cultures and languages. About 10 million Czechs and 5 million Slovaks lived in Czechoslovakia. Czechs lived mainly in the western part of the country and Slovaks mainly in the east.

Czechoslovakia Splits

Many Slovaks believed that the Czechs ran Czechoslovakia. They were angry that the Czech part of the country was more prosperous. After 1990, some Slovak political leaders demanded independence from Czechoslovakia. The forces pushing for a split proved to be strong. On January 1, 1993, Czechoslovakia ceased to exist. In its place were the Czech Republic and Slovakia. The split took place peacefully.

Vaclav Havel became the first president of the new Czech Republic. He was saddened by the breakup. Yet he still was optimistic about the Czech Republic and Europe. "I'm driven by hope," he said. "Despite the dangers, this is the best chance of a lifetime that Europe may break out into peace."

Case Study Review

1. How did Vaclav Havel change the government when he was elected president of Czechoslovakia?

2. **Understanding Points of View** Many people are convinced that a united Czechoslovakia would have a stronger economy than a divided country. Still, Slovaks pushed for a breakup. Why do you think this was so?

REVIEWING CHAPTER 41

I. Reviewing Vocabulary

Match each word on the left with the correct definition on the right.

1. privatize
2. tariff
3. stalemate
4. civil disobedience

a. to end government control of factories, farms, and businesses and turn them over to private individuals
b. a form of protest that involves disobeying laws
c. a situation in which two sides oppose each other but neither can win
d. a tax on a product one country sells to another

II. Understanding the Chapter

Answer the questions below on a separate sheet of paper.

1. How did World War II help lead to the end of the European colonial empires?
2. Why is 1989 called the "Year of the People"?
3. Why was the EU an important step forward for Europe?
4. Why did Czechoslovakia break up in the 1990s?

III. Building Skills: Reading a Pie Graph

Read the pie graphs on the next page about the West German and East German work forces. Then answer the questions that appear below the graphs.

IV. Working Together

Make a list of seven important events covered in this chapter. Put them in chronological, or time, order. Then create a time line that shows the date of the event and a brief description of it.

On Assignment. . .

Conducting an Interview: With a classmate, plan an interview with an "expert" on Europe. One of you should play the reporter and the other the expert. Plan questions and answers about the events covered in this chapter.

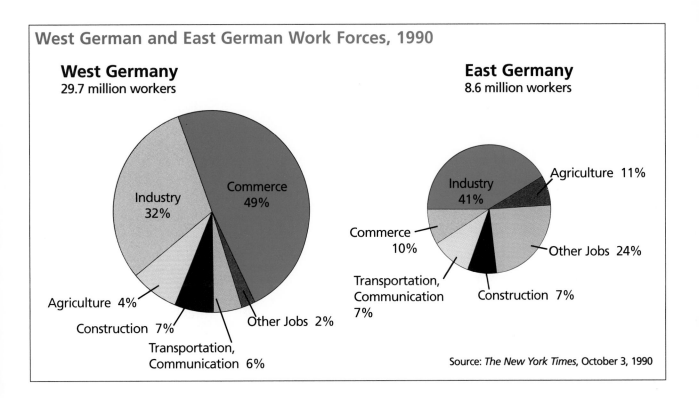

West German and East German Work Forces, 1990

West Germany
29.7 million workers

Commerce 49%
Industry 32%
Agriculture 4%
Construction 7%
Transportation, Communication 6%
Other Jobs 2%

East Germany
8.6 million workers

Industry 41%
Agriculture 11%
Commerce 10%
Transportation, Communication 7%
Other Jobs 24%
Construction 7%

Source: *The New York Times*, October 3, 1990

1. Which Germany had a larger proportion of workers in agriculture?

2. In which Germany was a majority of workers employed in commerce, transportation, and communications?

3. Which Germany had more workers in construction?

4. How many workers did Germany have? What percentage of them lived in West Germany? What percentage lived in East Germany?

CHAPTER 42

The Heritage of Russia and the Eurasian Heartland

What are the historical roots of Russia and the Eurasian Heartland?

Bound to the land by law, Russia's serfs lived in poverty and misery. Here, Russian peasants are shown in their rural village in the 1870s.

On Assignment...

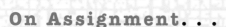

Writing a Journal Entry: Many people keep journals of their daily experiences. The entries they make tell about what they have done or what they are thinking at the time. After reading this chapter, you will be asked to write journal entries for people who have lived in Russia and in the Eurasian Heartland. Look for topic suggestions in the boxes as you read the chapter.

Looking at Key Terms

- **tsar** a term for a king of Russia
- **autocracy** a form of government in which the ruler has almost complete power over the people
- **modernize** to bring up to date
- **assassinate** to kill an important person
- **revolution** an attempt to overthrow a political system
- **socialism** the belief that the government should own a country's factories and farms and that people should share wealth equally
- **provisional** temporary
- **purge** to remove people who are considered undesirable

SECTION 1

Russia Takes Shape

How did a few scattered farming communities along the Dnieper River become a center of Russian power?

More than a thousand years ago, a people called the East Slavs lived on the fertile Russian steppe. Many were farmers. They were skilled at many crafts and at making iron. The East Slavs built many towns that were protected from raiders by wooden stockades.

Gradually, a center of power developed around Kiev (kee•EHF), a town on the Dnieper (d'NEYE•pehr) River. Today Kiev is the capital of Ukraine. Most people in Kiev were farmers. However, trade was very important and helped the region prosper.

Much of the trade was with the Byzantine Empire, Kiev's neighbor to the south. Every year hundreds of boats sailed down the Dnieper River to the Black Sea and on to Constantinople. Kievan merchants unloaded furs, wax, honey, grain, forest products, and slaves. They exchanged them for wines, perfumes, and other luxuries.

Kiev Converts to Christianity

One event in the 800s had a tremendous impact on Russian history. Russian traders brought back the Christian religion from Constantinople. Once Christianity was introduced, it spread rapidly among the poor people. In 988, Prince Vladimir of Kiev converted to Christianity, which he made the official religion of his land.

Over several centuries the new church developed into the Russian Orthodox Church. The religious texts of this church were written in a new alphabet called the Cyrillic (suh•RIHL•ihk) alphabet. It was based on the Greek alphabet but created especially for the language of the East Slavs.

On Assignment...

Imagine that you were living in Kievan Russia during the years of the Mongol conquest. Describe in your journal what was happening to your country.

Today Russian, Ukrainian, and Belarusian all are written with the Cyrillic alphabet.

The Mongol Conquest

Kievan Russia was at its most powerful in the 1000s and 1100s. Then its power was gradually weakened by disputes and fighting between princes from different cities. It also faced continual attacks from nomadic peoples moving westward out of Asia. Even at the height of its power, Kiev struggled to protect itself against these warlike groups.

In the 1200s, the Mongols appeared out of Asia to attack Kiev. The Mongols already had conquered a huge empire in Asia. They were by far the most powerful enemy that Kievan Russia had ever seen.

The Mongols moved through Kievan territory destroying everything in their path. A traveler a few years after the Mongol invasion found only 200 houses still standing in Kiev. He wrote that the city "has been reduced to nothing." The Mongols enslaved thousands of people and left the country in ruins.

Mongol rule was a disaster for Russia. It lasted for more than 200 years, and it separated Russia from Europe. The Mongols placed high taxes on the people and cruelly punished anyone who refused to obey.

Section 1 Review

1. What form of Christianity did Kievan Russia adopt?
2. **Drawing Conclusions** Why was the Mongol conquest such a disaster for Kievan Russia?

SECTION 2

The Rise of the Tsars

How did the Russian tsars throw off the rule of the Mongols and take control of a vast area of Eurasia?

The princes of a Russian state called Moscow gradually gained power over the surrounding states. Moscow thrived because it was near several important rivers and was well placed for trade.

Over several centuries, Moscow grew by seizing the territory of weaker Russian states. As it grew, the power of its princes also grew. Gradually, the princes of Moscow began to push back the Mongol invaders.

The Russian Orthodox Church established its headquarters in Moscow in the 1320s. Over time, the Russian Orthodox Church became a central part of the Russian national identity.

By the mid-1400s, Moscow was a large and powerful state. Its prince was Ivan III. Ivan came to the throne in 1462. Over the next 43 years, he tripled the size of Russia. He defeated Moscow's remaining Russian rivals. In 1480, he was strong enough to declare his independence from the Mongols. When Ivan died, he left behind a powerful and independent Russia.

Russia's First Tsar

Ivan's grandson was Ivan IV. He is called Ivan the Terrible because of his cruelty. His goal was to be an all-powerful ruler. When

Movement Over hundreds of years, the princes of Moscow took control of a great deal of territory. Under which ruler did Russian territory extend to the Caspian Sea?

Ivan was 13, he decided to execute a close adviser whom he disliked. This was the beginning of a long series of executions. In 1547, Ivan had himself crowned **tsar**, or emperor, of Russia.

Ivan the Terrible increased his strength by breaking the strength of Russia's nobles. He killed and tortured those who dared to oppose him. Ivan even killed his own son to be sure his hold on power was complete.

Ivan the Terrible finished the job of making the Russian monarchy an **autocracy**. In an autocracy, the ruler has almost complete power over the people. The law does not limit what an autocratic ruler can do.

Serfdom

Serfdom in Russia developed over a period of about 150 years. Serfdom guaranteed that Russia's nobles would have workers on their estates. Serfdom also made it easier for the government to tax the peasants. Russian serfs could not move, marry, or learn to read without their landlord's permission. They could be drafted into the army and had to pay very heavy taxes.

Serfdom kept Russia's peasants under control. It also left them ignorant and poor. Serfdom was a cruel system that damaged Russian life for centuries. (See Chapter 38 to review serfdom in Western Europe.)

Russia Expands

As Russia became more powerful, it began to grow. There were few natural boundaries to stop that expansion. Ivan the Terrible pushed Russia's borders southward to the shores of the Caspian Sea. He also expanded into Asia.

Russian expansion continued through the 1800s. It made Russia by far the largest country in the world. It also made Russia an empire in which only half the people were Russian. Over 100 non-Russian groups lived within its borders.

No matter how big Russia grew, it could not overcome a major problem. By the 1500s, Russia lagged behind the countries of Western Europe. It trailed them in technology and in economic strength. Russia's military forces also were weak compared to Europe's forces.

Determined to spread Western ways to Russia, Peter the Great took some bold steps. Here he cuts off the sleeves of his nobles' robes to force them to adopt Western dress.

Peter the Great

The first tsar to try to get Russia to catch up with the West was Peter I, known to history as Peter the Great. Peter was a giant of a man—tall, muscular, and strong. During his 43 years as tsar, he helped make Russia a leading power.

Peter wanted to **modernize** Russia, or bring it up to date, so that it could compete with the European powers.

Peter made many reforms. He brought Western experts to Russia and sent Russians to study in Europe. He established schools and new industries.

Peter built a new capital city on the Baltic Sea called St. Petersburg. He said that his new city was his "window on the West." Peter hoped having such a window would help Russia learn from the West.

During his long reign, Peter expanded Russia's territory. However, his many wars left Russia's people poor and exhausted. Thousands of peasants died in the building of St. Petersburg.

Catherine the Great

Catherine the Great ruled Russia from 1762 to 1796. Like Peter, Catherine was a strong leader. During her reign, Catherine further expanded Russia's borders. Catherine built new schools and introduced reforms in government.

However, Catherine's wars, new palaces, and other projects were expensive. Again, the common people suffered. The greatest peasant rebellion in Russia's history took place during her reign. Catherine had the rebellion put down with great cruelty.

Section 2 Review

1. How did serfdom limit freedom in Russia?
2. **Making Inferences** Why might ordinary Russians not have liked Peter the Great or Catherine the Great?

SECTION 3

The Fall of the Tsars

What led to the fall of the Russian tsars?

Between 1853 and 1856, Russia fought and lost the Crimean War against Britain and France. This defeat made Russia's leaders realize the need for reforms that would modernize Russia.

In 1861, Tsar Alexander II finally freed Russia's serfs. This huge step set free 20 million peasants. However, nothing was done to raise their standard of living. Some of Alexander II's reforms were reversed after he was **assassinated**, or killed, in 1881.

Russia's Artistic Achievements

The 1800s saw a great flowering of Russian art and culture. Russia produced some of the world's greatest writers. Among them were Alexander Pushkin, Fyodor Dostoyevsky (dohs•tuh•YEHV•skee), and Leo Tolstoy. Russia also produced some of the world's greatest composers, opera singers, and ballet dancers. Russians made outstanding contributions in every area of culture.

The Revolutionary Movement

Despite the reforms of the 1800s, Russia remained an autocratic state. Most of its people were very poor. Some young Russians decided that the country needed a **revolution**. They wanted to overthrow Russia's political system and replace it with a new one.

Many of Russia's revolutionaries believed in **socialism**. In a socialist system, the government owns the country's factories and farms and runs the economy. Its goal is to share all wealth equally.

Russian revolutionaries had to operate in secret to avoid arrest. By the early 1900s, there were several revolutionary groups. One extreme party was the Bolsheviks, led by Vladimir Lenin.

Take notes on the events of 1914 to 1917. Then make entries in your diary that describe what happened in Russia at that time.

In 1904, Russia went to war with Japan. This war caused great hardship at home. On January 22, 1905, a large crowd of workers and their families gathered in St. Petersburg to ask Tsar Nicholas II for help. Soldiers fired on the crowd, killing hundreds of people. That day is called Bloody Sunday.

Bloody Sunday sparked the Revolution of 1905. The tsar was able to put down the revolution. However, he had to agree to some reforms.

The Russian Revolution

Nicholas II tried to ignore Russia's problems. When World War I broke out in 1914, Russia was not prepared. Its armies suffered many defeats. By early 1917, more than 8 million soldiers had been killed or wounded, or were missing. At home, people were cold and hungry. They began to turn against the tsar.

The March Revolution

In March 1917, a week of demonstrations caused the tsar's government to collapse. Nicholas II was forced to give up the throne. He was replaced by a government called the **Provisional** Government. This temporary government wanted Russia to be democratic and to have a modern capitalist economy. The new government immediately passed laws that guaranteed civil rights and ended discrimination.

During the next eight months, the new government was unable to restore order in Russia. Russian troops suffered defeats at the front. The government was losing support among the people.

After the Bolsheviks seized control of the Russian government in 1917, a unit of soldiers paraded through the streets of Moscow under a banner that simply reads "Communism."

The Bolshevik Revolution

The Bolshevik party, led by Lenin, took advantage of the situation. Lenin's party had support among workers in the big cities and among soldiers. However, most Russians supported other parties.

In November, the Bolsheviks staged an armed uprising. Bolshevik forces arrested leaders of the Provisional Government. Russia's first experiment with democracy was over. A long period of dictatorship was about to begin.

Section 3 Review

1. What was Tsar Alexander II's greatest reform?
2. **Analyzing Information** How did World War I help lead to the revolutions of 1917?

SECTION 4

A Brief History of the Soviet Union

How did the Communists create the Soviet Union?

The Bolsheviks were followers of a German thinker named Karl Marx. His version of socialism was called communism. According to Marx, capitalism created a few rich owners and many poor workers. Eventually the workers would overthrow the capitalists and establish a Communist system. Everyone would be treated equally and poverty would be abolished.

Communist Dictatorship

As soon as the Bolsheviks seized power, they began to build a dictatorship. Their opponents ranged from supporters of the tsar to other socialists. The result was a civil

Karl Marx's theory of communism was more successful in Russia than in Western Europe. To Communists, the free enterprise system was doomed.

war. It lasted from 1918 to 1921. Millions of people died. The Bolsheviks won the civil war. In 1922, they renamed the country the Union of Soviet Socialist Republics, or the Soviet Union.

Under Lenin, the secret police hunted down anyone who opposed the government. Lenin's government took control of the country's large industries. However, it was not strong enough to take over the whole economy. Most of the Soviet people were peasant farmers. They were allowed to keep farming their land and sell what they grew.

The Struggle for Power

Lenin led the Communist party until his death in 1924. A struggle for power followed. Joseph Stalin won this struggle. By 1929, Stalin was the leader of the Communist party and the dictator of the Soviet Union.

The Drive to Build Industry

Communist party leaders agreed that in order for communism to succeed, a country needed modern industry. However, because the Soviet Union was mainly a country of

Describe in your diary or journal how Stalin's policies affected the Soviet people.

poor farmers, the leaders agreed that a complete change must be made. Stalin decided to industrialize the country in ten years.

This drive to build industry used brutal methods. Beginning in 1929, the government seized all land from the peasants. They were forced to move to large farms where hundreds of families worked together.

Farmers who resisted were shot or sent to slave labor camps. Millions of people suffered. In the early 1930s, at least five million farmers died of starvation.

The Soviet government used all of its resources to build industry. Workers received low salaries. Housing conditions were terrible. The standard of living fell drastically.

The drive to build industry lasted through the 1930s. It made the Soviet Union the world's second largest industrial power, behind the United States. The price was great hardship for the Soviet people.

Stalin's Reign of Terror

In the mid-1930s, Stalin began a campaign of terror that took millions of lives. That event is known as the Great **Purge**. During this time, Stalin had the secret police arrest millions of people. Among those arrested were most of the Communist party's leaders and the country's top generals. Stalin feared that they might try to seize power from him.

At least one million people were shot. Millions more were sent to slave labor camps, where a great many died.

In 1941, the Soviet Union was drawn into World War II by a German attack. A terrible four-year struggle followed. At least 20 million Soviet citizens died during the war.

Stalin's Successors

Stalin died in 1953. After a power struggle, Nikita Khrushchev (KROOSH•chehf) took

The mighty fall. A statue of Lenin erected in Hungary in 1971 was pulled down in 1990 when Hungary rejected communism.

power. However, Khrushchev was not an absolute dictator like Stalin. His power depended on support from other top Communist party officials.

Khrushchev introduced reforms that improved the life of the Soviet people. Their standard of living rose. Artists and writers had more freedom to express themselves. However, the Soviet Union still was a Communist dictatorship. In 1964, party bosses opposed to Khrushchev's reforms removed him from power.

The Soviet leader for the next eighteen years was Leonid Brezhnev (BREZH•nef). Under Brezhnev, no reforms took place. The Soviet economy weakened. Corruption and crime increased. When Brezhnev died in 1982, the Soviet Union badly needed reforms and new policies.

Section 4 Review

1. Why did Stalin try to modernize Russia's industries?

2. **Formulating Questions** If you could ask Joseph Stalin one question, what would it be?

Reform and Collapse

In 1985, Mikhail Gorbachev became the Soviet Union's new leader. Gorbachev believed that the country needed major reforms to solve its problems.

Gorbachev soon ran into trouble. He tried to combine two opposing elements. One element was the Soviet Union's Communist dictatorship. The other element was the system of freedom in Western Europe and the United States.

When communism collapsed in the Soviet Union, it took with it the career of Mikhail Gorbachev, left. The first leader of the newly independent Russia was Boris Yeltsin, right.

One Gorbachev reform called for elections to a new Soviet parliament. These would be real elections. Previously, the Soviets had held elections with only one candidate for each office. Yet at the same time, Gorbachev intended that the Communist party's dictatorship should continue.

When the new parliament was elected, many non-Communists won seats. The parliament immediately became difficult for Gorbachev to control. Other groups in Soviet society also became more difficult to control. Among the most important were several non-Russian ethnic groups. They began threatening to leave the Soviet Union and set up their own governments.

Gorbachev also was unable to improve the Soviet economy. In August 1991, several top party officials tried to overthrow Gorbachev. The army refused to obey the plotters, and the plot failed.

However, Gorbachev could not save the Soviet Union. By the end of the year, the Soviet Union had been divided into 15 new nations. A new era in the history of the Eurasian Heartland had begun.

Case Study Review

1. How did Mikhail Gorbachev attempt to reform the Soviet government?
2. **Analyzing Information** How did attempts at reform lead to the collapse of the Soviet Union?

I. Reviewing Vocabulary

Match each word on the left with the correct definition on the right.

1. assassinate
2. modernize
3. autocracy
4. provisional

a. to bring up to date
b. a form of government in which the ruler has almost complete power over the people
c. temporary
d. to kill an important person

II. Understanding the Chapter

Answer the questions below on a separate sheet of paper.

1. What was the goal of Peter the Great and how did he try to accomplish it?
2. How did the Bolshevik party come to power?
3. What means did Stalin use to modernize the Soviet Union?
4. What happened during the Great Purge?

III. Building Skills: Comparing and Contrasting

Answer the questions below on a separate sheet of paper.

1. What goal did Peter the Great and Stalin have in common?
2. How was government under the Russian tsars similar to the government under the Communists in the Soviet Union?
3. What was the main difference between Khrushchev and Brezhnev?

IV. Working Together

In a small group, make a list of the different rulers mentioned in this chapter. Arrange them in chronological, or time, order under the heading "Important Rulers in Russia's History." Consult a reference book in your library. Have each person in the group write a one-page summary of the importance of one Russian or Soviet ruler from your list. Assemble your summaries into a reference book for your classroom.

On Assignment . . .

Writing a Journal Entry: Take the journal entries you have written and arrange them in chronological order. Then put them together in pamphlet form. Put your journal on display for your classmates to read.

CHAPTER 43

Changing Patterns of Life in Russia and the Eurasian Heartland

How has life changed in Russia and the Eurasian Heartland since the fall of the Soviet Union?

With historic St. Basil's cathedral in the background, democracy demonstrators carry the banner of the Russian republic through Red Square in a 1991 demonstration.

On Assignment...

Creating an Atlas: As you read this chapter, you will sketch maps of the places being discussed. Look for suggestions about what maps to sketch in the On Assignment boxes throughout the chapter. At the end of the chapter, you will put the map sketches together and create your own atlas of Russia and the Heartland. You can use this atlas for review purposes.

Looking at Key Terms

- **convenience** something that saves work or makes a person's life easier
- **hostile** very unfriendly or opposed to something
- **nationalism** devotion to one's country
- **suppress** to put down by force
- **genocide** the destruction of a national or ethnic group
- **secede** to break away from a country or another political unit
- **divert** to channel in another direction

Changing Patterns in Russia

What problems do Russians today have to overcome?

When the 1900s began, most Russians were peasant farmers living in small villages. In the late 1920s, the Soviet government began to build industries. Millions of people moved to the cities to work in these industries.

By the middle of the century, about half of Russia's people lived in cities. Today about three out of four Russians live in urban areas.

Moscow is Russia's capital and its largest and most important city. It is home to more than 10.5 million people. The offices of the government, called the Kremlin, are located in Moscow.

Russia's second largest city is St. Petersburg. St. Petersburg, which was built under the direction of Tsar Peter the Great, is considered one of the most beautiful cities in the world. It contains many museums and art galleries. The most famous of these is the Hermitage (HERM•uh•tihj), which is located in the former Winter Palace of the tsars.

The area that includes Moscow and St. Petersburg is one of Russia's largest industrial regions. It is a highly populated area and is connected by railroads, rivers, and canals to the sources of raw materials. The Volga and other rivers link Moscow to the sea. As a result, goods flow steadily in and out of Moscow and St. Petersburg.

SOME FACTS ABOUT RUSSIA AND THE HEARTLAND

COUNTRY	CAPITAL CITY	POPULATION (in millions)	AREA (square miles)	PER CAPITA INCOME
Armenia	Yerevan	3.5	11,500	$4,710
Azerbaijan	Baku	7.1	33,400	3,750
Belarus	Minsk	10.3	80,200	5,960
Georgia	Tbilisi	5.5	26,900	4,410
Kazakstan	Almaty	16.9	1,049,200	3,720
Kyrgyzstan	Bishkek	4.5	76,600	3,030
Moldova	Chisinau	4.4	13,000	3,830
Russia	Moscow	149.3	6,592,800	5,810
Tajikistan	Dushanbe	5.5	55,300	2,340
Turkmenistan	Ashgabat	3.9	188,500	3,370
Ukraine	Kiev	52.1	233,100	4,700
Uzbekistan	Tashkent	21.3	172,700	2,750

One country, Russia, dominates the Heartland in population and area. Which country is the next largest in area? Which has the next largest population? Estonia, Latvia, and Lithuania are included in the chart on page 537.

Women in Russian Society

The Soviet era had a great impact on the role of women. The Soviet state needed millions of women workers. They were used in new industries, on building projects, and on farms.

This need created new opportunities for many women. Women entered professions such as medicine and engineering. By the end of the Soviet era, most Russian women worked outside the home.

These new opportunities for women, though, came at a high price. Men continued to hold most of the high-ranking jobs. Most Russian women also worked double shifts. They worked a full day on the job and then did housework and cared for their children.

Russian women did not have private cars, supermarkets, and other **conveniences** to help them with their many tasks. Such time-savers could have made their lives easier. Since 1991, hard economic times have added to the burdens of Russian women.

Turning to Tradition

The Russian people face many challenges now that communism has fallen. They have turned to some of their oldest traditions to help them face these challenges.

The Russian Orthodox Church One of the most important of those traditions is the Russian Orthodox Church. Under communism, the state was **hostile** to religion. The government destroyed many houses of woship and made it difficult for people to practice religion. All religious groups suffered, including the Russian Orthodox Church.

Since the fall of communism, Russians have won freedom of religion. Many have returned to the Orthodox faith.

Russian Science Russians have many scientific achievements to their credit. Among the great Russian scientists of the pre-Soviet period was chemist Dmitry Mendeleyev (duh•MEET•ree men•duh•LAY•uhf). He developed the Periodic Table of the Elements.

The Soviet space program was highly successful. In 1957, the Soviets launched the first human-made satellite. They put the first human into space in 1961.

Science is one of many areas of Russian life that suffered during the early 1990s. The new government did not have the money to support scientific research. Some scientists left the country. Others moved into different types of work in order to make a living.

After years of persecution by the Communists, the Russian Orthodox Church began to grow again in the 1980s. Orthodox churches, such as this one in the village of Belaya, attract many worshipers.

Russian Nationalism **Nationalism**, or devotion to one's country, can be healthy or it can become extreme. In recent years, some Russian nationalists have become hostile toward other nations or ethnic groups. They talk of attacking their neighbors to regain territory lost with the collapse of the Soviet Union. Many extreme Russian nationalists are also opposed to democratic government. They say that it is too weak and call for a dictatorship to run the country. Many of Russia's neighbors worry about the growth of Russian nationalism.

Section 1 Review

1. What are Russia's two largest cities?
2. **Hypothesizing** Why did Russians return to religion after the collapse of communism?

SECTION 2

Changing Patterns in Western Eurasia

How are the republics of Western Eurasia facing life without the Soviet Union?

When the Soviet Union collapsed, three new independent countries emerged along Russia's southwestern border. They are Ukraine, Belarus, and Moldova. This region has no mountains or other natural borders. Instead, language and religion have made one area different from another.

Ukraine

Ukraine is the largest of these three countries. Ukraine has rich coal fields and important industries. However, Ukraine's greatest resource is its fertile farmland.

Ukraine has been under foreign control through most of its history. It was under Russian control for more than 300 years.

When the Russian empire collapsed in 1917, Ukraine briefly was independent. However, Bolshevik forces overran the country and brought it into the Soviet Union.

Ukrainian nationalism grew again in the 1980s. On December 1, 1991, Ukraine's people voted for independence. That vote helped lead to the breakup of the Soviet Union.

Belarus

Belarus is the smallest of the three Eastern Slav nations. Forests cover about a third of the country. They are vital to such industries as paper and furniture making.

Except for a short period in 1918, Belarusians have never been independent. Belarus has long been a battleground between Russia and Poland. Each country has tried to **suppress**, or put down by force, Belarusian national feeling. After the collapse of communism, Belarusians suddenly gained independence and a chance to build a national identity.

Moldova

Moldova is a small country squeezed between much stronger neighbors. The Moldovans speak a language that is closely related to the Romanian language. Before 1917, Romania and the Russian empire fought over Moldova. The struggle continued during the Soviet era.

While Moldova was under Soviet control, Russians and Ukrainians moved into the region. Today only two out of every three people in the country are Moldovan. Most of the rest are Russian or Ukrainian. Ethnic tensions are very high in Moldova.

Section 2 Review

1. How did Russia try to suppress nationalism in Belarus?
2. **Making Inferences** What kinds of problems can occur when many different languages are spoken in a country?

Changing Patterns in the Caucasus

How are ethnic conflicts endangering peace in the Caucasus?

Three small countries, Armenia, Azerbaijan (ah•zuhr•beye•JAHN), and Georgia, share the Caucasus region south of Russia. Over the centuries, Christian and Muslim forces have clashed there many times. Today, all three countries are threatened by violence among opposing ethnic groups.

Armenia

The Armenians are an ancient people. They trace their history to 900 B.C. Their capital, Yerevan, was founded in 782 B.C.

The Armenian people converted to Christianity about A.D. 300. Armenia's Muslim neighbors have been its enemies for centuries.

During World War I, the Turkish Ottoman Empire committed **genocide** against the Christian Armenians. The Turks murdered more than 1.5 million Armenians in 1915.

Since independence, Armenia has fought with Muslim Azerbaijan. The conflict is over a part of Azerbaijan that has many Armenian residents.

Azerbaijan

Azerbaijan is located on the western shores of the Caspian Sea. The area has been invaded by Arabs, Turks, and Russians. It came under Russian control in the 1800s.

Azerbaijan has large oil deposits. Its capital, Baku, is an important oil center.

The people of Azerbaijan are Muslim and have close religious ties to the people of Iran, which is just across Azerbaijan's southern border. Today Azerbaijan's most urgent problem is its dispute with Armenia.

Georgia

The Georgian people have lived in the Caucasus region since ancient times. Although they were surrounded by powerful neighbors, they remained independent for many centuries.

Georgia became part of the Russian empire in the early 1800s. Since gaining its

Ethnic violence has torn apart an area of Azerbaijan called Nagorno Karabakh. There ancient hatreds between Christians and Muslims have exploded into violence.

independence, Georgia has been torn by division. Non-Georgian minorities have fought to **secede** from the country and form their own countries.

Ethnic Troubles in the Caucasus

While the Caucasus has known many conflicts, some of the most bitter have been between Muslims and Christians. In recent years, the worst violence has been a war between Christian Armenia and Muslim Azerbaijan over Nagorno Karabakh (nah•GAWR•noh kahr•uh•BAHK). It is a beautiful mountain area about the size of Delaware. Most of its people are Armenian Christians. However, borders drawn during the Soviet era put the region in Azerbaijan. Azerbaijan is a mostly Muslim nation.

The cost of the war has been high to all sides. More than 20,000 people have been killed. At least one million are homeless. Armenia is short of food, fuel, and other goods. Azerbaijan has been unable to develop its oil riches.

Section 3 Review

1. What happened in Armenia in 1915?

2. **Formulating Questions** You are reporting on the conflict in Nagorno Karabakh for a U.S. newspaper. Make up three questions to ask each side that you think would best explain the nature of the conflict.

On Assignment. . .

Draw an outline map of Russia on a piece of paper. Place Moscow and St. Petersburg on your map. Refer to an atlas for the location of other large Russian cities. Put them on your map as well.

SECTION 4

Changing Patterns in Central Asia

What challenges do the people of the republics of Central Asia face?

Before the Communist takeover, Central Asia had a rich civilization. Important trade routes connected Central Asia with China and East Asia, Europe, and the Middle East. Cities on the trade route grew wealthy.

At the beginning of the 1900s, most people of Central Asia outside the cities were nomads. Both the nomads and city dwellers were devout Muslims.

The Soviets were hostile to religion. They attempted to stamp out Muslim culture. Many fine old buildings were torn down. Public celebrations glorified communism, not Islam.

With the fall of the Soviet Union, new countries became independent in Central Asia. The two largest Central Asian countries, Kazakstan and Uzbekistan, show how patterns of life changed in this region.

Kazakstan

Next to Russia, Kazakstan (kuh•zahk•STAHN) is the largest republic to emerge from the breakup of the Soviet Union. It is about twice the size of Alaska.

Kazakstan is a country in which no group is in the majority. The Kazaks (kuh•ZAKS) are the largest group. They are about 40 percent of the population. The Kazaks are Muslims. The second largest group of people in Kazakstan are Russians. They are almost 38 percent of the population.

Kazakstan has large oil deposits in and around the Caspian Sea. It also has high unemployment. Kazakstan's most serious problem is its environment. It was heavily polluted by industries built during the Soviet era and by Soviet nuclear weapons tests.

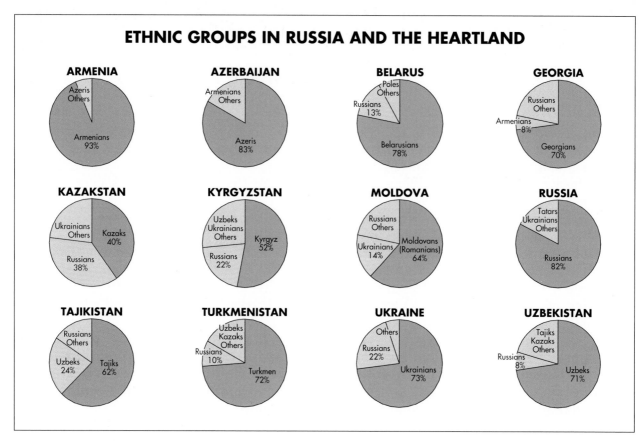

ETHNIC GROUPS IN RUSSIA AND THE HEARTLAND

ARMENIA
- Azeris
- Others
- Armenians 93%

AZERBAIJAN
- Armenians
- Others
- Azeris 83%

BELARUS
- Poles
- Others
- Russians 13%
- Belarusians 78%

GEORGIA
- Russians
- Others
- Armenians 8%
- Georgians 70%

KAZAKSTAN
- Ukrainians
- Others
- Kazaks 40%
- Russians 38%

KYRGYZSTAN
- Uzbeks
- Ukrainians
- Others
- Kyrgyz 52%
- Russians 22%

MOLDOVA
- Russians
- Others
- Ukrainians 14%
- Moldovans (Romanians) 64%

RUSSIA
- Tatars
- Ukrainians
- Others
- Russians 82%

TAJIKISTAN
- Russians
- Others
- Uzbeks 24%
- Tajiks 62%

TURKMENISTAN
- Uzbeks
- Kazaks
- Others
- Russians 10%
- Turkmen 72%

UKRAINE
- Others
- Russians 22%
- Ukrainians 73%

UZBEKISTAN
- Tajiks
- Kazaks
- Others
- Russians 8%
- Uzbeks 71%

A complex mix of ethnic groups lives in the nations of the Eurasian Heartland. In which of these nations is the major ethnic group a minority in its own nation?

Uzbekistan

Uzbekistan has even more serious problems with its environment. The worst environmental problem involves the Aral Sea. The Aral Sea is a salt lake with no outlet. The Soviet government **diverted** water from the rivers that flow into the Aral Sea. Instead of reaching the Aral, the water now goes to irrigate cotton fields. Without its water supply, the Aral Sea started to dry up. Winds then blew the salty sands from the dry sea bottom across the countryside. The salt ruined large areas of farmland.

On Assignment . . .

Review this chapter and make a list of some of the trouble spots in the Eurasian Heartland. Then draw an outline map of Russia and the Heartland and locate these trouble spots on it. Write short explanations to accompany your map.

Section 4 Review

1. What problem is facing the Aral Sea and the area around it?

2. **Cause and Effect** How does pollution in Central Asia affect life today?

Ethnic Tensions in Crimea

The collapse of the Soviet Union brought to the surface ethnic tensions all over the Heartland. New national borders split some ethnic groups into two or more countries. New countries crammed together ethnic groups that have long-standing tensions. Millions of people who had been Soviet citizens suddenly became ethnic minorities.

The Crimea in Dispute

The Crimea has played an important role in Russian history. During the Crimean War, Britain, France, Italy, and Turkey attacked Russia's Crimean port of Sevastopol. Only when the city was virtually destroyed did its garrison surrender.

During World War II, a mighty German army attacked Sevastopol. This time, the city held out for 248 days.

Near the end of World War II, Soviet, British, and U.S. leaders met at the Crimean resort of Yalta for a conference. The Yalta Conference had a large influence on how Europe was divided after World War II.

Russian or Ukrainian?

The Soviet Union was divided into 15 parts, called republics. Until 1954, the Crimea was part of Russia. In 1954, the Soviets decided to attach the Crimea to Ukraine. The decision was not considered important because the 15 republics were tightly controlled by the Soviet government in Moscow.

When the Soviet Union collapsed, the borders of the republics suddenly became important. They had become the borders of independent nations. The new borders left the Crimea in Ukraine.

The problem was that about two thirds of the Crimea's population was Russian. About 25 percent was Ukrainian. Nine percent belong to other groups.

Crimea's Russians do not want to be part of Ukraine. They want to secede from Ukraine and rejoin Russia. One Crimean Russian explained how his people feel. "Most people who live here have always considered themselves Russian. They always thought they lived in Russia. Now suddenly, it turns out they are in Ukraine."

Case Study Review

1. Why are Russia and Ukraine arguing over Crimea?

2. **Interpreting a Quotation** What does the Crimean resident mean by the following statement: "They always thought they lived in Russia. Now suddenly, it turns out they are in Ukraine"?

REVIEWING CHAPTER 43

I. Reviewing Vocabulary

Match each word on the left with the correct definition on the right.

1. convenience
2. hostile
3. suppress
4. secede

a. very unfriendly or opposed to something
b. to put down by force
c. to break away from a country or another political unit
d. something that saves work or makes a person's life easier

II. Understanding the Chapter

Answer the questions below on a separate sheet of paper.

1. What caused Russia to change from a rural country to an urban country?
2. What is the source of the dispute between Armenia and Azerbaijan?
3. What has happened to the Aral Sea in recent years and why has it happened?
4. Why are Russia and Ukraine arguing over the Crimean peninsula?

III. Building Skills: Distinguishing Fact From Opinion

Tell whether the following statements are facts or opinions. If they are opinions, rewrite the sentences to make them factual.

1. By opposing religion, the Communists caused the downfall of the Soviet Union.
2. Environmental damage in Central Asia caused the Aral Sea to dry up.
3. Russians have many scientific achievements to their credit, including the creation of the Periodic Table of the Elements.

IV. Working Together

Form a small group. Choose Russia or one of the countries of the Eurasian Heartland mentioned in this chapter. What is the major problem or issue facing that country? Discuss possible solutions to the problem. Reach agreement within the group on how you would deal with that problem if you led the country. Compare your solutions with those of other groups. Have the class vote to select the solution they think is most realistic.

On Assignment. . .

Creating an Atlas: Take the map sketches you have done for this chapter and staple them to form an atlas. Put your atlas on display in your classroom. Choose one of the sketches and discuss the theme that you have portrayed in it.

CHAPTER 44

Russia and the Heartland in the World Today

How are Russia and the new republics dealing with each other and with the outside world?

Trying to live in the rubble caused by ethnic fighting, residents of Grozny in Chechnya must climb a ladder to use a bridge. The bridge was destroyed after fighting in 1994.

Looking at Key Terms

- **foreign policy** the way in which a country deals with other countries
- **overthrow** to bring down from power by force
- **negotiation** the act of dealing or bargaining with someone else
- **nonaggression treaty** an agreement between countries not to take hostile action against one another
- **arms race** a contest between nations to build more powerful weapons
- **black market** a place or system in which goods are sold illegally
- **barter** the act of exchanging goods and services without using money

On Assignment...

Writing an Editorial: When you finish this chapter you will write a newspaper editorial about Russia's relationship with its neighbors and the rest of the world. You should understand how Russia dealt with other countries between 1917 and 1991. Then you can compare and contrast Soviet conduct before and after 1996.

SECTION 1

The Soviets and the World, 1917–1945

Why did the Soviets make a treaty with the Nazis?

In the highlands of Kazakstan, a teenage boy named Berik sits on a doorstep. He cannot see because he has been blind since birth. His entire face is swollen. It has been that way since the day Berik was born.

Berik is one of thousands of victims of Soviet nuclear tests. These tests were conducted up to 30 years before he was born. But their effects live on today in people such as Berik.

Nobody knows how many other victims there are. Scientists do know that between 1949 and 1989, the Soviet government performed 500 nuclear tests in the region. Many were above ground. The winds blew nuclear fallout from those tests into areas where people lived. Among those people were Berik's mother and father. Scientists think exposure to fallout caused many such problems.

A HISTORY OF SOVIET FOREIGN POLICY, 1917–1991

1917	Bolsheviks take over government
1919	Comintern is organized
1939	Stalin and Hitler sign nonaggression treaty
1939	Soviet Union invades Poland and Finland
1941	Germans attack Soviet Union
1942	Battle of Stalingrad
1945	Soviet armies overrun Eastern Europe
1948	Berlin airlift begins
1949	Soviet Union explodes atom bomb
1955	Warsaw Pact formed
1956	Soviets brutally put down Hungarian uprising
1961	Berlin Wall built
1962	Cuban Missile Crisis
1968	Soviet army invades Czechoslovakia
1979	Soviets invade Afghanistan
1989	Communism begins collapsing in Eastern Europe
1991	Soviet Union collapses

The last years of Communist rule were filled with foreign policy disasters. In what years did Soviet troops attempt to put down foreign uprisings?

Today, the nuclear tests no longer go on. But for Berik and many thousands of other Kazaks, it is too late.

Nuclear testing is one example of how little concern the Soviets showed for human life. For most of their history, the leaders of the Soviet Union believed they were in a life-and-death struggle with the non-Communist West. Almost any action was acceptable if it helped strengthen the Soviet Union.

Therefore, nuclear testing went on for years. This was true long after Soviet officials knew it was poisoning the air that Soviet citizens were breathing.

Spreading Communism

From its beginning in 1922, the Soviet Union showed this belief in a life-and-death struggle in their **foreign policy**. A foreign policy is the way a country deals with other countries.

The goal of communism was to destroy the capitalist system in other countries. To achieve this goal, the Soviet Union helped Communists in other countries who were trying to **overthrow** their governments, or bring them down by force.

In 1919, the Soviet Union set up an organization to promote Communist revolutions. It was called the Communist International, or Comintern for short. The Comintern worked in countries as far apart as Germany and China. However, all attempts at revolutions failed.

Treaty With Nazi Germany

After the Nazis came to power in Germany in 1933, the Soviet Union was in danger. The Soviet leaders expected that some day Nazi Germany would attack the Soviet Union.

In August 1939, the Soviet Union began secret **negotiations** with Nazi Germany. On August 23, 1939, Germany and the Soviet Union announced a **nonaggression treaty**. In this treaty, the two countries agreed not to take hostile actions against each other. The world was shocked. No one expected that two countries that had called each other enemies could reach such an agreement.

There was a secret part to the Nazi-Soviet pact. The two countries were going to destroy Poland. They had secretly agreed to divide Poland between themselves.

The Soviet Union at War

On September 1, 1939, the Germans invaded Poland. This was the beginning of

One of the bloodiest battles in history was fought at Stalingrad in 1942. After months of fighting from building to building, Soviet troops finally drove the Germans out of the city.

World War II. Shortly afterward, the Soviet Union took over eastern Poland.

The Soviet Union stayed out of World War II for almost two years. During that time, the Soviets sent the Nazis raw materials needed to wage war.

However, Hitler secretly was planning to attack the Soviet Union. On June 22, 1941, he launched his attack.

For the next four years, the Soviet Union fought for its survival. The Nazi-Soviet pact clearly had dissolved. The Soviets fought as part of an alliance that included Britain, France, and the United States.

The Soviet people fought with great heroism. By the time the fighting was over, 20 million Soviet citizens were dead. The fighting destroyed 1,100 cities, 70,000 villages, and 32,000 factories. The Russian people call this struggle their Great Patriotic War. Today, Russians look back at that war in horror at the suffering it caused.

Section 1 Review

1. What was the Comintern?
2. **Drawing Conclusions** What do you think was the reaction in the West to the Nazi-Soviet pact?

SECTION 2

Confronting the United States

How did the world come close to nuclear attack in the 1960s?

The **arms race** was one of the most dangerous parts of the Cold War between the Soviet Union and the United States. The "race" was a contest to build more powerful weapons. Each side in the Cold War built enough nuclear weapons to destroy the other many times over.

On Assignment...

For your editorial, take notes on the Comintern and the Nazi-Soviet treaty. What do they tell about the aims of Soviet foreign policy?

Crisis in Berlin

One place where Cold War tensions were very high was Berlin. The Soviet Union wanted to force the United States and its allies to leave West Berlin.

The Soviets were embarrassed because West Berlin was much more prosperous than East Berlin. Between 1945 and 1961, thousands of East Germans used Berlin to escape to the West. West Berlin was a daily reminder that life under democracy was better than life under communism.

In 1961, the Soviets built the Berlin Wall to stop East Germans from reaching West Berlin. They also hoped that the Wall would weaken the U.S. will to stay in Berlin. President John F. Kennedy made it clear that the United States was staying.

In October, a crisis developed. The Soviets interfered with U.S. government officials crossing from West to East Berlin. The Soviets had no right to stop these officials. During the crisis, U.S. and Soviet tanks met at a crossing point called Checkpoint Charlie. There they faced each other for 16 hours. Finally, the Soviet tanks left. Gradually the tensions cooled.

The Cuban Missile Crisis

The most serious Soviet-American clash took place in Cuba, an island 90 miles (145 km) from Florida. In 1959, a revolution had brought Fidel Castro to power in Cuba.

Castro was a Communist. He made Cuba an ally of the Soviet Union. In 1962, the Soviet Union decided to place nuclear missiles in Cuba. These missiles could threaten the eastern United States.

In October 1962, the United States learned about the Soviet plan when U.S. spy planes photographed Soviet missile bases. President Kennedy demanded that the Soviets remove the missiles. The United States then placed ships around Cuba to stop Soviet ships from reaching Cuba with supplies.

What would the Soviets do? If they tried to get through, there would be shooting. That could easily spark a Soviet-American war.

For 13 days, the world stood on the brink of nuclear war. Finally the Soviets backed down. They agreed to remove their missiles from Cuba.

Both sides were frightened that they had come so close to war. After the Cuban missile crisis, a direct telephone "hotline" was set up between the White House and the Soviet government.

The End of the Cold War

During the 1960s and 1970s, Soviet influence grew in several parts of the world. Several Arab countries in the Middle East were heavily armed with Soviet weapons. Communist parties controlled several countries in Asia and Africa.

Soviet policies changed as the Soviet economy showed signs of collapse in the 1980s. Soviet leaders wanted to improve relations with the United States and Western Europe. This would allow them to spend less on the military and more on solving their problems at home.

In 1987, the Soviet Union and the United States signed a treaty to reduce nuclear arms in Europe. In 1989, communism col-

On Assignment . . .

For your editorial on Soviet foreign policy, take notes on the crises in Berlin and in Cuba. Also take notes on Soviet foreign policy after 1985. You will want to discuss them when you write your editorial.

lapsed in the Soviet satellites. With the collapse of the Soviet Union in 1991, the Cold War ended. U.S. President George Bush spoke for a happy world when he said, "We have closed a chapter in history. The Cold War is over."

Section 2 Review

1. What was the Cuban missile crisis?
2. **Making Hypotheses** Why was the Cuban missile crisis so dangerous?

SECTION 3

Republics at Risk

What serious problems face the republics of the former Soviet Union today?

The collapse of the Soviet Union left many unsolved problems in the new nations of the Eurasian Heartland. It also created some new problems when the new countries argued over territory and other issues.

Nuclear Weapons

When the Soviet Union collapsed, most of its nuclear weapons were in Russia. However, some were also in Ukraine, Belarus, and Kazakstan.

The nuclear weapons in these three countries were a threat to world peace. In 1991, the Soviet Union and the United States signed an important treaty that called for large cuts in their nuclear weapons. A 1993 treaty between Russia and the United States called for even larger cuts.

Neither treaty could be put into effect while nuclear weapons remained in Ukraine, Belarus, and Kazakstan. All three countries also had to agree to give up their nuclear weapons.

It took several years to get them to agree to these conditions. These nations wanted nuclear weapons as protection against other new republics. However, by 1994, all three nations had agreed to give up nuclear weapons.

Ethnic Problems in Russia

When the Soviet Union existed, its powerful army and autocratic government prevented ethnic problems from surfacing. People who stirred ethnic protests were severely punished.

The collapse of the Soviet Union left most of the new countries of Eurasia with ethnic problems. Some groups wanted their own independent states. Others wanted borders redrawn so that they would be united with people in a neighboring country.

Russia had serious ethnic problems. Several minority ethnic groups demanded more control over their lives. Some of the strongest demands came from the Tatars. This group is descended from the Mongols, who had conquered Russia in the A.D. 1200s. In 1991, they made up about 4 percent of Russia's population.

Many Tatars live in a region of Russia just west of the Ural Mountains. The Tatars did not try to break completely with Russia. Instead, they pushed for more local control.

Revolt in Chechnya

A group called the Chechens did declare independence. The Chechens are a Muslim people who live in a region called Chechnya (CHECH•nee•uh) near the Caspian Sea. Chechnya contains some of the richest oil producing areas of Russia.

Over the years, the Chechens have had many conflicts with the Russians. During World War II, hundreds of thousands of Chechens were forcibly removed from their homes by the Soviet army and sent to live in Kazakstan. After the death of Stalin in 1953, the surviving Chechens returned home. However, the bitterness over their exile remained.

Nuclear weapons in new countries, such as Ukraine, pose a threat to world peace. Here, a nuclear warhead is taken from its launch site in Ukraine to be disarmed and destroyed.

The Chechens demanded independence from Russia in 1991. They refused any compromise short of complete independence.

In 1994, Russia sent 40,000 soldiers to Chechnya to end the independence movement. The Russians expected that this show of force would quickly end the uprising. Instead, they found themselves in a conflict that seemed to be unending.

Bloody fighting followed. In 1994 and 1995, more than 20,000 people were killed. Many cities and towns were destroyed.

After a long battle, Russian troops captured the region's capital, Grozny (GROHZ•nee). The Russians then took control of most of Chechnya. However, many people throughout the world criticized the Russian government for using brutal force. Many Russians were horrified and urged the Russian government to recognize Chechen independence. The government refused, fearing that if it gave in to the Chechens, minorities throughout the country would demand independence.

Although the big battles were over, Chechen rebels continued shooting at Russian soldiers. In 1996, Chechen rebels seized a Russian city near the Chechen border. They were only driven out after a fierce battle that killed many Chechens and Russians.

Crime Endangers Democracy

As the economy declined, many Russians became concerned that a rising tide of crime would overwhelm democracy. Many Russians became convinced that democratic government was not strong enough to deal with the Russian crime wave. Many Russians were terrified of crime and disgusted by the failure of the government to curb it.

During a 1996 test, the government sent a truck filled with valuable consumer goods across the country. At 22 of 24 checkpoints, the police stopped the truck, searched it, and demanded bribes to let the truck pass. The incident reinforced the view of many Russian citizens that the police are so corrupt that they cannot be trusted to protect the public. "Everything has a price," one government official said. "It's very bitter, but this is the way things are."

Russian President Boris Yeltsin became increasing concerned with the rise in crime. Yeltsin said, "Until we have rigidly enforced law and order, until we have protection of individual rights by the courts, including protection against corruption, then we cannot speak seriously of democracy."

Economic Hard Times

Almost every country of the Eurasian Heartland faced serious economic problems. All the new countries had to move from a Communist economic system to a free enterprise economic system.

In Russia, the new government stopped controlling prices. It sold state-owned factories and business to private individuals.

However, many people lost their jobs. Prices rose quickly. Millions of people could not afford to buy what they needed.

Outside the large cities, a thriving **black market** grew up to meet the needs of consumers. A black market is a place or system in which goods are sold illegally. In a black market, goods in short supply are sold for very high prices.

These situations caused the standard of living of most Russians to fall. Increasing numbers of Russians began to turn back to communism to improve economic conditions.

A System of Barter

In some parts of Russia, merchants accepted payment in other goods or services. Such a system is known as **barter**. In the city of Ulyanovsk (ool•YAH•nofsk), for example, a former radio equipment plant tried to stay in business after the government cut off its military contract. Now, instead of space communication equipment, it makes vacuum cleaners.

Vacuum cleaners are in great demand, but because money is in short supply, few people can afford to buy them. Instead, factory managers barter the vacuum cleaners for TVs and tape recorders produced at another local plant. Workers at the vacuum cleaner factory then receive TVs and tape recorders instead of their salaries. The factory also tries to sell the bartered products in a small store it runs. It advertises in local newspapers, paying the cost of the ads with vacuum cleaners, TVs, and tape recorders.

Section 3 Review

1. Why did some people in Ukraine, Belarus, and Kazakstan want to keep nuclear weapons?

2. **Predicting Consequences** If economic conditions continue to worsen in the Heartland, what do you think will happen?

An Environment in Ruins

The Kola Peninsula was a place of beauty. Pine forests stretched as far as the eye could see. Wildlife roamed these forests and fish swam in clear rivers and streams.

Today the Kola Peninsula is poisoned. Two huge plants that make the metal nickel from ore have polluted the region.

Dead stumps have replaced many forests. Fish are gone from the polluted streams. In some places, even the mice have been killed off. According to one scientist, "The soil will need 400 years to cleanse itself."

Workers in the region suffer from lung diseases and die at a young age. As one Russian official said, "What has happened to the Kola Peninsula is a disaster. We destroyed the health of the people. We destroyed nature."

Pollution from plants like this Siberian petrochemical plant shorten the lives of people who live nearby.

Chernobyl

Nothing better shows the impact of Soviet policies on its neighbors than the 1986 explosion at the Chernobyl (chehr•NOH•buhl) nuclear power plant in Ukraine. Nuclear particles spread into the atmosphere, where they traveled for thousands of miles. Then they fell to earth, poisoning the land.

About 5,000 people died as a result of the disaster. In Ukraine, at least one million people still live in areas poisoned by nuclear fallout. The situation is even more serious in Belarus, where winds carried much of the fallout from the explosion. Tens of thousands of acres of farmland have been poisoned by the fallout. About 20 percent of Belarus was poisoned by the Chernobyl accident.

The tragic stories of Chernobyl and the Kola Peninsula are among the worst in Eurasia. For decades, the Soviet government built without caring about what it was destroying. Today the people who live in the region must pay the price and try to fix the damage.

Case Study Review

1. What happened at Chernobyl?
2. **Interpreting a Quotation** Why did the Russian official say, "What has happened to the Kola Peninsula is a disaster"?

I. Reviewing Vocabulary

Match each word on the left with the correct definition on the right.

1. overthrow   **a.** the act of exchanging goods or services without using money
2. barter   **b.** to bring down from power by force
3. negotiation   **c.** the way in which countries deal with other countries
4. foreign policy   **d.** the act of dealing or bargaining with someone else

II. Understanding the Chapter

Answer the questions below on a separate sheet of paper.

1. How was Soviet foreign policy different from the foreign policies of other countries?
2. What damage did World War II do to the Soviet Union?
3. Why was it so important that Ukraine, Belarus, and Kazakstan give up their nuclear weapons?
4. What effect did Soviet policies have on Russia's environment?

III. Building Skills: Reading a Map

Study the map on pages 602–603 and answer the following questions.

1. What two countries border on the Aral Sea?
2. The Ural Mountains form the border between Europe and Asia. What two countries have territory in both Europe and Asia?
3. Which countries of the Eurasian Heartland border the Caspian Sea?
4. Which two rivers empty into the Caspian Sea?

IV. Working Together

Form a small group. Imagine that you are citizens of Russia or one of the other republics that emerged from the Soviet Union. Draw up a petition that asks the government to make at least one change in its policies. Decide together what request to make in your petition and how to phrase your request. Understand that your request should have some benefit for the government, as well as for your group. Choose a member of the group to read your petition aloud to the class.

On Assignment. . .

Writing an Editorial: Take the information that you have gathered and write an editorial about how the Soviet Union dealt with other nations. You should mention the Comintern as well as events such as the Nazi-Soviet pact and the Cuban missile crisis. You should also discuss Soviet actions with respect to the environment.

UNIT 6 REVIEW

I. Understanding the Unit

Answer the questions below on a separate sheet of paper.

1. How did ancient Greece influence the development of Europe?

2. (a) What was the Industrial Revolution and where did it begin? (b) How did it affect the way Europeans lived?

3. (a) What was the main cause of World War I? (b) What event started the war?

4. (a) What was the Cold War? (b) How did the Cold War begin? (c) How did it divide Europe?

5. (a) What major historical event occurred in Germany in 1989? (b) How did this event affect Germany and the rest of the world in the 1990s?

6. (a) Why were Russian people dissatisfied with their government by the end of the 1800s? (b) What were the goals of the Communist revolution?

7. Ethnic tension and nationalism are sources of much world conflict today. Give one example of fighting caused by ethnic tension in Europe and one example in the Eurasian Heartland. Briefly describe each one.

8. Describe three problems currently facing people in the Heartland.

II. Thinking Critically

Answer the questions below on a separate sheet of paper.

1. **Determining Cause and Effect** Physical features of a region often influence patterns of settlement. Why is Western Europe more densely populated than Eastern Europe or Eurasia? Describe two physical features that might account for the differences in population density.

2. **Making Inferences** Many times in history, members of one country or ethnic group have tried to destroy another country or ethnic group. The Holocaust during World War II was one of these times. What was the Holocaust? Why did it occur? What makes it unique in history?

III. Writing to Learn

On a separate sheet of paper, write a three-paragraph essay about the following topic.

Imagine you are an old woman or man living in Ukraine in the 1990s. Describe the changes that have taken place in your country since the turn of the century. How have these changes affected you and your family?

IV. Practicing Skills: Interpreting Pie Charts

Read the pie charts below. On a separate sheet of paper, answer the questions that follow.

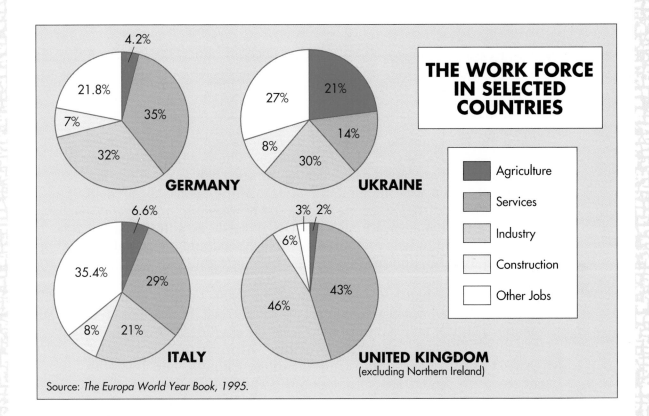

THE WORK FORCE IN SELECTED COUNTRIES

GERMANY: 4.2%, 21.8%, 7%, 32%, 35%

UKRAINE: 21%, 27%, 8%, 30%, 14%

ITALY: 6.6%, 35.4%, 8%, 21%, 29%

UNITED KINGDOM (excluding Northern Ireland): 3%, 2%, 6%, 46%, 43%

Key:
- Agriculture
- Services
- Industry
- Construction
- Other Jobs

Source: *The Europa World Year Book, 1995.*

1. (a) What five categories of jobs are listed in the key? (b) For which four countries is data provided?

2. (a) Which country has the greatest percentage of its work force in industry? (b) Which has the greatest percentage of its work force in services?

3. How does the information provided in the pie chart above support the following generalization: "Ukraine is the breadbasket of Eastern Europe."

V. Going Beyond the Unit

Work with two or three students to write an outline for a children's book about European or Russian history from ancient times to the present. Your book outline should be geared to children in approximately third grade. List chapter titles and provide a summary of what would be included in each chapter. Also list some photographs, maps, drawings, and other artwork you would include. Present your completed outline to the class.

The UN Works to Preserve the Peace

Looking at Key Terms

charter, humanitarian relief, General Assembly, Security Council, coalition

On June 25, 1945, the leaders of 51 nations signed a **charter**—a set of rules—for a new world organization. The organization's aim was to prevent destructive wars such as the one that was just ending. That organization was the United Nations. Many people throughout the world thought they were seeing the end of war.

Member nations agreed to ask the UN to settle disputes. The UN also was directed to help end disease, furnish food and aid to nations in times of disaster, and safeguard basic human rights.

Exactly 50 years after the signing of the UN charter, people saw that these hopes had been exaggerated. In 1992, famine, civil war, and bandits killed at least 40,000 people in the East African nation of Somalia. The UN stepped in to help with relief efforts. However, the UN couldn't protect volunteers providing **humanitarian relief**— free food and medicine. The United States, Canada, and Pakistan sent troops to protect the volunteers. But the violence among opposing Somali troops was too great. After 19 U.S. and 23 Pakistani peace-keepers were murdered, the UN withdrew its forces.

Maintaining the Peace

The UN is made up of two major bodies. The **General Assembly**, which has representatives from every member nation, debates problems that nations are experiencing. The other major body is the **Security Council**, which has 15 members. The Security Council is charged with maintaining peace in the world. It is the only part of the UN that can order force to be used against a member nation. The Security Council is still dominated by the victors of World War II— the United States, Britain, China, France, and Russia.

Publicized Defeats, Quiet Successes

The UN peace-keeping record has been good. Its greatest successes have been in stopping conflicts between smaller nations. Peace-keeping forces have kept fighters apart to give them time to work out a solution to their problem or to keep the war from spreading.

The UN sent peace-keeping forces to the Middle East in 1947 to help in dividing Palestine. When the creation of Israel led to war between Israel and the Arab nations, UN forces helped to restore

Established to preserve world peace, the UN has worked tirelessly to end local conflicts. The results have been mixed. At left, the United Nations Security Council meets.

peace. UN forces also helped to end the fighting between India and Pakistan in 1949. During the 1960s, the UN helped to restore peace to the Congo and Cyprus.

At other times, the UN has asked the major powers to use force against an outlaw member nation. In 1990, Iraq invaded the oil-rich country of Kuwait. Shortly after the invasion, the UN demanded that Iraq get out of Kuwait. When Kuwait refused, the UN took action. A **coalition**, or temporary alliance, of UN forces from the United States, Saudi Arabia, Egypt, Syria, Britain, and France attacked and swiftly defeated Iraq. Kuwait was restored to its people.

The UN has had important successes preserving the peace in troubled areas of the world. UN troops may not always succeed, but they have saved countless lives and helped countries solve their problems with words and not weapons.

Review

1. Why is the UN's role important in preserving world peace?
2. **Hypothesizing** List two reasons UN peace-keeping operations might succeed. List two reasons they might fail.

Taking Action: Creating an Advertisement

Next week, a big TV network will broadcast a special program called "Keeping the Peace Around the World." You have been asked to create a collage to advertise the special to other students in your school. Find pictures in books, magazines, and newspapers that show the work of the UN in preserving the peace. Use these pictures, as well as your own words and drawings, to create a collage that will make your fellow students want to watch the program.

REFERENCE SECTION

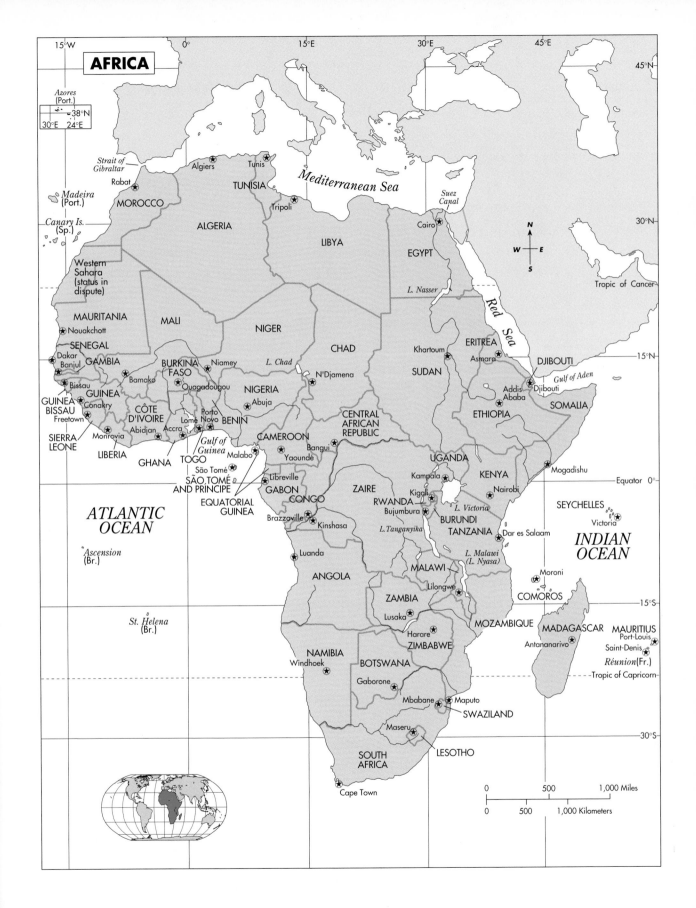

AFRICA

15°W · 0° · 15°E · 30°E · 45°E

45°N

Azores
(Port.)
~38°N
30°E · 24°E

Strait of
Gibraltar

Algiers ✪
Tunis ✪

Mediterranean Sea

Suez
Canal

Rabat ✪
TUNISIA
Tripoli ✪
Cairo ✪
30°N

Madeira
(Port.)
MOROCCO

Canary Is.
(Sp.)
ALGERIA
LIBYA
EGYPT

Tropic of Cancer

Western
Sahara
(status in
dispute)

L. Nasser

N
W · E
S

Red Sea

MAURITANIA
Nouakchott ✪
MALI
NIGER
CHAD
Khartoum ✪
ERITREA
Asmara ✪
DJIBOUTI
15°N

SENEGAL
Dakar ✪
Banjul ✪
GAMBIA
BURKINA
FASO
Niamey ✪
L. Chad
N'Djamena ✪
SUDAN
Addis
Ababa ✪
Djibouti ✪
Gulf of Aden

Bamako ✪
Ouagadougou ✪
NIGERIA
Abuja ✪
ETHIOPIA
SOMALIA

Bissau ✪
GUINEA
Conakry ✪
CÔTE
D'IVOIRE
Porto
Novo ✪
Lomé ✪
BENIN
CENTRAL
AFRICAN
REPUBLIC
GUINEA
BISSAU
Freetown ✪
Abidjan ✪
Accra ✪
CAMEROON
Bangui ✪
UGANDA
Mogadishu ✪
Equator 0°

SIERRA
LEONE
Monrovia ✪
GHANA
TOGO
Yaoundé ✪
Kampala ✪
KENYA
SEYCHELLES

LIBERIA
São Tomé ✪
Malabo ✪
Libreville ✪
Kigali ✪
Nairobi ✪
Victoria ✪

SÃO TOMÉ
AND PRÍNCIPE
GABON
ZAIRE
RWANDA
L. Victoria

EQUATORIAL
GUINEA
CONGO
Brazzaville ✪
Kinshasa ✪
BURUNDI
Bujumbura ✪
L. Tanganyika
TANZANIA
Dar es Salaam ✪

ATLANTIC
OCEAN
INDIAN
OCEAN

Ascension
(Br.)
Luanda ✪
L. Malawi
(L. Nyasa)
Moroni ✪

ANGOLA
MALAWI
COMOROS

St. Helena
(Br.)
Lilongwe ✪
MADAGASCAR
MAURITIUS

ZAMBIA
Lusaka ✪
MOZAMBIQUE
Antananarivo ✪
Port-Louis ✪
Saint-Denis ✪
15°S

NAMIBIA
Windhoek ✪
ZIMBABWE
Harare ✪
Réunion (Fr.)

BOTSWANA
Gaborone ✪
Tropic of Capricorn

Mbabane ✪
Maputo ✪
SWAZILAND
30°S

SOUTH
AFRICA
Maseru ✪
LESOTHO

Cape Town ✪

0 · 500 · 1,000 Miles
0 · 500 · 1,000 Kilometers

Map of Africa

593

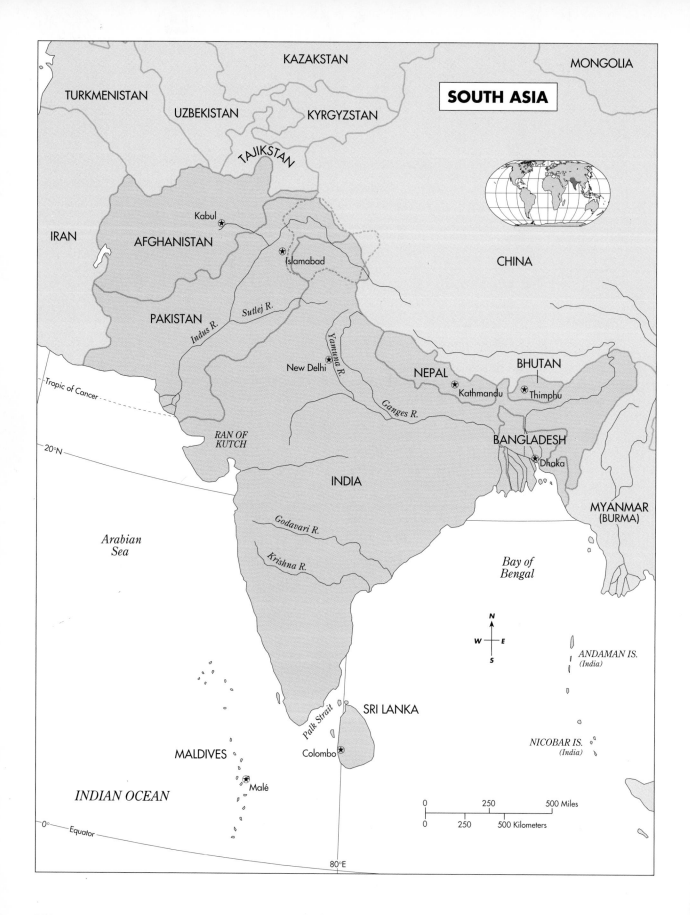

SOUTH ASIA

KAZAKSTAN

MONGOLIA

TURKMENISTAN

UZBEKISTAN

KYRGYZSTAN

TAJIKSTAN

IRAN

Kabul ✴

AFGHANISTAN

Islamabad ✴

CHINA

PAKISTAN

Sutlej R.

Indus R.

Yamuna R.

New Delhi ✴

NEPAL

BHUTAN

Kathmandu ✴

Thimphu ✴

Tropic of Cancer

Ganges R.

RAN OF KUTCH

20°N

BANGLADESH

Dhaka ✴

INDIA

MYANMAR (BURMA)

Godavari R.

Arabian Sea

Krishna R.

Bay of Bengal

N

W — E

S

ANDAMAN IS. (India)

MALDIVES

SRI LANKA

Colombo ✴

Palk Strait

NICOBAR IS. (India)

Malé ✴

INDIAN OCEAN

0° Equator

| 0 | | 250 | | 500 Miles |
| 0 | 250 | | 500 Kilometers | |

80°E

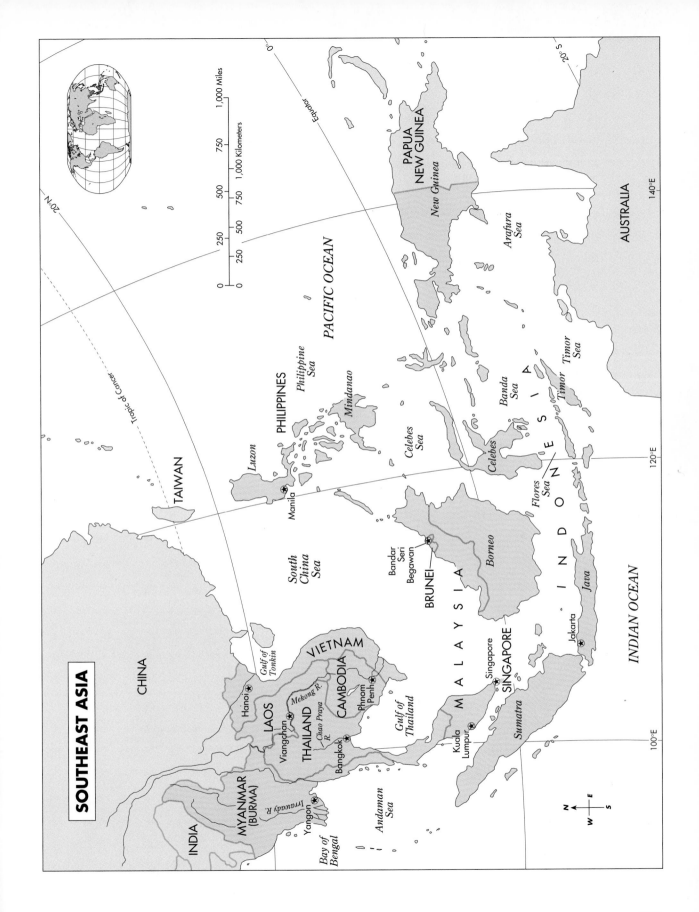

SOUTHEAST ASIA

CHINA

INDIA

MYANMAR (BURMA)

Irrawaddy R.

Yangon

Bay of Bengal

Andaman Sea

LAOS

Vientiane

THAILAND

Chao Praya R.

Bangkok

Mekong R.

VIETNAM

Hanoi

Gulf of Tonkin

CAMBODIA

Phnom Penh

Gulf of Thailand

MALAYSIA

Kuala Lumpur

SINGAPORE

Singapore

Sumatra

INDONESIA

South China Sea

TAIWAN

PHILIPPINES

Luzon

Manila

Mindanao

Philippine Sea

PACIFIC OCEAN

Celebes Sea

Celebes

BRUNEI

Bandar Seri Begawan

Borneo

Flores Sea

Banda Sea

Java

Jakarta

INDIAN OCEAN

Timor Sea

Timor

Arafura Sea

PAPUA NEW GUINEA

New Guinea

AUSTRALIA

Tropic of Cancer

20°N

Equator

20°S

100°E

120°E

140°E

1,000 Miles
750
500
250
0

1,000 Kilometers
750
500
250
0

N
E
S
W

Map of Southeast Asia

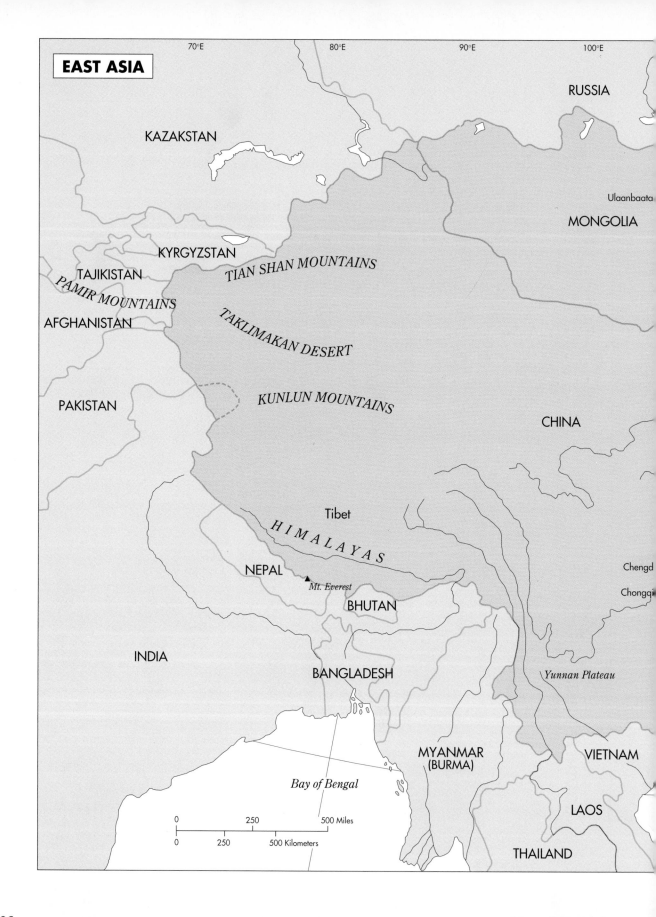

EAST ASIA

70°E   80°E   90°E   100°E

RUSSIA

KAZAKSTAN

Ulaanbaata

MONGOLIA

KYRGYZSTAN

TIAN SHAN MOUNTAINS

TAJIKISTAN

PAMIR MOUNTAINS

AFGHANISTAN

TAKLIMAKAN DESERT

PAKISTAN

KUNLUN MOUNTAINS

CHINA

Tibet

HIMALAYAS

Chengd

NEPAL

▲
Mt. Everest

Chonga

BHUTAN

INDIA

BANGLADESH

Yunnan Plateau

MYANMAR
(BURMA)

VIETNAM

Bay of Bengal

LAOS

| 0 | 250 | 500 Miles |

| 0 | 250 | 500 Kilometers |

THAILAND

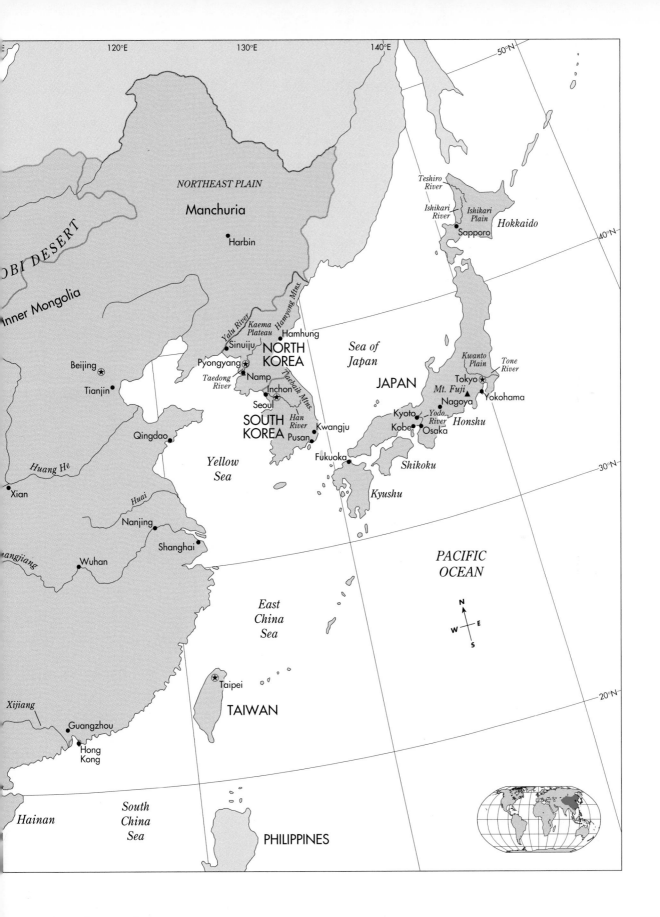

120°E   130°E   140°E   50°N

NORTHEAST PLAIN

Manchuria

GOBI DESERT

Inner Mongolia

Harbin

40°N

*Teshiro
River*

*Ishikari
River*

*Ishikari
Plain*

Sapporo

Hokkaido

Hamyong Mtns.

Yalu River

*Kaema
Plateau*

Hamhung

Sinuiju

**NORTH
KOREA**

*Sea of
Japan*

JAPAN

*Kwanto
Plain*

*Tone
River*

Beijing

Pyongyang

Tokyo

Tianjin

*Taedong
River*

Namp

Taebaik Mtns.

Inchon

Seoul

**SOUTH
KOREA**

*Han
River*

Kwangju

Pusan

Mt. Fuji

Nagoya

Yokohama

Kyoto

Kobe

*Yodo
River*

Osaka

Honshu

Qingdao

*Yellow
Sea*

Fukuoka

Shikoku

Huang He

Xian

30°N

Kyushu

Huai

Nanjing

Shanghai

*East
China
Sea*

*PACIFIC
OCEAN*

angjiang

Wuhan

N

W   E

S

20°N

Taipei

TAIWAN

Xijiang

Guangzhou

Hong
Kong

Hainan

*South
China
Sea*

PHILIPPINES

Map of East Asia

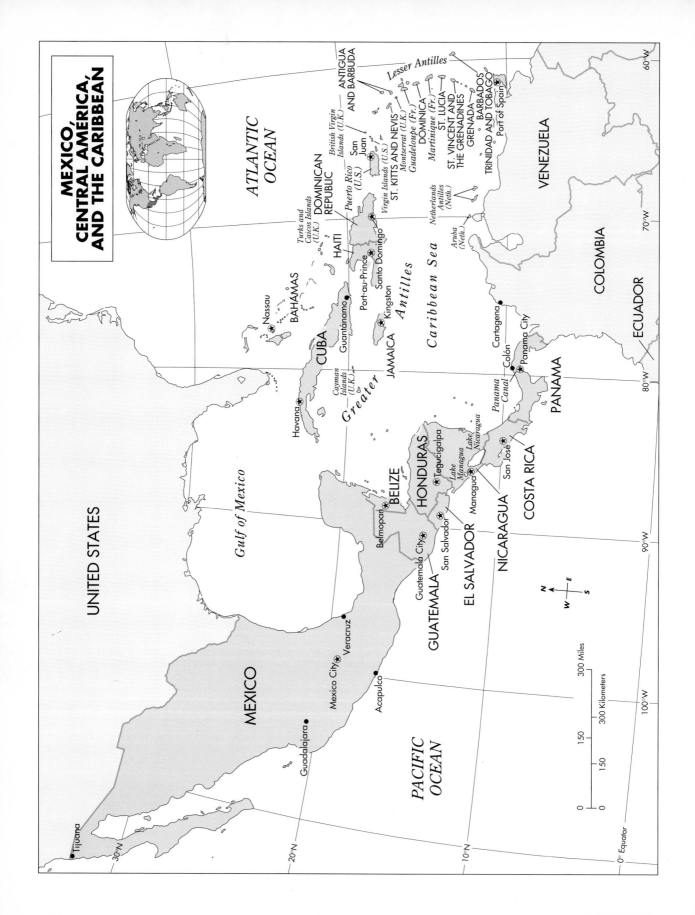

MEXICO, CENTRAL AMERICA, AND THE CARIBBEAN

ATLANTIC OCEAN

Lesser Antilles

ANTIGUA AND BARBUDA

British Virgin Islands (U.K.)

San Juan

ST. KITTS AND NEVIS
Montserrat (U.K.)
Guadeloupe (Fr.)
DOMINICA
Martinique (Fr.)
ST. LUCIA
ST. VINCENT AND THE GRENADINES
GRENADA
BARBADOS
TRINIDAD AND TOBAGO
Port of Spain

Puerto Rico (U.S.)
Virgin Islands (U.S.)

Netherlands Antilles (Neth.)

Aruba (Neth.)

VENEZUELA

70°W

COLOMBIA

ECUADOR

60°W

Turks and Caicos Islands (U.K.)

DOMINICAN REPUBLIC

HAITI

Port-au-Prince

Santo Domingo

BAHAMAS

Nassau

Caribbean Sea

Greater *Antilles*

Kingston

CUBA

Guantánamo

JAMAICA

Cayman Islands (U.K.)

Havana

Cartagena

Panama City

Colón

Panama Canal

PANAMA

80°W

UNITED STATES

Gulf of Mexico

Tegucigalpa

HONDURAS

BELIZE

Belmopan

Guatemala City

San Salvador

Lake Managua

Lake Nicaragua

Managua

San José

NICARAGUA

COSTA RICA

EL SALVADOR

GUATEMALA

90°W

N
E
W
S

300 Miles
300 Kilometers

0   150   150

MEXICO

Mexico City

Veracruz

Acapulco

Guadalajara

Tijuana

30°N

20°N

100°W

PACIFIC OCEAN

10°N

0° Equator

Map of Mexico, Central America, and the Caribbean

Caribbean Sea

ATLANTIC OCEAN

Caracas

VENEZUELA

GUYANA

SURINAME

Georgetown

French Guiana (Fr.)

Paramaribo

Cayenne

10°N

Bogotá

COLOMBIA

Quito

0° Equator

ECUADOR

Galapagos Is. (Ec.)

PERU

BRAZIL

Recife

Lima

10°S

La Paz

Brasília

BOLIVIA

Sucre

PARAGUAY

20°S

Tropic of Capricorn

Asunción

Rio de Janeiro

São Paulo

ATLANTIC OCEAN

CHILE

URUGUAY

30°S

Santiago

Buenos Aires

Montevideo

PACIFIC OCEAN

ARGENTINA

N

W   E

S

40°S

SOUTH AMERICA

0   300   600 Miles

0   300   600 Kilometers

Falkland Is. (U.K.)

50°S

100°W   90°W   80°W   70°W   60°W   50°W   40°W   30°W   20°W

Map of South America

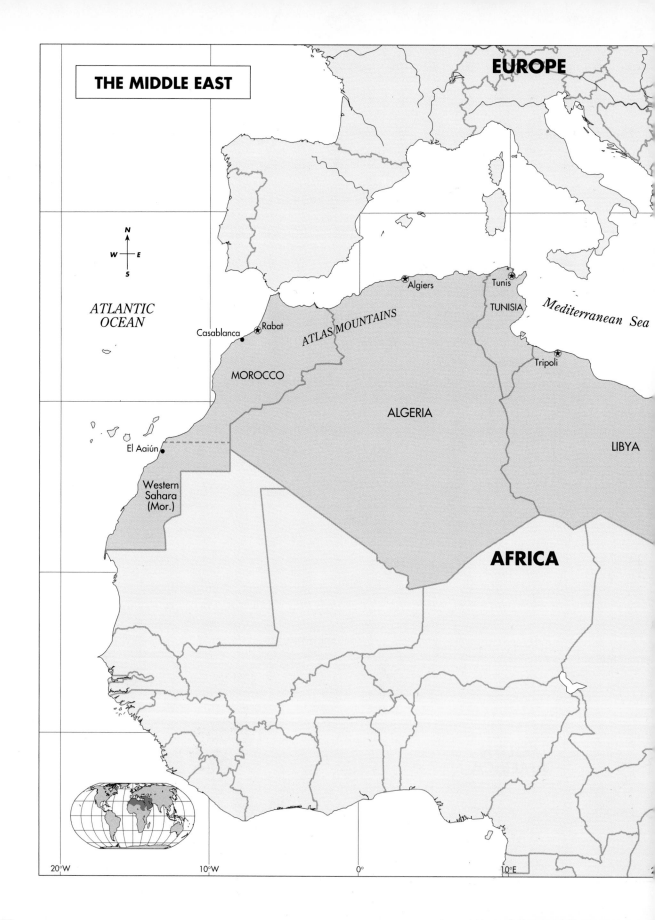

THE MIDDLE EAST

EUROPE

N
W · E
S

ATLANTIC
OCEAN

Mediterranean Sea

Algiers

Tunis

TUNISIA

Casablanca · ⊛Rabat

ATLAS MOUNTAINS

Tripoli

MOROCCO

ALGERIA

LIBYA

El Aaiún

Western
Sahara
(Mor.)

AFRICA

20°W   10°W   0°   10°E

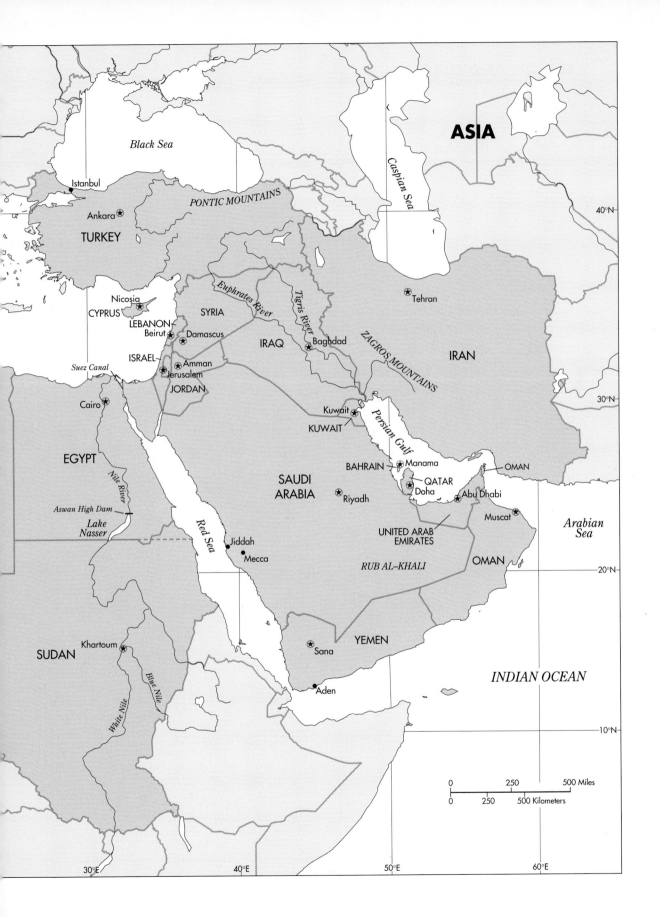

Map of the Middle East

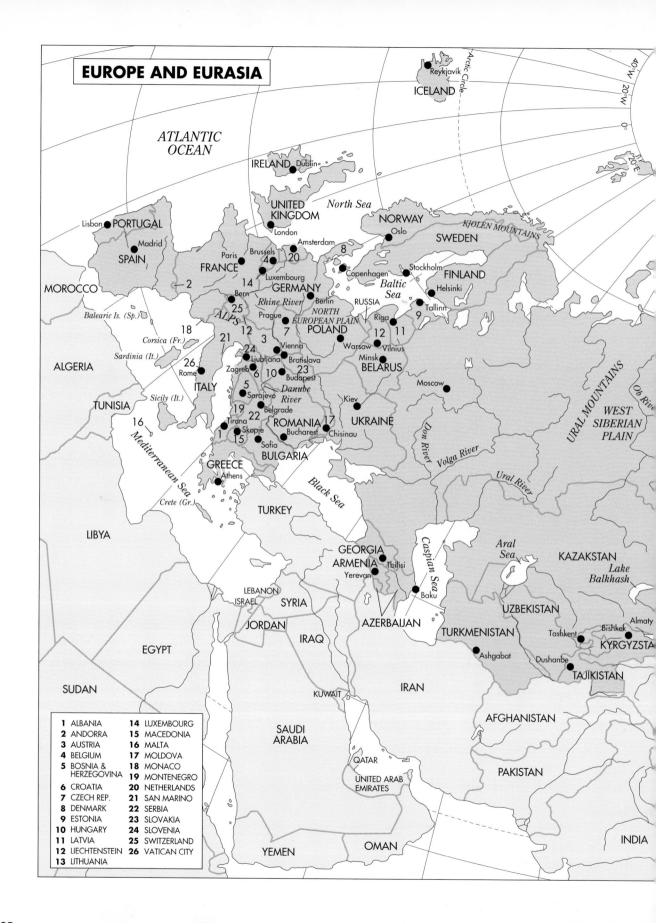

EUROPE AND EURASIA

ATLANTIC
OCEAN

Arctic Circle

Reykjavík
ICELAND

IRELAND Dublin

North Sea

UNITED
KINGDOM

London

NORWAY
Oslo

SWEDEN

KJØLEN MOUNTAINS

Lisbon PORTUGAL

Madrid

SPAIN

Paris Brussels
FRANCE 4 20

Amsterdam

8

Copenhagen

Stockholm

FINLAND

Helsinki

MOROCCO

2

14

Luxembourg

GERMANY

Berlin

RUSSIA

*Baltic
Sea*

Tallinn

Balearic Is. (Sp.)

Bern

25

Rhine River

Prague

NORTH
EUROPEAN PLAIN

Riga

9

Corsica (Fr.)

18

Sardinia (It.)

21

12

ALPS

3

7

POLAND

Warsaw

12 11

Vilnius

26

24

Vienna

Minsk

Rome

Ljubljana

Bratislava

23

BELARUS

ITALY

Zagreb

6

10

Budapest

Moscow

URAL MOUNTAINS

Ob River

WEST
SIBERIAN
PLAIN

5

Sarajevo

*Danube
River*

Kiev

Sicily (It.)

19

Belgrade

UKRAINE

TUNISIA

16

Tirana

22

ROMANIA

17

1

Skopje

Bucharest

Chisinau

Don River

Volga River

15

Sofia

ALGERIA

Mediterranean Sea

GREECE

BULGARIA

Ural River

Crete (Gr.)

Athens

Black Sea

LIBYA

TURKEY

GEORGIA

ARMENIA

Tbilisi

Caspian Sea

*Aral
Sea*

KAZAKSTAN

*Lake
Balkhash*

Yerevan

LEBANON

ISRAEL

SYRIA

Baku

AZERBAIJAN

UZBEKISTAN

JORDAN

IRAQ

TURKMENISTAN

Tashkent

Bishkek Almaty

KYRGYZSTA

EGYPT

IRAN

Ashgabat

Dushanbe

TAJIKISTAN

SUDAN

KUWAIT

SAUDI
ARABIA

QATAR

AFGHANISTAN

PAKISTAN

UNITED ARAB
EMIRATES

INDIA

YEMEN

OMAN

1 ALBANIA	**14** LUXEMBOURG
2 ANDORRA	**15** MACEDONIA
3 AUSTRIA	**16** MALTA
4 BELGIUM	**17** MOLDOVA
5 BOSNIA & HERZEGOVINA	**18** MONACO
	19 MONTENEGRO
6 CROATIA	**20** NETHERLANDS
7 CZECH REP.	**21** SAN MARINO
8 DENMARK	**22** SERBIA
9 ESTONIA	**23** SLOVAKIA
10 HUNGARY	**24** SLOVENIA
11 LATVIA	**25** SWITZERLAND
12 LIECHTENSTEIN	**26** VATICAN CITY
13 LITHUANIA	

Map of Europe and Eurasia

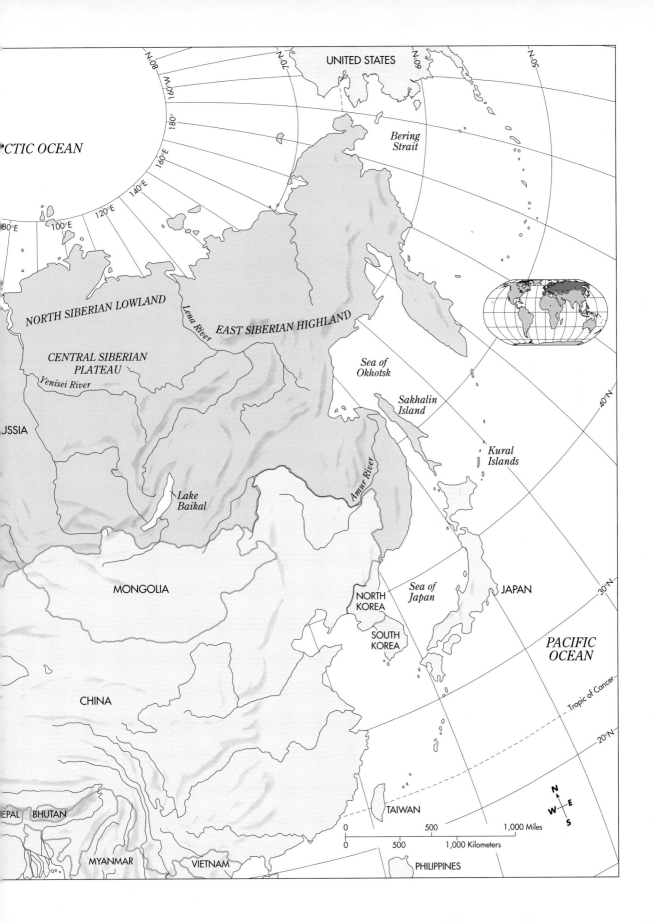

Map of Europe and Eurasia

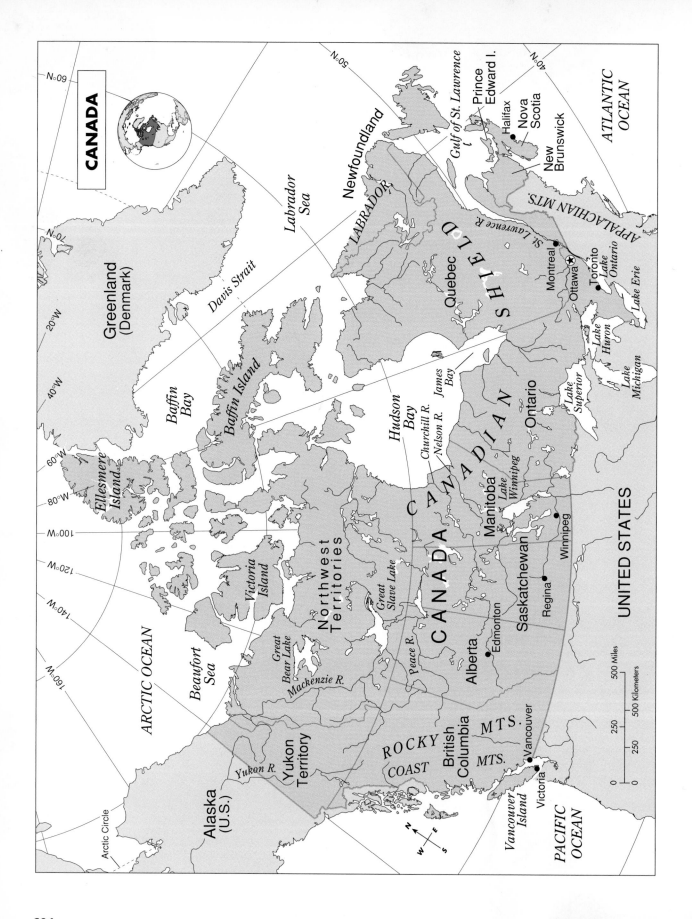

CANADA

Map of Canada

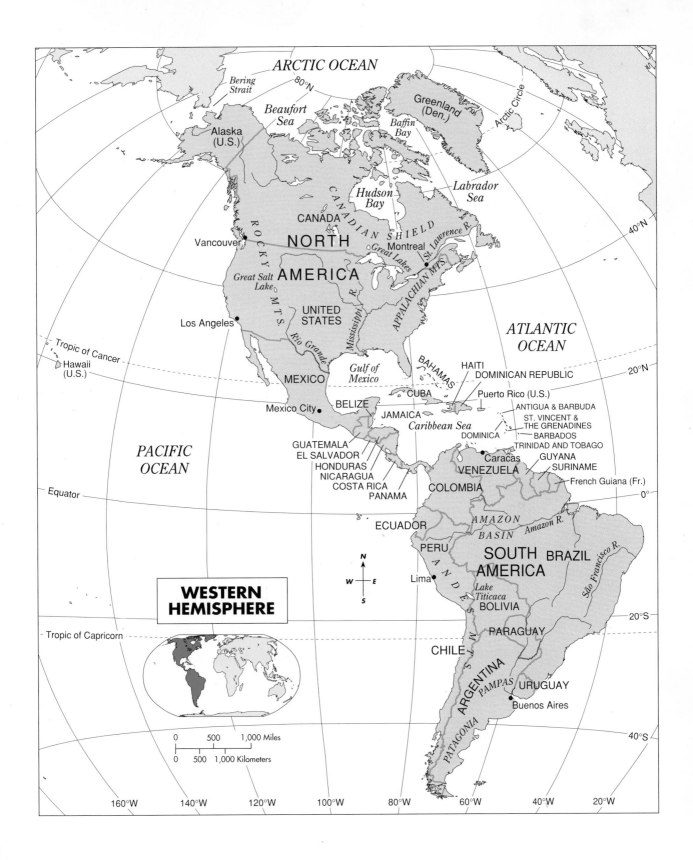

WESTERN HEMISPHERE

ARCTIC OCEAN

Bering Strait

Beaufort Sea

Alaska (U.S.)

Greenland (Den.)

Baffin Bay

Arctic Circle

80°N

Hudson Bay

Labrador Sea

CANADA

CANADIAN SHIELD

NORTH AMERICA

Vancouver

Montreal

Great Lakes

St. Lawrence R.

40°N

ROCKY MTS.

Great Salt Lake

UNITED STATES

Los Angeles

Mississippi R.

APPALACHIAN MTS.

ATLANTIC OCEAN

Tropic of Cancer

Rio Grande

BAHAMAS

HAITI

20°N

Hawaii (U.S.)

MEXICO

Gulf of Mexico

DOMINICAN REPUBLIC

CUBA

Puerto Rico (U.S.)

Mexico City

BELIZE

JAMAICA

ANTIGUA & BARBUDA

ST. VINCENT & THE GRENADINES

Caribbean Sea

DOMINICA

BARBADOS

GUATEMALA

EL SALVADOR

TRINIDAD AND TOBAGO

PACIFIC OCEAN

HONDURAS

NICARAGUA

Caracas

GUYANA

SURINAME

COSTA RICA

VENEZUELA

PANAMA

COLOMBIA

French Guiana (Fr.)

0°

Equator

ECUADOR

AMAZON BASIN

Amazon R.

PERU

SOUTH AMERICA

BRAZIL

São Francisco R.

N

W   E

Lima

ANDES

S

Lake Titicaca

BOLIVIA

20°S

Tropic of Capricorn

PARAGUAY

CHILE

ARGENTINA

PAMPAS

URUGUAY

Buenos Aires

PATAGONIA

40°S

0   500   1,000 Miles

0   500   1,000 Kilometers

160°W   140°W   120°W   100°W   80°W   60°W   40°W   20°W

Map of the Western Hemisphere

ARCTIC OCEAN

Arctic Circle

ICELAND

NORWAY

SWEDEN

FINLAND

UNITED
KINGDOM

DENMARK

15
21
24

U R A L   M O U N T A I N S

Volga R.

Moscow

R U S S I A

ASIA

IRELAND

London

28

GERMANY

POLAND

BELARUS

EUROPE

KAZAKSTAN

Aral Sea

Paris

23

13

35

UKRAINE

LUXEMBOURG

37

ALPS

4

19

30

26

Danube R.

Black Sea

CAUCASUS MTS.

Caspian Sea

UZBEKISTAN

KYRGYZSTAN

FRANCE

32

36

8

34

TURKMENISTAN

TAJIKISTA

PYRENEES

ITALY

12

9

17

3

PORTUGAL

2

27

33 39

1

25

GREECE

TURKEY

AZERBAIJAN

AFGHANISTAN

HIMALAY

11

SPAIN

5

CYPRUS

SYRIA

22

20

ZAGROS MTS.

IRAN

PAKISTAN

NEP

ATLAS MOUNTAINS

TUNISIA

Mediterranean Sea

IRAQ

JORDAN

MOROCCO

CANARY
ISLANDS
(Sp.)

Western
Sahara
(Mor.)

ALGERIA

LIBYA

EGYPT

Cairo

KUWAIT

SAUDI
ARABIA

6

29

INDI

CAPE
VERDE

MAURITANIA

S A H A R A

AFRICA

Nile R.

Red Sea

UNITED
ARAB
EMIRATES

OMAN

Bombay

MALI

NIGER

CHAD

SUDAN

ERITREA

YEMEN

Arabian
Sea

SENEGAL

16

18

GUINEA

BURKINA
FASO

CÔTE
D'IVOIRE

GHANA

BENIN

NIGERIA

Lagos

CAMEROON

CENTRAL
AFRICAN
REPUBLIC

DJIBOUTI

SIERRA LEONE

LIBERIA

38

14

GABON

CONGO

ZAIRE

Zaire R.

GREAT RIFT VALLEY

ETHIOPIA

UGANDA

SOMALIA

SRI
LANKA

SAO TOMÉ
AND PRINCIPE

31

10

KENYA

Nairobi

N
W E
S

TANZANIA

INDIAN
OCEAN

ANGOLA

MALAWI

Zambezi R.

ZAMBIA

ATLANTIC
OCEAN

NAMIBIA

ZIMBABWE

MOZAMBIQUE

MADAGASCAR

BOTSWANA

MAURITIUS

SWAZILAND

SOUTH
AFRICA

LESOTHO

Cape Town

20°W

0°

20°E

40°E

60°E

80°E

Map of the Eastern Hemisphere

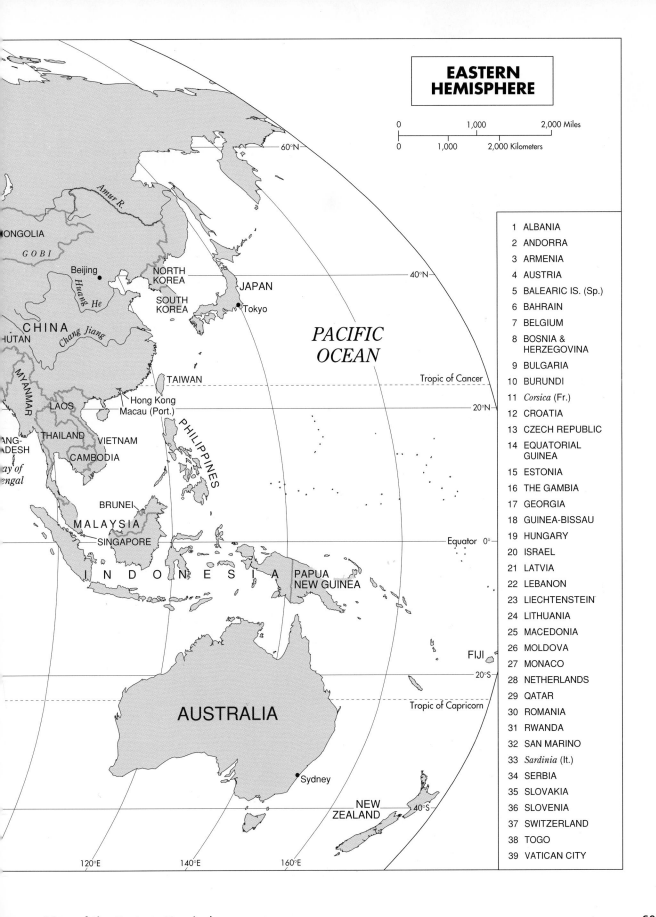

EASTERN HEMISPHERE

0 — 1,000 — 2,000 Miles
0 — 1,000 — 2,000 Kilometers

60°N

MONGOLIA

GOBI

Amur R.

Beijing

Huang He

Chang Jiang

CHINA

BHUTAN

NORTH KOREA

SOUTH KOREA

JAPAN

Tokyo

40°N

PACIFIC OCEAN

MYANMAR

LAOS

TAIWAN

Hong Kong
Macau (Port.)

Tropic of Cancer

20°N

BANG-
LADESH

THAILAND

VIETNAM

CAMBODIA

PHILIPPINES

Bay of
Bengal

BRUNEI

MALAYSIA

SINGAPORE

INDONESIA

PAPUA
NEW GUINEA

Equator 0°

FIJI

20°S

AUSTRALIA

Tropic of Capricorn

Sydney

NEW
ZEALAND

40°S

120°E   140°E   160°E

1	ALBANIA
2	ANDORRA
3	ARMENIA
4	AUSTRIA
5	BALEARIC IS. (Sp.)
6	BAHRAIN
7	BELGIUM
8	BOSNIA & HERZEGOVINA
9	BULGARIA
10	BURUNDI
11	*Corsica* (Fr.)
12	CROATIA
13	CZECH REPUBLIC
14	EQUATORIAL GUINEA
15	ESTONIA
16	THE GAMBIA
17	GEORGIA
18	GUINEA-BISSAU
19	HUNGARY
20	ISRAEL
21	LATVIA
22	LEBANON
23	LIECHTENSTEIN
24	LITHUANIA
25	MACEDONIA
26	MOLDOVA
27	MONACO
28	NETHERLANDS
29	QATAR
30	ROMANIA
31	RWANDA
32	SAN MARINO
33	*Sardinia* (It.)
34	SERBIA
35	SLOVAKIA
36	SLOVENIA
37	SWITZERLAND
38	TOGO
39	VATICAN CITY

Map of the Eastern Hemisphere

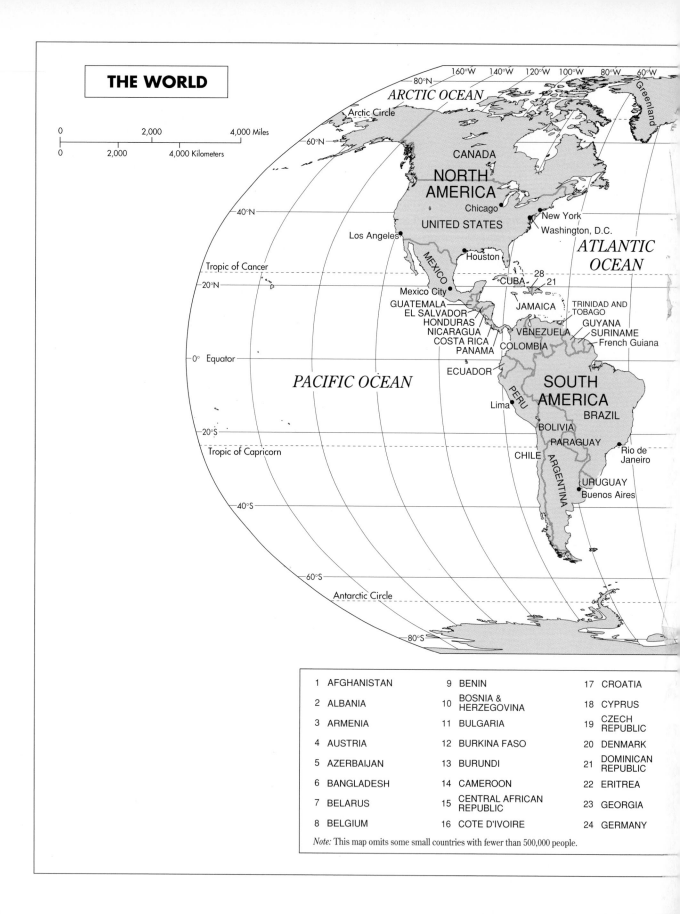

THE WORLD

0   2,000   4,000 Miles

0   2,000   4,000 Kilometers

ARCTIC OCEAN

Arctic Circle

Greenland

CANADA

NORTH AMERICA

Chicago

New York

Washington, D.C.

UNITED STATES

ATLANTIC OCEAN

Los Angeles

Houston

Tropic of Cancer

MEXICO

CUBA

28

21

Mexico City

JAMAICA

TRINIDAD AND TOBAGO

GUATEMALA

GUYANA

EL SALVADOR

HONDURAS

SURINAME

NICARAGUA

VENEZUELA

French Guiana

COSTA RICA

COLOMBIA

PANAMA

Equator

ECUADOR

SOUTH AMERICA

PACIFIC OCEAN

PERU

BRAZIL

Lima

BOLIVIA

PARAGUAY

Tropic of Capricorn

CHILE

Rio de Janeiro

ARGENTINA

URUGUAY

Buenos Aires

Antarctic Circle

1 AFGHANISTAN	9 BENIN	17 CROATIA
2 ALBANIA	10 BOSNIA & HERZEGOVINA	18 CYPRUS
3 ARMENIA	11 BULGARIA	19 CZECH REPUBLIC
4 AUSTRIA	12 BURKINA FASO	20 DENMARK
5 AZERBAIJAN	13 BURUNDI	21 DOMINICAN REPUBLIC
6 BANGLADESH	14 CAMEROON	22 ERITREA
7 BELARUS	15 CENTRAL AFRICAN REPUBLIC	23 GEORGIA
8 BELGIUM	16 COTE D'IVOIRE	24 GERMANY

Note: This map omits some small countries with fewer than 500,000 people.

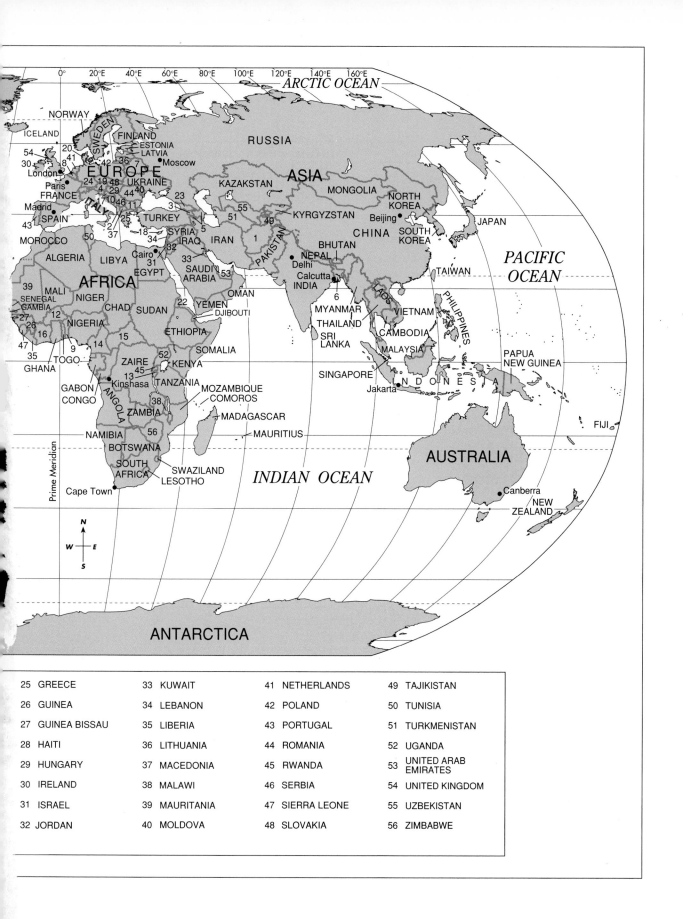

25	GREECE	33	KUWAIT	41	NETHERLANDS	49	TAJIKISTAN
26	GUINEA	34	LEBANON	42	POLAND	50	TUNISIA
27	GUINEA BISSAU	35	LIBERIA	43	PORTUGAL	51	TURKMENISTAN
28	HAITI	36	LITHUANIA	44	ROMANIA	52	UGANDA
29	HUNGARY	37	MACEDONIA	45	RWANDA	53	UNITED ARAB EMIRATES
30	IRELAND	38	MALAWI	46	SERBIA	54	UNITED KINGDOM
31	ISRAEL	39	MAURITANIA	47	SIERRA LEONE	55	UZBEKISTAN
32	JORDAN	40	MOLDOVA	48	SLOVAKIA	56	ZIMBABWE

GLOSSARY

A

absolute monarchy a system in which one person has total rule

affably in a friendly manner

age set in some African societies, a group made up of boys or girls the same age

allegations accusations without proof

alliance an agreement between two or more countries to help each other

animism the belief that spirits live in the natural world in such things as rocks, trees, and streams

anti-Semitism hatred of Jews

apartheid the South African policy of strict separation of the races

aqueduct (AK•wuh•dukt) a system of pipes that carry water to where it is needed

arms race a contest between nations to build more powerful weapons

assassinate to kill an important person

atoll a small coral island with a body of water at its center; most often found in the South Pacific

autocracy a form of government in which the ruler has almost complete power over the people

B

barter the act of exchanging goods and services without using money

bilingual speaking two languages

bilingualism the policy of recognizing two official languages

bio-prospecting payment by one country to another for the right to search for animals and plants that have medicinal or industrial value

black market a place or system in which goods are sold illegally

boycott a refusal to buy or use certain goods or services

Bundestag the lower house of the German parliament

bureaucracy a group of officials who do the daily chores of government

bustee a poor area of a city where people live in shacks

C

calligraphy the art of beautiful handwriting

canal a ditch made by humans to carry water

capitalism an economic system in which businesses are owned privately

capitalist system an economic system in which individuals make economic decisions

caravan a group of travelers who band together for safety

caste a social group based on birth; the system that separates Hindus by class and job

caudillo (kaw•DEE•yoh) a Spanish term for a military strongman

causeway a raised road across water or marshland

chaperon (SHAP•uh•rohn) an older person who goes with a boy and girl on a date to assure proper behavior

charter a set of rules for an organization

city-state a political unit made up of a town and the area around it

civil disobedience a form of protest that involves disobeying laws

civilian a citizen who does not belong to the military

civilization a highly organized group of people with their own culture

clan a group made up of many extended families

coalition a temporary alliance of nations or political parties

coexist to live peacefully side by side with others

Cold War the long period of hostility between Western and Communist countries that began after World War II

collaborate cooperate; work together

colonialism the policy of taking over foreign lands, usually to exploit them economically

colony a land that is controlled by another country

command economies economic systems in which the government makes economic decisions

commonwealth a self-governing state with close ties to another more powerful state

Commonwealth of Nations the group of nations that were once colonies of Great Britain

commune a large farm, with all land and property jointly owned and operated by the farmers

communication satellites human-made objects that orbit the earth, sending information vast distances

communism an economic system in which the government owns and controls most property and industry

competition the result of having more than one seller of a particular product in a market economy

concentration camps large prisons built by Germans to hold people they were going to kill

consensus an agreement reached by a group as a whole or by a majority

constitutional monarchy a system in which a monarch's power is limited by law

consumers people who buy and use products

convenience something that saves work or makes a person's life easier

cooperative farm a farm in which families join their lands and work together, sharing the output

corrupt dishonest

counterrevolutionary a person who does not support the reform movement, or revolution

coup a revolt, often by military leaders, against a nation's government

covenant an agreement or contract

Creole a person in Spanish Latin America whose parents or ancestors were Spanish

crisis a tense period or turning point

cultural diffusion the spread of new ideas and new ways of doing things from one society to others

cultural diversity having a variety of cultures

culture the way of life of a group of people, including their ideas, customs, skills, and arts

cuneiform the form of writing in ancient Sumer that had wedge-shaped characters

custody control over another person

cyclone a dangerous windstorm; often one that brings rain

D

daimyo a powerful local leader under the Japanese feudal system

delta a triangle of land that forms where a river meets the sea

demilitarized zone an area of land in which armed troops are not permitted

democracy government by most citizens

descendant a person who can trace his or her heritage to an individual or group

desertification a process that turns a dry grassland into desert through overgrazing and lack of rain

devout very religious

dialect a regional form of a language that has its own words, expressions, and pronunciations

dictatorship rule by a person who has total power

Diet Japan's two-house parliament

direct democracy a democracy in which every citizen votes on public issues, instead of electing representatives to vote on issues

dissent opposition to a government's policies

diverse different or varied

diversify to make more varied; to give additional options

divert to channel in another direction

divine godlike

drought a long period without rain

dynasty a family of rulers

E

efficient well run, without extra expenses

embargo a restriction on trade with another country

emigrate to leave one country permanently and settle in another

emir an Arab ruler

environment the surroundings in which people live

epic a long poem that tells the story of a hero

epidemic an outbreak of disease

ethnic group a group of people who share a common history, language, culture, and way of life

exile a person who lives in another country usually because of political disagreements

exported sent to other countries for sale

extended family the family unit in most traditional societies, consisting of three or four generations living in one household

extinct species, or separate kinds of animals and plants, that perish forever from the Earth

extract to remove or take from

F

fascism a system of dictatorship that stresses extreme nationalism

fault a crack in the earth's crust caused by movements in that crust

federal system a system in which power is divided between a central government and local governments

feudalism social system based on ties of loyalty and service

foreign policy the way in which a country deals with other countries

free enterprise an economic system in which individuals make economic decisions

fundamentalism a movement or point of view that opposes modern ideas and favors a return to strict religious values

futile useless

G

gangling tall, thin, and awkward

gendarmerie police force

General Assembly the body of the UN that has representatives from every member nation

genocide the deliberate destruction of a racial, national, or economic group

geothermal energy energy produced from heat within the earth

geyser a natural spring of hot water that shoots steam or hot water into the air from time to time

gilded covered with a thin layer of gold

glacier (GLAY•shur) a huge sheet of ice

gloated enjoyed someone else's pain or misfortune .

global village a term that refers to the entire modern world where diverse people communicate, share experiences, and depend on one another for resources

gong a round musical instrument that is struck

griot (GREE•oh) an African storyteller

guerrilla warfare hit-and-run attacks by small bands of fighters against a larger power

gunboat diplomacy a foreign policy that calls for threatening the use of military force to achieve a country's goals

H

headman the leader of a village

hereditary passed from one generation to another

hieroglyphics the form of writing in ancient Egypt that used characters that look like pictures

Holocaust the systematic slaughter of millions of Jews by the Nazis during World War II

hospitality generous treatment of guests

hostile very unfriendly or opposed to something

humanitarian relief the act of helping people; for example, giving free food and medicine to people who need it

hunger strike a refusal to eat; sometimes used as a tactic to pressure a government to meet a list of demands

hydroelectric power power created by the force of rushing water

hygiene personal cleanliness

I

illiterate unable to read or write

immigration coming to one country from another country

immune protected against a specific disease

imperialism a policy of conquering and taking over foreign territory

incense material that makes a scent when burned

incentive a reward offered to encourage people to take a desired action

indelible permanent

Industrial Revolution time of change from making goods by hand to making goods by machine

industrialize to develop industries

inexplicable not capable of being explained

insecticide a chemical that kills insects

interdependent the state of being dependent on one another for support or survival

Internet a network of computers around the world

intifada protests and attacks that began in 1987 by the Palestinians against Israeli rule in the West Bank and Gaza

investors people who put money into businesses in hopes of making a profit

irrigation a system of human-made ditches that carry water

K

kampung a village in Southeast Asia

kibbutz a farm where the land is owned by everyone who farms it

kneads massages or presses with the hands

Knesset the governing body of Israel

Koran the holy book of Islam

kowtow a ceremony in which a person bows down before a superior

L

lagoons bodies of water which are bounded by sandbars or coral reefs

lalang a kind of very tall, thick grass

lamenting feeling or expressing great sorrow

land reform a government policy that involves breaking up large estates and giving the land to peasants

landlocked having no outlet to the sea

lasers special light waves through which information can be sent

lassitude feeling of exhaustion or weakness

legacy something handed down from the past

liberation theology a belief that the Roman Catholic Church should take an active role in ending poverty in Latin America

literacy the ability to read and write

literate able to read and write

M

majority rule a government that reflects the wishes of most of its people, not just a few

mandate an area or country put under the protection of another; permission to rule

market economy a system in which prices are based on what people are willing to pay and companies make goods based on what people want to buy

martial arts arts and skills related to warfare

martial law temporary rule by the military

meditate to think deeply

mestizos people who are part Native American and part European

Middle Passage the journey across the Atlantic Ocean from West Africa to the Americas that was the route of the African American slave trade

midwife a person who helps women during childbirth

migrate to move from one place to another

militant a person who believes in using violence to promote a cause

minaret a large tower near a mosque from which Muslims are called to prayer

minority less than half

mission a religious settlement devoted to spreading Christianity

missionary a person who is sent to do religious work in a territory or foreign country

mixed economies economies in which both individuals and government make economic decisions

moderate less extreme in ideas or behavior

modernize to bring up to date

monarchy a form of government in which one person rules

monsoon a seasonal wind that brings wet or dry weather

monument something that is built to honor a person or event

Moorish of the Moors, especially those Muslim people of North Africa who invaded Spain in the 8th century

morality rules of proper conduct

mosaic a design made up of many small pieces of materials

mosque an Islamic house of worship

multilingual able to speak more than one language

multinational having operations in many countries

multiracial made up of many races

mummy a dead body treated with chemicals and wrapped so that it does not decay

mural a very large painting or photograph that is applied to a wall or ceiling

muted muffled or softer in sound

N

nation-state a unified country

nationalism the belief that a people should have their own government; a feeling of pride and loyalty to a nation

natural gas underground reserves of gas that can be used as fuel

negotiation the act of dealing or bargaining with someone else

neutrality a policy of refusing to take sides in a conflict

nirvana a state in which a person has achieved perfect happiness because he or she wants nothing

nomad a person who has no permanent home and moves from place to place

non-aligned nation a nation that claimed not to prefer one side over the other in the Cold War

non-alignment a policy of not being allied with other nations on a regular basis, but of deciding each question of foreign policy individually

nonaggression treaty an agreement between countries not to take hostile action against one another

nuclear family the family unit in most developed societies, consisting often of a father, mother, and children

nuclear umbrella the military protection provided to a nation by another nation that possesses nuclear weapons

O

oasis a place in the desert where water comes to the surface

oracle bones bones that the ancient Chinese used to predict the future

oral history history that is passed down verbally, rather than in writing

outback the dry lands of Australia where there are few settlers

overthrow to bring down from power by force

P

pact an agreement

pan-Africanism the belief that people of African descent have common interests and should work together for freedom

papyrus reeds that ancient Egyptians pounded flat to make paper for writing

parliamentary rule a system of government in which a nation's legislature chooses the country's leader

penal colony a colony for prisoners

peninsula a body of land surrounded on three sides by water

pension a regular payment to retired people

peon a poor person who works all his or her life for rich landowners

percussion instrument a musical instrument that is played by striking it

pharaoh a ruler of ancient Egypt

pigments substances used to give color

pilgrimage a journey that a believer makes to a religious site

plateau a flat area that is higher than the land that surrounds it

polygamy the practice of having more than one spouse

population density the number of people per square mile in an area

Prebend land owned by the Church of England

privatize to end government control of factories, farms, and businesses and turn them over to individuals

protectorate a country that is actually under the control of another country, although it is officially independent

proverb a short saying that expresses some well-known fact or common experience

province a territory governed as an administrative or political unit of a country

provisional temporary

public works projects done for the good of everyone, such as constructing roads and public buildings

purdah the practice of keeping women from public view

purge to remove people from a society who are considered undesirable

pyramid a large stone building with a square base and sides like triangles that rise to a point

Q

quality circles groups of workers that look for better ways to get jobs done

R

radical more extreme in ideas or behavior

raga one of the ancient melody patterns of Indian music

Ramadan the holiest month in the Islamic calendar

rapids a place where a river falls sharply and flows very quickly

Red Guards students, workers, and soldiers who rampaged through China in support of Mao's Cultural Revolution

refugee a person who has been forced to flee from his or her homeland for safety

regent someone who rules in the place of a child

reincarnation being reborn many times

republic a form of government in which citizens elect their leaders

revolt an uprising

revolution an attempt to overthrow a political system

rigid stiff; tightly controlled

Romance languages languages such as Italian and Spanish that developed from Latin

S

sabras Jewish people who were born in Israel

samurai a member of Japan's traditional warrior class

sanction the decision to cut off trade with a country until it changes its policies

sarong a simple wraparound dress or skirt

satellite a country controlled by another country; a spacecraft that orbits the earth

savannas (or **savannahs**) flat, treeless grasslands of warm regions

scribe the class of people in ancient Egypt whose job was to write

secede to break away from a country or another political unit

secular not related to religion

Security Council the body of the UN that has 15 members that are charged with maintaining world peace

self-sufficiency making do with one's own resources

serf a peasant during the Middle Ages who lived and worked on a manor

service occupations jobs that provide services to people; such as health care and teaching

shaman a priest or priestess who conducts ceremonies involving the worship of nature

shantytown a slum on the outskirts of a city

shogun a military leader who ruled in the name of the Japanese emperor

socialism the belief that the government should own a country's factories and farms and that people should share wealth equally

species separate kinds of animals and plants

squatter someone who settles on land without the right to do so

stalemate a situation in which two sides oppose each other but neither can win

steppe a large, treeless plain in the Eurasian Heartland that is very fertile

strait a narrow body of water that connects two larger bodies of water

strip-logging the practice of taking out narrow roadlike strips of a forest to help preserve it

stupa a dome-shaped burial mound that serves as a Buddhist holy site

subcontinent a large landmass that juts out from a continent

subsidy assistance that a government provides to consumers or industries

subsistence farming type of farming that produces just enough food for people to survive

sumo a Japanese form of wrestling

supply and demand an economic concept in which prices are based on what people are willing to pay and companies make goods based on what people want to buy

suppress to put down by force

suq a large market in the Middle East

sustainable development the practice of taking resources from rain forests in a way that doesn't destroy the environment

T

taiga a large forest of the Eurasian Heartland

tariff a tax on goods entering or leaving a country

temperate rain forests rain forests that receive moisture in the form of rain and fog; found in cooler regions than tropical rain forests

Timbuktu town in West Africa

trade deficit the result when a nation buys more from other nations than it sells to other nations

trade surplus the result when a nation sells more to other nations than it buys from other nations

tradition behavior handed down from generation to generation

trench a long, deep ditch

tribalism the allegiance of many Africans to their tribes

tributary a small river that flows into a larger river

tribute system an arrangement by which China collected payments from nearby nations

tropical rain forests dense woods that receive at least 80 inches (205 cm) of rain a year and have an average temperature of 80° F (27° C)

tropics lands that are near the equator

truce a halt to fighting in a war

tsar term for a king of Russia

tundra a level, treeless region with long winters

typhoon a fierce storm, like a hurricane

U

urban characteristic of a city or city life

urbanization the movement of people from the countryside to cities

V

vagrant a person who wanders from place to place

vassal under feudalism, a person who served a more powerful lord

viceroy a person who governs a colony as a representative of the king or queen

volcano a mountain with an opening near the top from which hot melted rocks, ash, and gases sometimes flow

W

warlord a local ruler and military leader

warm-water port a port that is ice-free all year

website an Internet home address

welfare state a government that assumes responsibility for the welfare of its citizens

work ethic the belief in the benefits of hard work

Z

zaibatsu giant family businesses in Japan which supposedly were broken up during the U.S. occupation

INDEX

A

Aborigines, 191-192, 193, 198
Absolute location, 6
Absolute monarchy, 519-520
Acadia, 390
Achebe, Chinua, 70
Acropolis, 514
Afghanistan, 156, 479
Africa
　arts in, 70-72, 74-77
　cities in, 23, 32, 34, 66-69
　colonial. *See* Colonialism in Africa
　countries of, 80-81
　economic systems in, 83-86
　education in, 65, 95-96
　environment in, 98-101
　ethnic groups in, 21, 63, 79, 82, 96-97
　famine in, 86, 97-98
　farming in, 22, 28, 29, 41, 45, 54, 67, 84-85, 86, 98
　foreign policy in, 93-94
　geography of, 14-20
　health in, 25, 42, 54, 94-95
　history of, 28-34, 44
　nationalism in, 55-57
　people of, 21-24
　political systems in, 79, 82-83
　refugees in, 96-97
　regional organizations in, 93
　slave trade in, 35-37
　traditional society in, 40-46
　See also specific countries
African National Congress (ANC), 57, 79, 90
Africans, in Latin America, 309, 310
Afro-Asiatic language, 24
Age set, 41
AIDS, 95
Aikido, 251
Ainu, 215
Akbar, 109, 129
Akkadians, 421
Albania, 544
Aleppo, Syria, 406

Alexander the Great, 422, 515
Alexander II of Russia, 564
Alexandria, Egypt, 414
Algeria, 17, 57, 63, 93, 410, 414, 436, 438, 476, 479
Algiers, 414, 436
Ali Jinnah, Muhammad, 152
Ali Khan, Liaquat, 152, 155
al-Jizah (Giza), Egypt, 414
Allah, 428
Alliances, European, 527, 531, 532
"All That You Have Given Me, Africa" (Kanié), 74-75
Alphabet
　Cyrillic, 561
　Phoenician, 421
Alpine Mountains (Alps), 502, 505, 506, 507
Amazon rain forest, 312, 370　·
Amazon River, 304, 305, 307, 312
American Colonization Society, 52
Anawrahta, King, 160
Andes Mountains, 304, 305, 307, 312, 314, 322, 334
Angkor Kingdom, 160-161
Angkor Wat, 108, 161, 175
Angola, 18, 24, 57
Animism, 162
Ankara, Turkey, 414
Anti-Semitism, 440, 517, 529
Apartheid, 11, 70-71, 72, 89-90
Aqueducts, 321, 515
Aquino, Benigno, 182
Aquino, Corazón, 182
Arabian Peninsula, 408, 411, 416, 428, 437
Arabic language, 24, 34, 411, 476
Arabs, 14, 21, 33-34, 35, 411, 428, 437, 440, 441, 470, 471, 474
Arabsat, 489
Arafat, Yasir, 472, 487
Aral Sea, 576
Architecture, Islamic, 140, 490
Arctic, 381, 383
Argentina, 305, 310, 335, 337-338, 345, 346, 352, 355, 356, 357

Arias, Oscar, 358
Armenia, 571, 574, 575
Armenians, 436, 438
Arms race, 582
Arts
　in Africa, 70-72, 74-77
　in China, 226-227, 262
　in Europe, 518, 538-539
　in Japan, 252-253
　in Latin America, 370-371, 376-377
　in Middle East, 443-446, 489-490
　in Russia, 564, 571
　in South Asia, 139-141
　in Southeast Asia, 143-146, 173-174
Aryans, 121, 124
Asia, 406, 431, 434
Askia Muhammad, 32, 44
Asoka, 128
Association of Southeast Asian Nations (ASEAN), 109, 183-184
Assyrians, 426
Aswan Dam, 17, 439, 480
Ataturk, Kemal, 438, 464
Athens, Greece, 498, 507, 514-515
Atlantic slave trade, 11, 35-36
Atlas Mountains, 16
Atolls, 196
Australia, 109, 188-189, 190, 191-192, 193, 194-195, 198
Austria-Hungary, 528, 541
Autocracy, 563
Axum, Kingdom of, 30-31
Ayatollah, 478, 485
Aymará, 313, 314-315
Ayutthaya Kingdom, 161
Azerbaijan, 571, 574, 575
Aztecs, 300, 320-321, 323-326

B

Babur, 129
Babylon, 421, 426
Baghdad, Iraq, 414, 415, 431, 486